BENJAM

INSTEAD OF A BOOK

BY A MAN TOO BUSY TO WRITE ONE

A FRAGMENTARY EXPOSITION OF

PHILOSOPHICAL ANARCHISM

Elibron Classics
www.elibron.com

Elibron Classics series.

© 2005 Adamant Media Corporation.

ISBN 1-4021-9845-0 (paperback)
ISBN 1-4021-3297-2 (hardcover)

This Elibron Classics Replica Edition is an unabridged facsimile
of the edition published in 1897 by Benj. R. Tucker,
New York.

Benj R Tucker

INSTEAD OF A BOOK

By A Man Too Busy to Write One

A FRAGMENTARY EXPOSITION OF

PHILOSOPHICAL ANARCHISM

CULLED FROM THE WRITINGS OF

BENJ. R. TUCKER

Editor of Liberty

Liberty, Not the Daughter, but the Mother of Order.—PROUDHON

SECOND EDITION

NEW YORK

BENJ. R. TUCKER, PUBLISHER

1897

CONTENTS.

PREFACE.

"INSTEAD of a book!" I hear the reader exclaim, as he picks up this volume and glances at its title; "why, it *is* a book." To all appearance, yes; essentially, no. It is, to be sure, an assemblage within a cover of printed sheets consecutively numbered; but this alone does not constitute a book. A book, properly speaking, is first of all a thing of unity and symmetry, of order and finish; it is a literary structure, each part of which is subordinated to the whole and created for it. To satisfy such a standard this volume does not pretend; it is not a structure, but an afterthought, a more or less coherent arrangement, each part of which was created almost without reference to any other. Yet not quite so, after all; otherwise even the smallest degree of coherence were scarcely possible.

The facts are these. In August, 1881, I started in Boston, in a very quiet way, a little fortnightly journal called *Liberty*. Its purpose was to contribute to the solution of social problems by carrying to a logical conclusion the battle against authority,—to aid in what Proudhon had called "the dissolution of government in the economic organism." Beyond the opportunity of thus contributing my mite I looked for little from my experiment. But, almost before I knew it, the tiny paper had begun to exert an influence of which I had not dreamed. It went the wide world over. In nearly every important city, and in many a country town, it found some mind ripe for its reception. Each of these minds became a centre of influence, and in considerably less than a year a specific movement had sprung into existence, under Proudhon's happily chosen name, Anarchism, of which *Liberty* was generally recognized as the organ. Since that time, through varying fortunes, the paper has gone on, with slow but steady growth, doing its quiet work. Books inspired by it, and other journals which it called into being, have made their appearance, not only in various parts of the United States, but in England, France, Germany, and at the antipodes. Anarchism is now one of the forces of the world. But its literature, voluminous as it already is, lacks a systematic text-book. I have often been urged to attempt the task of writing one. Thus far,

however, I have been too busy, and there is no prospect that I shall ever
be less so. Pending the arrival of the man having the requisite time,
means, and ability for the production of the desired book, it has been determined to put forth, as a sort of makeshift, this partial collection of my
writings for *Liberty*, giving them, by an attempt at classification, some
semblance of system ; the thought being that, if these writings, scattered
in bits here, there, and everywhere, have already influenced so many
minds, they ought in a compact and cumulative form to influence very
many more.

The volume opens with a paper on "State Socialism and Anarchism,"
which covers in a summary way nearly the entire scope of the work.
Following this is the main section, "The Individual, Society, and the
State," dealing with the fundamental principles of human association. In
the third and fourth sections application of these principles is made to the
two great economic factors, money and land. In these two sections,
moreover, as well as in the fifth and sixth, the various authoritarian social
solutions which go counter to these principles are dealt with,—namely,
Greenbackism, the Single Tax, State Socialism, and so-called "Communistic Anarchism." The seventh section treats of the methods by
which these principles can be realized ; and in the eighth are grouped numerous articles scarcely within the scheme of classification, but which it
has seemed best for various reasons to preserve. For the elaborate index
to the whole the readers are indebted to my friends Francis D. Tandy and
Henry Cohen, of Denver, Colo.

The matter in this volume is largely controversial. This has frequently
necessitated the reproduction of other articles than the author's (distinguished by a different type), in order to make the author's intelligible. A
volume thus made must be characterized by many faults, both of style
and substance. I am too busy, not only to write a book, but to satisfactorily revise this substitute. With but few and slight exceptions, the
articles stand as originally written. Much they contain that is personal
and irrelevant, and that would not have found its way into a book spe-
cially prepared. It would be strange, too, if in writings covering a period
of twelve years there were not some inconsistencies, especially in the
terminology and form of expression. For such, if any there be, and for
all minor weaknesses, I crave, because of the circumstances, a measure of
indulgence from the critic. But, on the other hand, I challenge the most
searching examination of the central positions taken. Undamaged by
the constant fire of twelve years of controversy, they are proof, in my
judgment, against the heaviest guns. Apologizing, therefore, for their
form only, and full of faith in their power, I offer these pages to the
public INSTEAD OF A BOOK.

B. R. T.

STATE SOCIALISM AND ANARCHISM:

HOW FAR THEY AGREE, AND WHEREIN THEY DIFFER.

STATE SOCIALISM AND ANARCHISM :*

HOW FAR THEY AGREE, AND WHEREIN THEY DIFFER.

PROBABLY no agitation has ever attained the magnitude, either in the number of its recruits or the area of its influence, which has been attained by Modern Socialism, and at the same time been so little understood and so misunderstood, not only by the hostile and the indifferent, but by the friendly, and even by the great mass of its adherents themselves. This unfortunate and highly dangerous state of things is due partly to the fact that the human relationships which this movement—if anything so chaotic can be called a movement—aims to transform, involve no special class or classes, but literally all mankind; partly to the fact that these relationships are infinitely more varied and complex in their nature than those with which any special reform has ever been called upon to

---

* In the summer of 1886, shortly after the bomb-throwing at Chicago, the author of this volume received an invitation from the editor of the *North American Review* to furnish him a paper on Anarchism. In response the above article was sent him. A few days later the author received a letter announcing the acceptance of his paper, the editor volunteering the declaration that it was the ablest article that he had received during his editorship of the *Review.* The next number of the *Review* bore the announcement, on the second page of its cover, that the article (giving its title and the name of the author) would appear at an early date. Month after month went by, and the article did not appear. Repeated letters of inquiry failed to bring any explanation. Finally, after nearly a year had elapsed, the author wrote to the editor that he had prepared the article, not to be pigeon-holed, but to be printed, and that he wished the matter to be acted upon immediately. In reply he received his manuscript and a check for seventy-five dollars. Thereupon he made a few slight changes in the article and delivered it on several occasions as a lecture, after which it was printed in *Liberty* of March 10, 1888.

deal; and partly to the fact that the great moulding forces of
society, the channels of information and enlightenment, are
well-nigh exclusively under the control of those whose immediate pecuniary interests are antagonistic to the bottom
claim of Socialism that labor should be put in possession of
its own.

Almost the only persons who may be said to comprehend
even approximately the significance, principles, and purposes
of Socialism are the chief leaders of the extreme wings of the
Socialistic forces, and perhaps a few of the money kings themselves. It is a subject of which it has lately become quite
the fashion for preacher, professor, and penny-a-liner to treat,
and, for the most part, woful work they have made with it,
exciting the derision and pity of those competent to judge.
That those prominent in the intermediate Socialistic divisions
do not fully understand what they are about is evident from
the positions they occupy. If they did ; if they were consistent, logical thinkers ; if they were what the French call *consequent* men,—their reasoning faculties would long since have
driven them to one extreme or the other.

For it is a curious fact that the two extremes of the vast
army now under consideration, though united, as has been
hinted above, by the common claim that labor shall be put in
possession of its own, are more diametrically opposed to each
other in their fundamental principles of social action and their
methods of reaching the ends aimed at than either is to their
common enemy, the existing society. They are based on two
principles the history of whose conflict is almost equivalent to
the history of the world since man came into it; and all intermediate parties, including that of the upholders of the existing society, are based upon a compromise between them. It
is clear, then, that any intelligent, deep-rooted opposition to
the prevailing order of things must come from one or the
other of these extremes, for anything from any other source,
far from being revolutionary in character, could be only in the
nature of such superficial modification as would be utterly
unable to concentrate upon itself the degree of attention and
interest now bestowed upon Modern Socialism.

The two principles referred to are AUTHORITY and LIBERTY,
and the names of the two schools of Socialistic thought which
fully and unreservedly represent one or the other of them are,
respectively, State Socialism and Anarchism. Whoso knows
what these two schools want and how they propose to get it
understands the Socialistic movement. For, just as it has
been said that there is no half-way house between Rome and

Reason, so it may be said that there is no half-way house between State Socialism and Anarchism. There are, in fact,
two currents steadily flowing from the centre of the Socialistic
forces which are concentrating them on the left and on the
right; and, if Socialism is to prevail, it is among the possibilities that, after this movement of separation has been completed and the existing order has been crushed out between
the two camps, the ultimate and bitterer conflict will be still
to come. In that case all the eight-hour men, all the trades-
unionists, all the Knights of Labor, all the land nationalizationists, all the greenbackers, and, in short, all the members of the
thousand and one different battalions belonging to the great
army of Labor, will have deserted their old posts, and, these
being arrayed on the one side and the other, the great battle
will begin. What a final victory for the State Socialists will
mean, and what a final victory for the Anarchists will mean,
it is the purpose of this paper to briefly state.

To do this intelligently, however, I must first describe the
ground common to both, the features that make Socialists of
each of them.

The economic principles of Modern Socialism are a logical
deduction from the principle laid down by Adam Smith in
the early chapters of his "Wealth of Nations,"— namely, that
labor is the true measure of price. But Adam Smith, after
stating this principle most clearly and concisely, immediately
abandoned all further consideration of it to devote himself to
showing what actually does measure price, and how, therefore,
wealth is at present distributed. Since his day nearly all the
political economists have followed his example by confining
their function to the description of society as it is, in its industrial and commercial phases. Socialism, on the contrary,
extends its function to the description of society as it should
be, and the discovery of the means of making it what it
should be. Half a century or more after Smith enunciated
the principle above stated, Socialism picked it up where he
had dropped it, and, in following it to its logical conclusions,
made it the basis of a new economic philosophy.

This seems to have been done independently by three different men, of three different nationalities, in three different
languages: Josiah Warren, an American; Pierre J. Proudhon, a
Frenchman; Karl Marx, a German Jew. That Warren and
Proudhon arrived at their conclusions singly and unaided is
certain; but whether Marx was not largely indebted to Proudhon for his economic ideas is questionable. However this may
be, Marx's presentation of the ideas was in so many respects

peculiarly his own that he is fairly entitled to the credit of originality. That the work of this interesting trio should have been done so nearly simultaneously would seem to indicate that Socialism was in the air, and that the time was ripe and the conditions favorable for the appearance of this new school of thought. So far as priority of time is concerned, the credit seems to belong to Warren, the American,—a fact which should be noted by the stump orators who are so fond of declaiming against Socialism as an imported article. Of the purest revolutionary blood, too, this Warren, for he descends from the Warren who fell at Bunker Hill.

From Smith's principle that labor is the true measure of price—or, as Warren phrased it, that cost is the proper limit of price—these three men made the following deductions : that the natural wage of labor is its product; that this wage, or product, is the only just source of income (leaving out, of course, gift, inheritance, etc.); that all who derive income from any other source abstract it directly or indirectly from the natural and just wage of labor; that this abstracting process generally takes one of three forms,—interest, rent, and profit; that these three constitute the trinity of usury, and are simply different methods of levying tribute for the use of capital; that, capital being simply stored-up labor which has already received its pay in full, its use ought to be gratuitous, on the principle that labor is the only basis of price; that the lender of capital is entitled to its return intact, and nothing more; that the only reason why the banker, the stockholder, the landlord, the manufacturer, and the merchant are able to exact usury from labor lies in the fact that they are backed by legal privilege, or monopoly; and that the only way to secure to labor the enjoyment of its entire product, or natural wage, is to strike down monopoly.

It must not be inferred that either Warren, Proudhon, or Marx used exactly this phraseology, or followed exactly this line of thought, but it indicates definitely enough the fundamental ground taken by all three, and their substantial thought up to the limit to which they went in common. And, lest I may be accused of stating the positions and arguments of these men incorrectly, it may be well to say in advance that I have viewed them broadly, and that, for the purpose of sharp, vivid, and emphatic comparison and contrast, I have taken considerable liberty with their thought by rearranging it in an order, and often in a phraseology, of my own, but, I am satisfied, without, in so doing, misrepresenting them in any essential particular.

It was at this point—the necessity of striking down monopoly—that came the parting of their ways. Here the road forked. They found that they must turn either to the right or to the left,—follow either the path of Authority or the path of Liberty. Marx went one way; Warren and Proudhon the other. Thus were born State Socialism and Anarchism.

First, then, State Socialism, which may be described as *the doctrine that all the affairs of men should be managed by the government, regardless of individual choice.*

Marx, its founder, concluded that the only way to abolish the class monopolies was to centralize and consolidate all industrial and commercial interests, all productive and distributive agencies, in one vast monopoly in the hands of the State. The government must become banker, manufacturer, farmer, carrier, and merchant, and in these capacities must suffer no competition. Land, tools, and all instruments of production must be wrested from individual hands, and made the property of the collectivity. To the individual can belong only the products to be consumed, not the means of producing them. A man may own his clothes and his food, but not the sewing-machine which makes his shirts or the spade which digs his potatoes. Product and capital are essentially different things; the former belongs to individuals, the latter to society. Society must seize the capital which belongs to it, by the ballot if it can, by revolution if it must. Once in possession of it, it must administer it on the majority principle, through its organ, the State, utilize it in production and distribution, fix all prices by the amount of labor involved, and employ the whole people in its workshops, farms, stores, etc. The nation must be transformed into a vast bureaucracy, and every individual into a State official. Everything must be done on the cost principle, the people having no motive to make a profit out of themselves. Individuals not being allowed to own capital, no one can employ another, or even himself. Every man will be a wage-receiver, and the State the only wage-payer. He who will not work for the State must starve, or, more likely, go to prison. All freedom of trade must disappear. Competition must be utterly wiped out. All industrial and commercial activity must be centred in one vast, enormous, all-inclusive monopoly. The remedy for *monopolies* is MONOPOLY.

Such is the economic programme of State Socialism as adopted from Karl Marx. The history of its growth and progress cannot be told here. In this country the parties that uphold it are known as the Socialistic Labor Party, which pretends to follow Karl Marx ; the Nationalists, who follow Karl

Marx filtered through Edward Bellamy ; and the Christian Socialists, who follow Karl Marx filtered through Jesus Christ.

What other applications this principle of Authority, once adopted in the economic sphere, will develop is very evident. It means the absolute control by the majority of all individual conduct. The right of such control is already admitted by the State Socialists, though they maintain that, as a matter of fact, the individual would be allowed a much larger liberty than he now enjoys. But he would only be allowed it ; he could not claim it as his own. There would be no foundation of society upon a guaranteed equality of the largest possible liberty. Such liberty as might exist would exist by sufferance and could be taken away at any moment. Constitutional guarantees would be of no avail. There would be but one article in the constitution of a State Socialistic country : " The right of the majority is absolute."

The claim of the State Socialists, however, that this right would not be exercised in matters pertaining to the individual in the more intimate and private relations of his life is not borne out by the history of governments. It has ever been the tendency of power to add to itself, to enlarge its sphere, to encroach beyond the limits set for it ; and where the habit of resisting such encroachment is not fostered, and the individual is not taught to be jealous of his rights, individuality gradually disappears and the government or State becomes the all-in-all. Control naturally accompanies responsibility. Under the system of State Socialism, therefore, which holds the community responsible for the health, wealth, and wisdom of the individual, it is evident that the community, through its majority expression, will insist more and more on prescribing the conditions of health, wealth, and wisdom, thus impairing and finally destroying individual independence and with it all sense of individual responsibility.

Whatever, then, the State Socialists may claim or disclaim, their system, if adopted, is doomed to end in a State religion, to the expense of which all must contribute and at the altar of which all must kneel ; a State school of medicine, by whose practitioners the sick must invariably be treated ; a State system of hygiene, prescribing what all must and must not eat, drink, wear, and do ; a State code of morals, which will not content itself with punishing crime, but will prohibit what the majority decide to be vice ; a State system of instruction, which will do away with all private schools, academies, and colleges ; a State nursery, in which all children must be brought up in common at the public expense; and, finally, a State family, with an attempt at stirpiculture, or scientific breeding, in which no man and woman will be allowed to have children if the State prohibits them and no man and woman can refuse to have children if the State orders them. Thus will Authority achieve its acme and Monopoly be carried to its highest power.

Such is the ideal of the logical State Socialist, such the goal which lies at the end of the road that Karl Marx took. Let us now follow the fortunes of Warren and Proudhon, who took the other road,—the road of Liberty.

This brings us to Anarchism, which may be described as *the doctrine that all the affairs of men should be managed by individuals or voluntary associations, and that the State should be abolished.*

When Warren and Proudhon, in prosecuting their search for justice to labor, came face to face with the obstacle of class monopolies, they saw that these monopolies rested upon Authority, and concluded that the thing to be done was, not to strengthen this Authority and thus make monopoly universal, but to utterly uproot Authority and give full sway to the opposite principle, Liberty, by making competition, the antithesis of monopoly, universal. They saw in competition the great leveller of prices to the labor cost of production. In this they agreed with the political economists. The query then naturally presented itself why all prices do not fall to labor cost ; where there is any room for incomes acquired otherwise than by labor; in a word, why the usurer, the receiver of interest, rent, and profit, exists. The answer was found in the present one-sidedness of competition. It was discovered that capital had so manipulated legislation that unlimited competition is allowed in supplying productive labor, thus keeping wages down to the starvation point, or as near it as practicable; that a great deal of competition is allowed in supplying distributive labor, or the labor of the mercantile classes, thus keeping, not the prices of goods, but the merchants actual profits on them, down to a point somewhat approximating equitable wages for the merchants' work; but that almost no competition at all is allowed in supplying capital, upon the aid of which both productive and distributive labor are dependent for their power of achievement, thus keeping the rate of interest on money and of house-rent and ground-rent at as high a point as the necessities of the people will bear.

On discovering this, Warren and Proudhon charged the political economists with being afraid of their own doctrine.

The Manchester men were accused of being inconsistent. They believed in liberty to compete with the laborer in order to reduce his wages, but not in liberty to compete with the capitalist in order to reduce his usury. *Laissez faire* was very good sauce for the goose, labor, but very poor sauce for the gander, capital. But how to correct this inconsistency, how to serve this gander with this sauce, how to put capital at the service of business men and laborers at cost, or free of usury, — that was the problem.

Marx, as we have seen, solved it by declaring capital to be a different thing from product, and maintaining that it belonged to society and should be seized by society and employed for the benefit of all alike. Proudhon scoffed at this distinction between capital and product. He maintained that capital and product are not different kinds of wealth, but simply alternate conditions or functions of the same wealth; that all wealth undergoes an incessant transformation from capital into product and from product back into capital, the process repeating itself interminably; that capital and product are purely social terms; that what is product to one man immediately becomes capital to another, and *vice versa;* that, if there were but one person in the world, all wealth would be to him at once capital and product; that the fruit of A's toil is his product, which, when sold to B, becomes B's capital (unless B is an unproductive consumer, in which case it is merely wasted wealth, outside the view of social economy); that a steam-engine is just as much product as a coat, and that a coat is just as much capital as a steam-engine; and that the same laws of equity govern the possession of the one that govern the possession of the other.

For these and other reasons Proudhon and Warren found themselves unable to sanction any such plan as the seizure of capital by society. But, though opposed to socializing the ownership of capital, they aimed nevertheless to socialize its effects by making its use beneficial to all instead of a means of impoverishing the many to enrich the few. And when the light burst in upon them, they saw that this could be done by subjecting capital to the natural law of competition, thus bringing the price of its use down to cost,—that is, to nothing beyond the expenses incidental to handling and transferring it. So they raised the banner of Absolute Free Trade; free trade at home, as well as with foreign countries; the logical carrying out of the Manchester doctrine; *laissez faire* the universal rule. Under this banner they began their fight upon monopolies, whether the all-inclusive monopoly of the

State Socialists, or the various class monopolies that now prevail.

Of the latter they distinguished four of principal importance : the money monopoly, the land monopoly, the tariff monopoly, and the patent monopoly.

First in the importance of its evil influence they considered the money monopoly, which consists of the privilege given by the government to certain individuals, or to individuals holding certain kinds of property, of issuing the circulating medium, a privilege which is now enforced in this country by a national tax of ten per cent. upon all other persons who attempt to furnish a circulating medium, and by State laws making it a criminal offence to issue notes as currency. It is claimed that the holders of this privilege control the rate of interest, the rate of rent of houses and buildings, and the prices of goods,—the first directly, and the second and third indirectly. For, say Proudhon and Warren, if the business of banking were made free to all, more and more persons would enter into it until the competition should become sharp enough to reduce the price of lending money to the labor cost, which statistics show to be less than three-fourths of one per cent. In that case the thousands of people who are now deterred from going into business by the ruinously high rates which they must pay for capital with which to start and carry on business will find their difficulties removed. If they have property which they do not desire to convert into money by sale, a bank will take it as collateral for a loan of a certain proportion of its market value at less than one per cent. discount. If they have no property, but are industrious, honest, and capable, they will generally be able to get their individual notes endorsed by a sufficient number of known and solvent parties; and on such business paper they will be able to get a loan at a bank on similarly favorable terms. Thus interest will fall at a blow. The banks will really not be lending capital at all, but will be doing business on the capital of their customers, the business consisting in an exchange of the known and widely available credits of the banks for the unknown and unavailable, but equally good, credits of the customers, and a charge therefor of less than one per cent., not as interest for the use of capital, but as pay for the labor of running the banks. This facility of acquiring capital will give an unheard-of impetus to business, and consequently create an unprecedented demand for labor,—a demand which will always be in excess of the supply, directly the contrary of the present condition of the labor market. Then will be seen an exemplification of the words of Richard Cobden that, when two laborers are after one employer, wages fall, but when two employers are after one laborer, wages rise. Labor will then be in a position to dictate its wages, and will thus secure its natural wage, its entire product. Thus the same blow that strikes interest down will send wages up. But this is not all. Down will go profits also. For merchants, instead of buying at high prices on credit, will borrow money of the banks at less than one per cent., buy at low prices for cash, and correspondingly reduce the prices of their goods to their customers. And with the rest will go house-rent. For no one who can borrow capital at one per cent. with which to build a house of his own will consent to pay rent to a landlord at a higher rate than that. Such is the vast claim made by Proudhon and Warren as to the results of the simple abolition of the money monopoly.

Second in importance comes the land monopoly, the evil effects of which are seen principally in exclusively agricultural countries, like Ireland. This monopoly consists in the enforcement by government of land titles which do not rest upon personal occupancy and cultivation. It was obvious to Warren and Proudhon that, as soon as individuals should no longer be protected by their fellows in anything but personal occupancy and cultivation of land, ground-rent would disappear, and so usury have one less leg to stand on. Their followers of to-day are disposed to modify this claim to the extent of admitting that the very small fraction of ground-rent which rests, not on monopoly, but on superiority of soil or site, will continue to exist for a time and perhaps forever, though tending constantly to a minimum under conditions of freedom. But the inequality of soils which gives rise to the economic rent of land, like the inequality of human skill which gives rise to the economic rent of ability, is not a cause for serious alarm even to the most thorough opponent of usury, as its nature is not that of a germ from which other and graver inequalities may spring, but rather that of a decaying branch which may finally wither and fall.

Third, the tariff monopoly, which consists in fostering production at high prices and under unfavorable conditions by visiting with the penalty of taxation those who patronize production at low prices and under favorable conditions. The evil to which this monopoly gives rise might more properly be called *mis*usury than usury, because it compels labor to pay, not exactly for the use of capital, but rather for the misuse of capital. The abolition of this monopoly would result in a great reduction in the prices of all articles taxed, and this saving to the laborers who consume these articles would be another step toward securing to the laborer his natural wage, his entire product. Proudhon admitted, however, that to abolish this monopoly before abolishing the money monopoly would be a cruel and disastrous policy, first, because the evil of scarcity of money, created by the money monopoly, would be intensified by the flow of money out of the country which would be involved in an excess of imports over exports, and, second, because that fraction of the laborers of the country which is now employed in the protected industries would be turned adrift to face starvation without the benefit of the insatiable demand for labor which a competitive money system would create. Free trade in money at home, making money and work abundant, was insisted upon by Proudhon as a prior condition of free trade in goods with foreign countries.

Fourth, the patent monopoly, which consists in protecting inventors and authors against competition for a period long enough to enable them to extort from the people a reward enormously in excess of the labor measure of their services,— in other words, in giving certain people a right of property for a term of years in laws and facts of Nature, and the power to exact tribute from others for the use of this natural wealth, which should be open to all. The abolition of this monopoly would fill its beneficiaries with a wholesome fear of competition which would cause them to be satisfied with pay for their services equal to that which other laborers get for theirs, and to secure it by placing their products and works on the market at the outset at prices so low that their lines of business would be no more tempting to competitors than any other lines.

The development of the economic programme which consists in the destruction of these monopolies and the substitution for them of the freest competition led its authors to a perception of the fact that all their thought rested upon a very fundamental principle, the freedom of the individual, his right of sovereignty over himself, his products, and his affairs, and of rebellion against the dictation of external authority. Just as the idea of taking capital away from individuals and giving it to the government started Marx in a path which ends in making the government everything and the individual nothing, so the idea of taking capital away from government-protected monopolies and putting it within easy reach of all individuals started Warren and Proudhon in a path which ends in making the individual everything and the government nothing. If the individual has a right to govern himself, all external government is tyranny.   Hence the necessity of abolishing the State.   This was the logical conclusion to which Warren and Proudhon were forced, and it became the fundamental article of their political philosophy.   It is the doctrine which Proudhon named An-archism, a word derived from the Greek, and meaning, not necessarily absence of order, as is generally supposed, but absence of rule.   The Anarchists are simply unterrified Jeffersonian Democrats. They believe that " the best government is that which governs least," and that that which governs least is no government at all.   Even the simple police function of protecting person and property they deny to governments supported by compulsory taxation.   Protection they look upon as a thing to be secured, as long as it is necessary, by voluntary association and coöperation for self-defence, or as a commodity to be purchased, like any other commodity, of those who offer the best article at the lowest price.   In their view it is in itself an invasion of the individual to compel him to pay for or suffer a protection against invasion that he has not asked for and does not desire.   And they further claim that protection will become a drug in the market, after poverty and consequently crime have disappeared through the realization of their economic programme.   Compulsory taxation is to them the life-principle of all the monopolies, and passive, but organized, resistance to the tax-collector they contemplate, when the proper time comes, as one of the most effective methods of accomplishing their purposes.

Their attitude on this is a key to their attitude on all other questions of a political or social nature.   In religion they are atheistic as far as their own opinions are concerned, for they look upon divine authority and the religious sanction of morality as the chief pretexts put forward by the privileged classes for the exercise of human authority.   " If God exists," said Proudhon, " he is man's enemy."   And, in contrast to Voltaire's famous epigram, " If God did not exist, it would be necessary to invent him," the great Russian Nihilist, Michael Bakounine, placed this antithetical proposition: " If God existed, it would be necessary to abolish him."   But although, viewing the divine hierarchy as a contradiction of Anarchy, they do not believe in it, the Anarchists none the less firmly believe in the liberty to believe in it.   Any denial of religious freedom they squarely oppose.

Upholding thus the right of every individual to be or select his own priest, they likewise uphold his right to be or select his own doctor.   No monopoly in theology, no monopoly in medicine. Competition everywhere and always ; spiritual advice and medical advice alike to stand or fall on their own merits. And not only in medicine, but in hygiene, must this principle of liberty be followed. The individual may decide for himself not only what to do to get well, but what to do to keep well. No external power must dictate to him what he must and must not eat, drink, wear, or do.

Nor does the Anarchistic scheme furnish any code of morals to be imposed upon the individual. " Mind your own business " is its only moral law. Interference with another's business is a crime and the only crime, and as such may properly be resisted. In accordance with this view the Anarchists look upon attempts to arbitrarily suppress vice as in themselves crimes. They believe liberty and the resultant social well-being to be a sure cure for all the vices. But they recognize the right of the drunkard, the gambler, the rake, and the harlot to live their lives until they shall freely choose to abandon them.

In the matter of the maintenance and rearing of children the Anarchists would neither institute the communistic nursery which the State Socialists favor nor keep the communistic school system which now prevails. The nurse and the teacher, like the doctor and the preacher, must be selected voluntarily, and their services must be paid for by those who patronize them. Parental rights must not be taken away, and parental responsibilities must not be foisted upon others.

Even in so delicate a matter as that of the relations of the sexes the Anarchists do not shrink from the application of their principle. They acknowledge and defend the right of any man and woman, or any men and women, to love each other for as long or as short a time as they can, will, or may. To them legal marriage and legal divorce are equal absurdities. They look forward to a time when every individual, whether man or woman, shall be self-supporting, and when each shall have an independent home of his or her own, whether it be a separate house or rooms in a house with others; when the love relations between these independent individuals shall be as varied as are individual inclinations and attractions; and when the children born of these relations shall belong exclusively to the mothers until old enough to belong to themselves.

Such are the main features of the Anarchistic social ideal. There is wide difference of opinion among those who hold it as to the best method of obtaining it. Time forbids the treatment of that phase of the subject here. I will simply call attention to the fact that it is an ideal utterly inconsistent

with that of those Communists who falsely call themselves
Anarchists while at the same time advocating a *régime* of
Archism fully as despotic as that of the State Socialists themselves. And it is an ideal that can be as little advanced by
the forcible expropriation recommended by John Most and
Prince Kropotkine as retarded by the brooms of those Mrs.
Partingtons of the bench who sentence them to prison; an
ideal which the martyrs of Chicago did far more to help by
their glorious death upon the gallows for the common cause
of Socialism than by their unfortunate advocacy during their
lives, in the name of Anarchism, of force as a revolutionary
agent and authority as a safeguard of the new social order.
The Anarchists believe in liberty both as end and means, and
are hostile to anything that antagonizes it.

I should not undertake to summarize this altogether too
summary exposition of Socialism from the standpoint of Anarchism, did I not find the task already accomplished for me by
a brilliant French journalist and historian, Ernest Lesigne, in
the form of a series of crisp antitheses; by reading which to
you as a conclusion of this lecture I hope to deepen the impression which it has been my endeavor to make.

" There are two Socialisms.

" One is communistic, the other solidaritarian.

" One is dictatorial, the other libertarian.

" One is metaphysical, the other positive.

" One is dogmatic, the other scientific.

" One is emotional, the other reflective.

" One is destructive, the other constructive.

" Both are in pursuit of the greatest possible welfare for
all.

" One aims to establish happiness for all, the other to enable
each to be happy in his own way.

" The first regards the State as a society *sui generis*, of an
especial essence, the product of a sort of divine right outside
of and above all society, with special rights and able to exact
special obediences; the second considers the State as an association like any other, generally managed worse than others.

" The first proclaims the sovereignty of the State, the second
recognizes no sort of sovereign.

" One wishes all monopolies to be held by the State; the
other wishes the abolition of all monopolies.

" One wishes the governed class to become the governing
class ; the other wishes the disappearance of classes.

" Both declare that the existing state of things cannot last.

" The first considers revolution as the indispensable agent of

evolution ; the second teaches that repression alone turns evolution into revolution.

" The first has faith in a cataclysm.

" The second knows that social progress will result from the
free play of individual efforts.

" Both understand that we are entering upon a new historic
phase.

" One wishes that there should be none but proletaires.

" The other wishes that there should be no more proletaires.

" The first wishes to take everything from everybody.

" The second wishes to leave each in possession of his own.

" The one wishes to expropriate everybody.

" The other wishes everybody to be a proprietor.

" The first says : ' Do as the government wishes.'

" The second says : ' Do as you wish yourself.'

" The former threatens with despotism.

" The latter promises liberty.

" The former makes the citizen the subject of the State.

" The latter makes the State the employee of the citizen.

" One proclaims that labor pains will be necessary to the
birth of the new world.

" The other declares that real progress will not cause suffering to any one.

" The first has confidence in social war.

" The other believes only in the works of peace.

" One aspires to command, to regulate, to legislate.

" The other wishes to attain the minimum of command, of
regulation, of legislation.

" One would be followed by the most atrocious of reactions.

" The other opens unlimited horizons to progress.

" The first will fail; the other will succeed.

" Both desire equality.

" One by lowering heads that are too high.

" The other by raising heads that are too low.

" One sees equality under a common yoke.

" The other will secure equality in complete liberty.

" One is intolerant, the other tolerant.

" One frightens, the other reassures.

" The first wishes to instruct everybody.

" The second wishes to enable everybody to instruct himself.

" The first wishes to support everybody.

" The second wishes to enable everybody to support himself.

" One says :

" The land to the State.

" The mine to the State.

"The tool to the State.

"The product to the State.

"The other says:

"The land to the cultivator.

"The mine to the miner.

"The tool to the laborer.

"The product to the producer.

"There are only these two Socialisms.

"One is the infancy of Socialism; the other is its manhood.

"One is already the past; the other is the future.

"One will give place to the other.

"To-day each of us must choose for one or the other of these two Socialisms, or else confess that he is not a Socialist."

THE INDIVIDUAL, SOCIETY, AND
THE STATE.

RELATION OF THE STATE TO THE INDIVIDUAL.*

[*Liberty*, November 15, 1890.]

LADIES AND GENTLEMEN:—Presumably the honor which you have done me in inviting me to address you to-day upon " The Relation of the State to the Individual" is due principally to the fact that circumstances have combined to make me somewhat conspicuous as an exponent of the theory of Modern Anarchism, —a theory which is coming to be more and more regarded as one of the few that are tenable as a basis of political and social life. In its name, then, I shall speak to you in discussing this question, which either underlies or closely touches almost every practical problem that confronts this generation. The future of the tariff, of taxation, of finance, of property, of woman, of marriage, of the family, of the suffrage, of education, of invention, of literature, of science, of the arts, of personal habits, of private character, of ethics, of religion, will be determined by the conclusion at which mankind shall arrive as to whether and how far the individual owes allegiance to the State.

Anarchism, in dealing with this subject, has found it necessary, first of all, to define its terms. Popular conceptions of the terminology of politics are incompatible with the rigorous exactness required in scientific investigation. To be sure, a departure from the popular use of language is accompanied by the risk of misconception by the multitude, who persistently ignore the new definitions; but, on the other hand, conformity thereto is attended by the still more deplorable alternative of confusion in the eyes of the competent, who would be justified in attributing inexactness of thought where there is inexactness of expression. Take the term "State," for instance, with which we are especially concerned to-day. It is a word

* An address delivered before the Unitarian Ministers' Institute, at the annual session held in Salem, Mass., October 14, 1890, at which addresses on the same subject were also delivered by Rev. W. D. P. Bliss, from the standpoint of Christian Socialism, and President E. Benjamin Andrews, of Brown University, from the standpoint of State regulation,

that is on every lip. But how many of those who use it have
any idea of what they mean by it? And, of the few who have,
how various are their conceptions! We designate by the term
"State" institutions that embody absolutism in its extreme
form and institutions that temper it with more or less liberality.
We apply the word alike to institutions that do nothing but
aggress and to institutions that, besides aggressing, to some extent protect and defend. But which is the State's essential
function, aggression or defence, few seem to know or care.
Some champions of the State evidently consider aggression its
principle, although they disguise it alike from themselves and
from the people under the term "administration," which they
wish to extend in every possible direction. Others, on the contrary, consider defence its principle, and wish to limit it accordingly to the performance of police duties. Still others
seem to think that it exists for both aggression and defence,
combined in varying proportions according to the momentary
interests, or maybe only whims, of those happening to control
it. Brought face to face with these diverse views, the Anarchists, whose mission in the world is the abolition of aggression
and all the evils that result therefrom, perceived that, to be
understood, they must attach some definite and avowed significance to the terms which they are obliged to employ, and especially to the words "State" and "government." Seeking,
then, the elements common to all the institutions to which the
name "State" has been applied, they have found them two in
number: first, aggression; second, the assumption of sole authority over a given area and all within it, exercised generally
for the double purpose of more complete oppression of its subjects and extension of its boundaries. That this second element is common to all States, I think, will not be denied,—at
least, I am not aware that any State has ever tolerated a rival
State within its borders; and it seems plain that any State
which should do so would thereby cease to be a State and to be
considered as such by any. The exercise of authority over
the same area by two States is a contradiction. That the first
element, aggression, has been and is common to all States will
probably be less generally admitted. Nevertheless, I shall not
attempt to re-enforce here the conclusion of Spencer, which is
gaining wider acceptance daily,—that the State had its origin
in aggression, and has continued as an aggressive institution
from its birth. Defence was an afterthought, prompted by necessity; and its introduction as a State function, though effected
doubtless with a view to the strengthening of the State, was
really and in principle the initiation of the State's destruction.

Its growth in importance is but an evidence of the tendency of progress toward the abolition of the State. Taking this view of the matter, the Anarchists contend that defence is not an essential of the State, but that aggression is. Now what is aggression? Aggression is simply another name for government. Aggression, invasion, government, are interconvertible terms. The essence of government is control, or the attempt to control. He who attempts to control another is a governor, an aggressor, an invader; and the nature of such invasion is not changed, whether it is made by one man upon another man, after the manner of the ordinary criminal, or by one man upon all other men, after the manner of an absolute monarch, or by all other men upon one man, after the manner of a modern democracy. On the other hand, he who resists another's attempt to control is not an aggressor, an invader, a governor, but simply a defender, a protector; and the nature of such resistance is not changed whether it be offered by one man to another man, as when one repels a criminal's onslaught, or by one man to all other men, as when one declines to obey an oppressive law, or by all other men to one man, as when a subject people rises against a despot, or as when the members of a community voluntarily unite to restrain a criminal. This distinction between invasion and resistance, between government and defence, is vital. Without it there can be no valid philosophy of politics. Upon this distinction and the other considerations just outlined, the Anarchists frame the desired definitions. This, then, is the Anarchistic definition of government: the subjection of the non-invasive individual to an external will. And this is the Anarchistic definition of the State: the embodiment of the principle of invasion in an individual, or a band of individuals, assuming to act as representatives or masters of the entire people within a given area. As to the meaning of the remaining term in the subject under discussion, the word "individual," I think there is little difficulty. Putting aside the subtleties in which certain metaphysicians have indulged, one may use this word without danger of being misunderstood. Whether the definitions thus arrived at prove generally acceptable or not is a matter of minor consequence. I submit that they are reached scientifically, and serve the purpose of a clear conveyance of thought. The Anarchists, having by their adoption taken due care to be explicit, are entitled to have their ideas judged in the light of these definitions.

Now comes the question proper : What relations should exist between the State and the individual? The general

method of determining these is to apply some theory of ethics
involving a basis of moral obligation. In this method the
Anarchists have no confidence. The idea of moral obligation, of inherent rights and duties, they totally discard.
They look upon all obligations, not as moral, but as social,
and even then not really as obligations except as these have
been consciously and voluntarily assumed. If a man makes
an agreement with men, the latter may combine to hold him
to his agreement ; but, in the absence of such agreement, no
man, so far as the Anarchists are aware, has made any agreement with God or with any other power of any order whatsoever. The Anarchists are not only utilitarians, but egoists
in the farthest and fullest sense. So far as inherent right is
concerned, might is its only measure. Any man, be his name
Bill Sykes or Alexander Romanoff, and any set of men,
whether the Chinese highbinders or the Congress of the
United States, have the right, if they have the power, to kill
or coerce other men and to make the entire world subservient
to their ends. Society's right to enslave the individual and
the individual's right to enslave society are unequal only because their powers are unequal. This position being subversive of all systems of religion and morality, of course I
cannot expect to win immediate assent thereto from the audience which I am addressing to-day; nor does the time at my
disposal allow me to sustain it by an elaborate, or even a summary, examination of the foundations of ethics. Those who
desire a greater familiarity with this particular phase of the
subject should read a profound German work, "*Der Einzige
und sein Eigenthum*," written years ago by a comparatively unknown author, Dr. Caspar Schmidt, whose *nom de plume* was
Max Stirner. Read only by a few scholars, the book is buried
in obscurity, but is destined to a resurrection that perhaps
will mark an epoch.

If this, then, were a question of right, it would be, according to the Anarchists, purely a question of strength. But,
fortunately, it is not a question of right : it is a question of
expediency, of knowledge, of science,—the science of living
together, the science of society. The history of humanity
has been largely one long and gradual discovery of the fact
that the individual is the gainer by society exactly in proportion as society is free, and of the law that the condition of a
permanent and harmonious society is the greatest amount of
individual liberty compatible with equality of liberty. The
average man of each new generation has said to himself more
clearly and consciously than his predecessor : " My neighbor

is not my enemy, but my friend, and I am his, if we would but mutually recognize the fact.   We help each other to a better, fuller, happier living ; and this service might be greatly increased if we would cease to restrict, hamper, and oppress each other.   Why can we not agree to let each live his own life,neither of us transgressing the limit that separates our individualities ? "   It is by this reasoning that mankind is approaching the real social contract, which is not, as Rousseau thought, the origin of society, but rather the outcome of a long social experience, the fruit of its follies and disasters.   It is obvious that this contract, this social law, developed to its perfection, excludes all aggression, all violation of equality of liberty, all invasion of every kind.   Considering this contract in connection with the Anarchistic definition of the State as the embodiment of the principle of invasion, we see that the State is antagonistic to society ; and, society being essential to individual life and development, the conclusion leaps to the eyes that the relation of the State to the individual and of the individual to the State must be one of hostility, enduring till the State shall perish.

" But," it will be asked of the Anarchists at this point in the argument, " what shall be done with those individuals who undoubtedly will persist in violating the social law by invading their neighbors ? "   The Anarchists answer that the abolition of the State will leave in existence a defensive association, resting no longer on a compulsory but on a voluntary basis, which will restrain invaders by any means that may prove necessary. " But that is what we have now," is the rejoinder.   " You really want, then, only a change of name ? "   Not so fast, please. Can it be soberly pretended for a moment that the State, even as it exists here in America, is purely a defensive institution ? Surely not, save by those who see of the State only its most palpable manifestation,—the policeman on the street-corner. And one would not have to watch him very closely to see the error of this claim.   Why, the very first act of the State, the compulsory assessment and collection of taxes, is itself an aggression, a violation of equal liberty, and, as such, vitiates every subsequent act, even those acts which would be purely defensive if paid for out of a treasury filled by voluntary contributions.   How is it possible to sanction, under the law of equal liberty, the confiscation of a man's earnings to pay for protection which he has not sought and does not desire ?   And, if this is an outrage, what name shall we give to such confiscation when the victim is given, instead of bread, a stone, instead of protection, oppression ?   To force a man to pay for

the violation of his own liberty is indeed an addition of insult
to injury. But that is exactly what the State is doing. Read
the "Congressional Record"; follow the proceedings of the
State legislatures ; examine our statute-books; test each act
separately by the law of equal liberty,—you will find that a
good nine-tenths of existing legislation serves, not to enforce
that fundamental social law, but either to prescribe the individual's personal habits, or, worse still, to create and sustain
commercial, industrial, financial, and proprietary monopolies
which deprive labor of a large part of the reward that it
would receive in a perfectly free market. "To be governed,"
says Proudhon, "is to be watched, inspected, spied, directed,
law-ridden, regulated, penned up, indoctrinated, preached at,
checked, appraised, sized, censured, commanded, by beings
who have neither title nor knowledge nor virtue. To be governed is to have every operation, every transaction, every
movement noted, registered, counted, rated, stamped, measured, numbered, assessed, licensed, refused, authorized, in-
dorsed, admonished, prevented, reformed, redressed, corrected.
To be governed is, under pretext of public utility and in the
name of the general interest, to be laid under contribution,
drilled, fleeced, exploited, monopolized, extorted from, exhausted, hoaxed, robbed ; then, upon the slightest resistance,
at the first word of complaint, to be repressed, fined, vilified,
annoyed, hunted down, pulled about, beaten, disarmed, bound,
imprisoned, shot, mitrailleused, judged, condemned, banished,
sacrificed, sold, betrayed, and, to crown all, ridiculed, derided,
outraged, dishonored." And I am sure I do not need to
point out to you the existing laws that correspond to and justify nearly every count in Proudhon's long indictment. How
thoughtless, then, to assert that the existing political order is
of a purely defensive character instead of the aggressive State
which the Anarchists aim to abolish !

This leads to another consideration that bears powerfully
upon the problem of the invasive individual, who is such a
bugbear to the opponents of Anarchism. Is it not such treatment as has just been described that is largely responsible for
his existence ? I have heard or read somewhere of an inscrip-
tion written for a certain charitable institution:

> " This hospital a pious person built,
> But first he made the poor wherewith to fill't."

And so, it seems to me, it is with our prisons. They are
filled with criminals which our virtuous State has made what

they are by its iniquitous laws, its grinding monopolies, and
the horrible social conditions that result from them.   We
enact many laws that manufacture criminals, and then a few
that punish them.   Is it too much to expect that the new
social conditions which must follow the abolition of all interference with the production and distribution of wealth will in
the end so change the habits and propensities of men that our
jails and prisons, our policemen and our soldiers,—in a word,
our whole machinery and outfit of defence,—will be superfluous?   That, at least, is the Anarchists' belief.   It sounds
Utopian, but it really rests on severely economic grounds.
To-day, however, time is lacking to explain the Anarchistic
view of the dependence of usury, and therefore of poverty,
upon monopolistic privilege, especially the banking privilege,
and to show how an intelligent minority, educated in the principle of Anarchism and determined to exercise that right to ignore the State upon which Spencer, in his " Social Statics," so
ably and admirably insists, might, by setting at defiance the
National and State banking prohibitions, and establishing a
Mutual Bank in competition with the existing monopolies, take
the first and most important step in the abolition of usury and
of the State.   Simple as such a step would seem, from it all
the rest would follow.

A half-hour is a very short time in which to discuss the
relation of the State to the individual, and I must ask your
pardon for the brevity of my dealing with a succession of considerations each of which needs an entire essay for its development.   If I have outlined the argument intelligibly, I
have accomplished all that I expected.   But, in the hope of im-
pressing the idea of the true social contract more vividly upon
your minds, in conclusion I shall take the liberty of reading
another page from Proudhon, to whom I am indebted for
most of what I know, or think I know, upon this subject.
Contrasting authority with free contract, he says, in his " General Idea of the Revolution of the Nineteenth Century " : —

"Of the distance that separates these two *régimes*, we may
judge by the difference in their styles.

" One of the most solemn moments in the evolution of
the principle of authority is that of the promulgation of the
Decalogue.   The voice of the angel commands the People,
prostrate at the foot of Sinai:—

" Thou shalt worship the Eternal, and only the Eternal.

" Thou shalt swear only by him.

" Thou shalt keep his holidays, and thou shalt pay his
tithes.

" Thou shalt honor thy father and thy mother.

" Thou shalt not kill.

" Thou shalt not steal.

" Thou shalt not commit adultery.

" Thou shalt not bear false witness.

" Thou shalt not covet or calumniate.

" For the Eternal ordains it, and it is the Eternal who has made you what you are. The Eternal is alone sovereign, alone wise, alone worthy; the Eternal punishes and rewards. It is in the power of the Eternal to render you happy or unhappy at his will.

" All legislations have adopted this style; all, speaking to man, employ the sovereign formula. The Hebrew commands in the future, the Latin in the imperative, the Greek in the infinitive. The moderns do not otherwise. The tribune of the parliament-house is a Sinai as infallible and as terrible as that of Moses; whatever the law may be, from whatever lips it may come, it is sacred once it has been proclaimed by that prophetic trumpet, which with us is the majority.

" Thou shalt not assemble.

" Thou shalt not print.

" Thou shalt not read.

" Thou shalt respect thy representatives and thy officials, which the hazard of the ballot or the good pleasure of the State shall have given you.

" Thou shalt obey the laws which they in their wisdom shall have made.

" Thou shalt pay thy taxes faithfully.

" And thou shalt love the Government, thy Lord and thy God, with all thy heart and with all thy soul and with all thy mind, because the Government knows better than thou what thou art, what thou art worth, what is good for thee, and because it has the power to chastise those who disobey its commandments, as well as to reward unto the fourth generation those who make themselves agreeable to it.

" With the Revolution it is quite different.

" The search for first causes and for final causes is eliminated from economic science as from the natural sciences.

" The idea of Progress replaces, in philosophy, that of the Absolute.

" Revolution succeeds Revelation.

" Reason, assisted by Experience, discloses to man the laws of Nature and Society; then it says to him:—

" These laws are those of necessity itself. No man has made them; no man imposes them upon you. They have been gradually discovered, and I exist only to bear testimony to them.

" If you observe them, you will be just and good.

" If you violate them, you will be unjust and wicked.

" I offer you no other motive.

" Already, among your fellows, several have recognized that justice is better, for each and for all, than iniquity; and they have agreed with each other to mutually keep faith and right,— that is, to respect the rules of transaction which the nature of things indicates to them as alone capable of assuring them, in the largest measure, well-being, security, peace.

" Do you wish to adhere to their compact, to form a part of their society ?

" Do you promise to respect the honor, the liberty, and the goods of your brothers ?

" Do you promise never to appropriate, either by violence, or by fraud, or by usury, or by speculation, the product or the possession of another ?

" Do you promise never to lie and deceive, either in justice, or in business, or in any of your transactions ?

" You are free to accept or to refuse.

" If you refuse, you become a part of the society of savages. Outside of the communion of the human race, you become an object of suspicion. Nothing protects you. At the slightest insult, the first comer may lift his hand against you without incurring any other accusation than that of cruelty needlessly practised upon a brute.

" On the contrary, if you swear to the compact, you become a part of the society of free men. All your brothers enter into an engagement with you, promise you fidelity, friendship, aid, service, exchange. In case of infraction, on their part or on yours, through negligence, passion, or malice, you are responsible to each other for the damage as well as the scandal and the insecurity of which you have been the cause : this responsibility may extend, according to the gravity of the perjury or the repetitions of the offence, even to excommunication and to death.

" The law is clear, the sanction still more so. Three articles, which make but one,—that is the whole social contract. Instead of making oath to God and his prince, the citizen swears upon his conscience, before his brothers, and before Humanity. Between these two oaths there is the same difference as between slavery and liberty, faith and science, courts and justice, usury and labor, government and economy, non-existence and being, God and man."

OUR PURPOSE.*

[*Liberty*, August 6, 1881.]

LIBERTY enters the field of journalism to speak for herself because she finds no one willing to speak for her. She hears no voice that always champions her ; she knows no pen that always writes in her defence ; she sees no hand that is always lifted to avenge her wrongs or vindicate her rights. Many claim to speak in her name, but few really understand her. Still fewer have the courage and the opportunity to consistently fight for her. Her battle, then, is her own to wage and win. She accepts it fearlessly and with a·determined spirit.

Her foe, Authority, takes many shapes, but, broadly speaking, her enemies divide themselves into three classes : first, those who abhor her both as a means and as an end of progress, opposing her openly, avowedly, sincerely, consistently, universally ; second, those who profess to believe in her as a means of progress, but who accept her only so far as they think she will subserve their own selfish interests, denying her and her blessings to the rest of the world ; third, those who distrust her as a means of progress, believing in her only as an end to be obtained by first trampling upon, violating, and outraging her. These three phases of opposition to Liberty are met in almost every sphere of thought and human activity. Good representatives of the first are seen in the Catholic Church and the Russian autocracy ; of the second, in the Protestant Church and the Manchester school of politics and political economy ; of the third, in the atheism of Gambetta and the socialism of Karl Marx.

Through these forms of authority another line of demarcation runs transversely, separating the divine from the human ; or, better still, the religious from the secular. Liberty's victory over the former is well-nigh achieved. Last century Voltaire brought the authority of the supernatural into disrepute. The Church has been declining ever since. Her teeth are drawn, and though she seems still to show here and there vigorous signs of life, she does so in the violence of the death-agony upon her, and soon her power will be felt no more. It is human authority that hereafter is to be dreaded, and the State, its organ, that in the future is to be feared. Those who have lost their faith in gods

---

* *Liberty's* salutatory.

only to put it in governments; those who have ceased to be Church-worshippers only to become State-worshippers; those who have abandoned pope for king or czar, and priest for president or parliament,—have indeed changed their battle-ground, but none the less are foes of Liberty still. The Church has become an object of derision; the State must be made equally so. The State is said by some to be a "necessary evil"; it must be made unnecessary. This century's battle, then, is with the State: the State, that debases man; the State, that prostitutes woman; the State, that corrupts children; the State, that trammels love; the State, that stifles thought; the State, that monopolizes land; the State, that limits credit; the State, that restricts exchange; the State, that gives idle capital the power of increase, and, through interest, rent, profit, and taxes, robs industrious labor of its products.

How the State does these things, and how it can be prevented from doing them, Liberty proposes to show in more detail hereafter in the prosecution of her pupose. Enough to say now that monopoly and privilege must be destroyed, opportunity afforded, and competition encouraged. This is Liberty's work, and "Down with Authority" her war-cry.

CONTRACT OR ORGANISM, WHAT'S THAT TO US?

[*Liberty*, July 30, 1887.]

SOME very interesting and valuable discussion is going on in the London *Jus* concerning the question of compulsory *versus* voluntary taxation. In the issue of June 17 there is a communication from F. W. Read, in which the following passage occurs:

The voluntary taxation proposal really means the dissolution of the State into its constituent atoms, and leaving them to recombine in some way or no way, just as it may happen. There would be nothing to prevent the existence of five or six "States" in England, and members of all these "States" might be living in the same house! The proposal is, it appears to me, the outcome of an idea in the minds of those who propound it that the State is, or ought to be, founded on contract, just as a joint-stock company is. It is a similar idea to the defunct "original contract" theory. It was thought the State must rest upon a contract. There had been no contract in historic times; it was therefore assumed that there had been a prehistoric contract. The voluntary taxationist says there never has been any contract; therefore the State has never had any ethical basis; therefore we will not make a contract. The explanation of the

whole matter, I believe, is that given by Mr. Wordsworth Donisthorpe,—
viz., that the State is a social organism, evolved as every other organism
is evolved, and not requiring any more than other organisms to be based
upon a contract either original or contemporary.

The idea that the voluntary taxationist objects to the State
precisely because it does not rest on contract, and wishes to
substitute contract for it, is strictly correct, and I am glad to
see (for the first time, if my memory serves me) an opponent
grasp it. But Mr. Read obscures his statement by his previous
remark that the proposal of voluntary taxation is "the outcome of an idea . . . that the State *is, or* ought to be, founded
on contract." This would be true if the words which I have
italicized should be omitted. It was the insertion of these
words that furnished the writer a basis for his otherwise
groundless analogy between the Anarchists and the followers
of Rousseau. The latter hold that the State originated in a
contract, and that the people of to-day, though they did not
make it, are bound by it. The Anarchists, on the contrary,
deny that any such contract was ever made ; declare that, had
one ever been made, it could not impose a shadow of obligation on those who had no hand in making it; and claim the
right to contract for themselves as they please. The position
that a man may make his own contracts, far from being
analogous to that which makes him subject to contracts made
by others, is its direct antithesis.

It is perfectly true that voluntary taxation would not
necessarily "prevent the existence of five or six 'States' in
England," and that "members of all these 'States' might be
living in the same house." But I see no reason for Mr. Read's
exclamation point after this remark. What of it ? There are
many more than five or six Churches in England, and it frequently happens that members of several of them live in the
same house. There are many more than five or six insurance
companies in England, and it is by no means uncommon for
members of the same family to insure their lives and goods
against accident or fire in different companies. Does any
harm come of it ? Why, then, should there not be a considerable number of defensive associations in England, in which
people, even members of the same family, might insure their
lives and goods against murderers or thieves ? Though Mr.
Read has grasped one idea of the voluntary taxationists, I fear
that he sees another much less clearly,—namely, the idea that
defence is a service, like any other service ; that it is labor both
useful and desired, and therefore an economic commodity sub-

ject to the law of supply and demand ; that in a free market this commodity would be furnished at the cost of production; that, competition prevailing, patronage would go to those who furnished the best article at the lowest price; that the production and sale of this commodity are now monopolized by the State; that the State, like almost all monopolists, charges exorbitant prices; that, like almost all monopolists, it supplies a worthless, or nearly worthless, article ; that, just as the monopolist of a food product often furnishes poison instead of nutriment, so the State takes advantage of its monopoly of defence to furnish invasion instead of protection ; that, just as the patrons of the one pay to be poisoned, so the patrons of the other pay to be enslaved ; and, finally, that the State exceeds all its fellow-monopolists in the extent of its villany because it enjoys the unique privilege of compelling all people to buy its product whether they want it or not. If, then, five or six "States" were to hang out their shingles, the people, I fancy, would be able to buy the very best kind of security at a reasonable price. And what is more,—the better their services, the less they would be needed ; so that the multiplication of "States" involves the abolition of the State.

All these considerations, however, are disposed of, in Mr. Read's opinion, by his final assertion that "the State is a social organism." He considers this "the explanation of the whole matter." But for the life of me I can see in it nothing but another irrelevant remark. Again I ask: What of it? Suppose the State is an organism,—what then ? What is the inference ? That the State is therefore permanent ? But what is history but a record of the dissolution of organisms and the birth and growth of others to be dissolved in turn ? Is the State exempt from this order ? If so, why? What proves it ? The State an organism? Yes ; so is a tiger. But unless I meet him when I haven't my gun, his organism will speedily disorganize. The State is a tiger seeking to devour the people, and they must either kill or cripple it. Their own safety depends upon it. But Mr. Read says it can't be done. "By no possibility can the power of the State be restrained." This must be very disappointing to Mr. Donisthorpe and *Jus*, who are working to restrain it. If Mr. Read is right, their occupation is gone. Is he right ? Unless he can demonstrate it, the voluntary taxationists and the Anarchists will continue their work, cheered by the belief that the compulsory and invasive State is doomed to die.

THE NATURE OF THE STATE.

[*Liberty*, October 22, 1887.]

BELOW is reprinted from the London *Jus* the reply of F. W. Read to the editorial in No. 104 of *Liberty*, entitled "Contract or Organism, What's That to Us?"

To the Editor of Jus :

SIR,—Referring to Mr. Tucker's criticisms on my letters in *Jus* dealing with Voluntary Taxation, the principle of a State organism seems to be at the bottom of the controversy. I will therefore deal with that first, although it comes last in Mr. Tucker's article. Mr. Tucker asks whether the State being an organism makes it permanent and exempt from dissolution. Certainly not ; I never said it did. But cannot Mr. Tucker see that dissolving an organism is something different from dissolving a collection of atoms with no organic structure ? If the people of a State had been thrown together yesterday or the day before, no particular harm would come from splitting them into numerous independent sections ; but when a people has grown together generation after generation, and century after century, to break up the adaptations and correlations that have been established can scarcely be productive of any good results. The tiger is an organism, says Mr. Tucker, but if shot he will be speedily disorganized. Quite so; but nobody supposes that the atoms of the tiger's body derive any benefit from the process. Why should the atoms of the body politic derive any advantage from the dissolution of the organism of which *they* form a part ? That Mr. Tucker should put the State on a level with churches and insurance companies is simply astounding. Does Mr. Tucker really think that five or six " States " could exist side by side with the same convenience as an equal number of churches ? The difficulty of determining what " State " an individual belonged to would be practically insuperable. How are assaults and robberies to be dealt with ? Is a man to be tried by the " State "of which he is a citizen, or by the " State " of the party aggrieved ? If by his own, how is a police officer of that " State " to know whether a certain individual belongs to it or not ? The difficulties are so enormous that the State would soon be reformed on the old lines. Another great difficulty would be that the State would find it impossible to make a contract. If the State is regarded as a mere collection of individuals, who will lend money on State security ? The reason the State is trusted at all is because it is regarded as something over and above the individuals who happen to compose it at any given time ; because we feel that, while individuals die, the State remains, and that the State will honor State contracts, even if made for purposes that are disapproved by those who are the atoms of the State organism. I have, indeed, heard it said that it would be a good thing if the State did find it impossible to pledge its credit; but good credit seems as useful to a State as to an individual. Again, is it no advantage to us to be able to make treaties with foreign countries ? But what country will make a treaty with a mere mass of individuals, a large portion of whom will be gone in ten years' time ?

But apart from the question of organism or no organism, does not history show us a continuous weakening of the State in some directions, and a continuous strengthening in other directions? We find a gradual disappearance of the desire "to furnish invasion instead of protection," and, as the State ceases to do so, the more truly strong does it become, and the more vigorously does it carry out what I regard as its ultimate function,—that of protecting some against the aggression of others.

One word in conclusion as to restraining the power of the State. Of course by restraint I mean legal restraint. For instance, you could not deprive the State of its taxing power by passing a law to that effect. The framers of the Act of Union between Great Britain and Ireland tried to restrain the power of the State to disestablish the Irish Church; but the Irish Church was disestablished for all that. What Individualists are trying to do is to show the State that, when it regulates factories and coal mines, and a thousand and one other things, it is acting against its own interests. When the State has learned the lesson, the meddling will cease. If Mr. Tucker chooses to call that restraining the State, he can do so; I don't.   Yours truly, etc.,   F. W. READ.

In answer to Mr. Read's statement (which, if, with all its implications, it were true, would be a valid and final answer to the Anarchists) that "dissolving an organism is something different from dissolving a collection of atoms with no organic structure," I cannot do better than quote the following passage from an article by J. Wm. Lloyd in No. 107 of *Liberty*:

It appears to me that this universe is but a vast aggregate of individuals; of individuals simple and primary, and of individuals complex, secondary, tertiary, etc., formed by the aggregation of primary individuals or of individuals of a lesser degree of complexity. Some of these individuals of a high degree of complexity are true individuals, *concrete*, so united that the lesser organisms included cannot exist apart from the main organism; while others are imperfect, *discrete*, the included organisms existing fairly well, quite as well, or better, apart than united. In the former class are included many of the higher forms of vegetable and animal life, including man, and in the latter are included many lower forms of vegetable and animal life (quack-grass, tape-worms, etc.), and most societary organisms, governments, nations, churches, armies, etc.

Taking this indisputable view of the matter, it becomes clear that Mr. Read's statement about "dissolving an organism" is untrue while the word organism remains unqualified by some adjective equivalent to Mr. Lloyd's *concrete*. The question, then, is whether the State is a concrete organism. The Anarchists claim that it is not. If Mr. Read thinks that it is, the *onus probandi* is upon him. I judge that his error arises from a confusion of the State with society. That society is a concrete organism the Anarchists do not deny; on the contrary, they insist upon it. Consequently they have no intention or desire to abolish it. They know that its life is inseparable from the lives of individuals; that it is impossible to destroy one without destroying the other. But, though society cannot be destroyed, it can be greatly hampered and impeded in its operations, much to the disadvantage of the individuals composing it, and it meets its chief impediment in the State. The State, unlike society, is a discrete organism. If it should be destroyed to-morrow, individuals would still continue to exist. Production, exchange, and association would go on as before, but much more freely, and all those social functions upon which the individual is dependent would operate in his behalf more usefully than ever. The individual is not related to the State as the tiger's paw is related to the tiger. Kill the tiger, and the tiger's paw no longer performs its office; kill the State, and the individual still lives and satisfies his wants. As for society, the Anarchists would not kill it if they could, and could not if they would.

Mr. Read finds it astounding that I should "put the State on a level with churches and insurance companies." I find his astonishment amusing. Believers in compulsory religious systems were astounded when it was first proposed to put the church on a level with other associations. Now the only astonishment is—at least in the United States—that the church is allowed to stay at any other level. But the political superstition has replaced the religious superstition, and Mr. Read is under its sway.

I do not think " that five or six ' States ' could exist side by side with " *quite* " the same convenience as an equal number of churches." In the relations with which States have to do there is more chance for friction than in the simply religious sphere. But, on the other hand, the friction resulting from a multiplicity of States would be but a mole-hill compared with the mountain of oppression and injustice which is gradually heaped up by a single compulsory State. It would not be necessary for a police officer of a voluntary " State " to know to what " State " a given individual belonged, or whether he belonged to any. Voluntary " States " could, and probably would, authorize their executives to proceed against invasion, no matter who the invader or invaded might be. Mr. Read will probably object that the " State " to which the invader belonged might regard his arrest as itself an invasion, and proceed against the " State " which arrested him. Anticipation of such conflicts would probably result exactly in those treaties between " States " which Mr. Read looks upon as so desirable, and even in the establishment of federal tribunals, as courts of last resort, by the co-operation of the various " States," on the same voluntary principle in accordance with which the " States " themselves were organized.

Voluntary taxation, far from impairing the " State's " credit,

would strengthen it. In the first place, the simplification of
its functions would greatly reduce, and perhaps entirely
abolish, its need to borrow, and the power to borrow is generally inversely proportional to the steadiness of the need.   It
is usually the inveterate borrower who lacks credit.   In the
second place, the power of the State to repudiate, and still
continue its business, is dependent upon its power of compulsory taxation. It knows that, when it can no longer
borrow, it can at least tax its citizens up to the limit of
revolution.   In the third place, the State is trusted, not because it is over and above individuals, but because the lender
presumes that it desires to maintain its credit and will therefore pay its debts. This desire for credit will be stronger in
a "State" supported by voluntary taxation than in the State
which enforces taxation.

All the objections brought forward by Mr. Read (except
the organism argument) are mere difficulties of administrative detail, to be overcome by ingenuity, patience, dis-
cretion, and expedients.   They are not logical difficulties, not
difficulties of principle. They seem "enormous" to him ; but
so seemed the difficulties of freedom of thought two centuries
ago.   What does he think of the difficulties of the existing
régime ? Apparently he is as blind to them as is the Roman
Catholic to the difficulties of a State religion.   All these
"enormous" difficulties which arise in the fancy of the
objectors to the voluntary principle will gradually vanish
under the influence of the economic changes and well-distributed prosperity which will follow the adoption of that
principle.   This is what Proudhon calls "the dissolution of
government in the economic organism." It is too vast a subject for consideration here, but, if Mr. Read wishes to understand the Anarchistic theory of the process, let him study that
most wonderful of all the wonderful books of Proudhon, the
" Idée Générale de la Révolution au Dix-Neuvième Siècle."

It is true that "history shows a continuous weakening of
the State in some directions, and a continuous strengthening
in other directions."   At least such is the tendency, broadly
speaking, though this continuity is sometimes broken by
periods of reaction. This tendency is simply the progress of
evolution towards Anarchy. The State invades less and less,
and protects more and more. It is exactly in the line of this
process, and at the end of it, that the Anarchists demand the
abandonment of the last citadel of invasion by the substitution of voluntary for compulsory taxation.   When this step
is taken, the " State " will achieve its maximum strength as a

protector against aggression, and will maintain it as long as its services are needed in that capacity.

If Mr. Read, in saying that the power of the State cannot be restrained, simply meant that it cannot be legally restrained, his remark had no fitness as an answer to Anarchists and voluntary taxationists. They do not propose to legally restrain it. They propose to create a public sentiment that will make it impossible for the State to collect taxes by force or in any other way invade the individual. Regarding the State as an instrument of aggression, they do not expect to convince it that aggression is against its interests, but they do expect to convince individuals that it is against their interests to be invaded. If by this means they succeed in stripping the State of its invasive powers, they will be satisfied, and it is immaterial to them whether the means is described by the word "restraint" or by some other word. In fact, I have striven in this discussion to accommodate myself to Mr. Read's phraseology. For myself I do not think it proper to call voluntary associations States, but, enclosing the word in quotation marks, I have so used it because Mr. Read set the example.

A MISINTERPRETATION OF ANARCHISM.

[*Liberty*, March 8, 1890.]

ONE of the most interesting papers that come to this office is the *Personal Rights Journal* of London. Largely written by men like J. H. Levy and Wordsworth Donisthorpe, it could not be otherwise. Virtually it champions the same political faith that finds an advocate in *Liberty*. It means by individualism what *Liberty* means by Anarchism. That it does not realize this fact, and that it assumes Anarchism to be something other than complete individualism, is the principal difference between us. This misunderstanding of Anarchism is very clearly and cleverly exhibited in a passage which I copy from a keen and thought-provoking lecture on "The Outcome of Individualism," delivered by J. H. Levy before the National Liberal Club on January 10, 1890, and printed in the *Personal Rights Journal* of January and February :

If we are suffering from a poison, we find it advantageous to take a second poison, which acts as an antidote to the first. But, if we are wise, we limit our dose of the second poison so that the toxic effects of both combined are at the minimum. If we take more of it, it produces toxic effects of its own beyond those necessary to counteract, so far as possible, the first poison. If we take less of it, the first poison, to some extent, will do its bad work unchecked. This illustrates the position of the Individualist, against the Socialist on the one side and the Anarchist on the other. I recognize that government is an evil. It always means the employment of force against our fellow-man, and—at the very best— his subjection, over a larger or smaller extent of the field of conduct, to the will of a majority of his fellow-citizens. But if this organized or reg- ularized interference were utterly abolished, he would not escape from aggression. He would, in such a society as ours, be liable to far more violence and fraud, which would be a much worse evil than the inter- vention of government needs be. But when government pushes its in- terference beyond the point of maintaining the widest liberty equally for all citizens, it is itself the aggressor, and none the less so because its motives are good.

Names aside, the thing that Individualism favors, accord- ing to the foregoing, is organization to maintain the widest liberty equally for all citizens. Well, that is precisely what Anarchism favors. Individualism does not want such organ- ization any longer than is necessary. Neither does Anarchism. Mr. Levy's assumption that Anarchism does not want such organization at all arises from his failure to recognize the Anarchistic definition of government. Government has been defined repeatedly in these columns as the subjection of the *non-invasive* individual to a will not his own. The subjection of the *invasive* individual is not government, but resistance to and protection from government. By these definitions govern- ment is always an evil, but resistance to it is never an evil or a poison. Call such resistance an antidote if you will, but remember that not all antidotes are poisonous. The worst that can be said of resistance or protection is, not that it is an evil, but that it is a loss of productive force in a necessary effort to overcome evil. It can be called an evil only in the sense that needful and not especially healthful labor can be called a curse. The poison illustration, good enough with Mr. Levy's definitions, has no force with the Anarchistic use of terms.

Government is invasion, and the State, as defined in the last issue of *Liberty*, is the embodiment of invasion in an indi- vidual, or band of individuals, assuming to act as representa- tives or masters of the entire people within a given area. The Anarchists are opposed to all government, and especially to the State as the worst governor and chief invader. From *Liberty's* standpoint, there are not three positions, but two : one, that of the authoritarian Socialists, favoring government and the State ; the other, that of the Individualists *and* Anarchists, against government and the State.

It is true that Mr. Levy expressly accords liberty of definition, and therefore I should not have said a word if he had simply stated the Individualist position without misinterpreting the Anarchist position. But in view of this misinterpretation, I must ask him to correct it, unless he can show that my criticism is invalid.

I may add, in conclusion, that very probably the disposition of the Individualist to give greater prominence than does the Anarchist to the necessity of organization for protection is due to the fact that he seems to see less clearly than the Anarchist that the necessity for defence against individual invaders is largely and perhaps, in the end, wholly due to the oppressions of the invasive State, and that when the State falls, criminals will begin to disappear.

MR. LEVY'S MAXIMUM.

[*Liberty*, November 1, 1890.]

"WHATEVER else Anarchism may mean, it means that State coercion of peaceable citizens, into co-operation in restraining the activity of Bill Sikes, is to be condemned and ought to be abolished. Anarchism implies the right of an individual to stand aside and see a man murdered or a woman raped. It implies the right of the would-be passive accomplice of aggression to escape all coercion. It is true the Anarchist may voluntarily co-operate to check aggression ; but also he may not. *Quâ* Anarchist, he is within his right in withholding such co-operation, in leaving others to bear the burden of resistance to aggression, or in leaving the aggressor to triumph unchecked. Individualism, on the other hand, would not only restrain the active invader up to the point necessary to restore freedom to others, but would also coerce the man who would otherwise be a passive witness of, or conniver at, aggression into co-operation against his more active colleague."

The foregoing paragraph occurs in an ably-written article by Mr. J. H. Levy in the *Personal Rights Journal.* The writer's evident intention was to put Anarchism in an unfavorable light by stating its principles, or one of them, in a very offensive way. At the same time it was his intention also to be fair,—

that is, not to distort the doctrine of Anarchism,—and *he has not distorted it.* I reprint the paragraph in editorial type for the purpose of giving it, as an Anarchist, my entire approval, barring the stigma sought to be conveyed by the words "accomplice" and "conniver." If a man will but state the truth as I see it, he may state it as baldly as he pleases ; I will accept it still. The Anarchists are not afraid of their principles. It is far more satisfactory to have one's position stated baldly and accurately by an opponent who understands it than in a genial, milk-and-water, and inaccurate fashion by an ignoramus.

It is agreed, then, that, in Anarchism's view, an individual has a right to stand aside and see a man murdered. And pray, why not ? If it is justifiable to collar a man who is minding his own business and force him into a fight, why may we not also collar him for the purpose of forcing him to help us to coerce a parent into educating his child, or to commit any other act of invasion that may seem to us for the general good ? I can see no ethical distinction here whatever. It is true that Mr. Levy, in the succeeding paragraph, justifies the collaring of the non-co-operative individual on the ground of necessity. (I note here that this is the same ground on which Citizen Most proposes to collar the non-co-operator in his communistic enterprises and make him work for love instead of wages.) But some other motive than necessity must have been in Mr. Levy's mind, unconsciously, when he wrote the paragraph which I have quoted. Else why does he deny that the non-co-operator is "within his right " ? I can understand the man who in a crisis justifies no matter what form of compulsion on the ground of sheer necessity, but I cannot understand the man who denies the right of the individual thus coerced to resist such compulsion and insist on pursuing his own independent course. It is precisely this denial, however, that Mr. Levy makes ; otherwise his phrase "within his right " is meaningless.

But however this may be, let us look at the plea of necessity. Mr. Levy claims that the coercion of the peaceful non-co-operator is necessary. Necessary to what? Necessary, answers Mr. Levy, "in order that freedom may be at the maximum." Supposing for the moment that this is true, another inquiry suggests itself : Is the absolute maximum of freedom an end to be attained *at any cost ?* I regard liberty as the chief essential to man's happiness, and therefore as the most important thing in the world, and I certainly want as much of it as I can get. But I cannot see that it concerns me

much whether the aggregate amount of liberty enjoyed by all
individuals added together is at its maximum or a little below
it, if I, as one individual, am to have little or none of this aggregate.   If, however, I am to have as much liberty as others,
and if others are to have as much as I, then, feeling secure in
what we have, it will behoove us all undoubtedly to try to
attain the maximum of liberty compatible with this condition
of equality.   Which brings us back to the familiar law of
equal liberty,—the greatest amount of individual liberty compatible with the equality of liberty.   But this maximum of
liberty is a very different thing from that which is to be attained, according to the hypothesis, only by violating equality
of liberty.   For, certainly, to coerce the peaceful non-co-operator is to violate equality of liberty.   If my neighbor believes
in co-operation and I do not, and if he has liberty to choose
to co-operate while I have no liberty to choose not to co-operate, then there is no equality of liberty between us.   Mr.
Levy's position is analogous to that of a man who should
propose to despoil certain individuals of peacefully and honestly acquired wealth on the ground that such spoliation is
necessary in order that wealth may be at the maximum.   Of
course Mr. Levy would answer to this that the hypothesis is
absurd, and that the maximum could not be so attained ; but
he clearly would have to admit, if pressed, that, even if it
could, the end is not important enough to justify such means.
To be logical he must make the same admission regarding
his own proposition.

But, after all, is the hypothesis any more absurd in the one
case than in the other ?   I think not.   It seems to me just as
impossible to attain the maximum of liberty by depriving
people of their liberty as to attain the maximum of wealth by
depriving people of their wealth.   In fact, it seems to me that
in both cases the means is absolutely destructive of the end.
Mr. Levy wishes to restrict the functions of government ;
now, the compulsory co-operation that he advocates is the
chief obstacle in the way of such restriction.   To be sure,
government restricted by the removal of this obstacle would
no longer be government, as Mr. Levy is " quick-witted
enough to see " (to return the compliment which he pays the
Anarchists).   But what of that ?   It would still be a power
for preventing those invasive acts which the people are practically agreed in wanting to prevent.   If it should attempt to
go beyond this, it would be promptly checked by a diminution
of the supplies.   The power to cut off the supplies is the
most effective weapon against tyranny.   To say, as Mr. Levy

does, that "taxation must be coextensive with government" is not the proper way to put it.   It is government (or, rather, the State) that must and will be coextensive with taxation. When compulsory taxation is abolished, there will be no State, and the defensive institution that will succeed it will be steadily deterred from becoming an invasive institution through fear that the voluntary contributions will fall off. This constant motive for a voluntary defensive institution to keep itself trimmed down to the popular demand is itself the best possible safeguard against the bugbear of multitudinous rival political agencies which seems to haunt Mr. Levy.   He says that the voluntary taxationists are victims of an illusion. The charge might be made against himself with much more reason.

My chief interest in Mr. Levy's article, however, is excited by his valid criticism of those Individualists who accept voluntary taxation, but stop short, or think they stop short, of Anarchism, and I shall wait with much curiosity to see what Mr. Greevz Fisher, and especially Mr. Auberon Herbert, will have to say in reply.

On the whole, Anarchists have more reason to be grateful to Mr. Levy for his article than to complain of it.   It is at least an appeal for intellectual consistency on this subject, and as such it renders unquestionable service to the cause of plumbline Anarchism.

RESISTANCE TO TAXATION.

[*Liberty*, March 26, 1887.]

To the Editor of Liberty :
I have lately been involved in several discussions leading out of your refusal to pay your poll-tax, and I would like to get from you your reasons, so far as they are public property, for that action.   It seems to me that any good object could have been better and more easily obtained by compromising with the law, except the object of propagandism, and that in attaining that object you were going beyond the *right* into paths where you could not bid any one follow who was trying to live square with the truth, so far as we may know it.

It seems to me that we owe our taxes to the State, whether we believe in it or not, so long as we remain within its borders, for the benefits which we willingly or unwillingly derive from it; that the only right course to be pursued is to leave any State whose laws we can no longer obey without violence to our own reason, and, if necessary, people a desert island for ourselves ; for in staying in it and refusing to obey its authority, we are denying the right of others to combine on any system which they may deem right, and in trying to compel them to give up their contract, we are as far from right as they in trying to compel us to pay the taxes in which we do not believe.

I think that you neglect the grand race experience which has given us our present governments when you wage war upon them all, and that a compromise with existing circumstances is as much a part of the right as following our own reason, for the existent is the induction of the race, and so long as our individual reasons are not all concordant it is entitled to its share of consideration, and those who leave it out do, in so far, *wrong*.

Even granting strict individualism to be the ultimate goal of the race development, still you seem to me positively on a false path when you attempt—as your emphatic denial of all authority of existing government implies—to violently substitute the end of development for its beginning.

I think that these are my main points of objection, and hope that you will pardon my impertinence in addressing you, which did not come from any idle argumentative curiosity, but a genuine search for the truth, if it exists; and so I ventured to address you, as you by your action seem to me to accept the burden of proof in your contest with the existent.

                    Yours truly,   FREDERIC A. C. PERRINE.
7 ATLANTIC ST., NEWARK, N. J., November 11, 1886.

Mr. Perrine's criticism is an entirely pertinent one, and of the sort that I like to answer, though in this instance circumstances have delayed the appearance of his letter. The gist of his position—in fact, the whole of his argument—is contained in his second paragraph, and is based on the assumption that the State is precisely the thing which the Anarchists say it is not,—namely, a voluntary association of contracting individuals. Were it really such, I should have no quarrel with it, and I should admit the truth of Mr. Perrine's remarks. For certainly such voluntary association would be entitled to enforce whatever regulations the contracting parties might agree upon within the limits of whatever territory, or divisions of territory, had been brought into the association by these parties as individual occupiers thereof, and no non-contracting party would have a right to enter or remain in this domain except upon such terms as the association might impose. But if, somewhere between these divisions of territory, had lived, prior to the formation of the association, some individual on his homestead, who for any reason, wise or foolish, had declined to join in forming the association, the contracting parties would have had no right to evict him, compel him to join, make him pay for any incidental benefits that he might derive from proximity to their association, or restrict him in the exercise of any previously-enjoyed right to prevent him from reaping these benefits. Now, voluntary association necessarily involving the right of secession, any seceding member would naturally fall back into the position and upon the rights of the individual above described, who refused to join at all. So much, then, for the attitude of the individual toward any voluntary association surrounding him, his support thereof evidently depending upon his approval or disapproval of its objects, his view of its efficiency in attaining them, and his estimate of the advantages and disadvantages involved in joining, seceding, or abstaining. But no individual to-day finds himself under any such circumstances. The States in the midst of which he lives cover all the ground there is, affording him no escape, and are not voluntary associations, but gigantic usurpations. There is not one of them which did not result from the agreement of a larger or smaller number of individuals, inspired sometimes no doubt by kindly, but oftener by malevolent, designs, to declare all the territory and persons within certain boundaries a nation which every one of these persons must support, and to whose will, expressed through its sovereign legislators and administrators no matter how chosen, every one of them must submit. Such an institution is sheer tyranny, and has no rights which any individual is bound to respect; on the contrary, every individual who understands his rights and values his liberties will do his best to overthrow it. I think it must now be plain to Mr. Perrine why I do not feel bound either to pay taxes or to emigrate. Whether I will pay them or not is another question,— one of expediency. My object in refusing has been, as Mr. Perrine suggests, propagandism, and in the receipt of Mr. Perrine's letter I find evidence of the adaptation of this policy to that end. Propagandism is the only motive that I can urge for isolated individual resistance to taxation. But out of propagandism by this and many other methods I expect there ultimately will develop the organization of a determined body of men and women who will effectively, though passively, resist taxation, not simply for propagandism, but to directly cripple their oppressors. This is the extent of the only "violent substitution of end for beginning" which I can plead guilty of advocating, and, if the end can be "better and more easily obtained" in any other way, I should like to have it pointed out. The "grand race experience" which Mr. Perrine thinks I neglect is a very imposing phrase, on hearing which one is moved to lie down in prostrate submission ; but whoever first chances to take a closer look will see that it is but one of those spooks of which Tak Kak* tells us. Nearly

---

*A writer for *Liberty* who has devoted much space to exposition of the philosophy of Egoism.

all the evils with which mankind was ever afflicted were products of this "grand race experience," and I am not aware that any were ever abolished by showing it any unnecessary reverence. We will bow to it when we must ; we will "compromise with existing circumstances " when we have to ; but at all other times we will follow our reason and the plumb-line.

A PUPPET FOR A GOD.

[*Liberty*, April 9, 1887.]

To the Editor of Liberty :

Please accept my thanks for your candid answer to my letter of November 11, 1886. It contains, however, some points which do not seem to me conclusive. The first position to which I object is your statement that voluntary association necessarily involves the right of secession ; hereby you deny the right of any people to combine on a constitution which denies that right of secession, and in doing so attempt to force upon them your own idea of right. You assume the case of a new State attempting to impose its laws upon a former settler in the country, and say that they have no right to do so ; I agree with you, but have I not as much reason for assuming a State including no previous settler's homestead and voluntarily agreeing to waive all right of secession from the vote of the majority ? In any such State I claim, then, that any member becoming an Anarchist, or holding any views differing from those of the general body, is only right in applying them within the laws of the majority.

Such seems to me to represent the condition of these United States ; there is very little, if any, record of any man denying the right of the majority at their foundation, and, in the absence of any such denial, we are forced to the conclusion that the association and the passage of the majority rules were voluntary, and, as I said before, resistance to their government beyond the legal means by an inhabitant is practically denying the right of the others to waive the right of secession on entering into a contract. The denial of any such right seems to me to be irrational.

Of course, none of this applies to the Indians, who never did and never will come into the government. I do not, however, think that their case invalidates the argument.

In the second place. I object to your quotation of my phrase, " grand race experience," as grandiloquent. If we have anything grand, it is this " race experience " ; denying its grandeur. you either deny the grandeur and dignity of Man, or else, as you seem to do, you look back fondly to some past happy state in some " Happy Valley " of Eden from which man has been falling till now he can say. "All the evils with which mankind was ever afflicted were products of this 'grand race experience.' " It does indeed seem to me to be to you a " spook " and more : an ogre, The Devil going about devouring all good, rather than, as it seems to me, the manifestation of Divinity,—the divinity of Man, which has produced, not alone the evil in us, but has produced us as we are, with all our good and ill combined.

It is the force which is as surely leading us up to Anarchy and beyond as it has led us from the star-dust into manhood. It is the personifica- tion of our evolution, and, while no man may either advance or retard that evolution to any very considerable extent, still it seems to me that much more can be accomplished by acting with it than across its path, even though we may seem to be steering straight towards the harbor for which it is tacking.

The other night I attended a meeting of the Commonwealth Club of New York City, and there listened to the reading and discussion of a paper by Mr. Bishop, of the *Post*, on the effects of bribery at elections, concerning the amount of which Mr. Wm. M. Ivins had given so many startling figures at an earlier meeting. Mr. Bishop recited the long list of party leaders, and characterized them in their professions and prac- tices.

The whole unsavory story, only too familiar to us all, did not daunt him in his belief that the government is a part of the true curve of de- velopment, but only incited the proposal of a remedy, which consisted in substituting the State for the party machine in the distribution of the ballots and in the enactment of more stringent bribery and undue influ- ence acts,—in fact, a series of laws similar to those English laws of Sir Henry James, which are in force there at the present time and which seem to act to a certain extent beneficially.

In closing, after recognizing the difficulty in passing any reform measures, he quoted Gladstone's memorable appeal to the future for his vindication, claiming a common cause with all reformers and with Time, which is fighting for them.

The reading of this paper was followed by an address from Mr. Simon Sterne, advocating the minority representation of Mill, and one by Mr. Turner, who appealed for an open ballot.

Immediately Mr. Ivins rose, and, after showing that no open ballot could be free, as even asking a man for his vote is a form of coercion, proceeded on the lines of Mr. Bishop's closing quotation to show that the reform then proposed was but a link in the long chain which is leading us irresistibly onward ; that not in State supervision, or in minority repre- sentation, or in any measure at present proposed, was there an adequate solution of the problem, but that they were each logical steps in prog- ress,—progress which may end in a State Socialism or in Anarchy or in what not, but at any rate in *The* End which is right and inevitable. We cannot any of us turn far aside the course of this progress, however we may act. We can but put our shoulder to the wheel and give a little push onwards according to our little strength. Except at great epochs, the extremists diminish their effect by diminishing their leverage ; the steady, every-day workers who strive for the right along the existing lines purify the moral tone of the times and pave the way for those great revolutions when the world seems to advance by great bounds into the future.

Should we not, then, strike hands with these men of the Common- wealth Club, and, burying our differences of ultimate aims, if differences exist, work in and for the present?

I sat at that dinner with Republicans and Democrats, Free Traders and Protectionists, all absorbed with the one idea of advancement and working for that idea with heart and soul. Their influence will be felt, felt not only now, but in the future, even the future of a happy Anarchy; reaching out

after and touching that state before some of its more uncompromising
adherents.

When the days are ripe for a revolution, *then* let there be no compromise; the compromise will come in spite of us. But to fly against the
wall of an indolent public sentiment is folly, while each man, Anarchist
or not, can do something towards the purification of the existent order of
things, or at least should withhold the hand of hindrance from earnest
workers in that field.   FREDERIC A. C. PERRINE.
7 ATLANTIC STREET, NEWARK, N. J., April 1, 1887.

When I said, in my previous reply to Mr. Perrine, that voluntary association necessarily involves the right of secession,
I did not deny the right of any individuals to go through the
form of constituting themselves an association in which each
member waives the right of secession. · My assertion was
simply meant to carry the idea that such a constitution, if any
should be so idle as to adopt it, would be a mere *form*, which
every decent man who was a party to it would hasten to violate and tread under foot as soon as he appreciated the enormity of his folly. Contract is a very serviceable and most
important tool, but its usefulness has its limits ; no man can
employ it for the abdication of his manhood. To indefinitely
waive one's right of secession is to make one's self a slave.
Now, no man can make himself so much a slave as to forfeit
the right to issue his own emancipation proclamation. Individuality and its right of assertion are indestructible except
by death. Hence any signer of such a constitution as that
supposed who should afterwards become an Anarchist would
be fully justified in the use of any means that would protect
him from attempts to coerce him in the name of that constitution. But even if this were not so ; if men were really
under obligation to keep impossible contracts,—there would
still be no inference to be drawn therefrom regarding the relations of the United States to its so-called citizens. To assert
that the United States constitution is similar to that of the
hypothesis is an extremely wild remark. Mr. Perrine can
readily find this out by reading Lysander Spooner's " Letter
to Grover Cleveland." That masterly document will tell him
what the United States constitution is and just how binding
it is on anybody. But if the United States constitution were
a voluntary contract of the nature described above, it would
still remain for Mr. Perrine to tell us why those who failed
to repudiate it are bound, by such failure, to comply with it,
or why the assent of those who entered into it is binding upon
people who were then unborn, or what right the contracting
parties, if there were any, had to claim jurisdiction and sov-

ereign power over that vast section of the planet which has
since been known as the United States of America and over
all the persons contained therein, instead of over themselves
simply and such lands as they personally occupied and used.
These are points which he utterly ignores. His reasoning
consists of independent propositions between which there are
no logical links. Now, as to the "grand race experience."
It is perfectly true that, if we have anything grand, it is this,
but it is no less true that, if we have anything base, it is this.
It is *all* we have, and, being all, includes all, both grand and
base. I do not deny man's grandeur, neither do I deny his
degradation; consequently I neither accept nor reject all that
he has been and done. I try to use my reason for the purpose
of discrimination, instead of blindly obeying any divinity, even
that of man. We should not worship this race experience by
imitation and repetition, but should strive to profit by its mistakes and avoid them in future. Far from believing in any
Edenic state, I yield to no man in my strict adherence to the
theory of evolution, but evolution is "leading us up to Anarchy" simply because it has already led us in nearly every
other direction and made a failure of it. Evolution like nature, of which it is the instrument or process, is extremely
wasteful and short-sighted. Let us not imitate its wastefulness
or even tolerate it if we can help it ; let us rather use our
brains for the guidance of evolution in the path of economy.
Evolution left to itself will sooner or later eliminate every
other social form and leave us Anarchy. But evolution
guided will try to discover the common element in its past
failures, summarily reject everything having this element, and
straightway accept Anarchy, which has it not. Because we
are the products of evolution we are not therefore to be its
puppets. On the contrary, as our intelligence grows, we are to
be more and more its masters. It is just because we let it
master us, just because we strive to act with it rather than
across its path, just because we dilly-dally and shilly-shally
and fritter away our time, for instance, over secret ballots,
open ballots, and the like, instead of treating the whole matter
of the suffrage from the standpoint of principle, that we do indeed "pave the way," much to our sorrow, "for those great
revolutions" and "great epochs" when extremists suddenly
get the upper hand. Great epochs, indeed ! Great disasters
rather, which it behooves us vigilantly to avoid. But how ?
By being extremists now. If there were more extremists in
evolutionary periods, there would be no revolutionary periods.
There is no lesson more important for mankind to learn than

that. Until it is learned, Mr. Perrine will talk in vain about
the divinity of man, for every day will make it more patent
that his god is but a jumping-jack.

MR. PERRINE'S DIFFICULTIES.

[*Liberty*, July 16, 1887.]

To the Editor of Liberty :
I suppose I should feel completely swamped by the great waves of
satire which have rolled over my head from all directions but the front.
Still I feel able to lift my hand, and make the motion of scissors.
I have had the fallacy of a part of my argument so clearly pointed out
to me by another than *Liberty* that I did not think it would be necessary
for its editor to go so far around my position as to deny the sanctity of
contract in order to refute me.
Indeed, my only hope of *Liberty* now is that it will define some of its
own positions.
I have heard a great deal of "spooks" and "plumb-lines," but I cannot clearly see the reason that contract has ceased being a "plumb-
line" and become a "spook," unless we have to allow that much liberty
for an argument.
Will you please explain what safety there may be in an individualistic
community where it becomes each man's duty to break all contracts as
soon as he has become convinced that they were made foolishly ?
Again, it being the duty of the individuals to break contracts made
with each other, I cannot clearly see how it becomes an act of despicable despotism for the Republic to break contracts made with the Crow
Indians, unless the ideal community is that in which we all become despicable despots and where we amuse ourselves by calling each other
nard names.
Indeed, as I have said twice before, you seem to me to deny to others
the right to make and carry out their own contracts unless these contracts meet with your approval.
I am aware now of my error in assuming that the authority of the
State rested historically on any social contract, and those points which
were brought in in your reply as secondary are the main objections to
my position.
The true authority of the State rests, as Hearn shows in his "Aryan
Household," not on contract, but on its development ; a point at which
I hinted, but did not clearly develop.
However, I do not feel warranted in entering with you into any discussion from that standpoint till I am able to find out more clearly what
Liberty means by *development*. In your reply to me, you seem to think
of it as a sort of cut-and-try process ; this may be a Boston idea absorbed from the "Monday Lectures," but I think that it is hardly warranted by either Darwin or Spencer.
I tried in both of my letters to insist on the existence of a general line
of development which is almost outside the power of individuals, and
which is optimistic. By its being "optimistic" I mean that, on the

principle of the survival of the fittest, our present condition is the best that it is possible for us to have attained.   You do not deny man's divinity, " neither do you deny his degradation "; from what has man been degraded ?   You do not accept an Edenic state ; then what do you mean by " man's degradation "?

The idea of development which admits of a degradation and which expects *Liberty's* followers to arrest the " wasteful process " which has already made trial of everything else, and is now in despair about to make the experiment of Anarchy is something so new to me that I must ask for a more complete exposition of the system.

NEWARK, N. J.   FREDERIC A. C. PERRINE.

Mr. Perrine should read more carefully.   I have never said that it is " each man's duty to break all contracts as soon as he has become convinced that they were made foolishly." What I said was that, if a man should sign a contract to part with his liberty forever, he would violate it as soon as he saw the enormity of his folly.   Because I believe that some promises are better broken than kept, it does not follow that I think it wise always to break a foolish promise.   On the contrary, I deem the keeping of promises such an important matter that only in the extremest cases would I approve their violation. It is of such vital consequence ti at associates should be able to rely upon each other that it is better never to do anything to weaken this confidence except when it can be maintained only at the expense of some consideration of even greater importance.   I mean by evolution just what Darwin means by it, —namely, the process of selection by which, out of all the variations that occur from any cause whatever, only those are preserved which are best adapted to the environment.   Inasmuch as the variations that perish vastly outnumber those that survive, this process is extremely wasteful, but human intelligence can greatly lessen the waste.   I am perfectly willing to admit its optimism, if by optimism is meant the doctrine that everything is for the best *under the circumstances.*   Optimism so defined is nothing more than the doctrine of necessity. As to the word " degradation," evidently Mr. Perrine is unaware of all its meanings.   By its derivation it implies descent from something higher, but it is also used by the best English writers to express a low condition regardless of what preceded it.   It was in the latter sense that I used it.

WHERE WE STAND.

[*Liberty*, August 19, 1882.]

MR. B. W. BALL writes the best articles that appear in the
" Index," which is not saying much, and among the best that
appear in any of the weeklies, which is saying a good deal.
We were the more gratified, therefore, to find him treating in
a recent number the incipient, but increasing, opposition to the
existence of the State.   He at least is clear-sighted enough
not to underrate the importance of the advent into social and
political agitation of so straightforward, consistent, unterrified,
determined, and, withal, philosophically rooted a factor as
modern Anarchism, although his editorial chief, Mr. Under-
wood, declares that the issue which the Anarchists present
" admits of no discussion."

But even Mr. Ball shows, by his article on "Anti-State Theorists," that, despite his promptness to discover and be im-
pressed by the appearance of this new movement, he has as yet
studied it too superficially to know anything of the groundwork
of the thought which produced, animates, and guides it.   Indeed this first shot of his flies so wide of the mark that certain incidental phrases indicative of the object of his aim
were needed to reassure us that Anarchism really was his target.
In a word, he has opened fire on the Anarchists without inquiring where we stand.

Where, then, does he suppose us to stand?   His central
argument against us, stated briefly, is this : Where crime exists,
force must exist to repress it.   Who denies it ?   Certainly not
Liberty; certainly not the Anarchists.   Anarchism is not a
revival of non-resistance, although there may be non-resistants
in its ranks.   The direction of Mr. Ball's attack implies that
we would let robbery, rape, and murder make havoc in the
community without lifting a finger to stay their brutal, bloody
work.   On the contrary, we are the sternest enemies of invasion of person and property, and, although chiefly busy in
destroying the causes thereof, have no scruples against such
heroic treatment of its immediate manifestations as circumstances and wisdom may dictate.   It is true that we look forward to the ultimate disappearance of the necessity of force
even for the purpose of repressing crime, but this, though involved in it as a necessary result, is by no means a necessary
condition of the abolition of the State.

In opposing the State, therefore, we do not deny Mr. Ball's

proposition, but distinctly affirm and emphasize it. We make war upon the State as the chief invader of person and property, as the cause of substantially all the crime and misery that exist, as itself the most gigantic criminal extant. It manufactures criminals much faster than it punishes them. It exists to create and sustain the privileges which produce economic and social chaos. It is the sole support of the monopolies which concentrate wealth and learning in the hands of a few and disperse poverty and ignorance among the masses, to the increase of which inequality the increase of crime is directly proportional. It protects a minority in plundering the majority by methods too subtle to be understood by the victims, and then punishes such unruly members of the majority as attempt to plunder others by methods too simple and straightforward to be recognized by the State as legitimate, crowning its outrages by deluding scholars and philosophers of Mr. Ball's stamp into pleading, as an excuse for its infamous existence, the necessity of repressing the crime which it steadily creates.

Mr. Ball,—to his honor be it said,—during anti-slavery days, was a steadfast abolitionist. He earnestly desired the abolition of slavery. Doubtless he remembers how often he was met with the argument that slavery was necessary to keep the unlettered blacks out of mischief, and that it would be unsafe to give freedom to such a mass of ignorance. Mr. Ball in those days saw through the sophistry of such reasoning, and knew that those who urged it did so to give some color of moral justification to their conduct in living in luxury on the enforced toil of slaves. He probably was wont to answer them something after this fashion: "It is the institution of slavery that keeps the blacks in ignorance, and to justify slavery on the ground of their ignorance is to reason in a circle and beg the very question at issue."

To-day Mr. Ball—again to his honor be it said—is a religious abolitionist. He earnestly desires the abolition, or at least the disappearance, of the Church. How frequently he must meet or hear of priests who, while willing to privately admit that the doctrines of the Church are a bundle of delusions, argue that the Church is necessary to keep the superstition-ridden masses in order, and that their release from the mental subjection in which it holds them would be equivalent to their precipitation into unbridled dissipation, libertinism, and ultimate ruin. Mr. Ball sees clearly through the fallacy of all such logic, and knows that those who use it do so to gain a moral footing on which to stand while collecting their fees from the poor

fools who know no better than to pay them. We can fancy
him replying with pardonable indignation: "Cunning knaves,
you know very well that it is your Church that saturates the
people with superstition, and that to justify its existence on
the ground of their superstition is to put the cart before the
horse and assume the very point in dispute."

Now, we Anarchists are political abolitionists. We earnestly
desire the abolition of the State. Our position on this question is parallel in most respects to those of the Church abolitionists and the slavery abolitionists. But in this case Mr.
Ball—to his disgrace be it said—takes the side of the tyrants
against the abolitionists, and raises the cry so frequently raised
against him: The State is necessary to keep thieves and murderers in subjection, and, were it not for the State, we should
all be garroted in the streets and have our throats cut in our
beds. As Mr. Ball saw through the sophistry of his opponents,
so we see through his, precisely similar to theirs, though we
know that not he, but the capitalists use it to blind the people
to the real object of the institution by which they are able to
extort from labor the bulk of its products. We answer him as
he did them, and in no very patient mood: Can you not see
that it is the State that creates the conditions which give birth
to thieves and murderers, and that to justify its existence on
the ground of the prevalence of theft and murder is a logical
process every whit as absurd as those used to defeat your
efforts to abolish slavery and the Church?

Once for all, then, we are not opposed to the punishment of
thieves and murderers; we are opposed to their manufacture.
Right here Mr. Ball must attack us, or not at all. When next
he writes on Anarchism, let him answer these questions :

Are not the laboring classes deprived of their earnings by
usury in its three forms,—interest, rent, and profit?

Is not such deprivation the principal cause of poverty ?

Is not poverty, directly or indirectly, the principal cause of
illegal crime ?

Is not usury dependent upon monopoly, and especially upon
the land and money monopolies ?

Could these monopolies exist without the State at their back ?

Does not by far the larger part of the work of the State consist in establishing and sustaining these monopolies and other
results of special legislation ?

Would not the abolition of these invasive functions of the
State lead gradually to the disappearance of crime ?

If so, would not the disappearance of crime render the protective functions of the State superfluous ?

In that case, would not the State have been entirely abolished ? *

Would not this be the realization of Anarchy and the fulfilment of Proudhon's prophecy of " the dissolution of government in the economic organism "?

To each of these questions we answer: Yes. That answer constitutes the ground on which we stand and from which we refuse to be drawn away. We invite Mr. Ball to meet us on it. and whip us if he can.

TU-WHIT ! TU-WHOO!

[*Liberty*, October 24, 1885.]

To the Editor of Liberty:

Will you give direct and explicit answers to the following questions ?

I certainly will, wherever the questions are direct and explicit.

Does Anarchism recognize the right of one individual or any number of individuals to determine what course of action is just or unjust for others ?

Yes, if by the word unjust is meant invasive; otherwise, no. Anarchism recognizes the right of one individual or any number of individuals to determine that no man shall invade the equal liberty of his fellow; beyond this it recognizes no right of control over individual conduct.

Does it recognize the right to restrain or control their actions, whatever they may be ?

See previous answer.

Does it recognize the right to arrest, try, convict, and punish for wrong doing ?

Yes, if by the words wrong doing is meant invasion; otherwise, no.

Does it believe in jury trial?

Anarchism, as such, neither believes nor disbelieves in jury

---

* In this series of questions the word " State " is used in a sense inclusive of voluntary protective associations, whereas in all other parts of this volume it is used in a sense exclusive thereof. Attention is called to this inconsistency in terminology, in order to prevent misunderstanding.

trial; it is a matter of expediency.   For myself, I am inclined
to favor it.

If so, how is the jury to be selected?

Another matter of expediency.   Speaking for myself again,
I think the jury should be selected by drawing twelve names
by lot from a wheel containing the names of all the citizens
in the community,—jury service, of course, not to be compulsory, though it may rightfully be made, if it should seem best,
a condition of membership in a voluntary association.

Does it propose prisons, or other places of confinement, for such as
prove unsafe?

Another matter of expediency.   If it can find no better instrument of resistance to invasion, Anarchism will use prisons.

Does it propose taxation to support the tribunals of justice, and these
places of confinement and restraint?

Anarchism proposes to deprive no individual of his property,
or any portion of it, without his consent, unless the individual
is an invader, in which case Anarchism will take enough of his
property from him to repair the damage done by his invasion.
Contribution to the support of certain things may, like jury
service, rightfully be made a condition of membership in a
voluntary association.

How is justice to be determined in a given case?

This question not being explicit, I cannot answer it explicitly.   I can only say that justice is to be determined on the
principle of the equal liberty of all, and by such mechanism as
may prove best fitted to secure its object.

Will Anarchists wait till all who know anything about it are agreed?

This question is grammatically defective.   It is not clear
what "it" refers to.   It may refer to justice in the previous
question, or it may refer to Anarchism, or it may refer to some
conception hidden in the recesses of the writer's brain.   At a
venture I will make this assertion, hoping it may hit tne mark.
When Anarchists are agreed in numbers sufficient to enable
them to accomplish whatever special work lies before them,
they will probably go about it.

Will they take the majority rule?   Or will they sustain a small fraction
in their findings?

Inasmuch as Anarchistic associations recognize the right of
secession, they may utilize the ballot, if they see fit to do so.
If the question decided by ballot is so vital that the minority

thinks it more important to carry out its own views than to preserve common action, the minority can withdraw. In no case can a minority, however small, be governed against its consent.

Does Anarchism mean the observance and enforcement of natural law, so far as can be discovered, or does it mean the opposite or something else ?

Anarchism does mean exactly the observance and enforcement of the natural law of Liberty, and it does not mean the opposite or anything else.

If it means that all such as do not conform to the natural law, as understood by the masses, shall be made to suffer through the machinery of organized authority, no matter under what name it goes, it is human government as really as anything we now have.

Anarchism knows nothing about " natural law as understood by the masses." It means the observance and enforcement by each individual of the natural law of Liberty as understood by himself. When a number of individuals who understand this natural law to mean the equal liberty of all organize on a voluntary basis to resist the invasion of this liberty, they form a very different thing from any human government we now have. They do not form a government at all ; they organize a rebellion against government. For government is invasion, and nothing else ; and resistance to invasion is the antithesis of government. All the organized governments of to day are such because they are invasive. In the first place, all their acts are indirectly invasive, because dependent upon the primary invasion called taxation ; and, in the second place, by far the greater number of their acts are directly invasive, because directed, not to the restraint of invaders, but to the denial of freedom to the people in their industrial, commercial, social, domestic, and individual lives. No man with brains in his head can honestly say that such institutions are identical in their nature with voluntary associations, supported by voluntary contributions, which confine themselves to resisting invasion.

If it means that the undeveloped and vicious shall not be interfered with, it means that the world shall suffer all the disorder and crime that depravity unhindered can consummate.

                                                    S. BLODGETT.
GRAHAMVILLE, FLORIDA.

I hope that my readers will take in Mr. Blodgett's final assertion in all its length and breadth and depth. Just see what it says. It says that penal institutions are the only promoters of virtue. Education goes for nothing ; example goes for

nothing ; public opinion goes for nothing; social ostracism
goes for nothing ; freedom goes for nothing ; competition
goes for nothing ; increase of material welfare goes for nothing;
decrease of temptation goes for nothing ; health goes for
nothing ; approximate equality of conditions goes for nothing :
all these are utterly powerless as preventives or curatives of
immorality.　The only forces on earth that tend to develop
the undeveloped and to make the vicious virtuous are our
judges, our jails, and our gibbets.　Mr. Blodgett, I believe,
repudiates the Christian doctrine that hell is the only safeguard
of religious morality, but he re-creates it by affirming that a
hell upon earth is the only safeguard of natural morality.

　Why do Mr. Blodgett and all those who agree with him so
persistently disregard the constructive side of Anarchism ? The
chief claim of Anarchism for its principles is that the abolition
of legal monopoly will so transform social conditions that ignorance, vice, and crime will gradually disappear.　However often
this may be stated and however definitely it may be elabor-
ated, the Blodgetts will approach you, apparently gravely unconscious that any remark has been made, and say : " If there
are no policemen, the criminal classes will run riot."　Tell
them that, when the system of commercial cannibalism which
rests on legal privilege disappears, cutthroats will disappear
with it, and they will not deny it or attempt to disprove it, but
they will first blink at you a moment with their owl-like eyes,
and then from out their mouths will come the old, familiar
hoot : " Tu-whit ! tu-whoo !　If a ruffian tries to cut your throat,
what are you going to do about it ?　Tu-whit ! tu-whoo ! "

RIGHTS AND DUTIES UNDER ANARCHY.

[*Liberty*, December 31, 1887.]

　OLD readers of this paper will remember the appearance in
its columns, about two years ago, of a series of questions propounded by the writer of the following letter and accompanied
by editorial answers.　To-day my interrogator questions me
further ; this time, however, no longer as a confident comba-
tant, but as an earnest inquirer.　As I replied to him then according to his pugnacity, so I reply to him now according to
his friendliness.

To the Editor of Liberty:
Will you please insert the following questions in your paper with your answers thereto, and oblige an ethical, political, and humanitarian student ?

1. Do you, as an Anarchist, believe any one human being ever has the right to judge for another what he ought or ought not to do ?

The terms of this question need definition. Assuming, however, the word "right" to be used in the sense of the limit which the principle of equal liberty logically places upon might, and the phrase "judge for another" to include not only the *formation* of judgment but the *enforcement* thereof, and the word "ought" to be equivalent to *must* or *shall*, I answer : Yes. But the only cases in which a human being ever has such right over another are those in which the other's doing or failure to do involves an overstepping of the limit upon might just referred to. That is what was meant when it was said in an early number of *Liberty* that "man's only duty is to respect others' rights." It might well have been added that man's only right over others is to enforce that duty.

2. Do you believe any number combined ever have such a right ?

Yes. The right of any number combined is whatever right the individuals combining possess and voluntarily delegate to it. It follows from this, and from the previous answer, that, as individuals sometimes have the right in question, so a number combined may have it.

3. Do you believe one, or any number, ever have the right to prevent another from doing as he pleases?

Yes. This question is answered by the two previous answers taken together.

4. Do you believe it admissible, as an Anarchist, to use what influence can be exerted without the aid of brute force to induce one to live as seems to you best ?
Please explain what influence, if any, you think might be employed in harmony with Anarchistic principles.

Yes. The influence of reason ; the influence of persuasion ; the influence of attraction ; the influence of education ; the influence of example ; the influence of public opinion ; the influence of social ostracism ; the influence of unhampered economic forces ; the influence of better prospects ; and doubtless other influences which do not now occur to me.

5. Do you believe there is such a thing as private ownership of property, viewed from an Anarchistic standpoint ? If so, please give a way or rule to determine whether one owns a thing or not.

Yes. Anarchism being neither more nor less than the principle of equal liberty, property, in an Anarchistic society, must

accord with this principle. The only form of property which
meets this condition is that which secures each in the possession of his own products, or of such products of others as he
may have obtained unconditionally without the use of fraud
or force, and in the realization of all titles to such products
which he may hold by virtue of free contract with others.
Possession, unvitiated by fraud or force, of values to which no
one else holds a title unvitiated by fraud or force, and the possession of similarly unvitiated titles to values, constitute the Anarchistic criterion of ownership. By fraud I do not mean
that which is simply contrary to equity, but deceit and false
pretence in all their forms.

6. Is it right to confine such as injure others and prove themselves unsafe to be at large ? If so, is there a way consistent with Anarchy to
determine the nature of the confinement, and how long it shall continue ?

Yes. Such confinement is sometimes right because it is
sometimes the wisest way of vindicating the right asserted in
the answer to the first question. There are many ways consistent with Anarchy of determining the nature and duration
of such confinement. Jury trial, in its original form, is one
way, and in my judgment the best way yet devised.

7. Are the good people under obligations to feed, clothe, and make
comfortable such as they find it necessary to confine ?

No. In other words, it is allowable to punish invaders by
torture. But, if the " good " people are not fiends, they are
not likely to defend themselves by torture until the penalties
of death and tolerable confinement have shown themselves
destitute of efficacy.

I ask these questions partly for myself, and partly because I believe
many others have met difficulties on the road to Anarchism which a
rational, lucid answer would remove.

Perhaps you have been over this ground many times, and may feel im-
patient to find any one as much in the dark as I, but all would-be reformers have to keep reiterating their position to all new-comers, and I trust
you will try and make everything clear to me, and to others who may be
as unfortunate as myself.   S. BLODGETT.

GRAHAMVILLE, FLORIDA.

Time and space are the only limits to my willingness to answer intelligent questions regarding that science whose rudiments I profess to teach, and I trust that my efforts, on this
occasion, may not prove entirely inadequate to the commendable end which my very welcome correspondent had in view.

MORE QUESTIONS.

[*Liberty*, January 28, 1888.]

To the Editor of Liberty:
I thank you for your courteous treatment of my questions in your issue of December 31, and, as you express a willingness in this direction, I will follow in the same line, and trust you will still think my questions are pertinent and proper.

Do you think property rights can inhere in anything not produced by the labor or aid of man ?

You say, " Anarchism being neither more nor less than the principle of equal liberty," etc.   Now, if government were so reformed as to confine its operations to the protection of "equal liberty," would you have any quarrel with it ?   If so, what and why ?

Will you please explain what " jury trial in its original form " was ?   I never knew that it was ever essentially different from what it is now.

S. BLODGETT.

I do not believe in any *inherent* right of property.   Property is a social convention, and may assume many forms.   Only that form of property can endure, however, which is based on the principle of equal liberty.   All other forms must result in misery, crime, and conflict.   The Anarchistic form of property has already been defined, in the previous answers to Mr. Blodgett, as " that which secures each in the possession of his own products, or of such products of others as he may have obtained unconditionally without the use of fraud or force, and in the realization of all titles to such products which he may hold by virtue of free contract with others."   It will be seen from this definition that Anarchistic property concerns only products.   But anything is a product upon which human labor has been expended, whether it be a piece of iron or a piece of land.*

If " government " confined itself to the protection of equal liberty, Anarchists would have no quarrel with it ; but such protection they do not call government.   Criticism of the Anarchistic idea which does not consider Anarchistic definitions is futile.   The Anarchist defines government as invasion, nothing more or less.   Protection against invasion, then, is the opposite of government.   Anarchists, in favoring the abolition of government. favor the abolition of invasion, not of protec-

---

* It should be stated, however, that in the case of land, or of any other material the supply of which is so limited that all cannot hold it in unlimited quantities, Anarchism undertakes to protect no titles except such as are based on actual occupancy and use.

tion against invasion.   It may tend to a clearer understanding
if I add that all States, to become non-invasive, must abandon
first the primary act of invasion upon which all of them rest,—
the collection of taxes by force,—and that Anarchists look upon the change in social conditions which will result when
economic freedom is allowed as far more efficiently protective
against invasion than any machinery of restraint, in the absence of economic freedom, possibly can be.

Jury trial in its original form differed from its present forms
both in the manner of selecting the jury and in the powers of
the jury selected. It was originally selected by drawing twelve
names from a wheel containing the names of the whole body
of citizens, instead of by putting a special panel of jurors
through a sifting process of examination ; and by its original
powers it was judge, not of the facts alone, as is generally the
case now, but of the law and the justice of the law and the extent and nature of the penalty.   More information regarding
this matter may be found in Lysander Spooner's pamphlet,
" Free Political Institutions."

MR. BLODGETT'S FINAL QUESTION.

[*Liberty*, April 28, 1888.]

To the Editor of Liberty :
  I have one more question, and it does not occur to me now that I shall
want to trouble you further in this way.
  You say: " I do not believe in any *inherent* right of property. Property
is a social convention."
  Now, does Anarchism recognize the propriety of compelling individuals
to regard social conventionalities ?

S. BLODGETT.
GRAHAMVILLE, FLORIDA.

  Readers who desire to refresh their minds regarding the series of questions which the above includes should consult Nos.
115 and 117.   The answer to the first question in No. 115 is
really an answer to the question now put.   There I said that
the only compulsion of individuals the propriety of which Anarchism recognizes is that which compels invasive individuals
to refrain from overstepping the principle of equal liberty.
Now, equal liberty itself being a social convention (for there
are no natural rights), it is obvious that Anarchism recognizes
the propriety of compelling individuals to regard *one* social
convention.   But it does not follow from this that it recognizes

the propriety of compelling individuals to regard *any and all* social conventions. Anarchism protects equal liberty (of which property based on labor is simply an expression in a particular sphere), not because it is a social convention, but because it is equal liberty,—that is, because it is Anarchism itself. Anarchism may properly protect itself, but there its mission ends. This self-protection it must effect through voluntary association, however, and not through government; for to protect equal liberty through government is to invade equal liberty.

TRYING TO BE AND NOT TO BE.

[*Liberty*, June 9, 1888.]

To the Editor of Liberty:

I do not write this with the idea that you will publish it, for the tardiness with which you inserted my last question indicates that you do not care for any more of me in your paper.   You are too good a reasoner to not know that, if it is proper to interfere to compel people "to regard *one* social convention," it is not improper to force another, or all, providing there is any satisfaction in doing so.   If "there are no natural rights," there is no occasion for conscientious or other scruples, providing the power exists. Therefore there is no guarantee that there will be even as much individuality permitted under Anarchistic rule as under the present plan, for the *principle* of human rights is now recognized, however far removed we may be from giving the true application.   The "equal liberty" "social convention" catch-phrase can be stamped out as coolly as any other.   There are but two views to take of any proposed action,—that of right and that of expediency,—and as you have knocked the idea of right out, the thing is narrowed to the lowest form of selfishness.   There certainly can be no more reason why Anarchists, who deny every obligation on the ground of right, should be consistent in standing by the platform put forward when weak, than that ordinary political parties should stand by their promises made when out of power.

I called "equal liberty" a "catch-phrase."   It sounds nice, but when we criticise it, it is hollow.   For instance, "equal liberty" may give every one the same opportunity to take freely from the same cabbage patch, the same meat barrel, and the same grain-bin.   So long as no one interferes with another, he is not overstepping the principle of "equal liberty," but when one undertakes to keep others away, he is, and you can only justify the proscription by saying that one ought to have liberty there, and the others had not,—that those who did nothing in the production ought not to have "equal liberty" to appropriate.   But if nobody has any "natural rights," then the thief not only does not interfere with the "equal liberty" of others, but he does them no wrong.   You have done well, considering your opportunity, but your cause is weak.   You are mired and tangled in the web you have been weaving beyond material help.   Still, I see a ray of hope for Anarchism.   Just unite with the Christian Science metaphysicians, and the amalgamation will be an improvement.   As I have looked it over, I am sure the chemical combination will be perfect, and the result will be the most pleasing nectar ever imbibed by suffering humanity.

S. BLODGETT.

As Mr. Blodgett says, it is as proper to enforce one social convention as another " providing there is any satisfaction in doing so." But Anarchists, from the very fact that they are Anarchists, take no satisfaction in enforcing any social convention except that of equal liberty, that being the essence of their creed. Now, Mr. Blodgett asked me to define the sphere of force as viewed by Anarchism ; he did not ask me to define any other view of it. To say that an Anarchist is entitled to enforce all social conventions is to say that he is entitled to cease to be an Anarchist, which nobody denies. But if he should cease to be an Anarchist, the remaining Anarchists would still be entitled to stop him from invading them. I hope that Mr. Blodgett is a good enough reasoner to perceive this distinction, but I fear that he is not.

It is true, also, that, if there are no natural rights, there is no occasion for conscientious scruples. But it is not true that there is no occasion for " other scruples." A scruple, according to Webster, is " hesitation as to action from the difficulty of determining what is right *or expedient*." Why should not disbelievers in natural rights hesitate on grounds of expediency ? In other words, why should they be unscrupulous ?

It is true, again, that Anarchism does not recognize the principle of human rights. But it recognizes human equality as a necessity of stable society. How, then, can it be charged with failing to guarantee individuality ?

It is true, further, that equal liberty can be stamped out as coolly as anything else. But people who believe in it will not be likely to stamp it out. And Anarchists believe in it.

It is true, still further, that there are only two standards of conduct,—right and expediency. But why does elimination of right narrow the thing down to the lowest form of selfishness ? Is expediency exclusive of the higher forms of selfishness ? I deem it expedient to be honest. Shall I not be honest, then, regardless of any idea of right ? Or is honesty the lowest form of selfishness ?

It is far from true, however, that Anarchists have no more reason to stand by their platform than ordinary politicians have to stand by theirs. Anarchists desire the advantages of harmonious society and know that consistent adherence to their platform is the only way to get them, while ordinary politicians desire only offices and " boodle," and make platforms simply to catch votes. Even if it were conceivable that

hypocrites should step upon the Anarchistic platform simply
for their temporary convenience, would that invalidate the
principle of Anarchism ? Does Mr. Blodgett reject all good
principles the moment they are embodied in party platforms
by political tricksters ?

General opportunity for all to take freely from the same
cabbage patch is not equal liberty.   As was happily pointed
out some time ago by a writer for the New York *Truth
Seeker*, whose article was copied into *Liberty*, equal liberty
does not mean equal slavery or equal invasion. It means the
largest amount of liberty compatible with equality and mu-
tuality of respect, on the part of individuals living in society,
for their respective spheres of action.   To appropriate the
cabbages which another has grown is not to respect his sphere
of action.   Hence equal liberty would recognize no such conduct as proper.

The sobriety with which Mr. Blodgett recently renewed his
questions led me to believe that he did not relish the admixture of satire with argument.   But the exquisite touch of
irony with which he concludes the present letter seems to indicate the contrary.   If so, let him say the word, and he shall
be accommodated.   The author of " Tu-Whit ! Tu-Whoo ! "
is not yet at his wits' end.

MR. BLODGETT'S EXPLANATION.

[*Liberty*, Aug. 4, 1888.]

To the Editor of Liberty:

I was honest in the questions I asked concerning the foundation on
which Anarchism is aiming to build.   I had thought considerably on the
matter, and read in *Liberty* as it came in my way, and while the ideal
was fair to look upon, it seemed to me one must have a loose method of
reasoning to suppose its practical realization possible.   I also found that
those of my acquaintance who favored the idea reasoned from the standpoint of an imaginary, instead of a real, humanity, which left their arguments on the subject of no practical value.

I desired to see what showing you could give, if put to the test.   I
was ready to become an Anarchist, if Anarchism could be made to appear sensible, though I own I believed you would make the failure you
have.   In one thing I have been disappointed and pleased.   You have
had the manliness to face the dilemma in which you found yourself, and
published my last question, and my summing-up, subsequently.   I will
give you credit for straight work, and this is more than I expected to be
able to do.

When I wrote my last, I thought I was done, whether you published
it or not, and I should have stopped there, if you had not published it,
or, if you had published it, and simply made comments thereon, no matter what those comments might have been ; but the challenge and threat
bring me out once more.   I will say on that, that I never thought of
finding fault or being displeased with your "Tu-Whit ! Tu-Whoo !" and
that I *do* " relish the admixture of satire with argument " on fitting occasions.   I am as much at home in a sea of controversy and irony as a
fish is in water, so there is no occasion for your holding up out of sympathy for me.   Just give me the intellectual thumps when you feel like it
and can, and you need take no pains to have them sugar-coated.

And now for a few words on your last remarks. You accept my statement that it is as proper to enforce one social convention as another, provided there is any satisfaction in doing so. I find the difference between
an Anarchist and a Governmentalist is nothing here.   If there is any
difference in the action of the two, it is not a difference in the principles
which control it.   There might be a difference in method, and a difference
in the *kind* of social conventions which they wish to enforce.   On both
of these points I suppose I should have some sympathy with Anarchists
like you.   But when we prevent another from doing as he otherwise
would, we govern him in that particular, and I see no advantage in denying it, or in trying to find another term to express the fact.   In my
judgment it is better to not attempt to beat around the bush, but to state
plainly the social conventions and rights (for such as me who believe in
rights) we wish to enforce, and such restrictions as we wish to free the
world from, and fight it out above board and on that line.

You say "opportunity for all to take freely from the same cabbage
patch is not equal liberty." If all have opportunity to take freely, I do
not know how any one can have any greater liberty, and if all have all
there is, it looks to me " equal."   And further ; I maintain that " equal
slavery " is equal liberty.   It is impossible to make one's slavery complete ; and no matter how small an amount of liberty is left, if the same
amount is left for all, it is " equal liberty."   Equal does not mean much
or little, but to be on a par with others.   " Equal liberty " is not the
phrase to express what you are after, and you will have to try again, or
let it go that your ideas are either muddled or inexpressible.

It is also puzzling to know what you mean by " invasion."   It cannot
be you mean invasion of rights, because you claim there are no
rights to invade. But perhaps you are having in view some "social convention" to be invaded.   In any case, "*equal* invasion" is "equal liberty."   Suppose you do not " respect another's sphere of action," that
want of respect does not limit his liberty ; it is not necessary for him to
respect yours, and that leaves " equal liberty " in that direction.

I am glad I opened this question as I did, for I think I get from
what you have written a clue to your bottom feelings on it ; and if I do,
we are not so far apart in aim as would appear, and I recognize that you
may be of value in the reform world.   I certainly hope that you may
assist in loosening the grip of Government prerogatives relating to matters purely personal. Here we can work together.   S. BLODGETT.

I am not conscious that I have shown any special courage
or honesty in my discussion with Mr. Blodgett ; perhaps this
is because I am unconscious of having been confronted with
any dilemma.   If I have been as badly worsted as he seems

to suppose, it is fortunate for my pride and mental peace that I do not know it. The "difference in the kind of social conventions which they wish to enforce" is the only difference I claim between Anarchists and Governmentalists; 't is quite difference enough,—in fact, exactly equal to the difference between liberty and authority. To use the word government as meaning the enforcement of such social conventions as are unnecessary to the preservation of equal liberty seems to me, not beating around the bush, but a clear definition of terms. Others may use the word differently, and I have no quarrel with them for doing so as long as they refrain from interpreting my statements by their definitions. " Opportunity for all to take freely from the same cabbage patch is not equal liberty," because it is incompatible with another liberty,—the liberty to keep. Equal liberty, in the property sphere, is such a balance between the liberty to take and the liberty to keep that the two liberties may coexist without conflict or invasion. In a certain verbal sense it may be claimed that equal slavery is equal liberty; but nearly every one except Mr. Blodgett realizes that he who favors equal slavery favors the greatest amount of slavery compatible with equality, while he who favors equal liberty favors the greatest amount of liberty compatible with equality. This is a case in which emphasis is everything. By "invasion" I mean the invasion of the individual sphere, which is bounded by the line inside of which liberty of action does not conflict with others' liberty of action. The upshot of this discussion seems to be, by his own confession, that heretofore Mr. Blodgett has misconceived the position of the Anarchists, whereas now he understands it. In that view of the matter I concede his victory ; for in all intellectual controversy he is the real victor who gains the most light.

A PLEA FOR NON-RESISTANCE.

[*Liberty*, February 11, 1888.]

To the Editor of Liberty :

I must take exception to the teaching that the infliction of injury upon aggressors is compatible with the principle of equal liberty to all.

First, with an argument which is no argument, yet which has its force to those who have observed the growth of new ideas in their own minds ; how there comes first a revulsion against what is, then strong sentiment in favor of the opposite, and last only, and often not then until long after, perhaps never, comes the possibility of rational justification of the sentiment.

Now, it is a matter of observation that liberty interpreted to include non-resistance meets with quick welcome in many minds that are looking for better things, while liberty interpreted to mean our own liberty to compel others is to the same minds an unintelligible formula.

And the reason of it would seem to be this,—that while the right to defence, and, if you will, to offence too, is equal to the power and the desire to defend or to offend, it has no more to do with the actions proper to man in a social state than the right of cannibalism, which undoubtedly also exists, when, having no other food, a man must feed on his companion or die himself. Saving that in this case, with the exercise of this right to eat him, a social condition with him no longer exists ; it is a revulsion to a state of warfare.

Who is to judge of where the right to equal liberty is infringed? If each one is judge, why may not the pickpocket say, " You have right to imprison me for picking your pocket, I claim that as my natural liberty and I willingly grant you the liberty of picking mine in return—if you can. The right to pick pockets is co-extensive with the power to pick pockets, and you are committing an aggression in imprisoning me, rather than I in picking your pocket."

There is a difference between resistance and retaliation, and between resistance and anticipatory violence. Resistance may consist in barring a door, or raising a wall against an armed attack, or on behalf of others we may resist by interposing our own person to receive the attack.

But when the attack is done and past, when the violence is over, when the murder perhaps is committed, by what right of resistance do we assume to retaliate in cold blood?

Do we assume that a man who has killed once will kill again? Such an assumption is wholly unjustifiable.

Or, if it be admitted that such an one is more likely to kill a second time, do we kill him on a possibility that lies wholly in the future?

Shall we say that he places himself outside of society, declares war upon it, and society in return makes warfare upon him and exterminates him? Who then is to judge of all the rest of us whether we are sufficiently socialized to be permitted to exist? If each is to retaliate where he conceives himself attacked, we remain in our present state of warfare.

Furthermore, if I see one coming in a threatening attitude, with drawn revolver, shall I shoot first and kill him if I can?

Doubtless I may, and take the chances of his killing me ; but, in doing so, I cease to admit that he is an associate ; I join battle with him ; I accept the fortune of war.

Briefly, the argument may be expressed thus: In a social state no individual can be regarded as outside the pale of society for any cause. Society must embrace all.

He that takes pleasure in aggression is either undeveloped or a reversion to a former type, or his apparent aggression is really an attempt to resist what he conceives to be an injury to himself.

In any of these cases counter-violence is wrong,—namely, it does not accomplish its purpose.

If the aggressor thinks he is injured, the reasonable course is to explain and apologize, even though no injury was meant.

If the aggression be prompted by the mere pleasure of aggression, the delight in violence or a past type, the reasonable course is to regard the aggressor as a diseased man, on a par with a lunatic, or delirium tremens patient. Confine him, but as medical treatment. **Bind him, with no personal hatred of him in the ascendant.** And, in confinement, so far from torturing him, treat him as are treated, or as ought to be treated, all sick and infirm, with the best food, with the best lodging, with kindness, with care, with love.

This, I say, is rational treatment.

It seems to me that the theory you advocate can produce nothing but what we see now.

The people at large, for that purpose, if for no other, a voluntary association, hanged the Chicago men. The people believed with undoubted sincerity that they were in danger from violence on the part of the victims. They investigated the justice of their belief by means which they thought adequate. They resisted by retaliatory violence.

How can you by your principles blame them ?

It seems to me, too, that the simple proposition is that to compel by violence is to govern, and that Anarchists, who protest against government, should begin by saying : We will govern nobody. We will do no violence.

If you care to print this, I ask one thing : Make no verbal criticisms. I am not a Christian, nor a teleologist, nor a moralist, and any slips of language must not be construed to mean that I am. Another thing I ask, subject to your approval. Do not refute me in the same issue. Perhaps I am wrong. If so, I wish to change my opinion. You, I assume, are as ready to change yours.

But it will take a little time for either of us.

JOHN BEVERLEY ROBINSON.

If I could see that my silence for a fortnight could help either Mr. Robinson or myself to a change of opinion, I would certainly grant his last request. But it seems to me that, if either of us is open to conviction, such would be the very course to delay the change. I change my opinion when an argument is opposed to it which I perceive to be valid and controlling. If it does not seem to me valid at first, it rarely seems otherwise after mere waiting. But if I try to answer it, I either destroy it because of its weakness, or cause its strength to be made more palpable by provoking its restatement in another and clearer form. I should think the same must hold in Mr. Robinson's case, if he is writing his mature thought; if he is not, I should advise him to let it mature first and print it afterwards. There is, no doubt, something to be said in favor of allowing intervals between statements of opposing views, but solely from the reader's standpoint, not from that of the disputants. Such a plan encourages thought and compels the reader to frame some sort of answer for himself pending the rejoinder of the other side. But in the conduct of a journal this consideration, important as it is, is not the only one to be thought of. There are others, and they all tell in favor of the method of immediate reply. First, there is the consideration

of space, one third of which can generally be saved by avoiding the necessity of restating the opponent's position.   Second,
there is the consideration of interest, which wanes when a discussion is prolonged by frequent delays.   Third, there is the
consideration arising out of the fact that every issue of a paper
is seen by hundreds of people who never see another.   It is
better that such should read both sides than but one.

Mr. Robinson's other request—that I make no verbal
criticism—is also hard to comply with.   How am I to avoid
a verbal criticism when he makes against Anarchists a charge
of inconsistency which can only be sustained by a definition
of government which Anarchists reject?   He says that the
essence of government is compulsion by violence.   If it is,
then of course Anarchists, always opposing government, must
always oppose violence.   But Anarchists do not so define
government.   To them the essence of government is invasion.
From the standpoint of this definition, why should Anarchists, protesting against invasion and determined not to be
invaded, not use violence against it, provided at any time
violence shall seem the most effective method of putting a
stop to it?

But it is not the most effective method, insists Mr. Robinson in another part of his article; "it does not accomplish its
purpose."   Ah! here we are on quite another ground.   The
claim no longer is that it is necessarily un-Anarchistic to use
violence, but that other influences than violence are more
potent to overcome invasion.   Exactly; that is the gospel
which *Liberty* has always preached.   I have never said anything to the contrary, and Mr. Robinson's criticism, so far as
it lies in this direction, seems to me *mal à propos*.   His article
is prompted by my answers to Mr. Blodgett in No. 115.   Mr.
Blodgett's questions were not as to what Anarchists would
find it best to do, but as to what their Anarchistic doctrine
logically binds them to do and avoid doing.   I confined my
attention strictly to the matter in hand, omitting extraneous
matters.   Mr. Robinson is not justified in drawing inferences from my omissions, especially inferences that are antagonistic to my definite assertions at other times.

Perhaps he will answer me, however, that there are certain
circumstances under which I think violence advisable.
Granted; but, according to his article, so does he.   These
circumstances, however, he distinguishes from the social state
as a state of warfare.   But so do I.   The question comes
upon what you are to do when a man makes war upon you.
Ward him off, says Mr. Robinson, but do not attack him in

turn to prevent a repetition of his attack. As a general policy, I agree ; as a rule without exceptions, I dissent.   Suppose a man tries to knock me down. I will parry his blows for a while, meanwhile trying to dissuade him from his purpose.   But suppose he does not desist, and I have to take a train to reach the bedside of my dying child. I straightway knock him down and take the train.   And if afterwards he repeats his attack again and again, and thereby continually takes my time away from the business of my life, I put him out of my way, in the most decent manner possible, but summarily and forever.   In other words, it is folly for people who desire to live in society to put up with the invasions of the incorrigible. Which does not alter the fact that with the corrigible it is not only good policy, but in accordance with the sentiments of highly-developed human beings, to be as gentle and kind as possible.

To describe such dealing with the incorrigible as the exercise of " our liberty to compel others " denotes an utter misconception.   It is simply the exercise of our liberty to keep others from compelling us.

But who is to judge where invasion begins ? asks Mr. Robinson.   Each for himself, and those to combine who agree, I answer.   It will be perpetual war, then ?   Not at all ; a war of short duration, at the worst.   I am well aware that there is a border-land between legitimate and invasive conduct over which there must be for a time more or less trouble.   But it is an ever-decreasing margin.   It has been narrowing ever since the idea of equal liberty first dawned upon the mind of man, and in proportion as this idea becomes clearer and the new social conditions which it involves become real will it contract towards the geometrical conception of a line.   And then the world will be at peace.   Meanwhile, if the pick-pocket continues his objectionable business, it will not be because of any such reasoning as Mr. Robinson puts into his mouth. He may so reason, but as a matter of fact he never does. Or, if he does, he is an exceptional pick-pocket.   The normal pick-pocket has no idea of equal liberty.   Whenever the idea dawns upon him, he will begin to feel a desire for its realization and to acquire a knowledge of what equal liberty is. Then he will see that it is exclusive of pocket-picking.   And so with the people who hanged the Chicago martyrs.   I have never blamed them in the usual sense of the word blame.   I charge them with committing gross outrage upon the principle of equal liberty, but not with knowing what they did.   When they become Anarchists, they will realize what they did, and

will do so no more. To this end my comrades and I are trying to enlighten them concerning the principle of equal liberty.
But we shall fail if we obscure the principle by denying or
concealing the lengths to which, in case of need, it allows us
to go lest people of tender sensibilities may infer that we are
in favor of always going to such lengths, regardless of circumstances.

LIBERTY AND AGGRESSION.

[*Liberty*, February 2, 1889.]

My dear Mr. Tucker:
    Liberty has done me a great service in carrying me from the metaphysical
speculations in which I was formerly interested into a vein of practical
thought which is more than a mere overflow of humanitarianism; which is
as closely logical and strictly scientific as any other practical investigation.
In spite of certain small criticisms which it would be petty to dwell upon,
it is the most advanced and most intellectual paper that I have seen. I
esteem it most highly.
    The particular matter upon which we have exchanged letters—the ques-
tion of non-resistance—is still in my mind, but it is hard for me to find
time to write anything for publication. Perhaps it is even premature.
    Of course I see very clearly that economically Anarchism is complete
without including any question as to force or no-force at all: but the importance of preaching one or the other as a means of obtaining or perpet-
uating Anarchy has not diminished in my mind.
    People invariably feel, if they do not ask: "How are you going to ac-
complish it?" And I think the question is valid.
    In every definition of liberty, or of aggression, there is a reference to a
certain limit beyond which liberty becomes aggression. How this limit is certainly determinable I have never seen any one attempt to show. As a matter
of fact, the history of liberty has been a record of the continual widening of
this limit. Once there was a time when religious heterodoxy was regarded as an aggression, not vainly I think you will admit when you remember how much our actions are influenced by our predisposing theories.
When it was commonly thought, even by transgressors themselves, that
nothing but the acceptance of certain dogmas prevented all men from becoming transgressors, it was not unreasonable to "resist the beginnings."
    So now when multitudes of good people regard the maintenance of the
State as essential to the preservation of security, it is no wonder that they
should easily be inflamed against those who openly antagonize the State.
Formerly to think heterodoxy was regarded as an aggression. Afterwards
thought was freed, but speech was limited. To speak of the forbidden
thing was then an aggression, and still is to some extent.
    What is the line? Where is the limit? Thought and speech can both
be absolutely free. Thinking or talking cannot really hurt anybody.
    But when we come to actions, where are we to stop?
    That this line which separates liberty from aggression should be drawn
seems to me essential to the working of the Anarchistic principle in actual

practice. As an illustration, you and Egoist in the last issue of *Liberty* consider each the other an aggressor in a certain case.

Is not government really a bungling attempt, but perhaps the best we could do up to this time, to settle the question, roughly and arbitrarily, between parties who each regarded themselves as within their right and the other as the aggressor?

So it would appear to me. Even the land laws and other laws which seem primary are, I think, only secondary. I am not profoundly versed in the history of law, but I am inclined to think that statutes and the generalizations of common law have sprung from the collocation of many individual decisions, each decision being the best that could be arrived at under the circumstances of the time.

If this is at all a fair description of what is,—that is, if law is a rough attempt to draw the line between liberty and aggression, and not a conscious deliberate fraud committed by the privileged against the oppressed (and I think the notion of the State being " a conspiracy " is as empty as the parallel notion of some of our secularist friends that the Church is a conspiracy of priests),—if the State is the result of attempts to determine the limit of liberty, no theory that dispenses with the State is complete unless it otherwise defines that limit.

The essence of aggression, the reason that it is forbidden, is that it causes pain. Pain, even when caused by, or a concomitant of, properly limited liberty, is in itself a wrong,—an antagonist of personal or social progress. If aggression were uniformly pleasant, it would be regarded as commendable.

So that if in the exercise of my liberty I give pain to anybody, in so far as I give pain I am committing an aggression. If I bathe naked before one who is shocked by such exhibition, doubtless his prudery is unjustifiable ; that, however, does not alter the fact that I have deliberately injured him,—I have committed an aggression.

In trying to logically define this limit, I have cast about in various directions. At one time it seemed that individual liberty included a right to all non-action. That is, that people have a right to say to any one : " You are injuring us by your proceedings ; you must stop "; but that they have no right to say : " It is essential to our happiness that you should do this or that."

I am not sure that this is not a correct idea, but the statement lacks precision, and I have not so far been able to attenuate it.

The best thought that I have yet had is that what is called " non-resistance " is the true guide. A better word would be " non-retaliation," yet even that is not quite right.

At the bottom there is a feeling that no one attacks another nowadays for fun. If a man attacks me, I immediately conclude that I have injured him, or that he thinks that I have injured him. If I could " paralyze him by a glance " or otherwise " resist " him without injuring him, I should hardly call it resistance. Usually, however, there are but two courses open. One a timely apology: the other a counter attack. If I adopt the latter and disable him or kill him, the question of who first aggressed is undetermined. I have assumed an aristocratic attitude of impeccability ; sociality does not exist.

As for those who take pleasure in aggression, it is an evanescent type. They are hospital subjects, reversions to an ancestral type, certainly not responsible individuals.

Briefly, the question of what constitutes aggression can be settled only by compact between individuals. In order to arrive at an understanding and form the compact, the opinion of the one that thinks he is encroached upon must be final if it cannot be removed by argument,—that is, by changing his convictions.

If any action is persisted in which any one conceives to be an aggression upon him, it virtually is an aggression ; and the friend of liberty is compelled to recognize it as such and to recede, rather than to inflict injury in continuing his course.

I trust that you will seize my idea. I do not regard this as final, but I think some clearly logical demarcation essential.

Sincerely yours, JOHN BEVERLEY ROBINSON.
67 LIBERTY STREET, NEW YORK, January 25, 1889.

While I should like to see the line between liberty and aggression drawn with scientific exactness, I cannot admit that such rigor of definition is essential to the realization of Anarchism. If, in spite of the lack of such a definition, the history of liberty has been, as Mr. Robinson truly says, " a record of the continual widening of this limit," there is no reason why this widening process should not go on until Anarchy becomes a fact. It is perfectly thinkable that, after the last inch of debatable ground shall have been adjudged to one side or the other, it may still be found impossible to scientifically formulate the rule by which this decision and its predecessors were arrived at.

The chief influence in narrowing the strip of debatable land is not so much the increasing exactness of the knowledge of what constitutes aggression as the growing conception that aggression is an evil to be avoided and that liberty is the condition of progress. The moment one abandons the idea that he was born to discover what is right and enforce it upon the rest of the world, he begins to feel an increasing disposition to let others alone and to refrain even from retaliation or resistance except in those emergencies which immediately and imperatively require it. This remains true even if aggression be defined in the extremely broad sense of the infliction of pain ; for the individual who traces the connection between liberty and the general welfare will be pained by few things so much as by the consciousness that his neighbors are curtailing their liberties out of consideration for his feelings, and such a man will never say to his neighbors, " Thus far and no farther," until they commit acts of direct and indubitable interference and trespass. The man who feels more pained at seeing his neighbor bathe naked than he would at the knowledge that he refrained from doing so in spite of his preference is invariably the man who believes in aggression and government as the basis of society and has not learned the lesson that " liberty is the mother of order."

This lesson, then, rather than an exact definition of aggression, is the essential condition of the development of Anarchism. Liberty has steadily taught this lesson, but has never professed an ability to define aggression, except in a very general way. We must trust to experience and the conclusions therefrom for the settlement of all doubtful cases.

As for States and Churches, I think there is more foundation than Mr. Robinson sees for the claim that they are conspiracies. Not that I fail to realize as fully as he that there are many good men in both whose intent is not at all to oppress or aggress. Doubtless there are many good and earnest priests whose sole aim is to teach religious truth as they see it and elevate human life, but has not Dr. McGlynn conclusively shown that the real power of control in the Church is always vested in an unscrupulous machine? That the State originated in aggression Herbert Spencer has proved. If it now pretends to exist for purposes of defence, it is because the advance of sociology has made such a pretence necessary to its preservation. Mistaking this pretence for reality, many good men enlist in the work of the State. But the fact remains that the State exists mainly to do the will of capital and secure it all the privileges it demands, and I cannot see that the combinations of capitalists who employ lobbyists to buy legislators deserve any milder title than " conspirators," or that the term " conspiracy " inaccurately expresses the nature of their machine, the State.

RULE OR RESISTANCE—WHICH?

[*Liberty*, December 26, 1891.]

To the Editor of Liberty:

Do you think that it is accurate to say, as *Liberty* has said recently, that Anarchism contemplates the use of police, jails, and other forms of force? Is it not rather that Anarchism contemplates that those who wish these means of protection shall pay for them themselves ; while those who prefer other means shall only pay for what they want ? (1)

Indeed, the whole teaching that it is expedient to use force against the invader, which, as you know, I have always had doubts about, seems to me to fall when Egoism is adopted as the basis of our thought. To describe a man as an invader seems a reminiscence of the doctrine of natural depravity. It fails to recognize that all desires stand upon a par, morally, and that it is for us to find the most convenient way of gratifying as much of everybody's desires as possible. To say that a certain formula proposed by us to this end is " justice," and that all who do not conform to it—all who are " unjust"—will be suppressed by us by violence, is precisely parallel to the course of those who say that their formula for the regulation of conduct is the measure of righteousness, and that they will suppress the "unrighteous" by violence. (2)

As I absorb the Egoistic sentiment, it begins to appear that the fundamental demand is not liberty, but the cessation of violence in the obtaining of gratification for desires.

By the cessation of violence we shall obtain liberty, but liberty is the end rather than the means. (3)

"We demand liberty," say the Anarchists. "Yes, but we see no reason why we should forego our desire to control you, by your own canons, if you are Egoists," replies the majority. "Truly," we answer, "but we point out to you that it is for your advantage to give us liberty." "At present we are satisfied of the contrary; we are satisfied that you wish to upset institutions that we wish to preserve," say they. "We do, indeed," we reply, "but we will not invade you, we will not prevent you from doing anything you wish, provided it does not tend to deter us from uninvasive activities." "We think," concludes the majority, "that in attempting to destroy what we wish to preserve you are invading us"; and how are we to establish the contrary except by laying down a practicable definition of invasion—one by which it can be demonstrated that using unoccupied but claimed land, for instance, is not invasive. (4)

No, it seems to me that no definition of invasion can be made; that it is a variable quantity, like liberty itself.

When you said, some time ago, that liberty was not a natural right, but a social contract, I think you covered the case. If, however, liberty is a matter of contract, is not invasion, which is the limit of liberty, also a matter of contract? (5)

What Anarchism really means is the demand for the rule of contract, rather than for the rule of violence.

"As Egoists, we Anarchists point out to you, the majority, that the pleasure of mankind in fighting for the sake of fighting is rapidly declining from disuse. We point out further that from any other point of view fighting is not to the interest of anybody; that desires can be gratified and the harmonization of clashing interests attained much more pleasurably without fighting." "That is true," the majority replies, for, though the majority really enjoys fighting for the fun of it, it has got to a point where it will not admit that it does, and to a point where it clearly perceives the costliness of the amusement.

"We propose then," the Anarchists continue, "not to settle differences by violence ; but to reach the best agreement that we can without violence. We propose this with the more confidence that you will accept it, because you yourselves are beginning to admit that the condition of existence for men is not the former ascetic suppression, but the gratification of desires. We therefore propose that you shall at once cease to repress by violence conduct which is not against your interests and which you now suppress only on account of a surviving belief that you are called upon to suppress it for the interest of the doers. Following that, we shall make other demands for the cessation of violence."

But, of course, in proposing contract instead of violence, it follows that we abjure violence as a principle ; we become what I think it is fair to call non-resistants. That is to say that, although we do not guarantee our actions should our fellows refuse to accept our proposal of the system of contract, we do not for a moment suppose that such possible reversions to violence are a part of the new system of contract. (6)

We must hold, as Egoists, that the gratification of the desires of "criminals" is no more subject to "moral" condemnation than our own actions, though from our point of view it may be regrettable ; and that by just as much as we permit ourselves to use violence to repress it, by just so much we fortify the continuation of the present reign of violence, and postpone the coming of the reign of contract.   Therefore it is that I call myself a non-resistant and regard non-resistance as the necessary implication for an Egoist who prefers contract to violence.

When I say non-resistance, I must explain that, so to speak, I do not mean non-resistance,—that is to say, I mean resistance by every means except counter-violence.

The editorials that have recently appeared in *Liberty* signed by Mr. Yarros have had to me a strongly moralistic flavor, as indeed it is inevitable they should have, from his avowed views ; I think Pentecost's views more in conformity with Egoism.   By the way, I should be glad if Mr. Yarros could explain the moralistic position more clearly in *Liberty* ; or if you and he could have a discussion of the merits of the matter.   JOHN BEVERLEY ROBINSON.

67 LIBERTY STREET, NEW YORK, December 10, 1891.

(1) I think it accurate to say that Anarchism contemplates anything and everything that does not contradict Anarchism. The writer whom *Liberty* criticised had virtually made it appear that police and jails do contradict Anarchism.   *Liberty* simply denies this, and in that sense contemplates police and jails.   Of course it does not contemplate the compulsory support of such institutions by non-invasive persons.

(2) When I describe a man as an invader, I cast no reflection upon him; I simply state a fact.   Nor do I assert for a moment the moral inferiority of the invader's desire.   I only declare the impossibility of simultaneously gratifying the invader's desire to invade and my desire to be let alone.   That these desires are morally equal I cheerfully admit, but they cannot be equally realized.   Since one must be subordinated to the other, I naturally prefer the subordination of the invader's, and am ready to co-operate with non-invasive persons to achieve that result.   I am not wedded to the term "justice," nor have I any objection to it.   If Mr. Robinson doesn't like it, let us say " equal liberty " instead.   Does he maintain that the use of force to secure equal liberty is precisely parallel to the use of force to destroy equal liberty ?   If so, I can only hope, for the sake of those who live in the houses which he builds, that his appreciation of an angle is keener in architecture than it is in sociology.

(3) If the invader, instead of chaining me to a post, barricades the highway, do I any the less lose my liberty of locomotion ?   Yet he has ceased to be violent.   We obtain liberty, not by the cessation of violence, but by the recognition, either voluntary or enforced, of equality of liberty.

(4) We are to establish the contrary by persistent inculcation

of the doctrine of equality of liberty, whereby finally the majority will be made to see in regard to existing forms of invasion what they have already been made to see in regard to its obsolete forms,—namely, that they are not seeking equality of liberty at all, but simply the subjection of all others to themselves.   Our sense of what constitutes invasion has been acquired by experience.   Additional experience is continually sharpening that sense.   Though we still draw the line by rule of thumb, we are drawing it more clearly every day.   It would be an advantage if we could frame a clear-cut generalization whereby to accelerate our progress.   But though we have it not, we still progress.

(5) Suppose it is ; what then ? Must I consent to be trampled upon simply because no contract has been made ?

(6) So the position of the non-resistant is that, when nobody attacks him, he won't resist.   "We are all Socialists now," said some Englishman not long ago.   Clearly we are all non-resistants now, according to Mr. Robinson.   I know of no one who proposes to resist when he isn't attacked, of no one who proposes to enforce a contract which nobody desires to violate. I tell Mr. Robinson, as I have told Mr. Pentecost, that the be-lievers in equal liberty ask nothing better than that all men should voluntarily act in accordance with the principle.   But it is a melancholy fact that many men are not willing so to act.   So far as our relations with such men are concerned, it is not a matter of contract, but of force.   Shall we consent to be ruled, or shall we refuse to be ruled ?   If we consent, are we Anarchists ?   If we refuse, are we Archists?   The whole question lies there, and Mr. Robinson fails to meet it.

THE ADVISABILITY OF VIOLENCE.

[*Liberty*, January 16, 1892.]

To the Editor of Liberty:

When you preach passive resistance, is it not precisely the same thing as what is commonly called non-resistance ?

When William Penn (or was it Fox ?) refused to take off his hat for the king it was certainly passive resistance ; but, as he made no attempt to punch the king's head, it is accounted as quite compatible with the Friends' non-resistance tenets. (1)

I do not think that any practical difference exists between passive re-sistance and non-resistance.   Yet you urge that in emergency violence must be resorted to.   Why ?   In what emergency ?   If violence is as a matter of principle advisable in certain cases, why not in other cases ?

Why not embrace the advocacy of violence of the Communists through-out? (2)

Intelligible enough as a political measure, Anarchism halts as a system of philosophy as long as it includes violence at all.   To people who think government exists to suppress robbery, it is sufficient to point out that government exists by robbery, and to enlarge upon the advantages that might be expected to follow the establishment of freedom of membership in political societies. (3)

But all this involves no question as to what constitutes invasion.   It is simply stated that each shall take such measures as he prefers to protect himself, and that each shall determine for himself what protection is.

If, however, we go further, and lay down a formula, however defensible the formula may be : and say that we will by violence enforce that formula, whether it be the formula of equal liberty or any other formula, I must maintain that the action is precisely parallel to the course of everybody in the past and present who have compelled others to regulate their conduct in accordance with other formulas, alleged to be moral, and held to be as irrefragable as you now hold the formula of equal liberty to be. (4)

"Do not pick people's pockets to make them pay for protection they don't want," is good enough as far as it goes.

It may perhaps be well to go no further.

But if we have to go further and ask, What is protection ? or, What is invasion ? the complement of protection, the only reply you can give is that invasion is infringing upon equal liberty.

Until some method is devised by which we can tell whether a given act does infringe upon equal liberty the definition is vain. (5)

For instance, in a state of liberty Mr. Yarros prints a book.   You copy it.   He organizes a society for the suppression of pirates and imprisons you.   Your friends organize and a battle ensues.

You will doubtless say that you would not advocate violence under such circumstances to either side.   I again ask, Why not ? (6)

Investigate your own principles and you will find that the recognition of equal liberty rests upon the recognition of contract as supplanting violence.   Although we may think it wise among cannibals to become cannibals ourselves ; although when forced to it we may degrade ourselves to use violence ; let us at least recognize that the state of affairs when every one shall do as he pleases can only occur when all lay aside violence and appeal only to reason.   Let us at least recognize that it is for us to totally abjure violence as a principle of action; and if we at any time deem ourselves compelled to do violence let us admit that we do it under protest and not from principle. (7)

JOHN BEVERLEY ROBINSON.

(1) The chief difference between passive resistance and non-resistance is this : passive resistance is regarded by its champions as a mere policy, while non-resistance is viewed by those who favor it as a principle or universal rule.   Believers in passive resistance consider it as generally more effective than active resistance, but think that there are certain cases in which the opposite is true ; believers in non-resistance consider either that it is immoral to actively resist or else that it is *always* unwise to do so.

(2) Because violence, like every other policy, is advisable when it will accomplish the desired end and inadvisable when it will not.

(3) Anarchism is philosophical, but it is not a system of philosophy. It is simply the fundamental principle in the science of political and social life. The believers in government are not as easily to be satisfied as Mr. Robinson thinks; and it is well that they are not. The considerations upon which he relies may convince them that government does not exist to suppress robbery, but will not convince them that abolition of the State will obviate the necessity of dealing violently with the other and more ordinary kinds of government of which common robbery is one. For, even though they be led to admit that the disappearance of the robber State must eventually induce the disappearance of all other robbers, they will remember that effects, however certain, are not always immediate, and that, pending the consummation, there are often serious difficulties that must be confronted.

(4) If Mr. Robinson still maintains that doing violence to those who let us alone is precisely parallel to doing violence to those who assault us, I can only modestly hint once more that I have a better eye for an angle than he has.

(5) Not so, by any means. As long as nearly all people are agreed in their identification of the great majority of actions as harmonious with or counter to equal liberty, and as long as an increasing number of people are extending this agreement in identification over a still larger field of conduct, the definition of invasion as the infringement of equal liberty, far from being vain, will remain an important factor in political progress.

(6) Because we see no imperative and overwhelming necessity for an immediate settlement of the question of copyright, and because we think that the verdict of reason is preferable to the verdict of violence in all doubtful cases where we can afford to wait.

(7) It seems that there are cases in which, according to Mr. Robinson, we may resort to violence. It is now my turn to ask, Why? If he favors violence in one case, why not in all? I can see why, but not from his standpoint. For my part, I don't care a straw whether, when Mr. Robinson sees fit to use violence, he acts under protest or from principle. The main question is: Does he think it wise under some circumstances to use violence, or is he so much of a practical Archist that he would not save his child from otherwise inevitable murder by splitting open the murderer's head?

MR. PENTECOST AN ABETTOR OF GOVERNMENT.

[*Liberty*, November 14, 1891.]

BECAUSE I claim and teach that Anarchism justifies the application of force to invasive men and condemns force only when applied to non-invasive men, Mr. Pentecost declares that the only difference between Anarchism on the one hand and Monarchism or Republicanism on the other is the difference between the popular conception of invasion and my own. If I were to assert that biology is the science which deals with the phenomena of living matter and excludes all phenomena of matter that is not living, and if Mr. Pentecost were to say that, assuming this, the only difference between the biological sciences and the abiological is the difference between the popular conception of life and my own, he would take a position precisely analogous to that which he takes on the subject of Anarchism, and the one position would be every whit as sensible and every whit as foolish as the other. The limit between invasion and non-invasion, like the limit between life and non-life, is not, at least in our present comprehension of it, a hard and fast line. But does it follow from this that invasion and non-invasion, life and non-life, are identical? Not at all. The indefinite character of the boundary does no more than show that a small proportion of the phenomena of society, like a small proportion of the phenomena of matter, still resist the respective distinguishing tests to which by far the greater portion of such phenomena have yielded and by which they have been classified. And however embarrassing in practice may be the reluctance of frontier phenomena to promptly arrange themselves on either side of the border in obedience to the tests, it is still more embarrassing in theory to attempt to frame any rational view of society or life without recognition of these tests, by which, broadly speaking, distinctions have been established. Some of the most manifest distinctions have never been sharply drawn.

If Mr. Pentecost will view the subject in this light and follow out the reasoning thus entered upon, he will soon discover that my conception or misconception of what constitutes invasion does not at all affect the scientific differentiation of Anarchism from Archism. I may err grievously in attributing an invasive or a non-invasive character to a given social phenomenon, and, if I act upon my error, I shall act Archistically; but the very fact that I am acting, not blindly and at hap-hazard, but in furtherance of an endeavor to conform to a generalization which is the product of long experience and accumulating evidence, adds infinitely to the probability that I shall discover my error. In trying to draw more clearly the line between invasion and non-invasion, all of us, myself included, are destined to make many mistakes, but by our very mistakes we shall approach our goal. Only Mr. Pentecost and those who think with him take themselves out of the path of progress by assuming that it is possible to live in harmony simply by ignoring the fact of friction and the causes thereof. The no-rule which Mr. Pentecost believes in would amount in practice to submission to the rule of the invasive man. No-rule, in the sense of no-force-in-any-case, is a self-contradiction. The man who attempts to practise it becomes an abettor of government by declining to resist it. So long as Mr. Pentecost is willing to let the criminal ride roughshod over him and me, his " preference not to be ruled at all " is nothing but a beatific revelling in sheerest moonshine and Utopia.

THE PHILOSOPHER OF THE DISEMBODIED.

[*Liberty*, June 8, 1889.]

CONNECTED with the Massachusetts branch of the National Woman Suffrage Association is a body of women calling itself the Boston Political Class, the object of which is the preparation of its members for the use of the ballot. On Thursday evening, May 30, this class was addressed in public by Dr. Wm. T. Harris, the Concord philosopher, on the subject of State Socialism, Anarchism, and free competition. Let me say, parenthetically, to these ladies that, if they really wish to learn how to use the ballot, they would do well to apply for instruction, not to Dr. Harris, but to ex-Supervisor Bill Simmons, or Johnny O'Brien of New York, or Senator Matthew Quay, or some leading Tammany brave, or any of the "bosses" who rule city, State, and nation ; for, the great object of the ballot being to test truth by counting noses and to prove your opponents wrong by showing them to be less numerous than your friends, and these men having practically demonstrated that they are masters of the art of rolling up majorities at the polls, they can teach the members of the Boston Political Class a trick or two by which they can gain numerical supremacy, while Dr. Harris, in the most favorable view of the case, can only elevate their intelligence and thereby fix them more hopelessly in a minority that must be vanquished in a contest where ballots instead of brains decide the victory.

But let that pass. I am not concerned now with these excellent ladies, but with Dr. Harris's excellent address ; for it was excellent, notwithstanding the fact that he intended it partly as a blow at Anarchism. Instead of being such a blow, the discourse was really an affirmation of Anarchism almost from beginning to end, at least in so far as it dealt with principles, and departed from Anarchism only in two or three mistaken attempts to illustrate the principles laid down and to identify existing society with them as expressive of them.

After positing the proposition that the object of society is the production of self-conscious intelligence in its highest form, or, in other words, the most perfect individuality, the lecturer spent the first half of his time in considering State Socialism from this standpoint. He had no difficulty in showing that the absorption of enterprise by the State is indeed a " looking backward,"—a very long look backward at that communism which was the only form of society known to primitive man ; at that communism which purchases material equality at the expense of the destruction of liberty ; at that communism out of which evolution, with its tendency toward individuality, has been gradually lifting mankind for thousands of years ; at that communism which, by subjecting the individual rights of life and property to industrial tyranny, thereby renders necessary a central political tyranny to at least partially secure the right to life and make possible the continuance of some semblance of social existence. The lecturer took the position that civil society is dependent upon freedom in production, distribution, and consumption, and that such freedom is utterly incompatible with State Socialism, which in its ultimate implies the absolute control of all these functions by arbitrary power as a substitute for economic law. Therefore Dr. Harris, setting great value upon civil society, has no use for State Socialism. Neither have the Anarchists. Thus far, then, the Anarchists and this teacher of the Boston Political Class walk hand in hand.

Dr. Harris, however, labors under a delusion that just at this point he parts company with us. As we follow his argument further, we shall see if this be true. The philosophy of society, he continued in substance, is coextensive with a ground covered by four institutions,—namely, the family, civil society, the State, and the Church. Proceeding then to define the specific purposes of these institutions, he declared that the object of the family is to assure the reproduction of individuals and prepare them, by guidance through childhood, to become reasonable beings ; that the object of civil society is to enable each individual to reap advantage from the powers of all other individuals through division of labor, free exchange, and other economic means ; that the object of the State is to protect each individual against aggression and secure him in his freedom as long as he observes the equal freedom of others ; and that the object of the Church (using the term in its broadest sense, and not as exclusively applicable to the various religious bodies) is to encourage the investigation and perfection of science, literature, the fine arts, and all those higher humanities that make life worth living and tend to the elevation and completion of self-conscious intelligence or individuality. Each of these objects, in the view of the lecturer, is necessary to the existence of any society worthy of the name, and the omission of any one of them disastrous. The State Socialists, he asserted truthfully, would ruin the whole structure by omitting civil society, whereas the Anarchists, he asserted erroneously, would equally ruin it by omitting the State. Right here lies Dr. Harris's error, and it is the most vulgar of all errors in criticism,—that of treating the ideas of others from the standpoint, not of their definitions, but of your own. Dr. Harris hears that the Anarchists wish to abolish the State, and straightway he jumps to the conclusion that they wish to abolish what he defines as the State. And this, too, in spite of the fact that, to my knowledge, he listened not long ago to the reading of a paper by an Anarchist from which it was clearly to be gathered that the Anarchists have no quarrel with any institution that contents itself with enforcing the law of equal freedom, and that they oppose the State only after first defining it as an institution that claims authority over the *non-aggressive* individual and enforces that authority by physical force or by means that are effective only because they can and will be backed by physical force if necessary. Far from omitting the State *as Dr. Harris defines it*, the Anarchists expressly favor such an institution, by whatever name it may be called, as long as its *raison d'être* continues ; and certainly Dr. Harris would not demand its preservation after it had become superfluous.

In principle, then, are not the Anarchists and Dr. Harris in agreement at every essential point? It certainly seems so. I do not know an Anarchist that would not accept every division of his social map.

Defining the object of the family as he defines it, the Anarchists believe in the family ; only they insist that free competition and experiment shall always be allowed in order that it may be determined *what form* of family best secures this object.

Defining the object of civil society as he defines it, the Anarchists believe in civil society ; only they insist that the freedom of civil society shall be complete instead of partial.

Defining the object of the State as he defines it, the Anarchists believe in the State ; only they insist that the greater part, if not all, of the necessity for its existence is the result of an artificial limitation of the freedom of civil society, and that the completion of industrial freedom may one day so harmonize individuals that it will no longer be necessary to provide a guarantee of political freedom.

Defining the object of the Church as he defines it, the Anarchists most certainly believe in the Church ; only they insist that all its work shall be purely voluntary, and that its discoveries and achievements, however beneficial, shall not be imposed upon the individual by authority.

But there is a point, unhappily, where the Anarchists and Dr. Harris do part company, and that point is reached when he declares or assumes or leaves it to be inferred that the present form of the family is the form that best secures the objects of the family, and that no attempt at any other form is to be tolerated, although evidence of the horrors engendered by the prevailing family life is being daily spread before our eyes in an ever-increasing volume ; that the present form of civil society is the embodiment of complete economic freedom, although it is undeniable that the most important freedoms, those without which all other freedoms are of little or no avail,—the freedom of banking and the freedom to take possession of unoccupied land,—exist nowhere in the civilized world ; that the existing State does nothing but enforce the law of equal freedom, although it is unquestionably based upon a compulsory tax that is itself a denial of equal freedom, and is daily adding to ponderous volumes of statutes the bulk of which are either sumptuary and meddlesome in character or devised in the interest of privilege and monopoly ; and that the existing Church carries on its work in accordance with the principle of free competition, in spite of the indubitable fact that, in its various fields of religion, science, literature, and the arts, it is endowed with innumerable immunities, favors, prerogatives, and licenses, with the extent and stringency of which it is still unsatisfied.

All these assumptions clearly show that Dr. Harris is a man of theory, and not of practice. He knows nothing but disembodied principles. Consequently, when the State Socialist proposes to embody a principle antagonistic to his, he recognizes it as such and demolishes it by well-directed arguments. But this same antagonistic principle, so far as it is already embodied, is unrecognizable by him. As soon as it becomes incarnate, he mistakes it for his own. No matter what shape it has taken, be it a banking monopoly, or a land monopoly, or a national post-office monopoly, or a common school system, or a compulsory tax, or a setting-up of non-aggressive individuals to be shot at by an enemy, he hastens to offer it one hand, while he waves the flag of free competition with the other. In consequence of its fleshly wrappings, he is constitutionally incapable of combating the *status quo*. For this reason he is not an altogether competent teacher, and is liable to confuse the minds of the ambitious ladies belonging to the Boston Political Class.

THE WOES OF AN ANARCHIST.

[*Liberty*, January 25, 1890.]

Sir:

That barrel-organ outside my window goes near to driving me mad (I mean madder than I was before). What am I to do? I cannot ask the State, as embodied in the person of a blue-coated gentleman at the corner, to move him on ; because I have given notice that I intend to move on the said blue-coated gentleman himself. In other words, I have given the State notice to quit. Ask the organ-grinder politely to carry his melody elsewhere? I have tried that, but he only executes a double-shuffle and puts out his tongue. Ought I to rush out and punch his head? But, firstly, that might be looked upon as an invasion of his personal liberty ; and, secondly, he might punch mine ; and the last state of this man would be worse than the first. Ought I to move out of the way myself? But I cannot conveniently take my house with me, or even my library. I tried another plan. I took out my cornet, and, standing by his side, executed a series of movements that would have moved the bowels of Cerberus. The only effect produced was a polite note from a neighbor (whom I respect) begging me to postpone my solo, as it interfered with the pleasing harmonies of the organ. Now Fate forbid that I should curtail the happiness of an esteemed fellow-streetsman. What then was I to do? I put on my hat and sallied forth into the streets with a heavy heart full of the difficulties of my individualist creed. The first person I met was a tramp who accosted me and exposed a tongue white with cancer,—whether real or artificial I do not know. It nearly made me sick, and I really do not think that persons ought to go about exposing disgusting objects with

a view to gain. I did not hand him the expected penny, but I briefly—
very briefly—expressed a hope that an infinite being would be pleased to
consign him to infinite torture, and passed on. I wandered through street
after street, all full of houses painted in different shades of custard-color,
toned with London fog, and all just sufficiently like one another to make
one wish that they were either quite alike or very different. And I
wondered whether something might not be done to compel all the owners
to paint at the same time and with the same tints. At last I reached
a place where the road was rendered impassable by a crowd which had
gathered to listen to an orator who was shouting from an inverted tub.
He was explaining that many years ago Jesus died to save sinners like us,
and therefore the best thing we could do was to deprive the publicans
of their licenses without compensation. I ventured to remark that,
although this might be perfectly true, still I wanted to get into the
country along the common highway, and that the crowd he had collected
prevented me from doing so. He replied that he knew my sort, whatever that may mean ; but his words seem to have acted like magic on his
hearers, for, although I did at last elbow my way through the throng, it
was not without damage to the aforementioned hat. It was a relief to reach
the country and to sit down by a stream and watch the children gathering
blackberries. I was, however, surprised to find that the berries were still
pink and far from ripe. "Why don't you wait till they are ripe?" I
asked. "Coz if we did there would be none left by then," was the somewhat puzzling reply. "But surely, if you *all* agreed to wait, it could be
managed," I said. "Oh yes, sir," responded a little girl, with a pitying
laugh at my simplicity, "but the others always come and gather them
just before they are ripe." I don't quite know who the others are, but
surely something ought to be done to put a stop to this extravagant haste
and ruinous competition. The result of the present system is that nobody
gets any ripe blackberries. I mentioned the subject to an old gentleman
who was fishing in the rivulet ; "Exactly so," said he, "it is just the
same with fish. You see there is a close season for salmon and some
sorts ; but those scoundrels are steadily destroying the rest by catching
the immature fish, instead of waiting till they are fit for anything. I suppose they think that they will not have the luck to catch them again, and
that a sprat in hand is worth a herring in a bush." I admitted the force
and beauty of the metaphor, and proceeded on my journey.

Beginning to feel hungry, I made tracks for the nearest village, where
I knew I should find an inn. A few hundred yards from the houses I
observed a party of hulking fellows stripping on the bank with a view to
a plunge and a swim. It struck me they were rather close to the road,
but I nevertheless thought it my duty to resent the interference of a policeman who appeared on the scene and rather roughly ordered the fellows
off. "I suppose," said I, "that free citizens have a right to wash in a free
stream." But the representative of law and order fixed upon me a pair of
boiled eyes, and, without trusting his tongue, pointed to a blackboard
stuck on a post some little way off. I guessed his meaning and went on.
When I reached the inn, I ordered a chop and potatoes and a pint of
bitter, and was surprised to find that some other persons were served
before me, although they had come in later. Presently I observed one
of them in the act of tipping the waiter. "Excuse me, sir," said I, "but
that is not fair ; you are bribing that man to give you an undue share of
attention. I presume you also tip porters at a railway station, and perhaps custom-house officers?" "Of course I do ; what's that to you?
Mind your own business," was the reply I received. I had evidently

made myself unpopular with these gentlemen. One of them was chewing a quid and spitting about the floor. One was walking up and down the room in a pair of creaking boots, and taking snuff the while ; and a third was voraciously tackling a steak, and removing lumps of gristle from his mouth to his plate in the palm of his hand. After each gulp of porter, he seemed to take a positive pride in yielding to the influences of flatulence in a series of reports which might have raised Lazarus. My own rations appeared at last, and I congratulated myself that, by the delay, I had been spared the torture of feeding in company with Æolus, who was already busy with the toothpick, when to my dismay he produced a small black clay pipe and proceeded to stuff it with black shag. "There is, I believe, a smoking-room in the house," I remarked deprecatingly ; "otherwise I would not ask you to allow me to finish my chop before lighting your pipe here ; don't you think tobacco rather spoils one's appetite ?" I thought I had spoken politely, but all the answer I got was this, "Look 'ere, governor, if this 'ere shanty ain't good enough for the like of you, you'd better walk on to the Star and Garter." And, awaiting my reply with an expression of mingled contempt and defiance, he proceeded to emphasize his argument by boisterously coughing across the table without so much as raising his hand. I am not particularly squeamish, but I draw the line at victuals that have been coughed over. To all practical purposes, my lunch was gone,—stolen. I looked round for sympathy, but the feeling of the company was clearly against me. The gentleman in the creaking boots laughed, and, walking up to the table, laid his hand upon it in the manner of an orator in labor. He paused to marshal his thoughts, and I had an opportunity of observing him with several senses at once. His nails were in deep mourning, his clothes reeked of stale tobacco and perspiration, and his breath of onions and beer. His face was broad and rubicund, but not ill-featured, and his expression bore the stamp of honesty and independence. No one could mistake him for other than he was,—a sturdy British farmer. After about half a minute's incubation, his ideas found utterance. "I'll tell you what it is, sir," he said, "I don't know who you are, but this is a free country, and it's market day an' all." I could not well dispute any of these propositions, and, inasmuch as they appeared to be conclusive to the minds of the company, my position was a difficult one. "I do not question your rights, friend," I ventured to say at last, "but I think a little consideration for other people's feelings. . . eh?" "Folks shouldn't have feelings that isn't usual and proper, and if they has, they should go where their feelings is usual and proper, that's me," was the reply ; and it is not without philosophy. The same idea had already dimly shimmered in my own mind ; besides, was I not an individualist ? "You are right, friend," said I, "so I will wish you good morning and betake myself elsewhere." "Good morning," said the farmer, offering his hand, and "Good riddance," added the gentleman with the toothpick.

As I emerged from the inn, not a little crest-fallen, a cat shot across the road followed by a yelping terrier, who in his turn was urged on by two rosy little boys. "Stop that game," I shouted, "what harm has pussy done you ?" The lads did stop, but the merry twinkle in their eyes betokened a fixed intention to renew the sport as soon as old Marplot was out of the way. But the incident was not thrown away on a pale man with a long black coat and a visage to match. "It is of no use, my dear sir," said he, shaking his head and smiling drearily, "it is the nature of the dog to worry cats ; and it is the nature of the boys to urge on the dog ; we are all born in sin and the children of wrath, I

used to enjoy cat-hunts myself before I was born again. You must educate, sir, educate before you can reform. Mark my words, sir, the
school-board is the ladder to the skies." " The school-board!" I ejacu-
lated ; "you do not mean to say you approve of State-regulated education ? May I ask whether you also approve of a State religion—a State
church?" I thought this was a poser, but I was mistaken.   " The two
things are not *in pari materia*," replied the Dissenting minister (for
there was no mistaking his species); "the established church is the upas-
tree which poisons the whole forest.   It was planted by the hand of a
deluded aristocracy. The school-board was planted by the people." " I
do not see that it much signifies who planted the tree, so long as it is
planted; but, avoiding metaphor, the point is this," said I emphatically :
"is one fraction of the population to dictate to the other fraction what
they are to believe, what they are to learn, what they are to do? And I
do not care whether the dictating fraction is the minority or the majority. The principle is the same—despotism." The man of God started.
"What!" he cried, "are we to have no laws? Is every man to do that
which is right in his own eyes? Are you aware, sir, that you are preaching ANARCHY?" It was now my turn to double. "Anarchy is a strong
expression," said I, most disingenuously: " all I meant to say is that
the less the State interferes between man and man, the better; surely
you will admit that?" And now I saw from my interlocutor's contracted
brow and compressed lips that an answer was forthcoming which would
knock all the wind out of me. And I was right. "Do you see that
house with the flags on the roof and that sculptured group over the entrance representing the World, the Flesh, and the Devil?" " I see the
house, but, if you will pardon me, I think the group is intended for the
Three Graces." The parson shot an angry glance at me ; he knew well
enough what the figures were meant for ; but even the godly have their
sense of grim humor. He continued: " That is the porch of Hell ; and
there at the corner yawns Hell itself: they are commonly called Old
Joe's Theatre of Varieties, and the Green Griffin : but we prefer to call
them by their right names " " Dear me !" I said, somewhat appalled by
the earnestness of his manner, " are they very dreadful places?" I was
beginning to feel quite " creepy," and could almost smell the brimstone.
But, without heeding my query, he continued: " Are we to look on with
folded hands, while innocent young girls crowd into that sink of iniquity,
listen to ribald and obscene songs, witness semi-nude and licentious
dances, meet with dissolute characters, and finally enter the jaws of the
Green Griffin to drink of the stream that maddens the soul, that deadens
the conscience, and that fires the passions?" Here he paused for breath,
and then in a sepulchral whisper he added : " And what follows ? What
follows?" This question he asked several times, each time in a lower
key, with his eyes fixed on mine as though he expected to read the
answer at the back of my skull on the inside. " I will tell you what follows," he continued, to my great relief ; "the end is Mrs. Fletcher's."
There was something so grotesque in this anti-climax that I gave sudden
vent to a short explosive laugh, like the snap of the electric spark. I
could not help it, and I was truly sorry to be so rude, and, in order to
avoid mutual embarrassment, I fairly bolted down the street, leaving my
teacher transfixed with pious horror. To a denizen of the village, doubtless, long association had imbued the name of Mrs. Fletcher with a lurid
connotation, like unto the soothing influence of that blessed word Mes-
opotamia,—only in the opposite direction.
    I was now in the position of the happy man of fiction " with a pocket

full of money and a cellar full of beer " ; only my cellar was nine miles
off and my money was inconvertible, to all practical intents and purposes.
There was no other inn ; I dare not try the Green Griffin, and I did not
know the way to " Mrs. Fletcher's." I wanted to get back to town. "Is
there a railway station anywhere near here?" I inquired of a bald-
headed man, who was removing flower-pots from his front parlor win-
dow-sill. "Railway station?" he repeated with a snigger, "not much ;
how should there be a railway station?" "And pray why not?" I
asked. "You may well ask," replied the bald-headed man ; "if you
knew these parts, you would know that half the land between here
and town belongs to Lord Brownmead ; and he opposed the bill which
the Company brought into Parliament ; so of course the lords threw it
out and refused the concession : that is why there is no railway station.
That is why you and I may walk or creep or go in balloons. I wonder
his lordship or his lordship's ancestors ever allowed the high road to be
made. Why should not you and I grub our way underground, like
moles ? It is good enough for us, I suppose. Railway station, indeed !"
And down came a flower-pot with a crash, just to accentuate the absurdity of the idea. "Lord Brownmead belongs to the Liberty and Property Defence League, you know, and he says no one has a right to interfere with his liberty to do what he likes with his own land. Quite right ;
quite right," he continued in the same tone of bitter irony, "nothing like
liberty and property !" This was an awkward dig for me. I had always
believed in liberty, and I was thinking of joining Lord Brownmead's
association. "Perhaps there is a tramway or some other sufficient means
of rapid communication," I suggested, "in which case it may be that a
railway is not imperatively necessary." "Perhaps there is," sneered
the little man, "perhaps there is ; only there isn't, don't you see, so
that's where it is ; and if you prefer walking or paying for a fly, I am
sure I have no objection. You have my full permission, and Lord
Brownmead's too ; only mind you don't take the short cut by the bridle-
path, because that is closed. It appears it is not a right of way. It is
private, quite private. Don't forget." I did not want the irascible little
man to take me for a toady, so I merely asked why there was no tramway. "Why?" he shouted, and I began to fear physical argument,
"why? because Lord Brownmead and the carriage-folk say that tramways
cut up the road and damage the wheels of their carriages : that's why.
Isn't it a sufficient reason for you ? We lower ten thousand must walk,
for fear the upper ten should have to pay for an extra coat of paint at
the carriage-builder's. That's reasonable, isn't it ?" "I do not know
that it is, my dear sir," I replied, "but after all you know we have a
right to use the common road in any way for which it was originally intended. They can do no more. And it does seem to me that a tramway monopolizes for the benefit of a class (a large class, I grant you)
more than its fair share of the common rights of way. Ordinary traffic
is very much impeded by it, and the rails do certainly cause damage and
annoyance to persons who never use the public vehicles. Trams may
be expedient, friend, but they certainly are not just." I thought this
would have wound up the little man for at least another quarter of an
hour, but who can read the human mind ? Not another word did he utter.
I fancy my last remark had satisfied him that I was a Tory or an aristocrat
or one of the carriage-folk, and consequently beneath contempt and outside the pale of reason. After an awkward pause, I ventured to say:
"Well, thank you, I wish you good morning," but even that elicited no
response, and I walked slowly off, feeling some slight loss of dignity.

I presently ascertained that coaches ran every two hours from the Green Griffin to the Royal Oak in London, a fact which the bald-headed man had maliciously (as I thought) concealed from me. The line had been established, as the barman of the Griffin told me, by Lord Brownmead himself some years ago and was maintained at considerable loss for the benefit of his tenantry and his poorer neighbors ; and, as some people thought, to make amends for his opposition to the tramway. " Sometimes," added the barman, "his lordship drives hisself, and then, O lor !" There could be no doubt from the gusto with which the last words were pronounced that this individual derived a more tangible joy from these occasions than mere sympathy with the honored guest who occupied a seat on the box next the distinguished whip : and I accordingly slipped half a crown into his hand *à propos de bottes*. He expressed no surprise whatever, but just as the coach was about to start, I found myself the pampered ward of a posse of ostlers, grooms, and hangers-on, who literally lifted me into the envied seat and evinced the most touching concern for my comfort and safety. My knees were swathed in rugs and the apron was firmly buckled across to keep me warm and dry, without any effort on my part, and as the leaders straightened out the traces and Lord Brownmead cracked the whip, half-a-dozen pair of eyes " looked towards me," while their owners drank what they were pleased to call my health, but which looked to me more like beer. As we dashed down the high street, a little man with a bald head cast a withering glance at the coach and its occupants, and, when his eyes met mine, his expression said as plain as words : " *I thought so.*" I soon forgot him, and fell to reflecting on the curious circumstance that it should be in the power of a few potmen and stablemen to sell a nobleman's company and conversation for the sûm of half a crown. Yet so it undoubtedly was. And yet, after all, it is hardly stranger than that these same potmen and millions more of their own class should have the power of selling to the highest bidder a six-hundred-and-seventieth part of kingly prerogative. The divine right of kings is just what it ever was,—the right of the strong to trample on the weak, the absolute despotism of the *effective* majority. Only to-day, instead of being conferred in its entirety on a single person, it is cut up into six hundred and seventy little bits, and sold in lots to the highest bidder, by a ring of five millions of potmen and their like.

Such is the new democracy, I thought, and I might possibly have built up an essay on the reflection, when I was suddenly roused from my reverie by a grunt from the box-seat. " I beg your pardon," said I, " I did not quite catch what you said."   " Fine bird," repeated his lordship in a louder grunt, and jerking his thumb in the direction of a distant coppice. " Begin to-morrow : capital prospect," he continued. " Begin what ?" I asked, a little ashamed of my stupidity. "October to-morrow," he replied ; "forgotten, eh ?"   "Oh, ah ! yes, of course, October the 1st, pheasant-shooting, I see," I replied, as soon as I caught his meaning. " Done any good this season, sir ?" he went on. " Good, how ? what good ? what in ? I don't quite understand," said I. " Moors, moors," explained Lord Brownmead ; " grouse, sir, grouse : are you . . . er . . . er ?" "Oh, I see, " I hastened to reply ; " you mean have I shot many grouse this season ; no. I have not been to Scotland this year ; besides, I am short-sighted and do not shoot at all." A man who did not shoot was hardly worth talking to, and a long silence ensued. At last our Jehu took pity on me. " Fish I suppose ; can't hunt all the year round." I replied that I did not care for fishing, and that I had no horses and could not afford to hunt. I was fast becoming an object of keen interest. My last admission was followed by a series of grunts at intervals of about half a minute, and at last with a zeal and earnestness which he had not yet exhibited, and in a louder key than heretofore, Lord Brownmead turned upon me with this query : " Then what the doose do you do to kill time, dammy ?" I explained that I should have no difficulty in killing double the quantity of that article, if I could get it. "Out of the 24 hours," said I, " which is the usual allowance in a day, I sleep 7, I work 7, I spend about 2 over my meals, and that only leaves 8 for recreation." "Ay, ay, but what do you mean by recreation, sir ? That's just it, dammy." "Oh, sometimes I go to the theatre, sometimes to some music-hall ; then I go and spend the evening with friends, and all that sort of thing." "Balls, eh?" "No, I am not fond of dancing." "Ha, humph ! that's better ; the tenth don't dance, you know ; never went to a prancing party in my life." " Then last night I went to the Agricultural Hall to hear Mr. Gladstone," I continued. "Eh ? what ? Mr. who ? Be good enough not to mention that man's name in my presence, sir. He's an underground fellow, sir, an underground fellow." I was evidently on thin ice ; so, in order to turn the conversation, I remarked : " Pretty country this, my lord." " Pretty country be damned !" was the amiable response ; " it is not like the same country since that infernal bill was passed." " Indeed ! What bill is that?" Lord Brownmead cast upon me a look of ineffable scorn. " What bill do you suppose, sir ? Are you a foreigner ? I should like to feed that fellow on hares and rabbits for the rest of his life, sir." " Has the Hares and Rabbits Act done much harm ?" I inquired. " Done much harm ? Has it revolutionized the country ? you mean ; has it ruined the agriculturist ? has it set class against class ? has it turned honest farmers into poachers and vermin ? See that spire in the trees over there ? Well, that poor devil used to live on his glebe ; he has about fifteen kids, all told ; he used to have rabbit pie every Sunday. And now there isn't a blessed rabbit in the place." I presumed he was speaking of the pastor and not the steeple, so I expressed sympathy with one who was so very much a father under the melancholy circumstances. "Still," said I, "the rabbits used to eat up a good deal of the crops, I am told." "Nonsense, sir, nonsense ! don't believe it," growled his lordship ; "they never ate a single blade more than they were worth ; and if they did, the devils got it back out of their rents." Most of my companion's neighbors appeared to be devils of one sort or another, but I think he was referring to the farmers on this occasion. " The devils have all got votes, sir, that's what it is ; they've all got votes. I remember the time when a decent tenant would as soon have shot his wife as a rabbit. The fact is, we are moving a deal too quickly; downhill too, and no brake on." I did not wish to express agreement with this sentiment, so I merely said : " I believe you are a member of the Liberty and Property DefenceLeague ?" "Very likely ; very likely ; if it is a good thing, got up to counteract that underground scoundrel. Yes, I think my secretary did put me down for £50 a year. He said they were going to block this Tenants' Compensation Bill, or something or other. Good society, very; ought to be supported by honest men." "Then would you not give a tenant compensation for unexhausted improvements ?" I asked. "Compensation !" bawled Lord Brownmead ; "compensation for what ? Good God ! If one of those fellows on my town property put up a conservatory, or raised his house a story, or built a new wing, do you suppose at the end of his lease he would ask for compensation ? He would think himself mad to do it,—mad, sir. And why should the country be different from the town ? eh ?   The devils go into the thing with their eyes open, I suppose.   A bargain's a bargain, isn't it ?   What do they mean by compensation?   I'd compensate them.   Clap them into the stocks. That's what they want.   Depend upon it, sir," he added, lowering his voice to a husky whisper, "the old man is an unscrupulous agitator, and if I had my way, I would lock him up.   If he's loose much longer, he will ruin the country.   Whoa, Jerry, steady my pet ; damn that horse ! " We were now drawing up at the Royal Oak, and, to say the truth, I was not altogether sorry to get out of the atmosphere of fine, old, crusted toryism, and walk along the street among my equals.   And yet, there was about the man a rugged horror of mean meddling and State coddling which one could not but respect.   " A bargain's a bargain."   Well, that is not very original ; but it argues a healthy moral tone.   The rabbit-pie argument struck me as rather weak, but, take him for all in all, I have met politicians who have disgusted me a good deal more than Lord Brownmead.

It was now dusk, and the evening papers were out.   I stopped to read the placards on the wall, giving a summary of the day's news.   There was nothing very new.   "Three children murdered by a mother." " Great fire in the Strand."   " Loss of the Seagull with all hands."   On looking into the details to which these announcements referred, I found that the mother of the children was a widow, who had insured the lives of her little ones in the London and County Fire Office for £10 each, and had then pushed them into a reservoir.   Her explanation that they had fallen in while playing would no doubt have met with general acceptance but for the discovery of marks of violence on the neck of the eldest daughter, who had evidently struggled resolutely for life.   Other evidence then cropped up, which made it certain that the children were victims of foul play.   The editor of the paper expressed himself to the effect that no insurance company ought to be allowed to insure the lives of children, thus putting temptation in the way of the poor.   Oddly enough, the fire in the Strand seemed to have resulted from a similar motive and a similar transaction.   A hairdresser had insured his fittings and stock for £150 and then set fire to his shop.   Commenting on this, the editor had nothing to say about the iniquity of tempting people to commit arson, but he thought the State should see that all buildings in a public street were provided with concrete floors and asbestos paint ; and that muslin curtains should be forbidden.   The Seagull, laden with coals for Gibraltar, had gone down within sight of land, off Holyhead, before assistance could be obtained.   It appears she had been insured in the Liverpool Mutual Marine Association for double the value of hull and cargo.   One of the crew had refused to go, on the ground that she was unseaworthy, and he was sentenced to fourteen days' imprisonment under the Merchant Shipping Act.   The editor was of opinion that, although he had been justly sentenced, still, he thought, this fearful fulfilment of his prognostication would have such an effect on the minds of the public that his further incarceration would be highly inexpedient, and might lead to rioting.   He was further of opinion that marine insurance ought to be entirely prohibited, except when undertaken by underwriters " in the usual way."   This article, I have since heard, made a great sensation at Lloyd's, and four thousand copies of the paper were gratuitously distributed in the neighborhood of the docks both in Liverpool and London. A committee is being formed for the purpose of urging Parliament to make all marine policies void, except those which have been made " in he usual way."   It is obvious that the crew of the Seagull have not died in vain. They have perished in the cause of an ancient monopoly. The public indignation at their cruel fate is being used as a handy hook on which to hang all '' newfangled systems of marine insurance which have not stood the test of time, and which have hardly yet seen the light of day.''

I had reached my own door when I was attracted by a shout and the wrangling of many angry voices round the corner of the street. Running round, I saw the *débris* of an overturned dog-cart. Several persons seemed to be engaged in an animated debate in a small circle, while the crowd played the *rôle* of a Greek chorus. The disputants appeared to be a young gentleman of mettle, in a high collar and dog-skin gloves, a broken-down solicitor's clerk, the usual policeman, and a workman in corduroys. It was easy to explain the construction of the group. The '' masher '' was obviously the owner of the ill-fated dog-cart ; the workman was the watchman in charge of the traction-engine, which was lying quietly at the side of the road with a red lamp at each side. The clerk was '' the man in the street,'' the *vir pietate gravis* called in as arbitrator by both disputants ; and the policeman was there as a matter of course. When I reached the spot and worked my way to the inner circle, the debate had reached this stage : '' I tell you, any well-bred horse would shy at a god-forsaken machine like that ; your people had no right to leave it there. I will make them pay for this.'' Workman—'' Well, them's my instructions ; here's my lights all a-burning, and you shouldn't drive horses like that in the streets of London. They'll shy at anything, and it ain't safe.'' Masher—'' I beg your pardon, I tell you any horse would shy at that : and what is more, I believe traction-engines are unlawful in the streets ; I know I have heard so.'' Clerk—'' Well, I can't quite say, but I think so. I know elephants are not allowed to go through the streets without a special license in the daytime, because our people had a case in which a man wanted to ride an elephant through the city and distribute colored leaflets, and the Bench said that ''. . . Policeman—'' Traction-engines isn't elephants ; we don't want to know about elephants ; which way was you coming when your horse caught sight of this engine ? That is what I want to get at.'' '' Straight up King Street, constable, and this fellow was fast asleep near the machine.'' '' No, I warn't fast asleep ; didn't I ketch 'old of the 'orse ? '' '' Oh, yes, you woke up, but you never gave any warning ; why didn't you shout out, Beware of the traction-engine ?'' '' What for ? ain't you got no eyes ? Am I to be shouting all day ? What is there worse about this 'ere engine than about a flappin' van ? Eh ? policeman, what is there worse, I say ?'' Policeman (firmly)—'' That's not the question. The question is, Was your lamp burning ? '' '' A course they was a-burnin' ; ain't they a-burnin' now ? '' Clerk (soothingly)— '' They were burning.'' Policeman (treading on clerk's toes)—'' What do you want here ? Be off. What have you got to do with it ? Off with you. Now, sir,'' turning to the owner of the broken dog-cart, '' was this man asleep on dooty ? '' '' Well, I cannot exactly swear he was asleep, but '' (contriving to slip something into the expectant hand of the officer), '' but I am sure he was not awake—not wide awake.'' '' Thank you, sir '', turning to the watchman, '' you see where you are now ; I shall report you asleep on dooty.'' '' But I warn't asleep, I tell you.'' '' You *was;* didn't you hear the gentleman say you wasn't awake ? '' This was the conclusion ; there was a slight and sullen murmur in the crowd ; but it died away. The incident was at an end ; law was vindicated ; justice was done. Yes, *done,* and no mistake ! But I left without any clear idea as to the right of an engine-owner to the use of the common roads. The story of the elephant seemed germane to the issue, but it was nipped in the bud. I went home, swallowed my dinner not without appetite, and set forth in search of entertainment.

There was a good deal of choice. There always is in London, except on Sundays ; and even then there is the choice between the church, the public-house, and the knocking-shop. There were the brothers Goliah, and the infant Samuel on the high rope, and Miss Lottie Luzone, the teetotautomaton, and John Ball the Stentor Comique, and the Sisters Delilah, and Signor Farini with his wonderful pigeons, and the Tiger-tamer of Bengal, and the Pearl family with their unequalled aquatic feats, and I don't know what else. While I was dwelling on the merits of these rival attractions, I heard a familiar voice at the door : "Come on, old fellow ; come to the National Liberal ; Stewart Headlam is going to open a debate on the County Council and the Music-halls. We will have a high old time. Come and speak." As a rule, I fear the Trocadero or the Aquarium would have prevailed over the great Liberal Club as a place of after-dinner entertainment ; but on this occasion I had a newly-aroused interest in all such questions as the one about to be discussed. So I put on my hat and jumped into the hansom which Jack had left at the door. *En passant,* you may have noticed that this is the second time I have recorded the fact that "I put on my hat." English novelists are very careful about this precaution. "He put on his hat and walked out of the room." "He wished her goodbye, and, putting on his hat, he went out as he had come in." There is never a word said about the hero's top-coat or his gloves, no matter how cold the weather may be, but the putting on of the hat is always carefully chronicled. Now, there is a reason for this. It is a well-established principle of English common law that, whenever a public disturbance or street *mêlée* or other shindy takes place, the representative of order shall single out a suitable scapegoat from among the crowd. In case of a mutiny in the Austrian army, I am told, it is usual to shoot every tenth man who is chosen by lot. But here in merry England the instructions are to look round for a man without a hat. When found, he is marched off to the police station with the approval of all concerned. It is part of our unwritten law. Some few months since the principle was actually applied in a *cause célèbre* by the magistrate himself. A journalist summoned no less a personage than the Duke of Cambridge for assault. The facts were not denied, and the witnesses were all agreed, when succor came from an unexpected quarter. "Is it a fact, as I have seen it stated in the papers," asked the worthy stipendiary, "is it a fact, I ask, that the plaintiff was without a hat ?" There was no gainsaying this. The prosecutor *was* hatless at the time of the alleged assault. That settled the matter ; and the Commander-in-chief of the British Army left the court (metaphorically speaking) without a stain on his character.

However, as I have said, I put on my hat, and off we drove to the conference-room of the big club with the odd name. "National" was first used as a political term by the late Benjamin Disraeli to signify the patriotic as opposed to the cosmopolitan and anti-national. "Liberal" was first used in a political sense about 1815, to denote the advocates of liberty as opposed to the "serviles" who believed in State-control. And yet the members of the club avowedly uphold State-interference in all things, and dub the doctrine of *laissez faire* the creed of selfishness. Still the building is a fine and commodious one, and what's in a name, after all ?

When we reached the political arena, Mr. Headlam, who is a Socialist, was in the middle of a very able individualistic harangue. Indeed, I have never heard the case for moral liberty better stated and more courageously advocated than on this occasion. I was anxious to hear what the censor party might have to say. I half-expected to see some weary ascetic—perhaps an austere cardinal—rise in his place and wade through some solemn passages from the sententious Hooker. I was agreeably disappointed when a chirpy little Scotchman with an amusing brogue and a moth-eaten appearance started off with prattle of this kind : "Gentlemen, there's no one loves liberty more than me. But we've got to draw a line at decency, you see. I've been elected to sit on the Council and to see that that line is drawn at the right place. That is my duty, and my duty I mean to do. Everything which is calculated to bring a blush to the cheek of a pure maiden must be put down. And there's another thing ; I say that music-halls where intoxicating liquors is sold must be put down. We are not going to tolerate places what incites to fornication and drunkenness. But at the same time we are no foes to liberty,—that is, liberty to do right, and that's the only liberty worth fighting for, depend upon it." Mr. McDoodle slapped his knee with emphatic violence and sat down. "I should like to ask the last speaker," said a thin gentleman in a back row, "whether it is altogether consistent for a State which has repealed every statute penalizing fornication itself to keep up a lot of little worrying measures for the purpose of penalizing conduct which may possibly lead to fornication. In other words, fornication is perfectly legal, but a song likely to lead to fornication is illegal. Is this consistent ?" "Allow me," shouted a stout man with a loud voice ; "perhaps, being a lawyer, I know more about these matters than Mr. McDoodle possibly can. The gentleman who asks the question is in error. His major premise is false. Fornication in this country is a misdemeanor, by 23 and 24 Vict. c. 32." "Pardon me," replied the voice in the back row, "I also am a lawyer, and I say that the Act you refer to does not make fornication a misdemeanor ; it refers only to conspiracy to induce a woman to commit the sin ; that is a very different matter." "I don't see that it is," replied the stout man, "for what is a conspiracy but an agreement to do wrong? Very well, then, an agreement between a man and a woman to do wrong is itself a conspiracy. And since they cannot commit this sin without agreement (if they do, of course it comes under another head), it follows that I am right." "Not at all," rejoined the lawyer at the back, "not at all ; I fear your ideas of conspiracy are a little mixed. If you will consult Stephen's Digest of the Criminal Law, which I hold in my hand, you will find these words : ' provided that an agreement between a man and a woman to commit fornication is not a conspiracy.' I suppose Mr. Justice Stephen may be taken to know something about the law." Chairman (coming to the rescue)—"I think, gentlemen, we are getting off the lines. Perhaps Mr. Gattie will favor us with a few words ?" "I confess, sir," responded that gentleman, "I confess I am in a difficulty. Are we discussing whether indecency is wrong or not ? Or is the question before the meeting whether Mr. McDoodle and his coadjutors are the proper persons to act as *censores morum?* My own views on these three points are these : that indecency, when properly defined, is wrong ; that Mr. McDoodle and his friends are not competent to define it, nor to suggest means for suppressing it ; and, finally, that the State had much better leave the settlement of the question to public opinion and the common sense and common taste of the people." A whirl of arguments, relevant and irrelevant, followed his speech, which contained references to a pretty wide field of State-interferences, showing their invariable and

inevitable failure all along the line. One apoplectic little man was loudly
demanding an answer to his question "whether we were going to allow
people to run down the street in a state of complete nudity." That is
what he wanted to know. Some one replied that in this climate the
danger was remote, and that the roughs would provide a sufficient de-
terrent. Some one else wanted to know whether it was decent to hawk
the *Pall Mall Gazette* in the streets, and a very earnest young man inquired whether his hearers had ever read the thirty-sixth chapter of
Genesis, and whether, if so, it was calculated to raise a blush to the
cheek of virtue. A wag replied : "There *is* no cheek about virtue."
And so the ball was kept rolling. And we left without having formed
the faintest idea as to whether the State should interfere with the amuse-
ments of the people or not ; whether it should limit its interference to
the enforcement of decency and propriety ; what those terms signify for
the practical purpose ; whether in any case it should delegate this duty to
local authorities, and, if so, to what authorities ; whether it should itself
take the initiative, or leave it to persons considering themselves injured';
whether such alleged injury should be direct or indirect, and, in either
case, what those expressions mean. However, a good deal of dust had
been kicked up, and even the most cocksure of those who had entered
the lists went out, I doubt not, with a conviction that there was a good
deal to be said on all sides of the question. That, in itself, was an unmixed good.

Walking home, in the neighborhood of Oxford Circus, a respectable
young woman asked if I would be good enough to tell her the nearest
way to Russell Square. She had hardly got the words out of her mouth,
when a policeman emerged from a doorway and charged her with solic-
itation, asking me to accompany them to the station and sign the
charge-sheet. Not being a member of the profession, of course the
young woman had neglected to "pay her footing"; hence the official
zeal. Old hands had with impunity accosted me at least a dozen times
in the same street. I ventured to remonstrate, when I was myself
charged with being drunk and attempting a rescue, and I should certainly have ended my day in a State-furnished apartment, had not another keeper of the Queen's peace come alongside and drawn away my
accuser, whispering something in his ear the while. I recognized the
features of an old acquaintance with whom I have an occasional glass at
the Bottle of Hay on my way home from the club.

I reached home at last, and the events of the day battled with one another for precedence in my dreams. Freedom, order ; order, freedom.
Which is it to be ? When I arose in the morning, I tried to record the
previous day's experiences just as they came to me, without offering any
dogmatic opinion as to the rights and the wrongs of the several cases
which arose. "I will send them," I said, "to the organ of philosophic
Anarchy in America, and, perhaps, in spite of their trivial character,
they may be deemed to present points worthy of comment." What
a pity it is that we cannot put our London fogs in a bag and send them
by parcel post to Boston for careful analysis !

WORDSWORTH DONISTHORPE.

LONDON, ENGLAND.

THE MORAL OF MR. DONISTHORPE'S WOES.

[*Liberty*, January 25, 1890.]

THE reader of Mr. Donisthorpe's article in this issue on
" The Woes of an Anarchist " may rise from its perusal with
a feeling of confusion equal to that manifested by the author,
but at least he will say to himself that for genuine humor he
has seldom read anything that equals it. For myself I have
read it twice in manuscript and twice in proof, and still wish
that I might prolong my life by the laughter that four more
readings would be sure to excite. Mr. Donisthorpe ought to
write a novel. But when he asks *Liberty* to comment on his
woes and dissipate the fog he condenses around himself, I am
at a loss to know how to answer him. For what is the moral
of this article, in which a day's events are made to tell with
equal vigor, now against State Socialism, now against capitalism, now against Anarchism, and now against Individualism ?
Simply this,—that in the mess in which we find ourselves, and
perhaps in any state of things, all social theories involve their
difficulties and disadvantages, and that there are some troubles
from which mankind can never escape. Well, the Anarchists,
despite the fact that Henry George calls them optimists, are
pessimistic enough to accept this moral fully. They never have
claimed that liberty will bring perfection ; they simply say
that its results are vastly preferable to those that follow authority. Under liberty Mr. Donisthorpe may have to listen for
some minutes every day to the barrel-organ (though I really
think that it will never lodge him in the mad-house), but at
least he will have the privilege of going to the music-hall in
the evening ; whereas, under authority, even in its most honest and consistent form, he will get rid of the barrel-organ only
at the expense of being deprived of the music-hall, and, in its
less honest, less consistent, and more probable form, he may
lose the music-hall at the same time that the is forced to endure the barrel-organ. As a choice of blessings, liberty is the
greater ; as a choice of evils, liberty is the smaller. Then liberty always, say the Anarchists. No use of force, except
against the invader ; and in those cases where it is difficult to
tell whether the alleged offender is an invader or not, still no
use of force except where the necessity of immediate solution
is so imperative that we must use it to save ourselves. And
in these few cases where we must use it, let us do so frankly
and squarely, acknowledging it as a matter of necessity, without

seeking to harmonize our action with any political ideal or constructing any far-fetched theory of a State or collectivity having prerogatives and rights superior to those of individuals and aggregations of individuals and exempted from the operation of the ethical principles which individuals are expected to observe. But to say all this to Mr. Donisthorpe is like carrying coals to Newcastle, despite his catalogue of doubts and woes. He knows as well as I do that "liberty is not the daughter, but the mother of order."

L'ÉTAT EST MORT ; VIVE L'ÉTAT !

[*Liberty*, May 24, 1890.]

To the Editor of Liberty :
Hooks-and-eyes are very useful. Hooks are useless ; eyes are useless. Yet in combination they are useful. This is co-operation. Where you have division of labor and consequent differentiation of function and, eventually, of structure, there is co-operation. Certain tribes of ants have working members and fighting members. The military caste are unable to collect food, which is provided for them by the other members of the community, in return for which they devote themselves to the defence of the whole society. But for these soldiers the society would perish. If either class perished, the other class would perish with it. It is the old fable of the belly and the limbs.

Division of labor does not always result in differentiation of structure. In the case of bees and many other insects we know that it does. Among mammals we have the well-marked structural division into males and females, but beyond this the tendency to fix structural changes is very slight. In races where caste prevails, the tendency is more marked. Even in England, where caste is extinct, it has been observed among the mining population of Northumbria. And the notorious short-sightedness of Germans has been set down to compulsory book-study.

As a general rule, we may neglect this effect of co-operation among human beings. The fact remains that the organized effort of 100 individuals is a very great deal more effective than the sum of the efforts of 100 unorganized individuals. Co-operation is an unmixed good. And the Ishmaelitic anarchy of the bumble-bee is uneconomic. Hostility to the principle of co-operation (upon which society is founded) is usually attributed by the ignorant to philosophical Anarchists. While Socialists never weary of pointing to the glorious triumphs of co-operation, and claiming them for Socialism. Wherever a number of persons join hands with the object of effecting a purpose otherwise unattainable, we have what is tantamount to a new force,—the force, of combination : and the persons so combining and regarded as a single body may be called by a name,—any name ; a Union, an Association, a Society, a Club, a Company, a Corporation, a State. I do not say all these terms denote precisely the same thing, but they all *connote* co-operation. I prefer to use the word Club to denote all such associations of men for a common purpose.

Let the State be now abolished for the purposes of this discussion. How do we stand ? We have by no means abolished all the clubs and companies in which citizens find themselves grouped and interbanded. There they all are, just as before. Let us examine some of them. Stay ; there are a number of new ones, suddenly sprung up out of the *débris* of the old State.

Here are some eighty men organized in the form of a cricket-club. They may not pitch the ball as they like, but only in accordance with rigid laws. They elect a king or captain, and they bind themselves to obey him in the field. A member is told off to field at long-on, although he may wish to field at point. He must obey the despot.

Here is a ring of horsemen. They ride races. They back their own horses. Disputes arise about fouling, or perhaps the course is a curve and some rider takes a short cut. Or the weights of the riders are unequal, and the heavier rider claims to equalize the weights. All such matters are laid before a committee, and rules are drawn up by which all the members of the little racing club pledge themselves to be bound. The club grows : other riding or racing men join it or adopt its rules. At last so good are its laws that they are adopted by all the racing fraternity in the island, and all racing disputes are settled by the rules of the Jockey Club. And even the judges of the land defer to them, and refer points of racing law to the Club.

Here again is a knot of whalers chatting on the beach of a stormy sea. Each trembles for the safety of his own vessel. He would give something to be rid of his uneasiness. All his eggs are in one basket. He would willingly distribute them over many baskets. He offers to take long odds that his own vessel is lost. He repeats the offer till the long odds cover the value of his ship and cargo, and perhaps profits and time. "Now," says he, "I am comfortable. It is true, I forfeit a small percentage ; but if my whole craft goes to the bottom, I lose nothing." He laughs and sings while the others go croaking about the sands, shaking their heads and looking fearfully at the breakers. At last they all follow his example, and the net result is a Mutual Marine Insurance Society. After a while they lay the odds, not with their own members only, but with others ; and the risk being over-estimated (naturally at first), they make large dividends. But now difficulties arise. The captain of a whaler has thrown cargo overboard in a heavy sea. The owner claims for the loss. The company declines to pay, on the ground that the loss was voluntarily caused by the captain and not by the hand of God or the king's enemies ; and that there would be no limit to jettison, if the claim were allowed. Other members meet with similar difficulties, and finally Rules are made which provide for all known contingencies. And when any dispute arises, the chosen Umpire, whether it be a mutual friend, or an agora-full of citizens, or a department of State, or any other person or body of persons, refers to the common practice and precedents so far as they apply. In other words, the Rules of the Insurance Society *are* the law of the land. In spite of the State, this is so to-day to a considerable extent : I may say, in all matters which have not been botched and cobbled by statute.

There is another class of club springing out of the altruistic sentiment. An old lady takes compassion on a starving cat (no uncommon sight in the West End of London after the Season). She puts a saucer of milk and some liver on the doorstep. She is soon recognized as a benefactress and the cats for a mile round swarm to her household. The saucers increase and multiply, and the liver is an item in her butcher's bill. The strain is too great to be borne single-handed. She issues a circular appeal, and she is surprised to find how many are willing to contribute a fair share, although their sympathy shrivels up before an unfair demand. They are willing to be taxed *pro rata*, but they will not bear the burden of other people's stinginess. "Let the poor cats bear it rather," say they. "What is everybody's business is nobody's business. It is very sad, but it cannot be helped. If we keep one cat, hundreds will starve ; so what's the use ?" But when once the club is started, nobody feels the burden ; the Cats' Home is built and endowed, and all goes well. Hospitals, infirmaries, alms-houses, orphanages, spring up all round. At first they are reckless and indiscriminate, and become the prey of impostors and able-bodied vagrants. Then Rules are framed ; the Charity Organization Society co-ordinates and directs public benevolence. And those rules of prudence and economy are copied and adopted in many respects by those who administer the State Poor Law.

Then we have associations of persons who agree on important points of science or politics. They wish to make others think with them, in order that society may be pleasanter and more congenial for themselves. They would button-hole every man in the street and argue the question out with him ; but the process is too lengthy and wearisome. They club together and form such institutions as the British and Foreign Bible Society, which has spent seven million pounds in disseminating untruths all over the world. We have the Cobden Club, which is slowly and sadly dying of inconsistency after a career of merited success. We have scientific societies of all descriptions that never ask or expect a penny reward for all their outlay, beyond making other people wiser and pleasanter neighbors.

Finally, we have societies banded together to do battle against rivals on the principle of "Union is strength." These clubs are defensive or aggressive. The latter class includes all trading associations, the object of which is to make profits by out-manœuvring competitors. The former or defensive class includes all the political societies formed for the purpose of resisting the State,—the most aggressive club in existence. Over one hundred of these "protection societies" of one sort and another are now federated under the hegemony of the Liberty and Property Defence League.

Now we have agreed that the State is to be abolished. What is the result ? Here are Watch Committees formed in the great towns to prevent and to insure against burglars, thieves, and like marauders. How they are to be constituted I do not clearly know ; neither do I know the limits of their functions. Here again is a Mutual Inquest Society to provide for the examination of dead persons before burial or cremation, in order to make murder as unprofitable a business as possible. Here is a Vigilance Association sending out detectives for the purpose of discovering and lynching the unsocial wretches who knowingly travel in public conveyances with infectious diseases on them. Here is a journal supported by consumers for the advertisement of adulterating dealers. And here again is a Filibustering Company got up by adventurous traders of the old East India Company stamp for the purpose of carrying trade into foreign countries with or without the consent of the invaded parties. Here is a Statistical Society devising Rules to make it unpleasant for those who evade registration and the census, and offering inducement to all who furnish the required information. What sort of organization (if any) will be formed for the enforcement (not necessarily by *brute-force*) of contract?

Or will there be many such organizations dealing with different classes of contract? Will there be a Woman's League to boycott any man who has abused the confidence of a woman and violated his pledges? How will it try and sanction cases of breach of promise?

Above all, how is this powerful Company for the defence of the country against foreign invaders to be constituted? And what safeguards will its members provide against the tyranny of the officials? When a Senator proposed to limit the standing army of the United States to three thousand, George Washington agreed, on condition that the honorable member would arrange that the country should never be invaded by more than two thousand. Frankenstein created a Monster he could not lay. This will be a nut for Anarchists of the future to crack.

And now, to revert to the Vigilance Society formed for lynching persons who travel about in public places with small-pox and scarletina, what rules will they make for their own guidance? Suppose they dub every unvaccinated person a "focus of infection," shall we witness the establishment of an Anti-Vigilance Society to punch the heads of the detectives who punch the heads of the "foci of infection"? Remember, we have both these societies in full working order to-day. One is called the State, and the other is the Anti-Vaccination Society.

The questions which I should wish to ask, and which I should wish Mr. Herbert Spencer, Mr. Auberon Herbert, Mr. Benjamin Tucker, and Mr. Victor Yarros to answer, are chiefly these two :

1. How far may voluntary co-operators invade the liberty of others? And what is to prevent such invasion under a system of Anarchy?

2. Is compulsory co-operation ever desirable? And what form (if any) should such compulsion take?

The existing State is obviously only a conglomeration of several large societies which would exist separately or collectively in its absence ; if the State were abolished, these associations would necessarily spring up out of its ruins, just as the nations of Europe sprang out of the ruins of the Roman Empire. They would apparently lack the power of compulsion. No one would be compelled to join against his will. Take the ordinary case of a gas-lit street. Would a voluntary gas-committee be willing to light the street without somehow taxing all the dwellers in the street? If yes, then there is inequity. The generous and public-spirited pay for the stingy and mean. But if no, then how is the taxing to be accomplished? And where is the line to be drawn? If you compel A to pay for lighting the street when he swears he prefers it dark (a householder may really prefer a dark street to a light one, if he goes to bed at sunset and wants the traffic to be diverted into other streets to insure his peace) ; then you will compel him to subscribe to the Watch fund, though his house is burglar-proof ; and to the fire brigade, though his house is fire-proof ; and to the prisons as part of the plant and tools of the Watch Committee ; and, it may logically be urged, to the churches and schools as part also of such plant and tools for the prevention of certain crimes.

Moreover, if you compel him to subscribe for the gas in the street, you must make him pay his share of the street itself (paving, repairing, and cleansing) ; and if the street, then the highway ; and if the highway, then the railway, and the canal, and the bridges, and even the harbors and light-houses and other common apparatus of transport and locomotion.

Personally, as an individualist, I would not compel a citizen to subscribe to *common* benefits, even though he necessarily shares them. But what I want the four lights of Anarchy above-named to tell me is : How are we to remove the injustice of allowing one man to enjoy what another has earned ? My questions are quite distinct. Thus an army under the system of conscription is a case of compulsory co-operation : a band of brigands is a case of voluntary co-operation. I hate both. I would join a voluntary association directed against either or both. Neither do I put these questions in order to cast doubts on the feasibility of Anarchy at the present time. I ask merely for information from those who are, in my opinion, best able to give it.

WORDSWORTH DONISTHORPE.

LONDON, ENGLAND.

VOLUNTARY CO-OPERATION.

[*Liberty*, May 24, 1890.]

IT is questionable whether Herbert Spencer will relish Mr. Donisthorpe's classification of him as one of four lights of Anarchy. I think he would be justified in putting in a disclaimer. No doubt Anarchy is immeasurably indebted to Mr. Spencer for a phenomenally clear exposition of its bottom truths. But he entertains heresies on the very questions which Mr. Donisthorpe raises that debar him from recognition as an Anarchist. His belief in compulsory taxation and his acceptance of the majority principle, not as a temporary necessity, but as permanently warranted within a certain sphere, show him to be unfaithful to his principle of equal liberty, as Mr. Donisthorpe has convincingly demonstrated in his recent book on " Individualism." I am sure that his answers to Mr. Donisthorpe's questions would widely differ from any that Mr. Yarros or myself could possibly make.

When it comes to Auberon Herbert, the community of thought is closer, as on practical issues he is pretty nearly at one with the attitude of *Liberty*. But I fancy that Mr. Donisthorpe would have difficulty in driving all three of us into the same corner. Before he had gone far, the ethical question of the nature of right would arise, and straightway Mr. Yarros and myself would be arrayed with Mr. Donisthorpe against Mr. Herbert.

As one of the two remaining "lights of Anarchy" appealed to, I will try to deal briefly with Mr. Donisthorpe's questions. To his first : " How far may voluntary co-operators invade the liberty of others ? " I answer : Not at all. Under this head I have previously made answer to Mr. Donisthorpe, and as to the adequacy or inadequacy of this answer he has as yet made no sign. For this reason I repeat my words. " Then liberty always, say the Anarchists. No use of force, except against the invader ; and in those cases where it is difficult to tell whether the alleged offender is an invader or not, still no use of force except where the necessity of immediate solution is so imperative that we must use it to save ourselves. And in these few cases where we must use it, let us do so frankly and squarely, acknowledging it as a matter of necessity, without seeking to harmonize our action with any political ideal or constructing any far-fetched theory of a State or collectivity having prerogatives and rights superior to those of individuals and aggregations of individuals and exempted from the operation of the ethical principles which individuals are expected to observe." This is the best rule that I can frame as a guide to voluntary co-operators. To apply it to only one of Mr. Donisthorpe's cases, I think that under a system of Anarchy, even if it were admitted that there was some ground for considering an unvaccinated person an invader, it would be generally recognized that such invasion was not of a character to require treatment by force, and that any attempt to treat it by force would be regarded as itself an invasion of a less doubtful and more immediate nature, requiring as such to be resisted.

But under a system of Anarchy how is such resistance to be made ? is Mr. Donisthorpe's second question. By another band of voluntary co-operators. But are we then, Mr. Donisthorpe will ask, to have innumerable bands of voluntary co-operators perpetually at war with each other ? Not at all. A system of Anarchy in actual operation implies a previous education of the people in the principles of Anarchy, and that in turn implies such a distrust and hatred of interference that the only band of voluntary co-operators which could gain support sufficient to enforce its will would be that which either entirely refrained from interference or reduced it to a minimum. This would be my answer to Mr. Donisthorpe, were I to admit his assumption of a state of Anarchy supervening upon a sudden collapse of Archy. But I really scout this assumption as absurd. Anarchists work for the abolition of the State, but by this they mean not its overthrow, but, as Proudhon put it, its dissolution in the economic organism. This being the case, the question before us is not, as Mr. Donisthorpe supposes, what measures and means of interference we are justified in instituting, but which ones of those already existing we should first lop off. And to this the Anarchists answer that unquestionably the first to go should be those that interfere most fundamentally with a free market, and that the economic and moral changes that would result from this would act as a solvent upon all the remaining forms of interference.

" Is compulsory co-operation ever desirable ? " Compulsory co-operation is simply one form of invading the liberty of others, and voluntary co-operators will not be justified in resorting to it—that is, in becoming compulsory co-operators— any more than resorting to any other form of invasion.

" How are we to remove the injustice of allowing one man to enjoy what another has earned ? " I do not expect it ever to be removed altogether. But I believe that for every dollar that would be enjoyed by tax-dodgers under Anarchy, a thousand dollars are now enjoyed by men who have got possession of the earnings of others through special industrial, commercial, and financial privileges granted them by authority in violation of a free market.

In regard to the various clubs referred to by Mr. Donisthorpe as based on an intolerance that is full of the spirit of interference, I can only say that probably they will cease to pattern after their great exemplar, the State, when the State shall no longer exist, and that meantime, if intolerant bigots choose to make petty tyranny a condition of association with them, we believers in liberty have the privilege of avoiding their society. Doesn't Mr. Donisthorpe suppose that we can stand it as long as they can ?

L'ÉTAT, C'EST L'ENNEMI.

[*Liberty*, February 26, 1887.]

Dear Tucker :

Since the occasion when you so arbitrarily side-tracked me in the editorial columns of *Liberty*,* certain notions of self-respect in connection with your attitude towards me have bid me pause whenever I attempted

---

* The writer of this letter, Mr. Henry Appleton, was one of *Liberty's* original editorial contributors, and remained such for five years. At the end of that time he publicly took a position not in harmony with that of the paper, on a point of great importance, and it became necessary that his editorial contributions should cease. At the same time he was cordially invited to freely make use of the other departments of the paper for the expression of his views. He never availed himself of this invitation further than to write the above letter, which, with the editor's reply, is included in this volume because, in spite of the personal nature of the controversy, important questions of principle are also dealt with.

to state my present position, and wherein I feel that I have outgrown the partial methods by which you seek to deal with existing social maladjustments.   I *did* send a communication to the *Truth Seeker*, but Macdonald, though he had just published your communication, chose to even out-do your side-tracking method of discipline by dumping me out of his columns altogether.   But, lest I should be suspected of sneaking out of the ranks through cowardice, policy, or some other unworthy consideration, I will waive my own personality in behalf of right thinking, and state my case as fully as space and the magnitude of the subject will permit.

Every subject dealing with radical reform has two main terms,—*viz.*, its basic philosophic statement and its resultant protest.   The basic statement, or affirmation, of our propaganda is the *Sovereignty of the Individual*, around which the whole science of Individualism is built,—conditioned by liberty and the cost principle. (1)   Its protest is aimed at arbitrary force which ignores individual consent, and the label which you borrowed from Proudhon by which to designate it is "Anarchism."

Fully at one with Josiah Warren's grand affirmation, I was as fully at one with the righteousness of your protest, and, paying little regard as to whether you grabbed the beast of authority by the head or the tail, pulled off my coat and went in with you to haul him out of his hole. Whether this business was called Anarchy or not was to me, for the time being, of little account, being sure that it was righteous and telling business.

But few numbers of *Liberty* had appeared, when the esteemed personal friends whom I had induced to subscribe for it all had me by the collar with this one question : " Well, allowing that your protest is all right, what have you to substitute for the existing order ?"

"Why," I replied, "the order contemplated grows out of the science of Individualism, the corner-stone of which is our basic philosophic affirmation."

" Oh, yes, I see," replied a Judge of the United States Circuit Court ; "then you and Tucker belong to an order of social scientists who put their protest ahead of their affirmation, and thus propose to move society tail-end-to. Where is your constructive side ? Give us that, and the protest, which is simply its logical deduction, will take care of itself."

I replied to him and others that the paper was small and new, but that the constructive end would certainly be held up on a level with the protesting.   So I set to work, and for a long time was bent upon making every article of mine bear upon our philosophy.   I think a review of the first volume of *Liberty* will show that nearly every article explaining its philosophy and method was from my pen. (2)

But the temptation to fight and kick and scratch and bite, instead of educate and construct, was constantly after me.   Many a resolve did I make to leave the fighting department to you, and attend strictly to the educational, but, alas ! proved too weak, till finally a well-developed habit of personal sparring, countering, dropping to avoid punishment, etc., resulted in something akin to outright "slugging," when the proprietor of the ring put me outside the ropes, while Sister Kelly flung after me the taunt of compromise, and Brother Lloyd cried out : Is this a free fight ? (3)

Now, friend Tucker, these not very enviable experiences were the result of one fatal mistake in the beginning of your work,—and one which a truly scientific propagandist should never fall victim to.   It is that you projected your propaganda from the *protest* rather than from the *basic affirmation* of *Liberty*.   The affirmation is primary, the protest is secondary. Though the protest logically leads back to the affirmation, the process is always the unnatural one of walking backwards. If you develop your propaganda logically from step to step, as projected from your affirmation, the protests go along with it and are always fortified in the accompanying philosophical base of supplies. Meanwhile education and construction are the natural work in hand. But if you start out by deploying recklessly ahead with your protest, the process of walking backwards to your base of supplies is so unnatural, and the temptation to fight instead of construct so great, that you soon fight yourself so far away from your supplies that the objector naturally cries out on every side : "Well, what have you behind you, whither would you lead us, and what shall protect us when you get there ?" You must therefore take every individual recruit back to your philosophical commissary department, where you do not take it with you. (4)

As to the term Anarchism, I have grown to be convinced that it is partial, vague, misleading, and not a comprehensive scientific complement of Individualism. If it means a protest against the existing political State, then I am, of course, an Anarchist. You say that it means more, and includes a protest against every invasion of individual right. But this is merely a convenient assumption, not warranted by its etymology, which is purely of political origin. Proudhon, from whom you borrowed it, used it only when speaking of political application of government. Most, Parsons, and Seymour base their protest against the existing political State on Communism, their model of social order. You base yours on voluntary co-operation of individual sovereigns,—*your* model. Now, if Anarchism is merely a protest against the existing State, then, as friend Morse truly says, you have no more right to say that they are not Anarchists than they have to say that you are not one. If you are all Anarchists, and become such from principles in direct antagonism to each other, then who is an Anarchist and who is not, and what reliability attaches to it as a scientific protest ? (5)

Moreover, every man has the right to be understood. If you stretch the scope of Anarchy beyond the political sphere, then it plainly comes to mean *without guiding principle,*—the very opposite of what Individualism logically leads to. Anarchy means opposed to the *archos,* or political leader, because the motive principle of politics is force. If you take the *archos* out of politics, he becomes the very thing you want as an Individualist, since he is a leader by voluntary selection. It will not do, then, to stretch the scope of Anarchism beyond political government, else you defeat your own purpose. It must, therefore, stay within the boundaries of politics, and, staying there, is only a partial and quite unscientific term to cover the whole protest which complements Individualism. (6)

When I am asked if I am an Anarchist, the person who asks it wants to know if I am the kind of person he thinks I am,—one believing in no guiding principle of social administration. In duty to myself I am obliged to say *no.* This is the eternal mischief which follows from defining one's self through his protest, rather than his affirmation. It is a position which everyone owes to himself to keep out of, where the protest is deduced from a philosophical system. All the Protestant sects define themselves by their affirmations and not by their protests, and so should all scientific systems of sociology. The protest is none the less strong—yea, far stronger—when carried along as a complement to the principles which create it, rather than as a main term,—the creature usurping the domain of its creator. (7)

As an Individualist, I find the political State a consequent rather than an antecedent. By making your protest your main term, the State must be made antecedent, which it is not. If you think the State the efficient cause of tyranny over individuals, I take it you are beclouded in a most radical delusion, into which I could easily turn a flood of light, had I not already encroached too much on your space. The State is a variable quantity,—expanding just in proportion as previous surrenders of individual sovereignty give it material. The initial cause is, however, the surrendering individual, the State being only possible after the surrender. Hence the individual is the proper objective point of reform. As he is reformed, the State disappears of itself. (8)

This subject is so rich in thought that I could fill the whole edition of *Liberty*, and then not have said half that is still pertinent to what I have begun. Having already spent too much of my life in fighting and trying to pull things around by the tail rather than by the head and heart, I propose to spend the remainder of it in constructive educational work. Fighting with tongue and pen is simply a process of spiritual killing, differing from other killing only in method. While there is so much pressing constructive work to be done, I prefer to leave the fighting line of propaganda to those whose temperament and constitution make them better fighters than builders. So go on kicking up the Anarchistic dust at the tail end of the beast of despotism, but pardon me if, having been a reform tail-twister all my life, I am trying to get a little nearer the head and horns of the beast and finish up my work on that end.

Unnatural government inevitably follows unnatural conditions, and mere scolding and kicking and protesting to all eternity will never change this stern law of nature by which she secures self-preservation. That diseased form of social administration known as the State belongs in nature to that diseased condition known as centralization, in place of localization. New York and other cities, the places where the State chiefly draws its material for rent, usury, and individual slavery in general, are ulcers on the face of this planet. Localize their populations over the soil, with individuals not only claiming, but *utilizing*, their right to the soil and other means of sovereignty, and nineteen-twentieths of the State in this country would cease to be. Yet thousands of miserable servile wretches in New York will go to labor meetings and shout, "The land belongs to the people!" while they cannot be coaxed or whipped out of this stinking nest of usury and political corruption, though you should offer them plenty of good land for nothing. In fact, large tracts across the river in New Jersey can be had for next to nothing, the young men of those sections preferring to let their fathers' homes and lands rot and run to waste in order to crowd into New York with the rest of the vulgar herd, with future visions of duplicated Jay Goulds in mind. I say that, until we can get more manly and sober incentive into individuals, the New Yorks and Chicagos will press and stink themselves into such intolerable political corruption and general demoralization that the merciful torch alone can rid humanity of them. To cry Anarchy in such communities is futile, unless you cry it in its worst sense, and that is already well-nigh realized.

Yet, friend Tucker, you have always treated with contempt my proposal to warn individuals to get out of these cities and colonize on the soil, under conditions that alone make voluntary government possible. You say great cities are blessings, and that the proper thing for these low-motived, noisy wretches who cry in labor meetings, "The land for the people!" is to stay right here and fight it out. You seem possessed with the unfortunate delusion that natural government is possible in this crowded hole, where even the rich sleep in brown-stone stalls, and the surroundings of great masses of the people are more than beastly. So long as industry, commerce, and domicile are centralized, the necessary conditions of individual sovereignty are physically impossible, while usury is invited, and the patched-up fraud which goes by the name of government becomes the necessary arrangement for holding the diseased conditions together, pending the inevitable day when fire and dynamite will come to remove these social ulcers, in order that the general body social may survive. I sincerely hope you will look into these matters more seriously, and insist on localization, the social expression of Individualism. (9)

The name Liberty, so artistically inscribed on your editorial shingle, expresses neither the affirmation nor the protest of our system, but is simply an auxiliary term between them. I think it unfortunate that your paper was not named "The Individualist," and I have in mind a name even nearer the centre than that. Had our propaganda been started on the centre from the first, we should probably have been far along in the constructive educational work, rather than come to whipping about in the tanglebrush of misunderstanding. But it is probably all for the best, and, whatever may be the mistakes of its pioneers, the new structure is bound by and by to take definite shape and avert the social suicide which the existing order is so rapidly precipitating. (10)

HENRY APPLETON.

The foregoing article has been in my hands some time, the pressure on these columns having compelled its postponement. To this delay of several weeks in publication, however, I am the more easily reconciled by the fact that its writer had himself affected its timeliness, nearly as much as was possible, by a delay of several months in its preparation. The "arbitrary side-tracking" of which he complains, and out of which it grows, occurred last August, and, if his defensive protest seems at all stale in February, it should be remembered that it would not have charmed by its freshness in January. But principles never grow old, and, looked at in their light, Mr. Appleton's words are as wise or as foolish to-day as they ever were or ever will be.

Speaking exactly, all voluntary acts are arbitrary, inasmuch as they are performed in the exercise of will, and in that sense of course the "side-tracking" of Mr. Appleton was an arbitrary act. But in no objectionable sense was it arbitrary, in no sense was it despotic. Mr. Appleton having announced that the principal object for which he and I had so long editorially co-operated had become to him a secondary and comparatively trivial object, it should have been evident to him, as it was to me and to nearly everybody else, that our co-operation in future could not be what it had been. After such a declaration, my act became a matter of course. Instead of being despotic, it was almost perfunctory. He took the side track himself ; I but officially registered his course.

I appreciate the spirit of condescension and self-abasement

which has finally permitted Mr. Appleton to continue controversy with so unworthy an antagonist as myself and to place himself on a level with that inferior race of beings who write for *Liberty* non-editorially, and in this obliteration of self I feebly emulate him by consenting to let him fill these columns with his defence or explanation after he had ignored the invitation which I had extended him to do so long enough to ascertain that he could not procure its publication elsewhere.

After these preliminaries, I may proceed to consider Mr. Appleton's arguments, numbering the points as I deal with them, to avoid the necessity of repeating the statements criticised.

(1) I do not admit anything, except the existence of the individual, as a condition of his sovereignty. To say that the sovereignty of the individual is conditioned by *Liberty* is simply another way of saying that it is conditioned by itself. To condition it by the cost principle is equivalent to instituting the cost principle by authority,—an attempted fusion of Anarchism with State Socialism which I have always understood Mr. Appleton to rebel against.

(2) To bear out this statement Mr. Appleton would have to prove himself the author of nearly every article that appeared in the first volume of *Liberty*, whereas, as a general thing, he wrote but one article for each number. Nine tenths of the editorial matter printed in *Liberty* has been written to explain its philosophy and method. It is true that Mr. Appleton has used the words philosophy and method oftener than any other writer, but mere repetition of the words is neither philosophical nor rationally methodical. I am far from saying here that Mr. Appleton's articles were not philosophical ; I am only insisting that their philosophical character was not due to the use of the word philosophy, and that others which used the word less frequently or not at all were quite as philosophical as his.

(3) Whatever fighting Mr. Appleton has done in *Liberty*, he has done of his own motion. It has always been his privilege to use these columns as freely as he chose (within certain limits of space) for "constructive educational work" on the basis of individual sovereignty. He has written as he pleased on what subjects he pleased, with seldom even a suggestion from me. In any conflict with me he has always been the attacking party.

(4) It is true that the affirmation of individual sovereignty is *logically* precedent to protest against authority as such. But

in practice they are inseparable.   To protest against the invasion of individual sovereignty is necessarily to affirm individual sovereignty.   The Anarchist always carries his base of
supplies with him.   He cannot fight away from it.   The
moment he does so he becomes an Archist.   This protest
contains all the affirmation that there is.   As I have pointed
out to Comrade Lloyd, Anarchy has no side that is affirmative in the sense of constructive.   Neither as Anarchists
nor—what is practically the same thing—as individual sovereigns have we any constructive work to do, though as progressive beings we have plenty of it.   But, if we had perfect
liberty, we might, if we chose, remain utterly inactive and still
be individual sovereigns.   Mr. Appleton's unenviable experiences are due to no mistake of mine, but to his own folly in
acknowledging the pertinence of the hackneyed cry for construction, which loses none of its nonsense on the lips of
a Circuit Court Judge.

(5) I have asked friend Morse whether he ever made the
statement here attributed to him, and he says that he never
did.   But I scarcely needed to ask him.   He and I have not
kept intellectual company these fifteen years to the end that
he should so misunderstand me.   He knows perfectly well
that I base my assertion that the Chicago Communists are not
Anarchists entirely on the ground that Anarchism means
a protest against every form of invasion.   (Whether this
definition is etymologically correct I will show in the next
paragraph.)   Those who protest against the existing political
State, with emphasis on the *existing*, are not Anarchists, but
Archists.   In objecting to a special form or method of invasion, they tacitly acknowledge the rightfulness of some
other form or method of invasion.   Proudhon never fought
any particular State ; he fought the institution itself, as
necessarily negative of individual sovereignty, whatever form
it may take.   His use of the word Anarchism shows that he
considered it coextensive with individual sovereignty.   If his
applications of it were directed against political government,
it was because he considered political government the only
invader of individual sovereignty worth talking about, having
no knowledge of Mr. Appleton's " comprehensive philosophy,"
which thinks it takes cognizance of a " vast mountain of government outside of the organized State."   The reason why
Most and Parsons are not Anarchists, while I am one, is because their Communism is another State, while my voluntary
co-operation is not a State at all.   It is a very easy matter to
tell who is an Anarchist and who is not.   One question will

always readily decide it.   Do you believe in any form of imposition upon the human will by force ?   If you do, you are
not an Anarchist.   If you do not, you are an Anarchist.   What
can any one ask more reliable, more scientific, than this ?

(6) Anarchy does not mean simply opposed to the *archos*,
or political leader.   It means opposed to *arche*.   Now, *archē*,
in the first instance, means *beginning, origin*.   From this it
comes to mean *a first principle, an element ;* then *first place,
supreme power, sovereignty, dominion, command, authority ;* and
finally *a sovereignty, an empire, a realm, a magistracy, a governmental office.*   Etymologically, then, the word anarchy may
have several meanings, among them, as Mr. Appleton says,
without guiding principle, and to this use of the word I have
never objected, always striving, on the contrary, to interpret
in accordance with their definition the thought of those who
so use it.   But the word Anarchy as a philosophical term and
the word Anarchist as the name of a philosophical sect were
first appropriated in the sense of opposition to dominion, to
authority, and are so held by right of occupancy, which fact
makes any other philosophical use of them improper and confusing.   Therefore, as Mr. Appleton does not make the political sphere coextensive with dominion or authority, he cannot
claim that Anarchy, when extended beyond the political sphere,
necessarily comes to mean *without guiding principle,* for it may
mean, and by appropriation does mean, *without dominion, without authority.*   Consequently it is a term which completely and
scientifically covers the individualistic protest.

(7) The misunderstandings of which Mr. Appleton has been
a victim are not the result of his defining himself through his
protest, for he would not have avoided them had he defined
himself through his affirmation and called himself an Individualist.   I could scarcely name a word that has been more
abused, misunderstood, and misinterpreted than Individualism.
Mr. Appleton makes so palpable a point against himself in instancing the Protestant sects that it is really laughable to see
him try to use it against me.   However it may be with the
Protestant sects, the one great Protestant body itself was born
of protest, suckled by protest, *named after protest,* and lived
on protest until the days of its usefulness were over.   If such
instances proved anything, plenty of them might be cited
against Mr. Appleton.   For example, taking one of more recent date, I might pertinently inquire which contributed most
to the freedom of the negro,—those who defined themselves
through their affirmations as the Liberty Party or as Colonizationists, or those who defined themselves through their protests

as the Anti-Slavery Society or as Abolitionists. Unquestionably the latter. And when human slavery in all its forms
shall have disappeared, I fancy that the credit of the victory
will be given quite as exclusively to the Anarchists, and that
these latter-day Colonizationists, of whom Mr. Appleton has
suddenly become so enamored, will be held as innocent of its
overthrow as are their predecessors and namesakes of the overthrow of chattel slavery.

(8) It is to be regretted that Mr. Appleton took up so much
space with other matters that he could not turn his " flood of
light " into my " delusion " that the State is the efficient cause
of tyranny over individuals ; for the question whether this is
a delusion or not is the very heart of the issue between us.
He has asserted that there is a vast mountain of government
outside of the organized State, and that our chief battle is
with that ; I, on the contrary, have maintained that practically
almost all the authority against which we have to contend is
exercised by the State, and that, when we have abolished the
State, the struggle for individual sovereignty will be well-nigh
over.   I have shown that Mr. Appleton, to maintain his position, must point out this vast mountain of government and tell
us definitely what it is and how it acts, and this is what the
readers of *Liberty* have been waiting to see him do.   But he
no more does it in his last article than in his first.   And his
only attempt to dispute my statement that the State is the
efficient cause of tyranny over individuals is confined to two or
three sentences which culminate in the conclusion that the
initial cause is the surrendering individual.   I have never denied it, and am charmed by the air of innocence with which
this substitution of *initial* for *efficient* is effected.   Of initial
causes finite intelligence knows nothing ; it can only know
causes as more or less remote.   But using the word initial in
the sense of remoter, I am willing to admit, for the sake of
the argument (though it is not a settled matter), that the
initial cause was the surrendering individual.   Mr. Appleton
doubtless means voluntarily surrendering individual, for compulsory surrender would imply the prior existence of a power
to exact it, or a primitive form of State.   But the State, having come into existence through such voluntary surrender,
becomes a positive, strong, growing, encroaching institution,
which expands, not by further voluntary surrenders, but by
exacting surrenders from its individual subjects, and which
contracts only as they successfully rebel.   That, at any rate, is
what it is to-day, and hence it is the *efficient* cause of tyranny.
The only sense, then, in which it is true that " the individual

is the proper objective point of reform" is this,—that he must be penetrated with the Anarchistic idea and taught to rebel. But this is not what Mr. Appleton means. If it were, his criticism would not be pertinent, for I have never advocated any other method of abolishing the State. The logic of his position compels another interpretation of his words,—namely, that the State cannot disappear until the individual is perfected. In saying which, Mr. Appleton joins hands with those wise persons who admit that Anarchy will be practicable when the millennium arrives. It is an utter abandonment of Anarchistic Socialism. No doubt it is true that, if the individual could perfect himself while the barriers to his perfection are standing, the State would afterwards disappear. Perhaps, too, he could go to heaven, if he could lift himself by his boot-straps.

(9) If one must favor colonization, or localization, as Mr. Appleton calls it, as a result of looking "seriously" into these matters, then he must have been trifling with them for a long time. He has combatted colonization in these columns more vigorously than ever I did or can, and not until comparatively lately did he write anything seeming to favor it. Even then he declared that he was not given over to the idea, and seemed only to be making a tentative venture into a region which he had not before explored. If he has since become a settler, it only indicates to my mind that he has not yet fathomed the real cause of the people's wretchedness. That cause is State interference with natural economic processes. The people are poor and robbed and enslaved, not because "industry, commerce, and domicile are centralized,"—in fact, such centralization has, on the whole, greatly benefited them,—but because the control of the conditions under which industry, commerce, and domicile are exercised and enjoyed is centralized. The localization needed is not the localization of persons in space, but of powers in persons,—that is, the restriction of power to self and the abolition of power over others. Government makes itself felt alike in country and in city, capital has its usurious grip on the farm as surely as on the workshop, and the oppressions and exactions of neither government nor capital can be avoided by migration. *L'État, c'est l'ennemi.* The State is the enemy, and the best means of fighting it can only be found in communities already existing. If there were no other reason for opposing colonization, this in itself would be sufficient.

(10) I do not know what Mr. Appleton means when he calls Liberty an auxiliary term between the affirmation and the

protest of our system, and I doubt if he knows himself. That it expresses practically the same idea as "The Individualist" and is a much better name for a paper I think most persons will agree.   If, "had our propaganda been started on the centre from the first, we should probably have been far along in constructive educational work," and if, assuming, that we are not far along in it, it is "probably all for the best," then it is probably all for the best that our propaganda was not started on the centre, assuming that it was not so started ; and in that case what is all this fuss about? Optimists should never complain.

A LIBERTARIAN'S PET DESPOTISMS.

[*Liberty*, January 1, 1887.]

" THERE is nothing any better than Liberty and nothing any worse than despotism, be it the theological despotism of the skies, the theocratic despotism of kings, or the democratic despotism of majorities ; and the labor reformer who starts out to combat the despotism of capital with other despotism no better lacks only power to be worse than the foe he encounters."   These are the words of my brother Pinney of the Winsted *Press*, Protectionist and Greenbacker,—that is, a man who combats the despotism of capital with that despotism which denies the liberty to buy foreign goods untaxed and that despotism which denies the liberty to issue notes to circulate as currency.   Mr. Pinney is driven into this inconsistency by his desire for high wages and an abundance of money, which he thinks it impossible to get except through tariff monopoly and money monopoly.   But religious despottism pleads a desire for salvation, and moral despotism pleads a desire for purity, and prohibitory despotism pleads a desire for sobriety.   Yet all these despotisms lead to hell, though all these hells are paved with good intentions ; and Mr. Pinney's hells are just as hot as any.   The above extract shows that he knows Liberty to be the true way of salvation.   Why, then, does he not steadily follow it ?

DEFENSIVE DESPOTISM.

[*Liberty*, January 22, 1887.]

MR. PINNEY, editor of an exceedingly bright paper, the Winsted *Press*, recently combated prohibition in the name of Liberty. Thereupon I showed him that his argument was equally good against his own advocacy of a tariff on imports and an exclusive government currency. Carefully avoiding any allusion to the analogy, Mr. Pinney now rejoins : " In brief, we are despotic because we believe it is our right to defend ourselves from foreign invaders on the one side and wild-cat swindlers on the other." Yes, just as despotic as the prohibitionists who believe it is their right to defend themselves from drunkards and rumsellers. In another column of the same issue of the *Press* I find a reference to a " logical Procrustean bed " kept in *Liberty's* office to which I fit my friends and foes by stretching out and lopping off their limbs. It is a subject on which the dismembered Mr. Pinney speaks feelingly.

STILL IN THE PROCRUSTEAN BED.

[*Liberty*, February 12, 1887.]

CONTINUING his controversy with me regarding the logic of the principle of liberty, Mr. Pinney of the Winsted *Press* says :

There is no analogy between prohibition and the tariff ; the tariff prohibits no man from indulging his desire to trade where he pleases. It is simply a tax. It is slightly analogous to a license tax for the privilege of selling liquor in a given territory, but prohibition, in theory if not in practice, is an entirely different matter.

This is a distinction without a difference. The so-called prohibitory liquor law prohibits no man, even theoretically, from indulging his desire to sell liquor ; it simply subjects the man so indulging to fine and imprisonment: The tax imposed by the tariff law and the fine imposed by the prohibitory law share alike the nature of a penalty, and are equally invasive of liberty. Mr. Pinney's argument, though of no real validity in any case, would present at least a *show* of reason in the mouth of a "revenue reformer"; but, coming from one who scorns

the idea of raising revenue by the tariff and who has declared
explicitly that he desires the tariff to be so effectively prohibitory that it shall yield no revenue at all, it lacks even the
appearance of logic.

Equally lame is Mr. Pinney's apology for a compulsory
money system.

> As for the exclusive government currency which we advocate, and
> which Mr. Tucker tortures into prohibition of individual property scrip,
> there is just as much analogy as there is between prohibition and the
> exclusive law-making, treaty-making, war-declaring, or any other powers
> delegated to government because government better than the individual
> can be intrusted with and make use of these powers.

Just as much, I agree ; and in this I can see a good reason
why Mr. Pinney, who started out with the proposition that
" there is nothing any better than liberty and nothing any
worse than despotism," should oppose law-making, treaty-
making, war-declaring, etc., but none whatever why he should
favor an exclusive government currency. How much " torture " it requires to extract the idea of " prohibition of individual property scrip" from the idea of an " *exclusive* government currency" our readers will need no help in deciding, unless
the word " exclusive " has acquired some new meaning as
unknown to them as it is to me.

But Mr. Pinney's brilliant ideas are not exhausted yet.   He
continues :

> Government prohibits the taking of private property for public uses
> without just compensation.   Therefore, if we fit Mr. Tucker's Procrus-
> tean bed, we cannot sustain this form of prohibition and consistently op-
> pose prohibition of liquor drinking ! This is consistency run mad, " anal-
> ogy " reduced to an absurdity. We are astonished that Mr. Tucker can
> be guilty of it.

So am I.   Or rather, I should be astonished if I had been
guilty of it.   But I haven't.   To say nothing of the fact that
the governmental prohibition here spoken of is a prohibition
laid by government upon itself, and that such prohibitions can
never be displeasing to an Anarchist, it is clear that the taking
of private property from persons who have violated the rights
of nobody is invasion, and to the prohibition of invasion no
friend of liberty has any objection.   Mr. Pinney has already
resorted to the plea of invasion as an excuse for his advocacy
of a tariff, and it would be a good defence if he could establish it.   But I have pointed out to him that the pretence that
the foreign merchant who sells goods to American citizens or
the individual who offers his I O U are invaders is as flimsy

as the prohibitionist's pretence that the rumseller and the drunkard are invaders. Neither invasion nor evasion will relieve Mr. Pinney of his dilemma. If he has no more effective weapons, what he dubs " Boston analogy " is in no danger from his assaults.

PINNEY STRUGGLING WITH PROCRUSTES.

[*Liberty*, March 12, 1887.]

It is the habit of the wild Westerner, whenever he cannot answer a Bostonian's arguments, to string long words into long sentences in mockery of certain fancied peculiarities of the Boston mind. Editor Pinney of the Winsted *Press* is not exactly a wild Westerner, but he lives just far enough beyond the confines of Massachusetts to enable him to resort to this device in order to obscure the otherwise obvious necessity of meeting me on reason's ground. His last reply to me fruitlessly fills two-thirds of one of his long columns with the sort of buncombe referred to, whereas that amount of space, duly applied to solid argument, might have sufficed to show one of us in error. Whatever the characteristics of Boston intellect, generically speaking, in the particular Bostonian with whom he is now confronted Mr. Pinney would see, were he a student of human nature, an extremely hard-headed individual, about whose mind there is nothing celestial or supermundane or æsthetic or aberrant, and whose only dialectics consists in searching faithfully for the fundamental weakness of his adversary's position and striking at it with swift precision, or else, finding none such, in acknowledging defeat. But human nature—at least, Boston human nature—being a puzzle to Mr. Pinney, he mistakes me for a quibbler, a disputatious advocate, and a lover of logomachy. Let us see, then, by whom logomachy was first employed in this discussion.

In an unguarded moment of righteous impatience with the folly of the prohibitionists Mr. Pinney had given utterance to some very extreme and Anarchistic doctrine. I applauded him, and ventured to call his attention to one or two forms of prohibition other than that of the liquor traffic, equally repugnant to his theory of liberty and yet championed by him. One of these was the tariff. He answered me that "there is no analogy between prohibition and the tariff ; the tariff pro-

hibits no man from indulging his desire to trade where he
pleases." Right here logomachy made its first appearance,
over the word "prohibit." I had cited two forms of State interference with trade, each of which in practice either annoys
it or hampers it or effectively prevents it, according to circumstances. This analogy in substantial results presented a difficulty, which Mr. Pinney tried to overcome by beginning a dispute over the meaning of the word "prohibit,"—a matter of
only formal moment so far as the present discussion is concerned. He declared that the tariff is not like the prohibitory
liquor law, inasmuch as it prohibits nobody from trading
where he pleases. A purely nominal distinction, if even that;
consequently Mr. Pinney, in passing it off as a real one, was
guilty of quibbling.

But I met Mr. Pinney on his own ground, allowing that,
speaking exactly, the tariff does not prohibit, but adding, on
the other hand, that neither does the so-called prohibitory
liquor law ; that both simply impose penalties on traders, in
the one case as a condition, in the other as a consequence, of
carrying on their trades. Hence my analogy still stood, and
I expected it to be grappled with. But no. Mr. Pinney, in
the very breath that he protests against quibbling, insists on
his quibble by asking if prison discipline is, then, so lax that
convicted liquor sellers can carry on their business within the
walls, and by supposing that I would still think prohibition
did not prohibit, if the extreme penalty for liquor selling were
decapitation. I do not dispute the fact that a man cannot
carry on the liquor business as long as he is in prison, nor can
Mr. Pinney dispute the fact that a man cannot sell certain
foreign goods in this country as long as he cannot raise the
money to pay the tariff ; and while I am confident that decapitation, if rigorously enforced, would stop the liquor traffic,
I am no less sure that the effect on foreign traffic would be
equally disastrous were decapitation to be enforced as a tax
upon importers. On Mr. Pinney's theory the prohibitory
liquor laws could be made non-prohibitory simply by changing the penalties from imprisonments to fines. The absurdity
of this is evident.

But, if I were to grant that Mr. Pinney's quibble shows that
there is no analogy between a prohibitory liquor law and
a revenue tariff (which I do not grant, but deny), it would
still remain for him to show that there is no analogy between
a prohibitory liquor law and such a tariff as he favors,—one so
high as to be absolutely prohibitory and yield no revenue at all,
—or else admit his inconsistency in opposing the former and

not the latter.   He has not attempted to meet this point, even with a quibble.

One other point, however, he does try to meet.   To my statement that his position on the abstract question of liberty involves logically opposition to government in all its functions he makes this answer :

> Between puritan meddling with a man's domestic affairs, and necessary government regulation of matters which the individual is incompetent to direct, yet which must be directed in order to secure to the individual his rightful liberty, there is a distance sufficiently large to give full play to our limited faculties.

But who is to judge what government regulation is "necessary" and decide what matters "the individual is incompetent to direct"?   The majority?   But the majority are just as likely to decide that prohibition is necessary and that the individual is incompetent to direct his appetite as that a tariff is necessary and that the individual is incompetent to make his own contracts.   Mr. Pinney, then, must submit to the will of the majority.   His original declaration, however, was that despotism was despotism, whether exercised by a monarch or a majority.   This drives him back upon liberty in all things. For just as he would object to the reign of a monarch disposed to administer affairs rationally and equitably simply because he was a monarch, so he must object to the reign of a majority, even though its administration were his ideal, simply because it is a majority.   Mr. Pinney is trying to serve both liberty and authority, and is making himself ridiculous in the attempt.

A BACK TOWN HEARD FROM.

[*Liberty*, August 13, 1887.]

THE Winsted *Press* makes a long leader to ridicule the Anarchists for favoring private enterprise in the letter-carrying business.   It grounds its ridicule on two claims,—first, that private enterprise would charge high rates of postage, and, second, that it would not furnish transportation to out-of-the-way points.   An indisputable fact has frequently been cited in *Liberty* which instantly and utterly overthrows both of these claims.   Its frequent citation, however, has had no effect upon the believers in a government postal monopoly. I do not expect another repetition to produce any effect upon the Winsted *Press;* still I shall try it.

Some half-dozen years ago, when letter postage was still three cents, Wells, Fargo & Co. were doing a large business in carrying letters throughout the Pacific States and Territories. Their rate was five cents, more than three of which they expended, as the legal monopoly required, in purchasing of the United States a stamped envelope in which to carry the letter intrusted to their care. That is to say, on every letter which they carried they had to pay a tax of more than three cents. Exclusive of this tax, Wells, Fargo & Co. got less than two cents for each letter which they carried, while the government got three cents for each letter which it carried itself, and more than three cents for each letter which Wells, Fargo & Co. carried. On the other hand, it cost every individual five cents to send by Wells, Fargo & Co., and only three to send by the government. Moreover, the area covered was one in which immensity of distance, sparseness of population, and irregularities of surface made out-of-the-way points unusually difficult of access. Still, in spite of all these advantages on the side of the government, its patronage steadily dwindled, while that of Wells, Fargo & Co. as steadily grew. Pecuniarily this, of course, was a benefit to the government. But for this very reason such a condition of affairs was all the more mortifying. Hence the postmaster-general sent a special commissioner to investigate the matter. He fulfilled his duty and reported to his superior that Wells, Fargo & Co. were complying with the law in every particular, and were taking away the business of the government by furnishing a prompter and securer mail service, not alone to principal points, but to more points and remoter points than were included in the government list of post-offices.

Whether this state of things still continues I do not know. I presume, however, that it does, though the adoption of two-cent postage may have changed it. In either case the fact is one that triumphs over all possible sarcasms. In view of it, what becomes of Editor Pinney's fear of ruinous rates of postage and his philanthropic anxiety on account of the dwellers in Wayback and Hunkertown?

IN FORM A REPLY, IN REALITY A SURRENDER.

[*Liberty*, September 10, 1887.]

APPRECIATING the necessity of at least seeming to meet the indisputable fact which I opposed to its championship of government postal monopoly, the Winsted *Press* presents the following ghost of an answer, which may be as convincing to the victims of political superstition as most materializations are to the victims of religious superstition, but which, like those materializations, is so imperceptible to the touch of the hard-headed investigator that, when he puts his hand upon it, he does not find it there.

The single instance of Wells, Fargo & Co., cited by B. R. Tucker to prove the advantage of private enterprise as a mail carrier, needs fuller explanation of correlated circumstances to show its true significance. As stated by Mr. Tucker, this company half a dozen years ago did a large business carrying letters throughout the Pacific States and Territories to distant and sparsely populated places for five cents per letter, paying more than three to the government in compliance with postal law and getting less than two for the trouble, and, though it cost the senders more, the service was enough better than government's to secure the greater part of the business.

This restatement of my statement is fair enough, except that it but dimly conveys the idea that Wells, Fargo & Co. were carrying, not only to distant and sparsely populated places, but to places thickly settled and easy of access, and were beating the government there also,—a fact of no little importance.

Several facts may explain this : 1. Undeveloped government service in a new country, distant from the seat of government.

Here the ghost appears, all form and no substance. "John Jones is a better messenger than John Smith," declares the Winsted *Press*, "because Jones can run over stony ground, while Smith cannot." "Indeed !" I answer ; "why, then, did Smith outrun Jones the other day in going from San Francisco to Wayback ?" "Oh ! that may be explained," the *Press* rejoins, "by the fact that the ground was stony." The *Press* had complained against the Anarchistic theory of free competition in postal service that private enterprise would not reach remote points, while government does reach them. I proved by facts that private enterprise was more successful than government in reaching remote points. What sense, then, is there in answering that these points are distant from the government's headquarters and that it had not developed its service? The whole point lies in the fact that private enterprise was the first to develop its service and the most successful in maintaining it at a high degree of efficiency.

2. Government competition which kept Wells & Fargo from charging monopoly prices.

If the object of a government postal service is to keep private enterprise from charging high prices, no more striking illustration of the stupid way in which government works to achieve its objects could be cited than its imposition of a tax of two (then three) cents a letter upon private postal companies. It is obvious that this tax was all that kept Wells, Fargo & Co. from reducing their letter-rate to three or even two cents, in which case the government probably would have lost the remnant of business which it still commanded. This is guarding against monopoly prices with a vengeance! The competitor, whether government or individual, who must tax his rival in order to live is no competitor at all, but a monopolist himself. It is not government competition that Anarchists are fighting, but government monopoly. It should be added, however, that, pending the transformation of governments into voluntary associations, even government competition is unfair, because an association supported by compulsory taxation could always, if it chose, carry the mails at less than cost and tax the deficit out of the people.

3. Other paying business which brought the company into contact with remote districts and warranted greater safeguards to conveyance than government then offered to its mail carriers.

Exactly. What does it prove? Why, that postal service and express service can be most advantageously run in conjunction, and that private enterprise was the first to find it out. This is one of the arguments which the Anarchists use.

4. A difference of two cents was not appreciated in a country where pennies were unknown.

Here the phantom attains the last degree of attenuation. If Mr. Pinney will call at the Winsted post-office, his postmaster will tell him—what common sense ought to have taught him—that of all the stamps used not over five per cent. are purchased singly, the rest being taken two, three, five, ten, a hundred, or a thousand at a time. Californians are said to be very reckless in the matter of petty expenditures, but I doubt if any large portion of them would carry their prodigality so far as to pay five dollars a hundred for stamps when they could get them at three dollars a hundred on the next corner.

These conditions do not exist elsewhere in this country at present. Therefore the illustration proves nothing.

Proves nothing ! Does it not prove that private enterprise outstripped the government under the conditions that then and there existed, which were difficult enough for both, but extraordinarily embarrassing for the former ?

We know that private enterprise does not afford express facilities to sparsely settled districts throughout the country.

I know nothing of the kind. The express companies cover practically the whole country. They charge high rates to points difficult of access ; but this is only just. The government postal rates, on the contrary, are unjust. It certainly is not fair that my neighbor, who sends a hundred letters to New York every year, should have to pay two cents each on them, though the cost of carriage is but one cent, simply because the government spends a dollar in carrying for me one letter a year to Wayback, for which I also pay two cents. It may be said, however, that where each individual charge is so small, a schedule of rates would cause more trouble and expense than saving ; in other words, that to keep books would be poor economy. Very likely ; and in that case no one would find it out sooner than the private mail companies. This, however, is not the case in the express business, where parcels of all sizes and weights are carried.

No more would it mail facilities. A remarkable exception only proves the rule. But, if private enterprise can and will do so much, why doesn't it do it now? The law stands no more in the way of Adams Express than it did in the way of the Wells & Fargo express.

This reminds me of the question with which Mr. Pinney closed his discussion with me regarding free money. He desired to know why the Anarchists did not start a free money system, saying that they ought to be shrewd enough to devise some way of evading the law. As if any competing business could be expected to succeed if it had to spend a fortune in contesting lawsuits or in paying a heavy tax to which its rival was not subject ! So handicapped, it could not possibly succeed unless its work was of such a nature as to admit the

widest range of variation in point of excellence.   This was
the case in the competition between Wells, Fargo & Co. and
the government.   The territory covered was so ill-adapted to
postal facilities that it afforded a wide margin for the display
of superiority, and Wells, Fargo & Co. took advantage of this
to such an extent that they beat the government in spite of
their handicap.   But in the territory covered by Adams Express it is essentially different.   There the postal service is so
simple a matter that the possible margin of superiority would
not warrant an extra charge of even one cent a letter.   But I
am told that Adams Express would be only too glad of the
chance to carry letters at one cent each, if there were no tax
to be paid on the business.   If the governmentalists think
that the United States can beat Adams Express, why do they
not dare to place the two on equal terms ?   That is a fair question.   But when a man's hands are tied, to ask him why he
doesn't fight is a coward's question.

FOOL VOTERS AND FOOL EDITORS.

[*Liberty*, August 4, 1883.]

UNCLE Sam carries one hundred pounds of newspapers two thousand
miles for two dollars, and still pays the railroad three times too much for
mail service.   An express company would charge twenty dollars for the
same service ; yet some people don't know why all express stockholders
are millionaires and the people getting poorer.   In fact, some people
don't know anything at all and don't want to.   It is very unfortunate
that such people have votes.— *The Anti-Monopolist.*

Yes, Uncle Sam carries one hundred pounds of newspapers
two thousand miles, not for two dollars, but for one dollar,
pays the railroad more than its services are worth, and loses
about five dollars a trip.

Yes, an express company would charge twenty dollars for the
same service, because it knows it would be folly to attempt to
compete with the one-dollar rate, and therefore charges for its
necessarily limited business such rates as those who desire a
guarantee of promptness and security are willing to pay.

Uncle Sam nevertheless continues to carry at the one-dollar
rate, knowing that this is a good way to induce the newspapers
to wink at his villainies, and that he can and does make up in
two ways his loss of five dollars a trip,—1, by carrying one
hundred pounds of letters two thousand miles for thirty-two

dollars and forbidding anybody else to carry them for less, although the express companies would be glad of the chance to do the same service for sixteen dollars ; and, 2, by taking toll from all purchasers of whiskey and tobacco at home, and of various other articles from foreign countries.

And yet some people don't know why the thousands of officeholders who are pulling away at the public teats are getting fat while the people are getting poorer. In fact, some people don't know anything at all except, as Josh Billings said, " a grate menny things that ain't so." It is very unfortunate that such people are intrusted with the editing of newspapers.

ERGO AND PRESTO !

[*Liberty*, July 7, 1888.]

IN Henry George may be seen a pronounced type of the not uncommon combination of philosopher and juggler. He possesses in a marked degree the faculty of luminous exposition of a fundamental principle, but this faculty he supplements with another no less developed,—that of so obscuring the connection between his fundamental principle and the false applications thereof which he attempts that only a mind accustomed to analysis can detect the flaw and the fraud. We see this in the numerous instances in which he has made a magnificent defence of the principle of individual liberty in theory, only to straightway deny it in practice, while at the same time palming off his denial upon an admiring following as a practical affirmation. Freedom of trade is the surest guarantee of prosperity ; *ergo*, there must be perfect liberty of banking ; *presto!* there shall be no issue of money save by the government. Here, by the sly divorce of money-issuing from banking, he seems to justify the most ruinous of monopolies by the principle of liberty. And this is but an abridgment of the road by which he reaches very many of his practical conclusions. His simplicity and clearness as a philosopher so win the confidence of his disciples that he can successfully play the *rôle* of a prestidigitator before their very eyes. They do not notice the transformation from logic to legerdemain. For a certain distance he proceeds carefully, surely, and straightforwardly by the method of *ergo;* and then, when the minds of his followers are no longer on the alert, *presto!* he suddenly shouts, and in a twinkling they are switched off upon the track

of error without a suspicion that they are not still bound direct
for truth. It is this power to prostitute a principle to the furtherance of its opposite, to use truth as a tool of falsehood,
that makes Mr. George one of the most dangerous men among
all those now posing as public teachers.

One of the latest and craftiest of his offences in this direction was committed in the *Standard* of June 23 in a discussion of the copyright problem. A correspondent having raised
the question of property in ideas, Mr. George discusses it
elaborately. Taking his stand upon the principle that productive labor is the true basis of the right of property, he argues through three columns, with all the consummate ability
for which credit is given him above, to the triumphant vindication of the position that there can rightfully be no such
thing as the exclusive ownership of an idea.

No man, he says, "can justly claim ownership in natural
laws, nor in any of the relations which may be perceived by
the human mind, nor in any of the potentialities which nature
holds for it. . . . Ownership comes from production.   It
cannot come from discovery. Discovery can give no right of
ownership. . . . No man can discover anything which, so
to speak, was not put there to be discovered, and which some
one else might not in time have discovered. If he finds it, it
was not lost. It, or its potentiality, existed before he came.
It was there to be found. . . . In the production of any material thing—a machine, for instance—there are two separable
parts,—the abstract idea or principle, which may be usually
expressed by drawing, by writing, or by word of mouth ; and
the concrete form of the particular machine itself, which
is produced by bringing together in certain relations certain
quantities and qualities of matter, such as wood, steel, brass,
brick, rubber, cloth, etc. There are two modes in which labor
goes to the making of the machine,—the one in ascertaining
the principle on which such machines can be made to work ;
the other in obtaining from their natural reservoirs and bringing together and fashioning into shape the quantities and
qualities of matter which in their combination constitute the
concrete machine. In the first mode labor is expended in discovery. In the second mode it is expended in production.
The work of discovery may be done once for all, as in the
case of the discovery in prehistoric time of the principle or
idea of the wheelbarrow. But the work of production is required afresh in the case of each particular thing. No matter
how many thousand millions of wheelbarrows have been produced, it requires fresh labor of production to make another

one. . . . The natural reward of labor expended in discovery is in the use that can be made of the discovery without interference with the right of any one else to use it.   But to this natural reward our patent laws endeavor to add an artificial reward.   Although the effect of giving to the discoverers of useful devices or processes an absolute right to their exclusive use would be to burden all industry with most grievous monopolies, and to greatly retard, if not put a stop to, further inventions, yet the theory of our patent laws is that we can stimulate discoveries by giving a modified right of ownership in their use for a term of years.   In this we seek by special laws to give a special reward to labor expended in discovery, which does not belong to it of natural right, and is of the nature of a bounty.   But as for labor expended in the second of these modes,—in the production of the machine by the bringing together in certain relations of certain quantities and qualities of matter,—we need no special laws to reward that. Absolute ownership attaches to the results of such labor, not by special law, but by common law.   And if all human laws were abolished, men would still hold that, whether it were a wheelbarrow or a phonograph, the concrete thing belonged to the man who produced it.   And this, not for a term of years, but in perpetuity.   It would pass at his death to his heirs or to those to whom he devised it."

The whole of the preceding paragraph is quoted from Mr. George's article.   I regard it as conclusive, unanswerable.   It proceeds, it will be noticed, entirely by the method of *ergo.* But it is time for the philosopher to disappear.   He has done his part of the work, which was the demolition of patents. Now it is the prestidigitator's turn.   It remains for him to justify copyright,—that is, property, not in the ideas set forth in a book, but in the manner of expressing them.   So juggler George steps upon the scene.   *Presto!* he exclaims : " Over and above any 'labor of discovery' expended in thinking out *what* to say, is the 'labor of production' expended on *how* to say it."   Observe how cunningly it is taken for granted here that the task of giving literary expression to an idea is labor of production rather than labor of discovery.   But is it so ? Right here comes in the juggler's trick ; we will subject it to the philosopher's test.   The latter has already been quoted : " *The work of discovery may be done once for all . . . but the work of production is required afresh in the case of each particular thing.*"   Can anything be plainer than that he who does the work of combining words for the expression of an idea saves just that amount of labor to all who thereafter choose

to use the same words in the same order to express the same
idea, and that this work, not being required afresh in each
particular case, is not work of production, and that, not being
work of production, it gives no right of property ? In quoting
Mr. George above I did not have to expend any labor on "how
to say " what he had already said. He had saved me that
trouble. I simply had to write and print the words on fresh
sheets of paper. These sheets of paper belong to me, just as
the sheets on which he wrote and printed belong to him. But
the particular combination of words belongs to neither of us.
He discovered it, it is true, but that fact gives him no right to
it. Why not ? Because, to use his own phrases, this combination of words "existed potentially before he came "; "it
was there to be found "; and if he had not found it, some one
else would or might have done so. The work of copying or
printing books is analogous to the production of wheelbarrows, but the original work of the author, whether in thinking
or composing, is analogous to the *invention* of the wheelbarrow ; and the same argument that demolishes the right of the
inventor demolishes the right of the author. The method of
expressing an idea is itself an idea, and therefore not appro-
priable.

The exposure is complete. But will Mr. George acknowledge it ? Not he. He will ignore it, as he has ignored similar
exposures in these columns of his juggling with the questions
of rent, interest, and money. The juggler never admits an
exposure. It would be ruinous to his business. He lies low
till the excitement has subsided, and then " bobs up serenely "
and suavely to hoodwink another crowd of greenhorns with
the same old tricks. Such has been juggler George's policy
heretofore ; such it will be hereafter.

THE RIGHT OF OWNERSHIP.

[*Liberty*, August 2, 1890.]

To the Editor of Liberty :
    Will you permit me to ask you for the definition, from an Anarchistic
standpoint, of the " Right of Ownership " ? What do you mean to convey when you say that a certain thing belongs to a certain person ?
    Before directing my attention to the study of the social question, I had
a rather confused notion of the meaning of this term. Ownership appeared to me a kind of amalgamation of wealth with the individual. This
conception could, of course, not be sustained in an analysis of the social

question and the distribution of wealth. For some time I could not obtain a clear notion as to what the term, as popularly used, really signifies, nor could I find a satisfactory definition in any of the books I had at command. The writers of dictionaries content themselves with quoting a number of synonyms which throw no light on the subject, and the writers on Political Economy seem not to bother themselves about such trifles. They need no solid foundations for their theories since they build their castles in the air. It is said that ownership is the "exclusive right of possession," but this explanation fails to meet the inquiry of him who can nowhere find a satisfactory explanation of the import of the term "right."

It is clear that a radical distinction exists between possession and ownership, though these concepts are in a measure related to each other. It seems reasonable, therefore, to expect to find a clue by examining the distinction that exists between the possessor and the owner of a thing. And this examination is not difficult. The owner of a thing which for some reason is in the possession of some one else may demand its return, and, if it is not returned willingly, *the aid of the law can be invoked.* This leads to the conclusion that the right of ownership is that relation between a thing and a person created by the social promise to guarantee possession.

This is the only definition that appears satisfactory to me. But it implies the existence of a social organization, however crude it may be. It implies that a supreme power will enforce the command : "Thou shalt not steal." And in the measure in which this social organization gains stability and in which this social power gains a more universal supremacy, the right of ownership will assume a more definite existence.

Now I can perhaps repeat my question in a way to be better understood. Has Anarchism a different conception of the right of ownership, or is this right altogether repudiated, or is it assumed that out of the ruins of government another social organization, wielding a supreme power, will arise? I can at present see no other alternative.

                                                    HUGO BILGRAM.

In discussing such a question as this, it is necessary at the start to put aside, as Mr. Bilgram doubtless does put aside, the intuitive idea of right, the conception of right as a standard which we are expected to observe from motives supposed to be superior to the consideration of our interests. When I speak of the "right of ownership," I do not use the word "right" in that sense at all. In the thought that I take to be fundamental in Mr. Bilgram's argument—namely, that there is no right, from the standpoint of society, other than social expediency—I fully concur. But I am equally certain that the standard of social expediency—that is to say, the facts as to what really is socially expedient, and the generalizations from those facts which we may call the laws of social expediency —exists apart from the decree of any social power whatever. In accordance with this view, the Anarchistic definition of the right of ownership, while closely related to Mr. Bilgram's, is such a modification of his that it does not carry the implication which his carries and which he points out. From an Anarchistic standpoint, the right of ownership is that control of a thing by a person which will receive either social sanction, or else unanimous individual sanction, when the laws of social expediency shall have been finally discovered. (Of course I might go farther and explain that Anarchism considers the greatest amount of liberty compatible with equality of liberty the fundamental law of social expediency, and that nearly all Anarchists consider labor to be the only basis of the right of ownership in harmony with that law ; but this is not essential to the definition, or to the refutation of Mr. Bilgram's point against Anarchism.)

It will be seen that the Anarchistic definition just given does not imply necessarily the existence of an organized or instituted social power to enforce the right of ownership. It contemplates a time when social sanction shall be superseded by unanimous individual sanction, thus rendering enforcement needless. But in such an event, by Mr. Bilgram's definition, the right of ownership would cease to exist. In other words, he seems to think that, if all men were to agree upon a property standard and should voluntarily observe it, property would then have no existence simply because of the absence of any institution to protect it. Now, in the view of the Anarchists, property would then exist in its perfection.

So I would answer Mr. Bilgram's question, as put in his concluding paragraph, as follows : Anarchism does not repudiate the right of ownership, but it has a conception thereof sufficiently different from Mr. Bilgram's to include the possibility of an end of that social organization which will arise, not out of the ruins of government, but out of the transformation of government into voluntary association for defence.

INDIVIDUAL SOVEREIGNTY OUR GOAL.

[*Liberty*, June 7, 1890.]

IN an unsigned article in the *Open Court* (written, I suspect by the editor) I find the following :

When Anarchists teach the sovereignty of the individual, we have to inform them that society is an organized whole. The individual is what he is through the community only, and he must obey the laws that govern the growth of communal life. The more voluntary this obedience is, the better it is for the community as well as for the individual himself. But if the individual does not voluntarily obey the laws of the community, so-

ciety has a right to enforce them.   There is no such thing as sovereignty
of the individual.

True, there is no such thing ; and we Anarchists mean that
there shall be such a thing.   The criticism of the *Open Court*
writer is doubtless valid against those Anarchists who premise
the sovereignty of the individual as a natural right to which
society has no right to do violence.   But I cannot understand
its force at all when offered, as it is, in comment on the declaration of " a leading Anarchist of Chicago " that the *goal* of
progress is individual sovereignty.

Anarchism of the " natural right " type is out of date.   The
Anarchism of to-day affirms the right of society to coerce the
individual and of the individual to coerce society so far as
either has the requisite power.   It is ready to admit all that
the *Open Court* writer claims in behalf of society, and then go
so far beyond him that it will take his breath away.

But, while admitting and affirming all this, Anarchism also
maintains (and this is its special mission) that an increasing
familiarity with sociology will convince both society and the
individual that *practical* individual sovereignty—that is, the
greatest amount of liberty compatible with equality of liberty
—is the law of social life, the only condition upon which human beings can live in harmony.   When this truth is ascertained and acted upon, then we shall have individual sovereignty in reality,—not as a sacred natural right vindicated,
but as a social expedient agreed upon, or we will even say
as a privilege conferred, if the *Open Court* writer prefers the
word as tending to tickle the vanity of his god, Society.   It
is in this sense that *Liberty* champions individual sovereignty.
The motto on our flag is not " Liberty a Natural Right," but
" Liberty the Mother of Order."

It is to be hoped that the *Open Court* writer will note this
before again giving voice to the commonplace twaddle about
Nationalism and Anarchism as extreme opposites both of
which are right and both wrong.   Anarchism is exactly as extreme, exactly as right, and exactly as wrong, as that "ideal
state of society " which the *Open Court* writer pictures,—" a
state in which there is as much order as possible and at the
same time as much individual liberty as possible."   In fact,
Anarchism finds itself exactly coextensive with the idea which
its critic thus expresses : " Wherever a nation is developing
in the line of progress, we shall always notice an increasing realization of these two apparently antagonistic principles,
—liberty and order."

NEW ABOLITION AND ITS NINE DEMANDS.

[*Liberty*, January 25, 1890.]

THE New Abolition Party, nominally of the United States, but really limited at present (pending the time when it is to 'sweep the country like a wave ") by the walls of the *Individualist* office at Denver, started out with eight demands ; and, taken as a whole, very good demands they were. Lately it has added a ninth ; just why, I don't know, unless New Abolition was jealous of Liberalism and bound to have as many demands. This explanation seems hardly reasonable, because in the case of Liberalism nine does not seem to have proved a magic number for demand purposes. However this may be, it is certain that the ninth demand is a square contradiction of some of the most important of its eight other demands, notably the fifth and seventh. The ninth demand is for "collective maintenance and control of all public highways, waterways, railways, canals, ditches, reservoirs, telegraphs, telephones, ferries, bridges, water works, gas works, parks, electric plants, etc., to be operated in the interest of the people." The seventh demand is for "immediate and unconditional repeal of all forms of compulsory taxation." The fifth demand is for "immediate and unconditional repeal of all statutes that in any way interfere with free trade between individuals of the same or of different countries." Suppose that Mr. Stuart (the father of New Abolition) and I live on the same side of a river. I have a boat ; Mr. Stuart has none. Mr. Stuart comes to me and says : " How much will you charge to row me across the river? " " Ten cents," I answer. " It is a bargain, " says Mr. Stuart, and he steps into the boat. But up steps at the same time the New Abolition party in the shape of a police-man (and it will have to take that shape, because in these mat-ters a demand without a blue coat on its back and a club in its hand is an ineffective demand) and says to me : " See here! stop that ! Don't you know that the New Abolition party, which at the last election 'swept the country like a wave,' in-undated your row-boat with the rest by instituting the ' collec-tive maintenance and control of all ferries '? If you attempt to row Mr. Stuart across the river, I shall confiscate your boat in the name of the law." And then, addressing Mr. Stuart, the policeman adds : " So you may as well get out of that boat and take the ferry-boat which the New Abolitionists have

already provided." "Officer, you are exceeding your duty,"
hotly replies Mr. Stuart ; "I have made a bargain with Mr.
Tucker, and, if you were at all qualified for your post, you
would know that the New Abolition party demanded, in the
platform upon which it 'swept the country like a wave,' the
'immediate and unconditional repeal of all statutes that in any
way interfere with free trade.'" "Yes," I say, hastening to put
in my oar (I use the word metaphorically, not referring at all
to my boat-oar), "and you would know too that this same triumphant party demanded the 'immediate and unconditional
repeal of all forms of compulsory taxation.' So I should like
to see you confiscate my boat." "Oh! you're a couple of
tom-noodles, way behind the times," retorts the policeman ;
"the demands of which you speak were numbered five and
seven ; but the demand in regard to ferries was a ninth and
later demand, which invalidated all previous demands that
conflicted with it." Mr. Stuart, being a law abiding citizen
and not one of those "Boston Anarchists" who do not believe in the State, sorrowfully steps from the boat inwardly
cursing his political offspring, takes the government ferry-boat
an hour later, and gets across the river just in time to lose
the benefit of a lecture by a "Boston Anarchist" on "The
Fate of the Individualist Who Threw a Sop to the Socialistic
Cerberus."

COMPULSORY EDUCATION NOT ANARCHISTIC.

[*Liberty*, August 6, 1892.]

A PUBLIC-SCHOOL teacher of my acquaintance, much interested in Anarchism and almost a convert thereto, finds himself under the necessity of considering the question of compulsory education from a new standpoint, and is puzzled by it.
In his quandary he submits to me the following questions :

1. If a parent starves, tortures, or mutilates his child, thus actively
aggressing upon it to its injury, is it just for other members of the group
to interfere to prevent such aggression ?

2. If a parent neglects to provide food, shelter, and clothing for his
child, thus neglecting the self-sacrifice implied by the second corollary of
the law of equal freedom, is it just for other members of the group to
interfere to compel him so to provide ?

3. If a parent wilfully aims to prevent his child from reaching mental
or moral, without regard to physical, maturity, is it just for other members of the group to interfere to prevent such aggression ?

4. If a parent neglects to provide opportunity for the child to reach mental maturity,—assuming that mental maturity can be defined,—is it just
for other members of the group to interfere to compel him so to provide?

5. *If it be granted* that a knowledge of reading and writing—*i.e.*, of
making and interpreting permanent signs of thought—is a *necessary* function of maturity, and if a parent neglects and refuses to provide or accept opportunity for his child to learn to read and write, is it just for
other members of the group to interfere to compel the parent so to provide or accept?

Before any of these questions can be answered with a straight
yes or no, it must first be ascertained whether the hypothetical
parent violates, by his hypothetical conduct, the equal freedom,
not of his child, but of other members of society. Not of his
child, I say; why? Because, the parent being an independent, responsible individual, and the child being a dependent,
irresponsible individual, it is obviously inequitable and virtually impossible that equal freedom should characterize the relations between them. In this child, however, who is one day
to pass from the condition of dependence and irresponsibility
to the condition of independence and responsibility, the other
members of society have an interest, and out of this consideration the question at once arises whether the parent who impairs
the conditions of this child's development thereby violates
the equal freedom of those mature individuals whom this development unquestionably affects.

Now it has been frequently pointed out in *Liberty*, in discussing the nature of invasion, that there are certain acts which
all see clearly as invasive and certain other acts which all see
clearly as non-invasive, and that these two classes comprise
vastly the larger part of human conduct, but that they are
separated from each other, not by a hard and fast line, but by
a strip of dark and doubtful territory, which shades off in
either direction into the regions of light and clearness by an
imperceptible gradation. In this strip of greater or less obscurity are included that minority of human actions which
give rise to most of our political differences, and in the thick
of its Cimmerian centre we find the conduct of parent toward
child.

We cannot, then, clearly identify the maltreatment of child
by parent as either invasive or non-invasive of the liberty of
third parties. In such a difficulty we must have recourse to
the policy presented by Anarchism for doubtful cases. As I
cannot state this policy better than I have stated it already, I
quote my own words from *Liberty*, No. 154:

"Then liberty always, say the Anarchists. No use of force,
except against the invader; and in those cases where it is diffi-

cult to tell whether the alleged offender is an invader or not, still
no use of force except where the necessity of immediate solution is so imperative that we must use it to save ourselves.
And in these few cases where we must use it, let us do so frankly
and squarely, acknowledging it as a matter of necessity, without seeking to harmonize our action with any political ideal or
constructing any far-fetched theory of a State or collectivity
having prerogatives and rights superior to those of individuals
and aggregations of individuals and exempted from the operation of the ethical principles which individuals are expected
to observe."

In other words, those of us who believe that liberty is the
great educator, the "mother of order," will, in case of doubt,
give the benefit to liberty, or non-interference, unless it is
plain that non-interference will result in certain and *immediate*
disaster, if not irretrievable, at any rate too grievous to be
borne.

Applying this rule to the subject under discussion, it is evident at once that mental and moral maltreatment of children,
since its effects are more or less remote, should not be met
with physical force, but that physical maltreatment, if sufficiently serious, may be so met.

In specific answer to my questioner, I would say that, if he
insists on the form of his questions, " Is it just ? " etc., I cannot
answer them at all, because it is impossible for me to decide
whether interference is just unless I can first decide whether or
no there has already been invasion. But if, instead of " Is it
just ? " he should ask in each case, " Is it Anarchistic policy ? "
I would then make reply as follows :

1. Yes.
2. Yes, in sufficiently serious cases.
3. No.
4. No.
5. No.

RELATIONS BETWEEN PARENTS AND CHILDREN.

[*Liberty*, September 3, 1892.]

THE wisdom of acts is measured by their consequences.

The individual's measure of consequences is proportionate to the circle
of his outlook. His horizons may lie so near that he can only measure
at short range. But, whether they be near or far, he can only judge

of consequences as approximately or remotely touching himself. His judgment may err ; his motive remains always the same, whether he be conscious of it or not.

That motive is necessarily egoistic, since no one deliberately chooses misery when happiness is open to him. Acts always resulting either indifferently or in furtherance of happiness or increase of misery, one who has power to decide and intelligence to determine probable consequences will certainly give preference to the course which will ultimately advance his own happiness.

The law of equal freedom, " Every one is free to do whatsoever he wills," appears to me to be the primary condition to happiness. If I fail to add the remainder of Herbert Spencer's celebrated law of equal freedom, I shall only risk being misinterpreted by persons who cannot understand that the opening affirmation includes what follows, since, if any one did infringe upon the freedom of another, all would not be equally free.

Liberty without intelligence rushes towards its own extinction continually, and continually rescues itself by the knowledge born of its pain.

Intelligence without liberty is a mere potentiality, a nest-full of unhatched eggs.

Progress, therefore, presupposes the union of intelligence and liberty : Freedom to act, wisdom to guide the action.

Equal freedom is the primary condition to happiness.

Intelligence is the primary condition to equality in freedom.

Liberty and intelligence acting and reacting upon each other produce growth.

Thus growth and happiness are seen to be, if not actually synonymous, almost inseparable companions.

Where equal freedom is rendered impossible by disproportion in degrees of development, the hope of the higher units lies in the education of the lower.

Children, because of their ignorance, are elements of inharmony, hindrances to equal freedom. To quicken the processes of their growth is to contribute towards the equalization of social forces.

Then, liberty being essential to growth, they must be left as free as is compatible with their own safety and the freedom of others.

Just here arises my difficulty, which I freely admit. For the enunciation of this principle is the opening of a Pandora's box, from which all things fly out excepting adult judgment.

Who shall decide upon the permissible degree of freedom ? Who shall adjust the child's freedom to its safety so that the two shall be delicately, flawlessly balanced ?

The fecundity of these questions is without limit. Of them are born controversies that plague all the unregenerate alike, whether they be philosophers or the humblest truth-seekers.

Christians escape this toilsome investigation. Their faith in rulership simplifies all the relations of life. Their conduct need not be consistent with equal freedom, since obedience, not liberty, is the basis of their ideal society.

Reluctantly I admit that during infancy and to some extent in childhood others must decide what is for a child's welfare.

The human babe is a pitiably helpless and lamentably ignorant animal. It does not even know when it is hungry, but seeks the maternal breast as a cure-all for every variety of physical uneasiness ; therefore the mother or nurse must inevitably decide for it even the quantity of

nourishment it may safely receive and the length of time that may inter-
vene between tenders of supplies. That these judgments are far from
infallible is well known.   One mother of five living children confessed
to me that she had lost one child, starved it in the process of learning
that her lactation furnished a substance little more nutritious than water.

Grown older, the babe does not know the danger of touching a red-
hot stove.   How should it know?   It is without experience.   The
mother's impulse is to rescue the tender, white baby-hand.   Is she wise
in interposing this restraint ?   I think she is not.   If the child is to have
bayoneted sentries always on guard between it and experience, it can
only grow surreptitiously.   I say "bayoneted" advisedly, since the
hand interposed between the baby and the stove not infrequently emphasizes its power with a blow which gives more pain than the burn
would have given, while its value as experience may be represented
by the minus sign.

The theory that it is the duty of parents to provide for the needs
of their young children, and of children to obey their parents, and,
in their age, to support them, is so generally accepted that I shall rouse
a storm of indignation by asserting that there are no duties.

While a cursory glance at the subject may seem to show a denial of
equal freedom in the refusal of a parent to support his child, a more
careful study will reveal the truth that, so long as he does not hinder the
activities of any one nor compel any other person or persons to undertake the task which he has relinquished, he cannot be said to violate the
law of equal freedom.   Therefore his associates may not compel him to
provide for his child, though they may forcibly prevent him from aggressing upon it.   They may prevent acts ; they may not compel the performance of actions.

It will, perhaps, be well to anticipate at this point a question sure to
be asked during the discussion.

Is it not aggression on the part of parents to usher into existence a
child for which they are either unable or unwilling to provide ?

Much may be said in reply.

First : In any association differences of opinion would arise as to
whether it was aggression or not ; these differences would imply doubt,
and the doubt would make forcible prevention, even if practicable, unjustifiable.

Second : This doubt would be strengthened by consideration of the fact
that no one could be able to predict with certainty nine months previous
to the birth of a child that at the time of its birth its parents would be unable to provide sustenance for it.

Third : It would be further strengthened by the knowledge that death
is always open to those who find life intolerable, and, so long as persons
seek to prolong existence, they cannot properly complain of those who
thrust it upon them.   A young babe does not question whether the milk
it feeds upon flows from its mother's breast or from the udder of a cow,
and should it, with dawning intelligence, feel disturbed in mind or dis-
tressed in body by reason of its relations towards its environments, it will,
by then, have learned the art of dying.

And now, having opened a gulf which swallows up duty, shall I be able
to allay the consternation of those who have substituted the worship of
this for their repudiated worship of another unsubstantial God ?

It has seemed to me that, generally speaking, people's love for their
children is in inverse proportion to their love of God and duty.   However
this may be,—and I will admit that, although parallel and pertinent, it is

not directly in the line of inquiry I am pursuing,—there is still left to us the certainty that increasing intelligence will more and more incline individuals to face the consequences of their own acts ; not for duty's sake, but in order to help establish and preserve that social harmony which will be necessary to their happiness.

Even in the present semi-barbarous condition of parental relations it is exceptional, unusual, for parents to abandon their children, and the two distinct incentives to such abandonment will be removed by social evolution, leaving the discussion of the obligation of parents to care for their children purely abstract and rather unprofitable, since no one will refuse to do so.

The two motives to which I refer are poverty and fear of social obloquy.   Married parents sometimes desert their children because they lack abundant means of subsistence ; unmarried parents occasionally not only desert their offspring, but deny them, in order to escape the malice of the unintelligent who believe that vice is susceptible of transmutation into virtue by the blessing of a priest, and virtue into vice by the absence of the miracle-working words.

Recognition of the law of equal freedom would nearly remove the first, render the second more endurable, and finally obliterate both, leaving parents without motive for the abandonment of offspring.

That parents usually find happiness in provision for the welfare of their young is well known.   Even the habits of the lower animals afford evidence sufficient to establish this position, and, for convenience, postulating it as a principle, I shall proceed to examine how far parents defeat their own aim by unintelligent pursuit of it.

Food is the first, because the indispensable, requisite to welfare, but unintelligent and indiscriminate feeding results in thousands of deaths annually and sows seeds of chronic invalidism in millions of young stomachs.

Clothing also is considered indispensable, and is so in rigorous climates, but the primary object of covering the body, which is surely to make it comfortable, is usually almost wholly forgotten in the effort to conform to accepted ideals of beauty,—ideals often involving peculiar departures from natural forms.

Shelter is a necessity which is often accompanied by such over-zealous inhospitality to fresh air as places choice between in-door and out-door life in uncertain balance.

But the sturdiest pursuits and the dreariest defeats and failures are found in educational endeavors.

The child comes into an unknown world.   His blinking eyes cannot decide which is nearer, the lighted taper on the table or the moon seen through the window.   He does not know that a Riverside orange is larger than the palm of his tiny hand until he has learned the truth by repeated efforts to grasp it.   He has all things to learn: ideas of dimension, weight, heat, moisture, density, resistance, gravitation,—all things in their interrelations and their relations to himself.   And what bungling assistance he receives in the bewildering path through this tangle of truth !

He learns that God sends the rain, the hail, and the snow down from the sky ; that his little sister was brought from heaven by an angel and deposited in a doctor's pill-bags.   The tie of relationship between her and himself remains a mystery.   Anthropomorphism lurks everywhere.   The unseen hand moves all things.   He asks many questions which his teachers cannot answer, and, unwilling to confess their ignorance, they constantly reiterate : "God did it," as if that were an answer.

Turning from unsuccessful inquiries concerning natural phenomena, perhaps the child perceives, in a dim way, his relations with the State, and, as God posed before him in the realm of philosophy and science, so do all replies to his questionings now end in omnipotent government.

"Why does no one prevent the man with a star from clubbing the other man?"

"Because he is a policeman."

"Who said that a policeman might strike people?"

"The government."

"What is the government?"

"The government is —— my son, you will learn when you are older."

"Who pays the policeman for clubbing the other man?"

"The government."

"Where does the government get the money?"

"You will learn when you are older."

Usually at the age of six years, or even earlier, a child's education is practically abandoned by its inefficient parents and intrusted to the church and the State.

The State uses money robbed from the parents to perpetuate its powers of robbery by instructing their children in its own interest.

The church, also, uses its power to perpetuate its power. And to these twin leeches, as "Ouida" has aptly designated them, to these self-interested robbers and murderers, are the tender minds of babies entrusted for education.

Herbert Spencer has shown that the status of women and children improves in proportion to the decline of militarism and the advance of industrialism.

The military spirit is encouraged in multifold ways by both church and State, and little children and women, in their pitiable ignorance, assist in weaving nets that shall trip their own unwary feet and those of other women and children that follow them.

A spirit of subordination is inculcated by both church and State, which contemplate without rebuke the brutalities of authority, excepting in some cases of extraordinary cruelty, and teach the helpless victims that it is their duty to submit.

The most commonplace tenets of the sepowers would seem absurd and outrageous if expounded to an unprepared adult mind and stripped of all those devices of language by which the various promptings of shame, good nature, ignorance, or deceit impel us to soften the truth.

Say to such an one:

"Murder by the State is laudable; murder by an individual is criminal.

"Robbery by the State is permissible; robbery by an individual is a serious offence against the person robbed and also against public welfare.

"Assault of the parent upon his child is justifiable; assault of the child upon the parent is intolerable."

He would not look upon you with the simple confidence of a puzzled child, attributing the apparent incompatibilities to the feebleness of his own understanding.

But to the child these bewildering social sophistries, flowing into his mind from sources that appeal to his trust, and presented with ambiguities of language that serve to increase its difficulties, must appear hopeless labyrinths of mystery.

Thus at every step from infancy to adult life the progress of the child is checked by the incapacity of those who desire to advance its welfare.

Inherited tendencies and the training which they themselves received incline parents to become inexorable masters and to commend most the conduct of that child which is easiest enslaved.

Parents beat their children, elder children beat younger brothers and sisters, and the wee ones avenge their wrongs vicariously by beating their dolls or their wooden horses.

Through individual revolts against the general barbarity, revolts of increasing frequency and power, humanity gradually evolves above actual application of its savage principles.   But these revolts against savagery, when led by emotion, often result nearly as disastrously as savagery itself.

Reason must be the basis of all enduring social growth.

When reason shall have learned to rebel against inequalities in liberties, and when this mental rebellion shall have become quite general, then will people have passed beyond danger of relapse into savagery.

Then parent and child shall not be master and slave, a relation distasteful to reasoning people, but they shall be friend and friend.   There will be no restraints imposed except such as are absolutely necessary, and these will not take the form of blows and will be removed as early as possible.

Examples of such restraints as I mean are :

Detention from the brink of a precipice or an open well or the track of a coming locomotive, or of one child from striking another.

Parents who recognize the fundamental principle of happiness through freedom and intelligence will, generally speaking, achieve results proportionate to the degree of their success in harmonizing their lives with this principle.   The greater their intelligence the higher perfection will they reach in the interpretation and application of the law of equal freedom, and in preparing their children to attain harmonious relations with their environment.

SUPPLEMENTARY.

How to make liars of children :

I have said that infants have all things to learn. It would seem, and would be, superfluous to repeat a fact so well known, were it not true that most people credit little children with so much more knowledge than they could possibly have acquired in the given time.   I have heard, not once but many times, mothers accuse young children of falsehood when I fully believed that the apparent misstatements were due in part to the little ones' weak grasp on the language which they attempted to speak, and partly to misinterpretation of facts.   Even grown-up people do not look upon the simplest incident from exactly the same point of view ; yet they expect from mere babes perfection of accuracy, and, being disappointed in this unreasonable expectation, accuse them of falsehood, and not infrequently worry them into admitting faults which have, in reality, no meaning to their dim understandings.   But after lying has come to have meaning, the little mind becomes indifferent to truthfulness, finding that punishment falls the same, whether it inspire truth or falsehood.

Thus the child is made a liar by its parents' ignorant endeavor to teach it regard for the truth.

But worse mistakes are made by those parents whose daily conversation with their children furnishes examples of untruthfulness.   Who has not been frightened into obedience by tales of a bogie-man, a Chinaman, a black man, or a Santa Claus with his rattan,—stories which do triple injury by fostering cowardice, class hatred, and lying ?

To teach a child to steal :

Carefully lock away from him all fruits and sweets. Allow him no money for personal expenses. If you miss anything, accuse him of having taken it. If you send him out to make purchases, count the change with suspicious care when he returns. If he has lost a few pennies, accuse him of having spent them for candy. If you never buy candy for him, this will teach him a means of supplying himself, and probably your next accusation will be true.

Strike children and they learn to strike each other ; scold them and they learn to quarrel ; give them drums and flags and uniforms and toy guns and they desire to become professional murderers. Open their letters, listen to their conversations with their young friends, pry into their little secrets, invade their private rooms without knocking, and you make them meddlers and disagreeable companions.

I have said that it is not the duty of children to obey their parents or to care for them in old age.

The following facts bear on this position :

The life of a child is usually merely incident to the pleasure of its parents, and is often an accident deeply deplored by both. Even when conception is desired, it is still for the pleasure of the parents. If it were possible, which it is not, to conceive of a life given solely for its own happiness, its parents taking no pleasure either in the sexual relation or in the hope of offspring, the child could incur no responsibility by the opinions or the acts of its parents.

After its birth the child does not say :

"Give me food, clothes, and shelter now in exchange for food, clothes, and shelter which I will give you in your old age," and, could he make such a contract, it would be void. A man cannot be bound by promises he made during his infancy.

The question of obedience I pass, since highly-evolved parents cannot be obeyed, because they will not command.

On careful thought the removal of the idea of duty will be seen to be less startling than it must at first appear to those who have accepted without question the dogmas of authority. Mr. Cowell has called my attention to the fact that the love which most people have for their parents or foster-parents is evidence that few wholly lack lovable attributes. During the long years of familiar companionship between parents and child ties are usually formed which cannot be broken while life lasts, not ties of duty but of affection ; these render mutual helpfulness a source of pleasure. If they be lacking, a self-respecting parent would choose the shelter of an almshouse rather than the grudging charity bestowed by his child under the spur of a belief in duty.

CLARA DIXON DAVIDSON.

COMPULSORY EDUCATION AND ANARCHISM.

[*Liberty*, September 3, 1892.]

To the Editor of Liberty:

While reading your lucid editorial on the above topic, some thoughts occurred to me which I venture to offer in the hope that they may serve to supplement what you have said in dealing with your scholastic friend's well-put queries.

I cannot help thinking that he had in mind a very un-Anarchistic condition of things when he formulated the questions. Why is compulsory education in vogue to-day? For whom is it intended? If society had been composed of well-to-do people having all the comforts, advantages, and opportunities of civilization that some only enjoy at present, would the idea of statutory compulsion in the bringing-up and education of children ever have been thought of, much less put into force? Are such legal regulations applied, practically, to the classes superior in fortune to the majority, in whose interest (?) the regulations are supposed to be made? I find myself dropping into the interrogative style, like our friendly inquirer, and while in it would like to ask him, though not wishing to usurp the functions of a father confessor, if he had not in view, perhaps vaguely and even unconsciously, when thinking over the matter that he embodied in the five points, a typical wage slave, underpaid, uneducated, unrefined, the victim of compulsory restrictions and stultifying law-made conditions, a man or woman without intelligence, whose narrow mental scope and abnormal moral nature are the result of circumstances produced by invasive tyranny,—in short, parents whose unfilial instincts and unsocial acts are the direct outcome of ages of legal oppression. To such persons only could the assumptions underlying the questions apply.

If our friend apprehends clearly the drift of the queries above and consequently answers them to our mutual satisfaction, he will then, I imagine, discard his third, fourth, and fifth questions as unnecessary and inapplicable to a truly Anarchist condition of society. It seems to me unwise to attempt to apply Anarchistic principles to one case of social relations, itself arising out of other relations, without at the same time tracing that case to its sources and there defining the bearings of the whole in relation to perfect liberty,—Anarchy. I would not turn aside to condemn some kinds of compulsory interference which are really attempts at *ameliorating* the conditions that more inimical invasion has brought about, but would rather strike straight at the previous and more vital violations of the law of equal freedom. Hence I agree with the editor when he answers No, No, No, to the last three problems, not only on the grounds he lays down, but also because I believe that the economic emancipation which would result from the adoption of Anarchy as a basic method in Society would speedily solve all such problems by relegating them to the Museum of Curiosities of the Ante-Revolution.

On grounds of sentiment, of sympathy, feeling, and humanity, which would probably be stronger and more generous under equal liberty than now, I would not hesitate to *act* in the circumstances supposed in the first and second questions, though such action would certainly not be dictated by the mere theory of Anarchism, but would be no more a violation of it than would a refusal in such cases to interfere.

The undoubted tendency of an adoption of Anarchy would be, however, to minimize the possibility of unsocial conduct of the character under discussion, if not to abolish it altogether.   Fraternally yours,
                                                                   WILLIAM BAILIE.

CHILDREN UNDER ANARCHY.

[*Liberty*, September 3, 1892.]

NEARLY the whole of this issue of *Liberty* is devoted to the important question of the status of the child under Anarchy. The long article by Clara Dixon Davidson has been in my desk, unopened, for several months. On examining it the other day, I was surprised and delighted to find that a woman had written such a bold, unprejudiced, unsentimental, and altogether rational essay on a subject which women are especially prone to treat emotionally. I am even shamed a little by the unhesitating way in which she eliminates from the problem the fancied right of the child to life. My own difficulties, I fear, have been largely due to a lingering trace of this superstition. The fact is that the child, like the adult, has no right to life at all. Under equal freedom, as it develops individuality and independence, it is entitled to immunity from assault or invasion, and that is all. If the parent neglects to support it, he does not thereby oblige any one else to support it. If others give it support, they do so voluntarily, as they might give support to a neglected animal ; there is no more obligation in the one case than in the other.

I also welcome as important Comrade Bailie's contribution to the discussion. In one view the question of the status of the child under Anarchy is a trivial one,—trivial because the bugbears that surround it are hypothetical monsters, and because such ugly realities as do actually confront it are put to rout by the new social conditions which Anarchy induces. Even at present comparatively few parents are disposed to abuse or neglect their children, and in the absence of poverty and false notions of virtue their number will be infinitesimal and may be safely neglected. The question is one that vanishes as we approach it.

The chief value of its discussion is found in the light which it throws on the matter of equal freedom. Hence I am glad that it was brought forward by my friend the school-teacher, whose questions I answered in No. 232, and who now rejoins with the following letter :

To the Editor of Liberty:

I gather from your editorial that it is Anarchistic policy for neighbors to interfere if a parent is about to chisel off the third finger of its child's left hand, even if he proposes to secure a well-healed stump. I think I know you well enough to say that it is not Anarchistic policy for neighbors to interfere if the parent, otherwise sane, proposes to treat his own finger so. Now, where is the criterion of these two cases? Why should the child's physical integrity be of more importance to neighbors than the father's? Do we not recognize some substitute for or remnant of the law of equal freedom, restraining the parent's absolute control over the mind, body, and life of his child? "Not for the child's sake," primarily, because all sane altruism is rooted in egoism : but it is Anarchistic policy to recognize and defend the child's right to physical integrity, in extreme cases.

Again, the reason why we draw the line of Anarchistic policy at interference with any but physical maltreatment is, if I am correct, that non-interference will result in disaster, too grievous to be borne, which will be an invasion of the equal freedom of adult neighbors,—all this only in the case of physical maltreatment. On this ground is laid down the general rule that mental and moral maltreatment of children by parents should not be met by neighbors with physical force. It seems obvious to me that this rule cannot be thus justified in considering the case of physical maltreatment instanced above, and the following case of mental-and-moral maltreatment : A parent, with the intention of ruining his child's future, surrounds it with temptations to debauchery such as will assuredly render it imbecile, if it survives to the normal age of maturity.—This seems to me more harmful to adult neighbors than even such mutilation as an eye put out.

To put my thesis most directly, I claim (I) to state the law of equal freedom as follows :

Every individual has a right to and must expect the results of his own nature.

Cor. 1. Every individual must refrain from invading his neighbor's rights.

Cor. 2. Every child has a right to such sacrifice on the part of its parent as will enable it to arrive at maturity.

And I claim (II) that it is Anarchistic policy to use physical force to prevent transgressions of either corollary of this law, where such transgressions are clear and unmistakable. The Egoistic basis of enforcing Cor. 2 is, as your editorial implies, the fact that its violation will result in shouldering off upon others some unwelcome consequence of the parents' (propagative) conduct.

It is not always possible to apply the theoretical deductions of science; but that need not deter her devotees from trying to state and prove, as completely as possible, the results of science. Here we are, confronted by the "Cimmerian darkness" of one of the most important problems in social ethics. If the statement of Cor. 2 above is not accurate, I ask you, as my first instructor in this subject, to tell me where it is inaccurate, and why : if it is accurate, it furnishes a basis for the relation between Family and Society as firm and clear as the Law of Equal Freedom does for Society alone. And we can set ourselves calmly to write down the particular equations that represent the several phases of child-guardianship.

G. W. E.

My friend misapprehends me. When the interference of third parties is justifiable, it is not so because of the superior importance of the child's physical integrity as compared with that of the parent who mutilates himself, but because the child is potentially an individual sovereign. The man who mutilates himself does not impair equal freedom in the slightest, but the parent who mutilates his child assaults a being which, though still limited in its freedom by its dependence, is daily growing into an independence which will establish its freedom on an equality with that of others. In this doubtful stage the advisability of interference is to be decided by necessity, since, so far as we can see at present, it cannot be decided by principle. It is necessary to stop the parent from cutting off his child's finger, because the danger is immediate and the evil certain and irremediable. It is not necessary to prescribe the conditions of virtue with which a parent shall surround his child, because the danger is remote (it being possible perhaps in time to induce the parent to change his course), the evil is uncertain (the child often proving sufficiently strong in character to rise above its conditions), and the results are not necessarily permanent (as later conditions may largely, if not entirely, counteract them). In the former case, physical force must be met with physical force. In the latter case, it is safer and better to meet moral (or immoral) force with moral force. I am afraid that my friend is not yet a sufficiently good Anarchist to appreciate the full significance of Proudhon's declaration that Liberty is the Mother of Order, and the importance of securing education through liberty wherever practicable instead of through compulsion.

I do not think that my friend's formulas are capable of scientific treatment. When he tells me that "every individual has a right to and must expect the results of his own nature," he lays down a proposition too vague for the purposes of science. I do not know what the words mean, and in any case I deny the alleged right. An individual has a right to the results of his own nature *if he can get them;* otherwise, not. Apart from this right of might, no individual has a right to anything, except as he creates his right by contract with his neighbor.

NOT A DECREE, BUT A PROPHECY.

[*Liberty*, April 28, 1888.]

HAVE I made a mistake in my Anarchism, or has the editor of *Liberty* himself tripped? At any rate, I must challenge the Anarchism of one sentence in his otherwise masterful paper upon "State Socialism and Anarchism." If I am wrong, I stand open to conviction. It is this: "They [Anarchists] look forward to a time . . . when the children born of these relations shall belong exclusively to the mothers until old enough to belong to themselves."

Now, that looks to me like an authoritarian statement that is in opposition to theoretical Anarchy, and also to nature. What is the matter with leaving the question of the control of those children to their two parents, to be settled between them,—allowing them to decide whether both, or only one, and which one, shall have control?

I may be wrong, but it seems to me extremely un-Anarchistic to thus bring up an extraneous, authoritarian, moral obligation, and use it to stifle an instinct which nature is doing her best to develop.

I would like to know whether the editor of *Liberty* momentarily forgot his creed that we must follow our natural desires, or if I have misunderstood his statement, or misapplied my own Anarchy.

Paternal love of offspring is, with a few exceptions, a comparatively late development in the evolution of the animal world, so late that there are tribes of the order of man, and individuals even among civilized nations, in whom it is not found. But the fact that it is a late development shows that it is going to develop still more. And under the eased economical conditions which Anarchy hopes to bring about, it would burst forth with still greater power. Is it wise to attempt to stifle that feeling —as it would be stifled—by the sweeping statement that its object should belong to some one else? Maternal love of offspring beautifies the woman's character, broadens and enriches her intellect. And as far as I have observed, paternal feeling, if it is listened to, indulged, and developed, has an equally good, though not just the same, effect upon the man's mind. Should he be deprived of all this good by having swept out of his hands all care for his children, and out of his heart all feeling that they are his, by being made to feel that they "belong exclusively to the mother"? It seems to me much more reasonable, much more natural, and very much more Anarchistic, to say that the child of Anarchistic parents belongs to both of them, if they both wish to have united control of it, and, if they don't wish this, that they can settle between themselves as to which one should have it. The question is one, I think, that could usually be settled amicably. But if some unusual occasion were to arise when all efforts to settle it amicably were to fail, when both parents would strongly desire the child and be equally competent to rear it, then, possibly, the fact that the mother has suffered the pain of child-birth might give her a little the stronger right. But I do not feel perfectly sure that that principle is right and just.

I would like to know if Mr. Tucker, upon further consideration, does not agree with me.

F. F. K.

I accept F. F. K.'s challenge, and, in defence of the Anarchism of the sentence objected to, I offer to submit the language in which it is phrased to any generally recognized authority in English, for the discovery of any authoritarian meaning possibly therein contained. F. F. K. seems to misunderstand the use of the word "shall." Now, it may be ascertained from any decent dictionary or grammar that this auxiliary is employed, not alone in the language of command, but also in the language of prophecy. Suppose I had said that the Anarchists look forward to a time when all men shall be honest. Would F. F. K. have suspected me of desiring or predicting a decree to that effect? I hardly think so. The conclusion would simply have been that I regarded honesty as destined to be accepted by mankind, at some future period, in the shaping of their lives. Why, then, should it be inferred from similar phraseology in regard to the control of children that I anticipate anything more than a general recognition, in the absence of contract, of the mother's superior claim, and a refusal on the part of defensive associations to protect any other claim than hers in cases of dispute not guarded against by specific contract? That is all that I meant, and that is all that my language implies. The language of prophecy doubtless had its source in authority, but to-day the idea of authority is so far disconnected from the prophetic form that philosophers and scientists who, reasoning from accepted data, use this form in mapping out for a space the course of evolution are not therefore accused of designs to impose their sovereign wills upon the human race. The editor of *Liberty* respectfully submits that he, too, may sometimes resort to the oracular style which the best English writers not unfrequently employ in speaking of futurity, without having it imputed to him on that account that he professes to speak either from a throne or from a tripod.

As to the charge of departure from the Anarchistic principle, it may be preferred, I think, against F. F. K. with much more reason than against me. To vest the control of anything indivisible in more than one person seems to me decidedly communistic. I perfectly agree that parents must be allowed to "decide whether both, or only one, and which one, shall have control." But if they are foolish enough to decide that both shall control, the affair is sure to end in government. Contract as they may in advance that both shall control, really no question of control arises until they disagree, and then it is a logical impossibility for both to control. One of the two will then control; or else there will be a compromise, in which case each will be controlled, just as the king who makes concessions governs and is governed, and as the members of a democracy govern and are governed. Liberty and individualism are lost sight of entirely.

I rejoice to know that the tendency of evolution is towards the increase of paternal love, it being no part of my intention to abolish, stifle, or ignore that highly commendable emotion.

I expect its influence in the future upon both child and parent
to be far greater and better than it ever has been in the past.
Upon the love of both father and mother for their offspring I
chiefly rely for that harmonious co-operation in the guidance
of their children's lives which is so much to be desired.   But
the important question, so far as Anarchy is concerned, is to
whom this guidance properly belongs when such co-operation
has proved impossible.   If that question is not settled in advance by contract, it will have to be settled by arbitration, and
the board of arbitration will be expected to decide in accordance with some principle.   In my judgment it will be recognized that the control of children is a species of property, and
that the superior labor title of the mother will secure her right
to the guardianship of her children unless she freely signs it
away.   With my present light, if I were on such a board of
arbitration, my vote would be for the mother every time.

For this declaration many of the friends of woman's emancipation (F. F. K., however, not among them) are ready to
abuse me roundly.   I had expected their approval rather.   For
years in their conventions I have seen this "crowning outrage," that woman is denied the control and keeping of her
children, reserved by them to be brought forward as a *coup de
grâce* for the annihilation of some especially obstinate opponent.   Now this control and keeping I grant her unreservedly,
and, lo! I am a cursed thing!

ANARCHY AND RAPE.

[*Liberty*, March 10, 1888.]

WITH a plentiful sprinkling of full-face Gothic exclamation
points and a series of hysterical shrieks, the *Journal of United
Labor*, organ of pious Powderly and pure Litchman, rushes
upon *Liberty* with the inquiry whether "Anarchy asks liberty
to ruin little girls."   *Liberty* is thus questioned simply because
it characterized those who petitioned the Massachusetts legislature for a further raise of the "age of consent" to sixteen
as "a bevy of impertinent and prudish women."   The answer
shall be direct and explicit.   Anarchy does not ask liberty to
ruin little girls, but it does ask liberty of sexual association
with girls already several years past the age of womanhood,
equipped by nature with the capacity of maternity, and even
acknowledged by the law to be competent to marry and begin

the rearing of a family.   To hold a man whose association
with such a girl has been sanctioned by her free consent and
even her ardent desire guilty of the crime of rape and to subject him to life imprisonment is an outrage to which a whole
font of exclamation points would do scant justice.   If there
are any mothers, as the *Journal of United Labor* pretends, who
look upon such an outrage as a protection against outrage,
they confess thereby not only their callous disregard of human
rights, but the imbecility of their daughters and their own responsibility for the training that has allowed them to grow up
in imbecility.   " Has Liberty a daughter ? " further inquires the
Journal of United Labor.   Why, certainly; Order is Liberty's
daughter, acknowledged as such from the first.   " Liberty not
the daughter, but the mother, of Order."   But it is needless to
raise the " age of consent " on account of Liberty's daughter.
Order fears no seducer.   When all daughters have such mothers and all mothers such daughters, the *Journal of United
Labor* may continue to regard them as the " worst of woman-
kind," but the powers of the seducer will be gone, no matter
what may be fixed as the " age of consent."   Because *Liberty*
holds this opinion and expresses it, Powderly and Litchman
profess to consider her a " disgrace to the press of America."
Really they do not so look upon her, but they are very anxious
to win popular approval by pandering to popular prejudices,
and so they took advantage of the opportunity which *Liberty's*
words gave them to pose as champions of outraged virtue
while endeavoring to identify Anarchism with wholesale rape
of the innocents.

AN UNFORTUNATE ANALOGY.

[*Liberty*, November 5, 1887.]

A QUESTION has arisen in England whether the public have
a right of access to the top of Latrigg in Keswick Vale, the
public claiming such right and certain landowners denying
it.   It is probable that the claim of the public is good, but, as
I am not informed regarding the basis of the landholders'
title in this particular case, it is not my purpose to discuss the
matter.   The London *Jus*, however, has discussed the matter,
and I refer to it only to expose an inconsistency into which
that journal has fallen.   It seems that Mr. Plimsoll, who
champions the claim of the public, has made this declaration :

" What Parliament has given Parliament can take away."
Not rightly, declares *Jus ;* and it imagines a case.

Suppose Parliament grants a life-pension to a distinguished general ;
suppose the next Parliament, being of another color, rejects the grant, will
Mr. Plimsoll pretend that in such a case Parliament would have the right
to take it away ? Not he ; no honest man could think so for a moment.
Private persons do not consider themselves entitled to take back that
which they have given to others, even without any consideration whatever.

True, so far as private persons are concerned. But private
persons do consider themselves entitled to take back that
which has been taken from them and given to others. If the
body politic, or State, which compels A to belong to it and
aid in supporting it, pledges a certain sum annually to B, and,
to meet this pledge, forcibly collects annually from A a proportional part of the sum, then A, when he becomes strong
enough, may not only decline to make any further annual
payments to B, but may take from B all that he has been
compelled to pay to him in the past. To-day, to be sure, A,
as soon as he acquires power, generally vitiates his claim
upon B by proceeding to pledge others in the same manner
in which others, when they were in power, had pledged him.
But this fact, being accidental rather than essential, has no
logical bearing upon the question of A's right to recover from
B. It follows, then, that private persons cannot be held to
the pledges of an association which forces them into its membership, and that Parliament, which represents the will of a
majority of the members of such an association, and of a
majority which necessarily varies continually in its make-up,
stands on a very different footing from that of private persons
in the matter of observing or violating contracts.

But suppose the position of *Jus* that they stand on the
same footing to be granted. What has *Jus* to say then?
This,—namely, that it finds itself in sympathy with Mr. Plimsoll and the people of Keswick in their desire to enjoy the
beautiful scenery of Latrigg ; that it believes the right of
way to such enjoyment was originally theirs ; and that the
sooner they recover it, the better. But how ? It has already
denied that " what Parliament has given Parliament can take
away " ; so it finds itself obliged to pick its way around this
difficulty by the following devious path :

If Parliament has given away to private persons that which ought to
have been retained in public hands for the public use and benefit, with or
without sufficient (or any) consideration, *then let the Nation keep faith
and buy it back.*

The italics are mine.   Bearing them in mind, let us return
to the analogy between Parliament and private persons.   Do
private persons, then, consider themselves entitled to *buy* back
that which they have given to others, on terms fixed by themselves, and whether the others desire to sell or not?   That the
private person who gives a thing to another and afterwards
compels the latter to sell it back to him is less a thief than he
would have been if he had taken it back without compensation is a principle unrecognized, so far as I know, either in
law or in political economy.   No more can be said of such a
robber than that he shows some consideration for his victim.
Then, if Parliament and private persons stand on the same
footing, whence does *Jus* derive the right of Parliament to
forcibly buy back what it has given away ?

Jus is a fine paper.   It maintains certain phases of Individualism with splendid force and vigor.   But it continually puts
itself into awkward situations simply by failing to be thorough
in its Individualism.   Here, for instance, it denies the right of
the State to take from the individual without compensation
what it has given him, but affirms the right of the State to
compel the individual to sell to it what it has given him.   In
a word, *Jus* is not Anarchistic.   It does not favor individual
liberty in all things.   It would confine interference with it
within much narrower limits than those generally set by
governmentalists, but, after all, like all other governmentalists,
it fixes the limits in accordance with arbitrary standards prescribing that interference must be carried on only by methods
and for purposes which it approves on grounds foreign to the
belief in liberty as the necessary condition of social harmony.

THE BOYCOTT AND ITS LIMIT.

[*Liberty*, December 3, 1887.]

LONDON *Jus* does not see clearly in the matter of boycotting.   "Every man," it says, "has a perfect right to refuse to
hold intercourse with any other man or class from whom he
chooses to keep aloof.   But where does liberty come in when
several persons conspire together to put pressure upon another
to induce or coerce him (by threats expressed or implied) to refrain also from intercourse with the boycotted man?   It is not
that the boycotted man has grounds of legal complaint against
those who voluntarily put him in coventry.   His complaint is

against those who compel (under whatsoever sanction) third persons to do likewise. Surely the distinction is specific." Specific, yes, but not rational. The line of real distinction does not run in the direction which *Jus* tries to give it. Its course does not lie between the second person and a third person, but between the threats of invasion and the threats of ostracism by which either the second or a third person is coerced or induced. All boycotting, no matter of what person, consists either in the utterance of a threat or in its execution. A man has a right to threaten what he has a right to execute. The boundary-line of justifiable boycotting is fixed by the nature of the threat used. B and C, laborers, are entitled to quit buying shoes of A, a manufacturer, for any reason whatever or for no reason at all. Therefore they are entitled to say to A : " If you do not discharge the non-union men in your employ, we will quit buying shoes of you." Similarly they are entitled to quit buying clothes of D, a tailor. Therefore they are entitled to say to D : " If you do not co-operate with us in endeavoring to induce A to discharge his non-union employees,—that is, if you do not quit buying shoes of him,— we will quit buying clothes of you." But B and C are not entitled to burn A's shop or D's shop. Hence they are not entitled to say to A that they will burn his shop unless he discharges his non-union employees, or to D that they will burn his shop unless he withdraws his patronage from A. Is it not clear that the rightful attitude of B and C depends wholly upon the question whether or not the attitude is invasive in itself, and not at all upon the question whether the object of it is A or D?

A CASE WHERE DISCUSSION CONVINCED.

[*Liberty*, February 11, 1888.]

ONE word as to boycotting itself. *Jus* was some weeks ago taken to task by the Boston *Liberty* for incorrectly defining the term. " The line of distinction," says *Liberty*, " does not run in the direction which *Jus* tries to give it. Its course does not lie between the second person and a third person, but between the threats of invasion and the threats of ostracism by which either the second or a third person is coerced or induced. All boycotting, no matter of what person, consists either in the utterance of a threat or in its execution. A man has a right to threaten what he has a right to execute. The boundary-line of justifiable boycotting is fixed by the nature of the threat used." This seems reasonable enough, and, until we see the contrary proved, we shall accept this view in preference

to that which we have put forward hitherto. At the same time, **we are**
not so absolutely convinced of its soundness as to close our eyes to the
fact that there may be a good deal said on the other side. The doctrine
of conspiracy enters in. That which may not be illegal or even wrong in
one person becomes both illegal and morally wrong in a crowd of persons.
—*Jus.*

Liberty would be unfair to *Jus* if it should not present
the evidence of that journal's fairness by printing its hand-
some acknowledgment of error regarding boycotting. *Jus* still
thinks, however, that something may be said on the other side,
and declares that there are some things that one person may
rightfully do which become illegal and immoral when done by
a crowd. I should like to have *Jus* give an instance. There
are some invasive acts or threats which cannot be executed by
individuals, but require crowds—or conspiracies, if you will—
for their accomplishment. But the guilt still arises from the
invasive character of the act, and not from the fact of conspiracy. No individual has a right to do any act which is
invasive, but any number of individuals may rightfully " conspire" to commit any act which is non-invasive. *Jus* acknowledges the force of *Liberty's* argument that A may as
properly boycott C as B. Further consideration, I think, will
compel it to acknowledge that A and B combined may as
properly boycott C as may A alone or B alone.

A SPIRIT MORE EVIL THAN ALCOHOL.

[*Liberty*, August 13, 1887.]

THE authority of learning, the tyranny of science, which
Bakounine foresaw, deprecated, and denounced, never found
blunter expression than in an article by T. B. Wakeman in
the August number of the *Freethinkers' Magazine* in which
the writer endeavors to prove, on scientific grounds alone,
that alcohol is an unmitigated evil, a poison that ought never
to be taken into the human system. My knowledge of chem-
istry and physiology is too limited to enable me to judge of
the scientific soundness of the attempted demonstration ; but
I do know that it is admirably well written, wonderfully attractive, powerfully plausible, important if true, and therefore worthy of answer by those who alone are competent to
answer it if it can be answered. Such an answer I hope to
see ; and, if it arrives, I shall weigh it against Mr. Wakeman's

argument, award a verdict for myself, and act upon it for myself,—if I am allowed to do so.

But it is plain that, if Mr. Wakeman's party gets into power,
no such privilege will be granted me. For, after having asserted most positively that this "verdict of science" can be
made so manifest that it will become a' "*personal* prohibition
law, which no person in his senses would violate any more than
he would cut his own throat," in which case its compulsory enforcement will be entirely unnecessary except upon persons out
of their senses, Mr. Wakeman goes on to say that it is the duty
of the lawyers (of whom he is one) to see to it that the manufacture, sale, and use of alcohol as a beverage shall be out-
lawed, proscribed, and prohibited just as arsenic is, and that,
like arsenic, it shall be sold only as a labelled poison.   Rather
a summary way, it seems to me, of cramming science down the
throats of people who like a glass of claret better! "Ah!"
some reader will say, "you forget that this compulsory absti-
nence is only to be enforced upon people out of their senses,
probably hopeless sots who are a public danger."

This consideration possibly would afford a grain of consola-
tion, had not Mr. Wakeman taken pains in another paragraph
to leave no one in doubt as to the meaning of the phrase "in
his senses."   It is not applicable, he declares, to any drinker
of alcohol who claims to "know when he has enough," for
"that very remark shows that alcohol has already stolen away
his brains."   His position, then, is that the law of total absti-
nence will enforce itself upon all men in their senses, for no
man in his senses will drink alcohol after hearing the verdict
of science ; but that men who drink alcohol, however moderately, are out of their senses, and must be "treated, by force
if necessary, as diseased lunatics."

Was any priest, any pope, any czar ever guilty of teaching
a more fanatical, more bigoted, more tyrannical doctrine?

Does Mr. Wakeman imagine that he can restore men to
their senses by any such disregard of their individualities?

Does he think that the way to strengthen the individual's
reason and will is to force them into disuse by substituting for
them the reason and will of a body of *savants*?

In that case I commend him to the words of Bakounine :
" A society which should obey legislation emanating from a scientific academy, not because it understood itself the rational
character of this legislation (in which case the existence of
the academy would become useless), but because this legislation, emanating from the academy, was imposed in the name
of a science which it venerated without comprehending,—such

a society would be a society, not of men, but of brutes. It would be a second edition of those missions in Paraguay which submitted so long to the government of the Jesuits. It would surely and rapidly descend to the lowest stage of idiocy."

The mightiest foe of the human mind is not alcohol, by any means. It is that spirit of arrogance which prompts the conclusion of Mr. Wakeman's essay, and which, encouraged, would induce a mental paralysis far more universal and far more hopeless than any that science will ever be able to trace to the spirit of alcohol.

A WORD ABOUT CAPITAL PUNISHMENT.

[*Liberty*, August 30, 1890.]

SINCE the execution of Kemmler, I have seen it stated repeatedly in the press, and especially in the reform press, and even in the Anarchistic press, that that execution was a murder. I have also seen it stated that capital punishment is murder in its worst form. I should like to know upon what principle of human society these assertions are based and justified.

If they are based on the principle that punishment inflicted by a compulsory institution which manufactures the criminals is worse than the crime punished, I can understand them and in some degree sympathize with them. But in that case I cannot see why *capital* punishment should be singled out for emphatic and exceptional denunciation. The same objection applies as clearly to punishment that simply takes away liberty as to punishment that takes away life.

The use of the word *capital* makes me suspect that this denunciation rests on some other ground than that which I have just suggested. But what is this ground?

If society has a right to protect itself against such men as Kemmler, as is admitted, why may it not do so in whatever way proves most effective? If it is urged that capital punishment is not the most effective way, such an argument, well sustained by facts, is pertinent and valid. This position also I can understand, and with it, if not laid down as too absolute a rule, I sympathize. But this is not to say that the society which inflicts capital punishment commits murder. Murder is an offensive act. The term cannot be applied legitimately to any defensive act. And capital punishment, however ineffective it may be and through whatever ignorance it may be resorted to, is a strictly defensive act,—at least in theory.   Of course compulsory institutions often make it a weapon of offence, but that does not affect the question of capital punishment *per se* as distinguished from other forms of punishment.

For one, I object to this distinction unless it is based on rational grounds.   In doing so, I am not moved by any desire to defend the horrors of the gallows, the guillotine, or the electric chair.   They are as repulsive to me as to any one. And the conduct of the physicians, the ministers, the newspapers, and the officials disgusts me.   These horrors all tell most powerfully against the expediency and efficiency of capital punishment.   But nevertheless they do not make it murder. I insist that there is nothing sacred in the life of an invader, and there is no valid principle of human society that forbids the invaded to protect themselves in whatever way they can.

NO PLACE FOR A PROMISE.

[*Liberty*, November 12, 1892.]

A *Promise*, according to the common acceptation of the term, is a *binding* declaration made by one person to another to do, or not to do, a certain act at some *future* time.   According to this definition, there can, I think, be no place for a promise in a *harmonious, progressive* world. Promises and progress are incompatible, unless all the parties are, at all times, as free to break them as they were to make them ; and this admission eliminates the binding element, and, therefore, destroys the popular meaning of a promise.

In a progressive world we know more to-morrow than we know to-day. Also harmony implies absence of external coercion ; for, all coercion being social discord, a promise that appears *just* and feels agreeable when measured with to-day's knowledge may appear unjust and become disagreeable when measured with the standard of to-morrow's knowledge ; and in so far as the fulfilment of a promise becomes disagreeable or impossible, it is an element of discord, and discord is the opposite of harmony.   H. OLERICH, JR.

HOLSTEIN, IOWA.

But it is equally true, my good friend, that the non-fulfilment of a promise is disagreeable to the promisee, and in so far it is an element of discord, and discord is the opposite of harmony.   You need not look for harmony until people are disposed to be harmonious.   But justice, or a close approximation thereto, can be secured even from ill-disposed people.   I have no doubt of the right of any man to whom, for a

consideration, a promise has been made, to insist, even by
force, upon the fulfilment of that promise, provided the promise be not one whose fulfilment would invade third parties.
And if the promisee has a right to use force himself for such
a purpose, he has a right to secure such co-operative force
from others as they are willing to extend. These others, in
turn, have a right to decide what sort of promises, if any, they
will help him to enforce. When it comes to the determination of this point, the question is one of policy solely; and
very likely it will be found that the best way to secure the
fulfilment of promises is to have it understood in advance
that the fulfilment is not to be enforced. But as a matter of
justice and liberty, it must always be remembered that a
promise is a two-sided affair. And in our anxiety to leave the
promisor his liberty, we must not forget the *superior* right of
the promisee. I say superior, because the man who fulfils a
promise, however unjust the contract, acts voluntarily, whereas the man who has received a promise is defrauded by its non-
fulfilment, invaded, deprived of a portion of his liberty against
his will.

ON PICKET DUTY.

Bullion thinks that "civilization consists in teaching men
to govern themselves and then letting them do it." A very
slight change suffices to make this stupid statement an entirely accurate one, after which it would read : "Civilization
consists in teaching men to govern themselves by letting them
do it."—*Liberty*, August 20, 1881.

People in general, and the governmental Socialists in particular, think they see a new argument in favor of their
beloved State in the assistance which it is rendering to the
suffering and starving victims of the Mississippi inundation.
Well, such work is better than forging new chains to keep the
people in subjection, we allow ; but it is not worth the price
that is paid for it. The people cannot afford to be enslaved
for the sake of being insured. If there were no other alternative, they would do better, on the whole, to take Nature's risks
and pay her penalties as best they might. But Liberty supplies
another alternative, and furnishes better insurance at cheaper
rates. The philosophy of voluntary mutualism is universal in
its application, not omitting the victims of natural disaster.

Mutual banking, by the organization of credit, will secure the greatest possible production of wealth and its most equitable distribution ; and mutual insurance, by the organization of risk, will do the utmost that can be done to mitigate and equalize the suffering arising from its accidental destruction. —*Liberty*, April 1, 1882.

Democracy has been defined as the principle that "one man is as good as another, if not a little better." Anarchy may be defined as the principle that one government is as bad as another, if not a little worse.—*Liberty*, May 12, 1883.

In a lecture in Milwaukee a short time ago Clara Neyman of New York said that "if women could have the right to vote, they would devise better means of reform than those of narrow prohibition." Yes, indeed ; there would be nothing narrow about their prohibition ; it would be of the broadest kind, including everything from murder to non-attendance at church.—*Liberty*, May 12, 1883.

Eighteen men and women who had been punished once for all the crimes they had ever been convicted of committing, and against whom there was no shred of evidence of having committed any new crime, or of harboring any intention of committing any new crime, were taken into custody by the New York police on Thursday, August 6, on no pretext whatever save that these persons had the reputation of being professional pick-pockets, and that it was the part of prudence to keep such characters in jail until after the Grant obsequies, when they might be arraigned in court and discharged for want of evidence against them. That is to say, eighteen persons, presumably innocent in the eye of the law, had to be deprived of their liberty and kept in dungeons for four days, in order that some hundreds of thousands of people, half of them numskulls and the other half hypocrites, might not be obliged to keep their hands on their pocket-books while they shed crocodile tears at the grave of one of the foremost abettors of theft and plunder which this century has produced. And the upholders of governments continue to prate of the insecurity that would prevail without them, and to boast of the maxim, while thus violating it, that "it is better that ninety-nine guilty men should escape than that one innocent man should suffer."—*Liberty*, August 15, 1885.

"Whenever it is proposed," writes W. J. Potter in the *Index*, "that the voluntary system for religion shall be adopted and trusted wholly, there are many timid folk who start up with the warning that religion would be imperilled. Such people do not appear to have much confidence in the power of religion to maintain itself in the world." By similar reasoning, how much confidence does Mr. Potter, who would prohibit people from reading literature that does not satisfy his standard of purity, who would prohibit people from drinking liquors that do not satisfy his standard of sobriety, who would compel people to be charitable by making them pay taxes for the support of alms-houses and hospitals, and who would compel people to be learned, and still other people to pay the expense of their learning,—how much confidence, I say, does Mr. Potter appear to have in the power of purity, temperance, benevolence, and education to maintain themselves in the world? Mr. Potter should learn of Auberon Herbert that "every measure to which a man objects is a Church-rate if you have the courage and the logic to see it."—*Liberty*, September 12, 1885.

" No man who puts any conscience into his voting, or who acts from proper self-respect," says the Boston *Herald*, " will consider himself bound to support a dishonest or unfit candidate merely because he was ' fairly nominated ' by the majority of his party." But the *Herald* believes that every man who puts any conscience into his conduct, or who acts from proper self-respect, should consider himself bound to support and obey a dishonest or unfit official merely because he was fairly elected by the majority of his countrymen. Where is the obligation in the latter case more than in the former ? " Our country, right or wrong," is as immoral a sentiment as " our party, right or wrong." The *Herald* and its mugwump friends should beware of their admissions. They will find that the "divine right to bolt " leads straight to Anarchy. —*Liberty*, September 12, 1885.

To the Czar of Russia is due the credit of applying practically to taxation the *reductio ad absurdum*. Heretofore all his subjects have enjoyed at least the highly estimable privilege of praying for their rights free of cost. Any morning any of them could put in as many petitions as they chose to Alexander himself or any of his ministers for relief from any grievance whatsoever. Now, however, this state of things is no more. The last liberty of the Russian has been taken from him. The right of petition has been made the subject of a tax. Before the aggrieved citizen can make his grievance officially known, he must pay sixty kopecks into the treasury of His Imperial Nibs for the purchase of a stamp to put upon his document.   Other sovereigns have taxed every other right under the sun, but it was left for Alexander III. to tax the right to demand your rights.   No citizen of Russia can now ask his "dear father" to let him alone without paying sixty kopecks an ask.   This is the act of a notoriously cruel despot. See now how much wiser the policy of a reputedly benevolent one, Dom Pedro of Brazil.   He also is the author of a novelty in taxation.   No Brazilian husband, who, becoming suspicious of his wife, detects her and her lover *in flagrante delicto*, can hereafter legally establish such discovery until he has first poured into the State's coffers a sum slightly exceeding two dollars and a half.   This is a use of tyranny that almost inclines me to wink at it.   Bleeding domestic tyrants is better business than political tyrants are wont to engage in.   If there must be a tax-gatherer, I shall vote for Dom Pedro.—*Liberty*, November 14, 1885.

The latest piece of governmental infernalism is the proposition to raise the "age of consent" to eighteen years.   It sounds quite harmless, and belongs to that class of measures which especially allure stiff-necked moralists, pious prudes, "respectable" radicals, and all the other divisions of the "unco guid."   But what does it mean ?   It means that, if a girl of seventeen, of mature and sane mind, whom even the law recognizes as a fit person to be married and the mother of a family, shall love a man and win his love in return, and if this mutual love, by the voluntary and deliberate act of both parties, shall find sexual expression outside of the "forms of law" made and provided by our stupid legislatures, the man may be found guilty of committing rape and sent to prison for twenty years.   Such is the real nature of this proposition, whatever attempts may be made to conceal it beneath the garments of sentimentalism and moralism.   It is an outrage on manhood, and on womanhood not only an outrage, but an insult.   And yet it is put forward in the interest of young girls' honor.   Honor, forsooth !   As if it were possible to more basely dishonor a woman already several years past the age at which Nature provided her with the power of motherhood than by telling her that she hasn't brains enough to decide whether and in what way she will become a mother !—*Liberty*, April 17, 1886.

In these days of boycott trials a great deal of nonsense is being talked and written regarding "blackmail."   This is a question which the principle of Liberty settles at once. It may be well to state the verdict boldly and baldly. Here it is : Any individual may place any condition he chooses, provided the condition be not in itself invasive, upon the doing or not doing of anything which he has a right to do or not do ; but no individual can rightfully be a party to any bargain which makes a necessarily invasive condition incumbent upon any of the contracting parties. From which it follows that an individual may rightfully " extort " money from another by " threatening " him with certain consequences, provided those consequences are of such a nature that he can cause them without infringing upon anybody's rights. Such " extortion " is generally rather mean business, but there are circumstances under which the most high-minded of men might resort to it without doing violence to his instincts, and under no circumstances is it invasive and therefore wrongful, unless the act threatened is invasive and therefore wrongful. Therefore to punish men who have taken money for lifting a boycott is oppression pure and simple. Whatever may be the " common law " or the " statute law " of blackmail, this—to use Mr. Spooner's phrase—is the *natural law* that governs it.—*Liberty*, July 31, 1886.

The methods pursued by District Assembly 49 of the Knights of Labor in the conduct of the recent strike have driven Mayor Hewitt and divers other capitalistic publicists into a state of frenzy, so that they now lose no opportunity to frantically declare that one set of men must not be permitted to deprive other sets of men of the right to labor. This is a white-bearded truth, but, when spoken in condemnation of the Knights of Labor for ordering members in one branch of industry to quit work for the purpose of strengthening strikers in another branch by more completely paralyzing business, it is given a tone of impertinence more often characteristic of callow juvenility than of venerable old age. I can't see for my life whose liberty is encroached upon by such a procedure. Certainly not that of the men ordered to quit, because they joined the Knights, a voluntary organization, for certain express purposes, of which this was one, and, when they no longer approve it, can secede from it and then work when and where they please. Certainly not, on the other hand, that of the employers who thus lose their workmen, because, if it is no invasion of liberty for the individual workman to leave his employer in obedience to any whim whatsoever, it is equally no invasion of liberty for a body of workmen to act likewise, even though they have no grievance against their employer. Who, then, are deprived of their liberty ? None. All this outcry simply voices the worry of the capitalists over the thought that laborers have learned one of their own tricks,— the art of creating a corner. The policy of District Assembly 49 (whether wise or foolish is another question) was simply one of cornering labor, which is much easier to justify than cornering capital, because the cornered labor is withheld from the market by its rightful owners, while the cornered capital is withheld by men who never could have obtained it except through State-granted privilege to extort and rob.—*Liberty*, March 12, 1887.

All the indignation that is rife over the decision of Worcester shoe manufacturers and Chicago master builders to employ only such men as will sign an agreement practically excluding them from their unions is very ill spent. These employers have a perfect right to hire men on whatever conditions the men will accept. If the latter accept cruel conditions, it is only because they are obliged to do so. What thus obliges them ? Law-sustained monopolies. Their relief lies, then, not in depriving employers of the right of contract, but in giving employees the same right of contract without crippling them in advance.—*Liberty*, May 28, 1887.

Judge McCarthy, of the Pennsylvania supreme court, having to pass upon the question whether, under the Pennsylvania liquor law, licenses should be granted in a certain county, decided against granting them because he was opposed to the law, saying in the opinion which he filed : " When laws are passed that seem to conflict with God's injunctions, we are not 'compelled to obey them." I'll warrant that that same judge, were an Anarchist, arraigned before him for the violation of some unjust statute, to claim that he followed either God's injunction or any other criterion of conduct in his eyes superior to the statute, would give the prisoner three months extra for his impudence.—*Liberty*, September 10, 1887.

The Providence *People* lays it down as one of three " fundamentals " that " every child should be guaranteed a free complete education, physically, mentally, morally, and industrially." What is a *complete* education ? Who's got one that he can guarantee ? Who, if he had one and nothing else, could afford to impart it to another free of charge ? Even if he could afford to, why should he do so ? Why should he not be paid for doing so ? If he is to be paid, who should pay him

except the recipient of the education or those upon whom
the recipient is directly dependent? Do not these questions
cut under the "fundamental" of the *People?*" Is it, then, a
fundamental, after all?—*Liberty*, December 3, 1887.

Not content with getting the "age of consent" raised from
ten to thirteen, a bevy of impertinent and prudish women
went up to the Massachusetts State House the other day and
asked that it be raised again,—this time to eighteen. When a
member of the legislative committee suggested that the age
be placed at thirty-five, since the offence aimed at was as
much a crime at thirty-five as eighteen, the petitioners did
not seem to be terrified by his logic. Evidently these ladies
are not afraid that their consent will ever be asked at all.—
Liberty, February 11, 1888.

At the end of a protest against the addition of the higher
branches of education to the curriculum of the public
schools, the Winsted *Press* says: "The common district
school, thoroughly well conducted, is good enough for common folks. Let the uncommon folks have uncommon schools
and pay for them." True enough; but, if common folks
should not be made to pay for uncommon schools, why
should uncommon folks be made to pay for common schools?
—*Liberty*, April 28, 1888.

A New Jersey court has decided that the will of a citizen
of that State, by which Henry George was given a large sum
of money for the circulation of his books, is invalid on the
ground that the bequest is not educational or charitable, but
intended for the spread of doctrines contrary to the law of
the land. Probably the judge who rendered this decision
thinks regarding the determination of economic truth, as Mr.
George thinks regarding the issue of money, the collection of
rents, the carrying of letters, the running of railroads, and
sundry other things, that it is "naturally a function of government." And really, if Mr. George is right, I do not see
why the judge is not right. Yet I agree that Mr. George has
correctly branded him as an "immortal ass."—*Liberty*, May
26, 1888.

A California friend sends me a copy of the *Weekly Star* of
San Francisco containing an article which, if a tenth part of
it be true, shows that city and State to be under the pestilent
control of a band of felons. At the end of the article the
writer, regardless of the fact that this state of things is the

direct outgrowth of the government of man by man, proposes to add to the powers of this government the exclusive management of the telegraph system, of the banking system, and of corporate enterprises, as well as a vast new field of judicature.   To this political servant, who has not even the grace to hide in the earth the talent intrusted to him, but insists on using it as a scourge upon mankind, the editor of the *Weekly Star* says : " Thou hast been *un*faithful over a few things ; I will make thee ruler over many things." I am not surprised to find from another column of the same paper that the editor looks upon Anarchists as pestilent mischief-makers and noisy blatherskites.—*Liberty,* July 7, 1888.

Colonel Ingersoll has recently promulgated the theory that the husband should never be released from the marriage contract unless the wife has violated it, but that the wife should be allowed a divorce merely for the asking.   Presumably this is intended for chivalry, but it really is an insult to every self-respecting woman.   It is a relic of the old theory that woman is an inferior being, with whom it is impossible for a man to treat as an equal.   No woman worthy of the name and fully understanding the nature of her act would ever consent to union with a man by any contract which would not secure his liberty equally with her own.—*Liberty,* August 18, 1888.

The theoretical position taken by Henry George in regard to competition is that free trade should prevail everywhere except in those lines of business where in the nature of things competition can exist only partially if at all, and that in such lines there should be a government monopoly. Yet in a recent speech in England he declared that it was not quite clear to him whether the sale of liquor should be free or monopolized by the government.   Mr. George, then, if honest and logical, must entertain a suspicion of the existence of some natural restriction upon competition in the sale of liquor.   Will he be so good as to point it out ?   No, he will not ; and for the reason that his professed criterion is simply a juggler's attempt to conceal under something that looks like a scientific formula his arbitrary method of deciding that in such a channel of enterprise there shall be free trade, and in such another there shall be none.—*Liberty,* February 2, 1889.

The allopathic physicians of Massachusetts, having worked in vain for several years to obtain a legal monopoly of the practice of medicine, have concluded that a sure half loaf is better than a steadily diminishing slice, and so have gone into partnership with one or two factions of the "quacks" to prevent all other "quacks" from following their profession. This year the allopaths have taken the homœopaths and eclectics into the ring, and by this political manœuvre they hope to secure the valuable privilege which they are aiming at, on the plea which privileged classes always make,—that of protecting the masses. The battle is being stubbornly fought at the State House, and at a recent hearing before the judiciary committee Geo. M. Stearns of Chicopee, who appeared for the "quacks," made one of the wittiest, keenest, and most uncompromising speeches in favor of absolute liberty in medicine that ever fell from a lawyer's lips. It is a pity that some of his clients who followed him were not equally consistent. For instance, Dr. J. Rhodes Buchanan, who is a sort of quack-in-chief, in the course of a long argument made to convince the committee of the right of the patient to choose his own doctor, declared that he would favor a bill which would make treatment of cancer with a knife malpractice. The old story again. In medicine as in theology orthodoxy is *my* doxy and heterodoxy is *your* doxy. This "quack," who is so outraged because the "regulars" propose to suppress him, clearly enough aches for a dictator's power that he may abolish the regulars. He reminds one of those Secularists whose indignation at being compelled to pay taxes for the support of churches in which they do not believe is only equalled by the delight which they take in compelling church-members to pay taxes for the support of schools to which they are opposed. And yet there are good friends of Liberty who insist that I, in condemning these people, show an inability to distinguish between friends and foes. The truth is that, unlike these critical comrades, I am not to be blinded to the distinction between friends and foes by a mere similarity of shibboleth.—*Liberty,* February 23, 1889.

While justly censuring the centralized authority which is the essence of the scheme upon which the Topolobampo colony is founded, the Chicago *Unity* says nevertheless that, since we are privileged to stay away, "Mr. Owen's plan is in this respect a great improvement on Nationalism, or other forms of State Socialism, which would oblige all citizens, though directly in opposition to their own convictions and wishes, to submit to the new despotism." This is very true ; but I wonder if *Unity* realizes that among these "other forms of State Socialism" which oblige all citizens to submit to their despotism in opposition to the citizens' wishes, and to which there-

fore Mr. Owen's plan, hideous as it is, is in this respect superior, is properly to be classed the existing United States government.—*Liberty*, May 16, 1891.

The original patent of the Bell Telephone Company expires
in March, 1893. "From personal tests in Boston," says an expert in this matter, "I know they have practical instrument
that are one hundred per cent. better than those in use now
They are keeping these instruments in reserve to meet the
competition of the future. The Western Union Telegraph
Company is doing the same thing." A paper called the *Canal
Dispatch*, commenting on this, indignantly complains that
"some of the glorious and useful instruments of the nineteenth century are lying under lock and key as the fruit of
'free competition.'" This indignation is righteous, but mis-
directed. It is not free competition that is keeping these improvements locked up, but that form of monopoly known as
property in ideas. As the expert points out, as soon as the
patent expires and competition arrives, the improvements will
be brought to light.—*Liberty*, May 16, 1891.

In an article justifying the prohibition of the liquor traffic,
the Atlantic (Iowa) *Investigator* says : "According to the
Anarchistic theory, the government has no right to prohibit
anything, but only has the right to interfere where a wrong has
been done, and then only to make the wrong-doer repair damages." I know not the source whence the *Investigator* derived
this notion of Anarchism, but it is certainly a mistaken one.
As to government, Anarchism holds that it has no business to
do anything whatsoever or even to exist ; but voluntary defensive associations acting on the Anarchistic principle would
not only demand redress for, but would prohibit, all clearly
invasive acts. They would not, however, prohibit non-invasive
acts, even though these acts create additional opportunity for
invasive persons to act invasively. For instance, they would
not prevent the buying and selling of liquor, even though it be
true that some people are invasive when under the influence
of liquor. The *Investigator* has failed to grasp the Anarchistic view. It makes the dividing line of Anarchism run
between prohibition of injury and compulsory redress, whereas
Anarchism really includes both. Its dividing line runs in an
entirely different direction, and separates invasion from non-
invasion. Let the *Investigator* try again.—*Liberty*, May 30,
1891.

The editor of the *Arena* longs for the " era of woman "
because, when it arrives, States being woman-governed instead
of man-governed, the " age of consent " will be placed at
eighteen years. Pointing to the example set in this respect
by Kansas and Wyoming, the States which come nearest to
being woman-governed, he says in rebuking italics : " *All the
other States trail the banner of morality in the dust before the dictates of man's bestiality.*" Mr. Flower supposes himself to be an
individualist, and sometimes writes in favor of individualism
in a way that commands my admiration. But I am curious
to know by what rule he applies the theory of individualism,
that he can bring himself to violate and deny the individuality of the girl who wrote " The Story of an African Farm,"
by favoring a law which would send to prison for twenty
years, as guilty of rape, any man with whom she might have
freely chosen, at the age when she began to write that book,
to enter into sexual relations. Had Olive Schreiner lived in
civilized Wyoming instead of semi-barbarous South Africa,
and had she chosen to practise the theories which she favors
in her book, she would indeed have been raped ; not however
by the lover of her choice, but by the women who deny her
the right of choice, and by the men like B. O. Flower, who
glory in this denial ; raped, not of virginity, that paltry,
tawdry, and overrated gewgaw, but of liberty, that priceless,
matchless jewel, which it is becoming fashionable to despise.
—*Liberty*, August 1, 1891.

For one I shall shed no tears if the New York law forbidding the publication of accounts of executions is rigorously
enforced and its violators severely punished. Much as I
value the liberty of the press, yes, *because* I value it, I should
like to see the knife of authority buried to the hilt in the ten-
derest part of the ordinarily truckling newspapers of New
York and then turned vigorously and mercilessly round. Perhaps, after that, Comstock laws, anti-lottery laws, and other
similar legal villainies would no longer be made possible by
the subservient hypocrites who cry out against oppressions
only when victimized themselves. For some time past the
New York *Sun* has been violating law with boasting and defiance, and yet, because in Tennessee a forcible attempt has
been made to prevent the employment of convicts in the
mines, and because in Kansas an Alliance judge has disobeyed
the decree of the supreme court, it solemnly declares that to
disregard law " is resistance to the will of the people, except
in the case of an unconstitutional statute, which is really no

law at all." The exception here entered by the *Sun* to save its own skin does not avail for that purpose. Who is to decide whether a statute is unconstitutional? The supreme court, the *Sun* will answer. But is the *Sun* prepared, in case the supreme court declares the law regarding executions constitutional, to condemn its own course in violating the law? I think not. But then it must allow to the Tennessee laborers and the Kansas judge the same liberty that it claims for itself. If the "higher law" doctrine is good for anything, it is good, not only against legislatures, but against supreme courts. On the other hand, if it is good for nothing, the *Sun* should take its own advice to other law-breakers, and, instead of violating the law regarding executions, should go to the ballot box and get it repealed. But the *Sun* will not be thus heedful of consistency. That jewel is not prized by hogs. The *Sun* is a hog, an organ of hogs, an apologist for hogs ; and I shall not grieve to see it butchered like a hog.—*Liberty,* August 1, 1891.

The Seattle *Post-Intelligencer* has a very clever man on its editorial staff. His editorials are far above the ordinary literary level of the journalist, are often sensible, and always show a decided inclination to serious consideration of the subjects with which they deal, and to independent and original thought. But occasionally his originality carries him too far. Witness the following original discovery, which he gave to the world unpatented in a recent editorial against woman suffrage: " Nobody who is not an Anarchist in theory, if not in practice, ever pretended that suffrage was a natural right ; but from the Anarchist point of view that suffrage is a natural right, you can just as easily argue, as Anarchists do, that ' property is robbery.' " If this editor had ever investigated Anarchism, of course he would know that most Anarchists do not believe in natural rights at all ; that not one of them considers suffrage a natural right ; that, on the other hand, they all agree on the central proposition that rule is evil, and on the corollary that it is none the better for being majority rule. Anarchism is as hostile to the ballot as peace is to gunpowder.—*Liberty,* August 29, 1891.

I wonder if the people of Massachusetts know that their law-makers made a law this year *punishing with imprisonment for life* every criminal or pauper who has the syphilis. Such is the astounding fact. To be more specific, the law provides that any inmate of a State penal or charitable institution who, at the expiration of his term of imprisonment, shall be afflicted with syphilis shall not be discharged, but shall be detained in the institution until cured. As syphilis is seldom cured, this means in most cases life-imprisonment. Hereafter, in Massachusetts, only the rich and the law-abiding are to be allowed to have the syphilis and liberty too.—*Liberty*, August 29, 1891.

A certain class of *littérateurs* are raising their voices against the "degradation of literature" which they see in the advertisement by the newspapers of " Mr. Howells's $10,000 novel." The question occurs to me : if literature suffers no degradation from Mr. Howells's receipt of $10,000 for the right to publish his novel serially, how can it be injured by the announcement of the fact? That the whole business is degrading to literature I have no doubt, but the real source of the degradation is the State-created monopoly which enables Mr. Howells to put such a price upon his work. And yet in the eyes of these offended *littérateurs* it is this monopoly that uplifts literature. It is creditable to their instincts, though not to their reason, that, having obtained for literature "the proud reward to which it is entitled," they are ashamed to let the public know the amount of this reward.—*Liberty*, November 7, 1891.

There has been a law on the Pennsylvania statute books since 1885 prohibiting the manufacture and sale of butterine. Under the decisions of the United States courts, however, producers outside the State are able to ship their goods into the State and sell them in the original packages. An increasing number of dealers buy these packages, open them, and retail from them in violation of the law. So prevalent has this practice become that the Pennsylvania butchers, who used to sell their fats to the butterine factories, and now have to sell them in Holland much less advantageously, are taking advantage of it to prosecute the guilty parties in the hope of securing a repeal of the obnoxious law. Meanwhile the dear and protected people, instead of eating sweet and wholesome butterine, are forced to eat strong butter, for which they pay a monopoly price to the protected farmers and dairymen. The people are protected in the right to be robbed, and the farmers and dairymen in the right to rob. All these protections should be wiped out. The only protection which honest people need is protection against that vast Society for the Creation of Theft which is euphemistically designated as the State.—*Liberty*, May 14, 1892.

Talk about bloodthirsty Anarchists! Listen to this. It is the editor of the *American Architect* who speaks. "So far as principle goes, we would like to see any interference with the employment of a man willing to work, any *request* or demand—direct or indirect—*for the discharge of a faithful workman,* or any attempt at coercion of a workman, by threats of any sort, to leave his work, PUNISHABLE WITH DEATH." Here we have Archism in full flower. If John Smith politely asks Jim Jones to discharge or not to employ industrious and faithful Sam Robinson, kill him. Such is capitalism's counsel to the courts. If it should be acted upon, I hold that the people would have better cause to charge the *Architect* editor with conspiracy to murder, find him guilty, and dynamite him, than had the State of Illinois to find a similar verdict against Spies and his comrades and hang them. I wonder if the *Architect* editor would be willing to see his principle carried out impartially. Fancy, for instance, the electrocution of Col. Eliot F. Shepard for blacklisting an industrious and faithful Fifth Avenue stage-driver on account of his use of profane language and asking the superintendents of horse-car lines not to employ him. If incendiary counsel shall bring on a bloody revolution, the chief sin thereof will lie upon the capitalists and their hired advocates, and bitterly will they pay the penalty. In these modern days there are many Foulons, some of whom may yet eat grass.—*Liberty,* May 21, 1892.

In the State of New York an unsuccessful attempt to commit suicide is punishable as a crime. It is proposed that Anarchists of foreign birth shall not be allowed to become citizens. Attorney-General Miller wishes suffrage to be made compulsory by the disfranchisement of all who neglect to use the ballot. The New York Health Inspectors, when on a fruit-condemning expedition the other day, after seizing a push-cart full of green peaches turned it over to two messenger-boys, in consequence of which some fifty urchins had a feast and possibly several funerals. A government that gives away the germs of disease which it will not allow others to sell ; a government that insists on disfranchising people who will not vote; a government that refuses to naturalize people who refuse to be naturalized ; a government that refuses life to people who refuse to live,—well, for a good farce such a government is certainly a good farce.—*Liberty,* August 13, 1892.

Another monopoly is threatened. At present, as is well known, Wagner's " Parsifal " can be performed only at Bayreuth. This music-drama is Madame Wagner's property, and she refuses to allow any one else to produce it. But in Austria, it seems, every copyrighted work becomes free ten years after the author's death. Next year, therefore, " Parsifal " can be performed in Austria by any one who chooses. Madame Wagner is moving heaven and earth to secure the passage of a new law in Austria in the interest of her monopoly, and it is said that she may succeed. If she does, then Austrians, like Frenchmen, Englishmen, Americans, and the people of all other nations who have chosen to make slaves of themselves, must continue to pay tribute, not only to Madame Wagner, but to hotel-keepers and railroad corporations, if they desire to witness a representation of the greatest achievement in musical composition yet attained. This situation illustrates another absurdity of property in ideas, to which attention has never been called in these columns. As long as Madame Wagner is allowed to retain her monopoly,—and·really if it is rightfully her property, it ought never to be taken from her,—the price which a man must pay to see " Parsifal " is proportionate to the distance between his residence and Bayreuth. The citizen of Bayreuth pays but five dollars for the privilege which must cost a citizen of the United States from two to four hundred dollars. And this because of one woman's will and the rest of the world's lack of will. It may be replied, of course, that the same situation exists regarding many works of art and nature, and cannot be avoided,—for instance, a painting by Titian or the falls of Niagara. This is unfortunately true ; but the only good reason for putting up with such a state of things is that we cannot help ourselves. We pay heavily to see Niagara Falls because we cannot reproduce Niagara Falls within walking distance of our homes. But is the fact that we must pay more for things we cannot duplicate a good reason for paying more for things that can be duplicated ?— *Liberty*, September 24, 1892.

The recent strike at Carmaux, France, was followed by an agitation for compulsory arbitration of disputes between capital and labor. There was a lively fight over it in the French Chamber, which fortunately had the good sense to vote the measure down. Of all the demands made upon government in the interest of labor this is perhaps the most foolish. I wonder if it has ever occurred to the laborers who make it that to grant their desire would be to deny that cherished right to strike upon which they have insisted so strenuously and for so many years. Suppose, for instance, a body of operatives decide to strike in defence of an interest which they deem vital and to maintain which they are prepared and determined to struggle to the end.   Immediately comes along the board of arbitration, which compels strikers and employers to present their case and then renders a decision.   Suppose the decision is adverse to the strikers.   They are bound to accept it, the arbitration being compulsory, or suffer the penalty, —for there is no law without a penalty.   What then has become of their right to strike ?   It has been destroyed.   They can ask for what they want ; a higher power immediately decides whether they can have it ; and from this decision there is no appeal.   Labor thus would be prohibited by law from struggling for its rights.   And yet labor is so short-sighted that it asks for this very prohibition !—*Liberty*, November 19, 1892.

MONEY AND INTEREST.

"WHO IS THE SOMEBODY?"

[*Liberty*, August 6, 1881.]

"SOMEBODY gets the surplus wealth that labor produces and does not consume. Who is the Somebody?" Such is the problem recently posited in the editorial columns of the New York *Truth*. Substantially the same question has been asked a great many times before, but, as might have been expected, this new form of putting it has created no small hubbub. *Truth's* columns are full of it ; other journals are taking it up ; clubs are organizing to discuss it ; the people are thinking about it ; students are pondering over it. For it is a most momentous question. A correct answer to it is unquestionably the first step in the settlement of the appalling problems of poverty, intemperance, ignorance, and crime. *Truth*, in selecting it as a subject on which to harp and hammer from day to day, shows itself a level-headed, far-sighted newspaper. But, important as it is, it is by no means a difficult question to one who really considers it before giving an answer, though the variety and absurdity of nearly all the replies thus far volunteered certainly tend to give an opposite impression.

What are the ways by which men gain possession of property ? Not many. Let us name them: work, gift, discovery, gaming, the various forms of illegal robbery by force or fraud, usury. Can men obtain wealth by any other than one or more of these methods ? Clearly, no. Whoever the Somebody may be, then, he must accumulate his riches in one of these ways. We will find him by the process of elimination.

Is the Somebody the laborer ? No ; at least not as laborer ; otherwise the question were absurd. Its premises exclude him. He gains a bare subsistence by his work ; no more. We are searching for his surplus product. He has it not.

Is the Somebody the beggar, the invalid, the cripple, the discoverer, the gambler, the highway robber, the burglar, the defaulter, the pickpocket, or the common swindler ? None of these, to any extent worth mentioning. The aggregate of wealth absorbed by these classes of our population compared

177

with the vast mass produced is a mere drop in the ocean, unworthy of consideration in studying a fundamental problem of political economy. These people get some wealth, it is true ; enough, probably, for their own purposes: but labor can spare them the whole of it, and never know the difference.

Then we have found him. Only the usurer remaining, he must be the Somebody whom we are looking for; he, and none other. But who is the usurer, and whence comes his power ? There are three forms of usury : interest on money, rent of land and houses, and profit in exchange. Whoever is in receipt of any of these is a usurer. And who is not ? Scarcely any one. The banker is a usurer ; the manufacturer is a usurer; the merchant is a usurer; the landlord is a usurer; and the workingman who puts his savings, if he has any, out at interest, or takes rent for his house or lot, if he owns one, or exchanges his labor for more than an equivalent,—he too is a usurer. The sin of usury is one under which all are concluded, and for which all are responsible. But all do not benefit by it. The vast majority suffer. Only the chief usurers accumu- late: in agricultural and thickly-settled countries, the landlords; in industrial and commercial countries, the bankers. Those are the Somebodies who swallow up the surplus wealth.

And where do the Somebodies get their power ? From monopoly. Here, as usual, the State is the chief of sinners. Usury rests on two great monopolies,—the monopoly of land and the monopoly of credit. Were it not for these, it would disappear. Ground-rent exists only because the State stands by to collect it and to protect land-titles rooted in force or fraud. Otherwise the land would be free to all, and no one could control more than he used. Interest and house-rent exist only because the State grants to a certain class of individuals and corporations the exclusive privilege of using its credit and theirs as a basis for the issuance of circulating currency. Otherwise credit would be free to all, and money, brought under the law of competition, would be issued at cost. Interest and rent gone, competition would leave little or no chance for profit in exchange except in business protected by tariff or patent laws. And there again the State has but to step aside to cause the last vestige of usury to disappear.

The usurer is the Somebody, and the State is his protector. Usury is the serpent gnawing at labor's vitals, and only liberty can detach and kill it. Give laborers their liberty, and they will keep their wealth. As for the Somebody, he, stripped of his power to steal, must either join their ranks or starve.

REFORM MADE RIDICULOUS.

[*Liberty*, September 17, 1881.]

ONE of the most noteworthy of Thomas Jefferson's sayings
was that he " had rather live under newspapers without a
government than under a government without newspapers."
The Czar of Russia proposes to make this alternative unnecessary by establishing a national weekly journal to be distributed
gratuitously in every village, whose carefully-concocted news
paragraphs, severely-sifted political items, and rose-tinted editorials shall be read aloud 'on Sundays by designated officials to the assembled multitudes. This absurd proposal is
no more absurd than that of a delegate to the State Convention of the Massachusetts Greenbackers, who desired that the
government should add to its functions that of the collection
of news to be furnished gratuitously to the daily journals.
And this again is no more absurd than some of the proposals
actually endorsed by a majority of the delegates to the same
convention, nearly all of whose measures and methods, in
fact, are quite of a piece with those of the aforesaid Czar.

For instance, one of the resolutions adopted (and we grieve
to say that it was introduced by no less a person than our
excellent and earnest friend, J. M. L. Babcock of Cambridge)
asks the legislature to compel all corporations to distribute their
profits in excess of six per cent. among their employees in the
proportion of the scale of wages. Saying nothing of the fact
that this resolution seriously offends liberty by denying that
the equitable distribution of property which the labor movement seeks must result, not from legislative enactment, but
from the free play of natural laws, it also offends equity by
admitting that capital is entitled to a portion of labor's
product, and that the producer is entitled to exact a profit
from the consumer ! Yet we are told that only one man in
that whole convention had the brains and the courage to rise
from his seat and proclaim the great truth that, if labor can
claim anything, it can and should claim ALL. What wonder
that this half-hearted, half-headed Greenback party excites
among intelligent people no sentiment higher than that of a
pity akin to contempt ! Mr. Babcock's resolution would take
the labor movement off of its basis of right, and degen-
erate it into an unprincipled scramble for spoils by which the
strongest would profit. Take the half-loaf who will ; we shall
never cease to reiterate that the whole loaf rightfully belongs

to those who raise the wheat from the soil, grind it into flour, and bake it into bread, and not the smallest taste of it to the sharpers who deceive the unthinking masses into granting them a monopoly of the opportunities of performing these industrial operations, which opportunities they in return rent back to the people on condition of receiving the other half of the loaf.

A DEFENCE OF CAPITAL.

[*Liberty*, October 1, 1881.]

My dear Mr. Tucker:

Why do you " grieve " at a difference of opinion between us ? Am I to be bribed to agree with a valued friend by the fear that he will grieve if I do not ? Liberty, I should say, imposes no such burden on freedom of thought, but rather rejoices in its fullest exercise.

I did not know that the " no-profit " theory had become so well established, or so generally accepted, as to render ridiculous any proposition not based upon it.

Yet that is the only point I understand you to urge against the measure I proposed. But I never could see that labor, in its unequal struggle for its rights, gained anything by extravagant claims. Whatever contributes to production is entitled to an equitable share in the distribution. In the production of a loaf of bread (the example which you set forth in a magnificent paragraph), the plough performs an important, if not indispensable service, and equitably comes in for a share of the loaf. Is that share to be a slice which compensates only for the wear and tear ? It seems to me that it should be slightly thicker, even if no more than "the ninth part of a hair." For suppose one man spends his life in making ploughs to be used by others who sow and harvest wheat. If he furnishes his ploughs only on condition that they be returned to him in as good state as when taken away, how is he to get his bread ? Labor, empty-handed, proposes to raise wheat ; but it can do nothing without a plough, and asks the loan of one from the man who made it. If this man receives nothing more than his plough again, he receives nothing for the product of his own labor, and is on the way to starvation. What proportion he ought to receive is another question, on which I do not enter here ; it may be ever so small, but it should be something.

Capital, we will agree, has hitherto had the lion's share ; why condemn a measure which simply proposes to restore to labor a portion at least of what it is entitled to ?

I say nothing on the theory of " natural laws," because I understood you to suggest that point only to waive it.

Cordially yours,

J. M. L. BABCOCK.*

---

* It should be stated that a few years after the date of this discussion Mr. Babcock abandoned the position here taken, became a thoroughgoing opponent of interest, and has remained such ever since.

"THE POSITION OF WILLIAM."

[From Ruskin's Letters to British Workmen.]

WHAT you call " wages," practically, is the quantity of food which the possessor of the land gives you to work for him. There is, finally, no " capital" but that. If all the money of all the capitalists in the whole world were destroyed—the notes and bills burnt, the gold irrecoverably buried, and all the machines and apparatus of manufactures crushed, by a mistake in signals, in one catastrophe—and nothing remained but the land, with its animals and vegetables, and buildings for shelter—the poorer population would be very little worse off than they are at this instant ; and their labor, instead of being "limited" by the destruction, would be greatly stimulated. They would feed themselves from the animals and growing crop ; heap here and there a few tons of ironstone together, build rough walls round them to get a blast, and in a fortnight they would have iron tools again, and be ploughing and fighting, just as usual. It is only we who had the capital who would suffer ; we should not be able to live idle, as we do now, and many of us—I, for instance—should starve at once ; but you, though little the worse, would none of you be the better eventually for our loss—or starvation. The removal of superfluous mouths would indeed benefit you somewhat for a time ; but you would soon replace them with hungrier ones ; and there are many of us who are quite worth our meat to you in different ways, which I will explain in due place ; also I will show you that our money is really likely to be useful to you in its accumulated form (besides that, in the instances when it has been won by work, it justly belongs to us), so only that you are careful never to let us persuade you into borrowing it and paying us interest for it. You will find a very amusing story, explaining your position in that case, at the one hundred and seventeenth page of the "Manual of Political Economy," published this year at Cambridge, for your early instruction, in an almost devotionally catechetical form, by Messrs. Macmillan.

Perhaps I had better quote it to you entire ; it is taken by the author " from the French."

"There was once in a village a poor carpenter who worked hard from morning till night. One day James thought to himself, 'With my hatchet, saw, and hammer I can only make coarse furniture, and can only get the pay for such. If I had a plane, I should please my customers more, and they would pay me more. Yes, I am resolved I will make myself a plane.' At the end of ten days James had in his possession an admirable plane which he valued all the more for having made it himself. Whilst he was reckoning all the profits which he expected to derive from the use of it, he was interrupted by William, a carpenter in the neighboring village. William, having admired the plane, was struck with the advantages which might be gained from it. He said to James :

" ' You must do me a service; lend me the plane for a year.' As might be expected, James cried out, ' How can you think of such a thing, William ? Well, if I do you this service, what will you do for me in return ?'

" W. 'Nothing. Don't you know that a loan ought to be gratuitous ?'

"*J.* 'I know nothing of the sort ; but I do know that if I were to lend you my plane for a year, it would be giving it to you. To tell you the truth, that was not what I made it for.'

"*W.* 'Very well, then ; I ask you to do me a service; what service do you ask me in return ?'

"*J.* 'First, then, in a year the plane will be done for. You must therefore give me another exactly like it.'

" *W.* 'That is perfectly just. I submit to these conditions. I think you must be satisfied with this, and can require nothi᾽g further.'

"*J.* 'I think otherwise. I made the plane for myself, and not for you. I expected to gain some advantage from it. I have made the plane for the purpose of improving my work and my condition ; if you merely return it to me in a year, it is you who will gain the profit of it, during the whole of that time. I am not bound to do you such a service without receiving anything in return. Therefore, if you wish for my plane besides the restoration already bargained for, you must give me a new plank as a compensation for the advantages of which I shall be deprived.'

" These terms were agreed to, but the singular part of it is that at the end of the year, when the plane came into James's possession, he lent it again ; recovered it, and lent it a third and fourth time. It has passed into the hands of his son, who still lends it. Let us examine this little story. The plane is the symbol of all capital, and the plank is the symbol of all interest."

If this be an abridgment, what a graceful piece of highly-wrought literature the original story must be ! I take the liberty of abridging it a little more.

James makes a plane, lends it to William on 1st of January for a year. William gives him a plank for the loan of it, wears it out, and makes another for James, which he gives him on 31st December. On 1st January he again borrows the new one ; and the arrangement is repeated continuously. The position of William therefore is that he makes a plane every 31st of December, lends it to James till the next day, and pays James a plank annually for the privilege of lending it to him on that evening. This, in future investigations of capital and interest, we will call, if you please, "The Position of William."

You may not at the first glance see where the fallacy lies (the writer of the story evidently counts on your not seeing it at all).

If James did not lend the plane to William, he could only get his gain of a plank by working with it himself and wearing it out himself. When he had worn it out at the end of the year, he would, therefore, have to make another for himself. William, working with it instead, gets the advantage instead, which he must, therefore, pay James his plank for; and return to James what James would, if he had not lent his plane, then have had—not a new plane, but the worn-out one. James must make a new one for himself, as he would have had to do if no William had existed ; and if William likes to borrow it again for another plank, all is fair.

That is to say, clearing the story of its nonsense, that James makes a plane annually and sells it to William for its proper price, which, in kind, is a new plank. But this arrangement has nothing whatever to do with principal or with interest. There are, indeed, many very subtle conditions involved in any sale ; one among which is the value of ideas; I will explain that value to you in the course of time (the article is not one which modern political economists have any familiarity with dealings in), and I will tell you somewhat also of the real nature of interest ; but if you will only get for the present a quite clear idea of " The Position of William," it is all I want of you.

CAPITAL'S CLAIM TO INCREASE.

[*Liberty*, October 1, 1881.]

Liberty's strictures, in her last issue, upon the proposal of the Massachusetts Greenbackers, adopted at their Worcester convention, to ask the legislature to compel all corporations to distribute their profits in excess of six per cent. among the employees in proportion to their wages has stirred up Mr. J. M. L. Babcock, the author of that singular project, to a defence of it. And in defending it against *Liberty*, he is obliged to do so in behalf of capital. It seems a little odd to find this long-time defender of the rights of labor in the *rôle* of champion of the claims of capital ; but we remember that he is one who follows the lead of justice as he sees it, take him where it may.

Before proceeding to the main question, he gives us two minor points to settle. First, he very pertinently asks why we " grieve " at his course. We answer by taking it all back. As he says, *Liberty* should rejoice, rather than grieve, at the honest exercise of the right to differ. When we hastily said otherwise, we said a very foolish thing. Yes, worse than that ; in so far we were false to our own standard. Mr. Babcock has *Liberty's* sincerest thanks for recalling her to her own position. May he and all never fail to sharply prod us, whenever they similarly catch us napping ! *

Second, he assumes that the profit idea cannot be ridiculous (as we pronounced it), since its converse is not well established or generally accepted. To say that the no-profit theory is not well established is to beg the principal question under discussion ; to say that, because the theory is not generally accepted, the few friends that it has are not entitled to ridi-

---

* Reading this paragraph eleven years later, I am inclined to regret that I wrote it. So few are the manifestations of good nature in my polemical writings, that I can ill afford to disown any of them; but it really seems that on this occasion I tried a little too hard to be fair. The grief for which I thus apologized was over the fact that Mr. Babcock held an opinion in favor of injustice,—not over the fact that, holding such an opinion, he gave expression to it.

cule the position of its enemies is not in accordance with the nature of ideas or the custom of Mr. Babcock. How often have we listened with delight to his sarcastic dissection and merciless exposure to the light of common sense of some popular and well-nigh universal delusion in religion, politics, finance, or social life! He is in the habit of holding ridiculous all those things, whoever supports them, which his own reason pronounces absurd. And he is right in doing so, and wrong in saying that we ought not to follow his example. So, while it is clear that on the first minor point Mr. Babcock has the better of *Liberty*, on the second *Liberty* as decidedly has the better of Mr. Babcock.

Now to the question proper. Labor, says our friend, never gains anything by extravagant claims. True ; and no claim is extravagant that does not exceed justice. But it is equally true that labor always loses by foolish concessions ; and in this industrial struggle every concession is foolish that falls short of justice. It is to be decided, then, not whether *Liberty's* claim for labor is extravagant, but whether it is just. "Whatever contributes to production is entitled to an equitable share in the distribution!" Wrong! *Whoever* contributes to production is alone so entitled. *What* has no rights that *Who* is bound to respect. *What* is a thing. *Who* is a person. Things have no claims ; they exist only to be claimed. The possession of a right cannot be predicated of dead material, but only of a living person. "In the production of a loaf of bread, the plough performs an important service, and equitably comes in for a share of the loaf." Absurd ! A plough cannot own bread, and, if it could, would be unable to eat it. A plough is a *What*, one of those things above mentioned, to which no rights are attributable.

Oh ! but we see. "Suppose one man spends his life in making ploughs to be used by others who sow and harvest wheat. If he furnishes his ploughs only on condition that they be returned to him in as good state as when taken away, how is he to get his bread?" It is the maker of the plough, then, and not the plough itself, that is entitled to a reward? *What* has given place to *Who*. Well, we'll not quarrel over that. The maker of the plough certainly is entitled to pay for his work. Full pay, paid once ; no more. That pay is the plough itself, or its equivalent in other marketable products, said equivalent being measured by the amount of labor employed in their production. But if he lends his plough and gets only his plough back, how is he to get his bread ? asks Mr. Babcock, much concerned. Ask us an easy one, if you please. We give

this one up. But why should he lend his plough ? Why does
he not sell it to the farmer, and use the proceeds to buy bread
of the baker ? See, Mr. Babcock ? If the lender of the plough
" receives nothing more than his plough again, he receives nothing for the product of his own labor, and is on the way to
starvation." Well, if the fool will not sell his plough, let him
starve. Who cares ? It's his own fault. How can he expect
to receive anything for the product of his own labor if he
refuses to permanently part with it ? Does Mr. Babcock propose to steadily add to this product at the expense of some
laborer, and meanwhile allow this idler, who has only made a
plough, to loaf on in luxury, for the balance of his life, on the
strength of his one achievement ? Certainly not, when our
friend understands himself. And then he will say with us
that the slice of bread which the plough-lender should receive
can be neither large nor small, but must be nothing.

To that end we commend to Mr. Babcock the words of
his own candidate for Secretary of State, nominated at the
Worcester convention, A. B. Brown, editor of *The Republic*,
who says : " The laborers of the world, instead of having only
a small fraction of the wealth in the world, should have all
the wealth. To effect this all monopolies should be termina-
ted,—whether they be monopolies of single individuals or
' majorities,'—and labor-cost must be recognized as the measure
and limit of price." If Mr. Brown sticks to these words, and
the Greenbackers to their platform, there is going to be a
collision, and Mr. Brown will keep the track. But lest Mr.
Brown's authority should not prove sufficient, we refer Mr.
Babcock further to one of his favorite authors, John Ruskin,
who argues this very point on Mr. Babcock's own ground,
except that he illustrates his position by a plane instead of a
plough. Mr. Babcock may find his words under the heading,
" The Position of William," immediately following his own
letter to us. If he succeeds in showing Mr. Brown's assertions
to be baseless and Mr. Ruskin's arguments to be illogical, he
may then come to *Liberty* for other foes to conquer. Till
then we shall be but an interested spectator of his contest.

A BASELESS CHARGE.

[*Liberty*, October 15, 1881.]

My dear Mr. Tucker:

It is entirely immaterial in this discussion whether my position is "odd" or otherwise. The question at issue must be settled, if settled at all, on its own merits ; and no prejudice either for or against capital can affect the argument. Let us burden it with no irrelevant matter.

My question was simply this : Is a man who loans a plough entitled in equity to compensation for its use ; and if not, why not ?

This question (I say it with all respect) you evade. But, until it is answered, no progress can be made in this inquiry. It is no answer to say, "Let him sell his plough." He does not sell it ; he loans it, as he has a natural right to do. Another borrows it, as he has a natural right to do. I repeat : Is it just to pay for its use ?

You gain nothing when you say, "Let him sell"; for, if I followed you there, it would only be to present the same question substantially in another form. You might then suggest another alternative, until we "swung round the circle," and came back to the first. So let us save time and meet it at once. If it cannot be met where I proposed it, I do not see that it can be answered anywhere. If your theory will not bear an application to the example I stated, what is it good for ? I have never seen a good reason why the plough-maker is not entitled to pay for the use of his plough.

You refer me to certain "authorities,"—Brown and Ruskin. I do not bow to authorities on questions of this nature ; and I supposed you did not. I ask for a reason, not a name. Brown's proposition, which I affirm as stoutly as he does, does not answer my question. Ruskin is equally remote. He concludes that the case he examines is one of sale and purchase. That is not the case I stated at all. If there be an answer to my question, I am sure you are capable of stating it.

Yours cordially,

J. M. L. BABCOCK.

We have no wish to waste these columns in repetition ; but this charge of evasion is a serious one, which can be thoroughly examined only by reviewing ground already traversed. One of the objects that we had in view in beginning the publication of this journal was the annihilation of usury. If in our first direct conflict with a supporter of usury we have been guilty of evasion, we are unfitted for our task, and ought to abandon it to hands more competent. But we unhesitatingly plead " not guilty."

Mr. Babcock argued that the man who makes a plough and lends it is entitled to a portion of the loaf subsequently produced in addition to the return of his plough intact. He now asserts that we answered this by saying, " Let him sell his plough." No, we did not. On the principle that only labor can be an equitable basis of price, we argued in reply as follows: "The maker of the plough certainly is entitled to pay for his work. Full pay, paid once ; no more. That pay is the plough itself, or its equivalent in other marketable products, said equivalent being measured by the amount of labor employed in their production." True or false, this answer is direct and tangible ; in no sense is it evasive. Then Mr. Babcock asked this other and distinct question: " If he furnishes his ploughs only on condition that they be returned to him in as good state as when taken away, how is he to get his bread ? " We replied that we did not know, and that, if he was such a fool as to do so, we did not care. Nothing evasive here, either ; on the contrary, utter frankness. Touched a little, however, by Mr. Babcock's sympathy with the usurer thus threatened with starvation, we ventured the suggestion that, instead of lending his plough to the farmer, he might sell it to him, and thus get money wherewith to buy bread of the baker. This advice was gratuitous, we know ; possibly it was impertinent, also ; but was it evasive ? Not in the least.

Finally, thinking that Mr. Babcock might agree, as we do, with Novalis that a man's belief gains quite infinitely the moment another mind is convinced thereof, we called his attention to two other minds in harmony with ours on the point now in dispute, A. B. Brown and John Ruskin. But not as authorities, in Mr. Babcock's sense of the word. Still, Mr. Brown being Mr. Babcock's candidate for Secretary of State, and party candidates being supposedly *representative* in things fundamental, we deemed it not out of place to cite a proposition from Mr. Brown that seemed to us, *on its face*, directly contradictory of Mr. Babcock. To our astonishment Mr. Babcock accepts it as not inconsistent with his position, at the same time declaring it irrelevant. Argument ends here. If we hold up two objects, one of which, to our eyes, is red and the other blue, and Mr. Babcock declares that both are red, it is useless to discuss the matter. One of us is color-blind. The ultimate verdict of mankind will decide which. In quoting from Mr. Ruskin, however, we did not ask Mr. Babcock to accept him as authority, but to point out the weakness of an argument drawn from an illustration similar to Mr. Babcock's. Mr. Babcock replies by denying the similarity, saying that Ruskin "concludes that the case he examines is one of sale and purchase." Let us see. Ruskin is examining a story told by Bastiat in illustration and defence of usury. After printing Bastiat's version of it, he abridges it thus, stripping away all mystifying clauses:

James makes a plane, lends it to William on 1st of January for a year. William gives him a plank for the loan of it, wears it out, and makes another for James, which he gives him on 31st December. On 1st January he again borrows the new one ; and the arrangement is repeated continuously. The position of William, therefore, is that he makes a plane every 31st of December ; lends it to James till the next day, and pays James a plank annually for the privilege of lending it to him on that evening.

Substitute in the foregoing "plough" for "plane," and "loaf" or "slice" for "plank," and the story differs in no essential point from Mr. Babcock's. How monstrously unjust the transaction is can be plainly seen. Ruskin next shows how this unjust transaction may be changed into a just one :

If James did not lend the plane to William, he could only get his gain of a plank by working with it himself and wearing it out himself. When he had worn it out at the end of the year, he would, therefore, have to make another for himself. William, working with it instead, gets the advantage instead, which he must, therefore, pay James his plank for ; and return to James what James would, if he had not lent his plane, then have had—not a new plane, but the worn-out one. James must make a new one for himself, as he would have had to do if no William had existed ; and if William likes to borrow it again for another plank, all is fair. That is to say, clearing the story of its nonsense, that James makes a plane annually and sells it to William for its proper price, which, in kind, is a new plank.

It is *this latter transaction,* wholly different from the former, that Ruskin pronounces a "sale," having "nothing whatever to do with principal or with interest." And yet, according to Mr. Babcock, "the case he examines [Bastiat's, of course] is one of sale and purchase." We understand now how it is that Mr. Babcock can charge us with evasion. He evidently conceives his method of meeting a point to be straightforward. If it be so, certainly ours is evasive. If, on the other hand, our course has been straightforward, evasion is too mild a term for his. It is better described as flat misstatement ; purely careless, of course, but scarcely less excusable than if wilful. Again we invite our friend to a *careful* examination (and refutation, if possible) of the arguments advanced.

ANOTHER ANSWER TO MR. BABCOCK.

[*Liberty*, November 12, 1881.]

Mr. Tucker :

In your issue of October 15, I notice a question by J. M. L. Babcock, and, although you have answered it, yet I beg to give my answer. The question is this : " Is a man who loans a plough entitled in equity to compensation for its use ? " My answer is, " Yes." Now, then, what of it ? Does that make something for nothing right ? Let us see. We must take it for granted that the loaning of the plough was a good business transaction. Such being the case, the man who borrows the plough must give good security that he will return the plough and pay for what he wears out. He must have the wealth or the credit to make the owner of the plough whole in case he should break or lose the plough. Now, I claim that this man, having the wealth or credit to secure a borrowed plough, could transmute that same credit or security into money, *without cost*, and with the money buy a plough, were it not for a monopoly of money. For a monopoly of money implies a monopoly of everything that money will buy.

If the people should give to landholders, as a right, what they now give to bondholders as a special privilege—why, you might loan ploughs for a price, but the price would not include a money cost, as is inevitable under our present monetary system.

Let us remember that an individual transaction under a system of monopoly does not represent nor illustrate the truth as it would be under a natural or just system. Again, superficial ideas do not always harmonize with the central truth.

Briefly, but truly yours,

APEX.

ATTENTION, "APEX!"

[*Liberty*, November 26, 1881.]

My dear Mr. Tucker :

Allow me just to say that " Apex " is in error in supposing he has answered my question. It appears by his own comment that his " Yes " means that the plough-lender is entitled to pay for the *wear and tear* of the plough. I asked : Is he entitled to pay for its *use ?* I marvel that he should overlook the distinction, for I had been careful to mark it in my first statement. When the question as I put it is answered in the affirmative, I shall be ready to answer the other, " What of it ? " But I am still left to the mournful impression that my question is not answered.

Yours cordially,

J. M. L. BABCOCK.

USURY.

[*Liberty*, November 26, 1881.]

PAYING money for the use of money is a great and barbarous wrong. It is also a stupendous absurdity. No one man can use money. The use of money involves its transfer from one to another. Therefore, as no one man can use money, it cannot be right and proper for any man to pay for the use of that which he cannot use. The people do use money; consequently, they should pay whatever the money may cost.

Money is necessarily a thing which belongs to society. This is one of the great truths of civilization which has been generally overlooked. For this whole question of the rightfulness of interest turns on the question, "What is money?" So long as the people shall continue to consider money as a thing of itself objectively—why, there is no hope for humanity.

All wealth is the product of labor, but no labor can produce money. There can be no money until some wealth has been produced, because money is a representative of wealth.

Money is a form of credit—credit in circulation. It is not a thing of substance. The great object of money is to exchange values. Now, value is an idea, and money is used to represent, count, and exchange values. The symbol or token of money is not the money itself. Therefore, as money is not a thing of substance, and cannot wear out, it is and ever must be a great wrong and an utter absurdity to give wealth for the use of an idea.

In equity compensation implies service or labor, and as money does not cost labor, why, labor cannot justly be demanded for its use.

But let us look at it practically. , The people use money; the people furnish the money; and, if the cost of issue is paid, there can be no other expense. The great difficulty touching this whole matter is a barbarous misconception of the nature of money and a more barbarous disposition to monopolize power and rob the weak. For—let us ask—who pays the great tax of interest? Not those who have and handle the money; not those who use the money; but the poor, the weak, the ignorant, the dupes of the ruling class. We can illustrate this by a fact of to-day. If five or more men having one hundred thousand dollars, *and no more*, organize and establish a national bank, just so soon as their bank is in operation they have the use and income of one hundred and ninety thousand dollars. Now, is it not clear that, this company having got ninety thousand dollars for nothing, somebody has lost that amount? For, if one man gets a dollar that he has not earned, some other man has earned a dollar that he has not got. That is as certain as that two and two make four.

If all men could use their own credit in the form of money, there could be no such thing as interest. Yet, to put this idea into practice, there must be organization and consolidation of credit. Commercial credit, to be good, must be known to be good. A man's credit may be good to the extent of a thousand dollars, but, that fact not being generally known, he must, as things are, exchange his credit for that which is known to be good, and pay a monopoly price for the privilege of using his own credit in the form of money.

Let us remember that no man can borrow money, as a good business transaction, under any system, unless he has the required security to make the lender whole in case he should lose the money. What a stupendous wrong is this—that a man having credit cannot use it, but must exchange it and pay a monopoly price, which is really for the privilege of using his own credit!

And again, he cannot pay this himself, but must compel the poor man to work out this tax ; the latter must pay this interest in the enhanced price of goods. I wonder if the people will always be thus blind and stupid !

So long as business men, as such, and laborers shall continue to permit the few shrewd moneyed men to monopolize commercial credit—that is, money—just so long will it be hard times for business and labor. What we want now is the organization of credit on a just and equal plan. William B. Greene solved this whole matter and summed it up in two words : " MUTUAL BANKING." That is what we want.

APEX.

<hr>

APEX OR BASIS.

[*Liberty*, December 10, 1881.]

" APEX " says that it is a barbarism to pay interest on money. That is another way of saying that a state of society in which wealth is not universalized is barbarous, since, in our present stage of evolution, those who have no capital of their own will be glad to borrow from those who have, and to pay interest for the use of the capital.

For it is really capital that is borrowed, and not money, the latter being only the means for obtaining the former, as money would be worthless if it could not be exchanged for the capital needed. We see already that, as the loanable capital of a country increases, the rate of interest diminishes, and when the accumulated wealth of the world becomes large enough no one will pay interest.

But to denounce the payment of interest to-day, and (if it could be done) to forbid the man of ability, but lacking means, borrowing the capital he needs, or, in other words, using his credit, would not tend to universalize wealth and so destroy usury ; but, on the other hand, it would discourage the production and accumulation of capital, since one of the principal incentives to that production is the use of capital to increase production and add to one's wealth. It is obvious that, unless the use of capital added to the productiveness of labor, no one would wish to borrow, and no usury could be had. It should not be forgotten, in considering this question, that, in the last analysis, reducing things to their simplest, individualized form, the possessor of capital has acquired it by a willingness to work harder than his fellows and to sacrifice his love of spending all he produces that he may have the aid of capital to increase his power of production. For example, two men work side by side ; one consumes all he produces, the other saves part of his product. In time the latter has saved enough to enable him to build or buy a tool by the aid of which he accomplishes four times as much work as before, and is able to go on adding to his accumulation. The one who has not saved, seeing the advantage of the use of capital, naturally desires to obtain the same benefit for himself ; but, not liking to save and wait until he can create capital, he proposes to borrow a portion of the capital of the other. By means of this borrowed capital he can quadruple h's product, and is very willing to give a part of his increased product to the neighbor who has befriended him. Would he not be a mean sneak if he were not glad to do so ? By the use of the borrowed capital he is not only enabled to pay for the advantage gained, but, by his greater power to produce, he can, in a short time, buy his own tools and no longer be forced to borrow.

Although our present system of business is vastly complicated, and we sometimes seem to borrow money merely, the actual transaction being kept out of sight, yet the case supposed is the real basis of all just payment of interest. I believe there will be a state of society in which money will not be necessary, but that state cannot be built up by commencing at the top. We must build from the foundation, understanding things as they are as well as knowing how they ought to be.

The question is asked—and it is a very important one, and, simple as it is at bottom, a complex one as it stands— *What is money ?* It would simplify this matter very much if all would agree to call coin, or money having value as merchandise, *money*, and paper, or representative money, *currency*, or notes. It is plain that the representative money is that which must be and is principally used in this country and in all commercial countries. Coin money derives its real value in exchange, and as a measure for the exchangeable value of other products, from the fact that it costs labor to produce it ; and, although government laws may foolishly try to make it pass for more than its cost value, they never succeed in doing so. No government ever has succeeded in overriding natural law, though they may and often do obstruct the operations of Nature's laws to the great detriment of Nature's children.

The simplest form of representative money, or currency, is furnished by Josiah Warren's labor note, which was substantially as follows (I quote from memory) :

For value received, I promise to pay bearer, on demand, one hour's labor, or ten pounds of corn.

JOSIAH WARREN.

MODERN TIMES, July 4, 1852.

So long as it was believed by his neighbors that the maker of such notes always had the corn on hand with which to redeem them (since their redemption in labor would rarely be practicable or desirable), they would pass current in that locality ; and, in fact, such " labor notes " did pass to a limited extent at Modern Times. Interesting as that experiment was, and showing clearly, as it does, the principle at the basis of all good currency, it could not be extended so as to satisfy the needs of a great commercial country, or, safely, of a large neighborhood.

But a currency, to be good, must possess precisely the qualifications and qualities of that labor note, with the addition of a guaranty, universally recognizable, that the notes actually do represent solid wealth with which they will be redeemed on demand. Now, there is one thing, and only one, that government can rightfully or usefully do in the way of interference with the currency, the ebb and flow of which is governed by natural laws altogether out of the reach of State or national governments ; and that is to issue all the notes used for currency on such terms that it shall be universally known truly to represent actual, movable capital (not land, which is not property in the true sense, and which cannot be carried off by any one wishing a note redeemed), pledged for its redemption. There should be no monopoly, but any and every person complying with the terms should be furnished with the national note. Of course, no one who had not the requisite capital could procure these notes, and rightly so, because notes made by those who have no capital would swindle the people. And, as our government has no property or capital, except the necessary tools for carrying on the affairs of the nation, and as government should have no debts and no gold and silver accumulated, it is obvious that it cannot properly make a good note beyond the amount which could be redeemed in payment of taxes. And, as taxes ought to be diminished and ultimately abolished, there is no valid basis for a government note to be used as currency. Neither will Mutual Banks answer any good purpose if the notes are based on land.

BASIS.*

The remarks that follow are not intended to debar " Apex " from answering his opponent in his own time and way, but simply to combat, from *Liberty's* standpoint, such of the positions taken by " Basis " as seem to need refutation.

The first error into which " Basis " falls is his identification of money with capital. Representative money is not capital ; it is only a title to capital. He who borrows a paper dollar from another simply borrows a title.† Consequently he takes from the lender nothing which the lender wishes to use ; unless, indeed, the lender desires to purchase capital with his dollar, in which case he will not lend it, or, if he does, will charge for the sacrifice of his opportunity,—a very different thing from usury, which is payment, not for the lender's sacrifice, but for the borrower's use; that is, not for a burden borne, but for a benefit conferred. Neither does the borrower of the dollar take from the person of whom he purchases capital with it anything which that person desires to use ; for, in ordinary commerce, the seller is either a manufacturer or a dealer, who produces or buys his stock for no other purpose than to sell it. And thence this dollar goes on transferring products for which the holders thereof have no use, until it reaches its issuer and final redeemer and is cancelled, depriving, in the course of its journey, no person of any opportunity, but, on the contrary,

---

* It is interesting to note that " Basis," abandoning later the theory of interest maintained by him in the above article, took the initiative in the formation of a society for the abolition of interest, and now considers such abolition essential to the solution of the social problem.

† Nevertheless, to everybody but the issuer, representative money is capital to all intents and purposes, because it will procure capital. But to the issuer it is not capital, because he issues it against security belonging not to himself but to the borrower, would not be able to issue it were it not for such security, and therefore parts with nothing in issuing it. Now the idea that ˌmoney is capital does not sustain the position of " Basis," unless it be taken to mean that money is capital to the issuer.

serving the needs of all through whose hands it passes. Hence borrowing a title to capital is a very different thing from borrowing capital itself. But under the system of organized credit contemplated by "Apex" no capable and deserving person would borrow even a title to capital. The so-called borrower would simply so change the face of his own title as to make it recognizable by the world at large, and at no other expense than the mere cost of the alteration. That is to say, the man having capital or good credit, who, under the system advocated by "Apex," should go to a credit-shop—in other words, a bank—and procure a certain amount of its notes by the ordinary processes of mortgaging property or getting endorsed commercial paper discounted, would only exchange his own personal credit—known only to his immediate friends and neighbors and the bank, and therefore useless in transactions with any other parties—for the bank's credit, known and receivable for products delivered throughout the State, or the nation, or perhaps the world. And for this convenience the bank would charge him only the labor-cost of its service in effecting the exchange of credits, instead of the ruinous rates of discount by which, under the present system of monopoly, privileged banks tax the producers of unprivileged property out of house and home. So that "Apex" really would have *no borrowing at all*, except in certain individual cases not worth considering ; and, therefore, when "Basis," answering "Apex," says that "it is really capital that is borrowed, and not money," he makes a remark for which there is no audible call.

The second error commited by "Basis" he commits in common with the economists in assuming that an increase of capital decreases the rate of interest and that nothing else can materially decrease it. The facts are just the contrary. The rate of interest may, and often does, decrease when the amount of capital has not increased ; the amount of capital may increase without decreasing the rate of interest, which may in fact increase at the same time ; and so far from the universalization of wealth being the sole means of abolishing interest, the abolition of interest is the *sine qua non* of the universalization of wealth.

Suppose, for instance, that the banking business of a nation is conducted by a system of banks chartered and regulated by the government, these banks issuing paper money based on specie, dollar for dollar. If now a certain number of these banks, by combining to buy up the national legislature, should secure the exclusive privilege of issuing two paper dollars for each specie dollar in their vaults, could they not afford to, and would they not in fact, materially reduce their rate of discount? Would not the competing banks be forced to reduce their rate in consequence? And would not this reduction lower the rate of interest throughout the nation? Undoubtedly; and yet the amount of capital in the country remains the same as before.

Suppose, further, that during the following year, in consequence of the stimulus given to business and production by this decrease in the rate of interest and also because of unusually favorable natural conditions, a great increase of wealth occurs. If then the banks of the nation, holding from the government a monopoly of the power to issue money, should combine to contract the volume of the currency, could they not, and would they not, raise the rate of interest thereby? Undoubtedly ; and yet the amount of capital in the country is greater than it ever was before.

But suppose, on the other hand, that all these banks, chartered and regulated by the government and issuing money dollar for dollar, had finally been allowed to issue paper beyond their capital based on the credit and guaranteed capital of their customers ; that their circulation, thus doubly secured, had become so popular that people preferred to pay their debts in coin instead of bank-notes, thus causing coin to flow into the vaults of the banks and add to their reserve ; that this addition had enabled them to add further to their circulation, until, by a continuation of the process, it at last amounted to eight times their original capital ; that by levying a high rate of interest on this they had bled the people nigh unto death ; that then the government had stepped in and said to the banks: "When you began, you received an annual interest of six per cent. on your capital ; you now receive nearly that rate on a circulation eight times your capital based really on the people's credit ; therefore at one-eighth of the original rate your annual profit would be as great as formerly ; henceforth your rate of discount must not exceed three-fourths of one per cent." Had all this happened (and with the exception of the last condition of the hypothesis similar cases have frequently happened), what would have been the result ? Proudhon shall answer for us. In the eighth letter of his immortal discussion with Bastiat on the question of interest he exhausts the whole subject of the relation of interest to capital ; and " Basis " cannot do better than read the whole of it. A brief extract, however, must suffice here. He is speaking of the Bank of France, which at that time (1849) was actually in almost the same situation as that described above. Supposing, as we have just done after him, a reduction of the rate of discount to three-fourths of one per cent., he then asks, as we do, what the result would be. These are his words in answer to Bastiat, the " Basis " of that discussion :

The fortune and destiny of the country are to-day in the hands of the Bank of France. If it would relieve industry and commerce by a decrease of its rate of discount proportional to the increase of its reserve ; in other words, if it would reduce the price of its credit to three-fourths of one per cent., which it must do in order to quit stealing,—this reduction would instantly produce, throughout the Republic and all Europe, incalculable results. They could not be enumerated in a volume ; I will confine myself to the indication of a few.

If, then, the credit of the Bank of France should be loaned at three-fourths of one per cent., ordinary bankers, notaries, capitalists, and even the stockholders of the bank itself would be immediately compelled by competition to reduce their interest, discount, and dividends to at least one per cent., including incidental expenses and brokerage. What harm, think you, would this reduction do to borrowers on personal credit, or to commerce and industry, who are forced to pay, by reason of this fact alone, an annual tax of at least two thousand millions?

If financial circulation could be effected at a rate of discount representing only the cost of administration, drafting, registration, etc., the interest charged on purchases and sales on credit would fall in its turn from six per cent. to zero,—that is to say, business would then be transacted on a cash basis ; there would be no more debts. Again, to how great a degree, think you, would that diminish the shameful number of suspensions, failures, and bankruptcies ?

But, as in society *net* product is undistinguishable from *raw* product, so in the light of the sum total of economic facts CAPITAL is undistinguishable from PRODUCT. These two terms do not, in reality, stand for two distinct things ; they designate relations only. Product is capital ; capital is product : there is a difference between them only in private economy ; none whatever in public economy. If, then, interest, after having fallen in the case of money to three-fourths of one per cent.,— that is, to zero, inasmuch as three-fourths of one per cent. represents only the service of the bank,—should fall to zero in the case of merchandise also, by analogy of principles and facts it would soon fall to zero in the case of real estate ; rent would disappear in becoming one with liquidation. Do you think, sir, that that would prevent people from living in houses and cultivating land ?

If, thanks to this radical reform in the machinery of circulation, labor was compelled to pay to capital only as much interest as would be a just reward for the service rendered by the capitalist, specie and real estate being deprived of their reproductive properties and valued only as *products*,—as things that can be consumed and replaced,—the favor with which specie and capital are now looked upon would be wholly transferred to products ; each individual, instead of restricting his consumption, would strive only to increase it. Whereas, at present, thanks to the restriction laid upon consumable products by interest, the means of consumption are always very much limited, then, on the contrary, production would be insufficient ; labor would then be secure in fact as well as in right,

The laboring class gaining at one stroke the five thousand millions, or thereabouts, now taken in the form of interest from the ten thousand millions which it produces, plus five thousand millions which this same interest deprives it of by destroying the demand for labor, plus five thousand millions which the parasites, cut off from a living, would then be compelled to produce, the national production would be doubled and the welfare of the laborer increased fourfold. And you, sir, whom the worship of interest does not prevent from lifting your thoughts to another world,—what say you to this improvement of affairs here below? Do you see now that it is not the multiplication of capital which decreases interest, but, on the contrary, that it is the decrease of interest which multiplies capital?

Now, this reduction of the rate of discount to the bank's service, and the results therefrom as above described, are precisely what would happen if the whole business of banking should be thrown open to free competition. It behooves "Basis" to examine this argument well; for, unless he can find a fatal flaw in it, he must stand convicted, in saying that "when the accumulated wealth of the world becomes large enough, no one will pay interest," of putting the cart before the horse.

"Basis" is in error a third time in assuming that "Apex" wishes to "forbid the man of ability, but lacking means, using his credit." It is precisely because such men are now virtually prohibited from using their credit that "Apex," and *Liberty* with him, complains. This singular misconception on the part of "Basis" indicates that he does not yet understand what he is fighting.

The fourth error for which "Basis" assumes responsibility is found in his statement that "in the last analysis the possessor of capital has acquired it by a willingness to work harder than his fellows and to sacrifice his love of spending all he produces that he may have the aid of capital to increase his power of production." A man who thoroughly means to tell the truth here reiterates one of the most devilish of the many infernal lies for which the economists have to answer. It is indeed true that the possessor of capital may, in rare cases, have acquired it by the method stated, though even then he could not be excused for making the capital so acquired a leech upon his fellow-men. But ninety-nine times in a hundred the modern possessor of any large amount of capital has acquired it, not "by a willingness to work harder than his fellows," but by a shrewdness in getting possession of a monopoly which makes it needless for him to do any *real* work at all; not by a willingness "to sacrifice his love of spending all he produces," but by a cleverness in procuring from the

government a privilege by which he is able to spend in wanton
luxury half of what a large number of other men produce.
The chief privilege to which we refer is that of selling the
people's credit for a price.

"Basis" is guilty of several other errors which we have not
space to discuss at length. He supposes that to confine the
term *money* to coin and to call all other money *currency* would
simplify matters, when in reality it is the insistence upon this
false distinction that is the prevailing cause of mystification.
If the idea of the royalty of gold and silver could be once
knocked out of the people's heads, and they could once un-
derstånd that no particular kind of merchandise is created by
nature for monetary purposes, they would settle this question
in a trice. Again, he seems to think that Josiah Warren based
his notes on corn. Nothing of the kind. Warren simply took
corn as his standard, but made *labor and all its products* his
basis. His labor notes were rarely redeemed in corn. If he
had made corn his exclusive basis, there would be no distinction in principle between him and the specie men. Perhaps
the central point in his monetary theory was his denial of the
idea that any one product of labor can properly be made the
only basis of money. To quote him in this connection at all
is the height of presumption on the part of " Basis." A charge
that his system, which recognized *cost* as the only ground of
price, even contemplated a promise to pay anything "for *value*
received," he would deem the climax of insult to his memory.
"Basis," in donning the garments of Josiah Warren to defend
the specie fraud, has "stolen the livery of heaven to serve the
devil in." " Basis " is wrong, too, in thinking that land is not
a good basis for currency. True, unimproved vacant land,
not having properly a market value, cannot properly give value
to anything that represents it ; but permanent improvements
on land, which should have a market value and carry with
them a title to possession, are an excellent basis for currency.
It is not the raw material of any product that fits it for a basis,
but the labor that has been expended in shaping the material.
As for the immovability of land unfitting it for a basis, it has
just the opposite effect. Here " Basis " is misled by the idea
that currency can be redeemed only in that on which it is based.

But this fertile subject has taken us farther than we intended
to follow it. So here, for the present, we will quit its company, meanwhile handing over " Basis " to the tender mercies
of " Apex," and heartily indorsing almost all that " Basis "
says at the close of his article concerning the true duty of
government, as long as it shall exist, regarding the currency.

"THE POSITION OF WILLIAM."

[*Liberty*, October 13, 1888.]

JOHN RUSKIN, in the first of his "Fors Clavigera" series of
letters to British workmen, opened what he had to say about
interest by picturing what he called "the position of William."
Bastiat, the French economist, had tried to show the nature
of capital and interest by a little story, in which a carpenter
named James made a plane in order to increase his productive
power, but, having made it, was induced by a fellow-carpenter
named William to lend it to him for a year in consideration of
receiving a new plane at the end of that time besides a plank
for the use of it. Having fulfilled these conditions at the end
of the first year, William borrowed the plane again on the
same terms at the beginning of the second, and year after year
the transaction was repeated to the third and fourth generations of the posterity of William and James. Ruskin disposed
of this plausible story in a sentence by pointing out that the
transactions of William and James amounted simply to this,—
that William made a plane every 31st December, lent it to
James till 1st January, and paid James a plank for the privilege of thus lending him the plane overnight.

Ruskin called this "the position of William," and, though
he threw down the gauntlet right and left, he never could find
an economist rash enough to undertake to dispute the justice
of his abridgment of Bastiat's tale. At last, however, one
has appeared. F. J. Stimson has discovered the fallacy in
"the position of William," and confidently tells the readers of
the *Quarterly Journal of Economics* that it lies in Ruskin's
tacit assumption that the plank which William paid James was
the only plank which the plane had enabled him to make
during the year. Mr. Stimson is so proud of this discovery
that he puts it in italics, but I am unable to see that it shows
anything except Mr. Stimson's failure to get down to the kernel
of the question at issue.

If Ruskin made the assumption attributed to him,—which is
improbable,—he did so because he knew perfectly well that the
number of planks which the plane enabled William to make
ought in equity to have had no influence upon the plane's selling or lending price, always provided the number was great
enough to make it worth while to have manufactured the plane
in the first place. If Mr. Stimson were half the economist

that Ruskin is, he would know that, in the absence of monopoly, the price of an article worth producing at all is governed, not by its utility, but by the cost of its production, and that James consequently, though his plane should enable William to make a million planks, could not sell or lend it for more than it cost him to make it, except he enjoyed a monopoly of the plane-making industry.

The fallacy in "the position of William" remains undiscovered. Perhaps a few more such failures to discover it as Mr. Stimson's may convince the people that there is no fallacy there to be discovered. On the whole, the original policy of James's friends was the safer one,—to ignore "the position of William" on the ground that his champion, Mr. Ruskin, is not an economist, but an artist.

ECONOMIC HODGE-PODGE.

[*Liberty*, October 8, 1887.]

It will be remembered that, when a correspondent of the *Standard* signing "Morris" asked Henry George one or two awkward questions regarding interest, and George tried to answer him by a silly and forced distinction between interest considered as the increase of capital and interest considered as payment for the use of a legal tender, John F. Kelly sent to the *Standard* a crushing reply to George, which the latter refused to print, and which subsequently appeared in No. 102 of *Liberty*. It may also be remembered that George's rejection of Kelly's article was grounded on the fact that since his own reply to "Morris" he had received several articles on the interest question, and that he could not afford space for the consideration of this subordinate matter while the all-important land question was yet to be settled.

I take it that the land battle has since been won, for in the *Standard* of September 3 nearly three columns—almost the entire department of "Queries and Answers" in that issue—are given to a defence of interest, in answer to the questions of two or three correspondents. The article is a long elaboration of the reply to "Morris," the root absurdity of which is rendered more intangible by a wall of words, and no one would know from reading it that the writer had ever heard of the considerations which Mr. Kelly arrayed against his position. It is true that at one or two points he verges upon them, but his words are a virtual admission of their validity and hence a reduction of interest to an unsubstantial form. He seems, therefore, to have written them without thought of Mr. Kelly; for, had he realized their effect, he could not—assuming his honesty—have prepared the article, which has no *raison d'être* except to prove that interest is a vital reality apart from money monopoly. On the other hand, assuming his dishonesty, the suspicion inevitably arises that he purposely smothered Mr. Kelly's article in order to subsequently juggle over the matter with less expert opponents. Unhappily this suspicion is not altogether unwarrantable in view of the tactics adopted by George in his treatment of the rent question.

The matter seems, too, to have taken on importance, as it is now acknowledged that " the theory of interest as propounded by Mr. George has been more severely and plausibly criticised than any other phase of the economic problem as he presents it." When we consider that George regards it as an economic law that interest varies inversely with so important a thing as rent, we see that he cannot consistently treat as unimportant any " plausible " argument urged in support of the theory that interest varies principally, not with rent, but with the economic conditions arising from a monopoly of the currency.

But, however the article may be accounted for, it is certainly before us, and Mr. George (through his sub-editor, Louis F. Post, for whose words in the " Queries and Answers " department he may fairly be held responsible), is discussing the interest question. We will see what he has to say.

It appears that all the trouble of the enemies of interest grows out of their view of it as exclusively incidental to borrowing and lending, whereas interest on borrowed capital is itself " incidental to real interest," which is " the increase that capital yields irrespective of borrowing and lending." This increase, Mr. George claims, is the work of time, and from this premise he reasons as follows:

The laborer who has capital ready when it is wanted, and thus, by saving time in making it, increases production, will get and ought to get some consideration,—higher wages, if you choose, or interest, as we call it, —just as the skilful printer who sets fifteen hundred ems an hour will get more for an hour's work than the less skilful printer who sets only a thousand. In the one case greater power due to skill, and in the other greater power due to capital, produce greater results in a given time; and in neither case is the increased compensation a deduction from the earnings of other men.

To make this analogy a fair one it must be assumed that skill is a product of labor, that it can be bought and sold, and

that its price is subject to the influence of competition ; otherwise, it furnishes no parallel to capital. With these assumptions the opponent of interest eagerly seizes upon the analogy
as entirely favorable to his own position and destructive of
Mr. George's. If the skilful printer produced his skill and
can sell it, and if other men can produce similar skill and sell
it, the price that will be paid for it will be limited, under free
competition, by the cost of production, and will bear no relation to the extra five hundred ems an hour. The case is precisely the same with capital. Where there is free competition
in the manufacture and sale of spades, the price of a spade
will be governed by the cost of its production, and not by the
value of the extra potatoes which the spade will enable its
purchaser to dig. Suppose, however, that the skilful printer
enjoyed a monopoly of skill. In that case, its price would no
longer be governed by the cost of production, but by its utility to the purchaser, and the monopolist would exact nearly
the whole of the extra five hundred ems, receiving which hourly
he would be able to live for the rest of his life without ever
picking up a type. Such a monopoly as this is now enjoyed
by the holders of capital in consequence of the currency
monopoly, and this is the reason, and the only reason, why
they are able to tax borrowers nearly up to the limit of the
advantage which the latter derive from having the capital. In
other words, increase which is purely the work of time bears a
price only because of monopoly. Abolish the monopoly, then,
and what becomes of Mr. George's " real interest " except as
a benefit enjoyed by all consumers in proportion to their consumption ? As far as the owner of the capital is concerned, it
vanishes at once, and Mr. George's wonderful distinction with it.

He tells us, nevertheless, that the capitalist's share of the
results of the increased power which capital gives the laborer
is " not a deduction from the earnings of other men." Indeed !
What are the normal earnings of other men ? Evidently what
they can produce with all the tools and advantages which
they can procure *in a free market* without force or fraud. If,
then, the capitalist, by abolishing the free market, compels
other men to procure their tools and advantages of him on less
favorable terms than they could get before, while it may be
better for them to come to his terms than to go without the
capital, does he not deduct from their earnings ?

But let us hear Mr. George further in regard to the great
value of time to the idler.

Suppose a natural spring free to all, and that Hodge carries a pail of
water from it to a place where he can build a fire and boil the water,

Having hung a kettle and poured the water into it, and arranged the fuel and started the fire, he has by his labor set natural forces at work in a certain direction ; and they are at work for him alone, because without his previous labor they would not be at work in that direction at all. Now he may go to sleep, or run off and play, or amuse himself in any way that he pleases ; and when an hour—a period of time—shall have elapsed, he will have, instead of a pail of cold water, a pot of boiling water. Is there no difference in value between that boiling water and the cold water of an hour before ? Would he exchange the pot of boiling water for a pail of cold water, even though the cold water were in the pot and the fire started ? Of course not, and no one would expect him to. And yet between the time when the fire is started and the time when the water boils he does no work. To what, then, is that difference in value due ? Is it not clearly due to the element of time ? Why does Hodge demand more than a pail of cold water for the pot of boiling water if it is not that the ultimate object of his original labor—the making of tea, for example— is nearer complete than it was an hour before, and that an even exchange of boiling water for cold water would delay him an hour, to which he will not submit unless he is paid for it? And why is Podge willing to give more than a pail of cold water for the pot of boiling water, if it is not that it gives him the benefit of an hour's time in production, and thus increases his productive power very much as greater skill would ? And if Podge gives to Hodge more than a pail of cold water for the pot of boiling water, does Podge lose anything that he had, or Hodge gain anything that he had not ? No. The effect of the transaction is a transfer for a consideration of the advantage in point of time that Hodge had, to Podge who had it not, as if a skilful compositor should, if he could, sell his skill to a less skilful member of the craft.

We will look a little into this economic Hodge-Podge. The illustration is vitiated from beginning to end by the neglect of the most important question involved in it,—namely, whether Hodge's idleness during the hour required for the boiling of the water is a matter of choice or of necessity. It was necessary to leave this out in order to give time the credit of boiling the water. Let us not leave it out, and see what will come of it. If Hodge's idleness is a matter of necessity, it is equivalent, from the economic standpoint, to labor, and counts as labor in the price of the boiling water. A storekeeper may spend only five hours in waiting *on* his customers, but, as he has to spend another five hours in waiting *for* them, he gets paid by them for ten hours' labor. His five hours' idleness counts as labor, because, to accommodate his customers, he has to give up what he could produce in those five hours if he could labor in them. Likewise, if Hodge, when boiling water for Podge, is obliged to spend an hour in idleness, he will charge Podge for the hour in the price which he sets on the boiling water. But it is Hodge himself, this disposition of himself, and not the abstraction, time, that gives the water its exchangeable value. The abstraction, time, is as truly at work when Hodge is bringing the water from the spring and starting the fire as when he is asleep waiting for the water to boil ; yet Mr. George would not dream of attributing the value of the water after it had been brought from the spring to the element of time. He would say that it was due entirely to the labor of Hodge. Properly speaking, time does not work at all, but, if the phrase is to be insisted on in economic discussion, it can be admitted only with some such qualification as the following : The services of time are venal only when rendered through human forces ; when rendered exclusively through the forces of nature, they are gratuitous.

That time does not give the boiling water any exchangeable value becomes still more evident when we start from the hypothesis that Hodge's idleness, instead of being a matter of necessity, is a matter of choice. In that case, if Hodge chooses to be idle, and still tries, in selling the boiling water to Podge, to charge him for this unnecessary idleness, the enterprising Dodge will step up and offer boiling water to Podge at a price lower than Hodge's, knowing that he can afford to do so by performing some productive labor while waiting for the water to boil, instead of loafing like Hodge. The effect of this will be that Hodge himself will go to work productively, and then will offer Podge a better bargain than Dodge has proposed, and so competition between Hodge and Dodge will go on until the price of the boiling water to Podge shall fall to the value of the labor expended by either Hodge or Dodge in bringing the water from the spring and starting the fire. Here, then, the exchangeable value of the boiling water which was said to be due to time has disappeared, and yet it takes just as much time to boil the water as it did in the first place.

Mr. George gets into difficulty in discussing this question of the increase of capital simply because he continually loses sight of the fact that competition lowers prices to the cost of production and thereby distributes this so-called product of capital among the whole people. He does not see that capital in the hands of labor is but the utilization of a natural force or opportunity, just as land is in the hands of labor, and that it is as proper in the one case as in the other that the benefits of such utilization of natural forces should be enjoyed by the whole body of consumers.

Mr. George truly says that rent is the price of monopoly. Suppose, now, that some one should answer him thus : You misconceive ; you clearly have leasing exclusively in mind, and suppose an unearned bonus for a lease, whereas rent of leased land is merely incidental to real rent, which is the superiority in location or fertility of one piece of land over another, irrespective of leasing. Mr. George would laugh at such an argument if offered in justification of the receipt and enjoyment of unearned increment or economic rent by the landlord. But he himself makes an equally ridiculous and precisely parallel argument in defence of the usurer when he says, in answer to those who assert that interest is the price of monopoly : " You misconceive ; you clearly have borrowing and lending exclusively in mind, and suppose an unearned bonus for a loan, whereas interest on borrowed capital is merely incidental to real interest, which is the increase that capital yields, irrespective of borrowing and lending."

The truth in both cases is just this,—that nature furnishes man immense forces with which to work in the shape of land and capital, that in a state of freedom these forces benefit each individual to the extent that he avails himself of them, and that any man or class getting a monopoly of either or both will put all other men in subjection and live in luxury on the products of their labor. But to justify a monopoly of either of these forces by the existence of the force itself, or to argue that without a monopoly of it any individual could get an income by lending it instead of by working with it, is equally absurd whether the argument be resorted to in the case of land or in the case of capital, in the case of rent or in the case of interest. If any one chooses to call the advantages of these forces to mankind rent in one case and interest in the other, I do not know that there is any serious objection to his doing so, provided he will remember that in practical economic discussion rent stands for the absorption of the advantages of land by the landlord, and interest for the absorption of the advantages of capital by the usurer.

The remainder of Mr. George's article rests entirely upon the time argument. Several new Hodge-Podge combinations are supposed by way of illustration, but in none of them is there any attempt to justify interest except as a reward of time. The inherent absurdity of this justification having been demonstrated above, all that is based upon it falls with it. The superstructure is a logical ruin ; it remains only to clear away the *débris*.

Hodge's boiling water is made a type of all those products of labor which afterwards increase in utility purely by natural forces, such as cattle, corn, etc.; and it may be admitted that, if time would add exchangeable value to the water while boil-

ing, it would do the same to corn while growing, and cattle
while multiplying.   But that it would do so under freedom
has already been disproved.   Starting from this, however, an
attempt is made to find in it an excuse for interest on products
which do not improve except as labor is applied to them, and
even on money itself.   Hodge's grain, after it has been growing for a month, is worth more than when it was first sown ;
therefore Podge, the shovel-maker, who supplies a market
which it takes a month to reach, is entitled to more pay for
his shovels at the end of that month than he would have been
had he sold them on the spot immediately after production ;
and therefore the banker who discounts at the time of production the note of Podge's distant customer maturing a month
later, thereby advancing ready money to Podge, will be entitled, at the end of the month, from Podge's customer, to
the extra value which the month's time is supposed to have
added to the shovels.

Here Mr. George not only builds on a rotten foundation,
but he mistakes foundation for superstructure.   Instead of
reasoning from Hodge to the banker he should have reasoned
from the banker to Hodge.   His first inquiry should have been
how much, in the absence of a monopoly in the banking
business, the banker could get for discounting for Podge
the note of his customer ; from which he could then have
ascertained how much extra payment Podge could get for his
month's delay in the shovel transaction, or Hodge for the
services of time in ripening his grain.   He would then have
discovered that the banker, who invests little or no capital of
his own, and, therefore, lends none to his customers, since the
security which they furnish him constitutes the capital upon
which he operates, is forced, in the absence of money monopoly, to reduce the price of his services to labor cost,
which the statistics of the banking business show to be much
less than one per cent.   As this fraction of one per cent.
represents simply the banker's wages and incidental expenses,
and is not payment for the use of capital, the element of
interest disappears from his transactions.   But, if Podge can
borrow money from the banker without interest, so can Podge's
customer ; therefore, should Podge attempt to exact from his
customer remuneration for the month's delay, the latter would
at once borrow the money and pay Podge spot cash.   Furthermore Podge, knowing this, and being able to get ready money
easily himself, and desiring, as a good man of business, to suit
his customer's convenience, would make no such attempt.   So
Podge's interest is gone as well as the banker's.   Hodge, then,

is the only usurer left. But is any one so innocent as to suppose that Dodge, or Lodge, or Modge will long continue to pay Hodge more for his grown grain than his sown grain, after any or all of them can get land free of rent and money free of interest, and thereby force time to work for them as well as for Hodge. Nobody who can get the services of time for nothing will be such a fool as to pay Hodge for them. Hodge, too, must say farewell to his interest as soon as the two great monopolies of land and money are abolished. *The rate of interest on money fixes the rate of interest on all other capital the production of which is subject to competition, and when the former disappears the latter disappears with it.*

Presumably to make his readers think that he has given due consideration to the important principle just elucidated, Mr. George adds, just after his hypothesis of the banker's transaction with Podge :

Of course there is discount *and* discount. I am speaking of a legitimate economic banking transaction. But frequently bank discounts are nothing more than taxation, due to the choking up of free exchange, in consequence of which an institution that controls the common medium of exchange can impose arbitrary conditions upon producers who must immediately use that common medium.

The evident purpose of the word "frequently" here is to carry the idea that, when a bank discount is a tax imposed by monopoly of the medium of exchange, it is simply a somewhat common exception to the general rule of "legitimate economic banking transactions." For it is necessary to have such a general rule in order to sustain the theory of interest on capital as a reward of time. The exact contrary, however, is the truth. Where money monopoly exists, it is the rule that bank discounts are taxes imposed by it, and when, in consequence of peculiar and abnormal circumstances, discount is not in the nature of a tax, it is a rare exception. The abolition of money monopoly would wipe out discount as a tax and, by adding to the steadiness of the market, make the cases where it is not a tax even fewer than now. Instead of legitimate, therefore, the banker's transaction with Podge, being exceptional in a free money market and a tax of the ordinary discount type in a restricted money market, is illegitimate if cited in defence of interest as a normal economic factor.

In the conclusion of his article Mr. George strives to show that interest would not enable its beneficiaries to live by the labor of others. But he only succeeds in showing, though in a very obscure, indefinite, and intangible fashion,—seemingly afraid to squarely enunciate it as a proposition,—that where there is no monopoly there will be little or no interest. Which is precisely our contention. But why, then, his long article ? If interest will disappear with monopoly, what will become of Hodge's reward for his time? If, on the other hand, Hodge is to be rewarded for his mere time, what will reward him save Podge's labor? There is no escape from this dilemma. The proposition that the man who for time spent in idleness receives the product of time employed in labor is a parasite up on the body industrial is one which an expert necromancer like Mr. George may juggle with before an audience of gaping Hodges and Podges, but can never successfully dispute with men who understand the rudiments of political economy.

AN UNWARRANTED QUESTION.

[*Liberty*, October 18, 1890.]

AUBERON HERBERT, in his paper, *Free Life*, asks me how I "justify a campaign against the right of men to lend and to borrow." I answer that I do not justify such a campaign, have never attempted to justify such a campaign, do not advocate such a campaign, in fact am ardently opposed to such a campaign. In turn, I ask Mr. Herbert how he justifies his apparent attribution to me of a wish to see such a campaign instituted.

It is true that I expect lending and borrowing to disappear, but not by any denial of the right to lend and borrow. On the contrary, I expect them to disappear by virtue of the affirmation and exercise of a right that is now denied,—namely, the right to use one's own credit, or to exchange it freely for another's, in such a way that one or the other of these credits may perform the function of a circulating medium, without the payment of any tax for the privilege. It has been repeatedly demonstrated in these columns that the exercise of such a right would accomplish the gradual extinction of interest without the aid of force, and the nature of this economic process has been described over and over again. This demonstration Mr. Herbert steadily ignores, and the position itself he never meets save by a sweeping denial, or by characterizing it as unphilosophical, or by substituting for it a man of straw of his own creation and then knocking it down.

The Anarchists assert that interest, however it may have originated, exists to-day only by virtue of the legal monopoly of the use of credit for currency purposes, and they trace the process, step by step, by which an abolition of that monopoly would gradually reduce interest to zero. Mr. Herbert never stops to analyze this process that he may find the weak spot in it and point it out ; he simply declares that interest, instead of resting on monopoly, is the natural, inevitable outcome of human convenience and the open market, and then wants to know how the Anarchists justify their attempt to abolish interest by force.

It is as if Mr. Herbert were to maintain (as I suppose he does maintain) that freedom in the domestic relation would gradually lessen and perhaps abolish licentiousness, and I were to answer him thus : " Oh, no, Mr. Herbert, you are un- philosophical ; prostitution does not rest on the compulsory marriage system, but is the natural, inevitable outcome of human convenience and desire ; how do you justify, I should like to know, a campaign against the right of men and women to traffic in the gratifications of the flesh ? " In such a case Mr. Herbert, I imagine, would say that I had studied his teaching very carelessly. And that is what I am forced to say of him, much against my will.

If it be true that interest will exist in the absence of mo- nopoly, then there is some flaw in the reasoning by which the Anarchists argue from the abolition of monopoly to the disap- pearance of interest, and it is incumbent upon Mr. Herbert to point this flaw out, or else admit his own error. It is almost incredible that an argument so often reiterated can have es- caped the attention of so old a reader of *Liberty* as Mr. Her- bert, but, lest he should plead this excuse, I will state that it is most elaborately and conclusively set forth in the pamphlet, " Mutual Banking," by Col. Wm. B. Greene. If, after master- ing the position, he thinks he can overthrow it, I shall be glad to meet him on that issue.

AN ALLEGED FLAW IN ANARCHY.

[*Liberty*, November 29, 1890.]

To the Editor of Liberty :

I am sorry if I have misinterpreted *Liberty*. I have not what I wrote before me, but I do not think I could have had the slightest intention of im- puting to *Liberty* a FORCE campaign against interest ; but I believed (am I wrong?) that I had seen both interest and rent denounced in *Liberty* as objectionable and opposed to the interests of society.   It was to this I was referring as a moral campaign.   My own position is that interest is both moral and useful, and often more than anything else a chance of a better future to workmen.   If workmen would give up punching the head of capital, and, instead of that little amusement, resolutely combine for the purpose of investing in industrial concerns, so as gradually to become the part-owner of the industrial machinery of the country, whilst they no longer remained wholly dependent upon wages, but partly upon wages, partly upon the return of invested money, I believe the great problem of our time would be approaching its solution.

As regards rent, I think that all Anarchists, including even sober-minded *Liberty*, use force to get rid of it.   The doctrine of use-possession seems almost framed for this purpose.   Even if it suits certain persons to sell me a hundred acres, and it suits me to buy it, and it suits other people to rent it from me,—as I understand, *Liberty* would not sanction the proceeding. We are all of us, in fact, to be treated as children, who don't know our own interests, and for whom somebody else is to judge.   You may reply that under the Anarchist system no action would be taken to prevent such an arrangement ; only that no action would be taken to prevent the tenants from establishing themselves as proprietors and ignoring their rent owed to me.   Good; but then how do you justify the fact that there is a proposed machinery (local juries, etc.) to secure the possessor who holds under use-possession in his holding and to prevent his disturbance by somebody else ?   Put these two opposed treatments together, and it means to say that a certain body of men have settled for others a form in which they may hold property, and a form in which they may not.   The desires and the conveniences of the persons themselves are set aside, and, as in old forms of government, a principle representing centralization and socialistic regulation obtains.   Is this Anarchy ?

AUBERON HERBERT.

Mr. Herbert's disclaimer is of course sufficient to establish the fact that he did not mean to charge me with an attempt to prohibit lending and borrowing.   But I must remind him that the charge which he made against me he made also at the same time against his correspondent, Mr. J. Armsden ; that Mr. Armsden interpreted it as I did and protested against its application to himself (though gratuitously allowing that it was justly applicable to me) ; and that Mr. Herbert made rejoinder, if my memory serves me, that he had misunderstood Mr. Armsden.   Now, I cannot see why Mr. Herbert should not admit in the same unqualified way that he misunderstood me, instead of suggesting that I misunderstood him.   But this is of little consequence ; I am satisfied to call it a case of mutual misunderstanding.

To avoid such misunderstanding in future, however, is of real importance ; and to that end I must further remind Mr. Herbert that, when I use the word *right*, I do so in one of two senses, which the context generally determines,—either in the moral sense of irresponsible prerogative, or in the social sense of accorded guarantee. Mr. Herbert, knowing that I am an Egoist, must be perfectly aware that it would be impossible for me to enter upon a moral campaign against any *special* right in the sense of irresponsible prerogative, for it is the Egoistic position either that no one has any rights whatever or —what amounts to the same thing—that every one has all rights. But it would be equally impossible for me to enter upon a moral campaign against a right in the sense of accorded guarantee, unless it were a case where I should consider myself justified, if it seemed expedient, in turning that moral campaign into a force campaign. For I could have no objection to any accorded guarantee save on the ground that the thing guaranteed was a privilege of invasion, and against invasion I am willing to use any weapons that will accomplish its destruction, preferring moral weapons in all cases where they are effective, but willing to resort to those of physical force whenever necessary. So Mr. Herbert is now duly cautioned not to charge me with maintaining, against any right whatever, a campaign which anything but expediency makes exclusively moral.

To go now from the general to the particular. I could not engage in any sort of campaign against the right to lend and borrow, because I do not consider that right a privilege of invasion. If, however, lending and borrowing should disappear in consequence of the overthrow of that form of invasion which consists of the monopoly of the right to issue notes as currency, that is not my affair.

It is the contention of the Anarchists that lending and borrowing, and consequently interest, will virtually disappear when banking is made free. Mr. Herbert's only answer to this is that he considers interest moral and useful. Does he mean by this that that is moral and useful which will disappear under free competition? Then why does he favor free competition? Or does he deny that interest will so disappear? Then let him disprove the Anarchists' definite and succinct argument that it will. In my last article, to which his present article is a reply, I strongly invited him to do this, but as usual he ignores the invitation. Nevertheless he and all his Individualistic friends will have to meet us on that issue sooner or later, and he may as well face the music at once.

Now, a word about rent. It is true that Anarchists, including sober-minded *Liberty*, do, in a sense, propose to get rid of ground-rent by force. That is to say, if landlords should try to evict occupants, the Anarchists advise the occupants to combine to maintain their ground by force whenever they see that they can do so successfully. But it is also true that the

Individualists, including sober-minded Mr. Herbert, propose to get rid of theft by force. "Even if it suits certain persons to sell me" Mr. Herbert's overcoat, "and it suits me to buy it, and it suits other people to rent it from me—as I understand," Mr. Herbert "would not sanction the proceeding. We are all of us, in fact, to be treated as children, who don't know our own interests, and for whom somebody else is to judge." The Anarchists justify the use of machinery (local juries, etc.) to adjust the property question involved in rent just as the Individualists justify similar machinery to adjust the property question involved in theft. And when the Individualists so adjust the property question involved in theft, this "means to say that a certain body of men have settled for others a form in which they may hold property and a form in which they may not," regardless of "the desires and conveniences of the persons themselves."

Yes, this is Anarchy, and this is Individualism. The trouble with Mr. Herbert is that he begs the question of property altogether, and insists on treating the land problem as if it were simply a question of buying and selling and lending and borrowing, to be settled simply by the open market. Here I meet him with the words of his more conservative brother in Individualism, Mr. J. H. Levy, editor of the *Personal Rights Journal*, who is trying to show Mr. Herbert that he ought to call himself an Anarchist instead of an Individualist. Mr. Levy says, and I say after him : "When we come to the question of the ethical basis of property, Mr. Herbert refers us to 'the open market.' But this is an evasion. The question is not whether we should be able to sell or acquire in 'the open market' anything which we rightfully possess, but how we come into rightful possession. And, if men differ on this, as they do most emphatically, how is this to be settled?"

SHALL THE TRANSFER PAPERS BE TAXED?

[*Liberty*, August 18, 1888.]

To the Editor of Liberty :

During the past six months I have read your paper searchingly, and greatly admire it in many respects, but as yet do not grasp your theory of interest. Can you give space for a few words to show from your standpoint the fallacy in the following ideas?

Interest I understand to be a payment, not for money, but for capital which the money represents; that is, for the use of the accumulated wealth of the race. As that is limited, while human wants are infinite, it would appear that there will always be a demand for more than exists. The simplest way of solving the difficulty would, therefore, be to put the social capital up and let open competition settle its price. Added accumulation means greater competition to let it, so that its price will be lowered year by year. But can that price ever become nothing so long as men have additional wants that capital can assist to fill ? Yet Mr. Westrup advocates a rate of interest based on the cost of issuing the money, —that is, allowing nothing for the capital. Is "stored labor" so plenty as to be cheaper than blackberries ?

For illustration, A has $1,000 worth of land, buildings, etc., in a farm, but sees that he can use $1,500 worth profitably. So he places a mortgage of $500 on the place and invests it in more property. Now to say that he should have that additional property merely for the cost of issuing the paper which represents it during the transfer would be like saying that, when he bought his house, he should have it merely for cost of the transfer papers,—the deeds, etc.,—paying nothing for the house itself.

In a line my query is : Where do your definitions of interest and discount on money diverge ? Yours truly,

J. HERBERT FOSTER.

MERIDEN, CONNECTICUT.

Discount is the sum deducted in advance from property temporarily transferred, by the owner thereof, as a condition of the transfer, regardless of the ground upon which such condition is demanded.

Interest is payment for the *use* of property, and, if paid in advance, is that portion of the discount exacted by the owner of the property temporarily transferred which he claims as payment for the benefit conferred upon the other party, as distinguished from that portion which he claims as payment for the burden borne by himself.

The opponents of interest desire, by reducing the rate of discount to cost, or price of burden borne, to thereby eliminate from discount all payment merely for benefit conferred.

But they are entirely innocent of any desire to abolish payment for burden borne, as it certainly would be abolished in the case supposed by Mr. Foster, were A to obtain his extra $500 worth of property simply by paying the cost of making out the transfer papers. A certainly could not thus obtain it under the system of credit proposed by the opponents of interest. His obligation is not discharged when he has paid over to the man of whom he buys the property the $500 which he has borrowed on mortgage. He still has to discharge the mortgage by paying to the lender of the money, at the expiration of the loan, in actual wealth or valid documentary claim upon wealth, the $500 which he borrowed. That is the time when he really pays for the property in which he invested. Now, the question is whether he shall pay simply the $500, which is supposed to represent the full value of the property at the time he made the investment, or whether he shall also pay a bonus for the use of the property up to the time when he finally pays for it. The opponents of interest say that he should not pay this bonus, because his use of the property has imposed no burden upon the lender of the money, and under free competition there is no price where there is no burden. They declare, not that he should not pay the $500, but that the only bonus he should pay is to be measured by the cost of making out the mortgage and other documents, including all the expenses incidental thereto.

The only reason why he now has to pay a bonus proportional to the benefit he derives from the use of the property is found in the fact that the lender of the money, or the original issuer of the money, from whom the lender procured it more or less directly, has secured a monopoly of money manufacture and can therefore proportion the price of his product to the necessities of his customers, instead of being forced by competition to limit it to the average cost of manufacture. In short, what the opponents of interest object to is, not payment for property purchased, but a *tax upon the transfer papers ;* and the very best of all arguments against interest, or payment for the use of property, is the fact that, at the present advanced stage in the operation of economic forces, it cannot exist to any great extent without taking this form of a *tax upon the transfer papers.*

SHALL THE TRANSFER PAPERS BE TAXED ? That is the question which *Liberty* asks, and Mr. Foster has already answered it in the negative by saying that open competition should be left to settle the price of capital. But when this open competition is secured, it will be found that, though there may be no limit to the desire for wealth, there is a limit at any given time to the capacity of the race to utilize capital, and that the amount of capital created will always tend to exceed this capacity. Then capital will seek employment and be glad to lend itself to labor for nothing, asking only to be kept intact, and reimbursed for the cost of the transfer papers. Such is the process by which interest, or payment for the *use* of property, not only will be lowered, but will entirely disappear.

MONEY AND CAPITAL.

[*Liberty*, December 1, 1888.]

To the Editor of Liberty:

I have read attentively Mr. Westrup's farther statement on mutual banking, but fail to see wherein he touches what is to my mind the vital point. He says that the system "would not be making use of capital that belonged to some one else." Then I cannot see how it would answer its purpose. The bank itself has no capital save the pledges advanced by borrowers, and if they take out no more than they put in, they make no gain, but are merely to the expense of the transaction. On the other hand, if they do take out more, some one else must have put it in. They do not increase their wealth by using their own property as a basis on which to make advances to themselves. It is only when some one else accepts it as a pledge on which to advance *his* property that they have made a gain. And if there is no one to be paid a dividend but "the same borrowers," that some one else will go unpaid.

The borrower's object is to get the use of additional capital, not of the money that represents it during the transfer. If he gets it, "some one [else] is deprived of the use of that much wealth," as two cannot use the same property at the same time. Our farmer worth $1,000, who borrowed $500 and invested it, found at the end of the transaction that he had at his disposal $1,500 worth of property. Now, where did the last $500 worth come from? Like all created things, its ownership vested rightfully in its creator; the farmer was not that creator, or he would not have had to borrow it. The bank, in issuing a volume of circulating medium, neither increased nor diminished the aggregate wealth of the country appreciably. It engaged in no "productive" industry. It did not create 500 dollars' nor 500 cents' worth of property. In fact, Mr. Westrup's rate of interest represents what it did create in additional value in making out the transfer papers,—a fraction of one per cent. of the $500. If, then, neither the bank nor the farmer created it, is it not clear that they "made use of capital that belonged to some one else"?

The distinction between owning property and merely having the use of it has been pointed out to me, but appears largely verbal, for the only value of property is the use thereof. At any rate, it seems clear that our farmer gets the use of $500 worth of property so long as he pays the expense of keeping $500 of circulating medium afloat. He uses his $1,000 worth of property as a guarantee to the producer of the $500 of value that the latter shall receive back his property intact, but with no payment for use.

If I have understood correctly the reply to my former letter, this is *Liberty*'s idea; but I do not see that Mr. Westrup coincides. However, if I am in error, I trust I am "open to conviction" and await further light.

J. HERBERT FOSTER.

Mr. Foster's difficulty arises from the futile attempt, which many others have made before him, to distinguish money from capital, the real fact being that money, though not capital in a material sense, is, in the economic sense and to all in-

tents and purposes, the most perfect and desirable form of
capital, for the reason that it is the only form of capital which
will at any time almost instantly procure all other forms of
capital.   Practically speaking, that man has capital who holds
an instantly convertible title to capital.*

If this be true, then Mr. Foster's claim that mutual banking involves the "making use of capital that belongs to some
one else" falls immediately.   Does he mean to say that, when
the borrower of a mutual bank's notes goes into the market
and buys capital with them, he is thereby keeping the seller
out of his capital?   If so, then Mr. Foster, when he pays his
butcher cash for a beefsteak for his to-morrow's breakfast, is
keeping his butcher out of his capital.   But does either he or
his butcher ever look at his conduct in that light?   If that is
being kept out of capital, then is the butcher only too glad to
be thus deprived.   He keeps a shop for the express purpose
of being kept out of his capital, and he feels that it's very
hard lines and a very dull season when he isn't kept out of it.
He knows that, when he sells a beefsteak to Mr. Foster for
cash, he parts with capital for which he has no use himself
and gets in exchange a title convertible whenever he may
choose into such capital as he has use for, and he knows further that he greatly benefits by the transaction.   The position
of Mr. Foster's butcher is precisely parallel to that of the
manufacturer of machinery who sells a plough or a press or
an engine to a borrower from a mutual bank.   Clearly, then,
Mr. Foster's sympathy for this manufacturer is misplaced.

Of course the position which I have just taken does not
hold with notes that will not command capital,—that is, that
are not readily received as money.   But that is not the point
under dispute.   When Mr. Foster shall question the solvency
of mutual money, I will meet him on that point also.   For
the present my sole contention against him is that the man
who exchanges a material value for good money is not thereby
kept out of his capital.

---

* This paragraph on the surface seems contradictory of the position
taken on a previous page in answer to "Basis." And in form and
terms it does contradict it. But a careful reading of both passages, in
connection with the accompanying explanatory sentences, will show that
there is no inconsistency between them.

"TO-DAY'S" VIEW OF INTEREST.

[*Liberty*, July 26, 1890.]

WHEN I saw the word " Interest " at the top of an article in a recent issue of *To-day*, I said to myself: This looks promising ; either the editor of *To-day* is about to remove the basis (so far as his paper is concerned) of Mr. Yarros's vigorous criticism upon journals of its class that they fail of influence because they neglect to show that individualism will redress economic grievances, or else he has discovered some vital flaw in the Anarchist economics and is about to save us further waste of energy by showing that economic liberty will not produce the results we predict from it. Fancy my disappointment when, on reading the article, I found it made up, seven eighths, of facts and historical remarks which would be more-interesting if less venerable, but which, though pertinent as throwing light upon the conditions under which interest arose, prevailed, and fluctuated, have not the remotest bearing upon the arguments of those who dispute the viability of interest to-day ; one-sixteenth, of the assertion of an economic truism, equally without significance in connection with those arguments ; and, one-sixteenth, of the assertion of an economic error, which assertion betrays no familiarity with those arguments (although it is within my knowledge that the editor of *To-day* possesses such familiarity in a considerable degree), and which error can be sufficiently refuted by stating it in a slightly different form.

The irrelevant facts I ignore. I do not care a copper whether interest was twelve per cent. in Aristotle's time or eighteen in Solon's ; whether Catholicism and Mohammedanism were united in their aversion to it ; whether Jew or Christian has been the greater usurer. The modern opponents of interest are perfectly willing to consider facts tending to refute their position, but no facts can have such a tendency unless they belong to one of two classes : first, facts showing that interest has generally (not sporadically) existed in a community in whose economy money was as important a factor as it is with us to-day and in whose laws there was no restriction upon its issue; or, second, facts showing that interest is sustained by causes that would still be effectively, invincibly operative after the abolition of the banking monopoly. I do not find any such facts among those cited by *To-day*. The array is formidable in appearance only. Possession of encyclopædic knowledge is a virtue which Spencer sometimes exaggerates into a vice, and a vice which some of his disciples too seldom reduce to the proportions of a virtue.

To the economic truism I will give a little more attention, its irrelevancy being less apparent. Here it is : " The existence of interest depends, of course, primarily upon the existence of private property." I call this a truism, though the word " primarily " introduces an element of error. If we are to inquire upon what interest *primarily* depends, we shall start upon an endless journey into the realm of metaphysics. But without entering that realm we certainly can go farther back in the series than private property and find that interest depends still more remotely upon the existence of human beings and even of the universe itself. However, interest undoubtedly depends upon private property, and, if this fact had any significance, I should not stop to trifle over the word " primarily." But it has no significance. It only seems to have significance because it carries, or seems to be supposed to carry, the implication that, if private property is a necessary condition of interest, interest is a necessary result of private property. The inference, of course, is wholly unwarranted by logic, but that it is intended appears from a remark almost immediately following : " Expectations have been entertained that it [interest] will eventually become zero ; but this stage will probably be reached only when economic products become common free property of the human race." The word " probably " leaves the writer, to be sure, a small logical loophole of escape, but it is not expected that the reader will notice it, the emphasis being all in the other direction. The reader is expected to look upon interest as a necessary result of private property simply because without private property there could be no interest. Now, my hat sometimes hangs upon a hook, and, if there were no hook, there could be no hanging hat ; but it by no means follows that because there is a hook there must be a hanging hat. Therefore, if I wanted to abolish hanging hats, it would be idle, irrelevant, and illogical to declare that I must first abolish hooks. Likewise it is idle, irrelevant, and illogical to declare that before interest can be abolished private property must be abolished. Take another illustration. If there were no winter, water-pipes would never freeze up, but it is not necessary to abolish winter to prevent this freezing. Human device has succeeded in preventing it as a general thing. Similarly, without private property there would be no borrowing of capital and therefore no interest ; but it is claimed that, without abolishing private property, a human device—namely, money and banking—will, if not restricted, prevent the necessity of borrowing capital as a general thing, and therefore virtually abolish interest ; though interest might still be paid in extraordinary cases, just as water-pipes still freeze up under extraordinary conditions. Is this claim true ? That is the only question.

This claim is met in the single relevant sixteenth of *To-day's* article,—that already referred to as an economic error. But it is met simply by denial, which is not disproof. I give the writer's words:

The most popular fallacy upon the subject now is that the rate of interest can be lowered by increasing the amount of currency. What men really wish to borrow usually is capital,—agencies of production, and money is only a means for the transfer of these. The amount of currency can have no effect upon the abundance of capital, and even an increase in the abundance of capital does not always lower the rate of interest; this is partly determined by the value of capital in use.

This paragraph, though introduced with a rather *nonchalant* air, seems to have been the objective point of the entire article. All the rest was apparently written to furnish an occasion for voicing the excessively silly notion that "the amount of currency can have no effect upon the abundance of capital." As I have already said, to show how silly it is, it is only necessary to slightly change the wording of the phrase. Let it be stated thus : "The *abolition* of currency can have no effect upon the abundance of capital." Of course, if the former statement is true, the latter follows. But the latter is *manifestly* absurd, and hence the former is false. To affirm it is to affirm that currency does not facilitate the distribution of wealth ; for if it does, then it increases the effective demand for wealth, and hence the production of wealth, and hence the abundance of capital. It is true that "an increase in the abundance of capital does not always lower the rate of interest." An extra horse attached to a heavy load does not always move the load. If the load is heavy enough, two extra horses will be required to move it. But it is always the tendency of the first extra horse to move it, whether he succeeds or not. In the same way, increase of capital always *tends* to lower interest up to the time when interest disappears entirely. But though increased capital lowers interest and increased currency increases capital, increased currency also acts directly in lowering interest before it has increased the amount of capital. It is here that the editor of *To-day* seems to show unfamiliarity with the position of the opponents of interest. It is true that what men really wish to get is capital,—the agencies of production. And it is precisely because money is "a means for the transfer of these" that the ability to issue money secured by their own property would make it unnecessary for them to borrow these agencies by enabling them to buy them. This raises a question which I have asked hundreds of times of defenders of interest and which has invariably proved a "poser." I will now put it to the editor of *To-day*. A is a farmer owning a farm. He mortgages his farm to a bank for $1,000, giving the bank a mortgage note for that sum and receiving in exchange the bank's notes for the same sum, which are secured by the mortgage. With the bank-notes A buys farming tools of B. The next day B uses the notes to buy of C the materials used in the manufacture of tools. The day after, C in turn pays them to D in exchange for something that he needs. At the end of a year, after a constant succession of exchanges, the notes are in the hands of Z, a dealer in farm produce. He pays them to A, who gives in return $1,000 worth of farm products which he has raised during the year. Then A carries the notes to the bank, receives in exchange for them his mortgage note, and the bank cancels the mortgage. Now, in this whole circle of transactions, has there been any lending of capital? If so, who was the lender? If not, who is entitled to any interest? I call upon the editor of *To-day* to answer this question. It is needless to assure him that it is vital.

"TO-DAY'S" EXCELLENT FOOLING.

[*Liberty*, August 16, 1890.]

To-day's rejoinder to my criticism of its article on interest is chiefly remarkable as an exhibition of dust-throwing. In the art of kicking up a dust the editor is an expert. Whenever he is asked an embarrassing question, he begins to show his skill in this direction. He reminds one of the clown at the circus when "stumped" by the ring-master to turn a double somersault over the elephant's back. He prances and dances, jabbers and gyrates, quotes Latin forwards and Greek backwards, declaims in the style of Dr. Johnson to the fishwife, sings algebraical formulæ to the music of the band, makes faces, makes puns, and makes an excellent fool of himself; and when at the end of all this enormous activity he slyly slips between the elephant's legs instead of leaping over his back, the hilarious crowd, if it does not forget his failure to perform the prescribed feat, at least good-humoredly forgives it. But I am not so good-natured. I admit that, as a clown, I find the editor interesting, but his performance, appropriate enough in a Barnum circus ring, is out of place in the economic arena. So I propose to ignore his three pages of antics and note only his ten-line slip between the elephant's legs, or, laying metaphor aside, his evasion of my question.

I had challenged him to point out any lending of capital in a typical banking transaction which I had described. He responds by asking me to define capital. This is the slip, the evasion, the postponement of the difficulty. He knows that, if he can draw me off into a discussion of the nature of capital, there will be an admirable opportunity for more clownishness, since there is no point in political economy that lends itself more completely to the sophist's art than this. But I am not to be turned aside. I stick to my question. In regard to the notion of capital the editor of *To-day* will find me, so far as the immediate question at issue is connected with it, the most pliable man in the world. I will take the definition, if he likes, that was given in the previous article in *To-day*. There it was said that money was one thing and capital another ; that capital consists of the agencies of production, while money is only a means for the transfer of these ; that what men really want is not money, but capital ; that it is for the use of capital that interest is paid ; and that this interest, this price for the use of capital, lowers, generally speaking, as capital becomes plentier, and probably cannot disappear unless abundance of capital shall reach the extreme of common property. Now I have shown (at least I shall so claim until my question is answered) that in the most ordinary form of transaction involving interest—namely, the discounting of notes—there is absolutely no lending of capital in the sense in which capital was used in *To-day's* first article, and the consequence, of course, is that that defence of interest which regards it as payment for the use of capital straightway falls to the ground. But if the editor of *To-day* does not like the view of capital that was given in the article criticised, he may take some other; I am perfectly willing. He may make a definition of his own. Whatever it may be, I, for the time being and for the purposes of this argument, shall say " Amen " to it. And after that I shall again press the question whether, in the transaction which I described, there was any lending of anything whatever. And if he shall then answer, as a paragraph in his latest article indicates, " Yes, the bank lent its notes to the farmer," I shall show conclusively that the bank did nothing of the kind. If I successfully maintain this contention, then it will be demonstrated that the interest paid in the transaction specified was not paid for the use of anything whatever, but was a tax levied by monopoly and *nothing else.*

Meantime it is comforting to reflect that my labor has not been entirely in vain. As a consequence of my criticism of *To-day's* article on interest, the editor has disowned it (though it appeared unsigned and in editorial type), characterized it as "trivial" (heaven knows it had the air of gravity !), and squarely contradicted its chief doctrinal assertion. This assertion was that "the amount of currency can have no effect upon the abundance of capital." It is contradicted in these terms : " Evidently money is a necessary element in the existing industrial plexus, and increase of capital is dependent upon the supply of a sufficient amount of money." After this I have hopes.

GOVERNMENT AND VALUE.

[*Liberty*, May 16, 1891.]

IN a letter to the London *Herald of Anarchy*, Mr. J. Greevz Fisher asserts that "government does not, and never can, fix the value of gold or any other commodity," and cannot even affect such value except by the slight additional demand which it creates as a consumer. It is true that government cannot *fix* the value of a commodity, because its influence is but one of several factors that combine to govern value. But its power to *affect* value is out of all proportion to the extent of its consumption. Government's consumption of commodities is an almost infinitesimal influence upon value in comparison with its prohibitory power. One of the chief factors in the constitution of value is, as Mr. Fisher himself states, utility ; and as long as governments exist, utility is largely dependent upon their arbitrary decrees. When government prohibits the manufacture and sale of liquor, does it not thereby reduce the value of everything that is used in such manufacture and sale ? If government were to allow theatrical performances on Sundays, would not the value of every building that contains a theatre rise ? Have not we, here in America, just seen the McKinley bill change the value of nearly every article that the people use ? If government were to decree

that all plates shall be made of tin, would not the value of tin
rise and the value of china fall? Unquestionably. Well, a
precisely parallel thing occurs when government decrees that
all money shall be made of or issued against gold or silver;
these metals immediately take on an artificial, government-
created value, because of the *new use* which arbitrary power
enables them to monopolize, and all other commodities, which
are at the same time forbidden to be put to this use, correspondingly lose value. How absurd, then, in view of these
indisputable facts, to assert that government can affect values
only in the ratio of its consumption! And yet Mr. Fisher
makes this assertion the starting-point of a lecture to the editor
of the *Herald of Anarchy* delivered in that dogmatic, know-
it-all style which only those are justified in assuming who
can sustain their statements by facts and logic.

THE POWER OF GOVERNMENT OVER VALUES.

[*Liberty*, June 27, 1891.]

To the Editor of Liberty:

In reference to your remarks upon my recent contribution to the London *Herald of Anarchy*, dogmatism of manner must often be adopted
to avoid verbosity; it is not necessarily an assumption of infallibility.

The action of governments with regard to gold is not truly analogous
in its economic effects to the prohibition of theatrical performances on
Sunday. In the last-named case, or in any similar case which we may
suppose, the effect is to diminish demand and to prolong or retard consumption. Thus, if we were prohibited from wearing shoes, boots, etc.,
on Sunday, or if every seventh person were prevented from using them,
then boots which now wear out in six months would last seven months,
and we may suppose theatres which now last seven years or seventy would
then be worn out in six or sixty. The immediate effect of opening theatres on Sunday would probably be to increase their value very greatly;
but eventually others would be built, and competition would reduce the
previously enhanced value. The residual enhancement of value would be
that resulting from the increased expense of producing the last increment
in the number of theatres which the market in its altered circumstances
could support. There is good reason to doubt whether this would be appreciable in the cases taken of articles of considerable durability. If the
government could reduce the consumption of food-stuffs, such as wheat,
and simultaneously of all substitutes, by one-seventh, it would be a very
different matter.

But in the case of gold the interference of governments in the present
day has little effect in increasing consumption. They do not collect it to
consume it, but simply to sell it. In this country, beyond specifying this
metal as the vehicle of value in contributing to the revenue, the interference appears to be limited to a restriction of the liberty of citizens to ex-

change promises of delivery of gold to bearer on demand. Bank-notes (or bills, as they seem to be called in your country) may only be issued by certain bankers, and by them only in a certain complex relation to the amount of gold they hold. But this is only a restriction in form, and not in quantity, because checks, drafts, and promissory notes other than to bearer on demand are issuable in unlimited quantity, subject to certain taxes—from which the other notes are not wholly exempt—and are transferable without further tax. What has this to do with the consumption of gold ? Next to nothing!

Now there is no legal obstacle, nothing, in fact, whatever except the inconveniences of bulk, fluctuation of value, and other inherent defects, to prevent the introduction and circulation of promises of wheat, cotton, oil, iron, or other commodity. This would not have any material effect upon the consumption, production, cost, or value of these commodities. Speculative sales of ''futures'' tend on the whole to steady values and to diminish the frequency and the intensity of gluts and famines.

Gold and silver are not used (in the sense of being consumed) by their circulation. They are merely conveyed, transferred, and exchanged more frequently. The fact that they are so often bought by people who do not themselves require to use them is not unique. Every merchant does the same with the commodity to which he devotes his attention.*

The peculiarity is that the trade in gold is familiar to every one. The portability, divisibility, and recognizability of this substance force it upon the attention of every one who avails himself of the services of others. The production and circulation of contracts for its future delivery are not unique. This is also done in the case of many other commodities. In both cases there is a very great convenience and economy ; and in both there is a very appreciable danger. Any such writings of individualists as may in any way give the impression that the free circulation of mutual indebtedness, miscalled '' mutual money,'' will be free from this element of danger are pernicious. Freedom to incur and to exchange debts is exceedingly desirable, but rather because they will encourage, purify, and chasten the spirit of enterprise than that they will in themselves bring very noticeable economic gain.

Apart from the wear and tear involved, neither the government nor any one else consumes one ha'penny worth more of gold by reason of its adoption in taxation and commerce as the most usual vehicle of value. Its use for this purpose may cause the world to hold a larger stock than it otherwise would; but this is in every way a benefit, because it steadies its value. If the metal were neglected, as platinum was until recently, then famine and glut might be observed. This would greatly lower the utility of gold as an intermediate exchange commodity, and would not help us to devise a substitute. It would throw upon every trade, including those who sell their own labor, a burden of doubt and uncertainty in estimating its fluctuations. The evil that government does by collecting needless millions is immeasurably greater than by its so-called maintenance of the gold standard.   Yours respectfully,

J. GREEVZ FISHER.

78 HARROGATE ROAD, LEEDS, ENGLAND.

---

* Division of labor originates in people making something they do not themselves want. It is further facilitated by selling this for one special commodity which is not directly wanted.

Dogmatism can be justified only by the event. In its use not only does nothing succeed *like* success, but nothing succeeds *but* success. And nothing fails like failure. If Mr. Fisher, in addressing the Anarchists upon finance as if they were babies and he a giant, shall succeed in making his assumed superiority felt as a reality, he will not only be forgiven for his dogmatism, but highly respected for his knowledge and power ; but if it shall appear that the ignorance and weakness are on his side rather than theirs, he will be covered not only with confusion by his error, but with ridicule by the collapse of his pretension. It is only just, however, to say that a comparison of his letter to *Liberty* with his letter to the *Herald of Anarchy* shows progress in the direction of modesty.

Already Mr. Fisher's pride has been followed by a fall. The central position taken by him at the start that government cannot affect the value of gold or any other commodity except by the slight additional demand which it creates as a consumer he has been forced to abandon at the first onslaught. If government were to allow the opening of theatres on Sunday, it would not thereby become a consumer of theatres itself (at least not in the economic sense; for, in the United States at any rate, our governors always go to the theatre as "deadheads "), and yet Mr. Fisher admits that in such a case the value of theatres would immediately rise very greatly. This admission is an abandonment of the position taken at first so confidently, and no other consideration can make it anything else. The fact that competition would soon arise to reduce the value does not alter the fact that for a time this action of government would materially raise it, which Mr. Fisher originally declared an impossibility. But even if such a plea had any pertinence, it could be promptly destroyed by a slight extension of the hypothesis. Suppose government, in addition to allowing the theatres now existing to open on Sunday, were to prohibit the establishment of any additional theatres. Then the value would not only go up, but stay up. It is hardly necessary to argue the matter further ; Mr. Fisher undoubtedly sees that he is wrong. The facts are too palpable and numerous. Why, since my comment of a month ago on Mr. Fisher's position, it has transpired that the cost of making twist drills in the United States has been increased *five hundred and twenty per cent.* by the McKinley bill. Government cannot affect value, indeed!

In the paragraph to which Mr. Fisher's letter is a rejoinder I said that "when government decrees that all money shall

be made of or issued against gold or silver, these metals immediately take on an artificial, government-created value, because
of the *new use* which arbitrary power enables them to monopolize." Mr. Fisher meets this by attempting to belittle the
restrictions placed upon the issue of paper money, as if all
vitally necessary liberty to compete with the gold-bugs were
even now allowed. Let me ask my opponent one question.
Does the law of England allow citizens to form a bank for the
issue of paper money against any property that they may see
fit to accept as security ; said bank perhaps owning no specie
whatever ; the paper money not redeemable in specie except
at the option of the bank; the customers of the bank mutually
pledging themselves to accept the bank's paper in lieu of gold
or silver coin of the same face value ; the paper being redeemable only at the maturity of the mortgage notes, and
then simply by a return of said notes and a release of the
mortgaged property,—is such an institution, I ask, allowed by
the law of England? If it is, then I have only to say that the
working people of England are very great fools not to take
advantage of this inestimable liberty, that the editor of the
Herald of Anarchy and his comrades have indeed nothing to
complain of in the matter of finance, and that they had better
turn their attention at once to the organization of such banks as
that which I have just described. But I am convinced that
Mr. Fisher will have to answer that these banks are illegal in
England; and in that case I tell him again that the present value
of gold is a monopoly value sustained by the exclusive monetary privilege given it by government. It may be true, as Mr.
Fisher says, that just as much gold would be used if it did not
possess this monopoly. But that has nothing to do with the
question. Take the illustration that I have already used in
this discussion when I said: "If government were to decree
that all plates shall be made of tin, would not the value of
tin rise and the value of china fall?" Now, if the supply of
tin were limited, and if nearly all the tin were used in making
plates, and if tin had no other use of great significance, it is
quite conceivable that, if the decree prohibiting the use of
china in making plates should be withdrawn, the same amount
of tin might continue to be used for the same purpose as
before, and yet the value of tin would fall tremendously in
consequence of the admitted competition of china. And similarly, if all property were to be admitted to competition with
gold in the matter of representation in the currency, it is possible that the same amount of gold would still be used as

money, but its value would decrease notably,—would fall,
that is to say, from its abnormal, artificial, government-created
value, to its normal, natural, open-market value.

FREE TRADE IN BANKING.

[*Liberty*, July 11, 1891.]

To the Editor of Liberty:

It is much to be regretted when *Liberty* is wounded in the house of her
friends. This is caused by those who regard liberty as a panacea for every
ill, or perhaps it would be better to say who regard the inevitable vicissi-
tudes and inequalities of life as evil. There is no more philosophical
reason for believing that all men can be equal, rich, and happy than for
believing that all animals can be equal, including, of course, that they
should all be equal to men.

Freedom is exceeding fair. It is by far the most excellent way. Under
liberty the very best possible results in every department of human activity, including commerce, will be obtained. But it won't make fools successful. One of its recommendations is that folly will more surely be
remedied by getting its medicine than by the grandmotherly plan of protection in all directions. In many cases cure is better than prevention.
Little burns, we may be sure, save many lives. (1)

It seems to be a fashion nowadays amongst reformers to rail at our
existing systems of currency and to regard government interference here
as greater and more pernicious than in many other matters. The truth,
however, is that there is scarcely anything which more completely illustrates the powerlessness of government to establish code in opposition to
custom than the unvarying failure of unsound currency enactments, and
the concomitant dwindling of monetary law into a mere specification of
truisms, a registration of established practice, or a system of licensing
certain individuals to carry on certain kinds of trade. But all these are
evils not perculiar to the money trade, nor do they here produce more injurious results than in the cases of priests, doctors, accountants, lawyers,
engineers, and other privileged faculties. (2)

Schemes to bring about the abolition of interest, especially when the authors promulgate this as a necessary consequence of free trade in banking,
are pernicious, and in their ultimate effect reactionary. Low rates of interest depend upon the magnitude of the mass of capital competing for investment rather than upon the presence or absence of the really trifling interference of governments with the modes in which debt may be incurred.
What is called free trade in banking actually means only unlimited liberty
to create debt. It is the erroneous labelling of debt as money which be-
gets most of the fallacies of currency-faddists, both coercionary and libera-
tionist. (3)

The principal error of the former is that they advocate schemes for the
growth and preferential marketing of government debt. The *ignis fatuus*
of some of the latter is a vision of people both using their property and
pledging it at the same time ; (4) while some go so far as to dream of
symbolical money of indefinite value. Thus we have Mr. Alfred B.
Westrup contributing " Citizens' Money " and " The Financial Problem,

both of which tacitly attempt to expound a method to enable every one to get into debt and keep there. (5)

The introduction to the first-named essay seems by implication to assert that the price of gold is too high, though no attempt is made to show how displacing it from currency would reduce the price as long as its cost and utility remain what they now are ; while the author himself appears to think that money can be made very much more plentiful and yet maintain its value, although he is contending that this value depends upon monopoly or scarcity. The last-named essay plainly assumes that by some such scheme poverty can be abolished. (6)

Banking is not the only financial operation in which government interferes. In the case of insurance companies, benefit societies, limited liability corporations, partnerships, trusts, insolvencies, and hundreds of other ways government is continually interfering. Most of this interference is well meant. Most, if not all, of it is actually injurious in itself, apart from the waste, the jobbery, and the imbecility of officialism it involves. These concomitant evils, though far greater than those directly resulting from the interference, had better for the time being be left out of sight. Their treatment belongs to the general subject of liberty, and they only incidentally pertain to the financial interference of government, as they do to all its other interference. Ignoring then the saving in cost, the immediate effect of the total abstention of government from its protection of the public from financial folly and roguery would be that a great crop of fresh schemes, bargains, and arrangements would offer themselves to those desirous of entrusting any of their wealth to the management of others. A very large proportion of these schemes—possibly the majority—would be unsound. (7) Amongst the unsound, unless its expounders grievously misrepresent it, would undoubtedly be found such mutual banking as is proposed by Mr. Westrup. He is altogether on a wrong tack. His whole talk is about money; but this term in his mouth means indebtedness, trust, credit, paper instruments binding some one to deliver something. Now, credit is not a representative of wealth, as Mr. Westrup so constantly declares. Mr. Westrup's money is a representative of a promise or debt. It may in many cases, as a matter of history, show that A has entrusted certain wealth to B ; but it does not guarantee that B has preserved it, and still less does it assure the holder that B can at call deliver or replace the borrowed articles, or any equal number of similar articles, or an equivalent value in some other articles. (8) As Mr. Donisthorpe insists in his " Principles of Plutology " (p. 136): " There is [at each moment] a certain amount of every valuable commodity in existence, neither more nor less ; nor can it be increased by a single atom though the whole population suddenly, as if by inspiration, began craving and yearning for it." (9) Again, what is there to show that any necessity exists, as Mr. Westrup asserts, for enabling all wealth to be represented by money ? If I give a man a loaf for sweeping my door-step, the loaf does not represent the work, nor does the work represent the loaf. All we know is that I desire the sweeping more than I desire the loaf, and the laborer desires the loaf more than his ease or idleness. If I give a guinea for a hat, this guinea does not represent the particular hat or any hat. It does not represent it while in my possession before the exchange, nor in the hatter's possession after the exchange. Gold is valuable ; it does not merely represent value. The value represents an estimate of the comparative labor necessary to produce the last increment needful to replenish the stock of gold at a rate equivalent to its consumption,—this consumption depending upon the comparative utility of gold in relation to its own value and that of other commodities. Or at a given hat-shop it represents an estimate of the cost of bringing as much more gold to the place as equivalent to the cost of bringing another hat to the shop. (10)

Mr. Westrup's fallacious analysis of commerce dogs his steps in every process of his reasoning. The gravest evils of the interference of government in monetary matters are little more than its cost and the deadening influence of fancied protection. The reform which monetary liberty would secure would not include any redistribution of the products of labor. This depends partly upon the possibility of the laborer possessing the skill of a speculator and of a producer and exercising both at the same time, and partly upon the enormously disproportionate share of taxation which he has to bear. These and many other evils, in so far as they are increased by government, depend not upon arbitrary money, but upon the arbitrary alienation of the substance of the citizen. It is a most trivial incident that the plunder is nominally priced in and redeemed by one commodity. The evil is that it should be taken. The form makes but an infinitesimal difference.

Mr. Westrup would do well to ask himself these questions, and, in answering them, to assign the grounds upon which he proceeds in arriving at the conclusions. (11)

1. Would the value of gold be (*a*) increased (*b*) reduced by mutual banking ? And what percentage ?

2. Is gold the only commodity produced and bought by people who don't want to consume it ?

3. Would gold lose its pre-eminence as the commodity the value of which is most correctly estimated, and which it is therefore safest to buy at market value when disposing of our own or our purchased produce ?

4. What has the rate of interest to do with the net or residual increment of wealth remaining as a surplus after maintaining the population ? Is this less in the United Kingdom where interest is low than in the United States where interest is high ?

5. How could legislation maintain the value of gold if it became as abundant as copper ? Would the volume of money then be greater than now ? Would the rate of interest be affected by this alteration apart from the changes due to the act of transition from the present state of dear gold to the supposed state of cheap gold ?

6. How is the voluntary custom of selling preferentially for gold a monopoly ? Are cattle a monopoly where used as a medium of exchange ?

7. What analogy is there between a law to require the exclusive consumption of hand-made bricks and any laws specifying that the word Dollar in a bond shall imply a certain quantity of gold ? Does any government force anyone to consume gold in preference to any other commodity ? Does government consume gold in constructing its offices and defences, or does it merely swap it off for other commodities ? Is all silver or gold in the United States delivered to government as fast as made, or does government purchase it in the open market ?

Yours, etc.,

J. Greevz Fisher.

78 Harrogate Road, Leeds, England.

Pending the arrival of any answer Mr. Westrup may desire to make to the foregoing criticisms upon his pamphlets, for which purpose the columns of *Liberty* are open to him, I take

the liberty of offering some comments as well as answers to Mr.
Fisher's questions.

(1) I know of no friend of liberty who regards it as a
panacea for every ill, or claims that it will make fools successful, or believes that it will make all men equal, rich, and
perfectly happy. The Anarchists, it is true, believe that under
liberty the laborer's wages will buy back his product, and that
this will make men more nearly equal, will insure the industrious and the prudent against poverty, and will add to human
happiness. But between the fictitious claims which Mr.
Fisher scouts and the real claims which the Anarchists assert
it is easy to see the vast difference.

(2) I do not understand how "the unvarying failure of
unsound currency enactments" makes the interference of
government with finance seem less pernicious. In fact, it
drives me to precisely the opposite conclusion. In the phrase,
"concomitant dwindling of monetary law into a mere specification of truisms," Mr. Fisher repeats his attempt, of which I
complained in the last issue of *Liberty*, to belittle the restrictions placed upon the issue of paper money. When he has
answered the question which I have asked him regarding the
English banking laws, we can discuss the matter more intelligently. Meanwhile it is futile to try to make a monopoly seem
less than a monopoly by resorting to such a circumlocution as
"system of licensing individuals to carry on certain kinds of
trades," or to claim that the monopoly of a tool not only
common but indispensable to all trades is not more injurious
than the monopoly of a tool used by only one trade or a few
trades.

(3) It is true that if the mass of capital competing for
investment were increased, the rate of interest would fall. But
it is not true that scarcity of capital is the only factor that
keeps up the rate of interest? If I were free to use my capital
directly as a basis of credit or currency, the relief from the
necessity of borrowing additional capital from others would
decrease the borrowing demand, and therefore the rate of
interest. And if, as the Anarchists claim, this freedom to use
capital as a basis of credit should give an immense impetus to
business, and consequently cause an immense demand for
labor, and consequently increase productive power, and consequently augment the amount of capital, here another force
would be exercised to lower the rate of interest and cause it to
gradually vanish. Free trade in banking does not mean *only*
unlimited liberty to create debt; it means also vastly increased
ability to meet debt: and, so accompanied, the liberty to

create debt is one of the greatest blessings. It is not erroneous
to label evidence of debt as money. As Col. Wm. B. Greene well
said: "That is money which does the work of the tool money."
When evidence of debt circulates as a medium of exchange, to
all intents and purposes it is money. But this is of small consequence. The Anarchists do not insist on the word "money."
Suppose we call such evidence of debt *currency* (and surely it
is currency), what then? How does this change of name
affect the conclusions of the "currency-faddists"? Not in
the least, as far as I can see. By the way, it is not becoming
in a man who has, not simply one bee in his bonnet, but a
whole swarm of them, to talk flippantly of the "fads" of men
whose lives afford unquestionable evidence of their earnestness.

(4) Mr. Fisher seems to think it inherently impossible to use
one's property and at the same time pledge it. But what else
happens when a man, after mortgaging his house, continues to
live in it? This is an actual every-day occurrence, and mutual
banking only seeks to make it possible on easier terms,—the
terms that will prevail under competition instead of the terms
that do prevail under monopoly. The man who calls this
reality an *ignis fatuus* must be either impudent or ignorant.
Unfortunately it is true that some believers in mutual banking
do "dream of symbolical money of indefinite value," but
none of the standard expositions of the subject offer any such
fallacy ; and it is with these that Mr. Fisher must deal if he
desires to overthrow the mutual banking idea.

(5) Mr. Westrup's method, if I understand it, would not
"enable every one to get into debt and keep there," but rather
to get into debt and out again, greatly to the advantage of the
borrower and of society generally. Mr. Westrup does not
contemplate the issue of bank-notes against individual notes
that never mature.

(6) Mr. Fisher, in his remark that "no attempt is made to
show how displacing gold from currency would reduce the
price as long as its cost and utility remain what they now are,"
is no less absurd than he would be if he were to say that no
attempt is made to show how displacing flour as an ingredient
of bread would reduce the price of flour as long as its cost and
utility remain what they now are. The utility of flour consists in the fact that it is an ingredient of bread, and the main
utility of gold consists in the fact that it is used as currency.
To talk of displacing these utilities and at the same time keeping them what they now are is a contradiction in terms, of
which Mr. Fisher is guilty. But Mr. Westrup is guilty of no

contradiction at all in claiming that money can be made very
much more plentiful and yet maintain its value at the same
time that he contends that the present value of money is due
to its monopoly or scarcity. For to quote Colonel Greene
again:

All money is not the same money. There is one money of gold,
another of brass, another of leather, and another of paper ; and there is
a difference in the glory of these different kinds of money. There is one
money that is a commodity, having its exchangeable value determined by
the law of supply and demand, which money may be called (though somewhat barbarously) *merchandise-money;* as, for instance, gold, silver, brass,
bank-bills, etc.: there is another money, which is not a commodity,
whose exchangeable value is altogether independent of the law of supply
and demand, and which may be called *mutual money.* . . . If ordinary
bank-bills represented specie actually existing in the vaults of the bank,
no mere issue or withdrawal of them could effect a fall or rise in the value
of money: for every issue of a dollar-bill would correspond to the lock-
ing-up of a specie dollar in the banks' vaults ; and every cancelling of a
dollar-bill would correspond to the issue by the banks of a specie dollar.
It is by the exercise of *banking privileges*—that is, by the issue of bills
purporting to be, but which are not, convertible—that the banks effect a
depreciation in the price of the silver dollar. It is this FICTION (by which
legal value is assimilated to, and becomes, to all business intents and
purposes, actual value) that enables bank-notes to depreciate the silver
dollar. *Substitute* VERITY *in the place of fiction,* either by permitting the
banks to issue no more paper than they have specie in their vaults, or by
effecting an entire divorce between bank-paper and its pretended specie
basis, and the power of paper to depreciate specie is at an end. So long
as the fiction is kept up, the silver dollar is depreciated, and tends to
emigrate for the purpose of travelling in foreign parts ; but, the moment
the fiction is destroyed, the power of paper over metal ceases. By its
intrinsic nature specie is merchandise, having its value determined, as
such, by supply and demand ; but, on the contrary, paper money is, by
its intrinsic nature, *not* merchandise, but the means whereby merchandise
is exchanged, and, as such, ought always to be commensurate in quantity
with the amount of merchandise to be exchanged, be that amount great
or small. MUTUAL MONEY IS MEASURED BY SPECIE, BUT IS IN NO WAY
ASSIMILATED TO IT ; AND THEREFORE ITS ISSUE CAN HAVE NO EFFECT
WHATEVER TO CAUSE A RISE OR FALL IN THE PRICE OF THE PRECIOUS
METALS.

This is one of the most important truths in finance, and
perfectly accounts for Mr. Westrup's position. When he says
that money can be made very much more plentiful and yet
maintain its value, he is speaking of *mutual money;* when he
says that the present value of money depends upon monopoly
or scarcity, he is speaking of *merchandise money.*

(7) As sensibly might one say to Mr. Fisher, who is a stanch
opponent of government postal service, that " the immediate
effect of the total abstention of government from its protection of the public from the roguery of private mail-carriers

would be that a great crop of fresh schemes would offer themselves to those desirous of intrusting any of their letters to others to carry. A very large proportion of these schemes—possibly the majority—would be unsound." Well, what of it ? Are we on this account to give up freedom ? No, says Mr. Fisher. But, then, what is the force of the consideration ?

(8) Mr. Westrup's money not only shows that A has given B a conditional title to certain wealth, but guarantees that this wealth has been preserved. That is, it affords a guarantee so nearly perfect that it is acceptable. If you take a mortgage on a house and the owner insures it in your favor, the guarantee against loss by fire is not perfect, since the insurance company may fail, but it is good enough for practical purposes. Similarly, if B, the bank, advances money to A against a mortgage on the latter's stock of goods, it is within the bounds of possibility that A will sell the goods and disappear forever, but he will thus run the risk of severe penalties; and these penalties, coupled with B's caution, make a guarantee that practically serves. To be sure, Mr. Westrup's money does not assure the holder that the bank will deliver the borrowed articles on demand, but it does assure him that he can get similar articles or their equivalents on demand from any customers of the bank that have them for sale, because all these customers are pledged to take the bank's notes; to say nothing of the fact that the bank, though not bound to redeem on demand, is bound to redeem as fast as the mortgage notes mature.

(9) I perceive the perfect truth of Mr. Donisthorpe's remark, but I do not perceive its pertinence to the matter under discussion.

(10) Nor do I detect the bearing of the truisms which Mr. Fisher enunciates so solemnly. They certainly do not establish the absence of any necessity for enabling all wealth to be represented by money. This necessity is shown by the fact that, when the monetary privilege is conferred upon one form of wealth exclusively, the people have to obtain this form of wealth at rates that sooner or later send them into bankruptcy.

(11) I conclude by answering Mr. Fisher's questions.

The value of gold would be reduced by mutual banking, because it would thereby be stripped of that exclusive monetary utility conferred upon it by the State. The percentage of this reduction no one can tell in advance, any more than he can tell how much whiskey would fall in price if there were unrestricted competition in the sale of it.

Neither gold nor any other commodity is bought by people

who don't want to consume it or in some way cause others to consume it. Gold is in process of consumption when it is in use as currency.

Mutual banking might or might not cause gold to lose its pre-eminence as the most thoroughly constituted value. If it should do so, then some other commodity more constantly demanded and uniformly supplied would take the place of gold as a standard of value. It certainly is unscientific to impart a factitious, monopoly value to a commodity in order to make its value steady.

Other things being equal, the rate of interest is inversely proportional to the residual increment of wealth, for the reason that a low rate of interest (except when offered to an already bankrupted people) makes business active, causes a more universal employment of labor, and thereby adds to productive capacity. The residual increment is less in the United Kingdom, where interest is low, than in the United States, where interest is high, because other things are not equal. But in either country this increment would be greater than it now is if the rate of interest were to fall.

If gold became as abundant as copper, legislation, if it chose, could maintain its value by decreeing that we should drink only from gold goblets. If the value were maintained, the volume of money would be greater on account of the abundance of gold. This increase of volume would lower the rate of interest.

A *voluntary* custom of selling preferentially for gold would not be a monopoly, but there is no such voluntary custom. Where cattle are used voluntarily as a medium of exchange, they are not a monopoly ; but where there is a law that *only* cattle shall be so used, they are a monopoly.

It is not incumbent on Anarchists to show an analogy between a law to require the exclusive consumption of handmade bricks and any law specifying that the word Dollar in a bond shall imply a certain quantity of gold. But they are bound and ready to show an analogy between the first-named law and any laws prohibiting or taxing the issue of notes, of whatever description, intended for circulation as currency. Governments force people to consume gold, in the sense that they give people no alternative but that of abandoning the use of money. When government swaps off gold for other commodities, it thereby consumes it in the economic sense. The United States government purchases its gold and silver. It can hardly be said, however, that it purchases silver in an open market, because, being obliged by law to buy so many millions each month, it thereby creates an artificial market.

CURRENCY AND GOVERNMENT.

[*Liberty*, August 15, 1891.]

To the Editor of Liberty:

There is not the slightest analogy between allowing theatres to be consumed on Sundays and allowing silver or iron to be sold on the same terms as gold. Currency is only buying and selling; it is not consuming. The customary adoption of gold as currency and the endorsement of this custom by edict involves only a very insignificant increase in its consumption. Most other commodities waste much more than gold in the processes of stocking, marketing, and distributing from points of production to points of consumption. An admission that if government allowed an increase in the consumption of theatres it would raise the price, in no way affects any known proposal or enactment in regard to gold as currency, because currency laws have so little effect upon the consumption of gold. There are laws which possibly affect the value of the precious metals. There are such as prohibit mixing them freely in all proportions, producing utensils or other articles of consumption. Thus, if the removal of the present restrictions should lead to a larger consumption of silver in culinary articles, this would slightly raise the price of silver.

But what is the use of pursuing a false analogy? If government simply facilitated the sale of theatres, how would that affect their price in the market? A comparison of the effects of facilitating consumption does not illustrate the effects of facilitating exchanges. It is in the power of government to alter the values of the precious metals enormously within the areas of their dominion by prohibiting their importation or exportation or by duties or bounties. It will be time enough to discuss these matters when they are proposed. They are not analogous to the attempts to fix the value of silver by the schemes of the bi-metallists, and they have still less analogy to the statutes which are supposed to determine the value of gold, but which, as a matter of fact, do nothing of the sort. To state that one-fourth ounce of gold shall exchange for one-fourth ounce of gold is simply to cumber the statute book with a "chestnut." No government ever does stipulate "that all money shall be made of or issued against gold or silver," and it is in supposing that it does so that some of our comrades get wrong. What is called *money* in the above sentence means a bond or promise to deliver coin. There is nothing to prevent any one from issuing bonds or promises to deliver something else, such as petroleum, pig-iron, wheat, lard, and so on. If you promise delivery of petroleum on demand or at a date named, you only discharge your bond by legally tendering the petroleum as specified. The law of England allows this. To prevent it would disorganize all trade. What is prohibited is the production and issue of notes in one particular form,—namely, promises to pay gold to bearer on demand. It is a most vicious equivoque to call such instruments money, and to exclude checks, drafts, bills, notes, whether drawn for gold, silver, iron, lard, or even labor.

Space prohibits (even when a condensed statement, which will be misnamed dogmatism, is employed) showing that even under our truck laws no one is prohibited from using or taking as a payment, flour, bread, meat, calico, boots, and so on.

The analogy as to an enactment that all plates should be made of tin is equally misleading and unsound. Government does not enact that all marketable articles shall be made of gold, or that all articles capable of being sold for future delivery shall be made of gold. There is no benefit to this argument in confounding acts which would seriously affect consumption with acts which have little or no such effect. The gold embodied in coins is marketable stock; it is not in consumption, as the tin would be if it had a monopoly in plate production. We want plates to use; we carry coin always to sell. It is not withdrawn from the market so as to raise its price, but is constantly brought afresh to market so as equally to lower it. Besides this, the illustration assumes and implies that for gold there is no other use of great significance but coin-making. If this were so, then the Westrups, the Tarns, and the Tuckers would have the argument all on their own side. The fact is, however, that the gold mines are not kept open to supply coin, but to supply the arts.

There is yet another fallacy in our comrades' position. It would be no monetary disadvantage if the facts really were as they suppose. If gold were twice as dear, or twice as cheap, its merchants would make just the same profit, bankers and financiers would not lose or gain—neither would anybody except the producers and consumers of gold. Grocers' profits are not affected by the price of sugar, but the growers and users are both vitally concerned.

There would seem to be nothing whatever in English law to prevent the establishment of a bank without any specie issuing inconvertible paper, which the customers mutually agree to accept at par value, but there is little likelihood such a scheme would be workable. It would tax the powers of a very clever master of legal or Anarchical phraseology to specify upon the notes the responsibility of each customer and to preserve the power of these customers fulfilling their agreements. Before one could use such notes to buy a breakfast or a railway ticket there would have to be a rather involved and tedious disquisition upon economics. No Anarchist would propose to embody such arrangements in a statute like our limited liability laws. Such notes would therefore be simply of the nature of mortgage bonds, for which there would possibly be a market and a price. The price would probably be below rather than above par.

Free trade in gold and in credit is desirable. Its desirability is proportionate to the restrictions which exist, but these are not very great or grievous. The field for their discussion opens only when our comrades' present mists have rolled away. But they bear no comparison with acts for the purchase by government of great quantities of silver, acts for repairing worn gold coin at public expense, and, above all, acts for tariffs designed to hamper trade and acts for raising public revenue in general.

Let our comrades in *Liberty*, *Egoism*, and *The Herald of Anarchy* rise to more vital matters when they touch upon the economics of coercion. The evils of coinage are greatly overstated, and to them are attributed effects with which they have no connection.   J. GREEVZ FISHER.

78 HARROGATE ROAD, LEEDS, ENGLAND.

Mr. Fisher's article, printed above, is nothing but a string of assertions, most of which, as matters of fact, are untrue. The chief of these untruths is the statement that in exchanging gold we do not consume it. What is consumption? It is the act of destroying by use or waste. One of the uses of gold—and under the existing financial system its chief use—is to act as a medium of exchange, or else as the basis of such a medium. In performing this function it wears out ; in other words, it is consumed. Being given a monopoly of this use or function, it has an artificial value,—a value which it would not have if other articles, normally capable of this function, were not forbidden to compete with it. And these articles suffer from this restriction of competition in very much the same way that a theatre forbidden to give Sunday performances suffers if its rival is allowed the privilege. Mr. Fisher may deny the analogy as stoutly as he chooses ; it is none the less established. This analogy established, Mr. Fisher's position falls,—falls as surely as his other position has fallen : the position that government cannot affect values, which he at first laid down with as much contemptuous assurance as if no one could deny it without thereby proving himself a born fool. So there is no need to refute the rest of the assertions. I will simply enter a specific denial of some of them. It is untrue that gold is not withdrawn from the market to raise its price. It is untrue that the gold mines are kept open *principally* to supply the arts. It is untrue that, if gold were twice as dear or twice as cheap, bankers would not lose or gain ; the chief business of the banker is not to buy and sell gold, but to lend it. And I believe it to be untrue—though here I do not speak of what I positively know—that English law permits the establishment of such banks as Proudhon, Greene, and Spooner proposed. Mr. Fisher certainly should know more about this than I, but I doubt his statement, first, because I have found him in error so often ; second, because nine out of ten Massachusetts lawyers will tell you with supreme confidence that there is no law in Massachusetts prohibiting the use of notes and checks as currency (yet there is one of many years' standing, framed in plain terms, and often have I astonished lawyers of learning and ability by showing it to them) ; and, third, because I am sure that, if such banks were legal in England, they would have been started long ago.

THE EQUALIZATION OF WAGE AND PRODUCT.

[*Liberty*, August 22, 1891.]

To the Editor of Liberty :

One does not lay oneself open to a charge of disloyalty to the principles of liberty by guarding against extravagant hopes. It seems necessary to keep this in mind before saying a word against any anticipations formed by ardent and able advocates of liberty like yourself. It is a hyperbole (possibly open to misconstruction) to imply that some advocates of liberty regard it as a panacea for every ill. It therefore is a great advantage when its expected benefits are clearly defined as in your issue of the 11th. You believe that under liberty the laborer's wages will buy back his product. This is fortunately a definite issue. It implies that if there be a naked producer or a commodity the complete production of which, including all the outlay needful for its delivery to the consumer at the very moment when he needs to consume it, occupies·time and demands the empolyment of wealth in material, sustenance of producer, and tools, of none of which this producer is possessed, this pauper producer shall retain the full value of his product notwithstanding his partial dependence upon some one who provides the necessaries for his production in anticipation of his fruition. Is not this a fair and correct interpretation of your phrase? and supposing it to be so, does it not show that you expect too much?(1)

The facilitation of credit and the so-called circulation of debts as a substitute for currency, together with all schemes for mutual banking or schemes for the more rapid development of commerce, imply that valuables shall be temporarily placed at the disposal of others than their owners who meanwhile sustain a privation and also take a serious risk, but that these owners shall obtain no recompense beyond the bare return of their valuables unimpaired. (2) If a complex and therefore intricate scheme or calculation results in producing something out of nothing it opens a suspicion that there is some concealed flaw in the train of thought. Credit without remuneration, debt without cost, unlimited or very plentiful money without depreciation, are the desired and hoped results of the new schemes. It is most important to distinguish between demanding liberty to try these schemes, and pledging liberty to their success. Unfortunately it does not appear to be sufficient to call attention to this distinction. Ardent friends will often unite the cause of the fad with that of the principle unless the fad itself be destroyed. There are faddists who avoid this pitfall. (3) Thus there are some who advocate a reform of spelling, but as advocates of freedom decline to make even that hoped success of reformed spelling, or its hoped rapid progress under a free system of education, a plea or prop for arguments to emancipate teaching from government restriction, or for enforced alienation of citizens' property for its support. Teaching ought to be free not because it is argued that spelling would be reformed and the reform would be good, but simply that the reform may get a chance and if good may succeed. So government restriction on banking and credit ought not to be repealed because Westrup's or Greene's finance would prevail and bless the people, but so that this and any other device may be tested and if good succeed. (4)

As against the scheme itself the contention is that wealth originates solely in production, and that with plentiful production the wealth of the poor will increase even though the wealth of some rich people is vastly, and, as it is thought, inordinately increased. But this banking scheme does not add to production. (5) It is but a scheme for destroying one source of income of the rich or appropriating it to the poorer producer. Without any attempt at deduction experience dictates the induction that the chances are in favor of the man with a special faculty for successful financial *operations* rather than of students of principles. The man who can actually value a horse, a house, a crop of wheat, is more useful in pursuing his function as a speculator than a student who can ably analyze the components of value by prolonged and tardy research. The trader helps society most and at greater risk, so those of them who succeed have the greater gain, and it is probably cheaper to society to pay this figure for the organization of commerce than dabble in amateurish schemes. The experience of co-operation—both its successes and its failures seem to point in this direction in this country. (6)

Government interference in finance has broken down whenever it has done serious violence to sound economical principles. At present it does not do so. It needlessly coins some metal. This is in England unaccompanied with the gross error of buying and hoarding increasing quantities of a metal whose production has been greatly cheapened of late. Apart from the silver folly of your government the residual evils of government coinage are infinitesimal, and they are not commercial. They are confined to the loss arising from carrying on a productive or distributive process by government under monopoly rather than by free individuals in combination or separately under the economic control of competition. Here they end. It is pure fancy unsupported as yet by evidence or true analogy that they interfere with the movements of the metal, or materially coerce the markets into using an inferior commodity as its most reliable and most fluent investment. (7) There is not the slightest use for the purposes of this argument in comparing a law enforcing the use of golden drinking-vessels with any laws connected with the use of gold as currency. A true analogy would be found in studying the effect of monetizing iron by law. Such a law would not demonetize gold unless it were much more tyrannical in its mode of prescribing iron as a legal tender than our present law is in prescribing gold. (8) All government income, borrowings, taxes, postage, school pence, court fees, all government outlay in wages, war material, grants to localities, payment of interest upon debt and all accounts, court verdicts, official valuations, bankrupt statements, and so on, would be in terms of iron. But I should be free to promise future delivery, or acceptance of gold, or to sell my services or my products for gold as I now am to promise to give or take iron at an agreed time and place or to hire myself for iron or for board and lodging or any other mode of recompense I can get any one to agree upon. (9) Now it is quite likely the first effect of this would be to raise the price of iron and thereby lower the value of gold in comparison with iron, coal, and other economic components of the value of iron. It is also quite likely it would stimulate the production of iron. But both of these effects would combine to maintain a larger stock of iron hanging as a buffer between producer and consumer. This would steady value, but it would also in time counteract the first temporary effects of the supposed monetization of iron, and neither price nor production would continue to be excessive—with the sole exception of the small increase of consumption from wear and tear of coins. It would not in all probability displace gold as the money in the market, because government, instead of doing as it now does, registering, and taking praise for the best monetary substance, would attempt to monetize an ill-adapted commodity, a task beyond its strength, and would sustain defeat as it has often done when debasement or other anti-economic schemes were undertaken.

If as you assert the main utility of gold consists in the fact that it is used for currency, then your general position is impregnable. But that this is not sound is somewhat implied by Greene, who recognizes gold and silver as merchandise. "Specie is merchandise having its value determined, as such, by supply and demand." The words "as such" may simply imply "therefore" or may imply an idea on Greene's part that the value of specie as money was otherwise determined. But what evidence have we that the very frequent resale of gold—called its monetary circulation—is effectual in altering its price (wear and tear excepted)? Every time gold is bought in or gathered in taxes the tendency is to put up the price, and every time it is thrown into market or spent by government in outlay it tends to lower its value. These operations do not constitute a monopoly. Any one can buy and any one can sell gold coin. There is no monopoly in the matter. The monetary privilege is not a monopoly, and it grows in the open market, not in the fancied forcing-house of government. Greene alleges (in small caps) that mutual money would neither raise nor lower the price of specie. You hold that it would be tangibly reduced by mutual banking. Which is correct? (10) Comparing the reduction in value you anticipate with one which might arise in the price of whiskey if there were unrestricted competition in the sale of it, you overlook the fact that there is unrestricted competition in the sale of gold bullion and specie. Moreover, though we cannot tell by what amount the price of whiskey would be reduced by unrestricted competition, we can tell of what the fall would consist. It would be limited to such relinquishment of profit as would be forced upon the dealers by competition. If consumption increased, it might raise the price by its effect upon marginal or residual production yielding a diminished return, or it might be lowered by cheapening production by remunerating economic employment of capital. This is a false and inapplicable analogy. It is no more correct to say that gold is in the process of being consumed when it is in use as currency than to say that the inevitable waste or deterioration of commodities on the road from producer to consumer is economically an act of consumption. (11) Production is not complete until the commodity reaches the hands of a person who applies it to the direct gratification of some personal craving. The waste of gold in the function of currency is part of the cost which the consumer has to repay when that coin has been converted into a consumable product which he purchases. The only exception is that this cost may fall upon some other product when the less waste of gold is voluntarily substituted for the waste of any other commodity if one seeks to transport to a distant market mere value irrespective of its embodiment. It is as if one temporarily needed a certain weight to steady a machine, but was indifferent as to whether it was embodied in stone, iron, or gold, all of which he happens to have in stock, but which he can subsequently consume or sell unimpaired, and whose employment for this purpose only infinitesimally deteriorates the ponderable and does not impoverish his trade stock because it does not withdraw the ponderous article from inspection or sale.

It is not correct to reply to a monetary question by pointing out that government might keep gold as dear as it now is even if it were as cheaply produced as copper, by decreeing that we should drink only from gold goblets. If this could have such effect it would be inapplicable to this discussion, because it would be decreeing consumption while currency is not consumption, but only marketing. But it would fail, because of the durability of substance. Only by buying up the metal at the desired value could the value be maintained. No purchases of gold with gold would alter its value. Silver, copper, wheat would have to be used to buy up gold at the value it was desired to maintain, and of course no government would have the strength for this. (12) It must be remembered that miners would be sellers at cost. The United States government raises the price of silver now while it is a buyer. If it tipped it in mid-ocean it would then consume it in an economic sense. When it becomes a seller the price must fall. The fact that there is a possibility the law may change at any moment even now keeps the price from rising as it would if the silver were immediately consumed or destroyed instead of being hoarded. Surely it is a very palpable error to say that when government sells or spends gold it consumes it in an economic sense. If I swap a horse for a cow and kill and eat the cow, do I consume the horse? (13) I took the horse from the market when I bought it, and I return it to the market when I offer to sell it. The question of the metal has demanded so much elucidation that debts as commodities and as currency must wait a future communication.   J. GREEVZ FISHER.

78 HARROGATE ROAD, LEEDS, ENGLAND.

(1) No, this is not a correct interpretation of my phrase, because it is based upon a conception of the term product seriously differing from my own. If a laborer's product is looked upon as the entirety of that which he delivers to the consumer, then indeed Mr. Fisher's point is well taken, and to expect the laborer's wages to buy back his product is to expect too much. But that is not what is ordinarily meant by a laborer's product. A laborer's product is such portion of the value of that which he delivers to the consumer as his own labor has contributed. To expect the laborer's wages to buy this value back is to expect no more than simple equity. If some other laborer has contributed to the total value of the delivered article by making a tool which has been used in its manufacture by the laborer who delivers it, then the wages of the laborer who makes the tool should also buy back *his* product or due proportion of value, and would do so under liberty. But his portion of the value and therefore his wage would be measured by the wear and tear which the tool had suffered in this single act of manufacture, and not by any supposed benefit conferred by the use of the tool over and above its wear and tear. In other words, the tool-maker would simply sell that portion of the tool destroyed in the act of manufacture instead of lending the tool and receiving it again accompanied by a value which would more than restore it to its original condition. Mr. Fisher's interpretation rests, furthermore, on a misconception of the term wages. When a farmer hires a day-laborer for a dollar a day and his board, the board is as truly a part of the wages as is the dollar ; and when I say that the laborer's wages should buy back his product, I mean that the total amount which he receives for his labor, whether in advance or subsequently, and whether consumed before or after the performance of his labor, should be equal in market value to his total contribution to the product upon which he bestows his labor. Is this expecting too much? If so, might I ask to whom the excess of product over wage should equitably go?

(2) Every man who postpones consumption takes a risk. If

he keeps commodities which he does not wish to consume,
they may perish on his hands. If he exchanges them for
gold, the gold may decline in value. If he exchanges them
for government paper promising gold on demand, the paper
may decline in value. And if he exchanges them for mutual
money, this transaction, like the others (though in a smaller
degree, we claim), has its element of risk. But, as long as
merchants seem to think that they run less risk by temporarily
placing their valuables at the disposal of others than by retaining possession of them, the advocates of mutual money
will no more concern themselves about giving them recompense beyond the bare return of their valuables unimpaired
than the advocates of gold and government paper will concern
themselves to insure the constancy of the one or the solvency
of the other. As for the "something out of nothing" fallacy,
that is shared between God and the Shylocks, and, far from
being entertained by the friends of free banking, is their
special abomination. "Credit without remuneration!" shrieks
Mr. Fisher in horror. But, if credit is reciprocal, why should
there be remuneration? "Debt without cost!" But, if debt
is reciprocal, why should there be cost? "Unlimited or very
plentiful money without depreciation!" But if the contemplated addition to the volume of currency contemplates in
turn a broadening of the basis of currency, why should there
be depreciation? Free and mutual banking means simply
reciprocity of credit, reciprocity of debt, and an extension of
the currency basis. Mr. Fisher has been so inveterate a
drinker of bad economic whiskey that he has got the economic jim-jams and sees snakes on every hand.

(3) In applying it to his own views also, Mr. Fisher takes
the sting out of the word "fad." But it was and is my impression that he originally applied it to the views of the free
money advocates, not in the playful spirit in which all independent men call themselves "cranks," but in the contemptuous spirit in which they are given that appellation by the
mossbacks. And it was natural enough. In finance, Mr.
Fisher is a mossback. Contempt for contempt,—that's fair,
isn't it?

(4) It has been repeatedly stated in these columns that we
ask nothing but liberty. Given liberty, if we fail, we will sub-
side. Nevertheless, with Mr. Fisher's permission, we will
continue to put in our best licks for liberty in those directions
which seem to us most promising of good results. Meanwhile we accord to Mr. Fisher the privilege of rapping away
for spelling reform so long as he does it at his own expense,

which is not the case at present. (My readers may not see the point, but Mr. Fisher and my printers will.)

(5) This I deny. It is the especial claim of free banking that it will increase production. To make capital fluent is to make business active and to keep labor steadily employed at wages which will cause a tremendous effective demand for goods. If free banking were only a picayunish attempt to distribute more equitably the small amount of wealth now produced, I would not waste a moment's energy on it.

(6) Here we have a very good reason why I should continue to debate with Mr. Fisher rather than form a banking partnership with Mr. Westrup. Very likely the banking firm of Westrup, Tucker & Co. would come speedily to grief. But I am none the less interested in securing the greatest possible liberty for banking so that I may profit by the greater competition that would then be carried on between those born with a genius for finance. But what about Proudhon, Mr. Fisher? He was no amateur. He could value, not only a horse, but a railroad, the money kings utilized his business brains, his Manual for a Bourse Speculator served them as a guide, and, when he started his Banque du Peuple, it immediately assumed such proportions that Napoleon had to construct a crime for which to clap him into jail in order to save the Bank of France from this dangerous competitor. Amateur, indeed!

(7) On the contrary, there is an abundance of evidence. The suppression of Proudhon's bank was a coercion of the market. And in this country attempt after attempt has been made to introduce credit money outside of government and national bank channels, and the promptness of the suppression has always been proportional to the success of the attempt.

(8) Here Mr. Fisher becomes heretical. The champions of gold are proclaiming with one voice that the monetization of silver will prove the demonetization of gold.

(9) Just as free, and no more so. But this is no freedom at all. I tell Mr. Fisher again that it is a crime to issue and circulate as currency a note promising to deliver iron at a certain time. I know that it is a crime in this country, and I believe that the laws of England contain restrictions that accomplish virtually the same result.

(10) There is no contradiction between my position and Greene's. Greene held, as I hold, that the existing monopoly imparts an artificial value to gold, and that the abolition of the monopoly would take away this artificial value. But he also held, as I hold, that, after this reduction of value had been effected, the variations in the volume of mutual money

would be independent of the price of specie.   In other words,
this reduction of the value of gold from the artificial to the
normal point will be effected by the equal liberty given to
other commodities to serve as a basis of currency; but, this
liberty having been granted and having taken effect, the issue
of mutual money against these commodities, each note being
based on a specific portion of them, cannot affect the value of
any of these commodities, of which gold is one.   It is no answer to the charge of monopoly to say that any one can buy
and sell gold coin.   No one denies that.   The monopoly complained of is this,—that only holders of gold (and, in this country, of government bonds) can use their property as currency
or as a basis of currency.   Such a monopoly has even more
effect in enhancing the price of gold than would a monopoly
that should allow only certain persons to deal in gold.   The
price of gold is determined less by the number of persons dealing in it than by the ratio of the total supply to the total demand.   The monopoly that the Anarchists complain of is the
monopoly that increases the demand for gold by giving it the
currency function to the exclusion of other commodities.   If
my whiskey illustration isn't satisfactory, I will change it.   If
whiskey were the only alcoholic drink allowed to be used as a
beverage, it would command a higher price than it commands
now.   I should then tell Mr. Fisher that the value of whiskey
was artificial and that free rum would reduce it to its normal
point.   If he should then ask me what the normal point was,
I should answer that I had no means of knowing.   If he should
respond that the fall in whiskey resulting from free rum " would
be limited to such relinquishment of profit as would be forced
upon the dealers by competition," I should acquiesce with the
remark that the distance from London to Liverpool is equal
to the distance from Liverpool to London.

(11) It is Mr. Fisher's analogy, not mine, that is false and
inapplicable.   The proper analogy is not between gold and
the commodities carried, but between gold and the vehicle in
which they are carried.   The cargo of peaches that rots on its
way from California to New England may not be economically
consumed (though for my life I can't see why such consumption isn't as economic as the tipping of silver into the Atlantic
by the United States government, which Mr. Fisher considers
purely economic), but at any rate the wear of the car that
carries the cargo is an instance of economic consumption.
Now the gold that goes to California to pay for those peaches
and comes back to New England to pay for cotton cloth, and
thus goes back and forth as constantly as the railway car and

facilitates exchange equally with the railway car and wears
out in the process just as the railway car wears out, is in my
judgment consumed precisely as the railway car is consumed.
That only is a complete product, Mr. Fisher tells us, which is
in the hands of a person who applies it to the direct gratification of some personal craving. I suppose Mr. Fisher will not
deny that a railway car is a complete product. But if it can
be said to be in the hands of a person who applies it to the
direct gratification of some personal craving, then the same
can be said of gold.

(12) I did not mean to say for a moment that a government
could carry out such an arbitrary policy of fixing values to an
unlimited extent without a revolution, but only that as far as
the attempt should be made, the economic result, pending the
revolution, would be as stated.

(13) Yes, to a trifling extent. And if the horse were then
to be used to buy a sheep, and then to buy a dog, and then to
buy a cat, and then to buy a cigar, until finally he could not
be sold for enough oats to keep him from falling in his tracks,
it is my firm conviction that the horse in that case would be
economically consumed in fulfilling the function of currency.

A FALSE IDEA OF FREEDOM.

[*Liberty*, February 26, 1887.]

I MUST refer once more to the Winsted *Press* and its
editor. It is lamentable to see so bright a man as Mr. Pinney
wasting his nervous force in assaults on windmills. But it is
his habit, whenever he finds it necessary or thinks it timely to
say something in answer to free-money advocates, to set up a
windmill, label it free money, and attack that. An instance
of this occurs in a scolding article on the subject in his issue
of February 17, as the following sentence shows : "We had a
little taste of this *free* currency in the days of *State* wildcat
banking, when every little community had its *State* bank
issues." The italics are mine,—used to emphasize the substitution of the windmill State for the giant Freedom. How
could State bank issues be free money ? Monopoly is monopoly, whether granted by the United States or by a single
State, and the old State banking system was a thoroughly
monopolistic system. The unfairness and absurdity of Mr.
Pinney's remark become apparent with the reflection that the

principal English work relied upon by the friends of free money, Colonel Greene's "Mutual Banking," was written expressly in opposition to the then existing State banking system, years before the adoption of the national banking system. Mr. Pinney would not fall back upon this idiotic argument if he had a better one. That he has none is indicated by his saying of free money, as he says of free trade : " In theory the scheme is plausible. In practice it would probably be an abomination." Mr. Pinney's old conservative, cowardly, Calvinistic refuge ! When driven into a corner on a question which turns on the principle of Liberty, he has but one resort, which amounts practically to this : " Liberty is right in theory everywhere and always, but in certain cases it is not practical. In all cases where I want men to have it, it is practical ; but in those cases where I do not want men to have it, it is not practical." What Mr. Pinney wants and does not want depends upon mental habits and opinions acquired prior to that theoretical assent to the principle of liberty which the arguments of the Anarchists have wrung from him.

MONOPOLY, COMMUNISM, AND LIBERTY.

[*Liberty*, March 26, 1887.]

PINNEY of the Winsted *Press* grows worse and worse. It will be remembered that, in attacking the free-money theory, he said we had a taste of it in the day of State wildcat banking, when every little community had its State bank issues ; to which I made this answer : " How could State bank issues be free money ? Monopoly is monopoly, whether granted by the United States or by a single State, and the old State banking system was a thoroughly monopolistic system." This language clearly showed that the free-money objection to the old State banks as well as to the present national banks is not founded on any mistaken idea that in either case the government actually issues the money, but that in both cases alike the money is issued by a monopoly granted by the government. But Pinney, not daring to meet this, affects to ignore the real meaning of my words by assuming to interpret them as follows (thus giving new proof of my assertion that he wastes his strength in attacking windmills):

It is apparently Mr. Tucker's notion that State banks were an institution of the State. They were no more a government institution than

is a railroad company that receives its charters from the State and con-
ducts its business as a private corporation under State laws. . . . For
purposes of illustration, they answer well, and Mr. Tucker's effort to
lessen the force of the illustration by answering that they were institutions of the State, because they are called for convenience *State* banks, is
very near a resort to wilful falsehood.

What refreshing audacity ! Pinney knows perfectly well
that the advocates of free money are opposed to the national
banks as a monopoly enjoying a privilege granted by the gov
ernment ; yet these, like the old State banks, are no more a
government institution than such a railroad company as he
describes. Both national and State banks are law-created
and law-protected monopolies, and therefore not free. Anybody, it is true, could establish a State bank, and can establish a national bank, who can observe the prescribed conditions. *But the monopoly inheres in these compulsory conditions.*
The fact that national bank-notes can be issued only by those
who have government bonds and that State bank-notes could
be issued only by those who had specie makes both vitally and
equally objectionable from the standpoint of free and mutual
banking, the chief aim of which is to secure the right of all
wealth to monetization without prior conversion into some particular form of wealth limited in amount and without being
subjected to ruinous discounts. If Mr. Pinney does not know
this, he is not competent to discuss finance ; if he does know
it, it was a quibble and " very near a resort to wilful falsehood " for him to identify the old State banking system with
free banking.

But he has another objection to free money,—that it would
enable the man who has capital to monetize it, and so double
his advantages over the laborer who has none. Therefore he
would have the general government, which he calls the whole
people, " monetize their combined wealth and use it in the
form of currency, while at the same time the wealth remains
in its owner's hands for business purposes." This is Mr.
Pinney's polite and covert way of saying that he would have
those without property confiscate the goods of those who
have property. For no governmental mask, no fiction of the
" whole people," can disguise the plain fact that to compel
one man to put his property under pawn to secure money issued
by or to another man who has no property is robbery and
nothing else. Though you leave the property in the owner's
hands, there is a " grab " mortgage upon it in the hands of the
government, which can foreclose when it sees fit. Mr. Pinney
is on the rankest Communistic ground, and ought to declare
himself a State Socialist at once.

Certainly no one wishes more heartily than I that every industrious man was the owner of capital, and it is precisely to secure this result that I desire free money. I thought Mr. Pinney was a good enough Greenbacker to know (for the Greenbackers know some valuable truths, despite their fiat-money delusion) that the economic benefits of an abundance of good money in circulation are shared by all, and not reaped exclusively by the issuers. He has often clearly shown that the effect of such abundance is to raise the laborer's wages to an equivalence to his product, after which every laborer who wishes to possess capital will be able to accumulate it by his work. All that is wanted is a means of issuing such an abundance of money free of usury. Now, if they only had the liberty to do so, there are already enough large and small property-holders willing and anxious to issue money, to provide a far greater amount than is needed, and there would be sufficient competition among them to bring the price of issue down to cost,—that is, to abolish interest. Liberty avoids both forms of robbery,—monopoly on the one side and Communism on the other,—and secures all the beneficent results that are (falsely) claimed for either.

PINNEY HIS OWN PROCRUSTES.
[Liberty, April 23, 1887.]

HAVING exhausted the resources of sophistry, and unable longer to dodge the inexorable and Procrustean logic of Pinney the anti-Prohibitionist, Pinney the Protectionist has subsided, and is now playing possum in the Procrustean bed in which Pinney the anti-Prohibitionist has laid him. But Pinney the Greenbacker evidently hopes still, by some fortunate twist or double, to find an avenue of escape yet open, and thus avoid the necessity of doing the possum act twice. Accordingly, in his Winsted *Press* of April 7, he makes several frantic dashes into the dark, the first of which is as follows :

Our first objection to free money was that the great variety of issues, coupled with a questionable security, would limit circulation to local circuits and subject the bill-holder to harassing uncertainty as to the value of currency in his possession and to constant risk of loss. To illustrate this defect we mentioned the experience of the people with the old State bank bills, which experience, disastrous as it was, did not offer a fair parallel, simply and solely because it was not disastrous enough, the banks being limited and regulated in a measure by State laws and machinery to enforce contracts. Our Boston Procrustes thereupon plunged straight into trouble by denying the similitude, because forsooth the old banks were incorporated institutions not perfectly free to cheat their creditors, forgetting that, in so far as they differed from free banks, the difference in point of security, scope of credit, etc., was in our favor.

That is one way of putting it. Here is another. Free money advocates hold that security is one (*only* one) essential of good money, and that competition is sure to provide this essential, competition being simply natural selection or the survival of the fittest, and the fittest necessarily possessing the quality of security. But they have never held that it was impossible for monopoly to furnish a temporaily secure money. It may or may not do so, according to the prescribed conditions of its existence. Pending the universal bankruptcy and revolution to which it inevitably will lead if allowed to live long enough, the national bank monopoly furnishes a money tolerably well secured. But the old State bank monopoly furnished a money far inferior in point of security, not because it was a freer system,—for it was not,—not because the conditions of its existence were less artificially and compulsorily prescribed, —for they were not,—but because the conditions thus prescribed were less in accordance with wise business principles and administration. The element of competition, or natural selection, upon which the free money advocates rely for the supply of a money that combines security with all other necessary qualities, was just as much lacking from the old State bank system as it is from the present national bank system. Therefore, to say of the State banks that, " in so far as they differed from free banks, the difference in point of security, scope of credit, etc., was in their favor " is to beg the question entirely ; and accordingly, when Mr. Pinney, as sole proof of an assertion that free money would be unsafe money, offered the insecurity of the old State bank bills, I informed him that there was not the slightest pertinence in his illustration, whereby I plunged, not myself, but Mr. Pinney into trouble.

To get out of it he performs a double which eclipses all his previous evolutions. Finding that he must deal in some way with my statement that the monopoly of money inheres in the compulsory conditions of its issue, chief among which are the government bond basis in the national bank system and the specie basis in the old State bank system, he asks :

How then about your free banking? Are there not any "compulsory conditions?" Free bank notes can be issued only by those who have government bonds, or specie, or property of some sort, we suppose, so there are your "compulsory conditions," enforced by the business law of self-preservation (for State law is not to be mentioned in Anarchist ears), and " the monopoly inheres in these compulsory conditions." Behold, then, the new monopoly of those who have property !

To this absurdity there are two answers.   In the first place, it is not true that under a free banking system " notes can be issued only by those who have property of some sort."   They can be issued and offered in the market by anybody who desires.   To be sure, none will be taken except those issued by persons having either property or credit.   But there is no monopoly of issue or the right to issue, no denial of liberty. If Mr. Pinney should claim that this answer amounts to nothing because issue is valueless without circulation, I shall then remind him of my previous statement that the circulation of an abundance of cheap and sound money benefits those who use it no less than those who issue it, and tends to raise the laborer's wages to a level with his product,—a point which he carefully avoids in his last article, because he knows that he cannot dispute it, having frequently maintained the same thing himself.

But, in the second place, Mr. Pinney's argument that the possession of property is a necessary condition of the issue and circulation of money, and that therefore free money is as much a compulsory monopoly as that of the government which prescribes the possession of a certain kind of property as a condition of even the issue of money, is precisely on a par with—in fact, is a glaring instance of—the reasoning resorted to by those friends of despotism who deny political and social liberty on the ground of philosophical necessity. The moment any person, in the name of human freedom, claims the right to do anything which another person does not want him to do, you will hear the second person cry : " Freedom ! Impossible ! There's no such thing.   None of us are free.   Are we not all governed by circumstances, by our surroundings, by motives beyond our control ?   Bow, then, to the powers that be ! "   Boiled down, the argument of these people and of Mr. Pinney is this : " No one can do as he pleases.   Therefore you must do as we please."   It needs only to be stated in this bald form to be immediately rejected. Hence I shall attempt no further refutation of it.   Mr. Pinney will please bear in mind hereafter that, when I use the word monopoly, I refer not to such monopolies as result from nat- ural evolution independent of government, but to monopolies imposed by arbitrary human power.   He knew it very well before, but he must dodge, and this was the only dodge left. Let the reader note here, however, how his double undid him. He says that under free banking the condition of a secure basis for money would be "enforced by the business law of self-preservation," exactly the opposite of his original charge that free money would be unsafe.

But he is not yet done with this twaddle about "compulsory conditions." Read again :

Mr. Tucker cannot see that there is any difference in principle between a law which absolutely prohibits the sale of an article, and a law which taxes the seller of that article. The tax is a "compulsory condition" which prohibits till it is complied with. The possession of property is another compulsory condition which prohibits free banking till it is complied with. Therefore there is no difference between absolute prohibition of free banking and the monopolistic condition that practically prohibits a man from being a free banker unless he can put up the security.

Utter confusion again ! Mr. Pinney seems unable to distinguish between disabilities created by human meddlesomeness and those that are not. The law which prohibits a sale and the law which taxes the seller both belong to the former class ; the lack of property belongs to the latter, or rather, it belongs to the latter when conditions are normal. It is true that the lack of property which at present prevails arises in most cases out of this very denial of free banking, but I cannot believe that even Mr. Pinney would cap the climax of his absurdity by assigning as a reason for the further denial of free banking a condition of affairs which has grown out of its denial in the past. The number of people who now own property, and the amount of property which they own, are sufficient to insure us an abundance of money as soon as soon as its issue shall be allowed, and from the time this issue begins the total amount of property and the number of property-owners will steadily increase.

To my objection to his government money monopoly that it would be Communistic robbery to mortgage all the wealth of the nation to secure all the money of the nation, Mr. Pinney can only make answer that the possibility that the government would foreclose the mortgage—that is, increase taxation— would be very remote. As if any possibility could be considered remote which is within the power and for the interest of lawmakers to achieve, and as if it were not the end and aim of government to tax the people all that it possibly can !

TEN QUESTIONS BRIEFLY ANSWERED.

[*Liberty*, May 16, 1891.]

Liberty is asked by the Mutual Bank Propaganda of Chicago to answer the following questions, and takes pleasure in complying with the request.

" 1. Does the prohibitory tax of ten per cent. imposed by Congress on any issue of paper money other than is issued by the U. S. Treasury limit the volume of money? If not, why not?

Yes.

" 2. Whence did the State originally derive the ' right' to dictate what the people should use as money?"

From its power.

" 3. If an association or community voluntarily agree to use a certain money of their own device to facilitate the exchange of products and avoid high rates of interest, has the State the right to prohibit such voluntary association for mutual advantage?"

Only the right of might.

" 4. Do not restrictions as to what shall be used as money interfere with personal liberty?"

Yes.

" 5. Has the question of free trade in banking—*i.e.*, the absence of all interference on the part of the State with making and supplying money—ever been a matter of public discussion?"

Yes.

" 6. What effect does the volume of money have upon the rate of interest?"

I suppose the intention is to ask what effect changes in the volume of money have upon the rate of interest. Not necessarily any; but any arbitrary limitation of the volume of money that tends to keep it below the demand also tends to raise the rate of interest.

" 7. Can the business of banking and the supply of money be said to be under the operation of supply and demand where the State prohibits or restricts its issue, or dictates what shall be used as money?"

Inasmuch as they often *are* said to be so, they evidently *can be* said to be so, but whoever says them to be so lies.

" 8. Is there such a thing as a measure or standard of value? If so, how is it constituted, and what is its function?"

There is such a thing as a measure or standard of value whenever we use anything as such. It is constituted such either by force or by agreement. Its function is implied in its name—measure of value. Without the selection, deliberate or accidental, conscious or unconscious, of something as a standard of value, money is not only impossible, but unthinkable.

" 9. What becomes of the 'standard' or 'measure' of value during suspensions of specie payment?"

Nothing. It remains what it was before. Certain parties have refused to pay their debts ; that's all.

" 10. Are you in favor of tree trade in banking, including the issue of paper money? If not, why not?"

Yes.

A STANDARD OF VALUE A NECESSITY.

[*Liberty*, June 13, 1891.]

READERS of *Liberty* will remember an article in No. 184 on " The Functions of Money," reprinted from the Galveston *News*. In a letter to the *News* I commented upon this article as follows:

I entirely sympathize with your disposal of the *Evening Post's* attempt to belittle the function of money as a medium of exchange ; but do you go far enough when you content yourself with saying that a standard of value is highly desirable? Is it not absolutely necessary? Is money posible without it? If no standard is definitely adopted, and then if paper money is issued, does not the first commodity that the first note is exchanged for immediately become a standard of value? Is not the second holder of the note governed in making his next purchase by what he parted with in his previous sale? Of course it is a very poor standard that is thus arrived at, and one that must come in conflict with other standards adopted in the same indefinite way by other exchanges occurring independently but almost simultaneously with the first one above supposed. But so do gold and silver come in conflict now. Doesn't it all show that the idea of a standard is inseparable from money? Moreover, there is no danger in a standard. The whole trouble disappears with the abolition of the basis privilege.

The *News* printed my letter, and made the following rejoinder:

It will occur that in emphasizing one argument there is such need of passing others by with seeming unconcern that to some minds other truths seem slighted,—truths which also need emphasizing perhaps in an equal, or it may be, for useful practical reasons, in a superior degree.

The *News* aims at illustrating one thing at a time, but it is both recep-
tive and grateful to those correspondents who intelligently extend its
work and indicate useful subjects for discussion, giving their best thought
thereon.   A Boston reader, speaking of the standard of value, states an
undeniable truth to the effect that without a thing or things of value to
which paper money can be referred and which can ultimately be got for
it, such money would be untrustworthy or worthless.   The *News* in
a past article was discussing primary commerce and the transition to
indirect exchange.   No agreed standard for valuation is needed while
mere barter is the rule ; but it is indispensable as soon as circulating
notes are issued.   The vice of the greenback theory is that the notes do
not call for anything in particular, and so, if their volume be doubled,
their purchasing power must apparently decline one-half.   A note properly based on gold, silver, wheat, cotton, or other commodity has a
tangible security behind it.   The one thing may be better than the
other, but the principle is there in all.   It is, however, a notable truth
that the standard for valuation can be nothing better than an empirical
one.   Like mathematical quantities, value has no independent existence,
but, unlike mathematical quantities, value has not even existence as a
quality of one object.   It cannot be compared to a measure of length,
which posesses the quality of extension in itself.   Gold is assumed to
vary little in relation to other things, and they to vary much in relation
to gold.   Nobody can know how much gold does vary in the relation.
The notable steadiness is in the amount of labor which will produce a
given quantity and the length of time which it will last.   The basis of the
assumed steadiness of gold is thus found.   But if the standard for use in
making valuations be confessedly empirical and value an elusive quality
not of things separately, but of things in relation, there is a countervailing difference between a standard of length and a standard of value,
which results in disposing of the objection that the standard is empirical.
Why would it be a serious objection to a yardstick if it were longer or
shorter from day to day ?   Because thus the customer would get more or
less cloth than was intended.   But why is that ?   Because the function
of the yardstick is to measure for delivery as great a length of cloth as
its own length.   But now let us visit a bank or insurance office.   We
want a loan of circulating notes or a policy of insurance.   The property
offered as security is valued.   Assume that gold is taken as the standard,
and that the loan or the policy is for $600 on a valuation of $1000.   It
is no matter in these cases if the standard varies, provided it does not
vary to exceed the margin between the valuation and the obligation.   The
property pledged is merely security for the loan, or, in the case of insurance, the premium paid is a per cent. of the amount insured.   The
margin between the valuation and the loan is established to make the loan
abundantly safe.   The policy is safely written through the same expedient.   The empirical standard of value has a needful compensation about
it which the yardstick or other measure neither has nor needs,—*viz.*, the
valuing goods does not deliver them.   It is provisional.   In case of
default in paying back the loan, the goods are sold and the same money
borrowed is paid back, but the residue goes to the borrower.   It is therefore an efficient compensation for the lack of an invariable standard of
value that the actual standard in any case is simply used as a means of
estimating limits within which loans are safe.   All danger is avoided by
giving the borrower the familiar right in case of foreclosure.   It is sometimes a fine thing to discover distinctions, but it is a frequently a finer
thing to discover whether or not the distinctions affect the question.

While not hesitating for a moment to accept the *News's* explanation that, when hinting that a standard of value is not indispensable, it was speaking of barter only, I may point out nevertheless that there was a slip of the pen, and that the words actually used conveyed the idea that something more than barter was in view. Let me quote from the original article :

It is manifest that a medium of exchange is absolutely necessary to all trade beyond barter. A standard of value is highly desirable, but perhaps this is as much as can be safely asserted on that question.

It seems to me a fair interpretation of this language to claim the meaning that in *trade beyond barter* it is not sure that a standard of value is absolutely necessary. And this interpretation receives additional justification when it is remembered that the words were used in answer to the *Evening Post's* contention that, in comparing the two functions of *money*, its office of medium of exchange must be held inferior to its office of measuring values.

However, the *News* now makes it sufficiently clear that a standard of value is absolutely essential to money, thereby taking common ground with me against the position of Comrade Westrup. Still I cannot quite agree to all that it says in comment upon the Westrup view.

First, I question its admission that a measure of value differs from a measure of length in that the former is empirical. True, value is a relation ; but then, what is extension ? Is not that a relation also,—the relation of an object to space? If so, then the yardstick does not possess the quality of extension in itself, being as dependent for it upon space as gold is dependent for its value upon other commodities. But this is metaphysical and may lead us far ; therefore I do not insist, and pass on to a more important consideration.

Second, I question whether the *News's* "countervailing difference between a standard of length and a standard of value" establishes all that it claims. In the supposed case of a bank loan secured by mortgage, the margin between the valuation and the obligation practically secures the noteholder against loss from a decline in the value of the security, but it does not secure him against loss from a decline in the value of the standard, or make it impossible for him to profit by a rise in the value of the standard. Suppose that a farmer, having a farm worth $5000 in gold, mortgages it to a bank as security for a loan of $2500 in notes newly issued by the bank against this farm. With these notes he purchases implements from a manufacturer. When the mortgage expires a year later, the borrower fails to to lift it. Meanwhile gold has declined in value. The farm is sold under the hammer, and brings, instead of $5000 in gold, $6000 in gold. Of this sum $2500 is used to meet the notes held by the manufacturer who took them a year before in payment for the implements sold to the farmer. Now, can the manufacturer buy back his implements with $2500 in gold? Manifestly not, for by the hypothesis gold has gone down. Why, then, is not this manufacturer a sufferer from the variation in the standard of value, precisely as the man who buys cloth with a short yard-stick and sells it with a long one is a sufferer from the variation in the standard of length? The claim that a standard of value varies, and inflicts damage by its variations, is perfectly sound; but the same is true, not only of the standard of value, but of every valuable commodity as well. Even if there were no standard of value and therefore no money, still nothing could prevent a partial failure of the wheat crop from enhancing the value of every bushel of wheat. Such evils, so far as they arise from natural causes, are in the nature of inevitable disasters and must be borne. But they are of no force whatever as an argument against the adoption of a standard of value. If every yardstick in existence, instead of constantly remaining thirty-six inches long, were to vary from day to day within the limits of thirty-five and thirty-seven inches, we should still be better off than with no yardstick at all. But it would be no more foolish to abolish the yardstick because of such a defect than it would be to abolish the standard of value, and therefore money, simply because no commodity can be found for a standard which is not subject to the law of supply and demand.

A NECESSITY OR A DELUSION,—WHICH?

[*Liberty*, June 27, 1891.]

To the Editor of Liberty :

It is not only a delusion, but a misuse of language, to talk of a "standard of value." Give us a standard of pain or pleasure, and you may convince us that there can be a "standard of value." I am well aware of the difficulty of discussing this question, even with so precise an editor as Mr. Tucker ; but since he has called in question the views presented in my pamphlet, I feel called upon to lay before the readers of *Liberty* some additional arguments to show the correctness of what Mr. Tucker has honored me by calling "the Westrup view."

Let us consider for a moment the practical workings of a Mutual Bank, as near as we can foretell them.

The incentive to organize a Mutual Bank is the opportunity of borrowing money at a very low rate of interest and no additional expense. This desideratum is not confined to a few individuals, but is well-nigh universal. It follows, therefore, that the starting of a bank will draw to it a large number of people, embracing producers and dealers in almost, perhaps all, commodities. One of the conditions in obtaining the notes (paper money) of the Mutual Bank is that they will be taken in lieu of current money without variation in the price of the commodities by those who borrow them. This condition is just, and will be readily acquiesced in without a murmur. At the very outset of the Mutual Bank, then, we have at least dealers in most of the ordinary commodities who will accept its money in place of current money. This certainty of its redemption in commodities at their market-price in current money guarantees its circulation.

Strictly speaking, the Mutual Bank does not issue the money ; it simply furnishes it and is the custodian of the collateral pledged to insure its return. It is the borrowers who both issue and redeem.

The transaction between the bank and the borrower is of no interest to the public previous to the *issue* of any of the money by the borrower. Neither is it concerned with the transaction between the borrower and the bank after the former has *redeemed* all the money he borrowed.

Discussing theories is far less important than efforts to put in practice such momentous reforms as the application of the mutual feature to the supply of the medium of exchange. If Comrade Tucker really desires the establishment of Mutual Banks, it seems to me he would naturally discuss the practicability of such institutions. Let him point out wherein the above forecast is unsound. Let him show the necessity for a "standard of value " and suggest how to introduce one ; perhaps I may become converted. I shall most surely acknowledge my error if I am convinced, but I have no time or inclination to discuss any abstract theory about a "standard of value." The one question that seems to me of importance is the practicability of the Mutual Bank. If it is not practicable, why is it not so ? If it is, why waste time and space in discussing whether the first or the second or any other commodity exchanged becomes the "measure or standard of value "; especially as "the whole trouble disappears with the abolition of the basis privilege."

ALFRED B. WESTRUP.

Mr. Westrup's article sustains in the clearest manner my contention that money is impossible without a standard of value. Starting out to show that such a standard is a delusion, he does not succeed in writing four sentences descriptive of his proposed bank before he adopts that "delusion." He tells us that " one of the conditions in obtaining the notes (paper money) of the Mutual Bank is that they will be taken *in lieu of current money.*" What does this mean ? Why, simply that the patrons of the bank agree to take its notes as the equivalent of gold coin of the same face value. In other words, they agree to adopt gold as a standard of value. They will part with as much property in return for the notes as they would part with in return for gold. And if there were no such standard, the notes would not pass at all, because nobody would have any idea of the amount of property that he ought to exchange for them. The *naïveté* with which Mr. Westrup gives away his case shows triumphantly the puerility of his raillery at the idea of a standard of value.

Indeed, Comrade Westrup, I ask nothing better than to discuss the practicability of mutual banks. All the work that I have been doing for liberty these nineteen years has been directed steadily to the establishment of the conditions that alone will make them practicable. I have no occasion to show the necessity for a standard of value. Such necessity is already recognized by the people whom we are trying to convince of the truth of mutual banking. It is for you, who deny this necessity, to give your reasons. And in the very moment in which you undertake to tell us why you deny it, you admit it without knowing it. It would never have occurred to me to discuss the abstract theory of a standard of value. I regard it as too well settled. But when you, one of the most conspicuous and faithful apostles of mutual banking, begin to bring the theory into discredit and ridicule by basing your arguments in its favor on a childish attack against one of the simplest of financial truths, I am as much bound to repudiate your heresy as an engineer would be to disavow the calculations of a man who should begin an attempt to solve a difficult problem in engineering by denying the multiplication table.

I fully recognize Mr. Westrup's faithful work for freedom in finance and the ability with which he often defends it. In fact, it is my appreciation of him that has prevented me from criticising his error earlier. I did not wish to throw any obstacle in the path or in any way dampen the enthusiasm of this ardent propagandist. But when I see that admirable paper, *Egoism*, of San Francisco, putting forward those writings of Mr. Westrup which contain the objectionable heresy ;* and when I see that other admirable paper, *The Herald of Anarchy*, of London, led by his or similar ideas to advocate the issue of paper bearing on its face the natural prices of all commodities (!); and when I see Individualists holding Anarchism responsible for these absurdities and on the strength of them making effective attacks upon a financial theory which, when properly defended, is invulnerable,—it seems high time to declare that the free and mutual banking advocated by Proudhon, Greene, and Spooner never contemplated for a

---

* *Egoism* later saw its error, and recognized the necessity of a standard of value.

moment the desirability or the possibility of dispensing with a standard of value. If others think that a standard of value is a delusion, let them say so by all means; but let them not say so in the name of the financial theories and projects which the original advocates of mutual banking gave to the world.

ANARCHY'S NEW ALLY.

[*Liberty*, June 18, 1892.]

NATURAL science and technical skill, which have revolutionized so many things, may yet revolutionize political economy, and in a way little dreamed of. It has long been known that the water of the ocean contains gold and silver. The percentage of these metals, however, is so very small that at first thought it hardly seems worth noticing. And as a matter of fact little notice has been taken of it, but principally for the reason that the extraction of the metals by any advantageous method has been deemed an impossibility. Now comes the Fairy Electricity, whose wand has already achieved so many wonders, and promises us a new miracle, which, though possibly less strange in itself than some others, will be more far-reaching in its results than all the telegraphs and telephones and railways imaginable. She proposes, by stretching long series of iron plates across channels and through various parts of the seas and ocean and running an electric current though them, to precipitate the gold and silver from the water upon these plates. It is estimated that one-half of one horse power is all that is needed for the purpose, and that it will consequently be possible to get gold in this way at a cost equal to but one per cent. of its present value.

But where does the revolution in political economy come in ? some one may ask. Does the connection seem remote to you, my thoughtless friend ? Then think a bit and listen. Every ton of sea-water contains half a grain of gold and a grain and a half of silver. Has that an insignificant sound ? If so, let us appeal to mathematics. We shall find that, at the rate of half a grain of gold and a grain and a half of silver to each ton of sea-water, the entire seas and oceans of the world (I take the figures from a scientific journal) contain 21,595 *billion tons* of gold and 64,785 *billion tons* of silver. As good fish in the sea as ever were caught ? I should say so, and much better ! Why, this means, to speak at a venture, that there is *several billion times* as much gold in the water as has been extracted from the land up to date. Now, if this gold can be taken from the water, as is claimed, at the rate of a dollar's worth for a cent, soon it will be scarcely worth its weight in good rag-paper. The much defamed "rag baby" will be a very aristocratic personage beside it. In that case what will become of "the metal appointed by God in his goodness to serve as the currency of the world"? Would it be possible to more thoroughly revolutionize political economy than by dethroning gold? And could gold be more effectually dethroned than by reducing its value to insignificance? Its monetary privilege would disappear instantly and of necessity, and the era of free money would dawn, with all the tremendous blessings, physical, mental, and moral, that must follow in its wake. As Proudhon well says: "The demonetization of gold, the last idol of the Absolute, will be the greatest act of the revolution of the future."

All hail, then, Electricity! On with your magnificent work! Lend a hand, you believers in dynamite; we offer you a better saviour! This good fairy is carrying on a "propaganda by deed" that discounts all your Ravachols. Success to her! May she force gold, the last bulwark of Archism, to become, through offering itself for sacrifice on the altar of Liberty, the greatest of Anarchists, the final emancipator of the race!

Money, said Adam Smith, in one of those flashes of his intellectual genius which have so illuminated man's economic path, money is "a wagon-way through the air." If Electricity shall make of this wagon-way a railway, it will be the most signal, the most useful of her exploits.

ECONOMIC SUPERSTITION.

[*Liberty*, August 13, 1892.]

APROPOS of my editorial of a few weeks ago, forecasting the probable increase in the supply of gold through its extraction from the ocean and the consequences thereof, Comrade Koopman writes me : "If this is so, every craft that sails the ocean blue will carry an electrical centre-board to rake in the gold as it sails along. I am afraid, though, that the governments will betake themselves to platinum (I believe Russia tried it once) or some other figment, and so postpone their day of reckoning. But what a shaking-up a gold deluge will give them if it come! I hope we may be there to see." If the present adherence to gold were anything but a religion, there would be some ground for Comrade Koopman's fears. But, so far as the people is concerned, it is only a religion. To uproot the idea that gold is divinely appointed to serve as the money of the world is to destroy the godhead. In vain, after that, will the priests of plutocracy propose a change of deities. The people will say to them : "If you lied when you told us that gold was God, you are lying now when you place platinum on the celestial throne. No more idolatry for us ! Henceforth all property shall stand on an equality before the Bank. In demonetizing gold we monetize all wealth." The Anarchists are fighting the old, old battle,—the battle of reason against superstition. In the earlier phases of this battle, science, after a time, re-enforced the philosophers and gave the finishing stroke in the demolition of the theological god. Perhaps it is reserved for science to similarly re-enforce the Anarchists in their task of smashing the last of the idols. Of this, however, I am not as hopeful as I was. A fact has lately come to light that fills me with misgiving. No sooner is it proposed to begin the extraction of gold and silver from the ocean by the new and cheap method than a man pops up in England to say that he patented this method a year or two ago. If his patent is valid (and I see nothing to the contrary), this man is virtual owner of the entire 21 billion tons of gold and 64 billion tons of silver which the ocean contains. All the priests and bishops and archbishops and cardinals of finance must kneel to him as Pope. "Nearest, my God, to Thee," will be his hymn henceforth, or rather till some luckier individual shall discover a still cheaper way of securing the ocean's treasures and thereby become Pope in his stead. This one perfectly logical and appalling possibility ought to be sufficient in itself to sweep away as so much cobweb all the sophistry that has ever been devised in support of property in ideas. Gold, after all, is not the last of the idols ; in mental property it has a twin. And my remaining hope is that science, with its new discovery, may do double duty as an iconoclast, and destroy them both at one fell stroke.

A BOOK THAT IS NOT MILK FOR BABES.

[*Liberty*, November 23, 1889.]

THE most important book that has been published this year comes to *Liberty* from the press of the J. B. Lippincott Company, of Philadelphia. It is a little volume of something over a hundred very small pages, printed from very large type. For ten years to come it probably will be read by one person where "Looking Backward" is read by a thousand, but the economic teaching which it contains will do more in the long run to settle the labor question than will ever be done by "Looking Backward," "Progress and Poverty," and "The Co-operative Commonwealth" combined. Its title is "Involuntary Idleness: An Exposition of the Cause of the Discrepancy Existing between the Supply of, and the Demand for, Labor and Its Products." The book consists of a paper read at the meeting of the American Economic Association in Philadelphia on December 29, 1888, by Hugo Bilgram, the author of that admirable little pamphlet, "The Iron Law of Wages," with which most readers of *Liberty* are familiar. I am strongly inclined to hail Mr. Bilgram's new work as the best treatise on money and the relation of money to labor that has been written in the English language since Colonel William B. Greene published his "Mutual Banking."

The author prefaces his essay with a very convenient and carefully prepared skeleton of his argument, which I reproduce here, since it gives a much better idea of the book than any condensation that I might attempt:

The aim of the treatise is to search for the cause of the lack of employment, which is obviously due to the observed fact that the supply of commodities and services exceeds the demand, although reason dictates that supply and demand in general should be precisely equal. The factor destroying this natural equation is looked for among the conditions that regulate the distribution of wealth,—*i.e.*, its division into Rent, Interest, and Wages.

The arguments evolved by the discussion of the Rent question, which of late has excited much public interest, being unable to account for the apparent surfeit of all kinds of raw materials, the topic of rent is eliminated by assuming all local advantages to be equal.

At first an examination is made of the relation of capital to the productivity of labor, and that of interest on capital to the remuneration for labor, showing that high interest tends to reduce the productivity of, as well as the remuneration for, labor. Low wages being also concomitant with a scarcity of employment, it is inferred that a close relation exists between the economic cause of involuntary idleness and the law of interest.

Following this clue, the two separate meanings of the ambiguous word " Capital " are compared, showing that money, which can never be used in the act of production, cannot be capital when that term is used in its *concrete* sense ; and since capital is capable of producing a profit only when the same is used productively, the fact that interest is paid for money-loans, when that which is loaned cannot be used productively, must be traced to an independent cause. The usual argument that with money actual capital can be purchased is rejected, because money and capital would not be interchangeable if their economic properties were not homogeneous. This compels a search for a property inherent in money that can account for the willingness of borrowers to pay interest on money-loans.

It is then shown that interest on money-loans is paid because money affords special advantages as a medium of exchange, and the value of this property of money is traced to its ultimate utility, or, in other words, to the increment of productivity which the last addendum to the volume of money affords by facilitating the division of labor.

Returning to the question of interest on actual capital, —*i.e.*, the excess of value produced over the cost of production,—the question as to what determines the value of a product leads to the assertion that capital-profit must be due to an advantage which the producer possesses over the marginal producer. This is found to be due to the interest payable by the marginal producer on money-loans.

An ideal separation of the financial from the industrial world reveals a tendency of the industrial class to drift into bankruptcy by force of conditions over which they have no control. Those who are at the verge of bankruptcy being the marginal producers, others who are free of debt will reap a profit corresponding to the interest payable by the marginal producers on debts equal to the value of the capital they employ ; hence the rate of capital-profit will tend to become equal to the rate of interest payable on money-loans, and the power of money to command interest, instead of being the result, is in reality the cause of capital-profit.

The inability of the debtor class to meet their obligations increases the risk of business investments, and the accumulation of money in the hands of the financial class depriving the channels of commerce of the needed medium of exchange, a stagnation of business will ensue, which readily accounts for the accumulation of all kinds of products in the hands of the producers and for the consequent dearth of employment. The losses sustained by the lenders of money involve a separation of interest into two branches, risk-premium and interest proper, and considering that the risk-premiums equal the sum total of all relinquished debts, the law of interest is evolved by an analysis of the monetary circulation between the debtors and creditors.

This analysis leads to the inference that an expansion of the volume of money, by extending the issue of credit-money, will prevent business stagnation and involuntary idleness.

The objections usually urged against credit-money are considered and found untenable, the claim that interest naturally accrues to capital is disputed at each successive stand-point, and in the concluding remarks an explanation is given of the present excess of supply over the demand of commodities and service, confirming the conclusion that the correction of this abnormal state is contingent upon the financial measure suggested.

Admirably accurate as the foregoing is as an outline, it conveys only a faint idea of the beautifully calm, logical, and convincing way in which the argument is worked out and sus-

/

tained. It seems impossible that any unbiased mind should follow the author's reasoning carefully from the start to the finish and not accept the conclusion which he reaches in common with *Liberty*,—namely, that our financial legislation is the real seat of the prevailing social disorder, and that the only way to secure remunerative employment to all who are able and willing to work is to abolish the restrictions upon the issue of money.

Moreover, the author not only establishes the strength of his own position, but throws numerous and powerful sidelights upon the weaknesses of others. He shows the inadequacy of Henry George's theory as an explanation of enforced idleness, the futility of protection, tariff reform, factory acts, and anti-immigration laws as measures of relief from stagnation of commerce, and the absurdity of the fiat-money theorists and all who hold with them that the value of money is dependent upon its volume. If Mr. Lloyd, who lately proposed the use of communistic credit-money, will get Mr. Bilgram's book and carefully read pages 64–77 inclusive, I think he will be satisfied of the unsoundness of any credit-money system that does not specifically assure the ultimate redemption of each note by value pledged for its security.

Having thus declared my high appreciation of this book, I may add a word or two by way of criticism. The policy of the author in abandoning what he himself considers the true definition of the word *capital* and adopting the definition generally sanctioned by the economists is of very questionable utility. It is true that he does not allow this confessed misuse of a word to vitiate his argument, but it forces him nevertheless to separate capital from money ; and thereby he strengthens the hold of the delusion which is exploited so effectively by the champions of interest,—namely, that in an exchange of goods for money the man who parts with the goods is deprived of capital while the man who parts with the money is not. If Mr. Bilgram had used the word *capital* to mean what he thinks it means,—all wealth capable of bringing a revenue to its owner,—he would have deprived his opponents of their favorite device for confusing the popular mind.

But this is a question of words only. It involves no difference of idea between Mr. Bilgram and *Liberty*. On another point, however, there is *substantial* disagreement. When Mr. Bilgram proposes that the government shall carry on (and presumably monopolize, though this is not clearly stated) the business of issuing money, it is hardly necessary to say that

Liberty cannot follow him. It goes with him in his economy, but not in his politics. There are at least three valid reasons, and doubtless others also, why the government should do nothing of the kind.

First, the government is a tyrant living by theft, and therefore has no business to engage in any business.

Second, the government has none of the characteristics of a successful business man, being wasteful, careless, clumsy, and short-sighted in the extreme.

Third, the government is thoroughly irresponsible, having it in its power to effectively repudiate its obligations at any time.

With these qualificatious *Liberty* gives Mr. Bilgram's book enthusiastic welcome. Its high price, $1.00, will debar many from reading it ; but money cannot be expended more wisely than in learning the truth about money.

STATE BANKING VERSUS MUTUAL BANKING.

[*Liberty*, February 15, 1890.]

To the Editor of Liberty :

In view of the favorable criticism which "Involuntary Idleness" received at your hands, I gladly accept the invitation to state my reasons for advocating governmental management of the circulating medium, rather than free banking.

My studies have led me to the conviction that mutual banking cannot deprive capital of its power to bring unearned returns to its owner. Referring to my exposition of the monetary circulation between the financial and the industrial group, and the inevitable effects flowing from the power of money to bring a persistent revenue, it follows that a normal condition can only be attained if interest on money loans is reduced to the rate of risk, so that, in the aggregate, interest will just pay for the losses incurred by bad debts ; and this desideratum will not result from mutual banking.

The members of such banks must no doubt be in some way assessed to defray the expenses and losses incurred by the banking associations, and these assessments are virtually interest payable for the loan of mutual money. While these rates are lower than the current rates of the moneylenders, the mutual banks will be more and more patronized, which will have a depressing effect on the current rate of interest. But the increase of membership will cease as soon as the current rate has adapted itself to the rate payable to the mutual banks.

We must now assume that the assessments of the mutual banks are in substance equitably distributed among their members ; otherwise, such banks cannot compete against others who have adopted the more equitable rules. These assessments must obviously cover not only the expenses of the banks, but also occasional losses ; and that such losses should be assessed in proportion to the rate of risk attached to the security each "borrower" offers for the faithful redemption of his obligation requires here no explication.   But other outlays, such as the making of the notes, together with all the attending expenses, must also be paid by the members of the mutual banks, and this increases the interest virtually payable by the borrowers beyond the rate of risk.   Consequently competition will be incompetent to lower the current rate of interest to this desirable point.   Money-lenders will therefore still be able to obtain an income from the mere loan of money, and capital will continue to return interest to the wealthy.   The germ of the inequitable congestion of wealth will still linger after the introduction of mutual banking.

At this point the question arises as to who should pay for that part of the expenses of the financial system that relates to the production of the money tokens.   The answer is not difficult when it is considered that the benefit of the medium of exchange accrues to those who use it.   They should contribute, as near as possible, in the proportion in which their handling wears the tokens, for in the long run the cost of production will virtually resolve itself into the cost of replacement.   Not the borrowers, then, who as members of the mutual banks would be obliged to do so, but the people at large, in whose hands the money circulates, are in equity under the obligation of this expense.   And to accomplish this I see no other way than for the people to instruct their representatives to make the notes at public expense, distribute them according to the demand, and charge no cost to the borrowers exceeding the rate of risk attached to the securities offered by them.

I should of course never attempt to deny that mutual banking would be by far better than the present oppressive system.   But the question at issue is between mutual banking, which would not remove but only mitigate the source of involuntary idleness, and a system involving a complete eradication of the cause of the discrepancy of the supply and the demand of commodities.   My preference for the latter does, however, not imply that any restrictions should be placed upon mutual banking ; such institutions could for obvious reasons not compete against the government institution, and would fail to find a suitable soil for their growth.

Before concluding I also wish to meet the objection of the critic of "Involuntary Idleness" to the use of the word "Capital" in its concrete sense.   Having frequent occasion to refer to "labor products used for further production" in contradistinction to "money," I elected to use the shorter term "capital," especially as I had no need to refer, during the discussion, to its other and perhaps more appropriate meaning. I attempted to express thoughts, and made use of words as tools, the selection of which cannot commit me to any opinion.   In fact, I am convinced that "Capital" in contradistinction to "Wealth" must lose its significance in either of its concepts as soon as the people learn to make honest laws.

Yours truly,   HUGO BILGRAM.

PHILADELPHIA, January 18, 1890.

Mr. Bilgram, then, if I understand him, prefers government banking to mutual banking, because with the former the rate of discount would simply cover risk, all banking expenses being paid out of the public treasury, while with the latter the rate of discount would cover both risk and banking expenses, which in his opinion would place the burden of banking expenses upon the borrowers instead of upon the people. The answer to this is simple and decisive : the burden of discount, no matter what elements, many or few, may constitute it, falls *ultimately*, under any system, not on the borrowers, but on the people. Broadly speaking, all the interest paid is paid by the people. Under mutual banking the expenses of the banks would, it is true, be paid directly by the borrowers, but the latter would recover this from the people in the prices placed upon their products. And it seems to me much more scientific that the people should thus pay these expenses through the borrowers in the regular channels of exchange than that they should follow the communistic method of paying them through the public treasury.

Mr. Bilgram's statement that money-lenders who, besides being compensated for risk, are compensated for their labor as bankers and for their incidental expenses " thereby obtain an income from the mere loan of money " is incomprehensible to me. He might just as well say that under government banking the officials who should receive salaries from the treasury for carrying on the business would thereby obtain an income from the mere loan of money. Under a free system the banker is as simply and truly paid only the normal wage of his labor as is the official under a government system.

But, since Mr. Bilgram does not propose to place any restriction upon private banking, I have no quarrel with him. He is welcome to his opinion that private banking could not compete with the governmental institution. I stoutly maintain the contrary, and the very existence of the financial prohibitions is the best evidence that I am right. That which can succeed by intrinsic merit never seeks a legal bolster.

I am agreeably disappointed. In challenging Mr. Bilgram on this point, I, knowing his intellectual acumen, had braced myself to withstand the most vigorous onslaught possible against Anarchism in finance, but it was a needless strain. Mr. Bilgram has struck me with a feather.

MR. BILGRAM'S REJOINDER.

[*Liberty*, April 19, 1890.]

To the Editor of Liberty:

My rejoinder on your remarks on my last communication, in your issue of February 15, was unavoidably delayed.

Above all, I must admit an omission in my exposition, but, since it was on both sides of the question, the result remains unaffected. I had paid no attention to the labor involved in making loans. Including this admitted factor, my argument is this: The expenses of mutual banks may be divided into three categories,—*i.e.*, risks, cost of making loans, and cost of making the tokens. These three items are represented in the interest payable by the patrons of such banks, and, while they determine the current rate of interest, those who lend money which they have acquired have to bear only two of these items, and will obtain interest composed of the three, and consequently receive pay for work they have not performed. And capital having the power of bringing an unearned income as long as money is thus blessed, I still hold that justice is not attained until the gross interest is reduced to the rate of risk and cost of making loans, the cost of making the tokens being defrayed by public contributions.

It cannot be denied that "the burden of discount falls ultimately, not on the borrowers, but on the people"; the trouble is that the people are compelled to pay more than this discount, and my desire is that they should cease to pay this excess which now falls into the hands of the owners of capital.

Should the question of free banking become a political issue, I should heartily coöperate with you in furthering the object. But this does not prevent me from advocating a government issue, provided the borrowers are charged no more than risk and cost of making the loans, as a preferable measure. Yours truly,   HUGO BILGRAM.

PHILADELPHIA, March 31, 1890.

To the above there are at least two answers. The first is that that factor in the rate of interest which represents the cost of making tokens is so insignificant (probably less than one-tenth of one per cent., guessing at it) that the people could well afford (if there were no alternative) to let a few individuals profit to that extent rather than suffer the enormous evils that result from transferring enterprise from private to government control. I am not so enamored of *absolute* equality that I would sacrifice both hands rather than one finger.

The second answer is that no private money-lenders could, under a free system, reap even the small profit referred to. Mr. Bilgram speaks of "those who lend money which they have acquired." Acquired how? Any money which they have acquired must have originated with issuers who paid the cost of making the tokens, and every time it has changed hands the burden of this cost has been transferred with it. Is it likely that men who acquire money by paying this cost will lend it to others without exacting this cost? If they should, they would be working for others for nothing,—a very different thing from "receiving pay for work they had not performed." No man can lend money unless he either issues it himself and pays the cost of making the tokens, or else buys or borrows it from others to whom he must pay that cost.

FREE MONEY.

[*Liberty*, December 13, 1884.]

To the Editor of Liberty :

The "Picket Duty" remarks of November 22 in regard to the importance of "free money " (with which I mainly agree) impel me to say a few words upon the subject. It is desirable, it seems to me, that *Liberty* should give its ideas upon that subject in a more systematic form than it has yet done (1). To be sure, it is easy for those who think to see that, if all laws in regard to money were abolished, commerce would readily provide its instruments of exchange. This might be promissory notes, or warehouse receipts, bills of lading, etc.; but, whatever it might be, the Anarchist could not doubt it would be better than that ever issued under monopoly.

Theoretically, at least, *Liberty* has expressed the idea that any circulating medium should be made redeemable ; but in what? If in gold, or in gold and silver, does it not involve the principle of a *legal* tender, or of a tender of "common consent?" and they do not greatly differ (2). It seems to me that the great fraud in regard to money starts just here, and vitiates all forms of finance as of trade (3). I define money to be a commodity or representative of a commodity, accepted by or forced upon the common consent, as *an invariable ratio and medium of exchange.* Now, since the price of all things else is variable and subject to extreme fluctuations, the dollar in exchange, and especially where the exchange is suspended as in borrowing, or buying on credit, becomes, as friend Pink suggests, a "war club"- rather than a tool or instrument of commerce.

Pardon me if I inflict some technicalities upon the readers of *Liberty.* I would discard the use of the word *value* from questions of exchange, or else divide its several parts, as value in use, value in service and compensation, and value in exchange. But ratio is a much better word. I would then define the Ratio of Utility to be the proportion in which any thing or service effects useful ends, in sustaining human life or adding to human enjoyment, —a constant Ratio.

The Ratio of Service, the proportion in which different services, of the same duration in time, effect useful ends.

The Ratio of Exchange, the proportion in which one commodity or service will exchange for another service or commodity at the same time and place. This is a variable ratio, *whose* MEAN *is the ratio of service.*

I cannot stop now to argue the correctness of these definitions. It must be seen, unless a commodity could be found which would answer every useful purpose, and could be readily obtained by all, it could not be made a tender without inflicting great injustice on the many. But as such commodity cannot be found, a commodity, gold, has been assumed to have an invariable value, although the most variable in value of all the metals, and about the least useful ; of a limited and irregular production and widely varying demand. With the addition of silver to the standard, the great injustice to labor is only divided, not changed.

As defined above, the only invariable ratio is that of use. A pound of flour of the same quality will at all times and places satisfy the same demand for food. The hundredweight of coal will at all times and places give off the same amount of heat in combustion, etc., having no reference either to the money or labor cost. Now, since labor is the only thing which can procure or produce articles of use, that is naturally the controlling element in exchange, and the only thing that commands a stable price or furnishes a stable ratio.

Though gold is assumed as the standard of value, it is well known that for ages the " promise to pay " this has constituted mainly the currency and medium of exchange of most nations.

The method of issuing this promissory money has been a great injustice to industry, and its almost infinite extension of the usurpation of the gold-tender fraud is now robbing labor of a large share of its production by the control it gives to the usurer and speculator, who can make the rate low when produce is coming under their control, and high when it is being returned for use to the people ; and can make money scarce and dear when they loan it, and plenty and cheap when they gather it in.

I think I have shown that the base of the money evil lies mainly in the monstrous assumption that the value of one of the most variable of things should be assumed to be an *invariable quantity*, and the standard of measurement of all other things. A gum elastic yardstick or gallon measure, or a shifting scale-beam, would suggest far more equitable dealing.

I know of but one invariable standard, and that is labor ; but what is its unit ? And by what method shall it be expressed ? Can *Liberty* give us light upon this subject ? (4) I have yet seen no feasible method by which credit or debt can serve safely as money, nor any honest way in which fiat money can be put in circulation. It appears to me now that, while men seek credit, they will have to pay interest, and that only by restoring opportunity to those who are now denied it by our monopolies of land, of money, and of public franchises, and so relieving them of the necessity of borrowing, can we hope to mitigate the evils of our money and trade iniquities. (5)

Credit being an incompleted exchange, in which one of the equivalents is not transferred, if we are to acknowledge it as an economic transaction, I see not why we should not accept that also where neither of the equivalents are transferred, as in produce and stock-gambling. (6) McLeod, I think, saw this dilemma, and therefore holds that the negotiable promissory note is payment for the things for which it is given. Yet, nevertheless, at maturity it will require a transfer of the counterbalancing equivalent, just the same as if a mere book account.

Credit is doubtless necessary under an inverted system of industry, finance, and trade ; but I am unable to see that it has any place in an honest state of things, except to conserve value, as where one puts things in another's care. It is vastly convenient, no doubt, for the profit-monger and speculator, as for the usurer, and without it neither could well thrive. In agreeing with the Anarchists that the State should not interfere to prevent, regulate, or enforce credit contracts, perhaps I go beyond them in excluding it from any economic recognition whatever, except as a means of conserving goods from decay and depreciation, involving always a service for which the creditor should pay.

J. K. INGALLS.

(1) *Liberty* is published not so much to thoroughly inform its readers regarding the ideas which it advocates as to interest them to seek this thorough information through other channels. For instance, in regard to free money, there is a book—"Mutual Banking," by William B. Greene—which sets forth the evils of money monopoly and the blessings of gratuitous credit in a perfectly plain and convincing way to all who will take the pains to study and understand it. *Liberty* can only state baldly the principles which Greene advocates and hint at some of their results. Whomsoever such statements and hints serve to interest can and will secure the book of me for a small sum. Substantially the same views, presented in different ways, are to be found in the financial writings of Lysander Spooner, Stephen Pearl Andrews, Josiah Warren, and, above all, P. J. Proudhon, whose untranslated works contain untold treasures, which I hope some day to put within the reach of English readers.

(2) Yes, it does involve one of these, but between the two there is all the difference that there is between force and freedom, authority and liberty. And where the tender is one of "common consent," those who do not like it are at liberty to consent in common to use any other and better one that they can devise.

(3) It is difficult for me to see any fraud in promising to pay a certain thing in a certain time, or on demand, and keeping the promise. That is what we do when we issue redeemable money and afterwards redeem it. The fraud in regard to money consists not in this, but in limiting by law the security for these promises to pay to a special kind of property, limited in quantity and easily monopolizable.

(4) It is doubtful if there is anything more variable in its purchasing power than labor. The causes of this are partly natural, such as the changing conditions of production, and partly and principally artificial, such as the legal monopolies that impart fictitious values. But labor expended in certain directions is unquestionably more constant in its average results than when expended in other directions. Hence the advantage of using the commodities resulting from the former for the redemption of currency whenever redemption shall be de-

manded. Whether gold and silver are among these commodities is a question, not of principle, but of statistics. As a
matter of fact, the holders of good redeemable money seldom
ask for any other redemption than its acceptance in the market and its final cancellation by the issuer's restoration of the
securities on which it was issued. But in case any other redemption is desired, it is necessary to adopt for the purpose
some commodity easily transferable and most nearly invariable
in value.

(5) Does Mr. Ingalls mean that all money must be abolished?
I can see no other inference from his position. For there
are only two kinds of money,—commodity money and credit
money. The former he certainly does not believe in, the
latter he thinks fraudulent and unsafe. Are we, then, to stop
exchanging the products of our labor?

(6) It is clearly the right of every man to gamble if he
chooses to, and he has as good a right to make his bets on the
rise and fall of grain prices as on anything else ; only he must
not gamble with loaded dice, or be allowed special privileges
whereby he can control the price of grain. Hence, in a free
and open market, these transactions where neither equivaalent is transferred are legitimate enough. But they are unwise, because, apart from the winning or losing of the bet,
there is no advantage to be gained from them. Transactions,
on the other hand, in which only one equivalent is immediately transferred are frequently of the greatest advantage, as
they enable men to get possession of tools which they immediately need, but cannot immediately pay for. Of course the
promise to pay is liable to be more or less valuable at maturity than when issued, but so is the property originally
transferred. The borrower is no more exempt than the
lender from the variations in value. And the interests of the
holder of property who neither borrows nor lends is also just
as much affected by them. There is an element of chance in
all property relations. So far as this is due to monopoly and
privilege, we must do our best to abolish it ; so far as it is
natural and inevitable, we must get along with it as best we can,
but not be frightened by it into discarding credit and money,
the most potent instruments of association and civilization.

FREE MONEY FIRST.

[*Liberty*, March 27, 1886.]

J. M. M'GREGOR, a writer for the Detroit *Labor Leaf*, thinks free land the chief desideratum. And yet he acknowledges that the wage-worker can't go from any of our manufacturing centres to the western lands, because "such a move would involve a cash outlay of a thousand dollars, which he has not got, nor can he get it." It would seem, then, that free land, though greatly to be desired, is not as sorely needed here and now as free capital. And this same need of capital would be equally embarrassing if the eastern lands were free, for still more capital would be required to stock and work a farm than the wage-worker can command. Under our present money system he could not even get capital by putting up his farm as collateral, unless he would agree to pay a rate of interest that would eat him up in a few years. Therefore, free land is of little value to labor without free capital, while free capital would be of inestimable benefit to labor even if land should not be freed for some time to come. For with it labor could go into other industries on the spot and achieve its independence. Not free land, then, but free money is the chief desideratum. It is in the perception of this prime importance of the money question that the greenbackers, despite their utterly erroneous solution of it, show their marked superiority to the State Socialists and the land nationalizationists.

The craze to get people upon the land is one of the insanities that has dominated social reformers ever since social reform was first thought of. It is a great mistake. Of agriculture it is as true as of every other industry that there should be as few people engaged in it as possible,—that is, just enough to supply the world with all the agricultural products which it wants. The fewer farmers there are, after this point of necessary supply is reached, the more useful people there are to engage in other industries which have not yet reached this point, and to devise and work at new industries hitherto unthought of. It is altogether likely that we have too many farmers now. It is not best that any more of us should become farmers, even if every homestead could be made an Arcadia. The plough is very well in its way, and Arcadia was very well in its day. But the way of the plough is not as wide as the world, and the world has outgrown the day of Arcadia. Human life henceforth is to be, not a simple, but a complex thing. The wants and aspirations of mankind are daily multiplying. They can be satisfied only by the diversification of industry, which is the method of progress and the record of civilization. This is one of the great truths which Lysander Spooner has so long been shouting into unwilling ears. But the further diversification of industry in such a way as to benefit, no longer the few and the idle, but the many and the industrious, depends upon the control of capital by labor. And this, as Proudhon, Warren, Greene, and Spooner have shown, can be secured only by a free money system.

STOP THE MAIN LEAK FIRST.

[*Liberty*, May 1, 1886.]

IN answer to my article, " Free Money First," in *Liberty* of March 27, in which was discussed the comparative importance of the money and land questions, J. M. M'Gregor, of the Detroit *Labor Leaf*, says : " I grant free money first. I firmly believe free money will come first, too, though my critic and myself may be widely at variance in regard to what would constitute free money." I mean by free money the utter absence of restriction upon the issue of all money not fraudulent. If Mr. M'Gregor believes in this, I am heartily glad. I should like to be half as sure as he is that it really is coming first. From the present temper of the people it looks to me as if nothing *free* would come first. They seem to be bent on trying every form of compulsion. In this current Mr. M'Gregor is far to the fore with his scheme of land taxation on the Henry George plan, and although he may believe free money will be first in time, he clearly does not consider it first in importance. This last-mentioned priority he awards to land reform, and it was his position in that regard that my article was written to dispute.

The issue between us, thus confined, hangs upon the truth or falsity of Mr. M'Gregor's statement that " to-day landlordism, through rent and speculation, supports more idlers than any other system of profit-robbing known to our great commonwealth." I take it that Mr. M'Gregor, by " rent," means ground-rent exclusively, and, by the phrase " supports more idlers," means takes more from labor ; otherwise, his statement has no pertinence to his position. For all rent except ground-rent would be almost entirely and directly abolished by free money, and the evil of rent to labor depends, not so much on the number of idlers it supports, as on the aggregate amount and quality of support it gives them, whether they be many or few in number. Mr. M'Gregor's statement, then, amounts to this : that ground-rent takes more from labor than any other form of usury. It needs no statistics to disprove this. The principal forms of usury are interest on money loaned or invested, profits made in buying and selling, rent of buildings of all sorts, and ground-rent. A moment's reflection will show any one that the amount of loaned or invested capital bearing interest in this country to-day far exceeds in value the amount of land yielding rent. The item of interest alone is a much more serious burden on the people than that of ground-rent. Much less, then, does ground-rent equal interest *plus* profit *plus* rent of buildings. But to make Mr. M'Gregor's argument really valid it must exceed all these combined. For a true money reform, I repeat, would abolish almost entirely and directly every one of these forms of usury except ground-rent, while a true land reform would directly abolish only ground-rent. Therefore, unless labor pays more in ground-rent than in interest, profit, and rent of buildings combined, the money question is of more importance than the land question. There are countries where this is the case, but the United States is not one of them.

It should also be borne in mind that free money, in destroying the power to accumulate large fortunes in the ordinary industries of life, will put a very powerful check upon the scramble for corner-lots and other advantageous positions, and thereby have a considerable influence upon ground-rent itself.

" How can capital be free," asks Mr. M'Gregor, " when it cannot get rid of rent ? " It cannot be entirely free till it can get rid of rent ; but it will be infinitely freer if it gets rid of interest, profit, and rent of buildings and still keeps ground-rent than if it gets rid of ground-rent and keeps the other forms of usury. Give us free money, the first great step to Anarchy, and we'll attend to ground-rent afterwards.

AN INDISPENSABLE ACCIDENT.

[*Liberty*, June 28, 1884.]

THE persistent way in which Greenbackers dodge argument on the money question is very tiresome to a reasoning mortal. Let an Anarchist give a Greenbacker his idea of a good currency in the issue of which no government has any part, and it is ten to one that he will answer : " Oh, that's not money. It isn't legal tender. Money is that thing which the supreme law of the land declares to be legal tender for debts in the country where that law is supreme."

Brick Pomeroy made such an answer to Stephen Pearl Andrews recently, and appeared to think that he had said something final. Now, in the first place, this definition is not correct, for that is money which performs the functions of money, no matter who issues it. But even if it were correct, of what earthly consequence could it be? Names are nothing. Who cares whether the Anarchistic currency be called money or something else? Would it make exchange easy? Would it make production active? Would it measure prices accurately? Would it distribute wealth honestly? Those are the questions to be asked concerning it ; not whether it meets the arbitrary definition adopted by a given school. A system of finance capable of supplying a currency satisfying the above requirements is a solution of what is generally known as the money question ; and Greenbackers may as well quit now as later trying to bind people to this fact by paltry quibbling with words.

But after thus rebuking Brick Pomeroy's evasion of Mr. Andrews, something needs to be said in amendment of Mr. Andrews's position as stated by him in an admirable article on "The Nature of Money," published in the New York *Truth Seeker* of March 8, 1884. Mr. Andrews divides the properties of money into essentials, incidentals, and accidentals. The essential properties of money, he says,—those in the absence of which it is not money whatever else it may have, and in the possession of which it is money whatever else it may lack,—are those of measuring mutual estimates in an exchange, recording a commercial transaction, and inspiring confidence in a promise which it makes. All other properties of money Mr. Andrews considers either incidental or accidental, and among the accidental properties he mentions the

security or "collateral" which may back up and guarantee
money.

Now as an analysis made for the purpose of arriving at a
definition, this is entirely right. No exception can be taken
to it. But it is seriously to be feared that nearly every person
who reads it will infer that, because security or "collateral"
is an accidental feature of money it is an unimportant and
well-nigh useless one. And that is where the reader will make
a great mistake. It is true that money is money, with or without security, but it cannot be a perfect or reliable money in
the absence of security ; nay, it cannot be a money worth considering in this age. The advance from barter to unsecured
money is a much shorter and less important step logically than
that from unsecured money to secured money. The rude
vessel in which primitive men first managed to float upon the
water very likely had all the essentials of a boat, but it was
much nearer to no boat at all than it was to the stanch,
swift, and sumptuous Cunarder that now speeds its way across
the Atlantic in a week. It was a boat, sure enough ; but not
a boat in which a very timid or even moderately cautious
man would care to risk his life in more than five feet of
water beyond swimming distance from the shore. It had
all the essentials, but it lacked a great many accidentals.
Among them, for instance, a compass. A compass is not
an essential of a boat, but it is an essential of satisfactory
navigation. So security is not an essential of money, but
it is an essential of steady production and stable commerce.
A boat without a compass is almost sure to strike upon
the rocks. Likewise money without security is almost sure
to precipitate the people using it into general bankruptcy.
When products can be had for the writing of promises and the
idea gets abroad that such promises are good money whether
kept or not, the promisors are very likely to stop producing ;
and, if the process goes on long enough, it will be found at the
end that there are plenty of promises with which to buy, but
that there is nothing left to be bought, and that it will require
an infinite number of promises to buy an infinitesimal amount
of nothing. If, however, people find that their promises will
not be accepted unless accompanied by evidence of an intention and ability to keep them, and if this evidence is kept
definitely before all through some system of organized credit,
the promisors will actively bestir themselves to create the
means of keeping their promises; and the free circulation of
these promises, far from checking production, will vastly stimulate it, the result being, not bankruptcy, but universal wealth.

A money thus secured is fit for civilized people.   Any other money, though it have all the essentials, belongs to barbarians, and is hardly fit to buy the Indian's dug-out.

LELAND STANFORD'S LAND BANK.

[*Liberty*, June 7, 1890.]

THE introduction in congress by Leland Stanford of a bill proposing to issue one hundred millions or more of United States notes to holders of agricultural land, said notes to be secured by first mortgages on such land and to bear two per cent. interest, is one of the most notable events of this time, and its significance is increased by the statement of Stanford, in his speech supporting the bill, that its provisions will probably be extended ultimately to other kinds of property. This bill is pregnant with the economics (not the politics) of Anarchism.   It contains the germ of the social revolution.   It provides a system of governmental mutual banking.   If it were possible to honestly and efficiently execute its provisions, it would have only to be extended to other kinds of property and to gradually lower its rate of interest from two per cent. (an eminently safe figure to begin with) to one per cent., or one half of one per cent., or whatever figure might be found sufficient to cover the cost of operating the system, in order to steadily and surely transfer a good three-fourths of the income of idle capitalists to the pockets of the wage-workers of the country.   The author of this bill is so many times a millionaire that, even if every cent of his income were to be cut off, his principal would still be sufficient to support his family for generations to come, but it is none the less true that he has proposed a measure which, with the qualifications already specified, would ultimately make his descendants either paupers or toilers instead of gigantic parasites like himself.   In short, Leland Stanford has indicated the only blow (considered solely in its economic aspect) that can ever reach capitalism's heart.   From his seat in the United States Senate he has told the people of this country, in effect, that the fundamental economic teaching reiterated by *Liberty* from the day of its first publication is vitally true and sound.

Unhappily his bill is vitiated by the serious defect of governmentalism.   If it had simply abolished all the restrictions and taxes on banking, and had empowered all indi-

viduals and associations to do just what its passage would em-
power the government to do, it would not only have been
significant, but, adopted by congress, it would have been the
most tremendously and beneficially effective legislative measure ever recorded on a statute book. But, as it is, it is made
powerless for good by the virus of political corruption that
lurks within it. The bill, if passed, would be entrusted for
execution either to the existing financial cabal or to some
other that would become just as bad. All the beneficent
results that, as an economic measure, it is calculated to
achieve would be nearly counteracted, perhaps far more than
counteracted, by the cumulative evils *inherent* in State administration. It deprives itself, in advance, of the vitalizing
power of free competition. If the experiment should be tried,
the net result would probably be evil. It would fail, disastrously fail, and *the failure and disaster would be falsely and
stupidly attributed to its real virtue, its economic character.* For
perhaps another century free banking would have to bear the
odium of the evils generated by a form of governmental banking more or less similar to it economically. Some bad name
would be affixed to the Stanford notes, and this would replace
the *assignat*, the "wild cat," and the "rag baby," as a more
effective scarecrow. It would unendurably prolong the bray
of those financial asses of whom the most recent typical
example is furnished in the person of General M. M. Trumbull,
of Chicago.*

While hoping, then, that it may never pass, let us nevertheless make the most of its introduction by using it as a text
in our educational work. This may be done in one way by
showing its economic similarity to Anarchistic finance and by
disputing the astounding claim of originality put forward by
Stanford. In his Senate speech of May 23, he said : " There
is no analogy between this scheme for a government of
65,000,000 people, with its boundless resources, issuing its
money, secured directly by at least $2 for $1, on the best pos-

---

* At the time when this was written General Trumbull had just been
guilty, and not for the first time, of stupidly confusing mutual money with
fiat money, and as his ignorance of the difference between them was utterly without excuse and yet was given voice in that tone of superiority
which ignorance is wont to assume, it seemed proper to administer this
rebuke, which, though conceded to be just by some of General Trumbull's
best friends, was considered by others unduly severe. The writer is not
behind these last in his admiration of General Trumbull as a man and a
thinker. As a publicist he is usually and unusually witty and wise; only
when discussing finance does he utter absurdities that justify the epithet
above applied.

sible security that could be desired, and any other financial proposition that has ever been suggested." If Stanford said this honestly, his words show him to be both an intellectual pioneer and a literary laggard. More familiarity with the literature of the subject would show him that he has had several predecessors in this path. Col. William B. Greene used to say of Lysander Spooner's financial proposals that their only originality lay in the fact that he had taken out a patent on them. The only originality of Stanford's lies in the fact that it is made for a government of 65,000,000 of people. For governments of other sizes the same proposal has been made before. Parallel to it in all essentials, both economically and politically, are Proudhon's Bank of Exchange and the proposal of Hugo Bilgram. Parallel to it economically are Proudhon's Bank of the People, Greene's Mutual Banks, and Spooner's real estate mortgage banks. And the financial thought that underlies it is closely paralleled in the writings of Josiah Warren, Stephen Pearl Andrews, and John Ruskin. If Stanford will sit at the feet of any of these men for a time, he will rise a wiser and more modest man.

Like most serious matters, this affair has its amusing side. It is seen in the idolization of Stanford by the Greenbackers. This shows how ignorant these men are of their own principles. Misled by the resemblance of the proposed measure to Greenbackism in some incidental respects, they hurrah themselves hoarse over the California senator, blissfully unaware that his bill is utterly subversive of the sole essential of Greenbackism, —namely, the fiat idea. The Greenbacker is distinguished from all other men in this and only in this,—that in his eyes a dollar is a dollar because the government stamps it as such. Now in Stanford's eyes a dollar is a dollar because it is based upon and secured by a specific piece of property that will sell in the market for at least a certain number of grains of gold. Two views more antagonistic than these it would be impossible to cite. And yet the leading organs of Greenbackism apparently regard them as identical.

MUTUALISM IN THE SERVICE OF CAPITAL.

[*Liberty*, July 16, 1887]

In a long reply to Edward Atkinson's recent address before the Boston Labor Lyceum, Henry George's *Standard* impairs the effect of much sound and effective criticism by the following careless statement :

Mr. Atkinson does not even know the nature of his own business. He told his audience that his "regular work is to stop the cotton and woollen mills from being burned up." This is a grave blunder. Fire insurance companies are engaged in distributing losses by fire among the insured. As a statistician he knows that statistics show that in New Hampshire, when that State was boycotted by the insurance companies, the number of fires was reduced by thirty per cent. He does not save buildings from fire.

This is a gross slander of one of the most admirable institutions in America,—none the less admirable in essence because it happens in this instance to exist for the benefit of the capitalists. Mr. George unwarrantably assumes that Mr. Atkinson is engaged in an insurance business of the every-day sort. This is far from true. He is the president of an insurance company doing business on a principle which, if it should be adopted in the banking business, would do more to abolish poverty than all the nostrums imagined or imaginable, including the taxation of land values. This principle is the mutualistic, or cost, principle.

Some time ago a number of mill-owners decided that they would pay no more profits to insurance companies, inasmuch as they could insure themselves much more advantageously. So they formed a company of their own, into the treasury of which each mill pays annually a sum proportional to the amount for which it wishes to insure, receiving it back at the end of the year minus its proportion of the year's losses by fire paid by the company and of the cost of maintaining the company. It is obvious that by the adoption of this plan the mills would have saved largely, even if fires had continued to occur in them as frequently as before. But this is not all. By mutual agreement the mills place themselves, so far as protection against fire is concerned, under the supervision of the insurance company, which keeps inspectors to see that each mill avails itself of all the best means of preventing and extinguishing fire, and uses the utmost care in the matter. As a consequence the number of fires and the aggregate damage caused thereby has been reduced in a degree that would scarcely be credited ; the cost of insurance to these mills is now next to nothing, and this cost might be reduced still further by cutting down an enormous salary paid to Mr. Atkinson for services which not a few persons more industrious and capable than he are ready to perform for less money. Mr. Atkinson's insurance company, then, does save buildings from fire, and Mr. George's statement that it does not is as reckless as anything that Mr. Atkinson ever said to prove that the laboring man is an inhabitant of Paradise.

Moreover, it is the height of stupidity for any champion of labor to slur this insurance company, for it contains in germ the solution of the labor question. When workingmen and business men shall be allowed to organize their credit as these mill-owners have organized their insurance, the former will pay no more tribute to the credit-monger than the latter pay to the insurance-monger, and the one class will be as safe from bankruptcy as the other is from fire. Yet Mr. Atkinson, whose daily life should keep this truth perpetually before his mind, pretends that the laborer can achieve the social revolution by living on beef-bones and using water-gas as fuel. Can any one think him sincere ?

EDWARD ATKINSON'S EVOLUTION.

[*Liberty*, January 10, 1891.]

THE great central principle of Anarchistic economics—namely, the dethronement of gold and silver from their position of command over all other wealth by the destruction of their monopoly currency privilege—is rapidly forging to the front. The Farmers' Alliance sub-treasury scheme, unscientific and clumsy as it is, is a glance in this direction. The importance of Senator Stanford's land bill, more scientific and workable, but incomplete, and vicious because governmental, has already been emphasized in these columns. But most notable of all is the recent revolution in the financial attitude of Edward Atkinson, the most orthodox and cock-sure of American economists, who now swells with his voice the growing demand for a direct representation of all wealth in the currency.

In a series of articles in Bradstreet's and in an address before the Boston Boot and Shoe Club, this old-time foe of all paper money not based on specie ; this man who, fifteen or twenty years ago, stood up in the town hall of Brookline in a set debate with Col. Wm. B. Greene to combat the central principle of Mutual Banking ; this boor, who has never lost an opportunity of insulting Anarchism and Anarchists,—now comes forward to save the country with an elaborate financial scheme which he offers as original with himself, but which has really been Anarchistic thunder these many years, was first put forward in essence by Proudhon, the father of Anarchism, and was championed by Atkinson's old antagonist, Col. Wm. B. Greene, to the end of his life. Of course, all the papers are talking about it, and, on the principle that " everything goes " that comes from the great Atkinson, most of them give it a warm welcome, though precious few of them understand what it means. Those which probably do understand, like the New York *Evening Post*, content themselves for the present with a mild protest, reserving their heavier fire to be used in case the plan should seem likely to gain acceptance.

The proposal is briefly this : that the national banks of the country shall be divided into several districts, each district having a certain city as a banking centre ; that any bank may deposit with the clearing-house securities satisfactory to the clearing-house committee, and receive from the clearing-house certificates in the form of bank-notes of small denominations, to the extent of seventy-five per cent. of the value of the securities ; that these notes shall bear the bank's promise to pay on the back, and shall be redeemable on demand at the bank in legal-tender money, and, in case of failure on the bank's part to so redeem them, they shall be redeemable at the clearing-house ; and that this new circulating medium shall be exempt from the ten per cent. tax imposed upon State bank circulation.

Of course a scheme like this would not work the economic revolution which Anarchism expects from free banking. It does not destroy the monopoly of the right to bank ; it retains the control of the currency in the hands of a cabal ; it undertakes the redemption of the currency in legal-tender money, regardless of the fact that, if any large proportion of the country's wealth should become directly represented in the currency, there would not be sufficient legal-tender money to redeem it. It is dangerous in its feature of centralizing responsibility instead of localizing it, and it is defective in less important respects. I call attention to it and welcome it, because here for the first time Proudhon's doctrine of the republicanization of specie is soberly championed by a recognized econo mist. This fact alone makes it an important sign of the times.

I am surprised that its importance has not been fully appreciated by the Galveston *News*, which journal alone among the great dailies of the country is an exponent of rational finance. Its editor, in noticing Atkinson's scheme, instead of pointing out its introduction of a revolutionary principle, remarks that "the one infallible way to reach the ideal of a sound system of organized credit is to reach the ideal of a population correspondingly sound in character and intellect." This philistine utterance I hardly expected from such a quarter. It is undoubtedly true that a considerable degree of character and intellect is necessary to the successful organization of credit. But this truth is now a truism. There is another truth, not a truism, for the inculcation of which there is pressing need,— that credit, once organized, will do as much to develop character and intellect as the development of character and intellect ever did to organize credit. It was this truth, and the important bearing that the monetization of all wealth would have upon it, that I expected to see emphasized by the Galveston *News* in its comments upon Atkinson's proposal. I hoped and still hope, to hear it rejoice with *Liberty* that the man whose solutions of the labor problem have consisted mainly of nine-dollar suits and ten-cent meals and patent ovens has at last broached a measure that, instead of being beneath contempt, is worthy of profound consideration.

A GREENBACKER IN A CORNER.

[*Liberty*, August 9, 1884.]

To the Editor of Liberty:

In *Liberty* of June 28 you refer to a writer in the *Essex Statesman*, of whom you say that he "gets down to bottom truth" on the tariff question by averring that "Free Money" and "Free Trade" are corollaries of each other.

Every Greenbacker (I am one) of brains perceived this simple (I might say *axiomatic*) doctrine the moment he thought at all on it.

Monopoly of money is through interest; monopoly of trade is through taxing (tariffs) : so, if you would overthrow all monopoly, you have only to secure currency unloaded with interest, and their doom is recorded.

There is no more rational reformer in existence than the "Greenbacker" who is a Greenbacker in the only rational sense of the word,— that is, a believer in "a non-interest-bearing currency."

It is amusing, this prating of "secured money"! Liberty ought to see that a currency " based " on any " security " other than its inherent function and non-discountableness would rob those who used it.

If the whole community co-operate in its issue and use, and " fix " no limit to its quantity or use, such currency would be perfect as to all qualities, and rob none ; and such money is "full legal tender" under any name you choose to label it.

As I have taught this doctrine for more than ten years, I hope you will give a corner to this brief " brick " in *Liberty*.

E. H. BENTON.

WELLS MILLS (GEERE), NEB., July, 1884.

I have given Mr. Benton his " corner," and I think he will have difficulty in getting out of it. Let me suppose a case for him. A is a farmer, and owns a farm worth five thousand dollars. B keeps a bank of issue, and is known far and wide as a cautious and honest business man. C, D, E, etc., down to Z are each engaged in some one of the various pursuits of civilized life. A needs ready money. He mortgages his farm to B, and receives in return B's notes, in various denominations, to the amount of five thousand dollars, for which B charges A this transaction's just proportion of the expenses of running the bank, which would be a little less than one-half of one per cent. With these notes A buys various products which he needs of C, D, E, etc., down to Z, who in turn with the same notes buy products of each other, and in course of time come back to A with them to buy his farm produce. A, thus regaining possession of B's notes, returns them to B, who then cancels his mortgage on A's farm. All these parties, from A to Z, have been using for the performance of innumerable transactions B's notes based on A's farm,—that is, a currency based on some security "other than its inherent function and non-discountableness." They were able to perform them only because they all knew that the notes were thus secured. A knew it because he gave the mortgage ; B knew it because he took the mortgage ; C, D, E, etc., down to Z knew it because they knew that B never issued notes unless they were secured in this or some similar way. Now, *Liberty* is ready to see, as Mr. Benton says it *ought* to see, that any or all of these parties have been robbed by the use of this money when Mr. Benton shall demonstrate it by valid fact and argument. Until then he must stay in his corner.

A word as to the phrase " legal tender." That only is legal tender which the government prescribes as valid for the discharge of debt. Any currency not so prescribed is not legal tender, no matter how universal its use or how unlimited its issue, and to label it so is a confusion of terms.

Another word as to the term " Greenbacker." He is a

Greenbacker who subscribes to the platform of the Greenback party. The cardinal principle of that platform is that the government shall monopolize the manufacture of money, and that any one who, in rebellion against that sacred prerogative, may presume to issue currency on his own account shall therefor be taxed, or fined, or imprisoned, or hanged, or drawn and quartered, or submitted to any other punishment or torture which the government, in pursuit and exercise of its good pleasure, may see fit to impose upon him. Unless Mr. Benton believes in that, he is not a Greenbacker, and I am sure I am not, although, with Mr. Benton, I believe in a non-interest-bearing currency.

FREE MONEY AND THE COST PRINCIPLE.

[*Liberty*, December 1, 1888.]

To the Editor of Liberty:

I understand that the monopoly of money should be broken, and this would leave all persons who possessed property free to issue solvent notes thereon, the competition between them so reducing the rate of interest that it would enable would-be business people to borrow on advantageous terms. Now, to my mind this would do no good *unless* the new order of benefited business persons adopted the "*Cost principle*" in production and distribution, in order to break down the present bad arrangements in society that is composed of workers on one side and idlers and unproductive or useless persons on the other side.

If the *cost principle* was not in view, the result to my mind of "plentiful money" would only lead to a short briskness of trade and a speedy breakdown,—much speedier than now.

Neither do I think (in the absence of applying the cost principle) that competition among bankers would bring the issue down to cost through the sheer force of competition, because people would cease to go into the banking business if it did not yield the normal rate of interest on capital.

In conclusion, I must say I believe in the "*Cost* principle," and yet as an Anarchist there seems something arbitrary in it. It is the reconciliation of "Cost" and competition that my mind cannot yet grasp.

Yours faithfully,   FRANK A. MATTHEWS.

The Cost principle cannot fail to seem arbitrary to one who does not see that it can only be realized through economic processes that go into operation the moment liberty is allowed in finance. To see this it is necessary to understand the principles of mutual banking, which Mr. Matthews has not attentively studied. If he had, he would know that the establishment of a mutual bank does not require the investment of capital, inasmuch as the customers of the bank furnish all the

capital upon which the bank's notes are based, and that therefore the rate of discount charged by the bank for the service
of exchanging its notes for those of its customers is governed,
under competition, by the cost of that service, and not by the
rate of interest that capital commands. The relation is just
the contrary of Mr. Matthews's supposition. It is the rate of
interest on capital that is governed by the bank's rate of discount, for capitalists will not be able to lend their capital at
interest when people can get money at the bank without
interest with which to buy capital outright. It is this effect
of free and mutual banking upon the rate of interest on
capital that insures, or rather constitutes, the realization of
the Cost principle by economic processes. For the moment
interest and rent are eliminated as elements of price, and brisk
competition is assured by the ease of getting capital, profits
fall to the level of the manufacturer's or merchant's proper
wage. It is well, as Mr. Matthews says, to have the Cost
principle in view ; for it is doubtless true that the ease with
which society travels the path of progress is largely governed
by the clearness with which it foresees it. But, foresight or
no foresight, it " gets there just the same." The only foresight absolutely necessary to progress is foresight of the fact
that liberty is its single *essential* condition.

PROUDHON'S BANK.

[*Liberty*, September 20, 1884.]

WHILE the principle of equal representation of all available values by the
notes of the Exchange Bank is what I have advocated these thirty years, I
do not perceive how, in generalizing the system, as Proudhon would do
(I refer to the paragraphs translated by Greene), we are to avoid the
chances of forgery on the one side, and on the other of fraudulent issues
by the officers of the Bank.

Such a Bank, moreover, is equivalent to a general insurance policy on
the property of a country, and the true value of its notes must depend on
security against conflagrations and other catastrophes affecting real estate
as well as " personal property."

I hope that the first essays will be local and limited. I think the
commercial activity of modern civilization dangerously, if not fatally,
exaggerated and disproportioned to production. The Railroad is a revolver in the hands of a maniac, who has just about sense enough to shoot
himself. Even were we not, in our blind passion for rapid and facile
transportation, hanging ourselves by the slip-noose of monopoly, the impulse which railroads give to and towards *city* life, coming, as it has,
before the establishment of a conservative scavenger system, by which the

cream of soils would be restored to them, rapidly drains and wastes terra-solar vitality, and suffices soon to render America a desert.   The feasible check to this " *galloping consumption* " lies in *localizing the circuits* of pro-duction with manipulation and consumption in coöperative associations. The smaller the area in which such self-sufficing circuit is effected, the greater the economy of force in transportation.

> Men and Gods are too extense ;
> Could you slacken and condense ?

I suppose you see the correlation of this idea with that of the safety of Exchange Bank notes, as in a locally restricted commerce frauds could and would be promptly detected, and therefore would be seldom attempted.

EDGEWORTH.

Proudhon was accustomed to present his views of the way in which credit may be organized in two forms,—his Bank of Exchange and his Bank of the People. The latter was his real ideal ; the former he advocated whenever he wished to avoid the necessity of combating the objections of the govern-mentalists. The Bank of Exchange was to be simply the Bank of France transformed on the mutual principle. It is easy to see that the precautions against forgery and over-issue now used by the Bank of France would be equally valid after the transformation. But in the case of the Bank of the People, which involves the introduction of free competition into the banking business, these evils will have to be other-wise guarded against. The various ways of doing this are secondary considerations, having nothing to do with the prin-ciples of finance ; and human ingenuity, which has heretofore conquered much greater obstacles, will undoubtedly prove equal to the emergency. The more reputable banks would soon become distinguished from the others by some sort of voluntary organization and mutual inspection necessary to their own protection. The credit of all such as declined to submit to thorough examination by experts at any moment or to keep their books open for public inspection would be ruined, and these would receive no patronage. Probably also the better banks would combine in the use of a uniform bank-note paper difficult to counterfeit, which would be guarded most carefully and distributed to the various banks only so far as they could furnish security for it. In fact, any number of checks can be devised by experts that would secure the currency against all attempts at adulteration. There is little doubt that the first essays will be, as " Edgeworth " hopes, " local and limited." But I do not think the money so pro-duced will be nearly as safe as that which will result when the system has become widespread and its various branches organized in such a way that the best means of protection may be utilized at small expense.

WHY WAGES SHOULD ABSORB PROFITS.

[*Liberty*, July 16, 1887.]

Van Buren Denslow, discussing in the *Truth Seeker* the comparative rewards of labor and capital, points out that the present wage system divides profits almost evenly between the two, instancing the railways of Illinois, which pay annually in salaries and wages $81,936,170, and to capital, which Mr. Denslow defines as the "labor previously done in constructing and equipping the roads," $81,720,265. Then he remarks : "No system of intentional profit-sharing is more equal than this, provided we assent to the principle that a day's work already done and embodied in the form of capital is as well entitled to compensation for its use as a day's work not yet done, which we call labor." Exactly. But the principle referred to is the very thing which we Socialists deny, and until Mr. Denslow can meet and vanquish us on that point, he will in vain attempt to defend the existing or any other form of profit-sharing. The Socialists assert that "a day's work embodied in the form of capital" has already been fully rewarded by the ownership of that capital ; that, if the owner lends it to another to use and the user damages it, destroys it, or consumes any part of it, the owner is entitled to have this damage, destruction, or consumption made good ; and that, if the owner receives from the user any surplus beyond the return of his capital intact, his day's work is paid for a second time.

Perhaps Mr. Denslow will tell us, as we have so often been told before, that this day's work should be paid for a second and a third and a hundredth and a millionth time, because the capital which it produced and in which it is embodied increased the productivity of future labor. The fact that it did cause such an increase we grant; but that labor, where there is freedom, is or should be paid in proportion to its usefulness we deny. All useful qualities exist in nature, either actively or potentially, and their benefits, under freedom, are distributed by the natural law of free exchange among mankind. The laborer who brings any particular useful quality into action is paid according to the labor he has expended, but gets only his share, in common with all mankind, of the special usefulness of this product. It is true that the usefulness of his product has a tendency to enhance its price; but this tendency is immediately offset, wherever competition is possible,—and as long as there is a money monopoly there is no freedom of competition in any industry requiring capital,—by the rush of other laborers to create this product, which lasts until the price falls back to the normal wages of labor. Hence it is evident that the owner of the capital embodying the day's work above referred to cannot get his work paid for even a second time by selling his capital. Why, then, should he be able to get it paid for a second time and an infinite number of times by repeatedly lending his capital? Unless Mr. Denslow can give us some reason, he will have to admit that all profit-sharing is a humbug, and that the entire net product of industry should fall into the hands of labor not previously embodied in the form of capital,—in other words, that wages should entirely absorb profits.

A GREAT IDEA PERVERTED.

[*Liberty*, June 19, 1886.]

THE Knights of Labor Convention at Cleveland voted to petition Congress for the passage of an act which embodies in a very crude way the all-important principle that all property having due stability of value should be available as a basis of currency. The act provides for the establishment of loan offices in every county in the United States, which, under the administration of cashiers and tellers appointed by the Secretary of the Treasury, shall issue legal tender money, redeemable on demand in gold coin or its equivalent in lawful money of the United States, lending it at three per cent. a year to all who offer satisfactory security.

The Knights have got hold of a great idea here,—one which has in it more potency for the emancipation of labor than any other; but see now how they vitiate it and render it impracticable and worthless by their political and arbitrary methods of attempting its realization!

One section of the act, by forbidding all individuals or associations to issue money, makes a government monopoly of the banking business,—an outrageous denial of liberty!

Another section, instead of leaving the rate of discount to be governed by cost to which, were it not for the monopoly, competition would reduce it, arbitrarily fixes it at three per cent., thus recognizing labor's worst foe, usury. As three per cent. represents the average annual increase of wealth,—that is, the difference between the annual production and the annual consumption,—this section means that what ought to be labor's annual savings, and would be if usury did not abstract them from labor's pockets, shall be turned into the government treasury to be squandered as Congress and corrupt officials may see fit.

Another section establishes a uniform usury law for the entire country, providing that any person who shall lend money at *any other* rate than three per cent. shall forfeit to the borrower both principal and interest. Legislators have heretofore been satisfied to limit the rate of interest in one direction; but this limits it in both, subjecting the lender at two per cent. to the same forfeit that the lender at four must suffer.

This piece of tyranny, however, as well as numerous others in the act, are thrown entirely into the shade by a section providing that any person convicted of offering for sale gold and silver coin of the United States "shall forfeit as a fine his entire estate, goods, money, and property, or may be imprisoned at hard labor for fifty years, or suffer both fine and imprisonment, and in addition forever forfeit the right of citizenship in the United States." What an opportunity for Recorder Smythe, should this offence ever come within his jurisdiction ! His insane lust for cruelty, which lamented its inability to hang John Most for making an incendiary speech, might find greater gratification under this statute. Imagine him addressing the prisoner at the bar :

" John Jones, a jury of your peers has found you guilty of a most heinous crime. You have presumed to offer in the market-place and subject to sacrilege of barter our sacred cart-wheel, the emblem of civilization, the silver dollar of the United States. It is evident that you are a member of the dangerous classes. You are probably the greatest scoundrel that ever disgraced the face of the earth. It is a great pity that our too merciful law will not permit me to burn you at the stake. But as it will not, I must be contented, in the interest of law, order, and society, to go to the extreme verge of the latitude allowed me. Therefore, I impose upon you a fine equal to your entire estate, I sentence you to imprisonment at hard labor for fifty years, and I strip you forever of the right to vote me out of office."

A beautiful organization, these Knights of Labor, for an Anarchist to belong to !

ON PICKET DUTY.

THE outcry against middlemen is senseless. As E. H. Hey-
wood puts it, " Middlemen are as important as end men." And
they are as truly producers.   Distribution is a part of production.   Nothing is wholly produced until it is ready for use,
and nothing is ready for use until it has reached the place
where it is to be used.   Whoever brings it to that place is a
producer, and as such entitled to charge for his work.   The
trouble with middlemen is that they charge consumers not
only for their work, but for the use of their invested capital.
As it is, they are useful members of society.   Eliminate usury
from their methods, and they will become respectable members also.—*Liberty*, October 1, 1881.

Those who would have the usurer rewarded for rendering a
service always find it convenient to forget that the usurer's
victims would not need his service were it not that the laws
made at his bidding prevent them from serving themselves.—
Liberty, October 15, 1881.

Of the absolute correctness of the principle, and advisability
of the policy, of free trade there can be no reasonable doubt;
but it must be thorough-going free trade,—no such half-way
arrangement as that which the so-called " free traders " would
have us adopt.   David A. Wells, Professor Perry, and all the
economists of the Manchester school are fond of clamoring
for " free trade "; but an examination of their position always
shows them the most ardent advocates of monopoly in the
manufacture of money,—the bitterest opponents of free trade
in credit.   They agree and insist that it is nothing less than
tyranny for the government to clip a large slice out of the
foreign product which any one choses to import, but are unable to detect any violation of freedom in the exclusive license
given by the government to a conspiracy of note-shaving corporations called national banks, which are enabled by this
monopoly to clip anywhere from three to fifteen per cent. out
of the credit which the people are compelled to buy of them.
Such " free trade " as this is the most palpable sham to any
one who really looks into it.   It makes gold a privileged product, the king of commodities.   And as long as this royalty of
gold exists, the protectionists who make so much of the theory

of the "balance of trade" will occupy an invulnerable position. While gold is king, the nation which absorbs it—that is, the nation whose exports largely exceed its imports—will surely govern the world. But dethrone this worst of despots, and that country will be the most powerful which succeeds to the largest extent in getting rid of its gold in exchange for products more useful. In other words, the republicanization of specie must precede the freedom of trade.—*Liberty*, March 18, 1892.

Some nincompoop, writing to the Detroit *Spectator* in opposition to cheap money, says : "If low interest insured high wages, during times of business depression wages would be high, for then interest reaches its minimum." Another man unable to see below the surface of things and distinguish association from causation ! The friends of cheap money do not claim that low interest insures high wages. What they claim is that free competition in currency-issuing and the consequent activity of capital insure both low interest and high wages. They do not deny that low interest sometimes results from other causes and unaccompanied by any increase in wages. When the money monopolists through their privilege have bled the producers nearly all they can, hard times set in, business becomes very insecure, no one dares to venture in new directions or proceed much further in old directions, there is no demand for capital, and therefore interest falls ; but, there being a decrease in the volume of business, wages fall also. Suppose, now, that great leveller, bankruptcy, steps in to wipe out all existing claims, and economic life begins over again under a system of free banking. What happens then ? All capital is at once made available by the abundance of the currency, and the supply is so great that interest is kept very low ; but confidence being restored and the way being clear for all sorts of new enterprises, there is also a great demand for capital, and the consequent increase in the volume of business causes wages to rise to a very high point. When people are afraid to borrow, interest is low and wages are low; when people are anxious to borrow, but can find only a very little available capital in the market, interest is high and wages are low ; when people are both anxious to borrow and can readily do so, interest is low and wages are high, the only exception being that, when from some special cause labor is extraordinarily productive (as was the case in the early days of California), interest temporarily is high also.—*Liberty*, November 22, 1884.

"To produce wealth in the shape of coal," says Henry
George, "nothing is needed but a bed of coal and a man."
Yes, one thing else is needed,—a pick-axe. This neglect of
the pick-axe and of the means of obtaining it is a vital flaw in
Mr. George's economy. It leads him to say that "what hin-
ders the production of wealth is not the lack of money to pay
wages with, but the inability of men who are willing to work
to obtain access to natural opportunities." That this lack of
access, in the proportion that it exists, is a hinderance to production is indisputable, but in this country it is but a molehill
in labor's path compared with the mountain that confronts
labor in consequence of the lack of money. In fact, the lack
of access is largely due to the lack of money.—*Liberty*, July
30, 1887.

In disposing with his usual cleverness of the economists
apologies for interest G. Bernard Shaw takes a position upon
the money question not at all in harmony with the State Socialism toward which he usually inclines. He would be taken,
in fact, for a first-class Anarchist. Speaking of the tax which
the banker who has a monopoly levies upon all commerce, he
says : " Only by the freedom of other financiers to adopt his
system and tempt his customers by offering to share the advantage with them, can that advantage eventually be distributed throughout the community." *Only*, observe. No other
method will do it. Government monopoly will not do it.
Nothing but *laissez-faire*, free competition, free money, in short,
as far as it goes, pure Anarchism, can abolish interest on
money. When Mr. Shaw shall apply this principle in all
directions, he and *Liberty* will stand on the same platform.—
Liberty, September 24, 1887.

It is a common saying of George, McGlynn, Redpath, and
their allies that they, as distinguished from the State Socialists,
want less government instead of more, and that it is no part
of the function of government to interfere with production
and distribution except to the extent of assuming control of
the bounties of nature and of such industries as are naturally
and necessarily monopolies,—that is, such as are, in the nature
of things, beyond the reach of competition's influence. In the
latter category they place the conduct of railroads and telegraphs and the issue of money. Now, inasmuch as it takes an
enormous capital to build a railroad, and as strips of land three
thousand miles long by thirty feet wide are not to be picked
up every day, I can see some shadow of justification for the

claim that railroads are necessarily exempt to a marked extent from competition, although I do not think on that account that it will be necessary to hand them over to the government in order to secure their benefits for the people. Still, if I were to accept Mr. George's premise that industries which are necessarily monopolies should be managed by the State, I might possibly conclude that railroads and some other enterprises belong under that head. But how his premise is related to the issue of money I do not understand at all. That the issue of money is at present a monopoly I admit and insist, but it is such only because the State has laid violent hands upon it, either to hold for itself or to farm out as a privilege. If left free, there is nothing in its nature that necessarily exempts it from competition. It takes little or no capital to start a bank of issue whose operations may become world-wide, and, if a thousand banks should prove necessary to the prevention of exorbitant rates, it is as feasible to have them as to have one. Why, then, is the issue of money necessarily a monopoly, and as such to be entrusted exclusively to the State? I have asked Mr. George a great many questions in the last half-dozen years, not one of which has he ever condescended to answer. Therefore I scarcely dare hope that he will vouchsafe the important information which I now beg of him.—*Liberty*, October 8, 1887.

The different uses of the word "free" lead to many misunderstandings. For instance, a writer in the Denver *Arbitrator* gives the preference to free trade and free land over free money and free transportation on the ground that the former are "natural rights" while the latter are "privileges that can be conferred only by society." Here free money is evidently taken to mean the supply of money to the people free of cost by some external power. But it no more means that than free rum means the supply of rum free of cost. It means freedom to manufacture money and offer it in the market, and is a part of free trade itself. One may look upon free money and free trade as privileges, or as rights, or as simple equalities recognized by contract ; that is a matter of ethics and politics. But whichever way one views them, he must view both alike, for economically they are the same in principle. There is no possible justification for calling one a right and the other a privilege, and giving a preference to one or the other on the basis of that distinction.—*Liberty*, September 29, 1888.

"A right theory of the functions of money," writes Robert Ellis Thompson in the *Irish World*, " is of the first necessity for understanding the controversy between protection and free trade." This is an important truth, first expressed, I think, by Proudhon. It is precisely because Mr. Thompson does not understand the money question that he is a protectionist. Supposing that State control of money is a foregone conclusion, he sees as a logical result of this false premise that the State must also control the balance of trade. That his premise may be doubted does not seem to have occurred to him. " The most extreme free trader," he says, " opposes free trade in money." Evidently he is unaware that the extremity of free trade is not to be found in the New York *Evening Post.* The Anarchists are the extreme free traders; and they, to a man, favor free trade in money,—most of them, in fact, recognizing it as a necessary condition of free trade in products. For, as Mr. Thompson truly says, it is " the height of folly for a country to exchange industrial power for industrial products." In the absence of a tariff, the tendency would be to just that sort of exchange, provided the State should continue to deprive all products, save one or two, of the monetary function, and therefore of industrial power. Mr. Thompson, supposing this restriction of the monetary function to be necessary and wise, clings very sensibly to the tariff. He would have the State hem in industrial power and bar out industrial products. Of two wrongs he tries to make a right. The simpler way, involving no wrong at all, is to give industrial power to industrial products by endowing them with the monetary function, and then strike down all commercial barriers whatsoever.—*Liberty,* February 2, 1889.

LAND AND RENT.

"THE LAND FOR THE PEOPLE."

[*Liberty*, June 24, 1882.]

The Liverpool speech,* it seems, was delivered by Davitt in response to a challenge from the English press to explain the meaning of the phrase, "the land for the people." We hope they understand it now.

"The land for the people," according to Parnell, appears to mean a change of the present tenants into proprietors of the estates by allowing them to purchase on easy terms fixed by the State and perhaps with the State's aid, and a maintenance thereafter of the present landlord system, involving the collection of rents by law.

"The land for the people," according to Davitt, as explained at Liverpool, appears to mean a change of the whole agricultural population into tenants of the State, which is to become the sole proprietor by purchase from the present proprietors, and the maintenance thereafter of the present landlord system involving the collection of rents in the form of taxes.

"The land for the people," according to George, appears to be the same as according to Davitt, except that the State is to acquire the land by confiscation instead of by purchase, and that the amount of rental is to be fixed by a different method of valuation.

"The land for the people," according to *Liberty*, means the protection (by the State while it exists, and afterwards by such voluntary associations for the maintenance of justice as may be destined to succeed it) of all people who desire to cultivate land in the possession of whatever land they personally cultivate, without distinction between the existing classes of landlords, tenants, and laborers, and the positive refusal of the protecting power to lend its aid to the collection of any rent whatsoever; this state of things to be brought about by inducing the people to steadily refuse the payment

---

* The speech in which Michael Davitt, in the summer of 1882, first publicly endorsed the doctrine of land nationalization.

of rent and taxes, and thereby, as well as by all other means of passive and moral resistance, compel the State to repeal all the so-called land titles now existing.

Thus "the land for the people" according to *Liberty* is the only "land for the people" that means the abolition of land-lordism and the annihilation of rent;* and all of Henry George's talk about "peasant proprietorship necessarily meaning nothing more than an extension of the landlord class" is the veriest rot, which should be thrown back upon him by the charge that land nationalization means nothing more than a diminution of the landlord class and a concentration and hundred-fold multiplication of the landlord's power.

BASIC PRINCIPLES OF ECONOMICS: RENT.

[*Liberty*, October 3, 1885.]

In following up the issues made by Mr. Tucker in the August number of *Liberty*, I am not quixotic enough to defend Proudhon either against Mr. T. or against his own possible inconsistencies. Only two of his works (recommended by Mr. T.) have been open to me. What I have to say stands upon its own merits, appealing to reason and the instinct of justice.

1. "The fiction of the productivity of capital."

In productivity for human needs or desires, human activity is implied. No one pretends that capital or the results of past labor can in this point of view be independent of actual labor. Ripe grain or fruit in field or orchard is a capital; its use implies the labor of gathering and storing, milling, cooking, etc. But these consummating works would be impossible without the capital of the harvest, the result of previous culture, which, whether by the same or by different laborers, is equally an integrant factor in productivity and justly entitled to its proportionate share of the fruits.

Now, go back a year or more. Before the culture in question, capital existed as the result of clearing, fencing, ditching, manuring, etc., without which the culture would have been fruitless or impossible. Such previous works, then, are, equally with the two later, integrant of productivity, and have just claims to be satisfied in the repartition of the harvest. Previous to these three kinds of works, there has often been expenditure of effort in discovery or exploration, in conquest of territory, to which the State falls heir, and on the strength of which it levies tribute under title of entry fees or purchase-money.

In the precited series, the second term in order of succession has absorbed the first, so that the entry or purchase-fee is added to the claim for preparatory works, whose aggregate constitutes the basis of rentals.

---

* Meaning by rent monopolistic rent, paid by tenant to landlord; not economic rent, the advantage enjoyed by the occupant of superior land.

Mr. Tucker says that the "liquidation of this value, whether immediate or gradual, is a sale, and brings a right of ownership, which it is not in the nature of rent to do. To call this rent inaccurate." Now, this is a question of the use of language. Accuracy here, as I maintain, consists in the use of words in their usual sense. I protest against neologies, or arbitrary definitions, in economics that make words squint, as a perfidy of Socialism which engenders vain logomachies and retards the triumph of justice. The liquidation of the value precited, the result of preparatory works, may be effected either by sale or by rentals. Sale is often impossible or unfeasible ; it would be so at present for my own farm. Now, comes in the idea that each payment of rent shall constitute an instalment of purchase-money. This is Proudhon's theory of liquidation with a view to the independent proprietorship of the soil by its farmers. It is viable for rentals during a term of successive years, but is inapplicable to many cases like the following. By expenditure of unpaid labor during several years I have prepared a field for cotton culture. An immigrant, needing to realize the results of labor more promptly than would be possible if he began by performing upon forest land the kind of work I have already done, offers me a fourth of the crop for the use of my field. *This is rent.* The crop from which it is paid leaves the soil poorer in proportion, and the fences, etc., will need repair at an earlier period. Thus each crop may be estimated as lessening the original value of productivity by about one-tenth, sometimes as much as one-fourth. Now, the tenant profits three times as much as I do at the cost of my preparatory labors. The loss by cropping, of this value, is the just basis of rent, which leaves no proportion of purchase title to the tenant during one or a few seasons who does not manure or repair fences. The tenant who does this, and thus reproduces the original value, justly enters into proprietorship, and his rentals ought to be regarded as instalments of purchase-money. There lies the practical difference.

It is necessary to face the facts, and to avoid confusion by abstract terminology. There is just rent, and there is unjust rent, or the legal abuse of the rental system. Abate the public nuisance of legislation, and these matters are naturally arranged by contract between farmers.

The equitable relations between actual labor and the previous labors that constitute capital in the soil, or immovable upon it, vary with time, place, and circumstance. Rulings concerning them, reduced to the procrustean measures of law, if just for some cases, must be unjust for others. Private contracts only can approximate to justice ; and how nearly they do it is the affair of the contracting parties, defying all prescriptive formulas.   EDGEWORTH.

The two works which I recommended to Edgeworth are among Proudhon's best ; but they are very far from all that he has written, and it is very natural for the reader of a very small portion of his writings to draw inferences which he will find unwarranted when he reads more. This is due principally to Proudhon's habit of using words in different senses at different times, which I regard as unfortunate. Now, in the article which gave rise to this discussion, Edgeworth inferred (or seemed to infer), from the fact that some of Proudhon's transitional proposals allowed a share to capital for a time, that he contemplated as a permanent arrangement a division

of labor's earnings between labor and capital as two distinct
things.   Lest this might mislead, I took the liberty to correct
it, and to state that Proudhon thought labor the only legitimate title to wealth.

Now comes Edgeworth, and says that he meant by capital
only the result of preparatory labor, which is as much entitled to reward as any other.   Very good, say I ; no one
denies that.   But this is not what is ordinarily meant by the
" productivity of capital " ; and Edgeworth, by his own rule, is
bound to use words in their usual sense.   The usual sense of
this phrase, and the sense in which the economists use it, is
that capital has such an independent share in all production
that the owner of it may rightfully farm out the privilege
of using it, receive a steady income from it, have it restored
to him *intact* at the expiration of the lease, farm it out again
to somebody else, and go on in this way, he and his heirs
forever, living in a permanent state of idleness and luxury
simply from having performed a certain amount of " preparatory labor."   That is what Proudhon denounced as " the
fiction of the productivity of capital " ; and Edgeworth, in
interpreting the phrase otherwise, gives it a very unusual
sense, in violation of his own rule.

Moreover, what Edgeworth goes on to say about the proportional profits of landlord and tenant indicates that he has
very loose ideas about the proper reward of labor, whether
present or preparatory.   The scientific reward (and under absolutely free competition the actual reward is, in the long run,
almost identical with it) of labor is the product of an equal
amount of equally arduous labor.   The product of an hour
of Edgeworth's labor in preparing a field for cotton culture,
and the product of an hour of his tenant's labor in sowing
and harvesting the crop, ought each to exchange for the
product of an hour's labor of their neighbor the shoemaker,
or their neighbor the tailor, or their neighbor the grocer, or
their neighbor the doctor, provided the labor of all these parties is equally exhausting and implies equal amounts of acquired skill and equal outlays for tools and facilities.   Now,
supposing the cases of Edgeworth and his tenant to be representative and not isolated ; and supposing them to produce,
not for their own consumption, but for the purpose of sale,
which is the purpose of practically all production, it then
makes no difference to either of them whether their hour's
labor yields five pounds of cotton or fifteen.   In the one
case they can get no more shoes or clothes or groceries or
medical services for the fifteen pounds than they can in the

other for the five. The great body of landlords and tenants, like the great body of producers in any other industry, does not profit by an increased productivity in its special field of work, except to the extent that it consumes or repurchases its own product. The profit of this increase goes to the people at large, the consumers. So it is not true (assuming always a *régime* of free competition) that Edgeworth's tenant "profits three times as much" as Edgeworth because of the latter's preparatory labors. Neither of them profit thereby, but each gets an hour of some other man's labor for an hour of his own.

So much for the reward of labor in general. Now to get back to the question of rent.

If Edgeworth performs preparatory labor on a cotton field, the result of which would remain intact if the field lay idle, and that result is damaged by a tenant, the tenant ought to pay him for it on the basis of reward above defined. This does not bring a right of ownership to the tenant, to be sure, for the property has been destroyed and cannot be purchased. But the transaction, nevertheless, is in the nature of a sale, and not a payment for a loan. Every sale is an exchange of labor, and the tenant simply pays money representing his own labor for the result of Edgeworth's labor which he (the tenant) has destroyed in appropriating it to his own use. If the tenant does not damage the result of Edgeworth's preparatory labor, then, as Edgeworth admits, whatever money the tenant pays justly entitles him to that amount of ownership in the cotton field. Now, this money, paid over and above all damage, if it does not bring equivalent ownership, is payment for use, usury, and, in my terminology, rent. If Edgeworth prefers to use the word rent to signify all money paid to landlords as such by tenants as such for whatever reason, I shall think his use of the word inaccurate; but I shall not quarrel with him, and shall only protest when he interprets other men's thought by his own definitions, as he seemed to me to have done in Proudhon's case. If he will be similarly peaceful towards me in my use of the word, there will be no logomachy.

The difference between us is just this. Edgeworth says that from tenant to landlord there is payment for damage, and this is just rent; and there is payment for use, and that is unjust rent. I say there is payment for damage, and this is indemnification or sale, and is just; and there is payment for use, and that is rent, and is unjust. My use of the word is in accordance with the dictionary, and is more definite and discriminating than the other; moreover, I find it more effective in argument. Many a time has some small proprietor, troubled with qualms of conscience and anxious to justify the source of his income, exclaimed, on learning that I believe in payment for wear and tear : " Oh ! well, you believe in rent, after all ; it's only a question of how much rent ; " after which he would settle back, satisfied. I have always found that the only way to give such a man's conscience a chance to get a hold upon his thought and conduct was to insist on the narrower use of the word rent. It calls the attention much more vividly to the distinction between justice and injustice. If in this I am guilty of neology, I am no more so than in my use of the word Anarchy, which Edgeworth adopts with great enthusiasm and employs with great effect. If the " squint " is what he objects to, why does it annoy him in one case and please him in the other ?

I must add that, after what I said in my previous answer in opposition to legislative interference for the control of rents, etc., it seems hardly within the limits of fair discussion to hint that I am in favor of "procrustean measures of law." Certainly, Edgeworth does not directly say so, but in an article avowedly written in answer to me I cannot see how the remark is otherwise pertinent.

RENT : PARTING WORDS.

[*Liberty*, December 12, 1885.]

THE terminology employed by me in the preceding numbers of *Liberty* needs no defence, as I have used common words in their usual sense without regard to the technicalities of schoolmen.

My admission that payments by a tenant beyond restoration of all values removed by crops, and during the years of culture, should justly be reckoned as purchase money, has nothing to do with terminology; it employs no words in an unusual sense. Therein consists, however, my radical accord with Proudhon and other modern socialists, and it cuts to the root of the tribune paid to idle landlords. The rent on real estate in cities has a compound basis; for, in addition to the equivalent for repairs and taxes common between it and agricultural rent, it includes an increment that may or may not have been earned by the owner and which is generally due to the concurrence of many individuals actuated by commercial and other social interests. A vortex, the site of which is determined by some local advantage, sucks in the population and resources of a large area.

The ethical title to the unearned increment of market values in real estate reverts to the municipal autonomy (1), but its legal title is now vested with individuals, and is the unjust basis of fortunes, like that of the Astors in New York City. Such titles carry with them at least hygienic duties, and certain tenement blocks are fairly indictable under existing laws as public nuisances.

Market gardens near cities partake of this compound basis of values, but for agricultural lands generally labor is the only factor of value and title of rent. "Reduction to Procrustean codes of law of these relations between past and present labor which constitute capital in the soil" is an archonistic vice which I do not attribute to Mr. Tucker, but I perceive in his reply some twinges of conscience which accuse his semi-allegiance to "Pantarchate" doctrines. One of these he brings forward in the formula of exchange of labor, hour for hour; an arrangement the feasibility of which is narrowly limited in practice, and which, even when feasible, must be subordinate to personal contracts under individual sovereignty. (2) The pretension to generalize it is purely conventional and foreign to economic science. (3)

Aiming at equalitarian justice in labor exchange, Marx takes from statistical tables the average life of laborers in each department, including even the manipulation of poisons; then, if the span of life in these is reduced to, say five years, while in farm-work it is sixty, he makes one hour of the latter exchange for twelve of the former.

Is it necessary to expose the puerility of such speculative views? With a despotic capitalism will cease the necessity for murderous industries. Honest labor owns no fealty to the royalty of gold; hence will abandon the quicksilver works of the Rothschilds, which have for their chief object the extraction of gold, to be kept in vaults as the basis of currency. The Labor and Produce Exchange Bank annihilates at one blow the industrial and the financial slavery.

Honest labor has no use for those paralyzing paints which are compounded with white lead. It will forge its plows as they were forged before capitalism dictated that sharpening process, to the dust of which so many lives are sacrificed by artifical phthisis. I make bold to declare that not a single murderous function will remain after the emancipation from the prejudice of government, for the political and the economic despotisms are Siamese twins. But that will not equalize exchanges, hour for hour,— a system whose occasional feasibility cannot go behind personal contracts, and for Anarchists must be optional with individual sovereignty. It is a rickety child of the "Pantarchate," that needs to be bolstered with half a dozen ifs. Not only is it incalculable for exchanges between the simpler forms of labor and those requiring years of previous study, or a costly preparation; (4) but even in agriculture or mechanics, labor is little more than the zero that gives value to judgment and skill, without which its intervention is not only worthless, but often detrimental. (5) A mere plowman in my orchard may ruin my fruit crop by a day's faithful work, or a surgeon cripple me for life by an operation however well intended, and, mechanically, well performed. (6)

The employer is naturally and ethically the appraiser of work, and what he wants to know is, not the cost in time or pains, but the probable value of the result, before proposing terms to labor. (7) Then the estimate of costs enters into the laborer's answer, but, as he must often accept work the unforeseen costs of which exceed the compensation, it is unjust to restrict him from indemnifying himself on other occasions, by computing the value of his work to the employer. (8)

The "cost limit of price" doctrine is another economic fantasy (9) that flouts practical expediency, and, while qualifying particular estimates, can never become a general law.

The ethical validity of investment of past labor as the basis of rent does

not need to lean upon the broken reed that Mr. Tucker supplies in his "*if*
its result would remain intact, the field lying idle," etc. He knows it could
not remain intact, for such field would grow up in grubs and the fences
would decay during idleness; but it does not follow that the field would lie
idle because not rented, nor would my loss in that case be a just reason
why I should not share in the fructification of my past labor by another
man's actual labor. (10)   My illustration of the mechanism and conditions
of the productivity of capital stands for itself and by itself ; it is not a
gloze or commentary upon Proudhon.   His ideas and mine both harmonize with the facts of the case; that is our agreement: it is not an affair of
mere verbiage.

The field in question owed its whole productivity to my previous labor.
Other land contiguous was free to my tenant's occupation and use, but
though of equal original capacities was rejected by him as a non-value.
This is true of most agricultural land. Only by contiguity to cities, or
in certain exceptional sites, has land any appreciable value independent of
labor, in this country.

I stated that, in making a crop upon the basis of values accumulated in
the soil by my previous labor, the tenant, paying one-fourth, profited
three times as much by my previous labor as I did.   This is the conventional award to his season's labor ; it may be more or less than relative
justice, but conventional rules or customs are infinitely preferable to arith-
metical computations of a balance by the hours of labor.   Farmers are not
apt to be monomaniacs of bookkeeping.   Instead of *profited*, I might
have written shared.   The term profit touches a hyperæsthetic spot in the
socialist brain, and makes thought fly off at a tangent. (11)   Mr. Tucker's
commentary here is to me a mere muddle of phrases, which it does not
appear profitable to analyze.

There is no squint in our use of the word Anarchy.   There is a squint
in employing it as a synonym with confusion. (12)   EDGEWORTH.

(1) This smacks of Henry George. If the municipality is
an organization to which every person residing within a given
territory must belong and pay tribute, it is not a bit more defensible than the State itself,—in fact, is nothing but a small
State ; and to vest in it a title to any part of the value of real
estate is simply land nationalization on a small scale, which no
Anarchist can look upon with favor. If the municipality is
a voluntary organization, it can have no titles except what it
gets from the individuals composing it. If they choose to
transfer their "unearned increments" to the municipality, well
and good ; but any individual not choosing to do so ought to
be able to hold his "unearned increment" against the world.
If it is unearned, certainly his neighbors did not earn it. The
advent of Liberty will reduce all unearned increments to a
harmless minimum.

(2) There it is again. After admitting that I do not want
to impose this principle of exchange, why does Edgeworth remind me that it must be "subordinate," etc.? When forced
to a direct answer, he allows that I am not in favor of legal
regulation, but immediately he proceeds with his argument as

if I were. Logic commands him for a moment; then he lapses back into his instinctive inability to distinguish between a scientific principle and statute law.

(3) Who pretends to generalize it? Certainly no Anarchist. The pretension is that it will generalize itself as soon as monopoly is struck down. This generalization, far from being conventional, depends upon the abolition of conventions. Instead of being narrowly limited in practice, the labor measure of exchange will become, through Liberty, an almost universal fact.

(4) Why incalculable? Suppose a boy begins farm labor at fifteen years of age with a prospect of fifty years of work before him at one thousand dollars a year. Suppose another boy of the same age spends ten years and ten thousand dollars in studying medicine, and begins practice at twenty-five years of age with a prospect of forty years of work before him. Is it snch a difficult mathematical problem to find out how great a percentage the latter must add to his prices in order to get in forty years as much as the farmer gets in fifty, and ten thousand dollars besides? Any schoolboy could solve it. Of course, labor cannot be estimated with the same degree of accuracy under all circumstances; but with the cost principle as a guide a sufficient approximation to equity is secured, while without it there is nothing but haphazard, scramble, and extortion. Edgeworth is mistaken, by the way, regarding the paternity of this principle. It is not a child of the "Pantarchate," or at any rate only an adopted child, its real father having been Josiah Warren, who hated the "Pantarchate" most cordially.

(5) I have never maintained that judgment and skill are less important than labor; I have only maintained that neither judgment nor skill can be charged for in equity except so far as they have been acquired. Even then the payment is not for the judgment or skill, but for the labor of acquiring; and, in estimating the price, one hour of labor in acquiring judgment is to be considered equal,—not, as now, to one day, or week, or perhaps year of manual toil,—but to one hour of manual toil. The claim for judgment and skill is usually a mere pretext made to deceive the people into paying exorbitant prices, and will not bear analysis for a moment.

(6) What has this to do with the price of labor? Imagine Edgeworth or any other sensible man employing an incompetent surgeon because his services could be had for a dollar a day less than those of one more competent! The course for sensible and just men to follow is this: Employ the best

workmen you can find ; whomsoever you employ, pay them equitably ; if they damage you, insist that they shall make the damage good so far as possible ; but do not dock their wages on the supposition that they *may* damage you.

(7) On the contrary, the employee, the one who does the work, is naturally and ethically the appraiser of work, and all that the employer has to say is whether he will pay the price or not. Into his answer enters the estimate of the value of the result. Under the present system he offers less than cost, and the employee is forced to accept. But Liberty and competition will create such an enormous market for labor that no workman will be forced by his incompetency to work for less than cost, as he will always be in a position to resort to some simpler work for which he is competent and can obtain ade• quate pay.

(8) The old excuse : to pay Paul I must rob Peter.

(9) No, not *another;* the same old fantasy, if it be a fantasy. The fact that Edgeworth supposes the exchange of labor for labor to be a different thing from the "cost limit of price" doctrine shows how little he understands it.

(10) Edgeworth admitted in his previous article that he could ask nothing more than that his field should be restored to him intact, and that anything his tenant might pay in addition should be regarded as purchase-money ; now he not only wants his field restored intact, but insists on sharing in the results of his tenant's labor. I can follow in no such devious path as this.

(11) It would have made no difference to me had Edgeworth said "shared" instead of "profited." In that case I should simply have said that neither landlords nor tenants as such (where there is freedom of competition) *share* in the results of the extra fertility of soil due to preparatory labor, but that those results go to the consumers. And Edgeworth's reply would have been the same,—that my remarks were a "muddle of phrases." Such a reply admits of no discussion. Only our readers can judge of its justice. In saying that "farmers are not apt to be monomaniacs of bookkeeping," Edgeworth is probably not aware that he is calling Proudhon (with whom he so obstinately insists that he is in accord) hard names. The statement occurs over and over again in Proudhon's works that bookkeeping is the final arbiter in all economical discussion. He never tires of sounding its praises. And this great writer, whose "radical accord" with Edgeworth "is not a matter of mere verbiage," was one of the

most persistent champions of the cost principle and the exchange of labor hour for hour.

(12) I presume I am entirely safe in saying that the word Anarchy is used in the sense of confusion a thousand times where it is used once in the sense of Liberty. Therefore Edgeworth's closing assertion that "there is no squint in our use of the word Anarchy," and that "there is a squint in employing it as a synonym with confusion," shows how much reliance can be placed upon his opening assertion that in this discussion he has "used common words in their usual sense."

PROPERTY UNDER ANARCHISM.

[*Liberty*, July 12, 1890.]

THE current objection to Anarchism, that it would throw property titles and especially land titles into hopeless confusion, has originated an interesting discussion in *The Free Life* between Auberon Herbert, the editor, and Albert Tarn, an Anarchistic correspondent. Mr. Tarn is substantially right in the position that he takes; his weakness lies in confining himself to assertion,—a weakness of which Mr. Herbert promptly takes advantage.

Mr. Tarn's letter is as follows :

To the Editor of The Free Life :

SIR,—In your article on "The Great Question of Property" in last week's *Free Life* you speak of the weakness of the Anarchist position as involving either " hard crystalline customs very difficult to alter," or "some perpetually recurring form of scramble."

It seems strange that you can attribute to Anarchy just the very weaknesses that characterize our present property system. Why, it is now that we have "hard crystalline customs very difficult to alter," and a " perpetually recurring "—nay, a never-ceasing—" form of scramble."

Anarchists above all, though in favor of free competition, are averse to the eternal scramble which is now going on for the privileges which legal money and legal property confer, of living at ease at the expense of the masses.

Anarchy would sweep away such privileges, and, there being no longer any chance of obtaining them, people would simply work for their living and retain whatever they earn. There would be little or no quarrel about property, no revolutionary movements to try to get hold of it, no taxes, no State Socialism. Why, all your struggles to-day, not only in the workshop and counting-house, but in the political field, are caused by the stupid laws of property and money, which result in a never-ending scramble.

Anarchy means peace; it means every one getting what he's worth and no more,—no thieving at all, neither by landlords, usurers, lawyers, tax-collectors, nor even by pick-pockets and burglars when the present contrasts of wealth vanish.

Your property laws are just as stupid as any other laws.   They defeat their own ends.   Yours faithfully,

                                                    ALBERT TARN.

In Mr. Herbert's rejoinder the case against Anarchism is exceptionally well put, and for this reason among others I give it in full:

It is not enough for our correspondent, Mr. Tarn, to say that Anarchy does away with scramble; we want to know "the how" and "the why." Our contention is that under the law of the free market everybody knows, first, who owns a particular piece of property, and, secondly, the conditions under which property can be acquired.   All is clear and definite, and that clearness and definiteness are worth far more to the human race in the long run than any temporary advantage to be gained by forcible interferings with distribution.   On the other hand, we say that under Anarchy nobody would know to whom a piece of property belonged, and nobody would understand how it was to be transferred from A to B. Take any instance you like.   Anarchists generally define property by use and possession; that is, whoever uses and possesses is to be considered owner.   John Robins possesses a plot of three acres, and manages to feed two cows on it.   John Smith possesses neither land nor cow.   He comes to John Robins and says: "You are not really using and possessing these three acres; I shall take half of them."   Who on earth is to judge between these men?   Who is to say whether John Robins is really possessing or not?   Who is going to say to John Smith that he shall not get a bit of land by "scramble" from John Robins, seeing that under the Anarchist system that was the very way in which John Robins himself got these three acres from the big landowner, who, as he said at the time, was not truly owning, because he was not possessing.

Mr. Tarn finds fault with us for saying that Anarchy, or no fixed standard of acquiring or owning, must lead either to rigid crystalline custom or to scramble.   But is that not almost absolutely certain?   At first it must be scramble.   Everybody who could would take or keep on the plea of possession.   We presume even a weekly tenant could claim under the same plea.   But even when the first great scramble was over, the smaller scrambles would continue, — the innumerable adjustments between John Robins and John Smith having to be perpetually made.   But after a certain time the race would tire of scramble, as it always has done, and then what would happen?   Why, necessarily, that a community would silently frame for itself some law or custom that would decide all these disputed cases.   They would say that no man should hold more than two acres; or that no man should be disturbed after so many years' possession; or they would fix some other standard, which would tend to become rigid and crystalline, and be very difficult to alter, just because there was no machinery for altering it.

We say that our friends the Anarchists—with whom, when they are not on the side of violence, we have much in common—must make their position clear and definite about property.   They are as much opposed as we are to State-regulated property; they are as much in favor of individualistic property as we are; but they will not pay the price that has to be paid for individualistic property, and which alone can make it possible.   When once you are away from the open market, there are only two alternatives, —State regulation (or law) and scramble. Every form of property-holding, apart from the open market, will be found to be some modification of one of these two forms.

This criticism of Anarchism, reduced to its essence, is seen to be twofold. First, the complaint is that it has no fixed standard of acquiring or owning. Second, the complaint is that it necessarily results in a fixed standard of acquiring or owning. Evidently Mr. Herbert is a very hard man to please. Before he criticises Anarchism further, I must insist that he make up his mind whether he himself wants or does not want a fixed standard. And whatever his decision, his criticism falls. For if he wants a fixed standard, that which he may adopt is as liable to become a " rigid crystalline custom " as any that Anarchism may lead to. And if he does not want a fixed standard, then how can he complain of Anarchism for having none ?

If it were my main object to emerge from this dispute victorious, I might well leave Mr. Herbert in the queer predicament in which his logic has placed him. But as I am really anxious to win him to the Anarchistic view, I shall try to show him that the fear of scramble and rigidity with which Anarchism inspires him has little or no foundation.

Mr. Herbert, as I understand him, believes in voluntary association, voluntarily supported, for the defence of person and property. Very well ; let us suppose that he has won his battle, and that such a state of things exists. Suppose that all municipalities have adopted the voluntary principle, and that compulsory taxation has been abolished. Now, after this, let us suppose further that the Anarchistic view that occupancy and use should condition and limit landholding becomes the prevailing view. Evidently then these municipalities will proceed to formulate and enforce this view. What the formula will be no one can foresee. But continuing with our suppositions, we will say that they decide to protect no one in the possession of more than ten acres. In execution of this decision, they, on October 1, notify all holders of more than ten acres within their limits that, on and after the following January 1, they will cease to protect them in the possession of more than ten acres, and that, as a condition of receiving even that protection, each must make formal declaration on or before December 1 of the specific ten-acre plot within his present holding which he proposes to personally occupy and use after January 1. These declarations having been made, the municipalities publish them and at the same time notify landless persons

that out of the lands thus set free each may secure protection
in the possession of any amount up to ten acres after January
1 by appearing on December 15, at a certain hour, and making declaration of his choice and intention of occupancy.
Now, says Mr. Herbert, the scramble will begin. Well, perhaps it will. But what of it ? When a theatre advertises to
sell seats for a star performance at a certain hour, there is a
scramble to secure tickets. When a prosperous city announces that on a given day it will accept loans from individuals up to a certain aggregate on attractive terms, there is a
scramble to secure the bonds. As far as I know, nobody
complains of these scrambles as unfair. The scramble begins
and the scramble ends, and the matter is settled. Some inequality still remains, but it has been reduced to a minimum,
and everybody has had an equal chance with the rest. So it
will be with this land scramble. It may be conducted as
peacefully as any other scramble, and those who are frightened by the word are simply the victims of a huge bugbear.

And the terror of rigidity is equally groundless. This rule
of ten-acre possession, or any similar one that may be
adopted, is no more rigid crystalline custom than is Mr. Herbert's own rule of protecting titles transferred by purchase and
sale. Any rule is rigid less by the rigidity of its terms than
by the rigidity of its enforcement. Now it is precisely in the
tempering of the rigidity of enforcement that one of the chief
excellences of Anarchism consists. Mr. Herbert must remember that under Anarchism all rules and laws will be little
more than suggestions for the guidance of juries, and that all
disputes, whether about land or anything else, will be submitted to juries which will judge not only the facts, but the law,
the justice of the law, its applicability to the given circumstances, and the penalty or damage to be inflicted because of
its infraction. What better safeguard against rigidity could
there be than this ? "Machinery for altering" the law, indeed ! Why, under Anarchism the law will be so flexible that
it will shape itself to every emergency and need no alteration.
And it will then be regarded as *just* in proportion to its flexi-
bility, instead of as now in proportion to its rigidity.

MERE LAND NO SAVIOUR FOR LABOR.

[*Liberty*, May 7, 1887.]

HERE is a delicious bit of logic from Mr. George : " If capital, a mere creature of labor, is such an *oppressive* thing, its creator, *when free*, can strangle it by refusing to reproduce it." The italics are mine. If capital is oppressive, it must be oppressive of labor. What difference does it make, then, what labor can do when free ? The question is what it can do when oppressed by capital. Mr. George's next sentence, to be sure, indicates that the freedom he refers to is freedom from land monopoly. But this does not improve his situation. He is enough of an economist to be very well aware that, whether it has land or not, labor which can get no capital— that is, which is oppressed by capital — cannot, without accepting the alternative of starvation, refuse to reproduce capital for the capitalists.

It is one thing for Mr. George to sit in his sanctum and write of the ease with which a man whose sole possession is a bit of land can build a home and scratch a living ; for the man to do it is wholly another thing. The truth is that this man can do nothing of the sort until you devise some means of raising his wages above the cost of living. And you can only do this by increasing the demand for his labor. And you can only increase the demand for his labor by enabling more men to go into business. And you can only enable more men to go into business by enabling them to get capital without interest, which, in Mr. George's opinion, would be very wrong. And you can only enable them to get capital without interest by abolishing the money monopoly, which, by limiting the supply of money, enables its holders to exact interest. And when you have abolished the money monopoly, and when, in consequence, the wages of the man with the bit of land have begun to rise above the cost of living, the labor question will be nine-tenths solved. For then either this man will live better and better, or he will steadily lay up money, with which he can buy tools to compete with his employer or to till his bit of land with comfort and advantage. In short, he will be an independent man, receiving all that he produces or an equivalent thereof. How to make this the lot of all men is the labor question. Free land will not solve it. Free money, supplemented by free land, will,

HENRY GEORGE'S "SECONDARY FACTORS."

[*Liberty*, September 24, 1887.]

In trying to answer the argument that land is practically useless to labor unprovided with capital, Henry George declares that "labor and land, even in the absence of secondary factors obtained from their produce, have in their union to-day, as they had in the beginning, the potentiality of all that man ever has brought, or ever can bring, into being."

This is perfectly true ; in fact, none know it better than the men whom Mr. George thus attempts to meet.

But, as Cap'n Cuttle was in the habit of remarking, " the bearin' o' this ere hobserwation lies in the application on't," and in its application it has no force whatever. Mr. George uses it to prove that, if land were free, labor would settle on it, thus raising wages by relieving the labor market.

But labor would do no such thing.

The fact that a laborer, given a piece of land, can build a hut of mud, strike fire with flint and steel, scratch a living with his finger-nails, and thus begin life as a barbarian, even with the hope that in the course of a lifetime he may slightly improve his condition in consequence of having fashioned a few of the ruder of those implements which Mr. George styles "secondary factors" (and he could do no more than this without producing for exchange, which implies, not only better machinery, but an entrance into that capitalistic maelstrom which would sooner or later swallow him up),—this fact, I say, will never prove a temptation to the operative of the city, who, despite his wretchedness, knows something of the advantages of civilization and to some extent inevitably shares them.

Man does not live by bread alone.

The city laborer may live in a crowded tenement and breathe a tainted air ; he may sleep cold, dress in rags, and feed on crumbs ; but now and then he gets a glimpse at the morning paper, or, if not, then at the bulletin-board ; he meets his fellow-men face to face ; he knows by contact with the world more or less of what is going on in it ; he spends a few pennies occasionally for a gallery-ticket to the theatre or for some other luxury, even though he knows he "can't afford it"; he hears the music of the street bands ; he sees the pictures in the shop windows ; he goes to church if he is pious, or, if not, perhaps attends the meetings of the Anti-Poverty Society and listens to stump speeches by Henry George ; and, when all these fail him, he is indeed unfortunate if some fellow-laborer does not invite him to join him in a social glass over the nearest bar.

Not an ideal life, surely ; but he will shiver in his garret and slowly waste away from inanition ere he will exchange it for the semi-barbarous condition of the backwoodsman without an axe. And, were he to do otherwise, I would be the first to cry : The more fool he !

Mr. George's remedy is similar—at least for a part of mankind—to that which is attributed to the Nihilists, but which few of them ever believed in,—namely, the total destruction of the existing social order and the creation of a new one on its ruins.

Mr. George may as well understand first as last that labor will refuse to begin this world anew. It never will abandon even its present meagre enjoyment of the wealth and the means of wealth which have grown out of its ages of sorrow, suffering, and slavery. If Mr. George offers it land alone, it will turn its back upon him. It insists upon both land and tools. These it will get, either by the State Socialistic method of concentrating the titles to them in the hands of one vast monopoly, or by the Anarchistic method of abolishing all monopolies, and thereby distributing these titles gradually among laborers through the natural channels of free production and exchange.

THE STATE SOCIALISTS AND HENRY GEORGE.

[*Liberty*, September 24, 1887.]

JUST as I have more respect for the Roman Catholic Christian who believes in authority without qualification, than for the Protestant Christian who speaks in the name of liberty, but does not know the meaning of the word, so I have more respect for the State Socialist than for Henry George, and in the struggle between the two my sympathy is with the former. Nevertheless the State Socialists have only themselves to blame for the support they have hitherto extended to George, and the ridiculous figure that some of them now cut in their sackcloth and ashes is calculated to amuse. Burnette G. Haskell, for instance. In his *Labor Enquirer*, previous to the issue of August 20, he had been flying the following flag : " For President in 1888, Henry George." But in that issue, having heard of the New York schism, he lowered his colors and substituted the following : " For President in 1888, any man who will go as the servant of the people and not as their ' boss,' and who understands that poverty can only be abolished by the abolition of the competitive wage system and the inauguration of State Socialism." When Haskell hoisted George's name, did he not know that his candidate believed that poverty was not to be abolished by the abolition of the wage system ? If he did not know this, his knowledge of his candidate must have been limited indeed. If he did know it, the change of colors indicates, not the discarding of a leader, but a revolution in ideas. Yet Haskell is undoubtedly not conscious of any revolution in his ideas, and would admit none. All of which tends to show that he has no ideas definite enough to be revolutionized.

LIBERTY AND THE GEORGE THEORY.

[*Liberty*, November 5, 1887.]

THERE is much in Liberty to admire, and in Anarchism that I believe has a divine right of way. But I see little of these qualities in the criticisms made by Editor Tucker on the George movement, and much, as I think, of the exaggeration and inconsistency inherent in the Anarchistic temper and teachings.

You have " more respect," you say, " for the State Socialist than for Henry George," and " in the struggle between the two your sympathy is with the former." This is vague, to say the least ; and the meaning is not helped by the comparison with "the Roman Catholic who believes in authority without qualification, and the Protestant who speaks in the name of liberty, but does not know the meaning of the word." Such expressions seem to me to point no issue, but to dodge or confuse issues. The question is threefold, relating to tactics, spirit, and doctrine, which are not always one, or of the same relative importance. You do not say whether the expulsion of the Socialists was just, whether they acted in good faith as members of the United Labor party, or believed their doctrine had any logical filiation with its platform. This ought to have something to do with our "respect" and " sympathy." To hold to the belief of a Roman Catholic is one thing, and to enter an evangelical body as an emissary of the Pope is quite another. You seem to slur this issue in speaking merely of "the ridiculous figure the Socialists now cut in their sackcloth and ashes," for "ridiculous" is not a word of a very specific meaning. But your closing remark appears to be a contradiction of the first so praiseful of the simple stable views of the State Socialist ; for of the act of the *Labor Enquirer* in hoisting Henry George's name one day and pulling it down the next you say it shows, not a revolution in ideas, but that it had " no ideas definite enough to be revolutionized."

And do you really believe that Protestantism is not an advance on Roman Catholicism; that such men as Luther, Wesley, Channing, are not as "respectable" as the Roman pontiffs? Do you think the apostate or rebellious element in both Church and State is not as deserving of respect as the older body, simply because it does not reach the goal of freedom at a bound? Have you more sympathy with Asia than Europe, with Europe than America, with unqualified despotism than with a constitutional monarchy, with monarchy than with republicanism? And is there no room for theory or experiment between State Socialism and Anarchism, no foothold for large views and manly purposes? Are Henry George and his co-workers of the class who "speak in the name of liberty, but do not know the meaning of the word"? Is their talk and spirit rubbish by the side no tonly of Anarchism, but its opposite, State Socialism? Did liberty have nothing to do with the starting of "Progress and Poverty,"—that book that has set so many to thinking and acting, and has done more to popularize the science of political economy than the writings of any dozen men, if not of all men, on that theme? Had liberty nothing to do with the starting of the *Standard*, the Anti-Poverty Society, the anointing of McGlynn, Pentecost, Huntington, Redpath, McGuire, and the rest of the new apostolate of freedom? I am aware there are things connected with this reform to which exceptions can and must be made; but they do not prove it is not Liberty's offspring, an onward movement freighted with benefit for the race.

Of a piece with this criticism is another article in the same number, in which you go even farther, and say: "Mr. George may as well understand first as last that labor will refuse to begin this world anew. It never will abandon even its present meagre enjoyment of wealth and the means of wealth which have grown out of its ages of sorrow, suffering, and slavery. If Mr. George offers it land alone, it will turn its back upon him. It insists upon both land and tools." That is an astounding assertion that he asks labor to "begin this world anew," and to "abandon" what it already has, and ought to he backed by some show of argument; but I see none. How are the people to lose by being made their own landlords? How are they to be robbed of their present advantages in having the land made free? Your whole argument, filling a column, is that "the city operative will not be tempted to leave what he has for the semi-barbarous condition of the backwoodsman without an axe, building a hut of mud, striking fire with flint and steel, and scratching a living with his finger nails"! Now, if the vacant lots and tracts of land in and about all the cities are brought into use by being built upon or cultivated, will not the stimulus given to industry and the increased opportunity for employment resulting therefrom not only enable the operative to buy an axe, rake, hoe, hammer, saw, and even a horse and plough? And not only this, but to find a suitable patch of land without going so far beyond the boundaries of civilization as you imagine? But the idea is not that every one will become a farmer or landowner, but that the cheapening and freeing of this primary factor of production, the land, will make it possible for those of very limited means and resources to do more for themselves and for the world than now, besides rendering capital more active, more productive; the clear tendency of which would be to relieve the labor market, and make the demand for labor greater than the supply, and so raise wages and secure to labor its just reward. And you do not see how this is in the interest of freedom; how the freeing of land will enable men to become the possessors, not only of the tools they need, but of their individuality as well! Taking

taxes off industry, and substituting therefor the social values given to
land, you call retrogression, or rather "a remedy similar—for a part of
mankind at least—to that attributed to the Nihilists, the total destruction
of the existing social order, and the creation of a new one on its ruins"!
This is wild talk, and is none the less so because of the use of the feeble
adjective, "similar," and the halting phrase, "at least a part of mankind," which destroy the value of the comparison for the purpose of argument, and, like the words "respect," "sympathy," "ridiculous," and
"semi-barbarous," show that *Liberty*, the Anarchist organ *par excellence*,
may dogmatize instead of reason, and make personal dictum or caprice
the standard of right.

But there is something of more consequence than the vulnerable points
in *Liberty's* logic, for it goes deeper. Granting that this reform does
mean the creation of a new order involving losses and sacrifices to the
individual for a generation, is that its condemnation? Words cannot
express my astonishment at the manner in which *Liberty* tells its readers that the city operative cannot be tempted "to begin life as a barbarian, even with the hope that in the course of a lifetime he may slightly
improve his condition," for he would be a "fool" not to prefer to this
the city with its "street bands," "shop windows," "theatres," and
"churches," even though he have to "breathe tainted air" and "dress
in rags." Ah, it is indeed true, as you say, "man does not live by bread
alone," and for that reason he prefers pure air and independence along
with isolation and struggle, to tainted air and serfdom along with brass
bands and hand organs, gaudy windows, and Black Crook performances.
But is that "beginning life as a barbarian," no matter with implements
however rude, at places however remote from the centres of pride and
luxury, with fruits of toil however slow in ripening, if the persons are
moved by the thought of bettering, not their own condition merely, but
that of the world, of the generations to come? Have not the pioneers of
freedom, the vanguards of civilization, again and again "begun life as
the barbarian," so to speak? This reform, it is true, means "bread,"
but bread for all, though there be luxury for none. We know the advantages of city life, and for that reason we would deny ourselves those advantages in order that cities might spread and civilization expand.

We want the earth, but do not mean to run away with it; there will
still be plenty of room,—yes, more than before, far more. It will be the
beginning, not the end, of reform; not the last step, but a great stride
forward. Socialism and Anarchism will both have a better chance then
than now, if the insufficiency of the principle is proven. For it is Socialistic in asserting the common ownership of the soil and governmental
control of such things as are in their nature monopolies, while it is Anarchistic in leaving all else to the natural channels of free production and
exchange, to free contract and spontaneous co-operation.

                                                        T. W. CURTIS.

Mr. Curtis's criticisms are based upon a series of misappre-
hensions of *Liberty's* statements, and in one instance upon
something that looks very like deliberate misrepresentation.

In the first place, he misapprehends my expression of
greater respect for and sympathy with the State Socialists than
Henry George, seeming to think that this preference included
in its sweep not only matters of doctrine, but matters of
tactics and spirit. The form of my assertion shows that I

confined it to doctrine simply. The declaration was that I
have more respect for the State Socialists than for George,
"*just* as I have more respect for the Roman Catholic Christian,
who *believes* in authority without qualification, than for the
Protestant Christian, who speaks in the name of liberty, but
does not know the meaning of the word." No one but Mr.
Curtis would dream of inferring from these words that I prefer
the tactics and spirit of Torquemada to those of Channing.
I left tactics and spirit entirely aside in making the above
statement. In respect to conduct I asserted superiority neither
for the State Socialist nor for George. Whether the State Socialists went to George or he went to them, or which seceded from
or betrayed the other, are questions which interest me only in
a minor degree. To me reason is the highest and grandest
faculty of man; and I place George lower in my esteem than
the State Socialist, because I consider him the greater offender
against reason. This is the sense in which I prefer Catholicism
to Protestantism, Asia to Europe, and monarchy to republicanism. The Catholic, the Asiatic, and the monarch are more
logical, more consistent, more straightforward, less corkscrewy,
more strictly plumb-line than the Protestant, the European,
and the republican. This is not a novel idea, and I am at a
loss to account for Mr. Curtis's suprise over it. Did he never
hear that there is no half-way house between Rome and
Reason? Likewise there is no room for logical, consistent
theory or intelligent, systematic experiment between State
Socialism and Anarchism. There is plenty of room between
them to jumble theories and to experiment blindly, but that is
all. The pity is that room of this kind should be so popular.

Yes, Henry George and his co-workers are of that class who
"speak in the name of liberty, but do not know the meaning
of the word." Mr. George has no conception of liberty as a
universal social law. He happens to see that in some things it
would lead to good results, and therefore in those things favors
it. But it has never dawned upon his mind that disorder is
the inevitable fruit of every plant which has authority for its
root. As John F. Kelly says of him, " he is inclined to look
with favor on the principle of *laissez faire*, yet he will abandon
it at any moment, whenever regulation seems more likely to
produce immediate benefits, regardless of the evils thereby
produced by making the people less jealous of State interference." The nature of his belief in liberty is well illustrated
by his attitude on the tariff question. One would suppose from
his generalization that he has the utmost faith in freedom of
competition; but one does not realize how little this faith

amounts to until he hears him, after making loud free-trade
professions, propose to substitute a system of bounties for the
tariff system.   If such political and economic empiricism is
not rubbish beside the coherent proposals of either Anarchism or State Socialism, then I don't know chaff from wheat.

Liberty, of course, had something to do with the writing of
"Progress and Poverty." It also had something to do with the
framing of divorce laws as a relief from indissoluble marriage.
But the divorce laws, instead of being libertarian, are an
express recognition of the rightfulness of authority over the
sexual relations.   Similarly "Progress and Poverty" expressly
recognizes the rightfulness of authority over the cultivation
and use of land.   For some centuries now evolution has been
little else than the history of liberty ; nevertheless all its factors have not been children of liberty.

Mr. Curtis tries to convict me of contradiction by pointing
to my statement that Burnette Haskell, a State Socialist, has no
definite ideas.   This he thinks inconsistent with my praise of
the simple stable views of the State Socialist.   Here is where
the color of misrepresentation appears.   In order to make his
point Mr. Curtis is obliged to quote me incorrectly. He attributes to me the following phrase: "the ridiculous figure the
Socialists now cut in their sackcloth and ashes."   My real words
were: "the ridiculous figure that *some of them* now cut in their
sackcloth and ashes."   It makes all the difference whether in
this sentence I referred to the whole body of State Socialists
or only to a few individuals among them.   It was precisely
because I was about to criticise the conduct of one State
Socialist in order to show that he had no real idea of State
Socialism that I felt it necessary to preface my criticism by
separating doctrine from conduct and declaring my preference
for the State Socialist over George in the matter of doctrine.
But Mr. Curtis will have it that I took Haskell as a typical
State Socialist, even if he has to resort to misquotation to
prove it.

He next turns his attention to the editorial on "Secondary
Factors."   He thinks that my assertion that George asks labor
to "begin this world anew" ought to be backed by some show
of argument.   Gracious heavens !   I backed it at the beginning of my article by a quotation from George himself.   Dis-
lodged by his critics from one point after another, George had
declared that "labor and land, even in the absence of secondary factors obtained from their produce, have in their union to-
day, as they had in the beginning, the potentiality of all that
man ever has brought, or ever can bring, into being."   When

such words as these are used to prove that, if land were free, labor would settle on it, even without secondary factors,—that is, without tools,—what do they mean except that the laborer is expected to "begin this world anew"? But if this is not enough for Mr. Curtis, may I refer him to the debate between George and Shewitch, in which the former, being asked by the latter what would have become of Friday if Crusoe had fenced off half the island and turned him loose upon it without any tools, answered that Friday would have made some fish-hooks out of bones and gone fishing? Isn't that sufficiently primitive to substantiate my assertion, Mr. Curtis? Tell Mr. George that the laborer can do nothing without capital, and he will answer you substantially as follows: Originally there was nothing but a naked man and the naked land ; free the land, and then, if the laborer has no tools, he will again be a naked man on naked land and can do all that Adam did. When I point out that such a return to barbarism is on a par with the remedy attributed to the Nihilists, the total destruction of the existing social order, Mr. Curtis asserts that "this is wild talk ; " but his assertion, it seems to me, "ought to be backed by some show of argument."

He is sure, however, that there is no need of going to the backwoods. There is enough vacant land in the neighborhood of cities, he thinks, to employ the surplus workers, and thus relieve the labor market. But this land will not employ any workers that have no capital, and those that have capital can get the land now. Thus the old question comes back again. Make capital free by organizing credit on a mutual plan, and then these vacant lands will come into use, and then industry will be stimulated, and then operatives will be able to buy axes and rakes and hoes, and then they will be independent of their employers, and then the labor problem will be solved.

My worst offence Mr. Curtis reserves till the last. It consists in telling the workingman that he would be a fool not to prefer the street bands, the shop windows, the theatres, and the churches to a renewal of barbaric life. Mr. Curtis again misapprehends me in thinking that I commend the bands, the windows, etc. I said explicitly that there is nothing ideal about them. But society has come to be man's dearest possession, and the advantages and privileges which I cited, crude and vulgar and base as some of them are, represent society to the operative. He will not give them up, and I think he is wise. Pure air is good, but no one wants to breathe it long alone. Independence is good, but isolation is too heavy a price to pay for it. Both pure air and independence must be reconciled with society, or not many laborers will ever enjoy them. Luckily they can be and will be, though not by taxing land values. As for the idea that persons can be induced to become barbarians from altruistic motives in sufficient numbers to affect the labor market, it is one that I have no time to discuss. In one respect at least Mr. George is preferable to Mr. Curtis as an opponent : he usually deals in economic argument rather than sentimentalism.

A CRITICISM THAT DOES NOT APPLY.

[*Liberty*, July 16, 1887.]

To the Editor of Liberty :

It pains me to see your frequent attacks on Henry George, as they make the defenders of monopolies secure in the knowledge that there is discord in the ranks of the reformers. It appears to me—though I may be mistaken and will gladly accept arguments and refutation—that one important point of the land question has escaped your attention, just as the vital point of the money question does not seem to be clear to the editor of the *Standard.* It is my conviction that in a state of perfect liberty, assuming the existence of "intelligent egoism," the people will combine for mutual protection, and among other things will enter a social compact creating an equitable right of property. They will also protect their members in the possession of the land they till, or on which they ply their trade or build their homes. But since some land possesses advantages over other land, they will demand an equitable remuneration for this protection and renunciation, especially if it can be shown to cost the consumers of whatever is produced under these special advantages exactly as much as the holder of land is able to obtain as "rent" (Ricardo's "rent," John Stuart Mill's "unearned increment"). The community would therefore collect the rent in the form of taxes,—*i.e.*, equitable pay for the right of possession,—and, to be perfectly fair, should divide the proceeds among those consumers who, through the operation of the law of supply and demand, were forced to pay more than the average cost. But as such distribution would be practically impossible, the proceeds of this taxation should be used as nearly as possible to the advantage of those to whom it equitably belongs. Can you suggest a better disposal than Henry George does? If so, we are ready to hear. But please admit, or else refute, the statement that the collection of rent by the community would be the natural outgrowth of equitable social compact entered for the sake of order and peace in a state of perfect liberty among intelligently egoistical beings.

You cannot convince Henry George of the error of his position in relation to capital, if you deride the truths he advances together with his errors. Let us reason together, and I am sure we can ultimately unite on one platform,—*i.e.*, the abolition of *all unjust* laws, of which the permission given to individual persons of appropriating the unearned increment (which has a natural, not an artificial, origin) is not by any means the least.   EGOIST.

PHILADELPHIA, May 11, 1887.

My correspondent, who, by the way, is a highly intelligent man, and has a most clear understanding of the money question, should point out the truths that I have derided before accusing me of deriding any. I certainly never have derided the truth contained in Ricardo's theory of rent. What I have derided is Henry George's proposal that a majority of the people shall seize this rent by force and expend it for their own benefit, or perhaps for what they are pleased to consider the benefit of the minority. I have also derided many of the arguments by which Mr. George has attempted to justify this proposal, many of which he has used in favor of interest and other forms of robbery, and his ridiculous pretence that he is a champion of liberty. But I have never disputed that, under the system of land monopoly, certain individuals get, in the form of rent, a great deal that they never earned by their labor, or that it would be a great blessing if some plan should be devised and adopted whereby this could be prevented without violating the liberty of the individual. I am convinced, however, that the abolition of the money monopoly, and the refusal of protection to all land titles except those of occupiers, would, by the emancipation of the workingman from his present slavery to capital, reduce this evil to a very small fraction of its present proportions, especially in cities, and that the remaining fraction would be the cause of no more inequality than arises from the unearned increment derived by almost every industry from the aggregation of people or from that unearned increment of superior natural ability which, even under the operation of the cost principle, will probably always enable some individuals to get higher wages than the average rate. In all these cases the margin of difference will tend steadily to decrease, but it is not likely in any of them to disappear altogether. Whether, after the abolition of the State, voluntary co-operators will resort to communistic methods in the hope of banishing even these vestiges of inequality is a question for their own future consideration, and has nothing whatever to do with the scheme of Henry George. For my part, I should be inclined to regard such a course as a leap not from the frying-pan into the fire, but from a Turkish bath into the nethermost hell. I take no pleasure in attacking Mr. George, but shall probably pursue my present policy until he condescends to answer and refute my arguments, if he can, or gives some satisfactory reason for declining to do so.

LAND OCCUPANCY AND ITS CONDITIONS.

[*Liberty*, August 27, 1887.]

To the Editor of Liberty :

Your reply of July 16, 1887, to my letter is not at all satisfactory to me. I cannot with my best endeavor harmonize your statement : " I am convinced, however, that the abolition of the money monopoly and the refusal of protection to all land titles *except those of occupiers* would . . . reduce this evil to a very small fraction of its present proportions " (the italics are mine), with your opposition to *all* government. The natural inference of your statement is that you are in favor of protecting the occupier of land. Who is to give this protection ? Who is to wield this authority ? As regards the application of authority, I can see a distinction in degree only, none in principle, between the tacit, unwritten agreement of an uncultured tribe to ostracize the thief and wrong-doer and the despotic government of a tyrannical autocrat. Without authority of some kind rights cannot exist. The right of undisturbed possession, called ownership, is invariably the result of an agreement, by which all others not only abstain from taking possession, but even give assistance socially or physically, should any one trespass this agreement. But just therein consists the authority which the strong exercise over the weak, or the many over the few. In my opinion there can be no objection to such agreements or laws, when they are strictly based upon equity,—nay, they are the necessary basis of order and civilization ; they are, in fact, my ideal of a government. Only when they favor one class at the expense of another, when they are inequitable, can they become the instrument of oppression, and some men will find it to their supposed advantage to support such laws by fair or unfair means, most frequently by making use of the ignorance and superstition of the masses, who are known to fly to arms and shed their blood even for the most tyrannical dictator.

I understand you to favor the ownership of land based upon occupancy. You believe that under absolute individual freedom all men will abstain from disturbing the occupier of land in his possession. To this view I take exception. The choice spots will be coveted by others, and it is not human nature to relinquish any advantage without a sufficient cause. If you say the occupiers of these choice spots *should* be left undisturbed possessors without paying an equivalent for the *special* advantage they enjoy, you will find many of contrary opinion who must be coerced to this agreement. Egoism, when coupled with the knowledge that iniquity must inevitably lead to revolution, will accept as a most equitable condition that in which the recipient of the necessary protection pays to the protector the value of the right of undisturbed possession ; in which he returns to those who agree to abandon to him a special natural or local advantage its full value —*i.e.*, the unearned increment—as a compensation for the grant of the right of ownership.

The defence of occupying ownership of land seems to me at a par with the frequent retort to money reformers that everybody has an equal right to become a banker or a capitalist. An equitable relation will be prevented by the natural limitation of land in one, by the artifical limitation of the medium of exchange in the other case. You may perhaps have reason to object to applying the rent, after it has been collected, in the manner

suggested by Henry George; but I fail to see how you can reasonably oppose the collection of rent for the purpose of an equitable distribution.

EGOIST.

Egoist's acquaintance with *Liberty* is of comparatively recent date, but it is hard to understand how he could have
failed to find out from it that, in opposing all government, it so
defines the word as to exclude the very thing which Egoist
considers ideal government. It has been stated in these
columns I know not how many times that government,
Archism, invasion, are used here as equivalent terms; that
whoever invades, individual or State, governs and is an
Archist; and that whoever defends against invasion, individual or voluntary association, opposes government and is an
Anarchist. Now, a voluntary association doing equity would
not be an invader, but a defender against invasion, and might
include in its defensive operations the protection of the occupiers of land. With this explanation, does Egoist perceive
any lack of harmony in my statements? Assuming, then, protection by such a method, occupiers would be sure, no matter
how covetous others might be. But now the question recurs:
What is equity in the matter of land occupancy? I admit at
once that the enjoyment by individuals of increment which
they do not earn is not equity. On the other hand, I insist
that the confiscation of such increment by the State (not a
voluntary association) and its expenditure for public purposes,
while it might be a little nearer equity practically in that the
benefits would be enjoyed (after a fashion) by a larger number
of persons, would be exactly as far from it theoretically,
inasmuch as the increment no more belongs equally to the
public at large than to the individual land-holder, and would
still be a long way from it even practically, for the minority,
not being allowed to spend its share of the increment in its
own way, would be just as truly robbed as if not allowed to
spend it at all. A voluntary association in which the landholders should consent to contribute the increment to the association's treasury, and in which all the members should
agree to settle the method of its disposition by ballot, would
be equitable enough, but would be a short-sighted, wasteful,
and useless complication. A system of occupying ownership,
however, accompanied by no legal power to collect rent, but
coupled with the abolition of the State-guaranteed monopoly
of money, thus making capital readily available, would distribute the increment naturally and quietly among its rightful
owners. If it should not work perfect equity, it would at least
effect a sufficiently close approximation to it, and without

trespassing at all upon the individualities of any. Spots are
" choice " now very largely because of monopoly, and those
which, under a system of free land and free money, should still
remain choice for other reasons would shed their benefits upon
all, just in the same way that choice countries under free
trade will, as Henry George shows, make other countries
more prosperous. When people see that such would be the
result of this system, it is hardly likely that many of them will
have to be coerced into agreeing to it. I see no point to
Egoist's analogy in the first sentence of his last paragraph, unless he means to deny the right of the individual to become a
banker. A more pertinent analogy would be a comparison of
the George scheme for the confiscation of rent with a system
of individual banking of which the State should confiscate
the profits.

COMPETITIVE PROTECTION.

[*Liberty*, October 13, 1888.]

To the Editor of Liberty:
You have more than once expressed the view that in an Anarchistic
state even the police protection may be in private hands and subject to
competition, so that whoever needs protection may hire it from whichever person or company he chooses. Now, suppose two men wish to occupy the same piece of land and appeal to rival companies for protection.
What will be the result?
It appears to me that there will be interminable contention as long as
there is a plurality of protectors upon the same territory, and that ultimately all others must submit to, or be absorbed by, one, to which all who
need protection must apply. If I am right, then Anarchy is impossible,
and an equitable democratic government the only stable form of society.
Moreover, as it can be shown that the value of the protection to the possession of land equals its economic rent, free competition will make the
payment of this rent a condition of protection. Thus the payment of
rent would become an essential feature in the contract between the land-
holder and the government,—in other words, the payment of rent to the
people as a whole will become one of the features of that social system of
an intelligent people which must evolve from anarchy by the process of
natural selection.   EGOIST.

Under the influence of competition the best and cheapest
protector, like the best and cheapest tailor, would doubtless
get the greater part of the business. It is conceivable even
that he might get the whole of it. But if he should, it would
be by his virtue as a protector, not by his power as a tyrant.
He would be kept at his best by the possibility of competition

and the fear of it; and the source of power would always remain, not with him, but with his patrons, who would exercise it, not by voting him down or by forcibly putting another in his place, but by withdrawing their patronage. Such a state of things, far from showing the impossibility of Anarchy, would be Anarchy itself, and would have little or nothing in common with what now goes by the name of "equitable democratic government."

If "it can be shown that the value of the protection to the possession of land equals its economic rent," the demonstration will be interesting. To me it seems that the measure of such value must often include many other factors than economic rent. A man may own a home the economic rent of which is zero, but to which he is deeply attached by many tender memories. Is the value of protection in his possession of that home zero? But perhaps Egoist means the exchange value of protection. If so, I answer that, under free competition, the exchange value of protection, like the exchange value of everything else, would be its cost, which might in any given case be more or less than the economic rent. The condition of receiving protection would be the same as the condition of receiving beefsteak,—namely, ability and willingness to pay the cost thereof.

If I am right, the payment of rent, then, would not be an *essential* feature in the contract between the landholder and the protector. It is conceivable, however, though in my judgment unlikely, that it might be found an *advantageous* feature. If so, protectors adopting that form of contract would distance their competitors. But if one of these protectors should ever say to landholders : "Sign this contract; if you do not, I not only will refuse you protection, but I will myself invade you and annually confiscate a portion of your earnings equal to the economic rent of your land," I incline to the opinion that "intelligent people" would sooner or later, "by the process of natural selection," evolve into Anarchy by rallying around these landholders for the formation of a new social and protective system, which would subordinate the pooling of economic rents to the security of each individual in the possession of the raw materials which he uses and the disposition of the wealth which he thereby produces.

PROTECTION, AND ITS RELATION TO RENT.

[*Liberty*, October 27, 1888.]

To the Editor of Liberty :

Referring to your favored reply of October 13, I fail to find an answer to the question as to the result of the attempt of two rival protectors to secure to different persons the same territory. I cannot see how, under such conditions, a physical conflict can be avoided, (1) nor is it clear why the best and cheapest protector will be most patronized if he is not at the same time the strongest. It would be the power rather than the quality of protection that would secure patronage. (2) But if the tyrant by sophistry could convince the masses, as he now does, that his policy is to their benefit and could obtain their support, Anarchy would inevitably lead to despotism. (3) The present State, to my mind, is indeed the natural outgrowth of Anarchy, its absurd character, being due to shortsighted intelligence and sustained by a copious amount of sophistry. (4)

My remarks about equity do certainly not refer to what is now termed equity, but to the genuine article.

The statement that the value of the protection in the possession of land equals its economic rent I consider true, even if there is no direct labor of protection involved.

By rent I mean, of course, that which Ricardo terms rent,—*i. e.*, the difference between the productivity of a particular piece of land and the marginal productivity; the excess of the value of a product over the value of the labor producing it.

The observation regarding the sentimental value of protection is certainly out of place, since in economic discussion none other than exchange value can be considered. (5) Even in a society in which the policeman is superfluous, the value of protection in the possession of land can be shown to be equal to its economic rent. The right of possession to land consists in an agreement of the people to forego the special advantages which the use of such lands affords to an undisturbed possessor. It represents a giving-up, by the community, of that which they could obtain for themselves,—the cost of the community being certainly that which they have relinquished, and equals in value the special advantage which is the cause of rent. In view of this, it seems to me that affording this protection is to the community an expense equal to the rent. (6) Moreover, assuming that owing to the favorable locality or fertility (eliminating a difference of skill or other merit) the production on that land of one year's labor (say three hundred days) will exchange for five hundred days' of other men's labor who must work without such special advantages, it will be difficult to show that the occupier of that land is equitably entitled to this exchange value. (7) Those who buy his products really produce and actually pay the excess of two hundred days' labor. Are they not entitled to a distribution of this rent which they, in the course of exchange, have paid to him? If the people of a community are endowed with intelligent egoism, they cannot give that protection to any one who is not willing to pay the rent ; and, if the occupier refuses to do so, the right of occupation will simply be given to one who is willing. (8) This is no invasion, but a bargain. (9) What right has he to expect the community to secure him an opportunity to make inequitable exchanges, (10) when others are willing to pay the full value of the advantages offered, whereby equity is established? I can conceive of no other individualistic measure (11) by which the cost principle of value can be realized in those cases in which the cost of producing equal quantities is different on account of a variation of local opportunities than to add rent to the cost where the immediate cost is naturally less than the value of the product. All men are then upon an equitable plane regarding the gifts of nature; and none can, as none should in this respect, have an advantage that is not similarly enjoyed by all. (12)   EGOIST.

(1) A physical conflict may or may not occur. The probability of it is inversely proportional to the amount of education in economics and social science acquired by the people prior to the inauguration of the conditions supposed. If government should be abruptly and entirely abolished to-morrow, there would probably ensue a series of physical conflicts about land and many other things, ending in reaction and a revival of the old tyranny. But if the abolition of government shall take place gradually, beginning with the downfall of the money and land monopolies and extending thence into one field after another, it will be accompanied by such a constant acquisition and steady spreading of social truth that, when the time shall come to apply the voluntary principle in the supply of police protection, the people will rally as promptly and universally to the support of the protector who acts most nearly in accordance with the principles of social science as they now rally to the side of the assaulted man against his would-be murderer. In that case no serious conflict can arise.

(2) Egoist neglects to consider my statement in reply to him in the last issue of *Liberty*, to the effect that the source of the protector's power lies precisely in the patronage. The protector who is most patronized will, therefore, be the strongest; and the people will endow with their power the protector who is best fitted to use it in the administration of justice.

(3) That is to say, if the masses, or any large section of them, after having come to an understanding and acceptance of Anarchism, should then be induced by the sophistry of tyrants to reject it again, despotism would result. This is perfectly true. No Anarchist ever dreamed of denying it. Indeed, the Anarchist's only hope lies in his confidence that people who have once intelligently accepted his principle will "stay put."

(4) The present State cannot be an outgrowth of Anarchy, because Anarchy, in the philosophic sense of the word, has never existed. For Anarchy, after all, means something more than the possession of liberty. Just as Ruskin defines wealth as "the possession of the valuable by the valiant," so Anarchy may be defined as the possession of liberty by libertarians,—

that is, by those who know what liberty means. The barbaric liberty out of which the present State developed was not Anarchy in this sense at all, for those who possessed it had not the slightest conception of its blessings or of the line that divides it from tyranny.

(5) Nothing can have value in the absence of demand for it. Therefore the basis of the demand cannot be irrelevant in considering value. Now, it is manifest that the demand for protection in the possession of land does not rest solely upon excess of fertility or commercial advantage of situation. On the contrary, it rests, in an ever-rising degree and among an ever-increasing proportion of the people, upon the love of security and peace, the love of home, the love of beautiful scenery, and many other wholly sentimental motives. Inasmuch, then, as the strength of some of the motives for the demand of protection bears often no relation to economic rent. the value of such protection is not necessarily equal to economic rent. Which is the contrary of Egoist's proposition.

(6) All this legitimately follows, once having admitted Egoist's definition of the right of possession of land. But that definition rests on an assumption which Anarchists deny,—namely, that there is an entity known as the community which is the rightful owner of all land. Here we touch the central point of the discussion. Here I take issue with Egoist, and maintain that " the community " is a nonentity, that it has no existence, and that what is called the community is simply a combination of individuals having no prerogatives beyond those of the individuals themselves. This combination of individuals has no better title to the land than any single individual outside of it ; and the argument which Egoist uses in behalf of the community this outside individual, if he but had the strength to back it up, might cite with equal propriety in his own behalf. He might say : " The right of possession of land consists in an agreement on my part to forego the special advantages which the use of such land affords to an undisturbed possessor. It represents a giving-up, by me, of that which I could obtain for myself,—the cost to me being certainly that which I have relinquished, and equals in value the special advantage which is the cause of rent. In view of this, it seems to me that affording this protection is to me an expense equal to the rent." And thereupon he might proceed to collect this rent from the community as compensation for the protection which he afforded it in allowing it to occupy the land. But in his case the supposed condition is lacking ; he has not the strength necessary to enforce such an argu-

ment as this. The community, or combination of individuals, has this strength. Its only superiority to the single individual, then, in relation to the land, consists in the right of the strongest,—a perfectly valid right, I admit, but one which, if exercised, leads to serious results. If the community proposes to exercise its right of the strongest, why stop with the collection of economic rent? Why not make the individual its slave outright? Why not strip him of everything but the bare necessities of life? Why recognize him at all, in any way, except as a tool to be used in the interest of the community? In a word, why not do precisely what capitalism is doing now, or else what State Socialism proposes to do when it gets control of affairs? But if the community does not propose to go to this extreme ; if it proposes to recognize the individual and treat with him,—then it must forego entirely its right of the strongest, and be ready to contract on a basis of equality of rights, by which the individual's title to the land he uses and to what he gets out of it shall be held valid as against the world. Then, if the individual consents to pool his rent with others, well and good ; but, if not— why, then, he must be left alone. And it will not do for the community to turn upon him and demand the economic rent of his land as compensation for the "protection" which it affords him in thus letting him alone. As well might the burglar say to the householder : " Here, I can, if I choose, enter your house one of these fine nights and carry off your valuables ; I therefore demand that you immediately hand them over to me as compensation for the sacrifice which I make and the protection which I afford you in not doing so."

(7) Precisely as difficult as it would be to show that the man of superior skill (native, not acquired) who produces in the ratio of five hundred to another's three hundred is equitably entitled to this surplus exchange value. There is no more reason why we should pool the results of our lands than the results of our hands. And to *compel* such pooling is as meddlesome and tyrannical in one case as in the other. That school of Socialistic economists which carries Henry George's idea to its conclusions, confiscating not only rent but interest and profit and equalizing wages,—a school of which G. Bernard Shaw may be taken as a typical representative,—is more logical than the school to which Mr. George and Egoist belong, because it completes the application of the tyrannical principle.

(8) Here again we have the assumption of the community's superior title to the land.

(9) Yes, the bargain of the highwayman to deliver another's goods.

(10) The cultivator of land who does not ask protection does not expect the community to secure him the opportunity referred to. He simply expects the community not to deprive him of this opportunity. He does not say to the community: "Here! an invader is trying to oust me from my land ; come and help me to drive him off." He says to the community: "My right to this land is as good as yours. In fact it is better, for I am already occupying and cultivating it. I demand of you simply that you shall not disturb me. If you impose certain burdens upon me by threatening me with dispossession, I, being weaker than you, must of course submit temporarily. But in the mean time I shall teach the principle of liberty to the individuals of which you are composed, and by and by, when they see that you are oppressing me, they will espouse my cause, and your tyrannical yoke will speedily be lifted from my neck."

(11) No *other!* Is Egoist's measure individualistic, then? I have already pointed out its communistic and authoritarian character.

(12) If the cost principle of value cannot be realized otherwise than by compulsion, then it had better not be realized. For my part, I do not believe that it is possible or highly important to realize it *absolutely and completely.* But it is both possible and highly important to effect its approximate realization. So much can be effected without compulsion,—in fact, can only be effected by at least partial abolition of compulsion, —and so much will be sufficient. By far the larger part of the violations of the cost principle—probably nine-tenths—result from artificial, law-made inequalities ; only a small portion arise from natural inequalities. Abolish the artificial monopolies of money and land, and interest, profit, and the rent of buildings will almost entirely disappear ; ground rents will no longer flow into a few hands ; and practically the only inequality remaining will be the slight disparity of products due to superiority of soil and skill. Even this disparity will soon develop a tendency to decrease. Under the new economic conditions and enlarged opportunities resulting from freedom of credit and land classes will tend to disappear; great capacities will not be developed in a few at the expense of stunting those of the many ; talents will approximate towards equality, though their variety will be greater than ever ; freedom of locomotion will be vastly increased ; the toilers will no longer be anchored in such large numbers in the

present commercial centres, and thus made subservient to the city landlords; territories and resources never before utilized will become easy of access and development; and under all these influences the disparity above mentioned will decrease to a minimum. Probably it will never disappear entirely; on the other hand, it can never become intolerable. It must always remain a comparatively trivial consideration, certainly never to be weighed for a moment in the same scale with liberty.

LIBERTY AND LAND.

[*Liberty*, December 15, 1888.]

To the Editor of Liberty:

Encouraged by the prompt and considerate attention given to my letter (in your issue of October 27), I beg leave to continue the discussion, especially since some of your arguments are not at all clear to me.

You say that my definition of the right of possession of land rests on an assumption "that there is an entity known as the community, which is the rightful owner of all land." I do not understand what you mean by "rightful ownership." Ownership outside of a combination of individuals is to me as inconceivable as "distance" would be were there but one grain of matter in the universe. And regarding the community formed by a compact entered into or sanctioned by a dynamic majority of individuals as an entity, I can conceive only the physical relation of " possession " and that of " ability to maintain it " ; but " ownership " I can recognize only as the result of this ability of the community, applied for the benefit of individuals. Hence I deny that my definition is based upon the premise stated by you, unless you have a conception of the term " ownership " unknown to me. (1) If I had " the strength to back it up," all land would be mine, and egoism would prompt me to dominate over mankind as naturally as mankind now dominates over the animal kingdom. (2) But since my egoism is not coupled with such a power, submission to the stronger is a necessity which may be good or evil. "Community" I only mention in recognition of its supreme power. It can have and need have no title to the land while there is no other power capable of successfully disputing its possession, a title being nothing else than an effective promise of those who wield the supreme power. Nor can I agree that the right of the strongest will lead to serious results, except when applied to create an inequitable relation between individuals ; and for the same reason that I advocate the distribution of rent as conducive to the establishment of an equilibrium, I do object to the collection of any other tribute. (3) Suppose I were to discover a gold mine that would enable me to command, by one hour's work, one year's labor of other men: a refusal to pool the rent with others with the expectation to be let alone in the exclusive enjoyment of this mine would imply that I consider all others to be devoid of even a trace of egoism, which my experience forbids. (4) There is one vital difference between the advantage which a man possesses by reason of superior skill and that due to the possession of valuable local opportunities : the one is inseparably attached to the individual; the other can be transferred by a mere transfer of the possession of the territory.   The former will therefore always remain the individual's; the disposition of the latter will invariably be controlled by the strongest. (5)

If you can convince the majority that occupation is the proper title for the ownership of land, your measure will be adopted.   But local opportunities being of different values and the most valuable limited, those who are less liberally provided by the existing social conditions will covet the superior advantages possessed by others.   This dissatisfaction, this germ of social disturbances and revolutions, will grow as the existing valuable opportunities are more and more appropriated and those who must do without them increase in numbers.   Under such conditions it will be easy to convince the masses that, by giving the local opportunities to the highest bidder and equitably distributing the rent, all will feel that they have an equal share in the blessings of social peace and all egoism in that direction is as fully satisfied as any intelligent man can expect. (6)

As to the question of how to accomplish the end and what to do first, I agree with you when you wish the first blow directed against the monopolization of the medium of exchange ; I only hold that, if the social state following would not imply a nationalization of the rent, the measure would be incomplete. (7)

From all appearances the differences between us is this : You consider that the rule of the superior will invariably lead to serious results, and in this respect you place yourself in opposition to what must naturally result from an association of egoists, *i.e.*, the rule of the superior, while I hold that superior ability will always rule and that this rule will be beneficial if administered so that no individual has any reasonable cause for complaint, which implies that all have an equal share in the transferable opportunities.   I admit that what I consider a reasonable cause may not be so considered by others : the decision must be left to the intelligence of the people, as there is no other tribunal. (8)

EGOIST.

(1) It was only because I conceived it out of the question that Egoist, in maintaining that " the value of protection in the possession of land is equal to its economic rent," could be discussing value without regard to the law of equal liberty as a prior condition, or soberly advocating the exercise of the right of might regardless of equity, that I interpreted his words as implying a superiority *in equity* in the community's title to land over that of the individual,—a superiority other than that of might ; a superiority, in short, other than that by which the highwayman relieves the traveller of his goods.   I was bound to suppose (and later statements in his present letter seem to strengthen the supposition) that he looked upon the " giving up, by the community," of its right to land as the giving up of a superior equitable right ; for otherwise, in demanding value in return for this sacrifice, he would be compelled in logic to demand, on behalf of a burglar, value in return for the sacrifice made in declining to carry off

a householder's wealth by stealth. But Egoist repudiates this supposition (though he does not follow the logic of his repudiation), and I must take him at his word. He thus lays himself open to a retort which I could not otherwise have made. In his previous letter he criticised me for making sentiment a factor in the estimation of value. Whether or not this was a transgression, on my part, of the limits of economic discussion, he certainly has transgressed them much more seriously in making force such a factor. Exchange implies liberty ; where there is no liberty there is no exchange, but only robbery ; and robbery is foreign to political economy. At least one point, however, is gained. Between Egoist and myself all question of any superior *equitable* right of the community is put aside forever. Equity not considered, we agree that the land belongs to the man or body of men strong enough to hold it. And for all practical purposes his definition of "ownership" suits me, though I view ownership less as the "result of the ability of the community to maintain possession" and an application of this result "for the benefit of individuals," than as a result of the *inability* of the community to maintain itself in peace and security otherwise than by the recognition of only such relations between man and wealth as are in harmony with the law of equal liberty. In other words, ownership arises not from superiority of the community to the individual, but from the inferiority of the community to the facts and powers of nature.

(2) This would depend upon whether such domination would prove profitable or disastrous to Egoist. I contend that it would prove disastrous, and that experience would lead him to abandon such a policy if foresight should not prevent him from adopting it.

(3) Here we have an acknowledgment of a principle of equity and a contemplation of its observance by the mighty, which goes to sustain my original supposition, despite Egoist's protest. It implies an abandonment by the mighty of their right of domination and a willingness to contract with the weak. Now, I agree that the contracts thus entered into will not lead to serious results, unless they create inequitable relations between individuals. But the first of all equities is not equality of material well-being, but equality of liberty ; and if the contract places the former equality before the latter, it *will* lead to serious results, for it logically necessitates the arbitrary levelling of all material inequalities, whether these arise from differences of soil or differences of skill. To directly enforce equality of material well-being is meddlesome, invasive, and

offensive, but to directly enforce equality of liberty is simply protective and defensive. The latter is negative, and aims only to prevent the establishment of artificial inequalities ; the former is positive, and aims at direct and active abolition of natural inequalities. If the former is the true policy, then it is as equitable to enforce the pooling of interest, profit, and wages as the pooling of rent. If the latter is the true policy, we have only to see to it that no artificial barriers against individual initiative are constructed. Under such conditions, if the natural inequalities tend to disappear, as they surely will, then so much the better.

(4) Not at all. It would only imply that Egoist considers others wise enough to see that, from the standpoint of self-interest, even so great a natural inequality as is here supposed is preferable to an arbitrary distribution of the products of labor.

(5) In speaking of skill as "inseparably attached to the individual," Egoist surely does not mean to argue the impossibility of seizing and distributing the results of skill, for that would be a ridiculous contention. Then he can only mean that there is something sacred about the individual which the mighty are bound to respect. But this again is inconsistent with his theory of the right of might. If the strongest is to exercise his might, then he need stop at nothing but the impossible ; if, on the other hand, he contracts with the weaker on a basis of equal liberty, then both strong and weak must be left secure in their possession of the products of their labor, whether aided by superior skill or superior soil.

(6) This is not true, unless Malthusianism is true ; and, if Malthusianism is true, it is as true after the pooling of rent as before. If the encroachment of population over the limit of the earth's capacity is inevitable, then there is no solution of the social problem. Pooling the rent or organizing credit would only postpone the catastrophe. Sooner or later the masses would find nothing to share but the curses of war rather than the "blessings of peace," and at that stage it would matter but little to them whether they shared equally or unequally.

(7) And I only hold that, if in that case rent were to be nationalized by force, liberty would be incomplete ; and liberty must be complete, whatever happens.

(8) No, I too hold that superiority will always rule ; and it is only when real superiority is known and recognized as such, and therefore allowed to have its perfect work unresisted and unimpeded, that the minimum of evil will result. The really serious results are those that follow the attempts of inferiority,

mistaking itself for superiority, to fly in the face of the real article. In other words, when individuals or majorities, seeing that they are stronger for the time being than other individuals or minorities, suppose that they are therefore stronger than natural social laws and act in violation of them, disaster is sure to follow. These laws are the really mighty, and they will always prevail. The first of them is the law of equal liberty. It is by the observance of this law, I am persuaded, rather than by "an equal share in the transferable opportunities," that the ultimate "intelligence of the people" will remove "every reasonable cause of complaint."

RENT, AND ITS COLLECTION BY FORCE.

[*Liberty*, January 19, 1889.]

To the Editor of Liberty.

I must confess that I may not fully grasp what its advocates exactly mean by Anarchism. Referring to the reply to my letter, in the issue of December 15, I cannot harmonize the sentiments of an opponent of even a temporary monopoly of inventors and authors with the defence of an indefinite monopoly of the discoverer of a gold mine. Moreover, the reference to the "law of equal liberty" appears to me inconsistent with your standpoint. If I understand this law, it can be thus expressed : Given a community of intelligent beings, who wish to live in peace and enjoy a maximum of happiness, what must they do to attain this result ? Proposition : They must mutually combine and form such an agreement as will secure equal freedom to all ; and if any one takes liberties at the expense of others, he must be restrained, even by force, if necessary.

This, however, appears to me a sound democratic doctrine and a repudiation of the doctrine of non-interference. Without a forcible measure against transgressors, equal freedom is unattainable. Force, therefore, appears to be a most important factor in political economy, the creator of all rights. Now, in respect to rent, I would advocate compulsion against those only who violate the law of equal freedom in relation to local opportunities. Surely, if I had discovered a gold mine, unless I knew that the supreme power of society would protect me unconditionally in the sole possession, I would willingly give the economic rent, in order to prevent others, less blessed in the possession of natural opportunities, from doing that which their egoism would naturally prompt them to do. This you appear to recognize in your answer. (2) Only those who fail to see that peaceful enjoyment of man's labor depends upon social equality will expect to occupy land free, for the possession of which others are willing to give a consideration, and they must suffer the natural consequences, either by the invasion of the State, in confiscating rent, or by the more disastrous interference in the form of social disturbances and revolutions.

You are correct in surmising that I can recognize no right but that of might or ability, not referring, of course, to that concept of the ambiguous term "right" which is synonymous with righteousness; and as to that might which results from the social compact, I must accept it as a social right, whether or not it is in harmony with my notions of what it should be. This, however, does not prevent me from protesting and agitating against any of the laws that violate equity, being convinced that inequitable laws will bring disaster unless abolished before the oppression leads to extreme measures. Enlightened self-interest is no doubt the most forcible incentive to maintain equity, and history amply proves that the strong will never enter into a compact with the weak unless their power is threatened. This does not preclude the power of the weaker from being reinforced by the compassion of a portion of the strong; sentiment, in this sense, has often an indirect influence in the distribution of the social power. Our aim, as individualists, should therefore be to so direct the power of the State that it will maintain the equal liberty of all.

EGOIST.

I find so little attempt to meet the various considerations which I have advanced that I have not much to add by way of comment. The monopoly of mining gold at a particular point exists in the physical constitution of things, and a pooling of the results thereof (which would be a virtual destruction of the monopoly) can only be directly achieved in one of two ways,—mutual agreement or an invasion of liberty. The monopoly of inventors and authors, on the contrary, has no existence at all except by mutual agreement or an invasion of liberty. It seems to me the difference between the two is sufficiently clear. Egoist's statement of the law of equal liberty is satisfactory. Standing upon it, I would repel, by force if necessary, the confiscator of rent on the ground that he "takes a liberty at the expense of others." I have no objection to forcible measures against transgressors, but the question recurs as to who are the transgressors. If the piece of land which I am using happens to be better than my neighbor's, I do not consider myself a transgressor on that account; but if my neighbor digs some of my potatoes and carries them off, I certainly consider him a transgressor, even though he may name his plunder economic rent. But Egoist, viewing this case, considers me the transgressor and my neighbor the honest man. I believe that education in liberty will bring people to my view rather than his. If it doesn't, I shall have to succumb. It is to be noted that Egoist makes no further reference to my argument regarding skill. I urged that the levelling of inequalities in land logically leads to the levelling of inequalities in skill. Egoist replied that skill is inseparably attached to the individual, while land is not. I rejoined that the results of skill are not inseparably attached to the individual, and that the right of might recognizes nothing sacred about the individual. To this Egoist makes no reply. Hence my argument that the nationalization of rent logically involves the most complete State Socialism and minute regulation of the individual stands unassailed.

THE DISTRIBUTION OF RENT.

[*Liberty*, February 23, 1889.]

To the Editor of Liberty :

Before replying to your rejoinder regarding land *vs.* skill, I should be pleased to know whether in an Anarchistic state, in the event of a transgression of equal liberty, the injured party is to resent the act according to his judgment and caprice, or is repression to be exercised by an organized power according to rules determined by previous agreement? In the one case the unavoidable difference of opinions must be a source of interminable disturbances ; in the other, we have the operation of an organized society with laws and supreme power,—in fact, a political State. If an agreement exists, who is to execute its provisions? And if some refuse to assist, and shirk social duties, have they any claim to the assistance of the organization, have they any social rights? Until we have a clear understanding on these points, we might argue forever without avail.

Assuming that equal liberty can be attained only through some social compact, I fail to see a distinction between the monopoly of a gold-mine and that of an invention. The exclusive possession of either is the result of a social compact, all persons agreeing not to exploit the natural deposit of the precious metal, or to make use of the device suggested by the inventor. The monopoly of a gold-mine can, therefore, have no existence except by mutual agreement, or eventually a forcible prevention of those who claim equal liberty and attempt to extract gold from the same deposit. In like manner, every other peaceable enjoyment of a natural or local advantage is a result of mutual agreement, supported by the power without which the agreement would be a dead letter. The occupier of superior land or location is therefore indebted to society for the right of undisturbed possession, and a society of egoists will natually confer this right to the highest bidder, who will then, as now, determine the rent. An occupier is not a transgressor of equal liberty unless he claims and receives this right without giving an equivalent in return, and the return is equitable if it equals what others are willing to give for the same right.

If we keep this in view, I may be able to more intelligently convey my views on the land *vs.* skill question. The social agreement, and not the "physical constitution of things," is the factor determining the distribution of land, while the distribution of skill is absolutely independent of this agreement, depending upon the physical and mental constitution of men. Some men may have reason to be dissatisfied with the distribution of land, knowing that it can be changed, while a dissatisfaction with the distribution of skill is like the crying of a child because it cannot fly.

Having shown that a vital difference exists between land and skill, the distribution of the one being due to human laws, that of the other to natural laws, I wish to further demonstrate that only by inequitable, despotic laws can an equalization of natural opportunities be prevented.

In a state of liberty rent will invariably be offered, by the occupiers of the poorest land yet needed, for the possession of better or more favorably located land. Shall law forbid such offers, or invalidate contracts made in compliance therewith, incidentally suppressing competition ; shall it permit certain individuals, the so-called land-owners, to appropriate this rent ; or shall society so distribute it that no citizen has any reason to complain of political favoritism ? Is there a fourth possibility, and if not, which of the three is consistent with the law of equal freedom? Which tend to establish artificial inequalities? I reiterate my conviction that a nationalization of rent will be an inevitable result of the establishment of equal liberty.

If I were the possessor of land on which the productivity of labor exceeds that obtainable on land held by others, they would be willing to lease my land and pay a rent of nearly the excess of productivity. But since under the system of occupying land-ownership such a contract must be void, I shall never vacate the land, whatever inducements should be offered me ; for, upon leaving it, I and my descendants would forever receive for the same efforts a less return than if I had retained possession of the said land. If for any reason some valuable land should become vacant, the number of applicants would naturally be very large. Each would be willing to give very nearly the annual excess of productivity afforded by this land, in his competitive attempt to outbid others. Who shall become the future occupier ? Shall appointment decide, or shall the land be given to the highest bidder ? In the one case, favoritism would reign ; in the other, the nationalization of rent would be realized, which you condemn. Moreover, if production is carried on in groups, as it now is, who is the legal occupier of the land ? The employer, the manager, or the ensemble of those engaged in the co-operative work ? The latter appearing the only rational answer, it is natural that those in possession of the lesser opportunities will offer themselves to the favored groups for wages slightly greater than what they can obtain on the less favorable land and less than the members of the favored group would obtain as a share of their co-operation (which is only another form of an offer of rent). But as such an accession to a group would displace some of those previously employed, pushing them upon the less favorable land, such competitive applications will be resisted to the utmost, and competition would be harassed. A development of a class distinction could not be avoided.

The relation of social agreement to the distribution of the *products* of skill is totally different. An attempt to distribute by law the products of labor will discourage production, diminish happiness, and reduce the power to resist adverse influences, enabling those people to survive in the struggle for existence who encourage production by protecting the producer in the peaceable enjoyment of the fruits of his labor, provided he pays the value of that protection. EGOIST.

I cannot excuse Egoist, for several years a subscriber for *Liberty*, when he requires me to answer for the thousand-and-first time the questions which he puts to me in his opening paragraph. It has been stated and restated in these columns, until I have grown weary of the reiteration, that voluntary association for the purpose of preventing transgression of equal liberty will be perfectly in keeping with Anarchism, and will probably exist under Anarchism until it " costs more than it comes to "; that the provisions of such associations will be executed by such agents as it may select in accordance with such methods as it may prescribe, provided such methods do not themselves involve a transgression of the liberty of the innocent ; that such association will restrain only the criminal (meaning by criminal the transgressor of equal liberty) ; that non-membership and non-support of it is not a criminal act; but that such a course nevertheless deprives the non-member of any title to the benefits of the association, except such as come to him incidentally and unavoidably. It has also been repeatedly affirmed that, in proposing to abolish the State, the Anarchists expressly exclude from their definition of the State such associations as that just referred to, and that whoever excludes from his definition and championship of the State everything except such associations has no quarrel with the,Anarchists beyond a verbal one. I should trust that the "understanding on these points" is now clear, were it not that experience has convinced me that my command of the English language is not adequate to the construction of a foundation for such trust.

The fact that Egoist points out a similarity between the monopoly of a gold-mine and that of an invention by no means destroys *the* difference between them which I pointed out,— this difference being that, whereas in the former case it is impossible to prevent or nullify the monopoly without restricting the liberty of the monopolist, in the latter it is impossible to sustain it without restricting the liberty of the would-be competitors. To the Anarchist, who believes in the minimum of restriction upon liberty, this difference is a vital one,—quite sufficient to warrant him in refusing to prevent the one while refusing to sustain the other.

Egoist says that "an occupier is not a transgressor of equal liberty unless he claims and receives the right of undisturbed possession without giving an equivalent in return." Anarchism holds, on the contrary, in accordance with the principles stated at the outset of this rejoinder, that an occupier is not a transgressor even if, not claiming it or paying for it, he does receive this right. This question of "Liberty in the Incidental" has been elaborately and clearly discussed in these columns within a few months by J. Wm. Lloyd, and an extract in confirmation of his position has been reprinted from Humboldt. I refer Egoist to those articles.

The assertion that "the distribution of skill is absolutely independent of social agreement" is absolutely erroneous. In proof of this I need only call attention to the apprenticeship regulations of the trade unions and the various educational

systems that are or have been in vogue, not only as evidence
of what has already been done in the direction of controlling
the distribution of skill, but also as an indication of what
more may be done if State Socialism ever gets a chance to try
upon humanity the interesting experiments which it proposes.
On the other hand, the collection of rent by the collectivity
does not necessarily affect the distribution of land.   Land
titles will remain unchanged as long as the tax (or rent) shall
be paid.   But it does distribute the products resulting from
differences of land, and it is likewise possible to distribute the
products resulting from differences of skill.   Now until this
position is overthrown (and I defy any one to successfully dispute it), it is senseless to liken "dissatisfaction with the distribution of skill " to " the crying of a child because it cannot
fly."   The absurdity of this analogy, in which the possibility
of distributing products is ignored, would have been apparent if it had been immediately followed by the admission of
this possibility which Egoist places several paragraphs further
down.   To be sure, he declares even there that it is impossible,
but only in the sense in which Proudhon declares interest-
bearing property impossible,— that of producing anti-social
results which eventually kill it or compel its abandonment.
I contend that similarly anti-social results will follow any attempt to distribute by law the products arising from differences
of land ; and I ask, as I have asked before without obtaining
an answer, why the collectivity, if in its right of might it may
see fit to distribute the rent of land, may not find it equally
expedient to distribute the rent of skill ; why it may not reduce
all differences of wealth to an absolute level ; in short, why it
may not create the worst and most complete tyranny the world
has ever known ?

In regard to the attitude of Anarchistic associations towards
rent and its collection, I would say that they might, consistently with the law of equal freedom, except from their jurisdiction whatever cases or forms of transgression they should
not think it expedient to attempt to prevent.   These exceptions would probably be defined in their constitutions.   The
members could, if they saw fit, exempt the association from
enforcing gambling debts or rent contracts.   On the other
hand, an association organized on a different basis which should
enforce such debts or contracts would not thereby become itself a transgressor.   But any association would be a transgressor which should attempt to prevent the fulfilment of
rent contracts or to confiscate rent and distribute it.   Of the
three possibilities specified by Egoist the third is the only

one that tends to establish an artificial inequality ; and that
the worst of all inequalities,—the inequality of liberty, or
perhaps it would be more accurate to call it the equality of
slavery. The first or second would at the worst fail to entirely
abolish *natural* inequalities.

The possibility of valuable land becoming vacant is hardly
worth consideration. Still, if any occupant of valuable land
should be foolish enough to quit it without first selling it, the
estate would be liable to seizure by the first comer, who would
immediately have a footing similar to that of other landholders. If this be favoritism, I can only say that the world
is not destined to see the time when some things will not go
by favor.

Egoist's argument that free competition will tend to distribute rent by a readjustment of wages is exactly to my purpose. Have I not told him from the start that Anarchists
will gladly welcome any tendency to equality *through liberty ?*
But Egoist seems to object to reaching equality by this road.
It must be reached by law or not at all. If reached by competition, " competition would be harassed." In other words,
competition would harass competition. This wears the aspect
of another absurdity. It is very likely that competitors would
harass competitors, but competition without harassed competitors is scarcely thinkable. It is even not improbable that
" class distinctions " would be developed, as Egoist says.
Workers would find the places which their capacities, conditions, and inclinations qualify them to fill, and would thus be
classified, or divided into distinct classes. Does Egoist think
that in such an event life would not be worth living? Of
course the words " harass " and " class distinction " have an
ugly sound, and competition is decidedly more attractive when
associated instead with " excel " and " organization." But
Anarchists never recoil from disagreeable terms. Only their
opponents are to be frightened by words and phrases.

ECONOMIC RENT.

[*Liberty*, November 5, 1892.]

To the Editor of Liberty :
I have often seen it claimed that under the Anarchistic organization
of society economic rent would disappear, or be reduced to an insignificant amount. But I have never yet been satisfied with any explanation
of the way in which this is to be brought about.

Some speak as if the abolition of rent were to be an immediate result of the abolition of interest, apparently taking the ground that rent is a product of the selling price of land and the interest of money. But according to the accepted theory of economists (the only one that I have learned to understand), rent is the independent factor, and the selling price is the product of rent and interest.

I have also seen it claimed that under liberty there will be no great cities, and therefore no city prices for land. I can understand that liberty will make the masses richer, so that they will be better able to choose the home which pleases them; and that it will make them saner, so that they will better appreciate the attractions of country life. But cities will still offer the greatest opportunities for making money, and many social and æsthetic advantages. I cannot believe, therefore, that great cities will disappear.

As to the freeing of vacant land, I do not remember to have heard that this would destroy any but "speculative" rent. There might perhaps be a greater relief at first, while the vacant land was being taken up. But certainly within a short time—within a year, I should say—all land which had any special advantage over ordinary farming land would be occupied, and these special advantages would be in the hands of the occupiers.

On the other hand, it must be remembered that, if any economic rent is left, every advance in prosperity will naturally tend to increase this rent. And liberty is to cause an advance in prosperity.

Again, when vacant land is free, cities can be settled more compactly. This will intensify the peculiar advantages of city life, and thereby increase the demand for city and suburban land. The effect of free vacant land would, I imagine, be closely analogous to that of rapid transit, which was expected to decrease rent, but has instead increased it.

How, then, is economic rent to be got out of the way?

STEPHEN T. BYINGTON.

Liberty has never stood with those who profess to show on strictly economic grounds that economic rent *must* disappear or even decrease as a result of the application of the Anarchistic principle. It sees no chance for that factor in the human constitution which makes competition such a powerful influence—namely, the disposition to buy in the cheapest market—to act directly upon *economic* rent in a way to reduce it. This disposition to buy cheap, which in a free market is fatal to all other forms of usury, is on the contrary the mainstay of economic rent, whether the market be free or restricted. When, through freedom of banking, it shall become possible to furnish money at cost, no one will pay for money more than cost ; and hence interest on money, as well as on all capital consisting of commodities which money will buy and to the production of which there is no natural limit, will necessarily disappear. But the occupant of land who is enabled, by its superiority, to undersell his neighbor and at the same time to reap, through his greater volume of business, more profit than his neighbor, enjoys this economic rent precisely because of his opportunity to exploit the consumer's disposition to buy cheap. The effect of freedom is not felt here in the same way and with the same directness that it is felt elsewhere.

There are other grounds, however, some of them indirectly economic, some of them purely sentimental, which justify the belief of the Anarchist that a condition of freedom will gradually modify to a very appreciable extent the advantage enjoyed by the occupant of superior land. Take first one that is indirectly economic. I agree with my correspondent that great cities are not destined to disappear. But I believe also that they will be able to maintain their existence only by offering their advantages at a lower price than they now exact. When the laborer, in consequence of his increased wages and greater welfare resulting from the abolition of interest, shall enjoy a larger freedom of locomotion, shall be tied down less firmly to a particular employment, and shall be able to remove to the country with greater facility and in possession of more capital than he can now command, and when the country, partly because of this mobility of labor and partly because of the advances in science, shall continually offer a nearer approach to the undoubted privileges of city life, the representatives of commercial and other interests in the great cities will be able to hold their patrons about them only by lowering their prices and contenting themselves with smaller gains. In other words, economic rent will lessen. Here the disposition to buy cheap, not any special commodity, but an easy life, does exert an indirect and general influence upon economic rent. And, under this influence and yielding to it, the city may increase in prosperity simultaneously with the decline of economic rent. Nay, the increase in prosperity may accelerate this decline; for under liberty increased prosperity means also well-distributed prosperity, which means in turn a lowering of the barriers between classes and a consequent tendency to equalize the different localities of the city one with another.

Upon the sentimental grounds for believing in the evanescence of economic rent it is perhaps not worth while to dwell. I have an aversion to definite speculations based on hypothetical transformations in human nature. Yet I cannot doubt that the disappearance of interest will result in an attitude of hostility to usury in any form, which will ultimately cause any person who charges more than cost for any product to be regarded very much as we now regard a pickpocket. In this way, too, economic rent will suffer diminution.

I think my correspondent fails to understand what is meant

by the freeing of vacant land. It does not mean simply the freeing of unoccupied land. It means the freeing of all land not occupied *by the owner*. In other words, it means land ownership limited by occupancy and use. This would destroy not only speculative but monopolistic rent, leaving no rent except the economic form, which will be received, while it lasts, not as a sum paid by occupant to owner, but as an extra and usurious reward for labor performed under special advantages.

But even if economic rent had to be considered a permanency ; if the considerations which I have urged should prove of no avail against it,—it would be useless, tyrannical, and productive of further tyranny to confiscate it. In the first place, if I have a right to a share of the advantages that accrue from the possession of superior land, then that share is mine ; it is my property; it is like any other property of mine ; no man, no body of men, is entitled to decide how this property shall be used; and any man or body of men attempting so to decide deprives me of my property just as truly as the owner of the superior land deprives me of it if allowed to retain the economic rent. In fact, still assuming that this property is mine, I prefer, if I must be robbed of it, to be robbed by the land-owner, who is likely to spend it in some useful way, rather than by an institution called government, which probably will spend it for fireworks or something else which I equally disapprove. If the property is mine, I claim it, to do as I please with ; if it is not mine, it is impertinent, dishonest, and tyrannical for anybody to forcibly take it from the land-occupant on the pretence that it is mine and to spend it in my name. It is precisely this, however, that the Single-Taxers propose, and it is this that makes the Single Tax a State Socialistic measure. There was never anything more absurd than the supposition of some Single-Taxers that this tax can be harmonized with Anarchism.

But I now and then meet a Single-Taxer who allows that the government, after confiscating this economic rent, has no right to devote it to any so-called public purposes, but should distribute it to the people. Supposing the people to be entitled to the economic rent, this certainly looks on its face like a much saner and more honest proposition than that of the ordinary Single-Taxer. But the question at once arises: Who is to pay the government officials for their services in confiscating the economic rent and handing me my share of it ? And how much is to be paid them? And who is to decide these matters ? When I reflect that under such a Single-Tax system the occupants of superior land are likely to become the politicians and to tax back from the people to pay their salaries what the people have taxed out of them as economic rent, again I say that, even if a part of the economic rent is rightly mine, I prefer to leave it in the pocket of the land-owner, since it is bound to ultimately get back there. As M. Schneider, the Carnegie of France, said in a recent interview with a *Figaro* reporter: "Even if we were to have a collectivist system of society and my property should be confiscated, I believe that I am shrewd enough to find a way to feather my nest just the same." M. Schneider evidently understands State Socialism better than the State Socialists themselves. The Socialists and Single-Taxers will have attained their paradise when they are robbed by officials instead of by landlords and capitalists.

In my view it is idle to discuss what shall be done with the economic rent after it has been confiscated, for I distinctly deny the propriety of confiscating it at all. There are two ways, and only two, of effecting the distribution of wealth. One is to let it distribute itself in a free market in accordance with the natural operation of economic law ; the other is to distribute it arbitrarily by authority in accordance with statute law. One is Anarchism ; the other is State Socialism. The latter, in its worst and most probable form, is the exploitation of labor by officialdom, and at its best is a *régime* of spiritless equality secured at the expense of liberty and progress ; the former is a *régime* of liberty and progress, with as close an approximation to equality as is compatible therewith. And this is all the equality that we ought to have. A greater equality than is compatible with liberty is undesirable. The moment we invade liberty to secure equality we enter upon a road which knows no stopping-place short of the annihilation of all that is best in the human race. If absolute equality is the ideal ; if no man must have the slightest advantage over another,—then the man who achieves greater results through superiority of muscle or skill or brain must not be allowed to enjoy them. All that he produces in excess of that which the weakest and stupidest produce must be taken from him and distributed among his fellows. The economic rent, not of land only, but of strength and skill and intellect and superiority of every kind, must be confiscated. And a beautiful world it would be when absolute equality had been thus achieved ! Who would live in it ? Certainly no freeman.

Liberty will abolish interest ; it will abolish profit ; it will abolish monopolistic rent ; it will abolish taxation ; it will abolish the exploitation of labor ; it will abolish all means whereby any laborer can be deprived of any of his product; but it will not abolish the limited inequality between one laborer's product and another's.   Now, because it has not this power last named, there are people who say : We will have no liberty, for we must have absolute equality.   I am not of them.   If I can go through life free and rich, I shall not cry because my neighbor, equally free, is richer.   Liberty will ultimately make all men rich ; it will not make all men equally rich.   Authority may (and may not) make all men equally rich in purse ; it certainly will make them equally poor in all that makes life best worth living.

LIBERTY AND PROPERTY.

[*Liberty*, December 31, 1892.]

To the Editor of Liberty:

I can agree with much that you say in your answer to my letter in No. 244 of *Liberty*, but I do not think you have proved your case.

In the first place, I object to your assumption that the plan proposed by Anarchists would realize equal liberty with regard to the land.   You praise the idea of "letting wealth distribute itself in a free market."   I echo your praises ; but I cannot see that they are anything to the point of this discussion, for you do not offer a free market.

It is a part of my liberty to use any land that I can use.   When another man takes a piece of land for his own and warns me off it, he exceeds the limits of equal liberty towards me with respect to that land.   If equally valuable land were open to me, the importance of his invasion would be mainly theoretical ; but when he shuts me out of a corner lot on lower Broadway, and asks me to console myself by taking up a New England "abandoned farm," it seems to me that I am receiving a very practical injury.   It might be a sort of reason in his favor if he were putting the land to better use than I could.   His title rests simply on the fact that he was there first, either by accident or because he had better speculative foresight than I.   The presence of his improvements on the land is the result of his invasion, and therefore cannot justify it.

The case of the man who receives what you call " the economic rent of strength and skill" is not parallel, for he has not gained his advantage by hindering another from using the strength and skill which were within that other's reach.

Now, I say : " I am not willing to waive my rights in this land unless the holder will buy me off by paying a fair equivalent.   I see no way in which I can collect this equivalent by myself, or through an organization representing only a part of the people.   Therefore I consent that one board of authority shall assume to represent the whole people for this purpose, in order to prevent what seems to me a greater invasion on the part of the land-owner."   You say "I consent to this invasion on the part of a *bona fide* occupier, rather than to admit a compulsory tax ; for I think that the latter is in itself a greater invasion, and also that it would be an entering wedge for the whole mass of government." Each of us proposes to waive one part of equal liberty for the sake of preserving another part. The only question is on which side the maximum of liberty lies. Certainly any force which I might use in carrying out my principle would be "against force"; and I think that, if private possession of land is responsible for as much evil as I suppose, it constitutes an emergency great enough to justify me in overriding the opposition of those who do not agree with me.

I am not convinced by your objection that the single-tax money would be used up in paying tax-collectors' salaries. There is nothing to hinder paying them by voluntary taxation. If I were enacting a law to suit my own fancy, I would confiscate rent, and then let every one who chose draw his per capita share, with no deduction for salaries or anything else. But I should expect that comparatively few would choose to take out their shares under penalty of paying at retail prices for privileges which would be free, or below cost, to those who remained partners in the large fund. Collectors' salaries should be paid out of this large, undivided fund, which would be a voluntary tax on those who chose not to take out their shares. At any rate, whether this is possible or not, if the people believe that the advantages of confiscating rent are worth the sum spent for collection, they will be willing to pay that sum voluntarily ; if they do not believe so, they will not confiscate rent.

Of course distribution at so much per capita is a terribly wooden way of trying to give every man his own, and I should be glad of a better. Aside from that, I cannot see how my plan, if carried out in good faith, would disagree with the law of equal liberty. I expect you to answer that it could not be carried out in good faith.

Your editorial makes two points against the single tax. You say first that the money would be badly spent. I answer, then let us spend it better. Then you say, very soundly, that it is idle to discuss what shall be done with the confiscated rent when the question is as to the propriety of confiscating it at all. Your second point is that the single tax is authoritarian, and you favor liberty. I answer that you propose to use force to support the occupier of land in a plain invasion of my rights. You have no right to call that liberty. Perhaps it may be the nearest possible approach to liberty ; I think not.

As to the relief that your system might bring, I object to your "sentimental " ground for expecting rent to diminish. If I understand you, you expect the occupier of valuable ground to sell his goods below competitive prices. The result might be that some lucky ones would get special bargains, while their neighbors must go without, or that people would stand in line before this merchant's door till they had wasted time enough to make up the difference in price, or that he would employ extra men till the law of diminishing returns brought his prices up to an equality with others. In the first case the rent would simply be divided among a larger number, while others would be left out in the cold as much as before. In the second and third cases, it would be disposed of by what is equivalent to throwing it into the river. Neither way suits me. Of course, the result I should expect in practice would be a complex of the three in disguised forms.   STEPHEN T. BYINGTON.

Let me begin my brief rejoinder by expressing my appreciation of my opponent. Once in a great while one meets an adversary who confines himself to the question at issue, resorts to no evasion, reasons himself, and is willing to listen to reason. Such a man, I am sure, is Mr. Byington, though I know him only by his writings. It is pleasant to debate with him, after having had to deal so continually with the Merlinos, the Mosts, the Hudspeths, and the whole host of those who cannot think.

Mr. Byington's erroneous conclusions regarding the confiscation of economic rent are due, as I view it, to his confusion of liberties with rights, or, perhaps I might better say, to his foundation of equality of liberty upon a supposed equality of rights. I take issue with him at the very start by denying the dogma of equality of rights,—in fact, by denying rights altogether except those acquired by contract. In times past, when, though already an Egoist and knowing then as now that every man acts and always will act solely from an interest in self, I had not considered the bearing of Egoism upon the question of obligation, it was my habit to talk glibly and loosely of the right of man to the land. It was a bad habit, and I long ago sloughed it off. Man's only right over the land is his might over it. If his neighbor is mightier than he and takes the land from him, then the land is his neighbor's until the latter is dispossessed in turn by one mightier still. But while the danger of such dispossession continues there is no society, no security, no comfort. Hence men contract. They agree upon certain conditions of land ownership, and will protect no title in the absence of the conditions fixed upon. The object of this contract is *not to enable all to benefit equally from the land*, but to enable each to hold securely at his own disposal the results of his efforts expended upon such portion of the earth as he may possess under the conditions agreed upon. It is principally to secure this absolute control of the results of one's efforts that equality of liberty is instituted, not as a matter of right, but as a social convenience. I have always maintained that liberty is of greater importance than wealth,— in other words, that man derives more happiness from freedom than from luxury,—and this is true ; but there is another sense in which wealth, or, rather, property, is of greater importance than liberty. Man has but little to gain from liberty unless that liberty includes the liberty to control what he produces. One of the chief purposes of équal liberty is to secure this fundamental necessity of property, and, if property is not thereby secured, the temptation is to abandon the *régime* of contract and return to the reign of the strongest.

Now the difference between the equal liberty of the Anarchists and the system which Mr. Byington and the Single-

Taxers consider equal liberty is this : the former secures property, while the latter violates it.

The Anarchists say to the individual : " Occupancy and use is the only title to land in which we will protect you ; if you attempt to use land which another is occupying and using, we will protect him against you ; if another attempts to use land to which you lay claim, but which you are not occupying and using, we will not interfere with him ; but of such land as you occupy and use you are the sole master, and we will not ourselves take from you, or allow any one else to take from you, whatever you may get out of such land."

The Single-Taxers, on the other hand, say to the individual : " You may hold all the land you have inherited or bought, or may inherit or buy, and we will protect you in such holding ; but, if you produce more from your land than your neighbors produce from theirs, we will take from you the excess of your product over theirs and distribute it among them, or we will spend it in taking a free ride whenever we want to go anywhere, or we will make any use of it, wise or foolish, that may come into our heads."

The reader who compares these two positions will need no comment of mine to enable him to decide " on which side the maximum of liberty lies," and on which side property, or the individual control of product, is respected.

If Mr. Byington does not accept my view thus outlined, it is incumbent upon him to overthrow it by proving to me that man has a right to land ; if he does accept it, he must see that it completely disposes of his assertion that " when another man takes a piece of land for his own and warns me off it, he exceeds the limits of equal liberty toward me with respect to that land," upon which assertion all his argument rests.

I see an excellent opportunity for some interesting and forcible remarks in comment upon Mr. Byington's concluding paragraph, but, desiring to confine the discussion to essentials for the present, I refrain.

GOING TO PIECES ON THE ROCKS.

[*Liberty*, March 12, 1887.]

SOME of Henry George's correspondents have been pestering him a good deal lately with embarrassing questions as to what will become, under his system, of the home of a man who has built a house upon a bit of land which afterwards so rises in value that he cannot afford to pay the taxes on it. Unable to deny that such a man would be as summarily evicted by the government landlord as is the Irish farmer in arrears by the individual landlord, and yet afraid to squarely admit it, Mr. George has twisted and turned and doubled and dodged, attempting to shield himself by all sorts of irrelevant considerations, until at last he is reduced to asking in rejoinder if this argument has not "a great deal of the flavor of the Georgia deacon's denunciation of abolitionists because they wanted to deprive the widow Smith of her solitary 'nigger,' her only means of support." That is, Mr. George virtually asserts that the claim to own a human being is no more indefensible than the claim of the laborer to own the house he has built and to the unincumbered and indefinite use of whatever site he may have selected for it without dispossessing another. The editor of the *Standard* must have been reduced to sore straits when he resorted to this argument. With all his shuffling he has not yet escaped, and never can escape, the fact that, if government were to confiscate land values, any man would be liable to be turned out of doors, perhaps with compensation, perhaps without it, and thus deprived, maybe, of his dearest joy and subjected to irreparable loss, just because other men had settled in his vicinity or decided to run a railroad within two minutes' walk of his door. This in itself is enough to damn Mr. George's project. That boasted craft, Land Nationalization, is floundering among the rocks, and the rock of individual liberty and the inalienable homestead has just made an enormous hole in its unseaworthy bottom which will admit all the water necessary to sink it.

"SIMPLIFYING GOVERNMENT."

[*Liberty*, September 10, 1887.]

HENRY GEORGE'S correspondents continue to press him regarding the fate of the man whose home should so rise in value through increase of population that he would be taxed out of it. At first, it will be remembered, Mr. George coolly sneered at the objectors to this species of eviction as near relatives of those who objected to the abolition of slavery on the ground that it would "deprive the widow Smith of her only 'nigger.'" *Liberty* made some comments on this, which Mr.

George never noticed. Since their appearance, however, his analogy between property in "niggers" and a man's property in his house has lapsed, as President Cleveland would say, into a condition of "innocuous desuetude," and a new method of settling this difficulty has been evolved. A correspondent having supposed the case of a man whose neighborhood should become a business centre, and whose place of residence, therefore, as far as the land was concerned, should rise in value so that he could not afford or might not desire to pay the tax upon it, but, as far as his house was concerned, should almost entirely lose its value because of its unfitness for business purposes, Mr. George makes answer that the community very likely would give such a man a new house elsewhere to compensate him for being obliged to sell his house at a sacrifice. That this method has some advantages over the "nigger" argument I am not prepared to deny, but I am tempted to ask Mr. George whether this is one of the ways by which he proposes to "simplify government."

ON PICKET DUTY.

HENRY GEORGE, in the *Standard*, calls Dr. Cogswell of San Francisco, who has endowed a polytechnic college in that city, and for its maintenance has conveyed certain lands to trustees, a "philanthropist by proxy," on the ground that the people who pay rent for these lands are really taxed by Dr. Cogswell for the support of the college. But what are Henry George himself, by his theory, and his ideal State, by its practice, after realization, but "philanthropists by proxy"? What else, in fact, is the State as it now exists? (Oftener a cannibal than a philanthropist, to be sure, but in either case by proxy.) Does not Mr. George propose that the State shall tax individuals to secure "public improvements" which they may not consider such, or which they may consider less desirable to them than private improvements? Does he not propose that individuals shall "labor gratis" for the State, "whether they like it or not"? Does he not maintain that what the State "does with their labor is simply none of their business"? Mr. George's criticism of Dr. Cogswell is equally a criticism of every form of compulsory taxation, especially the taxation of land values. He has aptly and accurately described himself.—*Liberty*, April 23, 1887.

THERE must be a limitation to great fortunes, says Henry George, "but that limitation must be natural, not artificial. Such a limitation is offered by the land value tax." What in the name of sense is there about a tax that makes it natural as distinguished from artificial? If anything in the world is purely artificial, taxes are. And if they are collected by force, they are not only artificial, but arbitrary and tyrannical.— *Liberty*, May 7, 1887.

Henry George answers a correspondent who asks if under the system of taxing land values an enemy could not compel him to pay a higher tax on his land simply by making him an offer for the land in excess of the existing basis of taxation, by saying that no offers will change the basis of taxation unless they are made in good faith and for other than sentimental motives. It seems, then, that the tax assessors are to be inquisitors as well, armed with power to subject men to examination of their motives for desiring to effect any given transaction in land. What glorious days those will be for "boodlers"! What golden opportunities for fraud, favoritism, bribery, and corruption! And yet Mr. George will have it that he intends to reduce the power of government.—*Liberty*, May 28, 1887.

Henry George thinks the New York *Sun's* claim, that it is "for liberty first, last, and forever," pretty cool from a paper that supports a protective tariff. So it is. But the frigidity of this claim is even greater when it comes from a man who proposes on occasion to tax a man out of his home, and to "simplify" government by making it the owner of all railroads, telegraphs, gas-works, and water-works, so enlarging its revenues that all sorts of undreamed-of public improvements will become possible, and unnumbered public officials to administer them necessary.—*Liberty*, July 2, 1887.

The idiocy of the arguments employed by the daily press in discussing the labor question cannot well be exaggerated, but nevertheless it sometimes makes a point on Henry George which that gentleman cannot meet. For instance, the New York *World* lately pointed out that unearned increment attaches not only to land, but to almost every product of labor. "Newspapers," it said, "are made valuable properties by the increase of population." Mr. George seems to think this ridiculous, and inquires confidently whether the *World's* success is due to increase of population or to Pulitzer's business management. As if one cause excluded the other! Does

Mr. George believe, then, that Pulitzer's business management could have secured a million readers of the *World* if
there had been no people in New York? Of course not.
Then, to follow his own logic, Mr. George ought to discriminate in this case, as in the case of land, between the owner's
improvements and the community's improvements, and tax the
latter out of the owner's hands.—*Liberty,* July 2, 1887.

Henry George was recently reminded in these columns that
his own logic would compel him to lay a tax not only on land
values, but on all values growing out of increase of population, and newspaper properties were cited in illustration. A
correspondent of the *Standard* has made the same criticism,
instancing, instead of a newspaper, "Crusoe's boat, which rose
in value when a ship appeared on the horizon." To this correspondent Mr. George makes answer that, while Crusoe's
boat might have acquired a value when other people came,
"because value is a factor of trading, and, when there is no
one to trade with, there can be no value," yet "it by no
means follows that growth of population increases the value
of labor products; for a population of fifty will give as much
value to a desirable product as a population of a million." I
am ready to admit this of any article which can be readily produced by any and all who choose to produce it. But, as Mr.
George says, it is not true of land; and it is as emphatically
not true of every article in great demand which can be produced, in approximately equal quality and with approximately
equal expense, by only one or a few persons. There are many
such articles, and one of them is a popular newspaper. Such
articles are of small value where there are few people and of
immense value where there are many. This extra value is unearned increment, and ought to be taxed out of the individual's hands into those of the community if any unearned increment ought to be. Come, Mr. George, be honest! Let us
see whither your doctrine will lead us.—*Liberty,* July 30, 1887.

Cart and horse are all one to Henry George. He puts
either first to suit his fancy or the turn his questioner may
take, and no matter which he places in the lead, he "gets
there all the same"—on paper. When he is asked how taxation of land values will abolish poverty, he answers that the
rush of wage-laborers to the land will reduce the supply of
labor and send wages up. Then, when somebody else asks
him how wage-laborers will be able to rush to the land without money to take them there and capital to work the land

afterwards, he answers that wages will then be so high that the laborers will soon be able to save up money enough to start with. Sometimes, indeed, as if dimly perceiving the presence of some inconsistency lurking between these two propositions, he volunteers an additional suggestion that, after the lapse of a generation, he will be a phenomenally unfortunate young man who shall have no relatives or friends to help him start upon the land. But we are left as much in the dark as ever about the method by which these relatives or friends, during the generation which must elapse before the young men get to the land, are to save up anything to give these young men a start, in the absence of that increase of wages which can only come as a consequence of the young men having gone to the land. Mr. George, however, has still another resource in reserve, and, when forced to it, he trots it out,—namely, that, there being all grades between the rich and the very poor, those having enough to start themselves upon the land would do so, and the abjectly poor, no longer having them for competitors, would get higher wages. Of course one might ask why these diminutive capitalists, who even now can go to the land if they choose, since there is plenty to be had for but little more than the asking, refrain nevertheless from at once relieving an over-stocked labor market ; but it would do no good. You see, you can't stump Henry George. He always comes up blandly smiling. He knows he has a ready tongue and a facile pen, and on these he relies to carry him safely through the mazes of unreason.—*Liberty*, July 30, 1887.

The Providence *People* having declared that " every tax is in the nature of a tax to discourage industry," I asked it if that was the reason why it favored a tax on land values. It answers that it favors such a tax because it would discourage industry less than any other tax, and because some tax is necessary in order to govern people who cannot govern themselves. In other words, the *People* declares that it is necessary to discourage industry in order to suppress crime. Did it ever occur to the *People* that the discouragement of industry causes more crime than it suppresses, and that, if industry were not discouraged, there would be little or no crime to suppress ?—*Liberty*, October 8, 1887.

Perhaps no feature of Henry George's scheme is so often paraded before the public as a bait as the claim that with a tax levied on land values all other taxes will be abolished. But now it is stated in the *Standard* that, if any great fortunes remain after the adoption of the land tax, it will be " a mere detail to terminate them by a probate tax." This is offered for the benefit of those who believe that interest no less than rent causes concentration of wealth. To those who fear the effects upon home industry in case of an abolition of the tariff Mr. George hints that he will be perfectly agreeable to the offering of bounties to home industries. To be sure, he would pay the bounties out of the land tax ; but the use of the proceeds of the land tax for a new purpose, after existing governmental expenses had been met, would be equivalent to a new tax. So we already have three taxes in sight where there was to be but one,—the land tax, the probate tax, and the bounty tax. Presently, as new necessities arise, a fourth will loom up, and a fifth, and a sixth. Thus the grand work of "simplifying government" goes on.—*Liberty*, November 5, 1887.

"What gives value to land?" asks Rev. Hugh O. Pentecost. And he answers : " The presence of population—the community. Then rent, or the value of land, morally belongs to the community." What gives value to Mr. Pentecost's preaching? The presence of population—the community. Then Mr. Pentecost's salary, or the value of his preaching, morally belongs to the community.—*Liberty*, August 18, 1888.

SOCIALISM.

SOCIALISM : WHAT IT IS.

[*Liberty*, May 17, 1884.]

"Do you like the word *Socialism ?*" said a lady to me the other day ; "I fear I do not; somehow I shrink when I hear it. It is associated with so much that is bad ! Ought we to keep it ? "

The lady who asked this question is an earnest Anarchist, a firm friend of Liberty, and—it is almost superfluous to add—highly intelligent. Her words voice the feeling of many. But after all it is only a feeling, and will not stand the test of thought. " Yes," I answered, "it is a glorious word, much abused, violently distorted, stupidly misunderstood, but expressing better than any other the purpose of political and economic progress, the aim of the Revolution in this century, the recognition of the great truth that Liberty and Equality, through the law of Solidarity, will cause the welfare of each to contribute to the welfare of all. So good a word cannot be spared, must not be sacrified, shall not be stolen."

How can it be saved ? Only by lifting it out of the confusion which obscures it, so that all may see it clearly and definitely, and what it fundamentally means. Some writers make Socialism inclusive of all efforts to ameliorate social conditions. Proudhon is reputed to have said something of the kind. However that may be, the definition seems too broad. Etymologically it is not unwarrantable, but derivatively the word has a more technical and definite meaning.

To-day (pardon the paradox !) society is fundamentally anti social. The whole so-called social fabric rests on privilege and power, and is disordered and strained in every direction by the inequalities that necessarily result therefrom. The welfare of each, instead of contributing to that of all, as it naturally should and would, almost invariably detracts from that of all. Wealth is made by legal privilege a hook with which to filch from labor's pockets. Every man who gets rich thereby makes his neighbor poor. The better off one is, the worse off the rest are. As Ruskin says, "every grain of calculated Increment to the rich is balanced by its mathematical

equivalent of Decrement to the poor." The Laborer's Deficit
is precisely equal to the Capitalist's Efficit.

Now, Socialism wants to change all this. Socialism says
that what's one man's meat must no longer be another's poison; that no man shall be able to add to his riches except
by labor; that in adding to his riches by labor alone no man
makes another man poorer; that on the contrary every man
thus adding to his riches makes every other man richer; that
increase and concentration of wealth through labor tend to increase, cheapen, and vary production; that every increase of
capital in the hands of the laborer tends, in the absence of
legal monopoly, to put more products, better products, cheaper
products, and a greater variety of products within the reach
of every man who works; and that this fact means the physical,
mental, and moral perfecting of mankind, and the realization
of human fraternity. Is not that glorious? Shall a word
that means all that be cast aside simply because some have
tried to wed it with authority? By no means. The man who
subscribes to that, whatever he may think himself, whatever
he may call himself, however bitterly he may attack the thing
which he mistakes for Socialism, is himself a Socialist; and
the man who subscribes to its opposite and acts upon its opposite, however benevolent he may be, however wealthy he
may be, however pious he may be, whatever his station in
society, whatever his standing in the Church, whatever his
position in the State, is not a Socialist, but a Thief. For there
are at bottom but two classes,—the Socialists and the Thieves.
Socialism, practically, is war upon usury in all its forms, the
great Anti-Theft Movement of the nineteenth century; and
Socialists are the only people to whom the preachers of
morality have no right or occasion to cite the eighth commandment, "Thou shalt not steal!" That commandment is
Socialism's flag. Only not as a commandment, but as a law of
nature. Socialism does not order; it prophesies. It does
not say: "Thou shalt not steal!" It says: "When all men
have Liberty, thou wilt not steal."

Why, then, does my lady questioner shrink when she hears
the word *Socialism*? I will tell her. Because a large number
of people, who see the evils of usury and are desirous of destroying them, foolishly imagine they can do so by authority,
and accordingly are trying to abolish privilege by centring
all production and activity in the State to the destruction of
competition and its blessings, to the degradation of the individual, and to the putrefaction of Society. They are well-
meaning but misguided people, and their efforts are bound to

prove abortive. Their influence is mischievous principally in this : that a large number of other people, who have not yet seen the evils of usury and do not know that Liberty will destroy them, but nevertheless earnestly believe in Liberty for Liberty's sake, are led to mistake this effort to make the State the be-all and end-all of society for the whole of Socialism and the only Socialism, and, rightly horrified at it, to hold it up as such to the deserved scorn of mankind. But the very reasonable and just criticisms of the individualists of this stripe upon State Socialism, when analyzed, are found to be directed, not against the Socialism, but against the State. So far Liberty is with them. But Liberty insists on Socialism, nevertheless,—on true Socialism, Anarchistic Socialism : the prevalence on earth of Liberty, Equality, and Solidarity. From that my lady questioner will never shrink.

ARMIES THAT OVERLAP.

[*Liberty*, March 8, 1890.]

OF late the *Twentieth Century* has been doing a good deal in the way of definition. Now, definition is very particular business, and it seems to me that it is not always performed with due care in the *Twentieth Century* office.

Take this, for instance : A Socialist is "one who believes that each industry should be co-ordinated for the mutual benefit of all concerned under a government by physical force."

It is true that writers of reputation have given definitions of Socialism not differing in any essential from the foregoing, —among others, General Walker. But it has been elaborately proven in these columns that General Walker is utterly at sea when he talks about either Socialism or Anarchism. As a matter of fact this definition is fundamentally faulty, and correctly defines only State Socialism.

An analogous definition in another sphere would be this : Religion is belief in the Messiahship of Jesus. Supposing this to be a correct definition of the Christian religion, none the less it is manifestly incorrect as a definition of religion itself. The fact that Christianity has overshadowed all other forms of religion in this part of the world gives it no right to a monopoly of the religious idea. Similarly, the fact that State Socialism during the last decade or two has overshadowed other forms of Socialism gives it no right to a monopoly of the Socialistic idea.

Socialism, as such, implies neither liberty nor authority. The word itself implies nothing more than harmonious relationship. In fact, it is so broad a term that it is difficult of definition. I certainly lay claim to no special authority or competence in the matter. I simply maintain that the word Socialism having been applied for years, by common usage and consent, as a generic term to various schools of thought and opinion, those who try to define it are bound to seek the common element of all these schools and make it stand for that, and have no business to make it represent the specific nature of any one of them. The *Twentieth Century* definition will not stand this test at all.

Perhaps here is one that satisfies it : Socialism is the belief that progress is mainly to be effected by acting upon man through his environment rather than through man upon his environment.

I fancy that this will be criticised as too general, and I am inclined to accept the criticism. It manifestly includes all who have any title to be called Socialists, but possibly it does not exclude all who have no such title.

Let us narrow it a little : Socialism is the belief that the next important step in progress is a change in man's environment of an economic character that shall include the abolition of every privilege whereby the holder of wealth acquires an anti-social power to compel tribute.

I doubt not that this definition can be much improved, and suggestions looking to that end will be interesting ; but it is at least an attempt to cover all the forms of protest against the existing usurious economic system. I have always considered myself a member of the great body of Socialists, and I object to being read out of it or defined out of it by General Walker, Mr. Pentecost, or anybody else, simply because I am not a follower of Karl Marx.

Take now another *Twentieth Century* definition,—that of Anarchism. I have not the number of the paper in which it was given, and cannot quote it exactly. But it certainly made belief in co-operation an essential of Anarchism. This is as erroneous as the definition of Socialism. Co-operation is no more an essential of Anarchism than force is of Socialism. The fact that the majority of Anarchists believe in co-operation is not what makes them Anarchists, just as the fact that the majority of Socialists believe in force is not what makes them Socialists. Socialism is neither for nor against liberty ;

Anarchism is for liberty, and neither for nor against anything
else. Anarchy is the mother of co-operation,--yes, just as
liberty is the mother of order; but, as a matter of definition,
liberty is not order nor is Anarchism co-operation.

I define Anarchism as the belief in the greatest amount
of liberty compatible with equality of liberty ; or, in other
words, as the belief in every liberty except the liberty to
invade.

It will be observed that, according to the *Twentieth Century*
definitions, Socialism excludes Anarchists, while, according
to *Liberty's* definitions, a Socialist may or may not be an Anarchist, and an Anarchist may or may not be a Socialist.
Relaxing scientific exactness, it may be said, briefly and
broadly, that Socialism is a battle with usury and that Anarchism is a battle with authority. The two armies—Socialism
and Anarchism—are neither coextensive nor exclusive ; but
they overlap. The right wing of one is the left wing of the
other. The virtue and superiority of the Anarchistic Socialist—or Socialistic Anarchist, as he may prefer to call himself
—lies in the fact that he fights in the wing that is common to
both. Of course there is a sense in which every Anarchist may
be said to be a Socialist virtually, inasmuch as usury rests
on authority, and to destroy the latter is to destroy the former.
But it scarcely seems proper to give the name Socialist to one
who is such unconsciously, neither desiring, intending, nor
knowing it.

SOCIALISM AND THE LEXICOGRAPHERS.

[*Liberty*, January 30, 1892.]

LIBERTY is informed that the Collectivists expect to prove
their claim to a monopoly of the name Socialism by reference to the Century Dictionary as an indisputable authority.
They will find that the Anarchistic Socialists are not to be
stripped of one half of their title by the mere dictum of the
last lexicographer. If the dictionary-makers were in substantial agreement in making Socialism exclusive of Anarchism, the demand that Anarchists should cease to call themselves Socialists might be made with some grace. But that
there is no approach to unanimity among them on this point
will be seen from the following definitions of Socialism taken
from various cyclopædias and dictionaries, for the compilation

of which *Liberty* is largely indebted to the industry of Comrade Trinkaus.

Stormonth's Dictionary of the English Language:

That system which has for its object the reconstruction of society on the basis of a community of property, and association instead of competition in every branch of human industry ; communion.

Worcester:

The science of reconstructing society on entirely new bases, by substituting the principle of association for that of competition in every branch of human industry.

In the various forms under which society has existed, private property, individual industry and enterprise, and the right of marriage and the family have been recognized. Of late years several schemes of social arrangement have been proposed, in which one or all of these principles have been abandoned or modified. These schemes may be comprehended under the general term Socialism.

Allgemeine deutsche Real-Encyklopädie:

The body of teachings developed into a system which aim at removing the evils of existing society by the establishment of a social order based on a new distribution of wealth, labor, and industry, and thereby creating the lasting welfare of all, but especially of the classes without capital, within a general grand development of humanity.

Globe Encyclopædia:

A term which is practically synonymous with Communism, though, strictly speaking, there is distinction between the two words, which is explained in the article " Communism."

Communism means the negation of private property ; it describes a society in which the land and instruments of production would be held as joint property and used for the common account, industry being regulated by a magistrate, and the produce being publicly divided in equal shares, or according to wants, or on some other principle of distributive justice.

Socialism does not necessarily involve the abolition of private property ; it merely insists . . . that the land and instruments of production should be the property of the association or government.

Webster:

A theory or system of social reform which contemplates a complete reconstruction of society, with a more just and equitable distribution of labor.

Encyclopædia Americana:

Socialism, in general, may be described as that movement which seeks by economic changes to destroy the existing inequalities of the world's social conditions. . . . Into all Socialistic schemes the idea of governmental change enters, with this radical difference, however : some Socialists rely upon the final abolition of existing forms of government and seek the establishment of a pure democracy, while others insist upon giving to government a paternal form, thus increasing its function instead of diminishing it.

Encyclopædia Britannica :

A new form of social organization, based on a fundamental change in the economic order of society. Socialists believe that the present economic order, in which industry is carried on by private competitive capital, must and ought to pass away, and that the normal economic order of the future will be one with collective means of production and associated labor working for the general good. [The " Britannica," in the same article, cataloguing the varieties of Socialism, includes in the list Anarchism, of which it calls Proudhon the acknowledged father.]

Meyer's Konversations-Lexicon :

Literally a system of social organization, commonly a designation for all those teachings and aspirations which contemplate a radical change of the existing social and economical order, in favor of a new order more in harmony with the requirements of the general welfare and the sense of justice than the existing order.

Sanders's Wörterbuch der deutscher Sprache :

A system according to which civil society is to be founded on the community of labor and the proportional distribution of the product.

Johnson's Universal Cyclopædia :

Socialism holds an intermediate position between pure Communism and simple co-operation. Unlike Communism, it does not advocate the absolute abolition of property, but aims simply at a more just and equitable distribution of it. Every man according to his capacity, and every capacity according to its work, is the great maxim laid down by Saint Simon, and to carry out this maxim is the great goal of all Socialistic movements.

Chambers's Encyclopædia :

The name given to a class of opinions opposed to the present organization of society, and which seeks to introduce a new distribution of property and labor, in which organized co-operation rather than competition should be the dominating principle.

American Cyclopædia :

The doctrine that society ought to be organized on more harmonious and equitable principles. Communism and co-operation are its principal divisions or varieties. Communism and Socialism are sometimes used as synonymous ; but generally the former term refers to the plans of social reform based on or embracing the doctrine of a complete community of goods. Co-operation is understood to be that branch of Socialism which is engaged exclusively with theories of labor and methods of distributing profits, and which advocates a combination of many to gain advantages not to be realized by individuals. Viewed as a whole, Socialistic doctrines have dealt with everything that enters into the life of the individual, the family, the Church, or the State, whether industrially, morally, or spiritually.

Universal Cyclopædia :

A system which, in opposition to the competitive system at present prevailing, seeks to reorganize society on the basis, in the main, of a certain secularism in religion, of community of interest, and in co-operation in labor for the common good.

Blackie's Modern Cyclopædia :

The name applied to various theories of social organization, having for their common aim the abolition of that individual action on which modern societies depend, and the substitution of a regulated system of co-operative action. The word Socialism, which originated among the English Communists, and was assumed by them to designate their own doctrines, is now employed in a larger sense, not necessarily implying communism, or the entire abolition of private property, but applied to any system which requires that the land and the instruments of production shall be the property not of individuals, but of communities, or associations, with the view to an equitable distribution of the products.

Lalor's Cyclopædia of Political Science :

An analysis of this word may be reduced to this: In every human society, whether it advances or retrogrades, modifications more or less profound are always going on,—modifications which are more or less perceptible, and which, with or without the knowledge of such society, act upon its economy. Apparently such a society remains the same; but in reality it is daily affected by changes of which it becomes entirely conscious only after time has fixed them in the habits and customs of the people, and marked them by its sanction. This is the course of civilizations which are being perfected, or which are declining. The honor of a generation is to add something to the inheritance it has received, and to transmit it improved to the generation which comes after it. To employ what has been acquired as an instrument of new acquisition, to advance from the verified to the unknown,—such is the idea of progress as it presents itself to well-ordered minds. But such is not the idea of the Socialists. In their eyes the situation given is a false one, and the process too simple. Reforms in detail do not seem to them worthy of attention. They have plans of their own, the first condition of which is to make a tabula rasa of everything that exists, to cast aside existing laws, manners, customs, and all the guarantees of personal property. It seems to them that we have lived thus far under the empire of a misconception, which it is urgent should cease; our globe, according to them, is an anticipated hell, and our civilization a coarse outline only. What is the remedy ? There is only one,—to try the treatment of which the Socialists hold the secret. That treatment varies according to the sect. There are Socialists with mild remedies and Socialists with violent remedies ; the only difficulty is in the choice. But, with all their differences, there is one point on which they agree,—the formal condemnation of human societies as they are at present constituted, and the necessity of erecting on the ruins an order of things more conformable to the instincts of man and to his destiny here below.

Century Dictionary :

Any theory or system of social organization which would abolish, entirely or in great part, the individual effort and competition on which modern society rests, and substitute for it co-operative action, would introduce a more perfect and equal distribution of the products of labor, and would make land and capital, as the instruments and means of production, the joint possession of the members of the community.

Littre's Dictionary of the French Language :

A system which, subordinating political reforms, offers a plan of social reforms. Communism, Mutualism, Saint-Simonism, Fourierism, are Socialisms.

Poitevin :

A political doctrine tending to establish *égalitaire* association as the basis of government.

Dictionary of the French Academy :

The doctrine of those who desire to change the condition of society and reconstruct it on an entirely new plan.

Cassell & Co.'s Encyclopædic Dictionary (1887):

Scientific Socialism embraces :

(1) *Collectivism :* An ideal Socialistic state of society, in which the functions of the government will include the organization of all the industries of the country. In a Collectivist State every person would be a State official, and the State would be coextensive with the whole people.

(2) *Anarchism* (meaning mistrust of government and not abandonment of social order) would secure individual liberty against encroachment on the part of the State in the Socialistic commonwealth. They are divided into Mutualists, who hope to attain their ends by banks of exchange and free currency, and Communists, whose motto is, "From every man according to his capacity, to every man according to his needs."

From this interesting assortment of broad-gauge and narrow-gauge definitions the Anarchists can glean as much encouragement as the Collectivists. None of them are authoritative. The makers of dictionaries are dependent upon specialists for their definitions. A specialist's definition may be true or it may be erroneous. But its truth cannot be increased or its error diminished by its acceptance by the lexicographer. Each definition must stand on its own merits. With this remark as a preface, I offer once more the definition of Socialism which I printed in these columns nearly two years ago, and am willing to leave it to the reader whether it meets the requirements of a scientific definition more or less satisfactorily than the definitions in the dictionaries :

"Socialism is the belief that the next important step in progress is a change in man's environment of an economic character that shall include the abolition of every privilege whereby the holder of wealth acquires an anti-social power to compel tribute."

THE SIN OF HERBERT SPENCER.

[*Liberty*, May 17, 1884.]

Liberty welcomes and criticises in the same breath the series of papers by Herbert Spencer on "The New Toryism," "The Coming Slavery," "The Sins of Legislators," etc., now running in the *Popular Science Monthly* and the English *Contemporary Review.* They are very true, very important, and very misleading. They are true for the most part in what they say, and false and misleading in what they fail to say. Mr. Spencer convicts legislators of undeniable and enormous sins in meddling with and curtailing and destroying the people's rights. Their sins are sins of commission. But Mr. Spencer's sin of omission is quite as grave. He is one of those persons who are making a wholesale onslaught on Socialism as the incarnation of the doctrine of State omnipotence carried to its highest power. And I am not sure that he is quite honest in this. I begin to be a little suspicious of him. It seems as if he had forgotten the teachings of his earlier writings, and had become a champion of the capitalistic class. It will be noticed that in these later articles, amid his multitudinous illustrations (of which he is as prodigal as ever) of the evils of legislation, he in every instance cites some law passed, ostensibly at least, to protect labor, alleviate suffering, or promote the people's welfare. He demonstrates beyond dispute the lamentable failure in this direction. But never once does he call attention to the far more deadly and deep-seated evils growing out of the innumerable laws creating privilege and sustaining monopoly. You must not protect the weak against the strong, he seems to say, but freely supply all the weapons needed by the strong to oppress the weak. He is greatly shocked that the rich should be directly taxed to support the poor, but that the poor should be indirectly taxed and bled to make the rich richer does not outrage his delicate sensibilities in the least. Poverty is increased by the poor laws, says Mr. Spencer. Granted ; but what about the *rich* laws that caused and still cause the poverty to which the poor laws add ? That is by far the more important question ; yet Mr. Spencer tries to blink it out of sight.

A very acute criticism of Mr. Spencer's position has been made recently before the Manhattan Liberal Club by Stephen Pearl Andrews. He shows that Mr. Spencer is not the radical *laissez faire* philosopher which he pretends to be ; that the only true believers in *laissez faire* are the Anarchists ; that individualism must be supplemented by the doctrines of equity and courtesy ; and that, while State Socialism is just as dangerous and tyrannical as Mr. Spencer pictures it, " there is a higher and nobler form of Socialism which is not only not slavery, but which is our only means of rescue from all sorts and degrees of slavery." All this is straight to the mark,—telling thrusts, which Mr. Spencer can never parry.

But the English philosopher is doing good, after all. His disciples are men of independent mind, more numerous every day, who accept his fundamental truths and carry them to their logical conclusions. A notable instance is Auberon Herbert, formerly a member of the House of Commons, but now retired from political life. While an enthusiastic adherent of the Spencerian philosophy, he is fast outstripping his master. In a recent essay entitled "A Politician in Sight of Haven," written, as the London *Spectator* says, with an unsurpassable charm of style, Mr. Herbert explodes the majority lie, ridicules physical force as a solution of social problems, strips government of every function except the police, and recognizes even that only as an evil of brief necessity, and in conclusion proposes the adoption of *voluntary taxation* with a calmness and confidence which must have taken Mr. Spencer's breath away. To be sure, Mr. Herbert is as violent as his master against Socialism, but in his case only because he honestly supposes that compulsory Socialism is the only Socialism, and not at all from any sympathy with legal monopoly or capitalistic privilege in any form.

WILL PROFESSOR SUMNER CHOOSE?

[*Liberty*, November 14, 1885.]

PROFESSOR SUMNER, who occupies the chair of political economy at Yale, addressed last Sunday the New Haven Equal Rights Debating Club. He told the State Socialists and Communists of that city much wholesome truth. But, as far as I can learn from the newspaper reports, which may of course have left out, as usual, the most important things that the speaker said, he made no discrimination in his criticisms. He appears to have entirely ignored the fact that the Anarchistic Socialists are the most unflinching champions in existence of his own pet principle of *laissez faire*. He branded Socialism as the summit of absurdity, utterly failing to note that one great school of Socialism says "Amen" whenever he scolds government for invading the individual, and only regrets that he doesn't scold it oftener and more uniformly.

Referring to Karl Marx's position that the employee is forced to give up a part of his product to the employer (which, by the way, was Proudhon's position before it was Marx's, and Josiah Warren's before it was Proudhon's), Professor Sumner asked why the employee does not, then, go to work for himself, and answered the question very truthfully by saying that it is because he has no capital. But he did not proceed to tell why he has no capital and how he can get some. Yet this is the vital point in dispute between Anarchism and privilege, between Socialism and so-called political economy. He did indeed recommend the time-dishonored virtues of industry and economy as a means of getting capital, but every observing person knows that the most industrious and economical persons are precisely the ones who have no capital and can get none. Industry and economy will begin to accumulate capital when idleness and extravagance lose their power to steal it, and not before.

Professor Sumner also told Herr Most and his followers that their proposition to have the employee get capital by forcible seizure is the most short-sighted economic measure possible to conceive of. Here again he is entirely wise and sound. Not that there may not be circumstances when such seizure would be advisable as a political, war, or terroristic measure calculated to induce political changes that will give freedom to natural economic processes ; but as a directly economic measure it must always and inevitably be, not only futile, but reactionary. In opposition to all arbitrary distribution I stand with Professor Sumner with all my heart and mind. And so does every logical Anarchist.

But, if the employee cannot at present get capital by industry and economy, and if it will do him no good to get it by force, how is he to get it with benefit to himself and injury to no other ? Why don't you tell us that, Professor Sumner ? You did, to be sure, send a stray shot somewhere near the mark when, in answer to a question why shoemakers have no shoes, you said that, where such a condition of things prevailed, it was due to some evil work of the government,—said evil work being manifest at present in the currency and taxation. But what is the precise nature of the evils thus manifest ? Tell me that definitely, and then I will tell you whe   r you are a consistent man.

I fancy that, if I should ask you what the great evil in our taxation is, you would answer that it is the protective tariff. Now, the protective tariff is an evil certainly, and an outrage; but, so far as it affects the power of the laborer to accumulate capital, it is a comparatively small one. In fact, its abolition, unaccompanied by the abolition of the banking monopoly, would take away from very large classes of laborers not only what little chance they now have of getting capital, but also their power of sustaining the lives of themselves and their families. The amount abstracted from labor's pockets by the protective tariff and by all other methods of getting governmental revenue is simply one of the smaller drains on industry. The amount of capital which it is thus prevented from getting will hardly be worth considering until the larger drains are stopped. As far as taxation goes, the great evils involved in it are to be found, not in the material damage done to labor by a loss of earnings, but in the assumption of the right to take men's property without their consent, and in the use of this property to pay the salaries of the officials through whom, and the expenses of the machine through which, labor is oppressed and ground down. Are you heroic enough, Professor Sumner, to adopt this application of *laissez faire?* I summon you to it under penalty of conviction of an infidelity to logic which ought to oust you from your position as a teacher of youth.

If taxation, then (leaving out the enormous mischief that it does as an instrument of tyranny), is only one of the minor methods of keeping capital from labor, what evil is there in the currency that constitutes the major method ? Your answer to this question, Professor Sumner, will again test your consistency. But I am not so sure what it will be in this case as I was in the other. If you answer it as most of your fellow-professors would, you will say that the great evil in the currency is the robbery of labor through a dishonest silver dollar. But this is a greater bugbear than the protective tariff. The silver dollar is just as honest and just as dishonest as the gold dollar, and neither of them is dishonest or a robber of labor except so far as it is a monopoly dollar. Both, however being monopoly dollars, and all our other dollars being monopoly dollars, labor is being robbed by them all to an extent perfectly appalling. And right here is to be found the real reason why labor cannot get capital. It is because its wages are kept low and its credit rendered next to valueless by a financial system that makes the issue of currency a monopoly

374 INSTEAD OF A BOOK.

and a privilege, the result of which is the maintenance of interest, rent, and profits at rates ruinous to labor and destructive to business. And the only way that labor can ever get capital is by striking down this monopoly and making the issue of money as free as the manufacture of shoes. To demonetize silver or gold will not help labor; WHAT LABOR NEEDS IS THE MONETIZATION OF ALL MARKETABLE WEALTH. Or, at least, the *opportunity* of such monetization. This can only be secured by absolutely free competition in banking. Again I ask you, Professor Sumner, does your anxiety lest the individual be interfered with cover the field of finance? Are you willing that the individual shall be " let alone " in the exercise of his right to make his own money and offer it in open market to be taken by those who choose? To this test I send you a second summons under the same penalty that I have already hung over your head in case you fail to respond to the first. The columns of *Liberty* are open for your answer.

Before you make it, let me urge you to consistency. The battle between free trade and protection is simply one phase of the battle between Anarchism and State Socialism. To be a consistent free trader is to be an Anarchist; to be a consistent protectionist is to be a State Socialist. You are assailing that form of State Socialism known as protection with a vigor equalled by no other man, but you are rendering your blows of little effect by maintaining, or encouraging the belief that you maintain, those forms of State Socialism known as compulsory taxation and the banking monopoly. You assail Marx and Most mercilessly, but fail to protest against the most dangerous manifestations of their philosophy. Why pursue this confusing course? In reason's name, be one thing or the other! Cease your indiscriminate railing at Socialism, for to be consistent you must be Socialist yourself, either of the Anarchistic or the governmental sort: either be a State Socialist and denounce liberty everywhere and always, or be an Anarchist and denounce authority everywhere and always; else you must consent to be taken for what you will appear to be,—an impotent hybrid.

AFTER "FREIHEIT," "DER SOZIALIST."

[*Liberty*, April 28, 1888.]

THE first criticism upon *Libertas* * came from the Communists by the pen of Herr Most. That I have answered, and Herr Most promises a rejoinder in *Freiheit.* Meanwhile there comes an attack from another quarter,—from the camp of the State Socialists. In their official organ, *Der Sozialist,* one of its regular writers, J. G., devotes two columns to comments upon my paper, "State Socialism and Anarchism." Under the heading "Consistent Anarchists" he first institutes a contrast between the Anarchists and the Communists who call themselves Anarchists, which is complimentary to the former's consistency, logic, and frankness, and then proceeds to demolish the logical Anarchists by charges of absurdity, nonsense, and ignorance, ringing about all the changes on these substantives and their kindred adjectives that the rich German vocabulary will allow. Now, I submit that, if the Anarchists are such ignoramuses, they do not deserve two columns of attention in *Der Sozialist;* on the other hand, if they merit a two-column examination, they merit it in the form of argument instead of contemptuous assertions coupled with a reference to Marx's works which reminds one very much of the way in which Henry George refers his State Socialistic critics to "Progress and Poverty." To tell the Anarchists that they do not know the meaning of the terms value, price, product, and capital, that economic conceptions find no lodgment in their brains, and that their statements of the position of the State Socialists are misrepresentations, is not to answer them. An answer involves analysis and comparison. To answer an argument is to separate it into its parts, to show the inconsistency between them, and the inconsistency between some or all of them and already established truths. But in J. G.'s article there is nothing of this, or next to nothing.

The nearest approach to a tangible criticism that I can find is the statement that I attribute to Marx a conception of the State entirely foreign to the sense in which he used the term ; that he did not believe in the old patriarchal and absolute State, but looked upon State and society as one. Yes, he re-

---

* A German edition of *Liberty* that was published for a time under the Latin title, *Libertas.*

garded them as one in the sense that the lamb and the lion are one after the lion has eaten the lamb. Marx's unity of State and society resembles the unity of husband and wife in the eyes of the law. Husband and wife are one, and that one is the husband ; so, in Marx's view, State and society are one, but that one is the State. If Marx had made the State and society one *and that one society*, the Anarchists would have little or no quarrel with him. For to the Anarchists society simply means the sum total of those relations between individuals which grow up through natural processes unimpeded by external, constituted, authoritative power. That this is not what Marx meant by the State is evident from the fact that his plan involved the establishment and maintenance of Socialism—that is, the seizure of capital and its public administration—by authoritative power, no less authoritative because democratic instead of patriarchal. It is this dependence of Marx's system upon authority that I insist upon in my paper, and if I misrepresent him in this I do so in common with all the State Socialistic journals and all the State Socialistic platforms. But it is no misrepresentation ; otherwise, what is the significance of the sneers at individual sovereignty which J. G., a follower of Marx, indulges in near the end of his article ? Has individual sovereignty any alternative but authority ? If it has, what is it ? If it has not, and if Marx and his followers are opposed to it, then they are necessarily champions of authority.

But we will glance at one more of J. G.'s "answers." This individual sovereignty that you claim, he says, is what we already have, and is the cause of all our woe. Again assertion, without analysis or comparison, and put forward in total neglect of my argument. I started out with the proposition that what we already have is a mixture of individual sovereignty and authority, the former prevailing in some directions, the latter in others ; and I argued that the cause of all our woe was not the individual sovereignty, but the authority. This I showed by specifying the most important barriers which authority had erected to prevent the free play of natural economic processes, and describing how these processes would abolish all forms of usury—that is, substantially all our woe—if these barriers should be removed. Is this argument met by argument? Not a bit of it. Humph ! says J. G., that is nothing but " Proudhonism chewed over," and Marx disposed of that long ago. To which I might reply that the contents of *Der Sozialist* are nothing but " Marxism chewed over," and Proudhon disposed of that long ago. When I can see that this style of reply is effective in settling controversy, I will resort to it,

Till then I prefer to see it monopolized by the State Socialists. This form of monopoly Anarchists would sooner permit
than destroy.

STATE SOCIALISM AND LIBERTY.

[*Liberty*, February 21, 1891.]

To the Editor of Liberty:

An Anarchist paper defines an Individualist to be "one who believes
in the principle of recognizing the right of every non-aggressive individual
to the full control of his person and property." Is this the meaning of
the word as you understand it? If so, and if it is correct, Individualism
and Socialism are reconcilable, since the aim of the latter is the obtain-
ment of the condition sought by the former. Though the methods of
Socialists may conflict in effect with the principle of Individualism, they
accord with it fundamentally, do they not? From all the works I can find
on modern Socialism, or Nationalism, I understand its object to be the
protection of each individual in the privilege of enjoying his rights,—*i.e.*,
to form a condition whereby equal freedom may be enjoyed, by forbidding
the invasion, and all acts of men, which affect to a disadvantage, directly
or indirectly, the person or property of any non-aggressive individual.
The means proposed by Socialists may fail in effect to form such a condition, but still a Socialist may be an Individualist. I understand how
the nationalization of industries may stop the invasion of the greedy monopolists of interest, unfair profits, and rents, but I have never learned
from *Liberty* or any other champion of Anarchism how the same could
invade the liberty of any individual but the aggressive and the tyrannical.
The protection of the weak and innocent against the strong and avari-
cious necessarily involves compulsion, whether by the will of the people
as typified by a system of democratic government or by their will as
idealized by Anarchists. A defence of a crime involves compulsion of
some sort, whether the force of a superstitious law or the power of popular Anarchy. How, then, does Anarchism conflict with Socialism or
Individualism as above defined? Yours,

WILLIS HUDSPETH.

ATLANTIC, IOWA, February 11, 1891.

The definition offered of Individualism might not be accepted by all Individualists, but it will do very well as a definition of Anarchism. When my correspondent speaks of Socialism I understand him to mean State Socialism and Nationalism,
and not that Anarchistic Socialism which *Liberty* represents.
I shall answer him on this supposition. He wishes to know,
then, how State Socialism and Nationalism would restrict the
non-aggressive individual in the full control of his person and
property. In a thousand and one ways. I will tell him one,
and leave him to find out the thousand. The principal plank

in the platform of State Socialism and Nationalism is the confiscation of *all* capital by the State. What becomes, in that case, of the property of any individual, whether he be aggressive or non-aggressive? What becomes also of private industry? Evidently it is totally destroyed. What becomes then of the personal liberty of those non-aggressive individuals who are thus prevented from carrying on business for themselves or from assuming relations between themselves as employer and employee if they prefer, and who are obliged to become employees of the State against their will? State Socialism and Nationalism mean the utter destruction of human liberty and private property.

ON PICKET DUTY.

IN a series of articles in the London *Commonweal*, Dr. Edward Aveling, newly-fledged disciple of Karl Marx, discusses economic questions. He concludes each article with what he calls " a concise definition of each of the terms mentioned." These two definitions stand side by side. " Natural object— that on which human labor has not been expended ; Product —a natural object on which human labor has been expended." A product, then, is something on which human labor has not been expended on which human labor has been expended. Curious animal, a product ! No wonder the laborer is unable to hold on to it. More slippery than a greased pig, I should imagine. But this is a " scientific " definition, and I suppose it must be true. For its author, Dr. Aveling, is a scientist, and the subject of his articles is " Scientific Socialism," which he champions against us loose-thinking Anarchists.—*Liberty*, July 18, 1885.

At his Faneuil Hall meeting Dr. Aveling said : " With the abolition of private property in land, with the abolition of private property in raw material, with the abolition of private property in machinery, will come the abolition of private property in human lives." Never was truer word spoken. For with State property in land, with State property in raw material, with State property in machinery, would come State property in human lives. Such is the object of Dr. Aveling's State Socialism,—the obliteration of the individual life. Property in human lives ought to be as "private" as possible;

each individual (forgive the tautology) should own his own. But under State Socialism the ownership of each individual's life would be virtually vested in the body politic. Those who hold the property in the means of living will inevitably hold the property in life itself.—*Liberty*, October 30, 1886.

In a late number of *Liberty* H. M. Hyndman was rebuked for confounding the teachings of *Liberty* with those of Most. Now his paper, the London *Justice*, in commenting upon a recent article in *Liberty*, says : " Evidently the Liberty and Property Defence League, the Manchester school of economists, and the Anarchists are one and the same." This indicates advancing intelligence. Most is much nearer to Hyndman than to *Liberty*, and Anarchism is much nearer to the Manchester men than to Most. In principle, that is. *Liber ty's* aim—universal happiness—is that of all Socialists, in contrast with that of the Manchester men—luxury fed by misery. But its principle—individual sovereignty—is that of the Manchester men, in contrast with that of the Socialists—individual subordination. But individual sovereignty, *when logically carried out*, leads, not to luxury fed by misery, but to comfort for all industrious persons and death for all idle ones.—*Liberty*, November 20, 1886.

Every day I meet some new man who tells me that Anarchy is the ultimate, but that it is to be reached through State Socialism. The State Socialists are shrewd enough to encourage this folly, though they laugh in their sleeve as they do so. It is astonishing, therefore, that the usually cunning Powderly should be so honest and imprudent as to permit the utterance of the real truth about this matter in the editorial columns of the *Journal of the Knights of Labor.* "Oscar Wilde declares that Socialism will simply lead to individualism. That is like saying that the way from St. Louis to New York is through San Francisco, or that the sure way to whitewash a wall is to paint it black. The man who says that Socialism will fail and then the people will try individualism—*i.e.*, Anarchy—may be mistaken; the man who thinks they are one and the same thing is simply a fool."—*Liberty*, May 16, 1891.

COMMUNISM.

GENERAL WALKER AND THE ANARCHISTS.*

[*Liberty*, November 19, 1887.]

LADIES AND GENTLEMEN:—Some four years ago I had occasion to write a criticism of a work then new,—Professor Ely's " French and German Socialism in Modern Times,"—and I began it with these paragraphs :

It is becoming the fashion in these days for the parsons who are hired, either directly or indirectly, consciously or unconsciously, to whitewash the sins of the plutocrats, and for the professors who are hired, either directly or indirectly, consciously or unconsciously, to educate the sons of the plutocrats to continue in the transgressions of their fathers,—it is becoming the fashion for these to preach sermons, deliver lectures, or write books on Socialism, Communism, Anarchism, and the various other phases of the modern labor movement. So general, indeed, has become the practice that any one of them who has not done something in this line begins to feel a vague sense of delinquency in the discharge of his obligations to his employer, and consequently scarce a week passes that does not inflict upon a suffering public from these gentlemen some fresh clerical or professorial analysis, classification, interpretation, and explanation of the ominous overhanging social clouds which conceal the thunderbolt that, unless the light of Liberty and Equity dissipates them in time, is to destroy their masters' houses.

The attitudes assumed are as various as the authors are numerous. Some are as lowering as the clouds themselves ; others as beaming as the noonday sun. One would annihilate with the violence of his fulminations ; another would melt with the warmth of his flattery and the persuasiveness of conciliation. These foolishly betray their spirit of hatred by threats and denunciation ; those shrewdly conceal it behind fine words and honeyed phrases. The latest manifestation coming to our notice is of the professedly disinterested order. Richard T. Ely, associate professor of political economy in the Johns Hopkins University at Baltimore and lecturer on political economy in Cornell University, Ithaca, N. Y., comes to the front with a small volume on " French and German Socialism in Modern Times," the chapters of which, now somewhat rewritten, were originally so many lectures to the students under his charge, and substantially (not literally) announces himself as follows : " Attention ! Behold ! I am come to do a service to the friends of law and order by expounding the plans and purposes of the honest but mistaken enemies of law and order. But, whereas nearly all my predecessors in this field have been

---

* An address delivered before the Boston Anarchists' Club on November 6, 1887.

unfair and partial, I intend to be fair and impartial." And we are bound
to say that this pretence has been maintained so successfully throughout
the book that it can hardly fail to mislead every reader who has not in advance the good fortune to know more than the author about his subject.

I quote these paragraphs at the beginning of this paper, because I was forcibly reminded of them on reading the other
day in the Boston *Post* a long and very interesting report of
an address on " Anarchism and Socialism," delivered the previous evening before the Trinity Club of this city by General
Francis A. Walker, president of the Massachusetts Institute
of Technology. The tone of the address, like that of Professor Ely's book, was seemingly so fair ; there was such an apparent effort to carefully discriminate between the different
schools of Socialism, and to bestow words of praise wherever,
in the speaker's judgment, such were deserved ; and a disposition was so frankly exhibited to find important elements of
truth in Socialistic teachings,—that I myself, usually so wary
and so doubtful of the possibility of any good issuing from the
Nazareth of orthodox political economy, was misled, not indeed into acquiescence in the speaker's errors, which were
many and egregious, but into a belief in his honesty of purpose and his genuine desire to understand his opponents and
represent them accurately. This man, said I to myself, is
ready to be set right.

So I wrote him a letter, asking the privilege of an hour's interview. The request was phrased as politely as my knowledge of English and of the requirements of courtesy would
permit. I congratulated General Walker on his evident disposition to be fair, but hinted as delicately as I could that
certain things had escaped him and certain others had misled
him. I assured him that I had no expectation of converting
him to my views, but was confident that I could give him a
better understanding of Anarchism. I told him that, if necessary, I would give him references among the foremost
Socialists of America as to my competency to accurately represent Anarchism, and added that for three years I was a
regular student in the educational institution of which he is
now at the head.

A day or two later I received this reply :

MASSACHUSETTS INSTITUTE OF TECHNOLOGY,
BOSTON, October 27, 1887.

DEAR SIR :—Your letter of the 25th inst. is received.

I regret that I have not time to go into the subject of Anarchism, as
you propose. The report of my speech before the Trinity Club, on the
24th, was altogether unauthorized. I was assured that I was addressing

a private club, informally ; and, at the last, only assented to the title of the lecture being mentioned.

I dare say the report was also incorrect. Such reports generally are. I have not read it.

Respectfully yours,

FRANCIS A. WALKER.

This letter completely dissolved my illusion. It showed me at once that General Walker's fairness, like that of his brother economist, Professor Ely, lay entirely on the surface,—the only difference between them, perhaps, being that, while Professor Ely falsified deliberately and with knowledge of the truth, General Walker spoke in ignorance, though posing as a teacher, and became a hypocrite only after the fact, by refusing to know the truth or have it pointed out to him. Here is a man, famous as an economist, with a reputation to sustain, who has time to prepare and deliver, or else to deliver without preparation, before a private club, on the uppermost and most important question of the day, an address so long that even an inadequate report of it filled a column and a half in the Boston *Post*, but has not one hour in which to listen to proof offered in substantiation of a charge of gross error preferred against him by one who for fifteen years has made this question a subject of special study.

It will not do for him to plead in excuse that the *Post's* report, which he has not read, may be incorrect, and that therefore the charge of error may be based on statements unwarrantably attributed to him. It so happens that it falls to my lot as a daily journalist to revise and prepare for publication reports of all descriptions to the number of several hundred a week, and in consequence I know an intelligent report when I see one as infallibly as a painter knows a good picture when he sees one. In the report in question there may be minor inaccuracies ; as to that I cannot say : but as a whole it is a report of uncommon excellence and intelligence. Given a report containing a mass of errors, if these errors are the reporter's, they will be a jumble ; if, on the other hand, they bear a definite relation to each other and proceed from a common and fundamental error, it is sure that they are not the reporter's errors, but the lecturer's. In this case the error fallen into at the start is so consistently held to and so frequently repeated that it would be contrary to the law of chances to hold the reporter responsible for it ; General Walker must answer for it himself. And as he will not listen to a private demonstration offered in a friendly spirit, I am compelled to submit him to a public demonstration offered in a somewhat antagonistic spirit.

What, then, is the fundamental error into which General Walker falls? It is this,—that, in trying, as he claims, to set Anarchism before his hearers as it is seen by its most intelligent advocates, he discriminates between men of whom he instances Prince Kropotkine as typical, as intelligent exponents of scientific Anarchy on the one hand, and, on the other hand, men like the seven under sentence at Chicago as unintelligent, ignorant, ruffianly scoundrels, who call themselves Anarchists, but are not Anarchists.

Now, I perfectly agree with General Walker that the Chicago men call themselves Anarchists, but are not Anarchists. And inasmuch as my subject compels me to say something in criticism of these men's opinions and inasmuch also as five days hence they are to die upon the gallows, victims of a tyranny as cruel, as heartless, as horrible, as blind as any that ever bloodied history's pages, you will excuse me, I am sure, if I interrupt my argument, almost before beginning it, long enough to qualify my criticism in advance by a word of tribute and a declaration of fellowship. Instead of ruffianly scoun· drels, these men are noble-hearted heroes deeply in love with order, peace, and harmony,—loving these so deeply, in fact, that they have not remained contented with any platonic affection worshipping them as ideals ever distant, but have given their lives to a determined effort to win and enjoy them to the fullest. I differ with them vitally in opinion ; I disapprove utterly their methods ; I dispute emphatically their Anarchism : but as brothers, as dear comrades, animated by the same love, and working, in the broad sense, in a common cause than which there never was a grander, I give them both my hands and my heart in them. Far be it from me to shirk in the slightest the solidarity that unites us. Were I to do so, for trivial ends or from ignoble fears, I should despise myself as a coward. For these brave men I have no apologies to make ; I am proud of their courage, I glory in their devotion. If they shall be murdered on Friday next, I fear that the vile deed will prove fraught with consequences from which, if its perpetrators could foresee them, even they, brutes as they are, would recoil in horror and dismay.

I say, however, with General Walker, that these men are not Anarchists, though they call themselves so. But if I prove that Prince Kropotkine agrees with them exactly, both as to the form of social organization to be striven for and as to the methods by which to strive for and sustain it, I show thereby that, as they are not Anarchists, he is not one, that General Walker's discrimination is therefore a false one, and that, in making it, he showed utter ignorance of the nature of Anarchism proper. Now, precisely that I propose to prove.

To this end the first question to be asked is : What is the Socialistic creed of the Chicago men ? It is a very simple one, consisting of two articles : 1, that all natural wealth and products of labor should be held in common, produced by each according to his powers and distributed to each according to his needs, through the administrative mechanism and under the administrative control of workingmen's societies organized by trades ; 2, that every individual should have perfect liberty in all things except the liberty to produce for himself and to exchange with his neighbors outside the channels of the prescribed mechanism. Not stopping to consider here how much any liberties would be worth without the liberty to produce and exchange, I proceed to the second question : How do the Chicago men propose that their creed shall be realized ? The answer to this is simpler still, consisting of but one article : that the working people should arm themselves, rise in revolution, forcibly expropriate every proprietor, and then form the necessary workingmen's societies, whose first duty should be to feed, clothe, and shelter the masses out of the common stock, whose second duty should be to organize production for the renewal of the stock, and whose third duty should be to suppress by whatever heroic measures all rebellious individuals who should at any time practically assert their right to produce and exchange for themselves. The literature circulated by this school is now so well known that I do not need to make quotations from it to show that its teachings are as I have stated. I assume that this will not be disputed. It remains to consider whether Kropotkine's teachings materially differ from them. I claim that they do not, and, as Kropotkine's writings are less familiar to Americans, it is necessary to prove this claim by quotations. His chief work is written in French, a volume of some 350 pages entitled " Paroles d'un Révolté " (" Words of a Rebel "). The title of the closing chapter is " Expropriation." From that chapter I now translate and quote as follows :

We have to put an end to the iniquities, the vices, the crimes which result from the idle existence of some and the economic, intellectual, and moral servitude of others. The problem is an immense one. But, since past centuries have left this problem to our generation; since we find ourselves under the historical necessity of working for its complete solution,— we must accept the task. Moreover, we are no longer obliged to grope in

the dark for the solution.   It has been imposed upon us by history, simultaneously with the problem; it has been and is being stated boldly in all
European countries, and it sums up the economic and intellectual development of our century.   It is Expropriation; it is Anarchy.

If social wealth remains in the hands of the few who possess it to-day; if
the workshop, the dockyard, and the factory remain the property of the
employer; if the railways, the means of transportation, continue in the
hands of the companies and the individuals who have monopolized them;
if the houses of the cities as well as the country-seats of the lords remain
in possession of their actual proprietors, instead of being placed, from the
beginning of the revolution, at the gratuitous disposition of all laborers; if
all accumulated treasure, whether in the banks or in the houses of the
wealthy, does not immediately go back to the collectivity—since all have
contributed to produce it; if the insurgent people do not take possession
of all the goods and provisions amassed in the great cities and do not organize to put them within the reach of all who need them ; if the land,
finally, remains the property of the bankers and usurers,—to whom it
belongs to-day, in fact, if not in law,—and if the great tracts of real estate
are not taken away from the great proprietors, to be put within the reach
of all who wish to labor on the soil; if, further, there is established a
governing class to dictate to a governed class,—the insurrection will not be
a revolution, and everything will have to be begun over again. . . .

Expropriation,—that, then, is the watchword which is imposed upon the
next revolution, under penalty of failing in its historic mission.   The
complete expropriation of all who have the means of exploiting human
beings.   The return to common ownership by the nation of all that can
serve in the hands of any one for the exploitation of others.

This extract covers all the doctrines of the Chicago men,
does it not ?   That it covers common property and distribution according to needs no one can question.   That it covers
the denial of the right of individual production and exchange
is equally clear.   Kropotkine says, it is true, that he would
allow the individual access to the land ; but as he proposes to
strip him of capital entirely, and as he declares a few pages
further on that without capital agriculture is impossible, it follows that such access is an empty privilege not at all equivalent to the liberty of individual production.   But one point
remains,—that of the method of expropriation by force ; and
if any one still feels any doubt of Kropotkine's belief in that,
let me remove it by one more quotation :

We must see clearly in private property what it really is, a conscious or
unconscious robbery of the substance of all, and seize it joyfully for the
common benefit when the hour of revendication shall strike.   In all former
revolutions, when it was a question of replacing a king of the elder branch
by a king of the younger branch or of substituting lawyers for lawyers in
the "best of republics," proprietors succeeded proprietors and the social
régime had not to change.   Accordingly the placards, "Death to robbers !" which were placed at the entrance of every palace were in perfect
harmony with the current morality, and many a poor devil caught touching a coin of the king, or perhaps even the bread of the baker, was shot
as an example of the justice administered by the people.

The worthy national guard, incarnating in himself all the infamous solemnity of the laws which the monopolists had framed for the defence of their property, pointed with pride to the body stretched across the steps of the palace, and his comrades hailed him as an avenger of the law. Those placards of 1830 and 1848 will not be seen again upon the walls of insurgent cities. No robbery is possible where all belongs to all. "Take and do not waste, for it is all yours, and you will need it." But destroy without delay all that should be overthrown, the bastilles and the prisons, the forts turned against the cities and the unhealthy quarters in which you have so long breathed an atmosphere charged with poison. Install yourselves in the palaces and mansions, and make a bonfire of the piles of bricks and rotten wood of which the sinks in which you have lived were constructed. The instinct of destruction, so natural and so just because it is at the same time the instinct of renovation, will find ample room for satisfaction.

Nothing more incendiary than that was ever uttered in the Haymarket or on the lake front at Chicago by the most rabid agitator of that volcanic city. And if further proof were needed, it could readily be found in the columns of Kropotkine's paper, Le Révolté, in which he lately lauded to the skies as a legitimate act of propagandism the conduct of a member of his party named Duval, who, after a fashion externally indistinguishable from that of a burglar, broke into a house in Paris and plundered it, and who afterwards vindicated his course in court as deliberately entered upon in pursuance of his principles.

In view of these things, I submit that General Walker has no warrant whatever for referring to such men as Kropotkine as true Anarchists and "among the best men in the world," while in the same breath he declares (I use his words as reported in the Post) that "the mobs at the Haymarket were composed of pickpockets, housebreakers, and hoodlums," and that "the ruffians who are called Anarchists who formed the mob in the Haymarket in Chicago were not Anarchists." If Kropotkine is an Anarchist, then the Chicago men are Anarchists; if the Chicago men are not Anarchists, then Kropotkine is not an Anarchist. If the Chicago men are pickpockets and housebreakers, then Kropotkine is a pickpocket and housebreaker; if Kropotkine is not a pickpocket and housebreaker, then the Chicago men are not pickpockets and housebreakers. The truth is that neither of them are housebreakers in the ordinary sense of the term, but that both of them, in advocating and executing the measures that they do, however unjustifiable these may be from the standpoint of justice and reason, are actuated by the highest and most humane motives. And as to their Anarchism, neither of them are Anarchists. For Anarchism means absolute liberty, nothing more, nothing less. Both Kropotkine and the Chicago men deny liberty in production and exchange, the most important of all liberties,—without which, in fact, all other liberties are of no value or next to none. Both should be called, instead of Anarchists, Revolutionary Communists.

In making this discrimination which does not discriminate, General Walker showed that he does not know what Anarchism is. Had he known, he would have drawn his line of discrimination in a very different direction,—between real Anarchists like P. J. Proudhon, Josiah Warren, Lysander Spooner, and their followers, who believe in the liberty of production and exchange, and miscalled Anarchists like Kropotkine *and* the Chicago men, who deny that liberty. But of the true Anarchism he seems never to have heard. For he says:

> All Anarchistic philosophy presumes the Communistic reorganization of society. No Anarchist claims that the principles of Anarchy can be applied to the present or capitalistic state of society. Prince Kropotkine, in common with other Anarchistic writers, claims that the next move of society will be free Communism. We must understand that Anarchism means Communism.

So far is this from true, that Communism was rejected and despised by the original Anarchist, Proudhon, as it has been by his followers to this day. Anarchism would to-day be utterly separate from Communism if the Jurassian Federation in Switzerland, a Communistic branch of the International, had not broken from the main body in 1873 and usurped the name of Anarchism for its own propaganda, which propaganda, having been carried on with great energy from that day to this, has given General Walker and many others an erroneous idea of Anarchism. To correct this idea we must go to the fountain-head.

In 1840 Proudhon published his first important work, "What is Property? or, An Inquiry into the Principle of Right and of Government." In it the following passage may be found:

> What is to be the form of government in the future? I hear some of my younger readers reply: "Why, how can you ask such a question? You are a republican."—"A republican! Yes; but that word specifies nothing. *Res publica;* that is, the public thing. Now, whoever is interested in public affairs—no matter under what form of government—may call himself a republican. Even kings are republicans."—"Well, you are a democrat?"—"No."—"What! you would have a monarchy?"—"No."—"A constitutionalist?"—"God forbid!"—"You are then an aristocrat?"—"Not at all."—"You want a mixed government?"—"Still less."—"What are you, then?'—"I am an Anarchist."
> "Oh! I understand you; you speak satirically. This is a hit at

the government."—" By no means. I have just given you my serious and well-considered profession of faith. Although a firm friend of order, I am (in the full force of the term) an Anarchist. Listen to me."

He then traces in a few pages the decline of the principle of authority, and arrives at the conclusion that, " in a given society, the authority of man over man is inversely proportional to the stage of intellectual development which that society has reached"; that, "just as the right of force and the right of artifice retreat before the steady advance of justice, and must finally be extinguished in equality, so the sovereignty of the will yields to the sovereignty of the reason, and must at last be lost in scientific Socialism"; and that, "as man seeks justice in equality, so society seeks order in Anarchy."

This is the first instance on record, so far as I have been able to discover, of the use of the word Anarchy to denote, not political chaos, but the ideal form of society to which evolution tends. These words made Proudhon the father of the Anarchistic school of Socialism. His use of the word and its adoption by his followers gave it its true standing in political and scientific terminology. Proudhon, then, being the Anarchist *par excellence*, let us examine his attitude towards Communism in order to test thereby General Walker's assertion that "all Anarchistic philosophy presumes the Communistic reorganization of society" and that "Anarchism means Communism."

It probably will surprise many who know nothing of Proudhon save his declaration that "property is robbery" to learn that he was perhaps the most vigorous hater of Communism that ever lived on this planet. But the apparent inconsistency vanishes when you read his book and find that by property he means simply legally privileged wealth or the power of usury, and not at all the possession by the laborer of his products. Of such possession he was a stanch defender. Bearing this in mind, listen now to the few paragraphs which I shall read from "What is Property?" and which are separated only by a dozen pages from what I have already quoted from the same work :

I ought not to conceal the fact that property and communism have been considered always the only possible forms of society. This deplorable error has been the life of property. The disadvantages of communism are so obvious that its critics never have needed to employ much eloquence to thoroughly disgust men with it. The irreparability of the injustice which it causes, the violence which it does to attractions and repulsions, the yoke of iron which it fastens upon the will, the moral torture to which it subjects the conscience, the debilitating effect which it has upon society ; and, to sum it all up, the pious and stupid uniformity which it enforces upon the free, active, reasoning, unsubmissive personality of man have shocked common sense, and condemned communism by an irrevocable decree.

The authorities and examples cited in its favor disprove it. The communistic republic of Plato involved slavery ; that of Lycurgus employed Helots, whose duty it was to produce for their masters, thus enabling the latter to devote themselves exclusively to athletic sports and to war. Even J. J. Rousseau—confounding communism and equality—has said somewhere that, without slavery, he did not think equality of conditions possible. The communities of the early Church did not last the first century out, and soon degenerated into monasteries. In those of the Jesuits of Paraguay, the condition of the blacks is said by all travellers to be as miserable as that of slaves; and it is a fact that the good Fathers were obliged to surround themselves with ditches and walls to prevent their new converts from escaping. The followers of Babœuf—guided by a lofty horror of property rather than by any definite belief—were ruined by exaggeration of their principles; the St. Simonians, lumping communism and inequality, passed away like a masquerade. The greatest danger to which society is exposed to-day is that of another shipwreck on this rock.

Singularly enough, systematic communism—the deliberate negation of property—is conceived under the direct influence of the proprietary prejudice; and property is the basis of all communistic theories.

The members of a community, it is true, have no private property; but the community is proprietor, and proprietor not only of the goods, but of the persons and wills. In consequence of this principle of absolute property, labor, which should be only a condition imposed upon man by Nature, becomes in all communities a human commandment, and therefore odious. Passive obedience, irreconcilable with a reflecting will, is strictly enforced. Fidelity to regulations, which are always defective, however wise they may be thought, allows of no complaint. Life, talent, and all the human faculties are the property of the State, which has the right to use them as it pleases for the common good. Private associations are sternly prohibited, in spite of the likes and dislikes of different natures, because to tolerate them would be to introduce small communities within the large one, and consequently private property ; the strong work for the weak, although this ought to be left to benevolence, and not enforced, advised, or enjoined; the industrious work for the lazy, although this is unjust ; the clever work for the foolish, although this is absurd ; and, finally, man — casting aside his personality, his spontaneity, his genius, and his affections—humbly annihilates himself at the feet of the majestic and inflexible Commune !

Communism is inequality, but not as property is. Property is the exploitation of the weak by the strong. Communism is the exploitation of the strong by the weak. In property, inequality of conditions is the result of force, under whatever name it be disguised: physical and mental force; force of events, chance, *fortune ;* force of accumulated property, etc. In communism, inequality springs from placing mediocrity on a level with excellence. This damaging equation is repellent to the conscience, and causes merit to complain ; for, although it may be the duty of the strong to aid the weak, they prefer to do it out of generosity,—they never will endure a comparison. Give them equal opportunities of labor, and equal wages, but never allow their jealousy to be awakened by mutual suspicion of unfaithfulness in the performance of the common task.

Communism is oppression and slavery. Man is very willing to obey the law of duty, serve his country, and oblige his friends ; but he wishes to labor when he pleases, where he pleases, and as much as he pleases. He wishes to dispose of his own time, to be governed only by necessity, to choose his friendships, his recreation, and his discipline ; to act from judgment, not by command ; to sacrifice himself through selfishness, not through servile obligation.   Communism is essentially opposed to the free exercise of our faculties, to our noblest desires, to our deepest feelings. Any plan which could be devised for reconciling it with the demands of the individual reason and will would end only in changing the thing while preserving the name.   Now, if we are honest truth-seekers, we shall avoid disputes about words.

Thus, communism violates the sovereignty of the conscience, and equality : the first, by restricting spontaneity of mind and heart, and freedom of thought and action ; the second, by placing labor and laziness, skill and stupidity, and even vice and virtue on an equality in point of comfort.   For the rest, if property is impossible on account of the desire to accumulate, communism would soon become so through the desire to shirk.

This extract sufficiently disposes of General Walker's claim. He probably has never read it.   In fact, I should judge from his address to the Trinity Club that his sole knowledge of Anarchism was derived from one very mild article written by Prince Kropotkine for the *Nineteenth Century.*   I think I have proven what I started to prove,—that his discriminations between Anarchists have no existence outside of his own imagination, and that he knows next to nothing of this subject, upon which he professes to teach others.   His address contained a number of other errors which I might as easily expose, had not this paper already extended beyond the limits originally set for it.   Time also forbids me to explain the true idea of Anarchism.   That I must leave for some future occasion.   The lesson that I have endeavored to teach to-day I find stated by General Walker.   He says : " Even our public speakers themselves exhibit a gross ignorance of the principles of Anarchism and Socialism as they are held by large bodies of intelligent men."   Of all his remarks to the Trinity Club, that was nearly the only one the truth of which he succeeded in establishing; and that one he established, not by argument, but by the object-teacher's method of personal illustration and example.

HERR MOST ON "LIBERTAS."

[*Liberty*, April 14, 1888.]

It is due to John Most to say that, in his paper *Freiheit,* he has greeted the appearance of *Libertas* in a spirit of entire fairness and liberality, at the same time that he has not hesitated to point out those of its features to which he cannot award approval. Besides giving liberal extracts from the first number, duly credited, he devotes nearly a column and a half to a review of its merits and demerits, which is hearty in its commendation and frank in its criticism. Barring the use in one sentence of the word "hypocritical," his article is free from those abusive epithets of which he has heretofore made me a target. With this preface of thanks for both his praise and his censure, I propose to briefly examine the latter in the same spirit in which it is offered.

Herr Most's opinion of *Libertas* may be thus summed up,— that it is thoroughly sound in its antagonism to the State and utterly unsound in its championship of private property. Whether *Libertas* champions private property depends entirely on the definition given to that term. Defining it with Prou- dhon as the sum total of legal privileges bestowed upon the holders of wealth, *Libertas* agrees with Proudhon that property is robbery. But using the word in the commoner acceptation, as denoting the laborer's individual possession of his product or of his proportional share of the joint product of himself and others, *Libertas* holds that property is liberty. And when- ever Proudhon, for the time being, uses the word in the latter sense, he too upholds property. But it is precisely in this sense of individual as opposed to communistic possession that Herr Most opposes property. Hence, when he prints as a motto (as he often does) Proudhon's phrase "Property is robbery," he virtually misrepresents that author by using his words as if they were intended to mean diametrically the opposite of what the author himself declared them to mean. If property, in the sense of individual possession, is liberty, then he who op- poses property necessarily upholds authority—that is, the State—in some form or other, and he who would deny both the State and property at once becomes thereby inconsistent and guilty of attempting the impossible.

The principal argument used by Herr Most against *Libertas* is that it ignores the necessity of production on the large scale now and hereafter,—a necessity which, in Herr Most's view, involves the exploitation of labor by capital wherever private property prevails. There is no foundation for this statement. *Libertas* does not for a moment deny or ignore the necessity of production on the large scale. It does, however, seriously question the claim that such production must always involve large concentration of capital, and emphatically denies that it necessarily involves labor's exploitation unless private property is abolished. As I have already said in these columns, "the main strength of the argument for State Socialism and Communism has always resided in the claim, till lately undisputed, that the permanent tendency of progress in the production and distribution of wealth is in the direction of more and more complicated and costly processes, requiring greater and greater concentration of capital and labor. But the idea is beginning to dawn upon minds—there are scientists who even profess to demonstrate it by facts—that the tendency referred to is but a phase of progress, and one which will not endure. On the contrary, a reversal of it is confidently looked for. Processes are expected to become cheaper, more compact, and more easily manageable, until they shall come again within the capacity of individuals and small combinations. Such a reversal has already been experienced in the course taken by improvements in implements and materials of destruction. Military progress was for a long time toward the complex, requiring immense armies and vast outlays. But the tendency of more recent discoveries and devices has been toward placing individuals on a par with armies by enabling them to wield powers which no aggregation of troops can withstand. Already, it is believed, Lieutenant Zalinski with his dynamite gun could shield any seaport against the entire British navy. With the supplanting of steam by electricity and other advances of which we know not, it seems more than likely that the constructive capacity of the individual will keep pace with his destructive. In that case what will become of State Socialism and Communism?" It behooves their advocates not to be so cock-sure as they have been heretofore of the correctness of this major premise of all their arguments.

But Herr Most may claim that in this reasoning the element of speculation and uncertainty is too large to warrant the placing of any weight upon it. Very well, then ; simply reaffirming my own confidence in it, I will let it go for what it is worth, and consider at once the question whether large concentration of capital for production on the large scale confronts us with the disagreeable alternative of either abolishing private property or continuing to hold labor under the capitalistic yoke. Herr Most promises that, if I will show him that the private property *régime* is compatible with production on the large scale without the exploitation of labor, he will stand by the side of *Libertas* in its favor. This promise contains a most significant admission. If Communism is really, as Herr Most generally claims, no infringement of liberty, and if in itself it is such a good and perfect thing, why abandon it for private property simply because the possibility of the latter's existence without the exploitation of labor has been demonstrated? To declare one's willingness to do so is plainly to affirm that, exploitation aside, private property is superior to Communism, and that, exploitation admitted, Communism is chosen only as the lesser evil. I take note of this admission, and pass on.

Right here, however, Herr Most qualifies his promise by placing another condition upon its fulfilment. I must not only demonstrate the proposition stipulated, but I must do so otherwise than by pointing to Proudhon's banking system. This complicates the problem. Show me that A is equal to B, says Herr Most, and I will uphold A ; only you must not show it by establishing that both A and B are equal to C. But perhaps the equality of both A and B to C is the only proof I have of the equality of A to B. Am I to be debarred, then, from making the demonstration simply because this form of logic is not agreeable to Herr Most? Not at all ; he is bound to show the flaw in the logic, or else accept its conclusion. His stipulation, then, that I must not point to Proudhon's banking system is ridiculous, inasmuch as this banking system, or at least its central principle, is essential to the demonstration of my position. I offer him this principle as conclusive proof ; he must show its error, or admit the claim. It cannot be brushed aside with a contemptuous wave of the hand.

Now, what is this principle? Simply the freedom of credit and the resultant organization thereof in such a way as to eliminate the element of the reward of capital from the production and distribution of wealth. Herr Most will not dispute, I think, that freedom of credit leaves private property intact and even increases the practicability of production on the large scale. The only question, then, is whether it will abolish usury ; for, if it will abolish usury, my position is established, usury being but another name for the exploitation of labor. The argument that it will effect such abolition, and the argument therefore which Herr Most is bound to destroy, he will find set forth in the latter half of my paper on " State Socialism and Anarchism," printed in the first issue of *Libertas*. If he makes no answer, the private property plank in the platform of *Libertas* remains unimpaired by his criticism ; if, on the other hand, he attempts an answer, then we shall see what there is further to be said.

But Herr Most's criticism is not aimed at the platform alone; he is especially severe upon the tactics of *Libertas*. It is here that he crosses the line of courteous criticism, and becomes abusive by characterizing as " hypocritical " the declaration of

Libertas that, as long as freedom of speech and of the press is not struck down, there should be no resort to physical force in the struggle against oppression. That *Libertas* is hypocritical in this position he infers from the fact that it now discountenances physical force, although five men have been murdered, others are in prison, and still others are in danger of imprisonment, for having exercised the right of free speech. Herr Most apparently forgets that *Freiheit* is still published in New York, the *Alarm* in Chicago, and *Liberty* and *Libertas* in Boston, and that all these papers, if not allowed to say everything they would like to, are able to say all that it is absolutely necessary to say in order to finally achieve their end, the triumph of liberty. It must not be inferred that, because *Libertas* thinks it may become advisable to use force to secure free speech, it would therefore sanction a bloody deluge as soon as free speech had been struck down in one, a dozen, or a hundred instances. Not until the gag had become completely efficacious would *Libertas* advise that last resort, the use of force. And this, far from showing hypocrisy, is the best evidence of the sincerity of this journal's utter disbelief in force as a solution of economic evils. If there is hypocrisy anywhere, it is on the side of those who, affecting to think force a deplorable thing only to be resorted to for purposes of defence, are eagerly watching for the commission of offences in the hope of finding a pretext for the inauguration of an era of terror and slaughter hitherto unparalleled in history.

STILL AVOIDING THE ISSUE.

[*Liberty*, May 12, 1888.]

As I expected, Herr Most, in his controversy with me upon private property, Communism, and the State, is as reluctant as ever to come to close quarters in an attempt to destroy my main position, and, for sole response to my challenge to do so, crouches behind the name of Marx, not daring even to attempt upon his own account the use of the weapons with which Marx has assailed it. Herr Most had promised to accept private property if I would show him that it is compatible with production on the large scale without the exploitation of labor. He warned me, to be sure, against showing this by Proudhon's banking system. But I answered that he is bound to accept my proposition on the strength of whatever proof I offer, or else demonstrate that the proof offered is no proof at all,—in other words, that he cannot reject my evidence without first refuting it. My proof, I then told him, consists precisely in that principle of freedom and organization of credit which is embodied in Proudhon's banking system and other systems of a similar nature, and I referred him to a recent essay in which I have explained the process whereby freely organized credit would abolish usury—that is, the exploitation of labor—and make production on the large scale easier than ever without interfering with the institution of private property.

Now it would naturally be assumed that, in answer to this, some examination would be made of the process referred to and the flaw in it be pointed out. But did Herr Most do anything of the kind ? Not he. His only answer is that Marx disposed of Proudhon's banking system long ago, that it is fifty years behind the times, and that it is not at all clear that there is any foundation for the claim that, with the prevailing inequalities of property, all could obtain credit. No, Herr Most, nor is it clear that any such claim was ever made by any sane champion of the organization of credit. The real claim is, not that all could straightway get credit if credit were not monopolized, but that, if all or a half or a quarter of such credit as could be at once obtained under a free system should be utilized, a tremendous impetus would thereby be given to production and enterprise which would gradually increase the demand for labor and therefore the rate of wages and therefore the number of people able to get credit, until at last every laborer would be able to say to his employer : " Here, boss, you are a good business manager, and I am willing to continue to work under your superintendence on a strictly equitable basis ; but, unless you are willing to content yourself with a share of our joint product proportional to your share of the labor and give me the balance for my share of the labor, I will work for you no longer, but will set up in business for myself on the capital which I can now obtain on my credit." Herr Most's misstatement of the claim made by the friends of free banking shows that he has no knowledge of their arguments or system, which probably explains his reluctance to discuss them otherwise than by reiteration of the magic name of Marx. Proudhon's banking system may be fifty years behind the times, but it is evidently far in advance of the point which Herr Most has reached in the path of economic investigation.

Even more careful is the wary editor of *Freiheit* to avoid

the following question, which I asked him *à propos* of his promise: "If Communism is really, as Herr Most generally claims, no infringement of liberty, and if in itself it is such a good and perfect thing, why abandon it for private property simply because the possibility of the latter's existence without the exploitation of labor has been demonstrated? To declare one's willingness to do so is plainly to affirm that, exploitation aside, private property is superior to Communism, and that, exploitation admitted, Communism is chosen only as the lesser evil." Herr Most knew that it would never do to admit that Communism curtails liberty. Yet he could not answer this question without admitting it. So he prudently let it alone.

But what, then, does he say in his three-column article?

Well, for one thing, he tries to make his readers think that I offered my incidental remarks, rather suggestive than conclusive, regarding the likelihood that the Communists' position, being based on a supposed necessity of great combinations in order to produce on the large scale, might soon be undermined by the tendency, of which symptoms are beginning to appear, towards a simplification and cheapening of machinery,—he tries to make his readers think, I say, that I offered these remarks as a necessary link in my argument. "On such grounds," he says, "we are expected to believe," etc., giving no hint of my express declaration that I offered this idea for what it was worth and not as essential to my position.

Nevertheless it is not easy to see why he should regard this thought as so utterly chimerical, when he finds it so easy, in order to show Communism to be practicable, to assume that the time is not far distant when wealth will be so abundant that individuals will not think of quarrelling over its possession, but will live as birds do in their hemp-seed. Of the two hypotheses the latter seems to me the more visionary. Certainly great strides are yet to be taken in labor-saving, and I do not doubt at all that a state of society will be attained in which every sound individual will be able to secure a comfortable existence by a very few hours of toil daily. But that there will ever be any such proportion between human labor and the objects of human consumption as now exists between bird labor and hemp-seed, or that land and other capital will ever be superabundant in the same sense that water, light, and air are superabundant, is inadmissible. If, however, the means of life shall ever become so utterly divorced from human toil that all men look on all wealth as air is now looked upon, I will then admit that, so far as material enjoyment is concerned, Communism will be practicable (I do not say advisable) without violation of liberty. Until then, I must insist that a State will be necessary to its realization and maintenance.

But, Herr Most asks me, if respect for private property is conceivable without a State, why is not Communism so conceivable? Simply because the only force ever necessary to secure respect for private property is the force of defence,—the force which protects the laborer in the possession of his product or in the free exchange thereof,—while the force required to secure Communism is the force of offence,—the force which compels the laborer to pool his product with the products of all and forbids him to sell his labor or his product. Now, force of offence is the principle of the State, while force of defence is one aspect of the principle of liberty. This is the reason why private property does not imply a State, while Communism does. Herr Most seems to be as ignorant of the real nature of the State as he is of Proudhon's banking system. In opposing it he acts, not as an intelligent foe of Authority, but simply as a rebel against the powers that be.

What is the use, in fact, of discussing with him at all? Does he not confess at the very outset of the article I am now examining that, although he has racked his brains, they refuse to perceive my distinction between the laborer's individual possession of his product and the sum total of legal privileges bestowed upon the holders of wealth? Is there any hope that such a mind will ever grasp an economic law? The reason he gives for his inability to recognize this distinction is his conviction that private possession and privilege are inseparable. The more one calls his own, he says, the less others will be able to possess. This is not true where all property rests on a labor title, and no other property do I favor. It is only true of the increase of property through usury. But usury, as has already been shown, rests on privilege. When the property of one increases through an advance in the productivity of his labor, the property of others, far from decreasing on that account, increases to an almost equal extent. This year A produces 100 in hats and B 100 in shoes. Each consumes 50 in his own product, and exchanges the remaining 50 for the other's remaining 50. Suppose that next year A's production remains the same, but that B's, with no extra labor, rises to 200. In that case A's remaining 50, instead of exchanging for B's remaining 50 as this year, will exchange for 100 in B's product. Under private possession, unaccompanied by usury, more for one man means, not less for another man, but more for all men. Where, then, is the privilege ?

But, after all, it makes very little difference to Herr Most what a man believes in economics. The test of fellowship with him lies in acceptance of dynamite as a cure-all. Though I should prove that my economic views, if realized, would turn our social system inside out, he would not therefore regard me as a revolutionist. He declares outright that I am no revolutionist, because the thought of the coming revolution (by dynamite, he means) makes my flesh creep. Well, I frankly confess that I take no pleasure in the thought of bloodshed and mutilation and death. At these things my feelings revolt. And if delight in them is a requisite of a revolutionist, then indeed I am no revolutionist. When revolutionist and cannibal become synonyms, count me out, if you please. But, though my feelings revolt, I am not mastered by them or made a coward by them. More than from dynamite and blood do I shrink from the thought of a permanent system of society involving the slow starvation of the most industrious and deserving of its members. If I should ever become convinced that the policy of bloodshed is necessary to end our social system, the loudest of to-day's shriekers for blood would not surpass me in the stoicism with which I would face the inevitable. Indeed, a plumb-liner to the last, I am confident that under such circumstances many who now think me chicken-hearted would condemn the stony-heartedness with which I should favor the utter sacrifice of every feeling of pity to the necessities of the terroristic policy. Neither fear nor sentimentalism, then, dictates my opposition to forcible methods. Such being the case, how stupid, how unfair, in Herr Most, to picture me as crossing myself at the mention of the word revolution simply because I steadfastly act on my well-known belief that force cannot substitute truth for a lie in political economy !

HERR MOST DISTILLED AND CONSUMED.

[*Liberty,* June 9, 1888.]

AFTER proclaiming, in *Freiheit* of May 19, his intention of proceeding to my final demolition, Herr Most, in *Freiheit* of May 26, closes his side of the controversy with me with such a homœopathic dilution of his preceding articles that it is

scarcely worth attention. Summarized, his positions are that
the controversy is unequal, because he quotes and then criticises, while I criticise without quotation; that I am the dodger,
not he, because the essential question is the private property
question, while I insist on discussing Proudhon's banking system ; that he has read *Liberty* for six years, and has found no
plausible defence of that system in its pages, and that the
statement in my last reply probably covers that system ; that
the system has been put into operation in Germany and elsewhere with no further effect than to enable the smaller *bourgeois* to hold out a little longer against the larger ; that I only
half understand Proudhon's works ; that, if I would read the
whole of *Freiheit* instead of only such portions as relate directly
to me, I might know something about the economics of Socialism ; that Proudhon's banking system has no longer a single
champion in Europe ; and that " if we are once through with
the political tyrants, then the economic ones will no longer be
dangerous to us, for the latter will surely have had their necks
broken with the former, especially since both kinds are essentially one and the same persons."

I answer, with like brevity and succinctness, that I have accurately represented Herr Most by restatements, while he has
*mis*represented me by garbled quotations ; that the essential
question is not the private property question, since Herr Most
promised to abandon Communism for private property on
being shown that the latter is compatible with production on
the large scale without the exploitation of labor, which immediately made the arguments on which the claim of such
compatibility rests the essential question ; that the principle
of Proudhon's banking system has been expounded repeatedly
in *Liberty,* and far more fully and adequately than in the present controversy ; that neither his system nor any similar system was ever put into unmolested operation, so far as I know,
and that, if my knowledge on this point is deficient, it is Herr
Most's business to supply the deficiency by distinct specification of facts ; that, other things being equal, those countries
and those periods have been the most prosperous in which
financial institutions have most nearly approached Proudhon's idea ; that to understand half of Proudhon's works is
better than to understand none of them ; that a number of intelligent persons whom I know, and who read *Freiheit* thoroughly, tell me that they have failed to derive any such benefit
from it as Herr Most promises me ; that within a very few
years a book of several hundred pages has been published in
Paris, ably stating and defending Proudhon's banking theories,

—"La Question Sociale," by Emile Chevalet ; that many
ideas of transcendent importance have been launched into the
world, only to lie dormant under the pressure of reaction for
long years before being revived and realized ; and that it is
quite true that economic privilege must disappear as a result of the abolition of political tyranny,—a fact which the Individualistic Anarchists have always relied on against the
"Communistic Anarchists," whose claim has steadily been
that to abolish the State is not enough, and that a separate
campaign against economic privilege is necessary. In this last
sentence of Herr Most's article he gives away his whole case.

SHOULD LABOR BE PAID OR NOT?

[*Liberty*, April 28, 1888.]

IN No. 121 of *Liberty*, criticising an attempt of Kropotkine
to identify Communism and Individualism, I charged him
with ignoring " the real question whether Communism will
permit the individual to labor independently, own tools, sell
his labor or his products, and buy the labor or products of
others." In Herr Most's eyes this is so outrageous that, in re-
printing it, he puts the words " the labor of others " in large
black type. Most being a Communist, he must, to be consistent, object to the purchase and sale of anything whatever ;
but why he should particularly object to the purchase and
sale of labor is more than I can understand. Really, in the
last analysis, labor is the only thing that has any title to be
bought or sold. Is there any just basis of price except
cost ? And is there anything that costs except labor or suffering (another name for labor) ? Labor should be paid ! Horrible, isn't it ? Why, I thought that the fact that it is not
paid was the whole grievance. " Unpaid labor " has been the
chief complaint of all Socialists, and that labor should get its
reward has been their chief contention. Suppose I had said
to Kropotkine that the real question is whether Communism
will permit individuals to exchange their labor or products on
their own terms. Would Herr Most have been so shocked ?
Would he have printed that in black type ? Yet in another
form I said precisely that.

If the men who oppose wages—that is, the purchase and
sale of labor—were capable of analyzing their thought and feelings, they would see that what really excites their anger is not

the fact that labor is bought and sold, but the fact that one class of men are dependent for their living upon the sale of their labor, while another class of men are relieved of the necessity of labor by being legally privileged to sell something that is not labor, and that, but for the privilege, would be enjoyed by all gratuitously. And to such a state of things I am as much opposed as any one. But the minute you remove privilege, the class that now enjoy it will be forced to sell their labor, and then, when there will be nothing but labor with which to buy labor, the distinction between wage-payers and wage-receivers will be wiped out, and every man will be a laborer exchanging with fellow-laborers. Not to abolish wages, but to make *every* man dependent upon wages and secure to every man his *whole* wages is the aim of Anarchistic Socialism. What Anarchistic Socialism aims to abolish is usury. It does not want to deprive labor of its reward ; it wants to deprive capital of its reward. It does not hold that labor should not be sold ; it holds that capital should not be hired at usury.

But, says Herr Most, this idea of a free labor market from which privilege is eliminated is nothing but "consistent Manchesterism." Well, what better can a man who professes Anarchism want than that ? For the principle of Manchesterism is liberty, and consistent Manchesterism is consistent adherence to liberty. The only inconsistency of the Manchester men lies in their infidelity to liberty in some of its phases. And this infidelity to liberty in some of its phases is precisely the fatal inconsistency of the *Freiheit* school,—the only difference between its adherents and the Manchester men being that in many of the phases in which the latter are infidel the former are faithful, while in many of those in which the latter are faithful the former are infidel. Yes, genuine Anarchism is consistent Manchesterism, and Communistic or pseudo-Anarchism is inconsistent Manchesterism. " I thank thee, Jew, for teaching me that word."

DOES COMPETITION MEAN WAR?

[*Liberty*, August 4, 1888.]

To the Editor of Liberty:

Your thought-provoking controversy with Herr Most suggests this question : Whether is Individualism or Communism more consistent with a society resting upon credit and mutual confidence, or, to put it another way, whether is competition or co-operation the truest expression of that mutual trust and fraternal good-will which alone can replace present forms of authority, usages and customs as the social bond of union?

The answer seems obvious enough. Competition, if it means anything at all, means war, and, so far from tending to enhance the growth of mutual confidence, must generate division and hostility among men. If egoistic liberty demands competition as its necessary corollary, every man becomes a social Ishmael. The state of veiled warfare thus implied where underhand cunning takes the place of open force is doubtless not without its attractions to many minds, but to propose mutual confidence as its regulative principle has all the appearance of making a declaration of war in terms of peace. No, surely credit and mutual confidence, with everything thereby implied, rightly belong to an order of things where unity and good-fellowship characterize all human relations, and would flourish best where co-operation finds its complete expression,—*viz.*, in Communism. W. T. HORN.

The supposition that competition means war rests upon old notions and false phrases that have been long current, but are rapidly passing into the limbo of exploded fallacies. Competition means war only when it is in some way restricted, either in scope or intensity,—that is, when it is not perfectly free competition; for then its benefits are won by one class at the expense of another, instead of by all at the expense of nature's forces. When universal and unrestricted, competition means the most perfect peace and the truest co-operation; for then it becomes simply a test of forces resulting in their most advantageous utilization. As soon as the demand for labor begins to exceed the supply, making it an easy matter for every one to get work at wages equal to his product, it is for the interest of all (including his immediate competitors) that the best man should win; which is another way of saying that, where freedom prevails, competition and co-operation are identical. For further proof and elaboration of this proposition I refer Mr. Horn to Andrews's "Science of Society" and Fowler's pamphlets on "Co-operation." The real problem, then, is to make the demand for labor greater than the supply, and this can only be done through competition in the supply of money or use of credit. This is abundantly shown in Greene's "Mutual Banking" and the financial writings of Proudhon and Spooner. My correspondent seems filled with the sentiment of good-fellowship, but ignorant of the science thereof, and even of the fact that there is such a science. He will find this science expounded in the works already named. If, after studying and mastering these, he still should have any doubts, *Liberty* will then try to set them at rest.

COMPETITION AND MONOPOLY CONFOUNDED.

[*Liberty*, September 1, 1888.]

To the Editor of Liberty:

Does competition mean war ? you ask, and then go on to answer:

"The supposition that competition means war rests upon old notions and false phrases that have been long current, but are rapidly passing into the limbo of exploded fallacies."

Pardon me, Mr. Tucker, but are you quite sure that the supposition in question rests upon nothing more than "old notions and false phrases"? Go out into the highways and byeways of the work-a-day world, look around you, and then tell us candidly if what you see there is likely to inspire any lover of his kind with a wish to foster competition.

Ah ! but you reply : "This is not *free* competition ; this is monopoly and privilege."

Exactly so, but what is monopoly but the very soul of competition ? I venture to submit that it is not for wealth *per se* men strive, but for the mastership it confers ; hence, if you deny the spoils of victory to the victor, you sheathe the sword forever. Monopolies and privileges of every kind are nothing more than resultants of a competition as *free* as nature could make it, for even the grand old Sphinx herself has not been able to evolve "equal liberty" from the free competition of unequal forces.

When the benefits of competition cease to "be won by one class at the expense of another," and when they are shared "by all at the expense of nature's forces," competition loses its *raison d'être* and dies.

When lower and semi-barbarous economic forms are subjected to the strong solvent action of higher ethical concepts, they disappear ; that is to say, when mutual confidence and good-fellowship prevail over hostility and love of mastership, competition must give place to co-operation ; hence, to my mind there is no escape from the conclusion that competition means war so long as it is the economic expression of hostility and mastership, and after that it will mean—nothing. "Equal liberty," however, would still remain, for what is it at bottom but community of interest?   W. T. HORN.

What the person who goes out into the work-a-day world will see there depends very much upon the power of his mental vision. If that is strong enough to enable him to see that the evils around him are caused by a prohibition of competition in certain directions, it is not unlikely that he will be filled with a "wish to foster competition." Such, however, will not be the case with a man who so misapprehends competition as to suppose that monopoly is its soul. Instead of its soul, it is its antithesis.

Whatever the reason for which men strive for wealth, as a general thing they get it, not by competition, but by the application of force to the suppression of certain kinds of competition,—in other words, by governmental institution and protection of monopoly.

Inasmuch as the monopolist is the victor, it is true that to deny him the spoils of victory is to sheathe the sword of *monopoly*. But you do not thereby sheathe the sword of competition (if you insist on calling it a sword), because competition yields no spoils to the victor, but only wages to the laborer.

When my correspondent says that all monopolies are "resultants of a competition as *free* as nature could make it," he makes competition inclusive of the struggle between invasive forces, whereas he ought to know that free competition, in the economic sense of the phrase, implies the suppression of invasive forces, leaving a free field for the exercise of those that are non-invasive.

If a man were to declare that, when the benefits of *labor* cease to be won by one class at the expense of another and when they are shared by all at the expense of nature's forces, *labor* loses its *raison d'être* and dies, his sanity would not long remain unquestioned; but the folly of such an utterance is not lessened an iota by the substitution of the word *competition* for the word *labor*. As long as the gastric juice continues to insist upon its rights, I fancy that neither labor nor competition will lack a *raison d'être*, even though the laborer and competitor should find himself under the necessity of wresting his "spoils" from the bosom of his mother earth instead of from the pocket of his brother man.

In Mrs. Glass's recipe for cooking a hare, the first thing was to catch the hare. So in Mr. Horn's recipe for the solution of economic forms in ethical concepts, the first thing is to get the concepts. Now, the concepts of mutual confidence and good-fellowship are not to be obtained by preaching,—otherwise the church militant would long ago have become the church triumphant; or by force,—otherwise progress would have gone hand in hand with authority instead of with liberty ; but only by unrestricted freedom,—that is, by competition, the necessary condition of confidence, fellowship, and co-operation, which can never come as long as monopoly, " the economic expression of hostility and mastership," continues to exist.

ON PICKET DUTY.

IN a speech recently delivered in Paris, Kropotkine said : " As the idea of the inviolability of the individual's home life has developed during the second half of our century, so the

idea of collective right to everything that serves in the production of wealth has developed in the masses. This is a fact ;
and whoever wants to live, as we do, with the life of the
people and follow its development will admit that this affirmation is but an accurate summary of popular aspirations."
Then Kropotkinian Anarchism means the liberty to eat, but
not to cook ; to drink, but not to brew; to wear, but not to
spin ; to dwell, but not to build ; to give, but not to sell or
buy ; to think, but not to print ; to speak, but not to hire a
hall ; to dance, but not to pay the fiddler. O Absurdity !
is there any length to which thou wilt not go ?—*Liberty*, July
3, 1886.

The Socialistic municipality of St. Etienne, France, has
abolished the common grave to which heretofore have been
consigned all bodies buried at the public expense. Why those
whose dearest wish is to institute Communism in everything
this side the grave should object to it in the grave itself is incomprehensible to an Anarchist. One would suppose that, if
Communism must be accepted at all, it would be found less
intolerable than anywhere else in the common du st of earth,
to which we all return. But it seems to be the aim of the
Communists and State Socialists to destroy all individuality
that exists and make a pretence of it after it has gone,—to
murder men and worship their ghosts.—*Liberty*, July 7, 1888.

Kropotkine, arguing in favor of Communism, says that he
has " always observed that workers with difficulty understand
the possibility of a wage-system of labor-checks and like artificial inventions of Socialists," but has been "struck on the
contrary by the easiness with which they always accept Communist principles." Was Kropotkine ever struck by the easiness with which simple-minded people accept the creation
theory and the difficulty with which they understand the possibility of evolution ? If so, did he ever use this fact as an
argument in favor of the creation hypothesis ? Just as it is
easier to rest satisfied with the statement, " Male and female
created he them," than to trace in the geological strata the
intricacies in the evolution of species, so it is easier to say that
every man shall have whatever he wants than to find the
economic law by which every man may get the equivalent of
his product. The ways of Faith are direct and easy to follow,
but their goal is a quagmire ; whereas the ways of Science,
however devious and difficult to tread, lead to solid ground at
last. Communism belongs to the Age of Faith, Anarchistic
Socialism to the Age of Science.—*Liberty*, September 15, 1888.

METHODS.

THE POWER OF PASSIVE RESISTANCE.

[*Liberty*, October 4, 1884.]

"EDGEWORTH" makes appeal to me through *Lucifer* to know how I propose to "starve out Uncle Sam." Light on this subject he would "rather have than roast beef and plum pudding for dinner *in sæculâ sæculorum*." It puzzles him to know whether by the clause "resistance to taxation" on the "sphynx head of *Liberty* on 'God and the State'" I mean that "true Anarchists should advertise their principles by allowing property to be seized by the sheriff and sold at auction, in order by such personal sacrifices to become known to each other as men and women of a common faith, true to that faith in the teeth of their interests and trustworthy for combined action." If I do mean this, he ventures to "doubt the policy of a test which depletes, not that enormous vampire, Uncle Sam, but our own little purses, so needful for our propaganda of ideas, several times a year, distrainment by the sheriff being in many parts of the country practically equivalent to tenfold taxes." If, on the other hand, I have in view a minority capable of "successfully withdrawing the supplies from Uncle Sam's treasury," he would like to inquire "how any minority, however respectable in numbers and intelligence, is to withstand the sheriff backed by the army, and to withhold tribute to the State."

Fair and pertinent questions these, which I take pleasure in answering. In the first place, then, the policy to be pursued by individual and isolated Anarchists is dependent upon circumstances. I, no more than "Edgeworth," believe in any foolish waste of needed material. It is not wise warfare to throw your ammunition to the enemy unless you throw it from the cannon's mouth. But if you can compel the enemy to waste his ammunition by drawing his fire on some thoroughly protected spot ; if you can, by annoying and goading and harassing him in all possible ways, drive him to the last resort of stripping bare his tyrannous and invasive purposes and put him in the attitude of a designing villain assailing honest men for purposes of plunder,—there is no better strategy. Let no Anarchist, then, place his property within reach of the sheriff's

clutch. But some year, when he feels exceptionally strong
and independent, when his conduct can impair no serious
personal obligations, when on the whole he would a little
rather go to jail than not, and when his property is in such
shape that he can successfully conceal it, let him declare to
the assessor property of a certain value, and then defy the col-
lector to collect. Or, if he have no property, let him decline
to pay his poll tax. The State will then be put to its trumps.
Of two things one,—either it will let him alone, and then he
will tell his neighbors all about it, resulting the next year in an
alarming disposition on their part to keep their own money in
their own pockets ; or else it will imprison him, and then by the
requisite legal processes he will demand and secure all the
rights of a civil prisoner and live thus a decently comfortable
life until the State shall get tired of supporting him and the
increasing number of persons who will follow his example. Unless, indeed, the State, in desperation, shall see fit to make its
laws regarding imprisonment for taxes more rigorous, and then,
if our Anarchist be a determined man, we shall find out how far
a republican government, "deriving its just powers from the
consent of the governed," is ready to go to procure that
" consent,"—whether it will stop at solitary confinement in a
dark cell or join with the Czar of Russia in administering torture by electricity. The farther it shall go the better it will
be for Anarchy, as every student of the history of reform well
knows. Who can estimate the power for propagandism of a
few cases of this kind, backed by a well-organized force of
agitators without the prison walls ? So much, then, for individual resistance.

But, if individuals can do so much, what shall be said of the
enormous and utterly irresistible power of a large and intelligent minority, comprising say one-fifth of the population in
any given locality ? I conceive that on this point I need do
no more than call " Edgeworth's " attention to the wonderfully instructive history of the Land League movement in
Ireland, the most potent and instantly effective revolutionary
force the world has ever known so long as it stood by its
original policy of " Pay No Rent," and which lost nearly all
its strength the day it abandoned that policy. " Oh, but it
did abandon it ? " " Edgeworth " will exclaim. Yes, but why ?
Because there the peasantry, instead of being an intelligent
minority following the lead of principles, were an ignorant,
though enthusiastic and earnest, body of men following blindly
the lead of unscrupulous politicians like Parnell, who really
wanted anything but the abolition of rent, but were willing to

temporarily exploit any sentiment or policy that would float them into power and influence. But it was pursued far enough to show that the British government was utterly powerless before it; and it is scarcely too much to say, in my opinion, that, had it been persisted in, there would not to-day be a landlord in Ireland. It is easier to resist taxes in this country than it is to resist rent in Ireland; and such a policy would be as much more potent here than there as the intelligence of the people is greater, providing always that you can enlist in it a sufficient number of earnest and determined men and women. If one-fifth of the people were to resist taxation, it would cost more to collect their taxes, or try to collect them, than the other four-fifths would consent to pay into the treasury. The force needed for this bloodless fight *Liberty* is slowly but surely recruiting, and sooner or later it will organize for action. Then, Tyranny and Monopoly, down goes your house!

"Passive resistance," said Ferdinand Lassalle, with an obtuseness thoroughly German, "is the resistance which does not resist." Never was there a greater mistake. It is the only resistance which in these days of military discipline resists with any result. There is not a tyrant in the civilized world to-day who would not do anything in his power to precipitate a bloody revolution rather than see himself confronted by any large fraction of his subjects determined not to obey. An insurrection is easily quelled; but no army is willing or able to train its guns on inoffensive people who do not even gather in the streets but stay at home and stand back on their rights. Neither the ballot nor the bayonet is to play any great part in the coming struggle; passive resistance and, in emergencies, the dynamite bomb in the hands of isolated individuals are the instruments by which the revolutionary force is destined to secure in the last great conflict the people's rights forever.*

---

* By "emergencies" something very serious is meant,—such, for instance, as the absolute suppression of freedom of speech and of the press.

THE IRISH SITUATION IN 1881.

[*Liberty*, October 29, 1881.]

IRELAND'S chief danger: the liability of her people — besotted with superstition; trampled on by tyranny; ground into the dust beneath the weight of two despotisms, one religious, the other political; victims, on the one hand, of as cruel a Church and, on the other, of as heartless a State as have ever blackened with ignorance or reddened with blood the records of civilized nations—to forget the wise advice of their cooler leaders, give full vent to the passions which their oppressors are aiming to foment, and rush headlong and blindly into riotous and ruinous revolution.

Ireland's true order: the wonderful Land League, the nearest approach, on a large scale, to perfect Anarchistic organization that the world has yet seen. An immense number of local groups, scattered over large sections of two continents separated by three thousand miles of ocean ; each group autonomous, each free; each composed of varying numbers of individuals of all ages, sexes, races, equally autonomous and free; each inspired by a common, central purpose; each supported entirely by voluntary contributions; each obeying its own judgment; each guided in the formation of its judgment and the choice of its conduct by the advice of a central council of picked men, having no power to enforce its orders except that inherent in the convincing logic of the reasons on which the orders are based; all coördinated and federated, with a minimum of machinery and without sacrifice of spontaneity, into a vast working unit, whose unparalleled power makes tyrants tremble and armies of no avail.

Ireland's shortest road to success: no payment of rent now *or hereafter;* no payment of compulsory taxes now or hereafter; utter disregard of the British parliament and its so-called laws; entire abstention from the polls henceforth; rigorous but non-invasive "boycotting" of deserters, cowards, traitors, and oppressors; vigorous, intelligent, fearless prosecution of the land agitation by voice and pen; passive but stubborn resistance to every offensive act of police or military; and, above all, universal readiness to go to prison, and promptness in filling the places made vacant by those who may be sent to prison. Open revolution, terrorism, and the policy above outlined, which is Liberty, are the three courses

from which Ireland now must choose one. Open revolution
on the battle-field means sure defeat and another century of
misery and oppression; terrorism, though preferable to revolution, means years of demoralizing intrigue, bloody plot, base
passion, and terrible revenges,—in short, all the horrors of a
long-continued national vendetta, with a doubtful issue at the
end; Liberty means certain, unhalting, and comparatively
bloodless victory, the dawn of the sun of justice, and perpetual peace and prosperity for a hitherto blighted land.

THE METHOD OF ANARCHY.

[*Liberty*, June 18, 1887.]

To the editor of the San Francisco *People* Anarchism is
evidently a new and puzzling doctrine. It having been propounded by an Anarchist from a public platform in that city
that Anarchism must come about by peaceful methods and
that physical force is never justifiable except in self-defence,
the *People* declares that, except physical force, it can see
but two methods of settling the labor question: one the voluntary surrender of privileges by the privileged class, which
it thinks ridiculous, and the other the ballot, which it rightly
describes as another form of force. Therefore the *People*,
supposing itself forced to choose between persuasion, the
ballot, and direct physical force, selects the last. If I were
forced to the alternative of leaving a question unsettled or
attempting one of three ineffectual means of settling it, I think
I should leave it unsettled. It would seem the wiser course
to accept the situation. But the situation is not so hopeless.
There is a fourth method of settling the difficulty, of which
the *People* seems never to have heard,—the method of
passive resistance, the most potent weapon ever wielded by
man against oppression. Power feeds on its spoils, and dies
when its victims refuse to be despoiled. They can't persuade
it to death; they can't vote it to death; they can't shoot it to
death; but they can always starve it to death. When a determined body of people, sufficiently strong in numbers and force
of character to command respect and make it unsafe to imprison them, shall agree to quietly close their doors in the
faces of the tax-collector and the rent-collector, and shall, by
issuing their own money in defiance of legal prohibition, at
the same time cease paying tribute to the money-lord, govern-

ment, with all the privileges which it grants and the monopolies which it sustains, will go by the board. Does the *People* think this impracticable? I call its attention, then, to the vast work that was done six years ago in Ireland by the old Irish Land League, in defiance of perhaps the most powerful government on earth, simply by shutting the door in the face of the rent-collector alone. Within a few short months from the inauguration of the "No-Rent" policy landlordry found itself upon the verge of dissolution. It was at its wits' end. Confronted by this intangible power, it knew not what to do. It wanted nothing so much as to madden the stubborn peasantry into becoming an actively belligerent mob which could be mowed down with Gatling guns. But, barring a paltry outbreak here and there, it was impossible to goad the farmers out of their quiescence, and the grip of the landlords grew weaker every day.

"Ah! but the movement failed," I can hear the *People* reply. Yes, it did fail; and why? Because the peasants were acting, not intelligently in obedience to their wisdom, but blindly in obedience to leaders who betrayed them at the critical moment. Thrown into jail by the government, these leaders, to secure their release, withdrew the "No-Rent Manifesto," which they had issued in the first place not with any intention of freeing the peasants from the burden of an "immoral tax," but simply to make them the tools of their political advancement. Had the people realized the power they were exercising and understood the economic situation, they would not have resumed the payment of rent at Parnell's bidding, and to-day they might have been free. The Anarchists do not propose to repeat their mistake. That is why they are devoting themselves entirely to the inculcation of principles, especially of economic principles. In steadfastly pursuing this course regardless of clamor, they alone are laying a sure foundation for the success of the revolution, though to the *People* of San Francisco, and to all people who are in such a devil of a hurry that they can't stop to think, they seem to be doing nothing at all.

THEORETICAL METHODS.

[*Liberty*, July 16, 1887.]

FROM the raw recruit in the Salvation Army up to the Theoretical Anarchist, none are lacking in "methods" whereby man may be saved. The
religious recruit who, perhaps, has just heard of Jesus is filled with sublime faith. In his exuberant optimism earth and heaven seem about to
unite, peace is to reign everywhere, and happiness fill every soul. But
one thing is lacking,—faith. So he sets out, like Bunyan's Christian,
steafast in purpose to convince the world that the *vade mecum* of temporal
and eternal success is but this one thing : Think as I do, and you will be
saved ! But, alas ! men have listened to the old song for centuries, and
heaven has not descended nor earth ascended to supernal bliss. Here, as
elsewhere, difference of views is a constant factor. What Proudhon calls
"the force of events" has led to wider and wider differentiation of character, and consequently of methods. We will leave the religionist to his theoretical method, and sadly smile as we pass by.

The statesman—from the public minister to the itinerant demagogue—
also has a method, a "Morrison's Pill" for all social ills. Having outgrown the delusion of the Fifth Monarchy men, who sought to intersect
the parallel lines of religion and politics, keeping one eye on earth and
the other wildly staring at the hollow vault that but re-echoed back their
loud appeals, the statesman sees but one method,—the ballot ! Eureka !
let workmen adopt political methods for economic ills, put We, Us & Co.
in office, and the problem is solved ! But again the constant factor appears ; in spite of harangues, preaching, and able editors, men will not
think alike. Here and there are those who assert that this mingling of
political and economic methods is but a repetition of the former folly.

The Prohibitionists see the world redeemed when all men abjure rum
or are unable to obtain it. If they perversely refuse to be virtuous, it is
proposed to inject virtue into them. The Socialists of the "orthodox"
stripe have been persistent, in season and out of season, in demonstrating
to the world that, when their "propaganda" has brought all men to one
way of thinking, incompetency will be able to select competency, or capacity, to run the social machine. The Co-operator also turns his little
"crank," and, in haste to realize results, gathers himself together and
starts a society in the South or West, where he proposes to socialize
"Millerism" within the State. But, again, to all these schemes the constant factor remains that the Apostle is only an apostle to the few.

And last, though not least, appears the Theoretical Anarchist, who,
while abjuring "systems," still as vociferously asserts the validity of his
unpatented "method," whereby the Millennium is to be inaugurated.
True, it has failed hitherto,—in Ireland, for instance ; but there the
"method," not "system," when it came to the test, found that existing
political methods had far greater attractions. Strange ! but "'twas ever
thus," and so it will be again while the State remains. Let us listen and
see if we do not catch the old, time-worn cadence, so long familiar to our
ears :

"Had the people realized the power they were exercising, and understood the economic situation, they would not have resumed the payment
of rent at Parnell's bidding, and to-day they might have been free."

Salvation Army hymn again ! "The force of events" within the State
will ever lead the attraction of State methods to predominate. The State
must go ! How ? I neither know nor care ; I have no patented or unpatented "method " to foist upon a long-suffering community. Let the
inevitable come as it will ; I can protest then as now. If the "brutal
Communists" of Chicago, as *Liberty* called them, had been more theoretical in their methods, they would not now be lying under the shadow
of the gallows for " conspiracy " to resist invasion of individual rights.

In fact, to realize "the method of Anarchy," I am forcibly reminded
of an incident which occurred when I risked my life to spread cheap labor
over the South. A young lieutenant was sent out with a platoon to
make a reconnaissance, and on his march came to a river which was not
fordable. Drilled in army methods, he followed his instructions to make
a requisition on the quartermaster if he needed anything. "Realizing
the power he was exercising and understanding the military situation,"
he sent in a requisition for a platoon of men eighteen feet high ! If he
had waited till the water had run by, he might have crossed easily, but
then, as now, nature and men remained constant factors.

Sadly,   DYER D. LUM.

It is no wonder that Mr. Lum feels sad. I should feel not
only sad, but ashamed, if the responsibility of the above article
rested on my shoulders. It is such a bundle of absurdities,
such a labyrinth of analogies that cross each other at every
turn, such an unmethodical mass of errors, that it is impossible
to pursue any method in answering it. There is so little
about it that is structural or organic that it must be dealt with
more or less at random. Perhaps I shall strike in a not altogether wrong direction if I point out to Mr. Lum that the
State which he is trying to abolish is not the State as institution, but simply the existing State. He is like the slave who
is so utterly destitute of an idea, so thoroughly incapable of a
generalization, in short, so entirely and exclusively practical,
that he cannot appreciate the remoter fact that his oppression
rests upon an almost universal belief in mastership, but can
see no further than the concrete master whose lash he feels.
If one of his fellows were to reason from the latter back to the
former and seek some method of striking at the foundation of
the tyranny, this slave would sneer at him, as Mr. Lum sneers
at the " Theoretical Anarchist " ; but to one of his fellows who
should snatch the lash from the master's hand and beat him
to death, though with no other thought than of straightway
kneeling to another master, this slave would lift his hat, as
Mr. Lum "lifted his hat to the thrower of the Chicago bomb."
I care as little as Mr. Lum how the State goes, but I insist
that it shall really go,—that it shall be abolished, not reformed.
That it cannot be abolished until there shall exist some considerable measure and solid weight of absolute and well-
grounded disbelief in it as an institution is a truth too nearly

axiomatic for demonstration. In the absence of such disbelief the existing State might be destroyed by the blindly rebellious or might fall through its own rottenness, but another
would at once arise in its stead. Why should it not, how
could it be otherwise, when all believe in the necessity of the
State ? Now, it is to create this measure and weight of disbelief that the "Theoretical Anarchist" is working. He is not
trying, like the religionist, to convert the whole world to his
way of thinking by a never-ending series of individual conver-
sions, or, like the politician, Prohibitionist, and Socialist, to
get a majority upon his side, or yet, like the Co-operator (whom
I am surprised to see cited as "theoretical"), to retire from
the busy world to build a play-house in the wilderness ; he is
simply addressing himself to such persons as are amenable to
reason to the end that these may unite and here and now enter
upon the work of laying the foundations of Liberty, knowing
that, these foundations once laid, the structure must rise upon
them, the work of all men's hands, as a matter of economic
necessity. This is a work that must be done sooner or later,
and the sooner the better. If, as Mr. Lum conceives, the
destruction of the existing State by force is inevitable, no fact
more than this should incite the "Theoretical Anarchist" to
immediately concentrate all his energies upon the work which
he has laid out. If ruin is to confront us so soon and surely,
all the greater need of seeing to it that Liberty, and not Authority, shall be the architect of the succeeding social structure. If Mr. Lum and his friends, the Communists of Chicago
(whose characterization as "brutal" Mr. Lum in the past,
when less anxious to score a point against me, has carefully
and correctly attributed to "X" instead of to *Liberty*), had
devoted one half the energy to this "theoretical" work that
they have expended in preaching the gospel of dynamite and
proclaiming "the logic of events," not only would none of
them "now be lying under the shadow of the gallows" (the
desirability of which position I do not perceive as clearly as
Mr. Lum), but very likely there would now be enough "Theoretical Anarchists" to begin some work similar to that which
C. T. Fowler is outlining in his luminous *Sun.* If Mr. Lum
can demonstrate the impossibility of creating such a force as
this, he will not only knock the bottom out of "Theoretical Anarchism," but he will reduce every species of Socialism to a
utopian dream. But until he can, it will be futile for him to
fight "Theoretical Anarchism" with analogies based on such
impossibilities as the recruiting of men eighteen feet high.
The two methods must be proved equally impossible before

the analogy will hold. I have not touched all the weak points, but perhaps I have said enough. At any rate, as Proudhon has been referred to, I cannot close more aptly than with these words from his "What is Property?" "There is one truth of which I am profoundly convinced,—nations live by absolute ideas, not by approximate and partial conceptions; therefore, men are needed who define principles, or at least test them in the fire of controversy. Such is the law,—the idea first, the pure idea, the understanding of the laws of God, the theory: practice follows with slow steps, cautious, attentive to the succession of events; sure to seize, towards this eternal meridian, the indications of supreme reason. The co-operation of theory and practice produces in humanity the realization of order,—the absolute truth. All of us, as long as we live, are called, each in proportion to his strength, to this sublime work. The only duty which it imposes upon us is to refrain from appropriating the truth to ourselves, either by concealing it, *or by accommodating it to the temper of the century*, or by using it for our own interests."

A SEED PLANTED.

[*Liberty*, May 26, 1888.]

Time: Thursday, May 17, 7.30 P.M.

Place: Residence of the editor of *Liberty*, 10 Garfield Ave., Crescent Beach, Revere (a town in the suburbs of Boston).

Dramatis Personæ: Charles F. Fenno, so-called tax-collector of Revere, and the editor of *Liberty*.

In answer to a knock the editor of *Liberty* opens his front door, and is accosted by a man whom he never met before, but who proves to be Fenno.

Fenno.—" Does Mr. Tucker live here?"

Editor of Liberty.—" That's my name, sir."

F.—" I came about a poll-tax."

E. of L.—" Well?"

F.—" Well, I came to collect it."

E. of L.—" Do I owe you anything?"

F.—" Why, yes."

E. of L.—" Did I ever agree to pay you anything?"

F.—" Well, no; but you were living here on the first of May last year, and the town taxed you one dollar."

E. of L.—" Oh! it isn't a matter of agreement, then?"

F.—" No, it's a matter of compulsion."

E. of L.—" But isn't that rather a mild word for it? I call it robbery."

F.—" Oh, well, you know the law; it says that all persons twenty years of age and upwards who are living in a town on the first day of May—"

E. of L.—" Yes, I know what the law says, but the law is the greatest of all robbers."

F.—" That may be. Anyhow, I want the money."

E. of L. (taking a dollar from his pocket and handing it to Fenno)—" Very well. I know you are stronger than I am, because you have a lot of other robbers at your back, and that you will be able to take this dollar from me if I refuse to hand it to you. If I did not know that you are stronger than I am, I should throw you down the steps. But because I know that you are stronger, I hand you the dollar just as I would hand it to any other highwayman. You have no more right to take it, however, than to enter the house and take everything else you can lay your hands on, and I don't see why you don't do so."

F.—" Have you your tax-bill with you?"

E. of L.—" I never take a receipt for money that is stolen from me."

F.—" Oh, that's it?"

E. of L.—" Yes, that's it."

And the door closed in Fenno's face.

He seemed a harmless and inoffensive individual, entirely ignorant of the outrageous nature of his conduct, and he is wondering yet, I presume, if not consulting with his fellow-citizens, upon what manner of crank it is that lives at No. 10 Garfield Ave., and whether it would not be the part of wisdom to lodge him straightway in a lunatic asylum.

THE "HOME GUARD" HEARD FROM.

[*Liberty*, June 23, 1888.]

THE last issue of the *Workmen's Advocate* contains the following communication:

To the Workmen's Advocate:

Oh! what a feeling of rapture came over me as I began reading the dialogue between Tucker and Fenno in the last number of *Liberty*. (Ego

Tucker needs no introduction; Fenno is the fiend who came to collect the poll-tax.) My thoughts went back to another age and to distant clime. I thought of John Hampden refusing to pay the ship-tax. I had often asked myself, who will be the leader in this, the struggle of the fourth estate? Where is the man who will dare resist oppression? I thought I was answered. *Here!* here was the man who would risk all for *Liberty! And although she slew him, still would he trust in her!*

But softly; as I read further, he takes the big iron dollar from his pocket and gives it to the minion.

Oh, ignominy! Instead of *refusing* to pay, he indulges in a little billingsgate,—a favorite pastime with him. He pays, and all is over. Our idol is but clay, and we must seek another leader. Is this what Ego Anarchists call "passive resistance"? If it is, it *is* certainly passive.

H. J. FRENCH.

DENVER, June 5.

When I published the poll-tax interview, I foresaw that it would call out some such rubbish as the above from my Socialistic critics. The fact that timely retreat often saves from defeat seldom saves the retreating soldier from the abuse of the "home guard." The "stay-at-homes" are great worshippers of glory, but are always willing to let others win it. To the man of peace the man who runs is never a hero, although the true soldier may know him for the bravest of the brave. After reading such a criticism as Mr. French's, well may one exclaim with Wilfrid Scawen Blunt: "What men call courage is the least noble thing of which they boast." To my mind there is no such depth of poltroonery as that of the man who does not dare to run. For he has not the real courage to obey his own judgment against that "spook," public opinion, above which his mind is not sufficiently emancipated to rise in scorn. Placed in a situation where, from the choice of one or the other horn of a dilemma, it must follow either that fools will think a man a coward or that wise men will think him a fool, I can conceive of no possible ground for hesitancy in the selection. I know my circumstances better than Mr. French can know them, and I do not permit him to be my judge. When I want glory, I know how to get it. But I am not working for glory. Like the base-ball player who sacrifices his individual record to the success of his club, I am "playing for my team",—that is, I am working for my cause. And I know that, on the whole, it was better for my cause that I should pay my tax this year than that I should refuse to pay it. Is this passive resistance? asks Mr. French. No; it is simply a protest for the purpose of propagandism. Passive resistants, no less than active resistants, have the right to choose when to resist.

Far be it from me to depreciate the services of the Hampdens and the martyrs reverenced by mankind. There are times when the course that such men follow is the best policy, and then their conduct is of the noblest. But there are times also when it is sheer lunacy, and then their conduct is not for sane men to admire. Did Mr. French ever hear of the Charge of the Light Brigade at Balaklava? And does he remember the comment of a military man who witnessed that memorable, that splendid, that insane exploit, fruitful in nothing save the slaughter of half a thousand men : "It is magnificent, but it is not war." The editor of *Liberty* is engaged in war.

COLONIZATION.

[*Liberty*, July 26, 1884.]

An excellently written article by E. C. Walker sets forth considerations in favor of isolated communities for reformatory purposes which are forcible and weighty, especially that of preventing, by the avoidance of social ostracism, the constant and serious drain upon the radical forces. Nevertheless, Réclus is right, all things considered. It is just because Mr. Walker's earnest desire for a fair practical test of Anarchistic principles cannot be fulfilled elsewhere than in the very heart of existing industrial and social life that all these community attempts are unwise. Reform communities will either be recruited from the salt of the earth, and then their success will not be taken as conclusive, because it will be said that their principles are applicable only among men and women wellnigh perfect ; or, with these elect, will be a large admixture of semi-lunatics among whom, when separated from the great mass of mankind and concentrated by themselves, society will be unendurable, practical work impossible, and Anarchy as chaotic as it is generally supposed to be. But in some large city fairly representative of the varied interests and characteristics of our heterogeneous civilization let a sufficiently large number of earnest and intelligent Anarchists, engaged in nearly all the different trades and professions, combine to carry on their production and distribution on the cost principle and to start a bank through which they can obtain a non-interest-bearing currency for the conduct of their commerce and dispose their steadily accumulating capital in new enterprises, the advantages of this system of affairs being open to all who should choose to offer their patronage,—what would be the

result ?   Why, soon the whole composite population, wise and
unwise, good, bad, and indifferent, would become interested
in what was going on under their very eyes, more and more of
them would actually take part in it, and in a few years, each
man reaping the fruit of his labor and no man able to live in
idleness on an income from capital, the whole city would become a great hive of Anarchistic workers, prosperous and free
individuals.   It is such results as this that I look forward to.
and it is for the accomplishment of such that I work.   Social
landscape gardening can come later if it will.   It has no interest for me now.   I care nothing for any reform that cannot
be effected right here in Boston among the every-day people
whom I meet upon the streets.

LABOR'S NEW FETICH.

[*Liberty*, August 23, 1884.]

GENERAL BUTLER'S long-expected letter [in acceptance of
the nomination for the presidency given him by the labor
party] is out at last.   The question now is how many it will
hoodwink.   Among these at least will not be *Liberty*.   Would
that as much could be asserted of all who think they believe
in *Liberty*.   But the political habit is a clinging one ; the fasci-
nations of political warfare seldom altogether lose their charm
over those who have once been under its influence ; traces of
faith in its efficacy still linger in the minds of those who suppose themselves emancipated ; the old majority superstition
yet taints the reformer's blood, and, in face of the evils that
threaten society's life, he appeals to its saving grace with the
same curious mixture of doubt and confidence that sometimes
leads a wavering and timorous Infidel, when brought face to
face with the fancied terrors of death, to re-embrace the theological superstition from which his good sense has once re-
volted and to declare his belief on the Lord Jesus, lest, as one
of them is said to have profanely put it, "there may be, after
all, a God, or a Christ, or a Hell, or some damned thing or
other."   To such as these, then, Butler will look for some of
his strength, and not be disappointed.
   The audacity of this demagogue's utterances, the fearlessness
with which he exposes such shams and frauds and tyrannies as
he does not himself champion, the fury of his onslaught on
those hypocrites in high places to dislodge whom for his own

benefit and glory he himself hypocritically espouses the cause of the people, all tend to fire such radical hearts as have no radical heads to guide them, and accordingly we see on every hand reformers of every stripe, through their press and on their platforms, enlisting in the service of this incarnation of reaction, this personification of absolutism, this total stranger to the principle of Liberty, this unscrupulous plunderer of labor, this servant of the fearful trinity of the people's enemies, being at once an insincere devotee of the Church, a steadfast lover of a mammoth and omnipotent State, and a bloated beneficiary of the exactions of Capital.

The platform announced in his letter is a ridiculous tissue of contradictions and absurdities. Anti-monopoly only in name, it sanctions innumerable monopolies and privileges, and avowedly favors class legislation. As far as it is not nondescript, it is the beginning of State Socialism,—that is, a long step towards the realization of the most gigantic and appalling monopoly ever conceived by the mind of man. One sentence in it, however, commands my approbation : " The laboring man votes for his Fetich, the Democratic party, and the farmer votes for his Fetich, the Republican party, and the result is that both are handed over as captives to the corruptionists and monopolists, whichever side wins. *Mark this : the laborers and the people never win !*" True, every word of it ! But why not go a little farther ? Suppose both laborer and farmer vote for their new Fetich, Ben Butler and his party of State Socialism, what will be the result then ? Will not both be handed over as captives to a band of corruptionists as much larger and greedier as the reach and resources of the government are made vaster, all in the service and pay, not of a number of distinct and relatively weak monopolies, but of one consolidated monopoly whose rapacity will know no bounds ? No doubt about it whatever. Let those who will, then, bow before this idol,— no Anarchistic knee shall bend. We Anarchists have not come for that. We come to shatter Fetiches, not to kneel before them,—no more before Fetich Butler than Fetich Blaine or Fetich Cleveland or Fetich St. John. We are here to let in the light of Liberty upon political superstition, and from that policy can result no captivity to corruption, no subserviency to monopoly, only *a world of free laborers controlling the products of their labor and growing richer every day.*

If *Liberty* has a weak-kneed friend who is contemplating a violation of his Anarchistic principles by voting *just for once,* may these golden words from John Morley's work on " Compromise " recall him to his better self :

A principle, if it be sound, represents one of the larger expediencies. To abandon that for the sake of some seeming expediency of the hour is to sacrifice the greater good for the less on no more creditable ground than that the less is nearer. It is better to wait, and to defer the realization of our ideas until we can realize them fully, than to defraud the future by truncating them, if truncate them we must, in order to secure a partial triumph for them in the immediate present. It is better to bear the burden of impracticableness than to stifle conviction and to pare away principle until it becomes mere hollowness and triviality. What is the sense and what is the morality of postponing the wider utility to the narrower? Nothing is so sure to impoverish an epoch, to deprive conduct of nobleness and character of elevation.

MR. PENTECOST'S BELIEF IN THE BALLOT.

[*Liberty*, January 19, 1889.]

I GREATLY admire Hugh O. Pentecost. He is a growing and a fair-minded man. His *Twentieth Century*, now published weekly in an enlarged form, is doing a useful work. He already accepts Anarchy as an ultimate, and the whole tenor of his writings is leading him on, it seems to me, to a casting-off of his devotion to the single-tax movement and to reforms still more distinctly State Socialistic, and to a direct advocacy of Anarchistic principles and methods. It is because I believe this that I feel like reasoning with him regarding a vital inconsistency in his discourse of January 13 on "Ballots or Bullets?" in which, moreover, the tendency referred to is marked.

After laying it down as a principle that force is never justifiable (and, by the way, I cannot accept so absolute a denial of force as this, though I heartily agree that force is futile in *almost all* circumstances), he goes on as follows : "If it is not justifiable for the establishment and maintenance of government, neither is it justifiable for the overthrow or modification of government. . . . The intellectual and moral process of regeneration is slower than force, but it is right ; and when the work is thus done, it has the merit of having been done properly and thoroughly." So far, excellent. But mark the next sentence : "The ballot is the people's agency even for correcting its own evils, and it seems to me a social crime to refrain from its use for regenerative purposes until it is absolutely demonstrated that it is a failure as an instrument for freedom."

Now, what is the ballot ? It is neither more nor less than a paper representative of the bayonet, the billy, and the bullet. It is a labor-saving device for ascertaining on which side force lies and bowing to the inevitable. The voice of the majority saves bloodshed, but it is no less the arbitrament of force than is the decree of the most absolute of despots backed by the most powerful of armies. Of course it may be claimed that the struggle to attain to the majority involves an incidental use of intellectual and moral processes ; but these influences would exert themselves still more powerfully in other channels if there were no such thing as the ballot, and, when used as subsidiary to the ballot, they represent only a striving for the time when physical force can be substituted for them. Reason devoted to politics fights for its own dethronement. The moment the minority becomes the majority, it ceases to reason and persuade, and begins to command and enforce and punish. If this be true,—and I think that Mr. Pentecost will have difficulty in gainsaying it,—it follows that to use the ballot for the modification of government is to use force for the modification of government ; which sequence makes it at once evident that Mr. Pentecost in his conclusion pronounces it a social crime to avoid that course which in his premise he declares unjustifiable.

It behooves Mr. Pentecost to examine this charge of inconsistency carefully, for his answer to it must deeply affect his career. If he finds that it is well-founded, the sincerity of his nature will oblige him to abandon all such political measures as the taxation of land values and the government ownership of banks and railroads and devote himself to Anarchism, which offers not only the goal that he seeks, but confines itself to those purely educational methods of reaching it with which he finds himself in sympathy

---

A PRINCIPLE OF SOCIAL THERAPEUTICS.

[*Liberty*, January 22, 1887.]

THE idea that Anarchy can be inaugurated by force is as fallacious as the idea that it can be sustained by force. Force cannot preserve Anarchy ; neither can it bring it. In fact, one of the inevitable influences of the use of force is to postpone Anarchy. The only thing that force can ever do for us is to save us from extinction, to give us a longer lease of life in which to try to secure Anarchy by the only methods that can

ever bring it.   But this advantage is always purchased at immense cost, and its attainment is always attended by frightful
risk.   The attempt should be made only when the risk of any
other course is greater.   When a physician sees that his patient's strength is being exhausted so rapidly by the intensity
of his agony that he will die of exhaustion before the medical
processes inaugurated have a chance to do their curative work,
he administers an opiate.   But a good physician is always loth
to do so, knowing that one of the influences of the opiate is to
interfere with and defeat the medical processes themselves.
He never does it except as a choice of evils.   It is the same
with the use of force, whether of the mob or of the State,
upon diseased society ; and not only those who prescribe its
indiscriminate use as a sovereign remedy and a permanent
tonic, but all who ever propose it as a cure, and even all who
would lightly and unnecessarily resort to it, not as a cure, but
as an expedient, *are social quacks.*

THE MORALITY OF TERRORISM.

[*Liberty*, May 7, 1887.]

E. BELFORT BAX has an article on "Legality" in the London *Commonweal,* which for the most part is by no means
bad.   He denies the obligation to respect legality as such, and
in the light of this denial discusses the policy of terrorism and
assassination.   Respecting this policy, he declares, as *Liberty*
has frequently declared before him, that it should be used
against the oppressors of mankind only when they have succeeded in hopelessly repressing all peaceful methods of agitation.   If he had stopped there, all would have been well.
But not satisfied with characterizing the policy as inexpedient
save under the conditions referred to, he must needs go further and brand it as immoral.   Then he becomes ridiculously
weak.   He is led to the conclusion that in Russia terrorism
is both morally justifiable and expedient ; that in Germany,
though morally justifiable, it is for various reasons inexpedient;
and that in England it is neither morally justifiable nor expedient.   *Liberty* agrees that terrorism is expedient in Russia
and inexpedient in Germany and England, but it will be many
years older than now before it assumes to set any limit on the
right of an invaded individual to choose his own methods of
defence.

The invader, whether an individual or a government, forfeits all claim to consideration from the invaded. This truth is independent of the character of the invasion. It makes no difference in what direction the individual finds his freedom arbitrarily limited; he has a right to vindicate it in any case, and he will be justified in vindicating it by whatever means are available. The right to take unoccupied land and cultivate it is as unquestionable as the right to speak one's thoughts, and resistance offered to any violation of the former is no less self-defence than resistance offered to the violation of the latter. In point of morality one is as good as the other. But with freedom of speech it is possible to obtain freedom of the land and all the other freedoms, while without it there is no hope save in terrorism. Hence the expediency—yes, the necessity—of terrorism to obtain the one; hence the uselessness and folly of employing it to obtain the other. So, when Mr. Bax says that the Russian who shall kill the Czar will act wisely, but that the Englishman who should kill Salisbury would act foolishly, he wins *Liberty's* approval; but when he makes this Russian a saint and this Englishman a knave, this approval must be accompanied by protest.

THE BEAST OF COMMUNISM.

[*Liberty*, March 27, 1886.]

HENRI ROCHEFORT is reported to have said to an interviewer the other day: "Anarchists are merely criminals. They are robbers. They want no government whatever, so that, when they meet you on the street, they can knock you down and rob you." This infamous and libellous charge is a very sweeping one; I only wish that I could honestly meet it with as sweeping a denial. And I can, if I restrict the word Anarchist as it always has been restricted in these columns, and as it ought to be restricted everywhere and always. Confining the word Anarchist so as to include none but those who deny all external authority over the individual, whether that of the present State or that of some industrial collectivity or commune which the future may produce, I can look Henri Rochefort in the face and say: "You lie!" For of all these men I do not recall even one who, in any ordinary sense of the term, can be justly styled a robber.

But unfortunately, in the minds of the people at large, this

word Anarchist is not yet thus restricted in meaning. This is
due principally to the fact that within a few years the word
has been usurped, in the face of all logic and consistency, by
a party of Communists who believe in a tyranny worse than
any that now exists, who deny to the laborer the individual
possession of his product, and who preach to their followers
the following doctrine: "Private property is your enemy; it is
the beast that is devouring you; all wealth belongs to everybody; take it wherever you can find it; have no scruples about
the means of taking it; use dynamite, the dagger, or the torch
to take it; kill innocent people to take it; but, at all events,
take it." This is the doctrine which they call Anarchy, and
this policy they dignify with the name of "propagandism by
deed."

Well, it has borne fruit with most horrible fecundity. To
be sure, it has gained a large mass of adherents, especially in
the Western cities, who are well-meaning men and women,
not yet become base enough to practise the theories which
they profess to have adopted. But it has also developed, and
among its immediate and foremost supporters, a gang of criminals whose deeds for the past two years rival in "pure cussed-
ness" any to be found in the history of crime. Were it not,
therefore, that I have first, last, and always repudiated these
pseudo-Anarchists and their theories, I should hang my head
in shame before Rochefort's charge at having to confess that
too many of them are not only robbers, but incendiaries and
murderers. But, knowing as I do that no *real* Anarchist has
any part or lot in these infamies, I do not confess the facts
with shame, but reiterate them with righteous wrath and indignation, in the interest of my cause, for the protection of its
friends, and to save the lives and possessions of any more
weak and innocent persons from being wantonly destroyed
or stolen by cold-blooded villains parading in the mask of
reform.

Yes, the time has come to speak. It is even well-nigh too
late. Within the past fortnight a young mother and her baby
boy have been burned to death under circumstances which
suggest to me the possibility that, had I made this statement
sooner, their lives would have been saved; and, as I now write
these lines, I fairly shudder at the thought that they may not
reach the public and the interested parties before some new
holocaust has added to the number of those who have already
fallen victims. Others who know the facts, well-meaning
editors of leading journals of so-called Communistic Anarchism, may, from a sense of mistaken party fealty, bear longer

the fearful responsibility of silence, if they will; for one I will not, cannot. I will take the other responsibility of exposure, which responsibility I personally and entirely assume, although the step is taken after conference upon its wisdom with some of the most trusted and active Anarchists in America.

Now, then, the facts. And they *are* facts, though I state them generally, without names, dates, or details.

The main fact is this : that for nearly two years a large num-'ier of the most active members of the German Group of the international Working People's Association in New York City, and of the Social Revolutionary Club, another German organization in that city, have been persistently engaged in getting money by insuring their property for amounts far in excess of the real value thereof, secretly removing everything that they could, setting fire to the premises, swearing to heavy losses, and exacting corresponding sums from the insurance companies. Explosion of kerosene lamps is usually the device which they employ. Some seven or eight fires, at least, of this sort were set in New York and Brooklyn in 1884 by members of the gang, netting the beneficiaries an aggregate profit of thousands of dollars. In 1885 nearly twenty more were set, with equally profitable results. The record for 1886 has reached six already, if not more. The business has been carried on with the most astonishing audacity. One of these men had his premises insured, fired them, and presented his bill of loss to the company within twenty-four hours after getting his policy, and before the agent had reported the policy to the company. The bill was paid, and a few months later the same fellow, under another name, played the game over again, though not quite so speedily. In one of the fires set in 1885 a woman and two children were burned to death. The two guilty parties in this case were members of the Bohemian Group and are now serving life sentences in prison. Another of the fires was started in a six-story tenement house, endangering the lives of hundreds, but fortunately injuring no one but the incendiary. In one case in 1886 the firemen have saved two women whom they found clinging to their bed-posts in a half-suffocated condition. In another a man, woman, and baby lost their lives. Three members of the gang are now in jail awaiting trial for murdering and robbing an old woman in Jersey City. Two others are in jail under heavy bail and awaiting trial for carrying concealed weapons and assaulting an officer. They were walking arsenals, and were found under circumstances which lead to the suspicion that they were about to perpetrate a robbery, if not a murder.

The profits accruing from this "propagandism by deed" are not even used for the benefit of the movement to which the criminals belong, but go to fill their own empty pockets, and are often spent in reckless, riotous living. The guilty parties are growing bolder and bolder, and, anticipating detection ultimately, a dozen or so of thém have agreed to commit perjury in order to involve the innocent as accomplices in their crimes. It is their boast that the active Anarchists shall all go to the gallows together.

It is only fair to John Most, editor of the *Freiheit*, to say that he had nothing to do with originating the plots of these criminals, and for a long time was unaware of what was going on ; but it is none the less true that, after he was made aware of these acts, he not only refused to repudiate them, but persisted in retaining as his right-hand men some of the worst of the gang. The facts have been coming to light one by one for some time, and the knowledge of them has been a torture to all decent men who have had any connection with the Communists. Justus Schwab, who is an exceptionally honest man, sickened long ago. He abandoned the business management of the *Freiheit*, summarily ejected all the criminals from his saloon with a warning not to visit it again, and served notice on his friend Most that he (Most) must entirely sever his connection with the villains or he (Schwab) would sever his connection with him. Thus called upon to choose, Most elected to lose Schwab and keep the criminals as his lieutenants. Perhaps he was too dependent on them to do otherwise. Now Schwab is posted in the *Freiheit* as a man with whom no Socialist should have anything to do. An erroneous conception of party duty has kept Schwab quiet so far as the public are concerned. I trust he will realize ere long that he cannot truly serve his party in any such way. It is high time that he threw off this yoke of party loyalty and spoke out like a man.

One of the most astonishing features of this abominable business has been the blindness of the police, the press, and the insurance companies. Although in a number of cases the criminals have been detected and arrested, the fact that these men all belong to one or two organizations and are acting in accordance with a course agreed upon has not dawned upon the mind of any detective or reporter, although it is an open secret among the German-speaking Socialists of New York. So far as the authorities or the newspapers have hitherto suspected, each of these offences is simply an isolated case of crime. How vigilantly our lives and possessions are protected by this

government of ours! One would think that the interests of
the insurance companies would prompt them at least to greater
vigilance. But they have been as blind as the rest, and
paid this extraordinary series of losses seemingly without a
question.

The attempt will doubtless be made in some quarters to vindicate these horrors as so many revolutionary acts. It will fail.
Private greed and popular vengeance have nothing in common. Even so rigid a Communistic journal as *Le Révolté*
pointed out some time ago that the Revolution can have no
solidarity with thieves. It was one thing to kill the Czar of
Russia, it is quite another to kill and rob an innocent old
woman; it was one thing for the striking miners of Decaze-
ville to take the life of the superintendent who had entered
into a conspiracy with the corporation to reduce the miners'
wages in consideration of a percentage, it is a far different
thing for lazy, selfish, cowardly brutes to set fire to a tenement
house containing hundreds of human beings. There are certain things which circumstances justify; there are certain
others which all lofty human instincts condemn. To the latter class belong these deeds of John Most's followers.

John Most has had a great deal to say about the "beast of
property." Property as it now exists, backed by legal privilege,
is unquestionably a horrible monster, causing untold and universal suffering; but I doubt if it can equal in essential cruelty
the act of a father who will insure the lives of his wife and
boy and conspire to cause their death that he may fill his
pockets with a few paltry dollars. Of such acts as that the
Beast of Communism seems to have a monopoly.

In conclusion, I appeal to every honorable newspaper in
America to lay these facts before its readers, placing the blame
where it belongs and distinguishing the innocent from the
guilty. And especially do I address the Anarchistic press.
Every Anarchistic journal ought to copy this exposure and
send it forth with the stamp of its approval. The cause is entering upon a serious crisis. The malicious and the ignorant
will do their utmost to damage it. Much will depend upon
the promptness with which good men and true separate themselves from common criminals. *He who is not against their
crimes is for them.*

TIME WILL TELL.

[*Liberty*, April 17, 1886.]

To the fearful charges of crime made in the last issue of *Liberty* against the " Communistic Anarchists " of New York and vicinity, John Most makes answer in *Freiheit*. After exhausting his choice vocabulary of epithets upon myself and parties whom he supposes to be behind me, he says that the press have ignored the charges as foolish ; that I could not know that such deeds have been done, because I live in Boston; that the two Bohemians referred to by me did not belong to the Bohemian group ; that Schwab left the *Freiheit*, not to separate himself from crime, but out of cowardice and fear of the police ; that he (Most) was never informed that such crimes had been perpetrated ; that, if he had been, he would have done nothing about it, because he never meddles with private matters that do not concern the party; and that he has not had criminals for lieutenants. I do not see why he did not add one more to his catalogue of lies by saying either that the crimes alleged by me were never committed, or that they were not committed by members of the organizations which I mentioned. Perhaps he was deterred from this by the memory that he has admitted in the presence of a dozen persons the perpetration of the crimes, and attempted to apologize for or excuse the guilty parties.

I do not propose to bandy words with John Most. It has never been my intention to try these charges, or prove them, in these columns. Sooner or later that will be done elsewhere. But I have nothing to retract. On the contrary, I reiterate all my charges as emphatically as before, and declare that I kept far inside of the horrible truth. Those who know me know that I would not make such charges lightly. I came into possession of certain facts, and I used such of them as I chose in what seemed the wisest way. I have done what I could to save the lives and possessions of unoffending people and to save Anarchy from being smirched by association, even in name, with crime and criminals. The poor fools who choose to attribute my course to jealousy, envy, revenge, or any other petty motive whatsoever, may wag their tongues as they will ; I wait for Time to do justice to the firebugs, to their friend, John Most, and to their enemy, myself. And I shall not wait in vain.

THE FACTS COMING TO LIGHT.

[*Liberty*, May 22, 1886.]

In a recent editorial, speaking of my accusations against the firebugs, I said : " It has never been my intention to try these charges, or prove them, in these columns. Sooner or later that will be done elsewhere." That I was not talking at random has since been shown by the appearance of a remarkable article in the New York *Sun*, of May 3, corroborating the charges in a way that defies all answer. After referring to *Liberty's* exposure and Most's answer thereto, the *Sun* says :

An attempt to verify Most's denial discloses a peculiar condition of things in Anarchistic circles here. There is internal dissension and discord, or rather there was, for a considerable number of the hundred or so members of the International Working People's Association have withdrawn from it. The cause of the secession lies in the facts which led *Liberty* to make its charges of incendiarism and rascality. These facts, which have been gleaned after considerable difficulty, show that the leading members of the International Working People's Association have been remarkably unlucky men. Taken in connection with Most's extraordinary doctrines, the curious fires from which these gentlemen have suffered are interesting. They have all originated in the upsetting, breaking, or exploding of kerosene oil lamps, and have resulted in more or less damage to the property of others than Anarchists, and in the collection of more or less insurance money each time by the persons in whose apartments the fires occurred.

Before taking up these occurrences in detail, it will be interesting to review rapidly various events in the past few years that may tend to throw light upon the German revolutionists of America.

After this historical review, the *Sun* describes the mechanical devices for carrying on " propaganda by deed," according to the instructions laid down by John Most in his pamphlet, " Revolutionary War Science," and proceeds as follows :

It is by no means asserted that Mr. Most has himself put into practical use any of his destructive devices, or even that his friends and followers have done so, but certain it is that the idea of "propaganda by deed " was received by several members of the International Working People's Association with enthusiasm. Earnest and eloquent in seconding and advocating Most's doctrines were Comrades J. C. Panzenbeck and Joseph Kaiser. These two are frequently mentioned in *Freiheit* as having partaken in the public discussions of the association, as well as having made set addresses on revolutionary topics. Among the radical Socialists of the city they are known as having extremely "radical " views upon their relation to society. Others who listened with marked attention to the seductive doctrine were Comrades Fritz C. Schaar, Wilhelm Scharff, Carl Heusler, Otto Nicolai, Hermann Wabnitz, Adolph Kramer, and Comrades Nolle, Weber, Kubitsch, and Beck. Some of these, as Schaär and Kubitsch and Beck, are acknowledged as members in *Freiheit* ; the others are well known as frequenters of the meetings now held in Coburger Hall, Stanton street, but formerly in a hall on Bond street, and in various other places where the association met to hear Most's harangues. Quiet inquiries in various quarters elicited the invariable response that all these men were Most's associates and members of either the International Working People's Association or the Social Revolutionary Club.

On the evening of May 14, 1883, Comrade Joseph Kaiser was so unfortunate as to suffer the ravages of a fire in his tenement at 432 East Fourteenth street. The fourth floor of this building was occupied by Adolph Kramer as a dwelling. Kaiser lived on the third floor, where the fire originated, owing, according to the story told to the firemen, to Mrs. Kaiser's accidentally letting a kerosene lamp fall. The building was damaged to the extent of $250. Mr. Kaiser's furniture naturally suffered some injury,—$25 worth, say the official records of the Fire Department. The insurance company which took the risk on the property, however, thought differently, and settled with the agitator for $278.68. The amount of the policy was $300, and it is a piece of good fortune that Mr. Kaiser had managed to secure the policy on May 7, a week preceding the calamity.

On November 27 John Charles Panzenbeck was then living at 406 East Sixty-third street. He or some resident of the building told the firemen that a picture fell from its place on the wall and knocked over a kerosene oil lamp. At any rate, the fire resulting from this or some other cause damaged the house to the extent of $1,000, but Caroline Yost, the owner, was amply insured. The contents of Panzenbeck's suite on the third floor were injured to the amount of several hundred dollars, he said. Some time in the first part of the month he had luckily taken out a policy for $700, and was paid nearly that amount as indemnity. Other tenants in the house lost from $50 to $100 each.

On the 29th of December, 1884, Wilhelm Scharff applied to one of the greatest companies in the city for a policy upon worldly goods contained in the fourth floor tenement of 400 East Fifty-ninth street. His application was successful, and after the lapse of a few days he found himself the holder of a document securing him against loss by fire to the extent of $500. This was peculiarly fortunate ; for, in the evening of January 5, 1885, six days after his application, a kerosene lamp upset in his apartments and fire broke out. The damage to the building, owned by John D. Hines, was not over $200. The record maker of the Fire Department thought Scharff's furniture was not injured over $200 worth, but the insurance company nevertheless were induced to settle for $456.25. An interesting feature of this case was that, when Scharff presented his bill of losses at the headquarters of the company, the day after the fire, his policy had not been registered. The money, however, was paid over.

Some time in this same year Carl Heusler, Social Democrat, established a small fancy-goods store at 137 Ludlow street. The building is a six-story tenement house, and was occupied in all apartments. On the evening of June 5, Mr. and Mrs. Heusler, after shutting up shop, entertained a few friends in the room back of the store. These people were Joseph Kaiser and his wife Mary, who lived at the time at 65 Walton street, Brooklyn ; Hermann Wabnitz of 61 East Eleventh street, Carl Baum of 98 Avenue B, and Otto Nicolai, the engineer of St. Charles Hotel. Shortly after nine o'clock a kerosene oil lamp exploded, and besides damaging the property caused severe but not dangerous injuries to the little party.

No one else in the building was hurt, though great exitement prevailed, and the fire was soon extinguished. Heusler's goods were insured, and a collection of upward of $300 was made from the company. Most of the unfortunate persons present, however, had to pass two or three weeks in the hospital, some going to Bellevue, others to the New York Hospital. Heusler had but recently stocked up his store, and did not resume business after this unfortunate event.

Long before this the International Working People's Association had suffered several secessions. Certain of the members became suspicious of their comrades, and preferred to withdraw from association with them. The seceders are one and all exceedingly reticent on the subject, and it was difficult to obtain information from them. This much, however, is certain : It was frequently asserted among the habitués of saloons where the advanced Socialists are in the habit of congregating that accidents to kerosene lamps were sometimes arranged with great skill; that the comrades were shrewd and successful in their onslaughts on capitalistic society. It was even asserted that the injuries received by the party in Heusler's back room were due to the premature appearance of the fire fiend, owing to carelessness in handling the materials or ignorance of the teachings of *Kriegswissenschaft*.

But these are not the only fires that have visited the agitators. On February 1, 1885, Adolph Kramer took possession of a tenement at 157 Ellery street, Brooklyn, in the house owned and in part occupied by Frederick Stuft. At ten o'clock in the evening of February 9 a kerosene oil lamp broke in his apartments, and an interesting conflagration was the result. Stuft's house was seriously damaged, over $300 worth, he says, and Kramer's furniture and belongings to an unknown amount. Mr. Kramer was paid $300 by the insurance company. It was not, however, until Kramer had been prosecuted ineffectually on a charge of incendiarism that he collected from the company.

In the autumn of the same year a similar accident happened in the tenement of a house on Clinton avenue, West Hoboken, occupied by Fritz C. Schaär. The house, owned by Mr. William Murphy, was so badly damaged that only the walls remained intact. Mr. Schaär was fortunately insured.

Mr. Murphy, owner, noted the fact that, when he arrived at the scene, the only thing burning was a bed, and that a strong odor of kerosene pervaded the entire building. But the odor may have been caused entirely by the lamp, and the lamp might have been placed accidentally near the bed before it broke.

Another unfortunate Anarchist was Louis Weber, who lived at 84 Avenue A. The lamp exploded in his tenement at 7.53 o'clock in the evening of November 30 last. His furniture was insured for $600.

Not long ago Wilhelm Scharff and Carl Wilmund were arrested for carrying concealed weapons with felonious intent. The circumstances are well known, although Scharff was then travelling under the alias Schliman, and was convicted under that name. He is at the penitentiary on Blackwell's Island, and Wilmund was sent to State prison for three and a half years by Recorder Smyth on Monday last. It may be remembered that a letter was found upon Wilmund in which he addressed himself to Most, offering his services in the cause of propaganda by deed.

The flaxen-haired Justus Schwab was approached. The reticence of this reformer is well known, and in this instance he preserved his character.

"I would rather have nothing further to say," remarked Mr. Schwab to the reporter; "you know how it is yourself?"

"But would you explain upon what grounds you ejected Wilhelm Scharff, alias Schliman, Adolph Kramer, and Joseph Kaiser from your saloon, and forbade their return?"

The muscular German drew himself up to his full height, and exclaimed sharply: "Where did you get those names?"

"From the official records of the Fire Department," replied the reporter.

The answer apparently failed to satisfy Mr. Schwab. However, he said:

"I turned them out because I had good reason to believe that they were immoral men, and that is reason enough for me."

An interesting interview was obtained with a young mechanic who is conversant with these affairs. He suggested a way in which such fires as have occurred might have been set, had the occupants so desired.

"They might take a lamp, filled wit. .il," he said, "and securely plug up the passage on the side of the burner intended for the escape of gases. Then, if the lamp be lighted and a candle placed so that the candle flame touches the oil chamber, gases will be quickly generated that, having no means of escape, will soon break the lamp and cause a fire. If the materials are skilfully placed, the breaking lamp will be sure to tip the candle off the table, so that its agency will not be suspected. This method may be made more sure by saturating strips of cloth with benzine and laying them from a point near the lamp to inflammable material elsewhere in the room. Benzine leaves no trace, and its fire-conducting qualities are so powerful that an experiment of this kind is perfectly sure of success. But if the parties at work are careless in handling the benzine, a conflagration may take place prematurely, and somebody will get hurt."

The article from the *Sun*, although it does not tell one-half the truth or the worst half, is a collation of names, dates, facts, and figures from official records sufficient to convince every fair-minded person that I told the truth about the scoundrels who are practising the precepts of John Most. They were sifted from an immense mass of material by weeks of tireless investigation pursued under great difficulties, and the writer would have been able to make his exposure much more complete had he not been hampered by the officials of the police and fire departments of New York, whose jealousy and pique at being outdone, and at the incidental revelation of their own stupidity, incompetence, and negligence, know no bounds. The work that he succeeded in doing, however, has thoroughly scared the firebugs, and they will probably discontinue their hellish practices. If not, the first attempt to renew them will be met by prompt and vigorous exposure. The charge made by *Freiheit* that Moritz Bachmann wrote the *Sun* article for money is utterly unfounded. It was written by a professional journalist not identified with the Anarchistic movement, and no one but himself received any pay for it or for the facts contained in it. Most's answer to the *Sun* is ridiculous and inadequate in the extreme. He says that he does not know whether the statements are true, and that, whether true or not, he does not know who the men mentioned are. Now, the greater number of these men have been mentioned in *Freiheit* as comrades from ten to fifty times each, and by a singular coincidence, in the very next column to that containing this audacious assertion, Panzenbeck, one of the first of the firebugs, is credited with a certain sum of money among the cash receipts. Most then asks, with characteristic assurance, if it is to be expected that Anarchists' houses will never take fire, and suggests the advisability of preparing a list of such capitalists' houses as have been burned. It will be time enough for Most to talk about this when he can find a society of one hundred capitalists even ten of whom (to say nothing of fifteen or twenty) have been so unfortunate as to lose their property by separate fires within a period of three years, and so prudent as in each case to take out an insurance policy somewhere from a week to a year before the occurrence of the calamity. And even then, would the fact that he could fasten such crimes upon the capitalists excuse the Communists for doing likewise?

LIBERTY AND VIOLENCE.

[*Liberty*, May 22, 1886.]

THE recent bomb-throwing at Chicago opens the whole question of the advisability of armed revolution. The right to resist oppression by violence is beyond doubt; it is only the policy of exercising this right that Anarchists at this juncture have to consider. In *Liberty's* view but one thing can justify its exercise on any large scale,—namely, the denial of free thought, free speech, and a free press. Even then its exercise would be unwise unless suppression were enforced so stringently that all other means of throwing it off had become hopeless. Bloodshed in itself is pure loss. When we must have freedom of agitation, and when nothing but bloodshed will secure it, then bloodshed is wise. But it must be remembered that it can never accomplish the Social Revolution proper; that that can never be accomplished except by means of agitation, investigation, experiment, and passive resistance; and that, after all the bloodshed, we shall be exactly where we were before, except in our possession of the power to use these means.

One thing the Chicago bomb-thrower established emphatically,—the superiority of dynamite to the Winchester rifle. No riot has occurred in this country in which so many policemen were killed and wounded at one time as by this single bomb; at least, so I am informed. As a true terrorist, the bomb-thrower made but one mistake,—in choosing a time when a crowd of working people were gathered upon whom the police could wreak their vengeance. If it becomes necessary to vindicate free speech by force, the work will have to consist of a series of acts of individual dynamiters. The days of armed revolution have gone by. It is too easily put down. On this point I may quote an instructive extract from a private letter written to me by Dr. Joseph H. Swain, of San Francisco, a few days before the Chicago troubles broke out :

For two or three weeks we have had labor orators from Oregon, Washington Territory, Colorado, Kansas, etc. They tell us that we are behind. In the places named labor societies are being organized and armed with Winchester rifles, while, as one of the fire-eaters said, we of San Francisco are not prepared to even lift a toothpick in a contest with capital. They claim there are many men already prepared for the coming conflict, and in Denver many women,—I think seventy,—all of whom are expert rifle*men*. They are urging the Socialists here to do the same. There is a good deal of secrecy. Some time ago it was said that the Knights of Labor Executive Committee ordered the local bodies to cease adding members or to go slow, the reason given being that men were joining before they understood the objects of the order. I think it was because revolutionists were joining. These men say that the Knights in the above States are Socialists. I think the trouble on the Gould line was caused by these revolutionary Knights. Powderly sees they are likely to swamp the order. Powderly is a good fellow, but doesn't understand the labor problem. He thinks the Knights could make money running Gould's railroad. One orator said revolutions started in conservative reform bodies, but soon the radicals took them out of their hands. The Socialists would do the same with this movement of the Knights. He said the Anarchists in Chicago were pretty good fellows. They predict an uprising within a year. I think there is great activity among these advocates of armed resistance. Their statement is that they must be armed to command the respect of the capitalists and to prevent an attack. Like Grant, they will have peace if they have to fight for it,—the peace of Warsaw. Which means, if they are armed, they can seize a railroad, and the owners won't dare to resist. As one speaker from Kansas said last night, the strikers had a right to prevent others from taking their places, for they had acquired a labor title to the road,— *i.e.*, were owners as well as the capitalists. He did not use the term labor title, but that was the idea. Of course, then, they will justify themselves in seizing the railroad, *their* property. If a conflict is precipitated it will be a severe blow to Liberty, and the fellows will find what fools they are, or were. They forget that it is brains, skill, long training, knowledge, and natural fitness that win in a contest of arms ; that the men so qualified are in the service of capital, and that they will lead other workingmen against these undisciplined bodies, so that workingmen will shoot down each other. Fatal error, to think they can intimidate the capitalists, who are mostly men of courage and superior to the masses, and as sincere in their opinions as to their rights to the property they control. Then, the rebels will be in small bodies and unable to concentrate, for the authorities will hold the depots and use trains, if they are run at all, to concentrate troops at given points, which the rebels will be unable to reach. This will afford the capitalists an excuse for a strong government, and progress will be retarded. The net gain will be money in the pockets of manufacturers of guns and other war munitions, and a strong government, with loss incalculable to the workers, who will lose some of the liberty they now have, and have to pay the cost of the war. If I could control the men in all these labor organizations, I could, without even lifting a toothpick other than to write with it, in a perfectly quiet way, bring capital to its knees ; or, if I thought it just and wise, force proprietors to sell their property at cost, or less. A resort to arms is suicidal to the side that initiates it. Moral force once clearly perceived as a social principle will be found to yield inexhaustible working power to defend natural rights. The simplicity of the thing is so apparent when you once strike a true lead that all brute force would cease. What a glorious chance the Irish had to rid themselves of landlords and politicians ! Had the no-rent policy been adhered to one year, the landlords would have been beggared. The price of land would have been discovered to have its only basis in monopoly, seizure, legal title. One such success would have opened the eyes of all civilized men to the weakness of brute force in a contest with moral force, and would have shown the ease with which governments could be rendered powerless. What a fraud and shadow they are, terrible only to childish men ! If there were a God, he would never forgive Parnell and the priests for furling the no-rent banner. If we could get but one such illustration of passive resistance on a large scale, Anarchy would be an accomplished fact.

I can add nothing to these wise words, nor can I make plainer their valuable lesson.

Leaving now our consideration of the actual throwing of the bomb, surrounding which, as I said, there is some doubt, let us glance a moment at what has happened since, regarding which there can be no doubt. The conduct during the last fortnight of the police, the courts, the pulpit, and the press, including many of the labor organs themselves, has been shameful in the extreme. Mammon's priests have foamed at the mouth ; the servants of Plutus who sit in editorial chairs have frothed at the point of the pen ; the stalwart graduates of the slums who are licensed and paid to swing shillalahs over the heads of unoffending citizens have shrieked for vengeance ; and wearers of judicial ermine on which there is room for no new spots have virtually declared their determination to know no bounds of right, mercy, or decency in dealing with any Anarchist who may be brought before them. Spies and Fielden have been arrested and held for murder, though they are not known to have done anything worse than to speak their minds ; nearly every one in Chicago who has dared to avow himself an Anarchist has been clapped into jail, and those who reach that haven without a broken head deem themselves peculiarly fortunate ; houses have been broken into and searched by wholesale ; the *Arbeiter Zeitung* and the *Alarm*, and, for aught I know, the *Budoucnost*, have been suppressed without a shadow of natural or legal right ; to be a German is to be looked upon with suspicion, and to be a Pole or Bohemian is to be afraid to show one's head ; and it has become exceedingly unsafe for the most respectable of men to stand upon the streets of Chicago and question the superiority of existing social and political systems to the Utopia of Sir Thomas More. Talk about the Communists being madmen ! *The authorities and their mouthpieces are the real madmen now.* One would think that the throwing of this bomb was the first act of violence ever committed under the sun. These lunatics seem to forget that they are the representatives and champions of a standing *régime* of violence,—a *régime* which is a perpetual menace levelled at every one who dares to claim his liberty ; a *régime* which ties the hands of laborers while a band of licensed robbers called capitalists pick their pockets. How can they expect aught but violence from their victims ? The fact is, there are two ways of inciting the suffering classes to violence : one is that of the so-called revolutionists, who directly advise them to use force ; the other, and by far the more dangerous, is that of the so-called friends of order who try to leave them no other hope than force. These two parties, though outwardly opposed, really play into each other's hands, to the damage of the real revolutionists and the real friends of order, who know that force settles nothing, and that no question is ever settled until it is settled right. *Just as truly as Liberty is the mother of order, is the State the mother of violence.*

CONVICTED BY A PACKED JURY.

[*Liberty*, September 18, 1886.]

UNJUST as the Chicago verdict was, the trial brought out certain facts regarding Illinois juries by which other communities might profit and at which Lysander Spooner must rejoice. In his great work, now out of print, " Trial by Jury," Mr. Spooner shows how the practice regarding jury trial has been turned by usurpation from the original theory, until it has lost altogether the three features that made it most potent as a safeguard of individual liberty. These three features were : 1, that the jury must be chosen by lot from a wheel containing the names of the whole body of citizens of the vicinity, instead of from a selected panel ; 2, that it must be judge, not only of the facts, but of the law and the justice of the law ; 3, that it must decide, not only the guilt or innocence of the accused, but, in case of guilt, the nature and severity of the penalty.

It appears from the charge of Judge Gary to the jury in the trial at Chicago that Illinois law has restored, nearly, if not quite intact, the second and third of these features. Said the judge :

> If the accused, or any of them, are found guilty by the jury, *they shall fix the punishment* by their verdict.

And further :

> The jury in a criminal case are, by the statutes of Illinois, made judges of the law and the evidence, and under these statutes it is the duty of the jury, after hearing the arguments of the counsel and the instructions of the court, to act upon the law and facts according to their best judgment of such law and such facts. *The jury are the judges of the law and the facts,* and you, as jurors, *have a right to disregard the instructions of the court,* provided you, upon your oaths, can say that you believe you know the law better than the court.

It is evident that in the hands of an unprejudiced jury endowed with such powers as these the life and liberty of a person unjustly accused would be well-nigh secure. The trouble in Chicago was the prejudice of the jury. And this jury was made up wholly of prejudiced men, simply because the first of the three safeguards referred to was not restored along with the second and third. If the twelve men composing it, instead of being sifted from a selected panel by a method of examination that enables the prosecution to practically pack the jury, had been chosen by lot from all the citizens of Chicago, there would have been a large percentage of workingmen among them, some or all of whom would undoubtedly have seen to it that no such fate was meted out to the eight prisoners as that under the awful shadow of which they now rest. But, as it was, the whole twelve men were men whose sympathies and interests ranged them on the side of capital and privilege, and they were determined from the start to hang the men who had questioned the sacred prerogatives of constituted power. It is needless to say that the State will never sound its own death-knell by restoring the safeguard that is still lacking, and that it never will be restored until the people themselves restore it by boycotting the State.

WHY EXPECT JUSTICE FROM THE STATE?

[*Liberty*, September 18, 1886.]

CHARLES T. FOWLER has written and *Lucifer* has published a very able article showing that the prosecution at Chicago was a prosecution of opinion and not of criminality, that the verdict was a verdict against Anarchy and not against bomb-throwing, and that the offence for which the victims are to be punished was not actual, but purely constructive. Setting aside the doubtless manufactured but certainly direct evidence put forward by the prosecution, of the man who swore that he saw Spies light the fuse and hand the bomb to Schnaubelt, and that then Schnaubelt threw it, Mr. Fowler's position is a sound one. Sound also is the position taken by "O," that the convictions were secured by a trick of the detectives. Sound also is my own position, that the convictions would have been impossible without a packed jury.

But, sound as all these positions are, what do they amount to? Something, perhaps, as so many instances of the infernalisms practised by the State; but nothing more. If urged in the hope that the State will ever do better, they are futile in the extreme. Is not the State an infernal institution? Why expect from it, then, anything but infernalisms? "Let the people of Chicago," says Mr. Fowler, "learn that there is no such thing as the crime of incendiary speech. . . . Then they will no longer prosecute Anarchy or persecute Anarchists, but hunt up the man who threw the bomb."

It is evident that Mr. Fowler here uses "the people of Chicago" as one with the State, because it is the State which is prosecuting Anarchy. But why should the State "hunt up the man who threw the bomb?" Why should it do anything in this matter but prosecute Anarchy? Is not Anarchy its deadliest foe? Is it to be expected that the State will pay heed to anything but its own existence and prosperity?

No whining, then! Let us not complain of the injustice practised by the State, except we do so for the sole purpose of exhibiting it to the people in its enormity and determining them to throw off its tyrannical yoke. One of the wisest comments that have been made upon the verdict is that of Louis Lingg, the maker of most of the bombs so prevalent in Chicago and the youngest of the convicted men. He is reported to have said, after the verdict, something like this:

"There is no reason to complain. Had I been in the judge's place and he in mine, I would have sent him to the gallows inside of twenty-four hours." The attitude of this brave Bohemian boy is superior to that of his older comrades. Louis Lingg understands the situation. He knows that Anarchy has challenged the State. He knows that the State has picked up the gauntlet. He knows that it is a duel to the death.

Both Lingg and his comrades, however, are fatally weak in that they do not really represent Anarchy. They have challenged in Anarchy's name, but to institute and secure one of the most revolting of Archies,— the Archy of compulsory Communism. They propose to win and uphold it by methods the most cruel and bloody. The strength of a righteous cause against tyranny lies in the fact that, as long as it remains itself innocent of offence, its persecution will bring it popular sympathy and aid. The so-called Anarchists of Chicago, by making their cause unrighteous, by announcing their readiness to commit any offences, however enormous, and by standing on a platform of Communistic tyranny, have cast aside this strength, alienated this popular sympathy for injured liberty, and thrown it upon the side of the enemy. And what is worse, by adopting the name of the real friends of Liberty and thus confusing the popular mind as to the character of Anarchy, they perhaps have made it possible for the enemy to carry out, *sustained by popular sanction*, what it dared not before attempt, *from fear of popular rebellion*,—the immediate suppression of the true Anarchists, who pursue Liberty as an end through Liberty as a means. If we could have gone on in our own way, we should have grown stronger and stronger, until the State would have had to face the alternative of frank surrender on the one hand, or, on the other, death in the last ditch through sacrificing popular support by assuming the offensive against innocent autonomists. As it is, the road to our sure triumph will probably be a much harder one to travel.

But what of the terrible predicament, it will be asked, in which these men who have injured our cause now find themselves ? The answer is ready. They are of the noble few who, however mistaken as to the way of obtaining it, desire universal human comfort and for it are willing to cast their lives into the balance ; we will snatch them, therefore, from the jaws of the wild beast, if we consistently can. To that end everything shall be done short of treason to our cause. But there we stop. If we cannot save these men except by resorting to their own erroneous methods and thus indefinitely postponing the objects we have in view, then the wild beast must have its prey. Nothing requires us to sacrifice that which is dearest to us to save misguided men from consequences which we did nothing to bring upon them. Those who think this cruelty may make the most of it. Call me brute, call me coward, call me "kid-gloved Anarchist," call me what you will, I stand to my post. I have yet to learn that it is any man's duty to sustain his reputation for bravery at the cost of his loyalty to truth. By my attitude upon that day—which, if its coming was inevitable, will come the sooner now—when I in turn shall find myself at close quarters with the wild beast, I consent to have my courage judged. For that day I wait. And while I wait I work.

THE LESSON OF THE HOUR.

[*Liberty*, September 24, 1887.]

UNLIKE some of my friends, I have never entertained any hope that the supreme court of Illinois would overturn the verdict against the condemned Socialists of Chicago ; and so, terrible as the recent news from that city is, I was not disappointed at it. But my heart grows heavier as the resources of defence diminish and the day approaches on which the brutal State proposes to execute upon these rash but noble men a base and far more rash revenge. To avert this act of madness and the unspeakable terrors to which it very possibly will lead, there remain but two cards yet to play in that game of statutory "justice" in which there is a percentage of chances in favor of the State that, if possessed by the backer of the games at Monte Carlo, would ruin him by driving all his victims to suicide. One of these cards is appeal to the supreme court of the United States ; the other is appeal to the governor of Illinois. Now, as experience teaches us that the ascending scale of judicial "supremacy" generally registers a corresponding increase of stupidity and cold-bloodedness, there seems little reason to expect more fairness from Washington than Ottawa ; and, unless Governor Oglesby is far less a tool of capital than the average Republican governor seeking political advancement, appeal to that quarter will be equally useless. Still no stone should be left unturned. Let ample funds flow in, in order that all that can be done may be done, regardless of cost ; and though capital's faintest whisper should sound louder in official ears than labor's mighty voice, let that voice give all its power to protest loud and long. Only so shall we have no error to regret.

Above all, we must not fail to learn the lesson of these troublous days. In all that *Liberty* has had to say about this sorry business from the first, the effort has been to make plain the folly of supposing the State to be at all concerned about justice. More than ever am I convinced of this after reading the long opinion of the Illinois judges. Their very able summary of the testimony offered at the trial confirms me in the opinion that *under the law as it stands* there was a sufficiency of evidence to convict the prisoners of murder. For it takes but precious little. For aught that I can see, the State's attorney has it in his power to hang thousands upon thousands of innocent citizens of Chicago as easily as he will hang the seven victims now under sentence. It is the infernal conspiracy law itself which is responsible for this iniquity; and this law, which passes almost without question, shows how inevitably the State becomes an instrument of tyranny. This monster cannot be reformed; *it must be killed*. But how ? Not by dynamite; that will not harm it. How, then ? By light ? It thrives in the darkness of its victims' ignorance; it and they must be flooded with the light of liberty. If the seven must die, such must be the lesson of their death.

CONVICTED FOR THEIR OPINIONS.

[*Liberty*, September 24, 1887.]

THE judges of the supreme court of Illinois are in accord with the Communists of Illinois upon at least one point. They say in their opinion: "Law and government cannot be abolished without revolution, bloodshed, and murder." Despite the sanction which the Communists thus receive from so exalted a quarter, Anarchists will continue to hold the contrary opinion, and to maintain that only under very rare and extreme circumstances is bloodshed essential to the abolition of government, that under other circumstances it can be no more than incidental to it, and that it will not be even that when there is a little more intelligence abroad regarding the principle of liberty, which, revolution or no revolution, must in any event be the chief factor in the abolition of government. Disregarding, however, the question whether the view of the judges and the Communists is correct or not, it is interesting to note the connection in which the former put it forward. Answering the claim of the counsel for the defence that one of the jurors was incompetent because he admitted a prejudice against Socialists, Communists, and Anarchists, the judges say that this is no disqualification; for, since Anarchism involves the destruction of law and government, which in turn involves revolution, bloodshed, and murder, and since Socialism or Communism involves a destruction of the right of private property, which in turn involves theft, "the prejudice which the ordinary citizen, who looks at things from a practical standpoint, would have against Anarchism and Communism would be nothing more than a prejudice against crime." After this judical declaration, will the jackals and jackasses of the capitalistic press dare to claim longer that the seven men under death sentence at Chicago were not tried and convicted for their opinions?

TO THE BREACH, COMRADES!

[*Liberty*, November 19, 1887.]

OF the tragedy just enacted at Chicago, what is there to say? Of a deed so foul perpetrated upon men so brave, what words are not inadequate to paint the blackness on the one hand and the glory on the other? My heart was never so full, my pen never so halt. As I write, the dying shout of noble Spies comes back to me from the scaffold: "At this moment our silence is more powerful than speech." But, who speaks or who keeps silent, all of us, I am certain, will from this time forth face the struggle before us with stouter hearts and firmer tread for the examples that have been set us by our murdered comrades. If we add to these a clearer vision, the result will not be doubtful.

And when it is achieved and history shall begin to make up its verdict, it will be seen and acknowledged that the John Browns of America's industrial revolution were hanged at Chicago on the Eleventh of November, 1887. The labor movement has had its Harper's Ferry; when will come the emancipation proclamation?

"Not good-by, but hail, brothers!" telegraphed Josephine Tilton to Albert Parsons on the morning of the fatal day;

"from the gallows trap the march shall be taken up. I will listen for the beating of the drum."

The drum-tap has sounded; the forlorn hope has charged; the needed breach has been opened; myriads are falling into line; if we will but make the most of the opportunity so dearly purchased, victory will be ours.

It shall be; it *must* be !

For, as Proudhon says, "like Nemesis of old, whom neither prayers nor threats could move, the Revolution advances, with sombre and inevitable tread, over the flowers with which its devotees strew its path, through the blood of its champions, and over the bodies of its enemies."

ON PICKET DUTY.

IT is one thing to admit the possibility of revolution; it is a second thing to point out that, in the presence of certain conditions and in the absence of certain other conditions, revolution is inevitable; it is a third and entirely different thing to so vividly " foresee " revolution that vision in every other direction becomes more and more obscure. When a man's " foresight " of revolution has arrived at this dazzling pitch, it is safe to conclude that in his heart of hearts he desires revolution, clings against his reason to a superstitious belief in its economic efficacy, and would openly urge it instead of " foreseeing " it, did he not know that he could not defend such a course against reasoning men. Knowing this, however, he contents himself with " foreseeing," but " foresees " so constantly and absorbingly that his prophecies have all the effect of preaching, while enabling him to dodge the preacher's responsibility.—*Liberty*, July 21, 1888.

Henry George's *Standard* makes a protest against the attitude of the Chicago authorities toward public meetings and processions. It is too late in the day, Mr. George, for you to pose as a champion of freedom of speech. You once had a chance to vindicate that cause such as comes to a man but once in a lifetime, and in the trial hour you not only failed the cause, but betrayed it. Let one of the meetings against the suppression of which you now protest be held; let some one present throw a bomb and kill an officer; let the speakers be arrested on a charge of murder; let a jury packed with the hirelings of capital convict them; let a judge sentence them to be hanged; let the supreme court formally sanction the whole; let a large portion of the people, hounded on by a bloodthirsty and prostituted press, clamor for these men's death; and let this culminate in the middle of a political campaign in which you are running for office: under these circumstances should we not see you do again what you have done once already,—declare that a supreme court can do no wrong, that in face of its opinion you recant yours, that the convicted men deserve to be hanged, and that you will not lift voice or pen to save them? We have known you, Henry George, in the past, and we know you for the future. The lamp holds out to burn, but for no such vile sinner as yourself. In vain your efforts to return to the fold. As Ingersoll says, " 'Twon't do."—*Liberty*, January 5, 1889.

Judge Gary, of Chicago, having to pass upon a " color-line case recently, rendered his decision in favor of the rights of the negro. But if Judge Gary had occupied the bench thirty years ago, and John Brown, who was so largely instrumental in accomplishing the revolution by virtue of which the black man is now able to vindicate his rights in court, had been brought before him on a charge of treason, it can scarcely be doubted that he would have sentenced his prisoner to be hanged with as little compunction as he showed in condemning Spies and his comrades to the gallows and with the same shedding of crocodile tears.—*Liberty*, January 19, 1889.

MISCELLANEOUS.

THE LESSON OF HOMESTEAD.

[*Liberty*, July 23, 1892.]

REGARDING methods, one of the truths that has been most steadily inculcated by this journal has been that social questions cannot be settled by force. Recent events have only confirmed this view. But when force comes, it sometimes leads incidentally to the teaching of other lessons than that of its own uselessness and becomes thereby to that extent useful. The appeal to force at Homestead affords a signal example of such incidental beneficence ; for it has forced the capitalistic papers of the country, and notably the New York *Sun*, to take up a bold defence of liberty in order to protect property. Now, all that Anarchism asks is liberty ; and when the enemies of liberty can find no way of saving their own interests except by an appeal to liberty, *Liberty* means to make a note of it and hold them to it.

Listen, therefore, to the New York *Sun* preaching the gospel of liberty. The passages here quoted are fair samples of its editorial columns for the last fortnight :

> If a man has labor to sell, he must find some one with money to buy it, or it is of no more use to him than unused capital is to Mr. Carnegie. If the man does not like the price offered, he can reject it. If the buyer does not like the price asked, he has the same liberty. Neither is obliged to accept the bargain, though both are under the same law which forces men to take what they can get. If the laborer does not want the work longer than he contracted to give it, he can throw it up, and the employer has the same right to dispense with the laborer. The workman can choose his employer, and the employer can choose his workmen. No law can take away that right from either. The workman can refuse to work and the employer to hire. Such is liberty.

> . . . .

> There are a good many fools and there are not a few scoundrels in the United States; but, even if the scoundrels could persuade the fools that violence is a friend of the workmen, the great majority of the American people, heartily despising the scoundrels and pitying the fools, would stand up . . . for the right of every citizen to enjoy his own property and select his own employees; for the right of every citizen to work for whom he chooses, and to belong or not to belong to a labor organization, as he chooses. By whatever folly or violence these rights are attacked, they are invincible while the present idea of civilization lasts.

453

Truth, every word! Golden truth! Anarchistic truth! But the bearing of this truth, as Cap'n Cuttle would say, lies in the application of it. Applied to the conduct of the Homestead strikers, this principle of equal liberty, of which the *Sun's* words are an expression, instead of condemning it as the *Sun* pretends, palliates and even excuses it ; for, before these strikers violated the equal liberty of others, their own right to equality of liberty had been wantonly and continuously violated. But, applied to the conduct of capitalists generally, it condemns it utterly, for the original violation of liberty in this matter is traceable directly to them.

This is no wild assertion, but a sober statement of fact, as I will explain. It is not enough, however true, to say that, "if a man has labor to sell, he must find some one with money to buy it"; it is necessary to add the much more important truth that, if a man has labor to sell, he has a right to a free market in which to sell it,—a market in which no one shall be prevented by restrictive laws from honestly obtaining the money to buy it. If the man with labor to sell has not this free market, then his liberty is violated and his property virtually taken from him. Now, such a market has constantly been denied, not only to the laborers at Homestead, but to the laborers of the entire civilized world. And the men who have denied it are the Andrew Carnegies. Capitalists of whom this Pittsburg forge-master is a typical representative have placed and kept upon the statute-books all sorts of prohibitions and taxes (of which the customs tariff is among the least harmful) designed to limit and effective in limiting the number of bidders for the labor of those who have labor to sell. If there were no tariffs on imported goods ; if titles to unoccupied land were not recognized by the State ; above all, if the right to issue money were not vested in a monopoly,—bidders for the labor of Carnegie's employees would become so numerous that the offer would soon equal the laborer's product. Now, to solemnly tell these men who are thus prevented by law from getting the wages which their labor would command in a free market that they have a right to reject any price that may be offered for their labor is undoubtedly to speak a formal truth, but it is also to utter a rotten commonplace and a cruel impertinence. Rather tell the capitalists that the laborer is entitled to a free market, and that they, in denying it to him, are guilty of criminal invasion. This would be not only a formal truth, but an opportune application of a vital principle.

Perhaps it will be claimed in answer to this that the laborers, being voters, are responsible for any monopolies that exist, and are thereby debarred from pleading them as an excuse for violating the liberty of their employers. This is only true to the extent to which we may consider these laborers as the "fools" persuaded by the capitalists who are the "scoundrels" that "violence (in the form of enforced monopoly) is a friend of the workmen"; which does not make it less unbecoming in the scoundrels to rebuke and punish the fools for any disastrous consequences that may arise out of this appalling combination of scoundrelism and folly.

Conspicuous among the scoundrels who have upheld these monopolies is the editor of the New York *Sun*. If he tells truth to-day, he tells it as the devil quotes scripture,—to suit his purpose. He will never consent to an application of equal liberty in the interest of labor, for he belongs to the brotherhood of thieves who prey upon labor. If he only would, we Anarchists would meet him with cheerful acquiescence in its fullest application in the interest of capital. Let Carnegie, Dana & Co. first see to it that every law in violation of equal liberty is removed from the statute-books. If, after that, any laborers shall interfere with the rights of their employers, or shall use force upon inoffensive "scabs," or shall attack their employers' watchmen, whether these be Pinkerton detectives, sheriff's deputies, or the State militia, I pledge myself that, as an Anarchist and in consequence of my Anarchistic faith, I will be among the first to volunteer as a member of a force to repress these disturbers of order and, if necessary, sweep them from the earth. But while these invasive laws remain, I must view every forcible conflict that arises as the consequence of an original violation of liberty on the part of the employing classes, and, if any sweeping is done, may the laborers hold the broom! Still, while my sympathies thus go with the under dog, I shall never cease to proclaim my conviction that the annihilation of neither party can secure justice, and that the only effective sweeping will be that which clears from the statute-book every restriction of the freedom of the market.

SAVE LABOR FROM ITS FRIENDS.

[*Liberty*, July 30, 1892.]

DURING the conflict now on between capital and labor, seldom a day passes without the shedding of blood. One of the most recent victims is a prominent leader of the forces of capital. The disaster that has befallen him has called out a display of grief on his behalf which, so far as it comes from the camp of labor, seems to me theatrical, and in which I certainly cannot share.   Henry C. Frick, like Charles A. Dana, the godfather of his two weeks-old son, is a conspicuous member of the brotherhood of thieves.   In joining this nefarious band he took his life in his hands, and he knew it.   It is but just to say that he has accepted his fate in the spirit of a bold bandit, without a cry or flinch.   His pluck excites my admiration, but his suffering moves me to less pity than I would feel for the most ordinary cur.   Why should I pity this man? What have he and I in common?   Does he aspire, as I do, to live in a society of mutually helpful equals?   On the contrary, it is his determination to live in luxury produced by the toil and suffering of men whose necks are under his heel.   He has deliberately chosen to live on terms of hostility with the greater part of the human race.   When such a man falls, my tears refuse to flow.   I am scarcely sorry that he is suffering ; I shall be still less sorry if he dies.

And yet I am very, very sorry that he has been shot.

Who is his assailant?   I do not know Alexander Berkman, but I believe that he is a man with whom I have much in common,—much more, at any rate, than with such a man as Frick.   It is altogether likely, despite the slanders in the newspapers, as insincere in their abuse as in their grief, that he would like to live on terms of equality with his fellows, doing his share of work for not more than his share of pay. There is little reason to doubt that his attitude toward the human race is one, not of hostility, but of intended helpfulness.   And yet, as one member of the human race, I freely confess that I am more desirous of being saved from friends like Berkman, to whom my heart goes out, than from enemies like Frick, from whom my heart withdraws.   The worst enemy of the human race is folly, and men like Berkman are its incarnation.   It would be comparatively easy to dispose of the Fricks if it were not for the Berkmans.   The latter are the hope of the former.   The strength of the Fricks rests on violence ; now it is to violence that the Berkmans appeal.   The peril of the Fricks lies in the spreading of the light ; violence is the power of darkness.   If the revolution comes by violence and in advance of light, the old struggle will have to be begun anew.   The hope of humanity lies in the avoidance of that revolution by force which the Berkmans are trying to precipitate.

No pity for Frick, no praise for Berkman,—such is the attitude of *Liberty* in the present crisis.

IS FRICK A SOLDIER OF LIBERTY?

[*Liberty*, August 20, 1892.]

To the Editor of Liberty:

In vain have I waited to hear from you a word of approval of the efforts of a man who lately has even risked his life in a fierce struggle for liberty. For even though Frick is one of the "Brotherhood of Thieves," he is now on the side of Liberty. Nor can I see that he is any more responsible for the existence of that "Brotherhood" than those that lead the contention against him. His only crime is that he is successful under present conditions. Of course, being an employer myself, my opinion may possibly be warped; but if Frick, in this particular case at least, has instituted a war against the oppressive monopoly of labor unions, defending liberty and independence, I do not see why Anarchists should condemn him therefor. Let the other side do the same,—*i.e.*, combat the iniquities of the present system by removing obstructions instead of increasing their number. I am sure, if the workmen should insist upon the proper remedy, the inequitable power of capital would soon be gone. If, however, these men do not understand the source of this power, is it fair to assume that the Fricks do? Is it true that all the workmen are fools, while all the Fricks are knaves? And, on that assumption, how is it possible to help those who resist the only measure that can help them,—*i.e.*, Liberty?

HUGO BILGRAM.

PHILADELPHIA, August 12, 1892.

When that most brilliant of Catholic journalists, Louis Veuillot, was once taunted by the Freethinkers in power because he, a Catholic and an unbeliever in liberty, had complained that the liberties of Catholics were denied, he thus made answer to his critics: "When I am not in power, I demand of you who are in power all possible liberties, because you believe in liberty; when I get into power, you shall have no liberties at all, because I do not believe in liberty." Veuillot was in religion what Frick is in political economy,—a believer in liberty for himself and his immediate allies, and in slavery for everybody else. Neither the Veuillots nor the Fricks have any use whatever for a society based throughout on equal liberty. Now when a man goes into a struggle in this Napoleonic style and in the course of it gets a knock-down blow, it is going too far to ask an Anarchist, a believer in equal liberty, to sympathize with or approve this would-be despot simply because at a particular moment in his struggle for unequal liberty he happens to defend a liberty which equal liberty recognizes.

But, Mr. Bilgram tells me, these union laborers are also struggling for unequal liberty ; why then sympathize with them ? True enough ; and their claim to sympathy is greatly lessened by their abominable authoritarianism. If it will comfort Mr. Bilgram, I take pleasure in assuring him that, if the time ever comes when these trade-union employees are thoroughly on top with their hands fastened upon their employers' throats, and when in consequence the employees begin to wax fat and the employers to grow wan and thin, much of my sympathy will be transferred from the employees to the employers. When both parties to a fight are wrong, whatever sympathy is felt goes naturally to the one that suffers most. Apart from this friendly feeling for the under dog, however, there is another consideration which mitigates the offence of the labor authoritarians as compared with that of the capitalist authoritarians. The latter, for the most part in knavery, set up authority as a weapon of aggression ; the former, for the most part in ignorance and following the latter's example, resort to authority originally as a weapon of defence. The difference is considerable.

Mr. Bilgram and I agree almost to a dot as to what constitutes the true solution of the difficulties at Homestead and of nearly all other labor difficulties whatsoever. I agree with him too that, if the workmen knew the remedy, they could apply it very quickly and effectively. But I do not think that the ignorance of the workmen implies a similar and equal ignorance on the part of the employers. For one thing, the employers, as a rule, are men of superior education and intellect. And for another thing, the creators of a scheme of aggression are much less likely to be innocent of evil intent than the victims. To be sure, there are many exceptions, and I have said nothing to the contrary. I am just as certain, for instance, that the employer, Hugo Bilgram, is not a knave as I am that Dana and Frick are knaves. If there were no such exceptions, then, as Mr. Bilgram says, the situation would be hopeless. It is on these exceptions that my hope rests. All the employers are not knaves, and all the workmen are not such fools that they cannot acquire wisdom ; and because of these two facts I see Light and Liberty ahead.

SHALL STRIKERS BE COURT-MARTIALLED ?

[*Liberty*, August 25, 1883.]

OF the multitude of novel and absurd and monstrous suggestions called forth from the newspapers by the telegraphers'
strike, none have equalled in novelty and absurdity and mon-
strosity the sober proposal of the editor of the New York
Nation, that unsentimental being who prides himself on his hard
head, that hereafter any and all employees of telegraph companies, railroad companies, and the post-office department who
may see fit to strike work without first getting the consent of
their employers be treated as are soldiers who desert or decline
to obey the commands of their superior officers ; in other
words (we suppose, though the *Nation* does not use these
other words), that they may be summarily court-martialled and
shot. The readers of *Liberty* not being noted for their
credulity, some of them may refuse to believe that a civilized
journal, especially one which claims to be of "the highest
order" and to represent "the best thought of the country and
time," has been guilty of uttering such a proposition ; therefore we print below an extract from a leader which appeared
in the *Nation* of July 19, and defy any one to gather any
other practical meaning from it than that which we have
stated.

The truth is that a society like ours, and like that of all commercial
nations, has become so dependent on the post-office, the railroads, and the
telegraph, that they may be said to stand to it in the relation of the
nerves to the human body. The loss even for a week of any one of them
means partial paralysis. The loss of all three would mean a total deprivation, for a longer or shorter period, of nearly everything which the community most values. It would mean a suspension of business and social
relations equal to that caused by a hostile invasion, barring the terror
and bloodshed. It is consequently something to which no country will
long allow itself to remain exposed. It cannot allow strikes of employees
in these great public services, any more than it can allow the corporations themselves to refuse to carry on their business as a means of ex-
tracting what they think fair rates of transportation. No Legislature
would permit this, and one or two more experiences like the railroad
strike will cause every Legislature to take measures against the other.
Telegraphers, railroad men, post-office clerks, and policemen fill places
in modern society very like that of soldiers. In fact, they together do
for society what soldiers used to do. They enable every man to come
and go freely on his lawful occasions, and transact his lawful business
without let or hinderance.

During the rebellion, when all of us, except the much-abused "copperheads," temporarily lost control of our reasoning faculties (we dare say that even the editor of the *Nation* at that time forgot himself and became sentimental for once), we got very angry with Carlyle for patly putting the American Iliad in a nutshell and epigrammatically establishing the substantial similarity between the condition of slave labor at the South and that of so-called "free" labor at the North. England's blunt old sham-hater was answered with much boisterous declamation about "freedom of contract," and his attention was proudly called to the fact that the laborer of the North could follow his own sweet will, leaving his employer when he saw fit, attaching himself to any other willing to hire him, or, if he preferred, setting up in business for himself and employing others. He was at liberty, it was loudly proclaimed by our abolitionists and free-traders, to work when he pleased, where he pleased, how he pleased, and on what terms he pleased, and no man could say him nay. What are we to think, then, when the chief newspaper exponent of the "freedom of contract" philosophy deliberately sacrifices the only answer that it could make to Carlyle's indictment by proposing the introduction of a military discipline into industry, which, in assimilating the laborer to the soldier, would make him—what the soldier is—a slave? Think? Simply this,— that the hypocritical thieves and tyrants who for years have been endeavoring to make their victims believe themselves freemen see that the game is nearly up, and that the time is fast approaching when they must take by the horns the bull of outraged industry, which, maddened by the discovery of its hitherto invisible chains, is making frantic efforts to burst them it knows not how. It is a point gained. An enemy in the open field is less formidable than one in ambush. When the capitalists shall be forced to show their true colors, the laborers will then know against whom they are fighting.

Fighting, did we say? Yes. For the laborer in these days *is* a soldier, though not in the sense which the *Nation* meant. His employer is not, as the *Nation* would have it, his superior officer, but simply a member of an opposing army. The whole industrial and commercial world is in a state of internecine war, in which the prolétaires are massed on one side and the proprietors on the other. This is the fact that justifies strikers in subjecting society to what the *Nation* calls a "partial paralysis." It is a war measure. The laborer sees that he does not get his due. He knows that the capitalists have been intrusted by society, through its external representative, the State, with privileges which enable them to control production and distribution ; and that, in abuse of these privileges, they have seen to it that the demand for labor should fall far below the supply, and have then taken advantage of the necessities of the laborer and reduced his wages. The laborer and his fellows, therefore, resort to the policy of uniting in such numbers in a refusal to work at the reduced rate that the demand for labor becomes very much greater than the supply, and then they take advantage of the necessities of the capitalists and society to secure a restoration of the old rate of wages, and perhaps an increase upon it. Be the game fair or foul, two can play at it ; and those who begin it should not complain when they get the worst of it. If society objects to being " paralyzed," it can very easily avoid it. All it needs to do is to adopt the advice which *Liberty* has long been offering it, and withdraw from the monopolists the privileges which it has granted them. Then, as Colonel William B. Greene has shown in his " Mutual Banking," as Lysander Spooner has shown in his works on finance, and as Proudhon has shown in his " Organization of Credit," capital will no longer be tied up by syndicates, but will become readily available for investment on easy terms; productive enterprise, taking new impetus, will soon assume enormous proportions ; the work to be done will always surpass the number of laborers to do it ; and, instead of the employers being able to say to the laborers, as the unsentimental *Nation* would like to have them, " Take what we offer you, or the troops shall be called out to shoot you down," the laborers will be able to say to their employers, " If you desire our services, you must give us in return an equivalent of their product,"—terms which the employers will be only too glad to accept. Such is the only solution of the problem of strikes, such the only way to turn the edge of Carlyle's biting satire.

CENSUS-TAKING FATAL TO MONOPOLY.

[*Liberty*, July 21, 1888.]

THE makers of party platforms, the writers of newspaper editorials, the pounders of pulpit-cushions, and the orators of the stump, who are just now blending their voices in frantic chorus to proclaim the foreign origin of evil and to advocate therefore the exclusion of the foreign element from American

soil, should study the figures compiled by Rev. Frederick
Howard Wines from the tenth census reports and presented
by him to the congress of the National Prison Association
lately held in Boston.   Such of these shriekers as are provided with thinkers may find in these statistics food for
thought.   From them it appears that, though the ratio of
crime among our foreign-born population is still very much
higher than the ratio among our native population, the former
ratio, which in 1850 was more than five times as high as the
latter, in 1880 was less than twice as high.   And it further
appears that, if crimes against person and property are alone
considered, the two ratios stand almost exactly on a level, and
that the ratio of foreign-born criminals tends to exceed that
of native criminals in proportion as the catalogue of "crimes"
is extended to cover so-called offences against public morals,
public policy, and society.   In other words, the percentage of
natives who steal, damage, burn, assault, kidnap, rape, and
kill is about as large as the percentage of foreigners of similarly invasive tendencies, and the percentage of foreign-born
law-breakers exceeds that of native law-breakers only because
the foreign-born are less disposed than the natives to obey
those laws which say that people shall not drink this or eat
that or smoke the other ; that they shall not love except
under prescribed forms and conditions ; that they shall not
dispose or expose their persons except as their rulers provide ;
that they shall not work or play on Sunday or blaspheme the
name of the Lord ; that they shall not gamble or swear ; that
they shall not sell certain articles at all, or buy certain others
without paying a tax for the privilege ; and that they shall not
mail, own, or read any obscene literature except the Bible.
That is to say, again, people who happen to have been born in
Europe are no more determined to invade their fellow-men
than are people who happen to have been born in America,
but that the latter are much more willing to be invaded and
trampled upon than any other people on earth.   Which speaks
very well, in *Liberty's* opinion, for the foreigners, and makes
it important for our own liberty and welfare to do everything
possible to encourage immigration.

  But, say the shriekers, these foreigners are Anarchists and
Socialists.   Well, there's some truth in that ; as a general
rule, the better people are, the more Anarchists and Socialists
will be found among them.   This, too, is a fact which the
tenth census proves.   The ratio of native criminals to native
population is as 1 to 949.   How about other nationalities ?
Listen to Rev. Mr. Wines :

From the West Indies, the number of prisoners is 1 in 117 of our West Indian population; from Spain, 1 in 165 of the Spaniards in this country; of the South Americans, 1 in 197; of the Chinese, 1 in 199; of the Italians, 1 in 260; of the Australians, 1 in 306; of the Irish, 1 in 350; of the Scotch, 1 in 411; of the French, 1 in 433; of the English, 1 in 456; of the British Americans, 1 in 590; of the Russians, 1 in 916; of the Germans, 1 in 949; of the Poles, 1 in 1033; of the Welsh, 1 in 1173; of the Belgians, 1 in 1195; of the Swiss, 1 in 1231; of the Hollanders, 1 in 1383; of the Scandinavians, 1 in 1539; and of the Austrians (including the Hungarians and Bohemians), 1 in 1936. The Hungarians and Bohemians make the best showing, in respect of crime, of any nationality; this is probably contrary to the popular opinion, which seems to have no better foundation than an unjust prejudice, founded in ignorance.

Now, in what class of foreigners *in this country* do the Anarchists and Socialists figure most largely. Certainly not among the Chinese or the Irish or the Cubans or the Spaniards or the Italians or the Australians or the Scotch or the French or the English or the Canadians. But these are the only foreigners except the Russians who make a poorer showing in point of criminality than the native Americans. To find in this country any considerable number of Anarchists and Socialists of foreign birth, we must go to the Russians, the Germans, the Poles, the Hungarians, and the Bohemians. The statistics show, however, that the Russians are almost as orderly as Americans, the Germans exactly as orderly, the Poles more orderly, and the Hungarians and Bohemians more than twice as orderly.

Moral: If the defenders of privilege desire to exclude from this country the opponents of privilege, they should see to it that Congress omits the taking of the eleventh census. For the eleventh census, if taken, will undoubtedly emphasize these two lessons of the tenth: first, that foreign immigration does not increase dishonesty and violence among us, but does increase the love of liberty; second, that the population of the world is gradually dividing into two classes,—Anarchists and criminals.

ANARCHY NECESSARILY ATHEISTIC.

[*Liberty*, January 9, 1886.]

To the Editor of Liberty :

If Anarchy, as you advocate it, is the abolition of all law and authority except the laws of self-government and self-restraint, and you believe that with these laws of self no man would injure his neighbor, how would such a condition of things, realizing the highest ideals of Socialism and negating all authority, differ from a society governed by the laws "*thou shalt love the Lord thy God with all thy heart, and thy neighbor as thyself,*" and affirming the authority of Christ? (1) If there is no real difference, what use in any negation?

But again: If Anarchy, as you advocate it, be the very highest ideal of Socialism, do you think it possible to make so great a transition as from the present condition of things to that ideal state, except by steps accomplished with more or less celerity? (2)

If not, why cannot all men who desire to change the present condition of things for a better one form parts of one great army, and advance as rapidly as possible towards the end? If part of the army halt when certain changes are effected, you are advanced with it so far, and part of your work is accomplished any way, and you have less to do. (3)

The practical question is: what shall we attack first with that amount and kind of force necessary to effect our purposes? The present system must be destroyed in detail, and a new one be supplied in detail. The job is too large to accomplish suddenly and at once.

Yours respectfully,
O. P. LEWIS.
BRIDGEPORT, CONN., December 3, 1885.

(1) A society negating all authority would differ from a society affirming the authority of Christ very much as white differs from black. Self-government is incompatible with government by the law, "thou shalt love the Lord thy God," for the reason that this law implies the existence of God, and God and Man are enemies. God, to be God, must be a governing power. His government cannot be administered directly by the individual, for the individual, and through the individual: if it could, it would at once obliterate individuality altogether. Hence the government of God, if administered at all, must be administered through his professed vicegerents on earth, the dignitaries of Church and State. How this hierarchy differs from Anarchy it is needless to point out.

(2) No.

(3) Because the great majority of the men whose hearts are filled with the "desire to change the present condition of things for a better one" are afflicted with an obscurity of mental vision which renders them incapable of distinguishing between advance and retrogression. Professing an aspiration for entire individual freedom, they aim to effect it by enlarging the sphere of government and restricting and restraining the individual through all sorts of new oppressions. No clear-sighted Anarchist can march with such an army. The farther he should go with it, the farther would he be from his goal, and, instead of having "less to do," he would have more to do and more to undo. Whenever *Liberty* hears of any demand for a real increase of freedom, it is prompt to encourage and sustain it, no matter what its source. It marches with any

wing of the army of freedom as far as that wing will go. But it sternly refuses to right about face. *Liberty* hates Catholicism and loves Free Thought; but, when it finds Catholicism advocating and Free Thought opposing the principle of voluntaryism in education, it sustains Catholicism against Free Thought. Likewise, when it finds Liberals and Socialists of all varieties favoring eight-hour laws, government monopoly of money, land nationalization, protection, prohibition, race proscription, State administration of railways, telegraphs, mines, and factories, woman suffrage, man suffrage, common schools, marriage laws, and compulsory taxation, it brands them one and all as false to the principle of freedom, refuses to follow them in their retrogressive course, and keeps its own eyes and steps carefully towards the front. It knows that the only way to achieve freedom is to begin to take it. It is an important question, as Mr. Lewis says, what we shall attack first. On this point *Liberty* has its opinion also. It believes that the first point of attack should be the power of legally privileged capital to increase without work. And as the monopoly of the issue of money is the chief bulwark of this power, it turns its heaviest guns upon that. But it is impossible to successfully attack the money monopoly or any other monopoly or privilege, unless the general principle of freedom be first established. That is the reason why *Liberty* makes this principle its own guide and its test of the course of others.

A FABLE FOR MALTHUSIANS.

[*Liberty*, July 31, 1886.]

OF all the astonishing arguments developed by the interesting Malthusian discussion now in progress in *Lucifer* and *Liberty* the most singular, surprising, and short-sighted is that advanced by E. C. Walker in maintaining the identity of political and domestic economy so far as the problem of population is concerned.

"The prosperity of the whole," he tells Miss Kelly, "exists only because of the prosperity of the parts."

"To speak of *domestic* economy," he tells Mr. J. F. Kelly, "as though it were something that could be considered apart from so-called national economy, is confusing and unautonomistic. There can be no 'public good' which is secured at the expense of the individual, at the sacrifice of the private

good. The 'population question' is nothing but a question
of the wisdom or unwisdom and the consequent happiness
or unhappiness of individuals and of families,—primarily, of
course, of individuals. Were Mr. Kelly and his *confrères* not
standing upon State Socialistic ground, they would never think
of advancing such a collectivist argument. Should any governmentalist say to Mr. Kelly that the 'public good' required
so and so, and that the individual must waive his rights when
confronted with the greater right of the majority, that gentleman would proceed to show his opponent that there was no
such thing as the 'public good,' save as it was the aggregation
of the individual goods, and what was required to augment
the 'public good' was to jealously preserve the rights and liberties of the individual."

This indicates the most blissful ignorance on Mr. Walker's
part of the real bearing of the point originally made against
him,—a point as indisputable as the sunlight, and which he had
only to admit frankly and unreservedly in order to stop the
"leak in the dykes that confined the waters of anti-Malthusian
eloquence," and thereby save himself the necessity of counter-
acting this leak by opening his own flood-gates. The point
referred to is this : that, in consequence of the "iron law of
wages" which prevails wherever monopoly prevails, a reduction of population cannot benefit the masses of laborers, and
hence, while monopoly lives, can be of little or no value in
political economy, although, if confined to a few families, it
may benefit the families in question, and therefore be good
domestic economy; the explanation of this being that small families means a reduction in the cost of living *for those families*,
and a reduction in the cost of living for even *one* family means,
under a monopolistic system, a reduction in the rate of wages
paid to *all* laborers. If Mr. Walker had understood this, he
never would have attempted to meet it with the specious statement (which to all Anarchists is the merest truism) that the
public good is only the aggregation of the individual goods.
Can he suppose that the Kellys and myself are so stupid that,
if we believed that Malthusianism would make all individuals
comfortable and happy, or would largely contribute to that
end, we would not be as ardent Malthusians as himself ? Mr.
Walker begs the question. He bases his argument on an un-
proven assumption of the very point which we dispute and
believe we disprove. The Kellys have expressly denied that
Malthusianism can benefit the aggregation of individuals, and
therefore the public. They have nowhere admitted that it
would benefit " the individual;" they have only admitted that

it might benefit "a few individuals;" and between these admissions there is a vast and vital difference.

Concerning the rights of the individual and the majority, neither Mr. Kelly nor Mr. Walker would say that "what was required to augment the 'public good' was to jealously preserve the rights and liberties of " *a few individuals* at the expense of others. So, in the matter of population, Mr. Kelly does not say that the public welfare is to be enhanced by reducing the size of a few families and thus making the individuals belonging to them comfortable at the expense of others. But Mr. Walker virtually does say so, and precisely there is his mistake. Thus Mr. Walker's own analogy convicts him of his error.

If he can be made to really see that under the present system small families must benefit *at the expense of others* if at all, I think he will be obliged in honesty to abandon his position that Malthusianism is good *political* economy. Will he excuse me, then, if I try to make this plain in a rather simple way?

I will suppose A, B, C, etc., to and including Y, to be day laborers, each having five children and each employed at wages barely sufficient to sustain such life as they are willing to endure rather than resort to forcible revolution and expropriation. Z is out of employment. He has four children, and sees the possibility of a fifth. Suddenly a happy thought strikes him. "As long as I have only four children, I can get work, for I can afford to work for less than Y with his five children. I will become a Malthusian,—no, a Neo-Malthusian,—and apply the preventive check." Counting the few dollars and cents still left in his pocket, he finds that he can keep his family in bread for two days longer and still have enough left to buy a copy of Dr. Foote's "Radical Remedy in Social Science" and a syringe of the most improved pattern. He makes these prudential purchases, and presents them to his good wife. Mrs. Z's eyes fairly dance with delight at the new vistas of joy that open before her, and I, for one, am sincerely glad for her. That night witnesses a renewal of the Zs' honeymoon. The next day, buoyant and hopeful, Z presents himself at the office of Mr. Gradgrind, Y's employer. " Y," says he, "works for you at a dollar and seventy-five cents a day ; I will do the same work at a dollar and a half." " You're the very man I'm after," says Gradgrind, rubbing his hands ; "come to work to-morrow." When Y puts on his coat to go home, he is handed his envelope containing his pay and his discharge.

Y, who has never been out of work long enough to read

Malthus, and to whom that famous parson's gospel would now come all too late, lies awake all night discussing the dismal prospect with Mrs. Y. Far from experiencing a second honeymoon, they begin to wish they had never known a first. " But we must live somehow," finally concludes Y ; "half a loaf is better than no bread ; to-morrow I will go to Mr. Gradgrind and offer to work for a dollar and a half." He carries out his resolve. This time Gradgrind's glee knows no bounds ; he takes Y back into his employ, and resolves thereafter to worship at the shrine of Parson Malthus. That night X finds himself in Y's predicament of the night before. Time goes on. Y's five children, not getting enough to eat, grow paler and thinner, and finally the youngest and frailest is carried off to the cemetery. The preventive check in the Z family has resulted in a positive check in the Y family.

Meanwhile there has been no interruption of the movement started by Z. A fate similar to Y's has overtaken X, W, V, and all their alphabetical predecessors, till now A, most unfortunate of all, finds himself thrown on a cold world with five starving children. What happens then ? Driven from half loaf to quarter loaf, A tries to underbid Z, and that prudent individual, who has enjoyed a temporary prosperity at the expense of his fellows, is at last forced down again to the general level in order to hold his place. The net result of his Malthusian experiment is that A is out of employment instead of himself, one child has not been born, twenty-four have died from hunger, wages have fallen to a dollar and a half, and Gradgrind, richer than ever, begins to think that cranks amount to something, and is shaking hands with Walker over the approaching millennium.

Ah ! a bloody millennium it will be, Mr. Gradgrind, if you and Mr. Walker keep on. Do you see what A is about ? Too proud to go to the poor-house, too honest to steal, he has wandered in despair over to the Haymarket (I forgot to say that Chicago is the scene of my tragedy), and there has learned from one Parsons that all wealth belongs to everybody, that each should seize what he can, and that he, A, and his hungry children, with twenty-five cents' worth of dynamite, may live and loaf like princes and Gradgrinds forever. Straightway some one hands him a bomb, and he flings it into a squad of police. "What then? The earth is but shivered into impalpable smoke by that Doom's-thunderpeal ; the sun misses one of his planets in space, and thenceforth there are no eclipses of the moon."

To what stern, ay ! to what singular realities has my allegory brought us! A bloody revolution, and Malthusianism to blame! Walker, the Malthusian, sharing with Gradgrind, the robber, the responsibility for Parsons, the dynamiter! Loud as Mr. Walker may declaim against forcible revolution (and he can do so none too loud for me), his voice is sounding deeper tones, which will push the people to it. I call the attention of the authorities to his incendiary Malthusian utterances.

Is it to be inferred, then, that I discountenance small families? By no means. I highly approve them. Z's conduct was right and wise. He acted within his right. And his act was perfectly innocent in itself. It was not his fault that it injured others ; it was the fault of the monopolistic system which shrewdly manages to keep the demand for labor below the supply. Z could not be expected to damage himself in order to refrain from damaging others, as long as his conduct was of such a character that it would not have damaged others except for the existence of an economic system for which he was in no special sense to blame. Nevertheless it will not do to wink out of sight the fact that he did damage others, or to fail to learn from it the folly of supposing that any reform is fundamental in political economy except the achievement of Liberty in our industrial and commercial life.

AUBERON HERBERT AND HIS WORK.

[*Liberty*, May 23, 1885.]

AUBERON HERBERT, whose essay, "A Politician in Sight of Haven," creates such an enthusiasm for Liberty in the minds of all thinking people who read it, has recently published still another book of similar purport and purpose. He calls it "The Right and Wrong of Compulsion by the State : A Statement of the Moral Principles of the Party of Individual Liberty, and the Political Measures Founded Upon Them." It consists of a series of papers written for Joseph Cowen's paper, the Newcastle *Chronicle*, supplemented by a letter to the London *Times* on the English factory acts. Dedicated to Mr. Cowen's constituents, "The Workmen of Tyneside," it appeals with equal force to workmen the world over, and their welfare and their children's will depend upon the readiness with which they accept and the bravery with which they adhere to its all-important counsel. The book is a magnificent assault on the majority idea, a searching exposure of the inherent evil of State systems, and a glorious assertion of the inestimable benefits of voluntary action and free competition, reaching its climax in the emphatic declaration that "this question of power exercised by some men over other men is the greatest of all questions, the one that concerns the very foundations of society," upon the answer to which "must ultimately depend all ideas of right and wrong." This is a bold and, at first sight, an astonishing claim; but it is a true one, nevertheless, and the fact that Mr. Herbert makes it so confidently shows that he is inspired by the same idea that gave birth to this journal, caused it to be christened *Liberty*, and determined it to labor first and foremost for Anarchy, or the Abolition of the State.

This is no fitful outburst on Mr. Herbert's part. He evidently has enlisted for a campaign which will end only with victory. The book in question seems to be the second in a series of "Anti-Force Papers," which promises to include special papers dealing more elaborately, but in the light of the same general principle, with the matters of compulsory taxation, compulsory education, land ownership, professional monopolies, prohibitory liquor laws, legislation against vice, State regulation of love regulations, etc., etc. I know no more inspiring spectacle in England than that of this man of exceptionally high social position doing battle almost single-handed with the giant monster, government, and showing in it a mental rigor and vigor and a wealth of moral fervor rarely equalled in any cause. Its only parallel at the present day is to be found in the splendid attitude of Mr. Ruskin, whose earnest eloquence in behalf of economic equity rivals Mr. Herbert's in behalf of individual liberty.

This thought leads to the other, that each of these men lacks the truth that the other possesses. Mr. Ruskin sees very clearly the economic principle which makes all forms of usury unrighteous and wages for work the only true method of sustaining life, but he never perceives for a moment that individual human beings have sovereign rights over themselves. Mr. Herbert proves beyond question that the government of man by man is utterly without justification, but is quite ignorant of the fact that interest, rent, and profits will find no place in the perfect economic order. Mr. Ruskin's error is by far the more serious of the two, because the realization of Mr. Herbert's ideas would inevitably result in the equity that Mr. Ruskin sees, whereas this equity can never be achieved for any length of time without an at least partial fulfilment of individual liberty. Nevertheless it cannot be gainsaid that Mr. Herbert's failure to see the economic results of his ideas considerably impairs his power of carrying them home to men's hearts. Unfortunately, there are many people whom the most perfect deductive reasoning fails to convince. The beauty of a great principle and its harmonizing influence wherever it touches they are unable to appreciate. They can only see certain great and manifest wrongs, and they demand that these shall be righted. Unless they are clearly shown the connection between these wrongs and their real causes, they are almost sure to associate them with imaginary causes and to try the most futile and sometimes disastrous remedies. Now, the one great wrong that these people see to-day is the fact that industry and poverty commonly go hand in hand and are associated in the same persons, and the one thing that they are determined upon, regardless of everything else whatsoever, is that hereafter those who do the work of this world shall enjoy the wealth of this world. It is a righteous determination, and in it is to be found the true significance of the State-Socialistic movement which Mr. Herbert very properly condemns and yet only half understands. To meet it is the first necessity incumbent upon the friends of Liberty. It is sure that the workers can never permanently secure themselves in the control of their products except through the method of Liberty; but it is almost equally sure that, unless they are shown what Liberty will do for them in this respect, they will try every other method before they try Liberty. The necessity of showing them this Mr. Herbert, to be sure, dimly sees, but, the light not having dawned on himself, he cannot show it to others. He has to content himself, therefore, with such inadequate, unscientific, and partially charitable proposals as the formation of voluntary associations to furnish work to the unemployed. The working people will never thus be satisfied, and they ought not to be.

But Mr. Herbert can satisfy them if he can convince them of all that is implied in his advocacy of "complete free trade in all things." To many special phases of this free trade he does call marked attention, but never, I believe, to the most important of all, free trade in banking. If he would only dwell upon the evils of the money-issuing monopoly and emphasize with his great power the fact that competition, in this as in other matters, would give us all that is needed of the best possible article at the lowest possible price, thereby steadily reducing interest and rent to zero, putting capital within the comfortable reach of all deserving and enterprising people, and causing the greatest liberation on record of heretofore restricted energies, the laborers might then begin to see that here lies their only hope ; that Liberty, after all, and not Government, is to be their saviour; that their first duty is to abolish the credit monopoly and let credit organize itself; that then they will have to ask nobody for work, but everybody will be asking work of them ; and that then, instead of having to take whatever pittance they can get, they will be in a position to exact wages equivalent to their product, under which condition of things the reign of justice will be upon us and labor will have its own. Then Mr. Herbert's work for Liberty will no longer be a struggle, but an unmixed pleasure. He will no longer have to breast the current by urging workmen to self-denial ; he can successfully appeal to their self-interest, the tide will turn, and he will be borne onward with it to the ends that he desires.

SOLUTIONS OF THE LABOR PROBLEM.

[*Liberty*, September 12, 1891.]

APROPOS of Labor Day, the Boston *Herald* printed in its issue of September 6 a collection of proposed solutions of the labor problem, received in response to a question which it had invited certain students and labor leaders to answer. The question was this : " How is a just distribution of the products of labor to be obtained ? " The answers were from two hundred to five hundred words in length ; below I give the essence of each :

George E. McNeill, general organizer of the Federation of Labor :—By a reduction of the hours of labor.

Edward Atkinson, political economist :—If laborers think themselves inadequately rewarded, they should work for themselves. The " scabs " should have unions of their own.

Edward S. Huntington, secretary of the First Nationalist Club :—By the organization of an all-inclusive trust by the laborers.

Albert Ross (Lynn Boyd Porter), novelist :—No individuals can justly distribute the products of other men's labor. Hence the State must do it.

Charles E. Bowers, Nationalist :—By national control and management of industries.

H. R. Legate, leader of the Third Party :—By public ownership of the means of production and distribution.

Henry Abrahams, secretary of the Boston Central Labor Union :—Organization of trades ; reduction of the hours of labor ; co-operation.

William H. Sayward, secretary of the National Association of Builders :—Absolute justice in distribution is unattainable. Improvement can be made by joint consideration and united action of laborers and employers.

M. J. Bishop, State worthy foreman, K. of L.:—By organizing and educating the people to demand control of the natural monopolies and the transportation of intelligence, passengers, and freight.

P. C. Kelly, secretary-treasurer of the State Assembly and D. A. 30, K. of L.:—By the nationalization of mines, railroads, telegraphs, telephones, and the levying of income taxes

W. J. Shields, ex-president of the United Brotherhood of Carpenters and Joiners : — The producers should free themselves from private control of all natural monopolies, and substitute government control and management.

George D. Moulton, Socialist :—By Socialism, to be reached through reduction of the hours of labor and a gradual increase of wages.

Harry Lloyd, president of the Carpenters' District Council :—By reduction of the hours of labor, destruction of the wage system, co-operation, profit-sharing, and government ownership of land, mines, and patents.

Some of the solutions proposed in the foregoing answers are as inadequate as Mrs. Partington's broom, others were buried by their authors in a flow of sentimentalism, and still others were presented so unsystematically and unscientifically that they could not influence reasoning minds.

Besides these, however, there were two answers that were analytical, that showed a true conception of the requirements of the problem, and that made a systematic attempt to meet them. I have no bump of modesty, and so am able to say unblushingly that one of these was written by Edward Bellamy and the other by myself. I give them in full :

Edward Bellamy, author of " Looking Backward " and founder of Nationalism :—Workmen will not receive a just proportion of the product of their labor until they receive the whole product. In order to receive the whole product, they must receive the profits which now go to the employers, in addition to their wages. In order to receive the profits which now go to the employers, they must become their own employers. The only way by which they can become their own employers is to assume through their salaried agents the conduct of industry as they have already (in this country) assumed the conduct of political affairs. The president, governor, and mayor do not make a profit on the business of the nation, State, or city, as employers do upon the industries which they manage. These and all other public officials receive salaries only, as agents, the business being conducted for the benefit of the people as the principals.

There is no more sense in permitting the industrial affairs of this country to be run for private profit than there would be in permitting their political affairs to be so exploited. Our industries are just as properly public business as our politics, and a great deal more important to us all.

As soon as the people wake up to the realization of this fact, there will be no labor question left. There will be no ground left for a dispute between workmen and capitalists, for every one will be at one and the same time employer and employee.

Benjamin R. Tucker, Anarchist :—A just distribution of the products of labor is to be obtained by destroying all sources of income except labor. These sources may be summed up in one word,—usury ; and the three principal forms of usury are interest, rent, and profit. These all rest upon legal privilege and monopoly, and the way to destroy them is to destroy legal privilege and monopoly. The worst monopoly of all is that of the power to issue money, which power is now restricted to the holders of a certain kind of property,—government bonds and gold and silver. If the holders of all kinds of property were equally privileged to issue money, not as legal tender, but acceptable only on its merits, competition would reduce the rate of discount, and therefore of interest on capital, to the mere cost of banking, which is much less than one per cent. And even this percentage would not be interest, properly speaking, but simply payment for the labor and expense of banking. When money could be had at such a rate and capital bought with it, of course no one would borrow capital at a higher rate. Free competition in banking would thus abolish interest, all rent except ground rent, and all profit on merchandise not enjoying the benefit of some special monopoly.

In the absence of monopoly of any kind, whatever the merchant "makes" out of his business is not strictly profit, but the wages of mercantile labor, determined by competition. This wage is what will remain after the abolition of the money monopoly, of all tariffs and taxes on industry and trade, and of all patents and copyrights.

That form of usury known as ground rent rests on land monopoly; that is, on government protection of land titles not based on personal occupancy and use. If this protection were withdrawn, landlordism would disappear, and ground rent would thereafter exist no longer in its monopolistic form, but only in its economic form ; in other words, the only existing rent would be the advantage accruing to the owner and occupier from superiority of soil or site.

The growing diversity of industry, coupled with the greater mobility that will be enjoyed by labor as soon as greater mobility is given to capital by the abolition of the monopolies, will have a strong and constant tendency to neutralize the existing inequalities of soil and site, and thus economic rent will gradually approach its vanishing point. Thus the whole ground is covered, and all forms of usury are abolished. All the drains upon labor being stopped, labor will be left in possession of its product, which is the solution of the problem. This solution is that which Anarchism offers.

The contrast between the robust uprightness and straightforwardness of these two answers and the flaccid incoherence of most of the others emphasizes my constant contention that the labor problem is to be settled between extreme State Socialism and extreme Anarchism, and that the struggle will become clear and direct in proportion as all compromises disappear and leave an open field. When this struggle comes, the weak point in Mr. Bellamy's position will be located. I point it out in advance. It lies in his enormous assumptions that laborers, in order to receive the profits which now go to the employers, *must* become their own employers, and that the *only* way by which they can do this is to assume through their salaried agents the conduct of industry. The Anarchistic solution shows that there is no such *must* and no such *only*. When interest, rent, and profit disappear under the influence of free money, free land, and free trade, it will make no difference whether men work for themselves, or are employed, or employ others. In any case they can get nothing but that wage for their labor which free competition determines. Therefore they need not become their own employers. Perhaps, however, they will prefer to do so. But in that case they need not assume the conduct of industry through their salaried agents. There is another way. Any of them that choose will be enabled through mutual banking to secure means of production whereby to conduct whatever industry they desire. This other way, being the way of liberty, is the better way, and is destined to triumph over Mr. Bellamy's way, which is the way of authority and coercion.

I have reserved to the last the only remaining answer among those printed in the *Herald*, that of Frank K. Foster, editor of the *Labor Leader*. This, too, I give in full, because of its significance.

The prime factors making toward the unjust distribution of the products of labor are profits, rent, and interest. In his direct relation to the employer, or buyer of labor,—not necessarily a capitalist,—the laborer has a remedy in every agency that gives him greater equality of bargaining power. The scope of this remedy is limited by the margin of profit on the joint product of the laborer and the " captains of industry." In this class of agencies are to be reckoned the trades unions, and their influences of agitation and education. Incidentally, the problems of immigration, of mobility of labor, and of the unwise and selfish competition (between the laborers themselves) for employment, are allied to this branch of the subject. Broadly speaking, in the field of adult labor, the principle of free association may be trusted to supply a remedy that shall adjust the supply of labor to meet the demand, and, by raising wages and regulating conditions, obtain for the laborer his just share of the profits of production. As wage earners, it is with this economic side of the question we have mainly to do.

The problems of rent and interest are not, in the same sense, class questions, for they affect the man who buys and the man who sells the commodity of labor. The wage earner, as a unit in the productive social system, is concerned, however, in the promotion of those reforms which will lessen the power of monopoly in land and money, and thus make a larger margin of profit upon production to be divided between himself and employer.

The taxation of land held for speculative purposes to its full market value, the abolition of special privileges granted by the State to bankers, and the repeal of tariff laws taxing the many for the enrichment of the few, are among the more, important remedies of this class.

Absolutely just distribution of the products of labor and absolute freedom from oppression by the possessors of power and pelf is only to be looked for in an ideal social state made up of creatures vastly different from the race in whose veins circulates the blood of old Adam.

It is surely a reasonable hope that justice and liberty may develop with the increasing years, and to my mind this development will come, not by legislative enactment, but through the broader avenue of the education and upbuilding of the individuals composing our complex civilization.

This remarkable utterance, in everything except its sentimental remark about " unwise and selfish competition " and its inconsistent adherence to the single-tax fallacy, is thoroughly Anarchistic, and shows that its author, not long ago a stanch State Socialist, has already accepted the " better way " of liberty.

KARL MARX AS FRIEND AND FOE.

[*Liberty*, April 14, 1883.]

By the death of Karl Marx the cause of labor has lost one of the most faithful friends it ever had. *Liberty* says thus much in hearty tribute to the sincerity and hearty steadfastness of the man who, perhaps to a greater extent than any other, represented, by nature and by doctrine, the principle of authority which we live to combat. Anarchism knew in him its bitterest enemy, and yet every Anarchist must hold his memory in respect. Strangely mingled feelings of admiration and abhorrence are simultaneously inspired in us by contemplation of this great man's career. Toward the two fundamental principles of the revolution of to-day he occupied an exactly contradictory attitude. Intense as was his love of equality, no less so was his hatred of liberty. The former found expression in one of the most masterly expositions of the infamous nature and office of capital ever put into print ; the latter in a sweeping scheme of State supremacy and absorption, involving a practical annihilation of the individual.

The enormous service done by the one was well-nigh neutralized by the injurious effects resulting from his advocacy of the other. For Karl Marx, the *égalitaire*, we feel the profoundest respect ; as for Karl Marx, the *autoritaire*, we must consider him an enemy. *Liberty* said as much in its first issue, and sees no reason to change its mind. He was an honest man, a strong man, a humanitarian, and the promulgator of much vitally important truth, but on the most vital question of politics and economy he was persistently and irretrievably mistaken.

We cannot, then, join in the thoughtless, indiscreet, and indiscriminate laudation of his memory indulged in so generally by the labor press and on the labor platform. Perhaps, however, we might pass it by without protest, did it not involve injustice and ingratitude to other and greater men. The extravagant claim of precedence as a radical political economist put forward for Karl Marx by his friends must not be allowed to overshadow the work of his superiors. We give an instance of this claim, taken from the resolutions passed unanimously by the great Cooper Union meeting held in honor of Marx : "In the field of economic social science he was the first to prove by statistical facts and by reasoning based upon universally recognized principles of political economy that capitalistic production must necessarily lead to the monopolizing and concentrating of all industry into the hands of a few, and thus, by robbing the working class of the fruits of their toil, reduce them to absolute slavery and degradation." These words were read to the audience in English by Philip Van Patten and in German by our worthy comrade, Justus Schwab. Is it possible that these men are so utterly unacquainted with the literature of Socialism that they do not know this statement to be false, and that the tendency and consequence of capitalistic production referred to were demonstrated to the world time and again during the twenty years preceding the publication of "Das Kapital," with a wealth of learning, a cogency and subtlety of reasoning, and an ardor of style to which Karl Marx could not so much as pretend? In the numerous works of P. J. Proudhon, published between 1840 and 1860, this notable truth was turned over and over and inside out until well-nigh every phase of it had been presented to the light.

What was the economic theory developed by Karl Marx ? That we may not be accused of stating it unfairly, we give below an admirable outline of it drawn by Benoit Malon, a prominent French Socialist, in sympathy with Marx's thought.

Aside from the special purpose which we have in quoting it, it is in itself well worth the space which it requires, being in the main a succinct and concise statement of the true principles of political economy :

All societies that have existed thus far in history have one common characteristic,—the struggle of classes. Revolutions have changed the conditions of this struggle, but have not suppressed it. Though the *bourgeoisie* has taken the place of feudalism, which was itself the successor of the old patrician order, and though slavery and serfdom have been succeeded by the *prolétariat*, the situation has retained these two distinctive characteristics,—" the merciless oppression and exploitation of the inferior class by the dominant class, and the struggle, either open or concealed, but deadly and constant, of the classes thus confronting each other."

The *bourgeoisie*, to obtain power, had to invoke political and economic liberty. In the name of the latter, which it has falsified, and aided by scientific and industrial progress, it has revolutionized production and inaugurated the system of capitalistic production under which all wealth appears as an immense accumulation of merchandise formed elementarily upon an isolated quantity of that wealth.

Everything destined for the satisfaction of a human need has a value of utility ; as merchandise it has a value of exchange. Value of exchange is the quantitative relation governing the equivalence and exchangeability of useful objects.

As the most eminent economists have shown, notably Ricardo, this quantitative relation, this measure of value, is time spent in labor. This, of course, can refer only to the amount of labor necessary upon an average and performed with average skill, mechanical facilities, and industry under the normal industrial conditions of the day.

It seems, therefore, that every one should be able to buy, in return for his labor, an amount of utilities and exchangeable values equivalent to those produced by him.

Nevertheless, such is not the case. " The accumulation of wealth at one of the poles of society keeps pace with the accumulation, at the other pole, of the misery, subjection, and moral degradation of the class from whose product capital is born."

How happens this ? Because, by a series of robberies which, though sometimes legal, are none the less real, the productive forces, as fast as they have come into play, have been appropriated by privileged persons who, thanks to this *instrumentum regni*, control labor and exploit laborers.

To-day he who is destined to become a capitalist goes into the market furnished with money. He first buys tools and raw materials, and then, in order to operate them, buys the workingman's power of labor, the sole source of value. He sets them to work. The total product goes into the capitalist's hands, who sells it for more than it cost him. Of the plus-value capital is born ; it increases in proportion to the quantity of plus-value or labor not paid for. All capital, then, is an accumulation of the surplus labor of another, or labor not paid for in wages.

For this singular state of things individuals are not to be held responsible ; it is the result of our capitalistic society, for all events, all individual acts are but the *processus* of inevitable forces slowly modifiable, since, ' when a society has succeeded in discovering the path of the natural law which governs its movement, it can neither clear it at a leap nor abolish

by decree the phases of its natural development. But it can shorten the
period of gestation and lessen the pains of delivery."

We cannot, then, go against the tendencies of a society, but only direct
them toward the general good. So capitalistic society goes on irresistibly concentrating capital.

To attempt to stop this movement would be puerile ; the necessary
step is to pass from the inevitable monopolization of the forces of production and circulation to their nationalization, and that by a series of
legal measures resulting from the capture of political power by the working classes.

In the meantime the evil will grow. By virtue of the law of wages the
increase in the productivity of labor by the perfecting of machinery increases the frequency of dull seasons and makes poverty more general by
diminishing the demand for and augmenting the supply of laborers.

That is easily understood.

For the natural production of values of utility determined and regulated
by real or fancied needs, which was in vogue until the eighteenth century,
is substituted the mercantile production of values of exchange,—a production without rule or measure, which runs after the buyer and stops in its
headlong course only when the markets of the world are gorged to over-
flowing. Then millions out of the hundreds of millions of *prolétaires*
who have been engaged in this production are thrown out of work and
their ranks are thinned by hunger, all in consequence of the superabun-
dance created by an unregulated production.

The new economic forces which the *bourgeoisie* has appropriated have
not completed their development, and even now the *bourgeois* envelope
of capitalistic production can no longer contain them. Just as industry
on a small scale was violently broken down because it obstructed production, so capitalistic privileges, beginning to obstruct the production which
they developed, will be broken down in their turn ; for the concentration
of the means of production and the socialization of labor are reaching a
point which renders them incompatible with their capitalistic envelope.

At this point the *prolétariat*, like the *bourgeoisie*, will seize political
power for the purpose of abolishing classes and socializing the forces of
production and circulation in the same order that they have been monopolized by capitalistic feudalism.

The foregoing is an admirable argument, and *Liberty* en-
dorses the whole of it, excepting a few phrases concerning the
nationalization of industry and the assumption of political
power by the working people ; but it contains literally nothing
in substantiation of the claim made for Marx in the Cooper
Institute resolutions. Proudhon was years before Marx with
nearly every link in this logical chain. We stand ready to give
volume, chapter, and page of his writings for the historical
persistence of class struggles in successive manifestations, for
the *bourgeoisie's* appeal to liberty and its infidelity thereto, for
the theory that labor is the source and measure of value, for
the laborer's inability to repurchase his product in consequence
of the privileged capitalist's practice of keeping back a part of
it from his wages, and for the process of the monopolistic concentration of capital and its disastrous results. The vital dif-

ference between Proudhon and Marx is to be found in the respective remedies which they proposed. Marx would nationalize the productive and distributive forces ; Proudhon would individualize and associate them. Marx would make the laborers political masters ; Proudhon would abolish political mastership entirely. Marx would abolish usury by having the State lay violent hands on all industry and business and conduct it on the cost principle ; Proudhon would abolish usury by disconnecting the State entirely from industry and business and forming a system of free banks which would furnish credit at cost to every industrious and deserving person, and thus place the means of production within the reach of all. Marx believed in compulsory majority rule ; Proudhon believed in the voluntary principle. In short, Marx was an *autoritaire ;* Proudhon was a champion of Liberty.

Call Marx, then, the father of State Socialism, if you will ; but we dispute his paternity of the general principles of economy on which all schools of Socialism agree. To be sure, it is not of the greatest consequence who was first with these doctrines. As Proudhon himself asks : " Do we eulogize the man who first perceives the dawn ? " But if any discrimination is to be made, let it be a just one. There is much, very much that can be truly said in honor of Karl Marx. Let us be satisfied with that, then, and not attempt to magnify his grandeur by denying, belittling, or ignoring the services of men greater than he.

DO THE KNIGHTS OF LABOR LOVE LIBERTY?

[*Liberty*, February 20, 1886.]

To the Editor of Liberty:

In *Liberty* of January 9 I see, in your notice of our friend, Henry Appleton, having become the editor of the *Newsman*, this precautionary language, or mild censure, from you to him : " Will he pardon me if I add that I look with grave doubts upon his advice to newsdealers to join the Knights of Labor ? His own powerful pen has often clearly pointed out in these columns the evils of that organization and of all others similar to it." And further on you say : " A significant hint of what may be expected from the Knights of Labor is to be found in the address of Grand Master Powderly, the head and front of that body, before its latest national convention. He said in most emphatic terms that it would not do for the organization to simply frown upon the use of dynamite, but that *any member hereafter advocating the use of dynamite must be summarily expelled.*"

Now, I do not know how much you know about the Knights of Labor, nor do I know how much our friend, Henry Appleton, knows about the Knights of Labor. But this much I am impelled to say after reading your reproving strictures,—that it is neither safe, prudent, or wise to condemn or censure any body of liberty-loving and earnestly truth-seeking people who are associated together to enlighten themselves as to what real Liberty is as well as to what are their most important and highest natural rights, duties, or privileges without a full knowledge of their objects, aims, and their methods to promote and achieve them. I can further confidently say that I have for more than forty years been an earnest seeker for these all-important natural scientific principles as taught or set forth by the most advanced individual thinkers or defenders of *Liberty*,—real *Anarchists*, if you please,—and I have found more persons holding said views and seeking the knowledge of these natural, inalienable laws or principles of scientific government among the members of this condemned association or school than I ever found outside of it. And I am confident that I can find more friends and earnest defenders of *Liberty* in its ranks than I can find outside of it. In fact, this school was founded to place Labor on a scientific basis and teach individual self-government at the expense of the individual without invading or infringing on the rights of others. Therefore, notwithstanding the opinions you have formed or the conclusions you may have arrived at in regard to this association or school, I fully indorse Friend Appleton's advice to the newsmen as well as all other useful workers who are in pursuit of Liberty, truth, justice, and a knowledge of their natural rights and highest duties. And although this association or school may be composed of a large majority of members who are laboring under the disadvantages of previous superstition, education, or training by the bossism of Church and State, nevertheless I esteem it the best opportunity, opening, or school in which to free them from said superstitions that I have ever met with, and for which the best minds in said school are constantly and earnestly laboring. And pardon me, Friend Tucker, for the suggestion that perhaps, if you knew more about their objects, aims, and methods, you might think better of them than you now do.

FAIR PLAY.

Criticism from a man like " Fair Play," whom I know to be a real knight of labor, whether nominally one or not, is always welcome in these columns, and will always deserve and secure my attention. In attending to it in this special case my first business is to repeat what I have said already,—that I misquoted Henry Appleton, that he has never advised newsdealers to join the Knights of Labor, and that he is as much opposed to the principles and purposes of that order as I am.

I don't pretend to know very much about the Knights of Labor, but I know enough to make it needless to know more. I know, for instance, their " Declaration of Principles," and my fatal objections to these principles, or most of them, no additional knowledge of the order could possibly obviate or in any way invalidate or weaken. Of them the preamble itself says: " Most of the objects herein set forth can only be obtained through legislation, and it is the duty of all to assist in

nominating and supporting with their votes only such candidates as will pledge their support to those measures, regardless
of party." Does "Fair Play" mean to tell me that he knows
of any "real Anarchist" who consents to stultify himself by
belonging to a society founded on that proposition? If he
does, I answer that that man either does not know what Anarchy means, or else is as false to his principles as would be
an Infidel who should subscribe to the creed of John Calvin.
Anarchy and this position are utterly irreconcilable; and no
man who understands both of them (with the possible exception of Stephen Pearl Andrews) would ever attempt to reconcile them.

But what are these objects which these "liberty-loving"
people expect to realize by that eminently Anarchistic weapon,
the ballot? The "Declaration" goes on to state them. "We
demand at the hands of the State" (think of an Anarchist
demanding anything of the State except its death!):

"That all lands now held for speculative purposes be taxed
to their full value." How long since taxation became an
Anarchistic measure? It is my impression that Anarchists
look upon taxation as the bottom tyranny of all.

"The enactment of laws to compel corporations to pay
their employees weekly in lawful money." Anarchism practically rests upon freedom of contract. Does not this impair
it? What party, outside of the makers of a contract, has any
right to decide its conditions?

"The enactment of laws providing for arbitration between
employers and employed, and to enforce the decision of the
arbitrators." That is, the State must fix the rate of wages
and the conditions of the performance of labor. The Anarchist who would indorse that must be a curiosity.

"The prohibition by law of the employment of children
under fifteen years of age in workshops, mines, and factories."
In other words, a boy of fourteen shall not be allowed to
choose his occupation. What Anarchist takes this position?

"That a graduated income tax be levied." How this would
lessen the sphere of government!

"The establishment of a national monetary system, in which
a circulating medium in necessary quantity shall issue direct
to the people without the intervention of banks; that all the
national issue shall be full legal tender in payment of all
debts, public and private; and that the government shall not
guarantee or recognize private banks, or create any banking
corporations." If "Fair Play" knows of any Anarchists who
have subscribed to this, I wish he would furnish their ad-

dresses. I should like to send them Colonel Greene's Mutual
Banking" and the keen and powerful chapter of Lysander
Spooner's " Letter to Grover Cleveland " which treats of the
congressional crime of altering contracts by legal-tender laws.
Perhaps they might thus be brought to their senses.

But need I, as I easily might, extend this list of tyrannical
measures to convince Friend " Fair Play " that, however much
I might know about the Knights of Labor, I could not think
better of them than I now do?

The trouble is that " Fair Play " and reformers generally do
not yet know what to make of such a phenomenon in journalism as a radical reform paper which, instead of offering the
right hand of fellowship to everything *calling itself* radical
and reformatory, adopts a principle for its compass and steers
a straight course by it. They all like it first-rate until its
course conflicts with theirs. Then they exclaim in horror. I
am sorry to thus shock them, but I cannot help it ; I must
keep straight on. When I launched this little newspaper craft,
I hoisted the flag of Liberty. I hoisted it not as a name
merely, but as a vital principle, by which I mean to live and
die. With the valued aid of " Fair Play " and others, added
to my own efforts, it has been kept flying steadily at the mast-
head. It has not been lowered an inch, and, while I have
strength to defend it, it never will be. And if any man attempts to pull it down, I care not who he may be, Knight of
Capital or Knight of Labor, I propose, at least with mental
and moral ammunition, to " shoot him on the spot."

PLAY-HOUSE PHILANTHROPY.

[*Liberty*, November 26, 1881.]

AMONG the ablest and most interesting contributions to the
columns of the *Irish World* are the sketches of one of its
staff correspondents, " Honorius," in which that writer, week
after week, with all the skill and strategy of a born general,
marshals anecdote, illustration, history, biography, fact, logic,
and the experiences of every-day life in impregnable line of
battle, and precipitates them upon the cohorts of organized
tyranny and theft, making irreparable breaches in their fortifi-
cations, and spreading havoc throughout their ranks. The
ingenuity which he displays in utilizing his material and turning everything to the account of his cause is marvellous. Out

of each new fact that falls under his notice, out of each new
character with whom he comes in contact, he develops some
fresh argument against the system of theft that underlies our
so-called "civilization," some novel application of the principles that must underlie the coming true society.

Unless we are greatly mistaken, the latest of his assaults will
not prove the least effective, since in it he has improved an
excellent opportunity to turn his guns upon enemies nearer
home, enemies in the guise of friends. He briefly tells the
story of the career of a Yorkshire factory-lord, one Sir Titus
Salt, who, through his fortunate discovery of the process of
manufacturing alpaca cloth, accumulated an enormous fortune,
which he expended in the establishment of institutions for the
benefit of his employees and in deeds of general philanthropy.
To this man he pays a tribute of praise for various virtues,
which, for aught we know, is well deserved. But he supplements it by forcible insistance on the fact that Sir Titus was
but a thief after all; that, however great his generosity of
heart, it was exercised in the distribution of other people's
earnings ; and that his title to exemption from the condemnation of honest men was no better than that of the more merciful of the Southern slave-owners. The importance of this
lesson it is impossible to overestimate. Gains are no less ill-
gotten because well-given. Philanthropy cannot palliate plunder. Robbery, though it be not born of rapacity, is robbery
still. This Sir Titus Salt but serves as a type of a large class of
individuals who are ever winning the applause and admiration
of a world too prone to accept benevolence and charity in the
stead of justice and righteousness.

Perhaps the most conspicuous example of the class referred
to now posing before the world is the man referred to by
" Honorius " in connection and comparison with Sir Titus,—
Godin of Guise, the famous founder of the *Familisterre*. "The
great Godin of Guise," " Honorius " styles him ; and it is precisely because this clear-headed writer, misinformed as to the
real facts, makes him the object of exaggerated and misplaced
adulation that the present article is written. Of Sir Titus Salt
we could not speak, but of the *Familisterre* and its founder
we can say somewhat that may interest and enlighten their
admirers. But first the words of " Honorius ":

Sir Titus Salt was the companion, as a noble-souled employer, to that
fellow-philanthropist, the great Godin of Guise, who founded the famous
social palace known as the *Familisterre*, although not so grand a character
as the renowned Frenchman. Titus Salt was a sectarian. His $80,000
church was for the "accommodation" of his own sect, and those who held

to other creeds found no place of worship from his money. Godin was a grand, liberal soul. Though educated a Catholic, he made the most liberal provision for every shade of belief among his working people, and he despised every form of narrowness and bigotry. Godin, too, was too noble a soul to descend to the arts of the politician, and would have despised himself had he solicited a vote from any of his people. So wonderful was the success of his industrial experiment at Guise that Louis Napoleon became jealous of the possibilities for labor which he had demonstrated, and that despicable fraud and royal scoundrel, "Louis the Little," repeatedly went out of his way to hamper his business, and even sought to disfranchise him.

Let us see how much of this is true,—if this man is really great, or only a pretender and a sham. It was once our privilege to visit the *Familisterre*. The visit extended through the better part of a week, and occurred at a very favorable time, including one of the two annual *fête* days (celebrating Education and Labor) peculiar to the institution. But the impression left on our mind was by no means favorable. The establishment seemed pervaded throughout by an atmosphere of supervision and routine, tempered here and there by awkward attempts at the picturesque. The air of buoyant contentment which the glowing accounts given of the Social Palace would lead one to expect did not characterize the members of the large household to any great extent. The workmen seemed to feel themselves and their class still the victims of oppression. A very slight acquaintance with them was sufficient to reveal the fact that their "boss" and "benefactor" does not appear as godlike in their eyes as in those that view him at a distance. In the presence of the inquiring observer their faces assumed an expression that seemed to say: "Oh, you think it's all very pretty, no doubt: no rags here, no dirt; everything clean and orderly, and a moderate degree of external comfort among us all. But all this has to be paid for by somebody, and it is the outside world that foots the bills. Our master has the reputation of being very kind and generous, but *he is our master*. We enjoy this material welfare at the expense of something of our independence. Besides, he's got a soft thing of it,—rolling up his millions year by year and excusing himself by distributing a certain proportion of his stealings among us; but he and the rest of us are living very largely on our fellow-laborers elsewhere, out of whose pockets these immense profits come."

And actual questioning proved that their faces told the truth. Inabilty to converse fluently in French prevented us from inquiring closely into details; but from an intelligent young Russian visiting the place at the same time and on much the same mission as ourselves, whose knowledge of French and English was excellent, we elicited information quite sufficient. The more intelligent of the workmen had told him confidentially just what we had read in their faces as stated above, not a few of them confessing that M. Godin, who at that time was a member of the National Chamber of Deputies, held his seat by a method strikingly similar to that which in Massachusetts the Boston *Herald* is wont to apologize for as "civilized bulldozing,"—that is, prior to election day he contrived to have it understood among his employees that a convenient opportunity would be found for the discharge of such of them as should fail to vote for him, no matter what their previous political affiliations or present political beliefs. And yet "Honorius" says (or seems to hint) that he is not ambitious, and "Honorius" is an honorable man. Hundreds and thousands of honorable men share the same delusion,—for a delusion it certainly is.

A strange sort of "philanthropist," this! A singular "nobility of soul" is M. Godin's! His religious liberality referred to by "Honorius" evidently does not extend into his business and politics. Here is a man, ingenious, shrewd, calculating, with large executive capacity and something of a taste for philosophy, who discovers an industrial process which, through a monopoly guaranteed by the patent laws, he is enabled to carry on at an enormous profit ; he employs hundreds of operatives ; for them and their families he builds a gigantic home, which he dignifies by the name of a palace, though it needs but a few bolts and bars to make it seem more like a prison, so cheerless, formal, and forbidding is its gloomy aspect ; he distributes among them a portion of the profits, perhaps to quiet his conscience, perhaps to become noted for fair ; dealing and philanthropy ; the balance—more than sufficient to satisfy the ordinary manufacturer subject to competition—he complacently pockets, putting forth, meanwhile, the ridiculous pretence that he holds this fund as a trustee ; finally, knowing nothing of Liberty and Equity and sneering at their defenders, he professes to think that he can regenerate the world by the fanciful and unsound schemes of education that he spends his leisure hours in devising and realizing, supporting them with wealth gained by theft, power gained by indirect bribery and bulldozing, and popularity gained by pretence and humbuggery. Nevertheless, for doing this the whole humanitarian world and not a few hard-headed reformers bow down and worship him: Even clear-sighted "Honorius" heaps honors on his head. But "Honorius" knows, and does not

---

fail to emphasize, the true lesson of the man's life, which is that the impending social revolution has certain fixed principles behind it ; that one of these principles is, " Thou shalt not steal " ; that any scheme by which a single individual becomes inordinately rich, whether as proprietor or trustee (unless the trust be purely voluntary), is necessarily carried on in violation of that principle ; and that whoever prosecutes it as in accordance with that principle thereby proves himself either too ignorant or too insincere to be allowed to serve, much less to lead, in the revolutionary movement. Such a man is of the plunderers, and should be with them. Idolsmashing is no enviable task ; but to unmask the pretensions of play-house philanthropists whose highest conception of distributive justice seems to be the sharing with a fortunate few of goods stolen from the many is a service that, however disagreeable, is of prime necessity in the realization of that Equity which distributes to each the product of his labor and that Liberty which renders it impossible for one to reap the profit of another's toil.

BEWARE OF BATTERSON!

[*Liberty*, March 6, 1886.]

GERTRUDE B. KELLY, who, by her articles in *Liberty*, has placed herself at a single bound among the foremost radical writers of this or any other country, exposes elsewhere in a masterful manner the unique scheme of one Batterson, an employer of labor in Westerly, R. I., which he calls co-operation. But there is one feature of this scheme, the most iniquitous of all, which needs still further emphasis. It is to be found in the provision which stipulates that no workman discharged for good cause or leaving the employ of the company without the written consent of the superintendent shall be allowed even that part of the annual dividend to labor to which he is entitled by such labor as he has already performed that year. In this lies cunningly hidden the whole motive of the plot. By promising to give labor at the end of the year the paltry sum of one third of such profits as are left after the stockholders have gobbled six per cent. on their investment, and adding that not even a proportional part of this dividend shall be given to labor if it quits work before the end of the year, this Batterson deprives the laborers of the only weapon of self-defence now within their reach,—the strike,—and leaves them utterly defenceless until they shall become intelligent enough to know the value and learn the use of Anarchistic methods and weapons.

Having got his laborers thus thoroughly in his power, and after waiting long enough to establish their confidence in him and his scheme, Batterson's next step will probably be to gradually screw down the wages. The laborers will have to submit to each reduction as it comes, or lose their dividend; and for the average laborer there is such a charm in the word "dividend" that he will go to the verge of starvation before giving it up. Now, of every dollar which Batterson thus manages to squeeze out of labor, only forty cents or less will come back to labor in the shape of dividend, the balance going into capital's pockets. Hence it is obvious that the reducing process will have to be kept up but a short time before capital's income will be larger and labor's income less than before the adoption of this philanthropic scheme of "co-operation." And, moreover, capital will thereby secure the additional advantage of feeling entirely independent of labor and will not have to lie awake nights in anticipation of a strike, knowing that, however rigorously it may apply the lash, its slaves will still be dumb.

Additional evidence that this is Batterson's plan is to be found in the further stipulation that no dividend will be allowed to superintendents, overseers, bookkeepers, clerks, or any employees except the manual laborers. Why? • *Because these never strike.* As it is not within their power to temporarily cripple his business, Batterson has no motive to offer them even a phantom dividend.

Altogether, this is one of the wiliest and foulest plots against industry ever hatched in the brain of a member of the robber class. But, though capital, by some such method as this, may succeed in suppressing strikes for a time, it will thereby only close the safety-valve; the great and final strike will be the more violent when it breaks out. If the laborers do not beware of Batterson now, the day will come when it will behoove Batterson to beware of them.

A GRATIFYING DISCOVERY.

[*Liberty*, May 31, 1884.]

Liberty made its first appearance in August, 1881. Of
that issue a great many sample copies were mailed to selected
addresses all over the world. Not one of these, however, was
sent from this office directly to Nantucket, for I had never
heard of a radical on that island. But, through some channel
or other, a copy found its way thither; for, before the second
number had been issued, an envelope bearing the Nantucket
postmark came to me containing a greeting for *Liberty*, than
which the paper has had none since more warm, more hearty,
more sympathetic, more intelligent, more appreciative.

But the letter was anonymous. Its style and language,
however, showed its writer to be a very superior person,
which fact, of course, added value to the substance of its
contents. The writer expressed his unqualified approval of
the political and social doctrines enunciated in the first number of *Liberty* (and certainly in no number since have those
doctrines been stated more boldly and nakedly than in that
one), saying that these views had been held by him for years,
and that the advent of an organ for their dissemination was
what he had long been waiting for. He gently chided *Liberty*, nevertheless, for its anti-religious attitude, not so much
apparently from any counter-attitude of his own or from any
personal sensitiveness in that direction, as from a feeling that
religious beliefs are essentially private in their nature and so
peculiar to the individuals holding them as to exempt them
from public consideration and criticism. After admonishing
Liberty to abandon this objectionable feature of its policy,
the letter closed by saying that I did not need to know the
writer's name, but, for the dollar enclosed, I might send the
paper regularly to "Post Office Box No. 22, Nantucket,
Mass."

Only the substance of the letter is given above, the manuscript having been inadvertently destroyed with an accumulation of others some time ago. To the given address *Liberty*
has regularly gone, and I never failed to wonder, when mail-
ing-day came, as to the identity of the mysterious Nan-
tucketer.

Lately came the revelation. It will be remembered that a
death occurred in Nantucket a few weeks ago which attracted

the attention of the whole country and occasioned columns of newspaper tribute and comment. In reading the various obituaries of the deceased, I learned that he was a man who had thought much and written radically on political subjects with a most decided trend toward complete individual liberty, that, nevertheless, he had been brought up in the Roman Catholic church, and to the end of his life was outwardly connected with it, though refusing on his death-bed to admit the priests to his presence for the administration of the sacrament; and that, though a member of a profession which necessarily made him a public man, he had always shunned publicity and notoriety in every way possible.

As these facts simultaneously presented themselves, the thought suddenly flashed upon my mind that I had found the holder of Box No. 22. Through a relative visiting Nantucket I instituted inquiries at the post-office on that island, and was promptly notified that the box in question had been rented for the past few years by the late Charles O'Conor. It was as I expected. The text of his letter, alas! is gone, but not its substance from my memory. The extracts from his published writings soon to appear in these columns will show how extreme a radical he was in his attitude towards governments, although in them he never expressed the fundamental thought acknowledged in his letter to me. Perhaps he regarded that as too strong meat for babes.

I am no hero-worshipper in the usual sense of that term, and among the friends of *Liberty* there are a number of humbler men than Charles O'Conor, whose approval I value even more highly than his; but none the less is it with extreme gratification that I now authoritatively record the fact that the great lawyer whose wonderful eloquence and searching intellectual power kept him for two decades the acknowledged head of the American bar, far from being the Bourbon which an ignorant and dishonest press has pictured him, was a thorough-going Anarchist.

CASES OF LAMENTABLE LONGEVITY.

[*Liberty*, March, 31, 1888.]

THE Emperor William is dead at the age of ninety-one. His was a long life, and that is the worst of it. Much may be forgiven to a tyrant who has the decency to die young.

But to the memory of one who thus prolongs and piles up the agony no mercy can be shown. As Brick Pomeroy says, there is such a thing as enough. In ninety-one years of such a man as William, Germany and the world had altogether too much. However, it is not kings alone that live too long. That awful fate sometimes befalls poets. Among others it has overtaken Walt Whitman. That he should live long enough to so far civilize his " barbaric yawp " as to sound it over the roofs of the world to bewail Germany's loss of her " faithful shepherd," and should do it too by the unseemly aid of the electric telegraph at the bidding of a capitalistic newspaper and presumably for hire, thus presenting the revolting spectacle of a once manly purity lapsing into prostitution in its old age, is indeed a woful example of superfluity of years. The propensity of poets of the people, once past their singing days, to lift their cracked voices in laudation of the oppressors of the people, burning what they once worshipped and worshipping what they once burned, tends to reconcile one to the otherwise unendurable thought that Shelley and Byron were scarcely suffered to outlive their boyhood. The fall of Russell Lowell was a terrible disappointment to those who never tire of reading the " Big'low Papers " and know " The Present Crisis " by heart, but the bitterness of their cup is honey beside the wormwood which all lovers of " Leaves of Grass " must have tasted when they read the lament of the Bard of Democracy over the death of the tyrant William. As one of his most enthusiastic admirers, I beseech Walt Whitman to let the rest be silence, and not again force upon us the haunting vision of what he once described, in the days when he still could write, as a " sad, hasty, unwaked somnambule, walking the dusk."

SPOONER MEMORIAL RESOLUTIONS.*

[*Liberty*, May 28, 1887.]

Resolved : That Lysander Spooner, to celebrate whose life and to lament whose death we meet to-day, built for himself, by his half century's study and promulgation of the science of justice, a monument which no words of ours, however elo-

---

* Offered by the author of this volume at the Lysander Spooner Memorial Services held in Wells Memorial Hall, Boston, on Sunday, May 29, 1887.

quent, can make more lasting or more lofty ; that each of his
fifty years and more of manhood work and warfare added so
massive a stone to the column of his high endeavor that now
it towers beyond our reach ; but that nevertheless it is meet,
for our own satisfaction and the world's welfare, that we
who knew him best should place on record and proclaim as
publicly as we may our admiration, honor, and reverence for
his exceptional character and career, our gratitude for the
wisdom which he has imparted to us, and our determination
so to spread the light for which we are thus indebted that
others may share with us the burden and the blessing of this
inextinguishable debt.

Resolved : That we recognize in Lysander Spooner a man
of intellect, a man of heart, and a man of will ; that as a man
of intellect his thought was keen, clear, penetrating, incisive,
logical, orderly, careful, convincing, and crushing, and set
forth withal in a style of singular strength, purity, and individuality which needed to employ none of the devices of
rhetoric to charm the intelligent reader ; that as a man of
heart he was a good hater and a good lover,—hating suffering, woe, want, injustice, cruelty, oppression, slavery, hypocrisy, and falsehood, and loving happiness, joy, prosperity,
justice, kindness, equality, liberty, sincerity, and truth ; that
as a man of will he was firm, pertinacious, tireless, obdurate,
sanguine, scornful, and sure ; and that all these virtues of
intellect, heart, and will lay hidden beneath a modesty of
demeanor, a simplicity of life, and a beaming majesty of
countenance which, combined with the venerable aspect of his
later years, gave him the appearance, as he walked our busy
streets, of some patriarch or philosopher of old, and made
him a personage delightful to meet and beautiful to look
upon.

Resolved : That, whether in his assaults upon religious
superstition, or in his battle with chattel slavery, or in his
challenge of the government postal monopoly, or in his many
onslaughts upon the banking monopoly, or in his vehement
appeal to the Irish peasantry to throw off the dominion of
privileged lords over themselves and their lands, or in his
denunciation of prohibitory laws, or in his dissection of the
protective tariff, or in his exposure of the ballot as an instrument of tyranny, or in his denial of the right to levy compulsory taxes, or in his demonstration that Constitutions and
statutes are binding upon nobody, or in the final concentration
of all his energies for the overthrow of the State itself, the
cause and sustenance of nearly all the evils against which he

had previously struggled, he ever showed himself the faithful soldier of Absolute Individual Liberty.

Resolved: That, while he fought this good fight and kept the faith, he did not finish his course, for his goal was in the eternities ; that, starting in his youth in pursuit of truth, he kept it up through a vigorous manhood, undeterred by poverty, neglect, or scorn, and in his later life relaxed his energies not one jot ; that his mental vigor seemed to grow as his physical powers declined ; that, although, counting his age by years, he was an octogenarian, we chiefly mourn his death, not as that of an old man who had completed his task, but as that of the youngest man among us,—youngest because, after all that he had done, he still had so much more laid out to do than any of us, and still was competent to do it ; that the best service that we can do his memory is to take up his work where he was forced to drop it, carry it on with all that we can summon of his energy and indomitable will, and, as old age creeps upon us, not lay the harness off, but, following his example and Emerson's advice, "obey the voice at eve obeyed at prime."

ON PICKET DUTY.

"Every man's labor," says the New York *Nation*, "is worth what some other man will do it equally well for, and no more." That is to say, if one man demands for his labor the whole product thereof, he cannot have it because some other man is satisfied to perform the same labor for half of the product. But in that case what becomes of the other half of the product ? Who is entitled to it, and what has he done to entitle him to it ? Every man's labor is worth what it produces, and would command that, if all men were free. "There is no natural rate for telegraphers any more than for bookkeepers or teamsters," continues the *Nation*. No more, truly ; but just as much. The natural rate of wages for ten hours of telegraphing or bookkeeping or teaming is as much money as will buy goods in the market for the production of which ten hours of equally tiresome and disagreeable labor were required. And this natural rate would be the actual rate if unlimited competition were allowed in everything. That competition is a potent factor in the regulation of wages we admit, but what we further assert is that, if competition were universal and applied to capitalists as well as laborers, it would regulate wages in accordance with equity. All that we ask is absolutely free play for the economists' boasted law of supply and demand. Why are the capitalists so afraid of the logical extension of their own doctrines?— *Liberty*, August 25, 1883.

Taking generals as they go, I have always held Robert E. Lee in moderately high esteem, but, if Jubal Early tells the truth, this opinion must be revised and perhaps reversed. Trying to relieve Lee from that horrible aspersion on his character which attributes to Grant's magnanimity at Appomattox Lee's retention of his sword, Early declares that Lee and all his officers were allowed by the express terms of the capitulation to retain their side-arms, and further (citing Dr. Jones's " Personal Reminiscences of General R. E. Lee ") that Lee once said to Jones and other friends, and in 1869 to Early himself, that, before going to meet Grant, he left orders with Longstreet and Gordon to hold their commands in readiness, as he was determined to cut his way through or perish in the attempt, if such terms were not granted as he thought his army entitled to demand." That is to say, General Lee, having determined that it would be folly to make his men fight longer for his cause, made up his mind to surrender, but decided at the same time that he would cause his men to die by the thousands rather than submit himself and his officers to a slight personal humiliation. He was willing to swallow the camel, but, rather than stomach the gnat, he would murder his fellow-men without compunction. All considerations fall before superstition, be the superstition religious, political, or military. The art of war, on which government finally rests, has, like government itself, its laws and regulations and customs, which, in the eyes of the military devotee, must be observed at all hazards. Beside them human life is a mere bagatelle. Man himself may be violated with impunity, but man-made laws and customs are inviolably enshrined in the Holy of Holies.—*Liberty*, April 11, 1885.

An idea for a cartoon, which *Puck* probably will not utilize: Grover Cleveland in the White House with his new and legal wife ; to the right, in a companion picture, George Q. Cannon in a prison cell; to the left of the White House, Maria Halpin, Cleveland's illegal wife, and their illegitimate son, dwelling as social outcasts in an abode of wretchedness and want because wilfully abandoned by the husband and father ; to the right of the prison, Cannon's illegal wives and

illegitimate children, dwelling in an abode of wretchedness
and want because the law has imprisoned the husband and
father instead of allowing him to live with and protect them ;
on the walls of the White House, illuminated texts concerning the purity of the home and exclusiveness of love, taken
from the president's message to congress on the Mormon
question ; on the walls of the prison cell, the constitutional
amendment forbidding the passage of laws abridging religious
freedom. Title for the cartoon : " Mormonism in Cleveland's
eyes, like the tariff in Hancock's, a purely local question."—
Liberty, June 19, 1886.

Work and Wages sneers at the paradise of cheapness of
which Edward Atkinson and other economists boast, but
which is achieved by the reduction of wages to a very low
point, as a fools' paradise. It is right. But its own paradise
of dearness, to be achieved by the determination of individuals to pay more than the market value for products and
thereby rob themselves, is equally a fools paradise, if not
more so. For, while it is true, as *Work and Wages* claims,
that cheapness is achieved at the cost of injury to health and
mind and morals and therefore to productive power, it is also
true, as the economists claim, that the payment of higher
than market prices causes a loss of capital, stifles enterprise,
and makes wages even lower than before. The wise men's
paradise is that in which the market value of products is equal
to the wages paid to the labor (of all sorts) expended in their
creation, and it can be achieved only by the total abolition of
those checks upon the supply of capital which States have
imposed and economists have justified for the purpose of
keeping wages at a point low enough to sustain capitalists in
luxury and yet not quite low enough to immediately " kill the
goose that lays the golden egg." In that paradise there will
be no sentimental endeavor to pay high prices, but all will
buy as cheaply as they can, the difference between that state
and this being the vital one that then the unimpeded circulation of capital will enable labor to buy its wages for much less
than it now pays for them. The tendency to cheapness of
product being thus balanced by a tendency to dearness of
labor, the displacement of monopoly and charity, those parents of pauperism, by competition and equity will give birth
to an entirely new economic condition in which industry and
comfort will be inseparable.—*Liberty*, May 28, 1887.

Jus, the London organ of semi-individualism, combats the
doctrine that surplus value—oftener called profits—belongs to

the laborer because he creates it, by arguing that the horse, by a parity of reasoning, is rightfully entitled to the surplus value which he creates for his owner. So he will be when he has the sense to claim and the power to take it ; for then the horse will be an individual, an ego. This sense and power the laborer is rapidly developing, with what results the world will presently see. The argument of *Jus* is based upon the assumption that certain men are born to be owned by other men, just as horses are. Thus its *reductio ad absurdum* turns upon itself ; it is hoist with its own petard.—*Liberty,* July 2, 1887.

In the silly speech which Colonel Ingersoll made at an informal session of the Republican convention at Chicago he declared that he favored protection of American industries because the Americans are the most ingenious people on the face of the earth. By the ordinary mind this will naturally be regarded as a reason why other people should be protected rather than the American. It requires the wit of an Ingersoll to see that it is either necessary or advisable to protect the ingenious against the dull-witted, the strong against the weak. —*Liberty,* July 7, 1888.

To Edward Atkinson's perfectly sound argument that the present accumulation of money in the United States treasury does not constitute a surplus revenue, inasmuch as there are $250,000,000 of demand notes outstanding against the United States for the payment of which no provision has been made, Henry George's *Standard* makes answer by asking if any private corporation would "ever acknowledge that it had any surplus revenue if it possessed an unlimited power of levying taxes on sixty odd millions of people." If Mr. Atkinson were not as blind as Mr. George himself to the wickedness of this power of taxation, he would doubtless retort with the question : "Would any highwayman ever acknowledge that he had any surplus revenue if he possessed an unlimited power of robbing travellers with impunity ?"—*Liberty,* July 7, 1888.

"There are two things needed in these days," says sagacious Edward Atkinson: "first, for rich men to find out how poor men live ; and, second, for poor men to know how rich men work." You are right, Mr. Atkinson ; and when the poor men once know this, the rich men will very speedily find themselves out of a job. It will be the greatest lock-out on record.— *Liberty,* August 4, 1888.

1350954R0

Printed in Great Britain by
Amazon.co.uk, Ltd.,
Marston Gate.